By reason of his elegance he resembles an image painted in a palace, though he is as majestic as the palace itself.

Robert Vavra's Classic Book of Horses

Introduction by
James A. Michener

Drawings by
John Fulton

Edited by
Mary Daniels

WILLIAM MORROW AND COMPANY, INC.

New York

The idea for this book was in part conceived by good friends and fellow horse lovers Deb Mihaloff and her husband Alan Kirshner of Markel Corporation. Markel's patronage of this project should not surprise anyone who is aware of their long-term dedication to the well-being of horses. Part of the proceeds from *Classic Book of Horses* will enable me to continue my long-running study of equine primitive social behavior. Each of the owners of the horses celebrated in this book has provided support for the equine behavior study, and it thrills Deb, Alan and me to know that the stallions, mares and geldings owned by these generous people are now a part of equine literature.

ROBERT VAVRA'S CLASSIC BOOK OF HORSES

ISBN 0-688-12019-9

Printed in Spain

First Edition

1 2 3 4 5 6 7 8 9 10

BOOK DESIGN BY ROBERT VAVRA

Production, Landmark/Markel: Dawn Colgin, Sue Ellen Witten, Carolyn Hunt, and Scott Sherman.
Typesetting and production, Fotographics: Jeff Piontkowski and Karen Crampton.
Printed and bound in Spain by Cayfosa, Barcelona.
Photographic laboratory associate: Rick Fabares.
Drawings by John Fulton.
Edited by Mary Daniels.
Typing: Bonita Walker.

During a lifetime of travel, I have visited few countries where the hoofprints of horses did not precede the footprints of man in establishing some civilization. One mystery that arises from my own country is the reason the original equine deserted the American continent, a journey that would eventually engage him in a peaceful association with man. This relationship would not only alter the world but endure until today. As I once wrote:

"Why did this stallion that had prospered so in Colorado desert his amiable homeland for Siberia? We do not know. Why did the finest animal America developed become discontented with the land of his origin? There is no answer. We know that when the horse negotiated the land bridge which he did with apparent ease and in considerable numbers, he found on the other end an opportunity for varied development that is one of the bright aspects of animal history. He wandered into France and became the mighty Percheron, and into Arabia, where he developed into a lovely poem of a horse, and into Africa, where he became the brilliant zebra, and into Scotland, where he bred selectively to form the massive Clydesdale. He would also journey into Spain, where his very name would become the designation for gentleman, a caballero, a man of the horse. There he would flourish mightily and serve the armies that would conquer much of the known world, and in 1519 he would leave Spain in small adventurous ships of conquest and land in Mexico, where he would thrive and develop special characteristics fitting him for a life on upland plains. In 1543 he would accompany Coronado on his quest for the golden cities of Quivira, and from later groups of horses brought by other Spaniards some would be stolen by Indians and a few would escape to become feral, once domesticated but now reverted to wildness. And from these varied sources would breed the animals that would return late in history, in the year 1768, to Colorado, the land from which they had sprung, making it for a few brief years the kingdom of the horse, the memorable epitome of all that was best in the relationship of horse and man."

As I have encountered horses in the lands I have visited, everywhere I have found men and women who have loved them. In this book Robert Vavra distinguishes many of these noble animals and the people who are devoted to them, and I know of no one more qualified to do so than he.

I met Robert Vavra more than thirty years ago, shortly after he arrived in Spain, when he was still more boy than man. Few of us who knew him in those days, including creative men like Ernest Hemingway, David Lean and Tom Lean, made his acquaintance without being impressed by his enthusiasm, his natural manner, his feeling for animals, and his personal style as a photographer. During my lifetime I have met dozens of writers and photographers in dozens of different countries, but I have encountered none who could both write and photograph with the artistry of Robert Vavra. While others who admired his work left Sevilla, I was so impressed by his distinct style and his sensitivity to people and places that one afternoon while I sat in his studio studying a batch of his recent photographs, it occurred to me that he might be just the person I had been looking for to help me with a book I had long planned but never written: a philosophical appreciation of the Spanish experience. To accomplish this I would need both words and photographs, and it seemed highly probable that Vavra could supply the latter. However, at this time I did not raise the question of our working together, because I was entwined with another subject which would absorb my attention for some years: a novel on the Holy Land.

In the spring of that year, 1960, I often accompanied Vavra to the wild marshes of the Guadalquivir where he was photographing and taking notes on the Spanish fighting bull, an animal he felt to be in danger of eventual extinction and about which he was preparing a book. During those delightful outings, I had the opportunity to appreciate his naturalist's eye as he pointed out creatures and told me of their ways, among them the Bee-eater and the Hoopoe, birds which would later become important in my own work.

It was not until 1966 that I managed to get back to Sevilla for Holy Week and its ensuing feria; now I was ready to devote uninterrupted time to the book on Spain, and I proposed to Vavra that he cooperate with me in an unusual way: "I want photographs but not the ordinary kind presented in the ordinary way. If I write about the cathedral at Toledo, I don't want the reader to see on the facing page a faithful shot of the cathedral's facade. I want you to roam Spain at the same time I do, you going your way, I going mine. When we're finished, we'll put the text and photographs together in some haphazard way, so that your portrait of a fighting bull might possibly face my words about the cathedral." Because of Vavra's special intuitions I never doubted that his photographs and my words would unite to form the impression I sought. When *Iberia* was published half my correspondents said, "I liked the pictures better than the text." The other half said, "When a man writes about the Toledo cathedral in an illustrated book, I expect to see a photograph of the cathedral." But all agreed that it was a happy union.

Though equus has fired the imaginations of painters from the prehistoric hunter-artists of Altamire to Leonardo da Vinci, Velázquez, Goya and Picasso, still, in the history of photography no cameraman has recorded the horse with such excitement and personal style as shown in these pages – pictures so exquisite they are of universal appeal. These photographs are works of art; they are interpretations of the horse as perceptive as those done by Stubbs and Remington. They are a joy to see because they evoke the inner nature of the horse.

Accompanying Vavra's words about the distinguished horses in the book are splendid sketches by that noted American artist John Fulton who is also doing all of the drawings for a book of mine now in progress. This combination of words and pictures is a fitting tribute to the animal that has more served man than any other creature on this planet.

James A. Michener
December 13, 1991

Robert Vavra's
Classic Book of Horses

the four winds are blowing

some horses

are coming

Teton Sioux — Song of the Horse Society

There was life in that silver

shroud.   Through its

beautiful transparency,

a pair of black, shiny hoofs

Around and around

he galloped, and sometimes

he jumped forward

and landed on stiff legs . . .

quivering . . . ears forward,

eyes rolling so that

the whites showed,

pretending to be afraid.

John Steinbeck

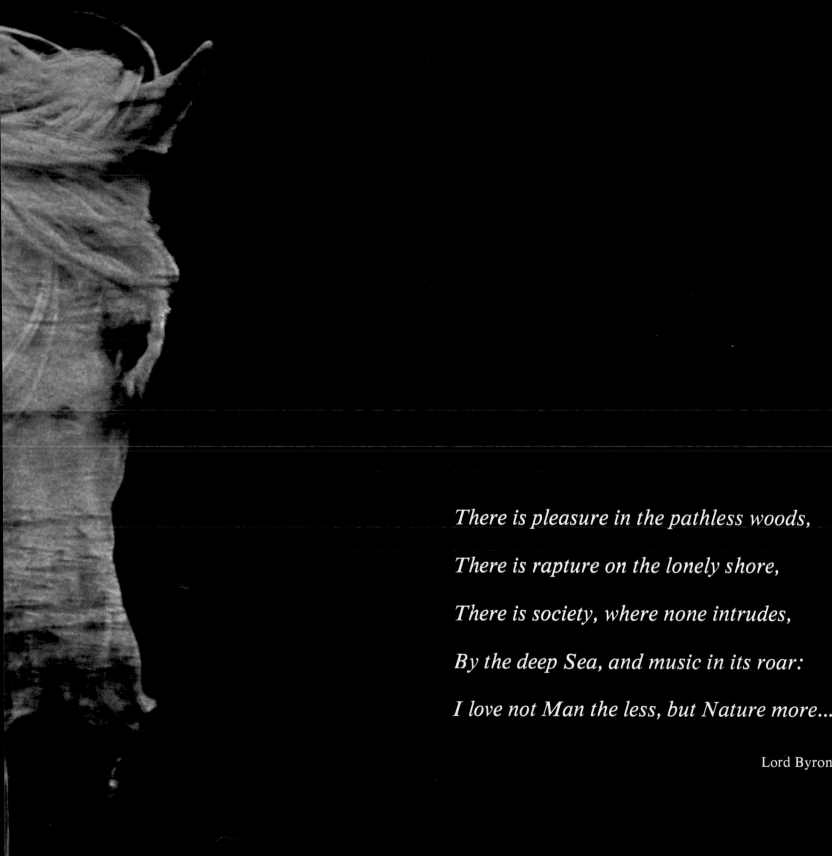

There is pleasure in the pathless woods,

There is rapture on the lonely shore,

There is society, where none intrudes,

By the deep Sea, and music in its roar:

I love not Man the less, but Nature more...

Lord Byron

From the

magic

of Aladdin

sprang

my strain,

and,

in part,

from

him

my name.

Trajan Tennent

Look for me by moonlight;

Watch for me by moonlight;

I'll come to thee by moonlight,

though hell should bar the way!

Alfred Noyes

I have never seen such a perfectly formed animal.

Beautiful and graceful like a gazelle, he burned hot and

wild with the deserts of Egypt in his soul.

Lynn V. Andrews

From the

city

of

Córdoba

came

my name,

Moorish

mosque

and Manolete's

fame.

Trajan Tennent

My horse be swift in flight.

Even like a bird;

My horse be swift in flight.

Bear me now in safety.

Far from the enemy arrows,

And you shall be rewarded

With streamers and ribbons red.

Sioux warrior's song to his horse

...the horse through all its trials had preserved the sweetness of paradise in its blood.

Johannes V. Jensen

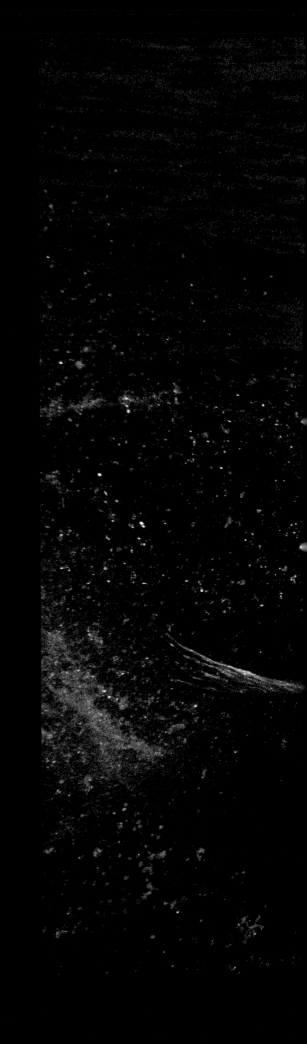

The stallion was surging on . . . his eyes open

against the spray. . . . A wall of steely flesh

broadside to the wave . . . that even the sea might

not conquer.

Charles Tenny Jackson

Now

I'm free.

The wind

is

free.

The

wind

is

me.

Trajan Tennent

Away, away, my steed and I,

Upon the pinions of the wind,

We sped like meteors through the sky,

When with its crackily sound the night

Is chequer'd with the northern light.

Lord Byron

We be of one blood, ye and I . . .

Rudyard Kipling

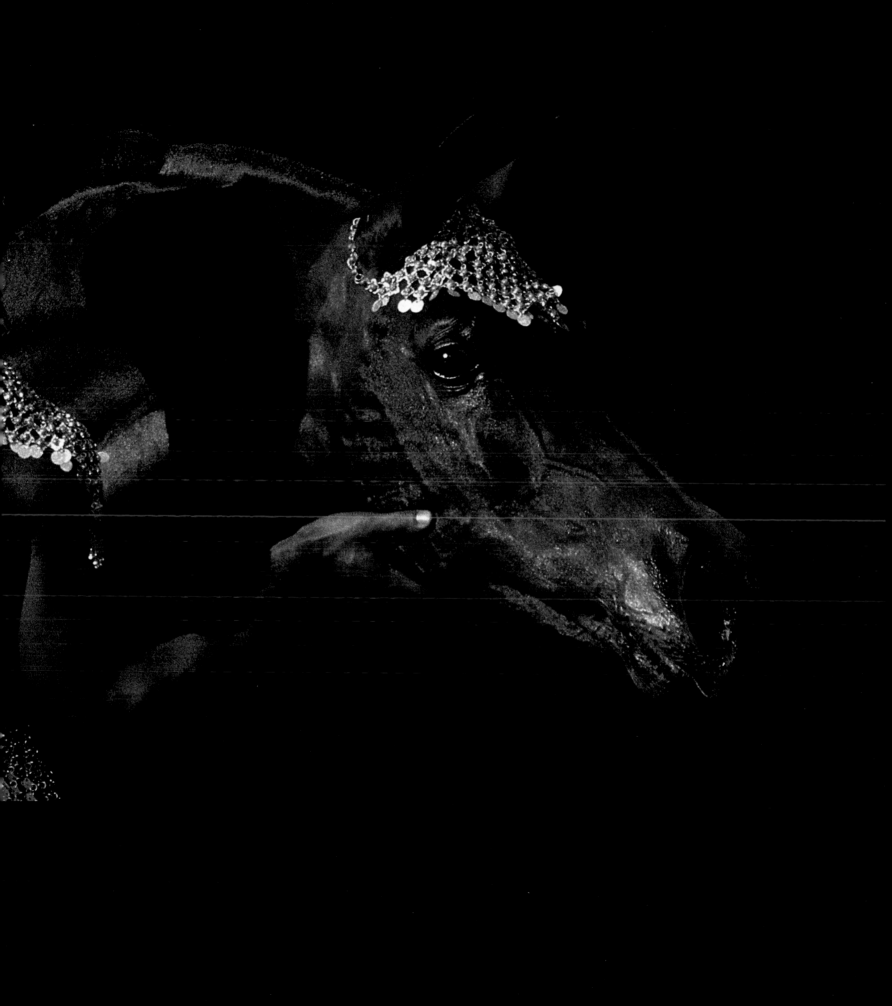

. . . stampeding horse that raves

. . . when it meets the sea at last

is swallowed outright by the waves!

Federico García Lorca

REFLECTIONS

Horses! Horses! What wonder, romance, pride, fear, adventure, warmth, excitement, heartbreak and happiness they bring into our lives. Because of their vitality, strength, size, physical ability to carry us, capacity to learn, unpredictability, dependency, moments of putting themselves and ourselves dangerously on the edge, closeness to nature which they allow us to share, and beauty, they enrich our lives as does no other animal.

Some months ago at the Los Angeles International Airport, James Michener and I were discussing this book and we concluded that it is all about the love, hope and dreams which to most of us are synonymous with horses. As with other things unexplainable in life, I can't really define why horses have always seemed as much a part of me as is my ability to hear, smell or see them in reality or in my imagination. Gazing into the past, in recalling my own childhood and the importance of equines in it, I remember Silver: When the colt Silver was given to me, Casablanca, Newmarket, Lisbon, Jerez de la Frontera, Paris and Querétero were merely romantic names in a geography book full of pale maps.

Silver, the only horse I ever owned, had just three legs, but oh, how we loved him! I was ten years old and my stallion was two inches high and cast in lead. On rainy days my twin, Ron, and I would play with our toy horses; to us they were as wild as any mustangs galloping free in Wyoming or Montana. And though Silver was a cripple, for us he would run as fast as Man O'War.

Then there were the herds of horses at Columbus Grammar School. Ron and I and all our friends would split into two bands, tossing our heads and voicing shrill whinnies and, since each troop had a lead stallion, fights were inevitable. Often these combats became so violent that a stallion's war cries turned into the sobs of a small boy.

However, there were also real horses in our lives during those years of the Second World War. They belonged to my Great Uncle Charlie Jankovsky, a wizened, brown Czech who had come to America sometime at the end of the last century, where he had worked like crazy in Wyoming as a tailor, saving almost every cent he ever made until he could retire in Long Beach, California. Uncle Charlie's dream was to own a ranch and to have some horses, and happily for him — and us! — he was able to make his dream come true. After purchasing six

hundred acres near Hemet, California, the first thing he did was to go to an auction and buy "livestock"; Polly was an old chestnut mare and Appaloosie was a sharp-looking Appaloosa. Uncle Charlie knew a lot about tailoring and saving money, but he always got taken at those auctions (even though my brothers and I were convinced he was a gypsy).

Our great uncle had bought Polly in foal with the promise that she has been bred to a prize Quarter Horse. This excited Ron and me so much that toward the end of the mare's pregnancy we talked our folks into spending as much time as possible at that old Last Gate Ranch that didn't have electricity or running water, and whose outhouse spider webs made us cautious about sitting on the seats. I can remember running down to the lower meadow the morning Polly had given birth. Her offspring, we were sure, would be as handsome a foal as the one in the film *Thunderhead* (which we had seen four times at the Alex Theater in Glendale). God, how sick we were when out of the sage brush stepped a baby mule! Polly died a year later.

Appaloosie was another problem. She shied so much that only my father could ride her, so Uncle Charlie went back to the auction and bought Gypsy, a coal black Morgan with a white star on her forehead. Soon enough, however, we found that not a fence on the ranch could hold that mare.

Once I remember Uncle Charlie got so mad at Gypsy that his brown face turned the color of split-pea soup. The mare leapt the barbed-wire right in front of the cabin and messed up the new pond and destroyed the water lilies that our great uncle had so carefully hauled in milk cans from Long Beach to Hemet. (Bringing those precious plants to the ranch the car had heated up twice and boiled over, but Uncle Charlie had refused to use water from his lovely lilies; he had preferred to walk a mile to the nearest farm.) I was scared and stood in the background when he tied Gypsy — our "Black Beauty" — to a tree and then beat her in the face with a bridle. It was an awful thing to see and it ruined the mare forever.

Chick was a small bay mare that also came from one of the auctions. How many owners she had had, and how many of them it had taken to spoil her, I don't know, but I never will forget sitting on Lizard Rock, above the outhouse, loading a B-B gun, talking with my mother who was currying Chick in the meadow, when the horse — for who knows what reason — whirled around, grabbed Mother by the shoulder, threw her on the ground and tried to trample her. If Dad hadn't raced up from the cabin to scare the mare away, I don't know what would have happened.

Later, as we drove Mother to the hospital, Dad said we shouldn't let Uncle Charlie's auction misfits ruin our love for horses. They really could be noble and beautiful animals, he told us, and to prove this, a few weeks later he took us to what was then the Kellogg Arabian Horse Farm near Pomona, California. To our twelve-year-old eyes, what could have been more beautiful than the Arab stallions and mares that were paraded before us in the golden light of that late California afternoon — certainly not Veronica Lake or even a Buick convertible. "How could anything be lovelier?" Ron and I wondered, "except maybe wild mustang stallions galloping free across the mesas of Colorado."

Not much later we had the chance to prove in person what we had heard so many times: that stallions were wild demons, couldn't be trusted and had to kept under lock and key. Ten miles from the Last Gate Ranch was a farm dedicated to the raising of Hereford cattle and Quarter Horses, where our uncle asked Dad to have a look at a Palomino stallion and to find out what kind of stud fee would be charged for covering either Chick or Gypsy. So early one morning we left the raw wilderness of the old Last Gate Ranch; my brothers Bill and Ron on one mare, and Dad and I on the other, we rode down the canyon, valley quail calling from the sage on either side of us, doves and jays taking off from dead branches of cottonwood trees that twisted silver against the sky. Finally, the dusty trail ended and we entered the neat white fences and lush green fields of the farm of the Palomino stallion.

While we boys stood outside with the mares, Dad went into the stable with a cowboy. All of a sudden we heard the banging of hoofs against wood and the battle screams of a horse. Bill ducked inside the building to have a look, returned shaking his head in respect, and then held the mares while Ron and I entered the cool darkness that housed not only the stallion, but the smells of fresh hay and horse sweat and manure — all lovely to our noses. "He's really a son-of-a-gun," the cowboy was saying to our dad. "Meaner than cat pee and twice as nasty." Then we knew why so few people in America had stallions for pleasure riding; it was like keeping a wild animal! Eyes rolled back, ears flat to his head, teeth bared, forelock tossing, the Palomino, like a dragon, thrust his head out of the box. "Stand back, fellas," warned the cowboy.

Later that night at the Last Gate Ranch, I couldn't get the stallion off my mind until I started for the outhouse and then stopped half-way along the path to unzip my pants; the nights in those mountains were so dark and the picture of the cougars trying to kill Flicka in the movie were still so vivid in my mind and imagination that every movement or owl's hoot from the oak trees sent chills up my back. After midnight, when the kerosene lamps had been turned off and everyone was in bed, when my father was snoring and the white-footed mice were scampering across the tin roof of the cabin, I remember thinking how sad it was that a stallion, except maybe in the movies or in a book, had to be such a wild beast, a savage to whom neither I nor any boy could be a friend. And yet, at the same time, I delighted in the thought of the Palomino's fiery display, for in truth, it was what I had always been told stallions were.

In the years that followed, I never lost my love for horses. Even today, in Sevilla, if I close my eyes and concentrate for a few minutes, I can brew up strong recollections of experiences with them from years ago. There was a rickety maze of corrals and loading ramps at a livestock auction near Downey, California, and we never passed it in our old Model T Ford without my father yielding to Ron's and my pleas to stop alongside the road. Then we boys would climb up on the fences and stare down at the nags nobody wanted and who, if they weren't sold for a few dollars at one of the auctions, would end up next door in billows of stinking smoke that rose from a glue factory. But we didn't see bony nags or notice those odors much, we just saw horses — horses! And how we loved that sight.

Mixed with those same childhood memories are scenes from Taft, California, a hick oil town on the edge of Steinbeck country, where my wonderful old grandmother Hamilton lived: On hot summer nights there was nothing to do but to go to the rollerskating rink and whirl around the warm cement to phonograph records of someone playing Strauss waltzes on a Hammond organ. In the daytime, however, even though the sun beat down with such intensity that the blacktop roads became soft underfoot, we would wander over to some nearby corrals and do nothing but look at the mares and geldings. Ron, my cousin Gary and I would have liked to ride those animals, but, like the grey lizards that basked in the sun out of reach of our hands, we were satisfied just to hang on the splintery fences and stare at the horses; to watch them, listen to them and smell them.

Not all those recollections, though, are as seemingly unexciting as were the inhabitants of those slipshod board corrals. I wouldn't trade anything for an experience at Uncle Charlie's ranch that flashes as dramatically before me today as it did in real life, more than forty years ago.

Dusk was settling as Ron and I left the North Forty where we had been twigging doves with a .22. Happy with having shot enough birds for supper, we walked in tired silence; the only sounds were our boots through the dry grass, the distant yapping of a coyote, and the chatter of a covey of quail going to roost in the surrounding oak trees. Then it came, like the cry of another child, from the canyon behind us — the scream of a mountain lion. We whirled around, shaking, white-faced, each knowing that there never was a recorded case of an unprovoked attack on man by a puma in the wild (but still fresh in our minds were those two big cats in the film *Thunderhead*, clinging like shadows to a tree, heads turning weasel-like, yellow eyes and fangs gleaming, ready to pounce on Flicka and her foal).

Suddenly, from the far side of the meadow, muffled sounds of hoofs thudded madly from the weeds and soft earth. "God!" I thought as I looked at the panicked expression on Ron's face. "A big cat's after the horses!"

Gypsy burst first through the shoulder-high sage at the clearing's edge, head high in fear, ears laid back, her mane rising and falling like a black wave as she galloped in violent surges, closer and closer. Behind came old Polly, then heavy in foal, and just as she passed us — "Boom" — into the air overhead burst a covey of what must have been almost a hundred quail. Ron and I exchanged glances; were we really at the Last Gate Ranch or were we slouched deeply into the cheap seats and darkness of the Alex Theater? But here the horses didn't whinny in fear, they just ran like crazy, flying toward the cabin as if the puma's claws were touching their flanks. "What shall we do?" Ron's voice was trembling.

"Mountain lions won't attack people," I answered. My hands were shaking so that one of the doves·dropped to the ground, but I was too frightened to stoop over and pick it up, sure the puma was crouching right then on one of the twisted limbs overhead. "But...but anyway," I whispered, "it might be a good idea to try to keep him from going after the horses." To which Ron emptied half his gun's magazine into the air, the shots ringing in lonely echoes off the granite boulders around the meadow.

Not many months after that experience, my Uncle Jim introduced us to a new kind of horse. That chestnut filly, coming out onto the Santa Anita Racetrack, sleek and gazelle-like, with large, lovely, dark doe eyes, and coils of charged-up muscle under her smooth coat — the beauty of that sight touched the deepest places of my soul. The infield grass was so green, the flowers so bright, and the silks of the jockeys so dazzling, that I grinned up at my handsome, silver-haired uncle and he smiled back because he knew that I then understood why he so loved the races. The horses were at the gate, they were inside while the world stood still for a moment, and then they were on the dirt, with the announcer's voice booming out to the purple haze beyond the track. Around the curve they glided, blossoms of color in the distance, swinging into the home stretch, coming so fast. Could horses move that fast? Each spread out in great strides, full drive, the jockeys pressed tightly to their mounts, the roar of the crowd suffocating the announcer's voice.

Strangely enough, in those early years I never learned to ride well; I was content just to look at horses. The explanation is simple, I suppose those misfits of Uncle Charlie's either had too many problems for us boys, or, like old Polly, they were nags. The other horses we rode were from one of the rental stables across from Griffith Park. Those plugs had long since been turned into walking robots and the only time they showed any life was when we turned them back toward the stables and then there was no stopping their mad, homeward gallops.

Soon sports, girls and studies just about crowded horses out of our lives. At college, however, some new stallions — Bucephalus, Alborak, Rocinante, Marengo — galloped from history into my imagination. To be honest, though, until shortly before coming to Spain, horses had been replaced in my world by other interests.

I was in Mexico one Sunday for a corrida when some friends introduced me to Carlos Arruza, a famous matador who, once he had retired from fighting bulls on foot in the ring, had turned to killing them from horseback in the classical tradition. The Andalusian mounts that Arruza used that afternoon were some of the most magnificent animals I had ever seen. They weren't large though they did have full chests, exceptionally long manes and tails, well-formed heads, and body conformation that although I knew little technically about such things seemed close to artistic perfection in their beauty. Two of Arruza's horses had unusually high and showy (but untrained, I was told) leg action. However, what most impressed me about those stallions was their gentle dispositions. At that time in America few stallions were kept for pleasure riding because they were generally considered dangerous. Thus, I assumed Arruza's horses were simply exceptionally beautiful and tame animals, and gave them little more thought. Also, this was the period in life when I was completely taken with what seemed to be the most impressive animals I had ever seen — fighting bulls — and I spent many free hours in Mexico studying their behavior and photographing them in the ring.

It was the fighting bull in 1958, when I was twenty-three years old, that brought me to Spain where I spent six years working on a naturalistic study of brave cattle. Not equipped with formal education for animal observation, I had to rely on the first lessons my father had given us in the ways of wild creatures which, along with an intense interest in nature, helped partly to overcome my lack of technical training by sometimes offering an open and fresh point of view.

During those wonderfully happy years in Andalusia, far from Uncle Charlie's Last Gate Ranch and the stockyards of Downey, I once again came in close contact with horses, spending day after day with the bulls. I then became obvious that Arruza's mounts had been no exceptions in their extreme beauty and their noble dispositions — Spanish horses were normally that way. It was also exciting to realize that most of the horses in America were, in one way or another, related to Andalusian stock taken to the New World by the Conquistadors. Even the racehorses we had watched with Uncle Jim at Santa Anita, Hollywood Park and Bay Meadows, as well as those I had seen in England and France, had backgrounds that could be traced in part to Spain and North Africa. The Wyoming mustangs my father had told us about, and the Quarter Horses I had known in Texas and Mexico all had some Spanish blood. So it seemed that most of the horses in my life were suddenly tied together in an intriguing manner.

During those first years in Spain, I had the good fortune to enjoy the friendship of a number of men who not only loved fighting bulls, but felt just as strongly for their horses. Of these, the one I recall with most affection is the late Juan Belmonte (the matador who, half a century ago, revolutionized bullfighting). Though thirty years have passed, I can still almost taste those cold bowls of *gazpacho* that were served to us by Asunción in the dining room of Belmonte's country house, Gómez Cardeña followed by afternoons of open-field testings of young bulls. In my mind, as well preserved as a fresh photograph, is the picture of Belmonte on a white gelding, far off in the distance, a white speck against a sea of grey-green olive trees, the portrait of happiness in the union of man and horse.

Those mornings and afternoons of *acoso y derribo* presented the opportunity to renew my interest in horses. Not content to photograph the testing from the edge of the field in the normal fashion, I asked Belmonte if there wasn't a new angle that could be used, a problem which he pondered on a number of occasions over coffee at the Café Los Corales in Sevilla. The first solution he suggested — with a slight smile on his rugged face — was to dig a hole a couple of meters deep at the edge of the field so that the action could be photographed from ground level. But I convinced him that the horses and cattle would flash by so fast there would barely be time to photograph them; those were the days before zoom lenses and motor drives were available to beginning photographers like me.

Then I remembered some pictures of an ox cart race in India that had been taken by the famous Hungarian woman photographer, Ylla, from the hood of a moving Land Rover. So, one morning at Los Corales, with much enthusiasm, I suggested the use of a Land Rover to Belmonte who, after he listened attentively to the plan, thought for a moment and then in his stutter asked, "B-b-but, won't that be dangerous? The field isn't as smooth as the Palmera Avenue, you know." It was then that I had to admit that Ylla had been killed during the cart race in India, thrown from the hood of the Land Rover when it hit a hole. "And you still want to do this?" he questioned. I smiled and nodded yes.

So arrived the opportunity of not only being able to photograph bulls from the hood of a fast-moving vehicle, but also to observe at close range the brilliant action of Spanish horses at work. Never had I seen such noble heads, curved necks, flowing manes, and natural gaits on animals anywhere. It was as though the stallions of the Prado had come to life before us.

In this way my childhood interest in horses was renewed in Spain, and it was thrilling to remember that wild Palomino stallion near Uncle Charlie's ranch and to imagine that hundreds of years ago his distant ancestors had grazed the same pastures and perhaps marshes through which I trudged while photographing fighting bulls. Thirty years ago those *marismas*, or marshes, were still untouched and wild, and frequently there was the opportunity to observe, hour after hour, semi-wild horses in games not completely unlike those played by Ron and me and our fourth-grade friends on the dusty grounds of Columbus Grammar School in Glendale, California.

In retrospect, years ago a decisive moment occurred that led to the doing of my equine books, but not until some time ago, on a flight from Denver to New York, did I fully realize its importance. James Michener and I were discussing moments of artistic expression in the performing arts which had most moved us, limiting ourselves to five performances each. At the head of my list, next to a magnificent *faena* by Curro Romero in Sevilla, Alicia Alonso dancing the dying swan, a dazzling trapeze performance by a troupe of Mexican flyers, Bjorling and Nillson singing Act Three from *Turandot*, I selected, without question, a performance by the Spanish Riding

School of Vienna during which a horse doing the extended trot had seemed to glide across the ring. The movements of the Lipizzaner — a direct descendant of the stallions of Andalusia — caused the kind of awe that touched emotions deeply enough to give me goosepimples.

I have often been asked which of my equine experiences is my favorite. Immediately I think of the birth of a foal that I photographed for *Equus*. When work on that book began, I didn't have the slightest hope of being able to include the birth of a foal in its pages. Experience from work on the bull book, when six weeks were spent before I was able to photograph a fighting cow giving birth, convinced me of the impossibility of harboring such a hope, especially since the actual full working days of photography on *Equus* would be limited to less than forty. "Horsey" friends were unanimous in their advice: "Concentrate on all phases of horse life, but completely dismiss the idea of including a birth in your book, an effort which will not only be a great waste of time, considering the almost impossibly short period you've allowed for photographing your book, but which can only end in disappointment."

One spring morning, after watching the breeding of a mare at El Hornillo, I decided to wander down to one of the lower pastures where the foals and their mothers were almost sure to be found. Just before leaving the dirt road to enter an olive grove, I met the *yeguero*, Alfonso, who was complaining that one of the ranch's nicest mares, Noticiera, was several days overdue in foaling. "I don't know what's wrong with her," he grumbled as he left me and plodded through the wild flowers that were still heavy with dew.

The clouds that had grayed the past week's skies had been blown from Andalusia. Somewhere ahead in the olive grove a nightingale was singing, accompanied by the faint, alluring sound of the mares' bells.

After reaching the herd, most of which were grazing in a field of mustard, the better part of an hour was spent photographing new foals at play. At about ten-thirty I decided to leave the yellow field; somewhere not far away the nightingale was still singing, and I wanted to try to get a close look at him. Of all the spring mornings spent on the book, this was perhaps the loveliest; the sky was so freshly blue, and dew was sparkling on the thousands of brilliant blossoms that spread out around the olive trees.

Locating the nightingale was not difficult, but staying with him as he tried to lure me from his nearby mate, who was sitting on a carefully woven, cone-shaped nest, was not easy. However, because there was nothing else to do — the sun was almost too high for good photography — I followed him.

After I wandered about a quarter of a mile, the bird's singing suddenly stopped and, as I swung around hoping to see his rust-colored body bursting in flight from one tree to another, I noticed a white horse spread out on the ground, almost hidden from view by low-hanging olive branches. At first, this sight did not rouse my curiosity; often mares could be seen stretched out in deep sleep, but usually somewhat earlier in the morning and closer to the herd. Approaching the white mare, I noticed that she was breathing heavily and that her eyes were not shut — she was also obviously pregnant, but so were a number of other females in the herd.

When Noticiera heard footsteps she lifted her head and swung it around to stare with large limpid eyes. Fourteen years old, the mother of nine foals, she was handsome for her age and, washed clean by the recent rain, looked beautifully white against the thousands of flowers that blossomed around her. As I walked toward her tail she stood up, and it was then the thought flashed: "She's giving birth!" But, as the mare turned around and started to graze, no secretion could be detected coming from below her tail. Still, I was terribly excited. Then, seeing Noticiera on her feet, I began to worry that if she was really in the process of giving birth my presence might disturb her. Mares, I knew, could postpone foaling for hours. Off somewhere in the grove, the nightingale had resumed singing and, trying to remember every landmark in sight — the grove was so extensive and each tree looked alike — I began walking in what seemed to be the bird's direction. I also checked my watch; I would give the mare fifteen minutes before returning to her.

I could barely contain the urge to turn back, as the nightingale's song grew louder. Reflecting on the existing birth photographs I had seen, before me appeared pictures of mares foaling at night, taken in boxes where the camera's flash gave a ghoulish cast to what should have been a beautiful scene; the blood and placenta always seemed like something out of front-page photographs of a car accident. I thought of another set of photographs where the photographer had been lucky enough to find a mare foaling during the daytime, but the morning had been so grey and the mare's sides had been so dirtied with mud that the pictures, though they were fine shots, somehow seemed tainted, and had none of the freshness and poetry of creation that vibrated from the animal and setting that waited so close to my lens.

When eight minutes had passed I turned around and rapidly but cautiously retraced my steps to one of the larger olive trees that stood not more than twenty feet from where I had left the mare. Through the leaves

Noticiera could be seen stretched out on the ground, a pair of small, blue hoof tips just emerging from below her tail! Obviously, before lying down she had expelled the birth water, and was now on her side, which would help to press the foal out. The mare sighed and her sides rocked with heavy breathing as she lifted her rear top leg into the air, straining to force out the baby horse that her belly had carried for nearly a year. Almost ten minutes passed before the foal, except for its hind legs, slid from its mother.

The foal, who had been sleeping inside his mother, was not only suddenly bumped awake as he slipped onto the ground, but was also shaken into consciousness by the terribly bright light around him. Front-lit, the scene was beautiful, but it became even more poetic when I moved around cautiously to the other side of the mare to photograph the back-lit foal. Noticiera, breathing hard, was still in too much of a trance from the birth to notice me. When the foal became more awake, he lifted his head and a front hoof to break the sac, which hung over his head like an Arab hood.

The foal's hind legs were still inside his mother. The sac membrane was strong and not easy for him to break. After about 10 minutes, Noticiera raised her head, glanced back at the foal and then, with a great effort, got to her feet as the foal's back legs slid free from her body. The mare turned around and looked curiously at the foal, as if to say, "Where did you come from?" before she briefly licked his muzzle, probably instinctively trying to remove any remaining birth fluid from his nose.

When the foal felt his mother's tongue he made a soft, bleating sound, which she answered. Seemingly stimulated by the brief licking, he feebly attempted to get up, which freed him from the sac. At this point, I was so caught up in experiencing the scene in front of me and enjoying photographing it, that I didn't have time to really reflect on my extraordinary luck.

After another few minutes had passed, the foal again tried to get up. Watching him and his mother, who had started to graze, it was suddenly obvious how completely exhausted the birth had left both of them. Occasionally mares who give birth for the first time are frightened by the foal, an apprehension which disappears as soon as the new baby gets to its feet and takes on the appearance of a horse, though a very miniature one. At times the foal's completely wide-eyed look fully expressed his reaction to the newness of absolutely everything around him. Each time he tried to get to his feet, to make work the legs that had never been used before, he rose slowly and then wavered before tumbling back to the ground, limbs spread in all directions.

Three-quarters of an hour passed before the foal was able to stand and maintain his balance. Taking a few wobbly steps this way and that, his long, slim legs seemed not at all sure of their course. It was a great effort for such a newborn animal, and each time he fell to the ground he had to stay there and rest, before making another attempt to stand. Shortly after he was able to keep his balance, one of the younger mares appeared through the trees and came curiously toward the foal. Noticiera, who had seemed to pay abnormally little attention to her new offspring (from the time she had licked his muzzle she had continued to graze), lifted her head in threat, ears flat back, neck outstretched, teeth showing, to discourage the young mare from approaching any closer. The foal's sense of balance was still so delicate it seemed that if the slightest breath of wind swept through the grove, he was sure to capsize.

As the mare grazed, the torn sac hung from under her tail. A few minutes later the afterbirth was cast out. Horses, unlike other animals, rarely eat their afterbirth. Then, the foal, who had been nosing around his mother's forelegs, sides and tail, knowing instinctively that somewhere there was something to be found and sucked, discovered one of Noticiera's bulging teats. In those moments the foal appeared to be in a vegetative state, barely able to make out forms, his muzzle testing rough and smooth surfaces, his ears, eyes and nose taking in stimuli that were all then unidentifiable to him. The mare, however, at precisely the wrong moment, took a step forward toward taller grass, and the foal lost contact with the udder. Those were anxious moments — I wanted to put down the camera, take hold of Noticiera's bell strap, grab the foal and press his muzzle to the mare's udder. Finally, though, he found the teat again and fastened on. A few minutes later he stopped drinking and lifted his tail to expel a thick, bad-smelling excrement, the digested product of the metabolism of eleven months as an embryo. I released the camera and let it swing from the shoulder strap. My watch showed a few minutes before noon. I had been with the mare for little more than an hour, and now she was moving off into the olive grove with the foal behind her, and what a handsome *potro* he was. It was then I named him — Potri — though Noticiero would be written on his pedigree. Walking back through the olive trees, I felt completely but joyfully spent as the nightingale sang somewhere ahead. Every minute of that walk through the grove I tried to enjoy, knowing that shortly my happiness would be blemished with the worry that the undeveloped film of the birth would be lost in the post or damaged in developing. However these worries, like most worries, were unfounded, and Potri's birth photographs became one of the most important sequences in *Equus*.

I can't remember ever not loving horses. It's as though I was born infatuated with how they look, feel, smell and sound. My father loved to tell us of his childhood in the American West; of having his small boy's eyes dazzled by the first electric light bulb turned on to illuminate the dusty streets of Cheyenne, Wyoming; of waiting in front of a saloon for a cowboy to ride up and say, "Hey, kid, hold my horse and I'll give you a nickel"; or of watching the overland stage pull into town, its team of horses lathered white under the load of exotic cargo and passengers brought to Cheyenne from "the outside world." He told of Indians coming into town to sell blankets and of Uncle John, his saddle-maker uncle, weaving out of saloons and along the wooden sidewalks after having been paid for one of the saddles that were fine enough to take him eventually to Hollywood where he would be employed by Gene Autry and Tom Mix. All of those precious memories from my father's treasure chest of experience were in some way related to horses and to the men who depended upon them.

My father's favorite story was about the outlaw Tom Horn. In the war between the cattlemen and the sheepmen, Horn had been contracted to gun down a sheep farmer and, in doing so, he mistakenly shot the teenage son of his intended victim. It was a famous court case with Horn counting on the support of the wealthy cattle ranchers to spring him from jail. My father told of walking the streets of Cheyenne with some other boys shortly before Horn was to have been hanged and of noticing several saddled, riderless horses tied, spaced along the way leading out of town, one of which was tethered to the schoolhouse hitching post.

"Let's play Tom Horn making his escape!" said my father to his friends, who for the next half hour ran around the rickety building, using their hands as imaginary guns while shouting "Bang! Bang!" and "You're dead!" At one point in the game, my father took the role of the hired killer and, as he sought a hiding place under the schoolhouse steps, discovered a neatly wrapped package that had been carefully wedged under one of the staircase's wooden supports. Removing the parcel from its hiding place, my father carefully untied the string and unfolded the newspaper to disclose two pearl-handled Colt forty-five pistols. Just then his older brother Frank appeared, rewrapped the guns, and ran off to show them to their Uncle Adolph. What happened to those pearl-handled Colt forty-fives, my father didn't know. Later, however, as a man, he deduced that the horses tied on the road out of town and the pistols

under the schoolhouse steps had been carefully placed there for Tom Horn's jail break. And it is here that can be seen the importance of the horse in the world just a single generation ago.

Today, when cowboys roar into Cheyenne on payday, they screech over-size pickup trucks to a halt and drop quarters into parking meters before going into bars. In my father's day, they galloped into town on horses and gave a coin to a small child who held their live transportation at the swinging doors of rowdy saloons in front of which Indians sold their wares. Now, when visitors come to Cheyenne, they arrive in jet aircraft or air-conditioned motor vehicles, and their dress does not distinguish them from the locals. In my father's time, they could only arrive by horseback or in horse-drawn carriages and wagons from which they disembarked among the town's inhabitants like a cageful of exotic tropical birds set free in a farmyard. Now, when a criminal tries to break out of jail, he might use a helicopter, hand grenades, and a submachine gun. Then, Tom Horn staked his life on a string of cow ponies and a pair of pearl-handled Colt forty-fives hidden under the rickety steps of a schoolhouse.

We forget just what a short time ago it was — barely yesterday — that man depended so totally on equines. Today, with the exception of the cattle horse, equines in America and most of the world are luxury items — used only for show, sport, and pleasure. They are dispensable.

History, however, testifies that man's association with horses exemplifies, perhaps, the most profound animal-human relationship in recorded experience. While dogs are said to be our "best friends," still the animal names etched in human history are those of horses: Bucephalus, Rosinante, Marengo, and Babieca. This fascination with equines is also illustrated by the abundance of horses in literature: Black Beauty, Flicka, Thunderhead, the Black Stallion, Smoky.

My own fascination with horses was, until not long ago, from a naturalist's and artist's point of view. These interests overpowered what most people find attractive in horses — the ability to ride them. It wasn't as though I didn't have the opportunity or wasn't coaxed by rider instructor friends in all parts of the world. "You sit well. You're a natural. Let me teach you." But years would pass before I would feel comfortable sitting on a horse. My time was spent looking at them through a camera or through binoculars in the wild, focusing on either their beauty or on their behavior. The manner in which animals, particularly horses, attend to their lives has forever intrigued me. When I was finishing some brief notes on the social behavior of horses, for possible use in the book *Equus*, I wrote to a friend, Carolyn Moyer, in

California, to see if she could locate any published material on the subject. My four-month study of horses in southern Spain had been so distracted by photography that I hoped the books she might find would confirm or refute some of the conclusions I had drawn.

"I have turned the local libraries upside down, looking for material on equine social behavior," wrote Carolyn, "including the University at Davis. I've found material on literally every aspect of horses but social behavior. This is unbelievable to me. They have entire tomes on conformation, breeding, training, showing, pathology, illness — you can also get the stud books for nearly every breed of horse in the world — and even biographies of famous horses. I though when I started the search that it would be a matter of culling out the best material for you, not desperately searching for anything on the subject. As far as published material goes, you are really in *terra incognita* with this one."

Fortunately, before *Equus* went to press, Dr. Patrick Duncan, an ecologist who leads a horse-study project in southern France, visited Sevilla and reviewed my notes. Shortly after leaving Spain he wrote to me: "Why has the horse, inspiration of so much creative art over millennia, been so little studied except in captivity or for breeding purposes? This lack of scientific attention is particularly striking when contrasted with the abundance of excellent new work on the behavior and ecology of exotic and distant species, such as the gorilla and lion (George Schaller), elephant (Iain and Oria Douglas-Hamilton) and chimpanzee (Jane Goodall)."

Carolyn Moyer's fruitless search in California, and my own fascination with horse behavior, decided me to expand my notes and include them in *Equus*. Once the book was published, however, it seemed to me that the reader could not really get a good picture of horse behavior if he had to depend on the text alone. So in 1977, I decided to do *Such Is the Real Nature of Horses*, a book on equine social behavior. There seemed only one sensible way to present horse behavior: to illustrate it with many photographs. When the reader reaches the last page of *Such Is the Real Nature of Horses* and reflects, for example, on eye-rolling, I hope that instead of the printed words on a page, memory will project in his mind a picture of a gray stallion, his head held high, with eyes completely turned so that the pupil is out of sight.

That book did not presume to reflect more than the most obvious forms of equine behavior. Patrick Duncan and his colleagues at Tour du Valat in the South of France were involved in a highly scientific study of interest to readers who desire academic and technical descriptions. Perhaps one reason books on horse behavior for the layman do not exist is the lack of locations for the study of horses in Europe and the United States, where they are of such interest to so many people. Equines must be living in herds at liberty or semi-liberty to behave as most of those which were photographed for *Such Is The Real Nature of Horses*. Wild horses, like the mustangs of North America, are so cagey that they make difficult subjects, although the late James D. Feist, Dale R. McCullough and Hope Ryden have make keen observations on their behavior.

I have the good fortune to spend some months each year in Spain, where horses are still kept in sizable herds, mainly by the Spanish military. Besides large herds of mares pastured together (in some cases more than 150 head), there are also groups of bachelor stallions that often held my interest for hours. Equine family units studied in different parts of the world include a herd of Przewalski's horses, Quarter Horses and Andalusians. The most explicit and vivid examples of social behavior of horses, however, were observed in southern France in the marshes of the Camargue.

After finishing *Such Is the Real Nature of Horses*, it seemed that the more I studied equine behavior, the more curious I became, so much so that I returned to the Camargue whenever the opportunity presented itself. The more I learned I realized that if humans knew more about equine communication that training would not only be easier on horses but also on people. *Such Is the Real Nature of Horses* apparently struck the right cord. *Life Magazine* excerpted eight pages from it, and the book, apart from having been done in American and British editions, was translated into Spanish, French, German, and Dutch.

During the past fifteen years I have been able to take time to continue my study of equine social behaviors thanks to some very generous horse lovers, among them Deedie Wrigley, Martha duPont, and William Shatner. Because of their support, further work was possible in Spain, France and most recently in Kenya with common zebra. From these observations we have learned fascinating things. For example, wild horses do not enjoy bashing one another. They know that serious battle can result in pain and loss of harem members. Permanent injury and death, greater risks, are undoubtedly beyond their comprehension. Thus, wild horses have devised all kinds of rituals and displays to avoid out-and-out combat. They have a breath-testing ceremony in which dominance and subordinance can be settled by this olfactory examination of one another. If this does not work, they seem capable of being able to sniff out dominance or subordinance from each other's flanks, at the same time possibly monitoring flank trembling. It is said that horses can sense fear in humans, which also seems to apply to their own relationships. However, if a dispute cannot be settled by breath- or flank-testing, there is the dung pile ritual in which the subordinate horse, when two rival males meet, always dungs first after which the dominant animal dungs on the same spot. In the rare instance of a standoff, the horses engage in simultaneous and parallel defecation. Fierce and bloody battle is not usual, but it is a possibility should these symbolic rituals and ceremonies fail.

Since horses are among the most social of animals, we are also learning much about the complicities of equine hierarchy. Flight distance is another subject that needs much more examination. In spite of their size and strength, horses are timid animals, and can be sent into blind panic by the most harmless stimulus if it is unknown or comes as a surprise.

Horse-to-horse communication is based primarily on silent signals. Head and body attitudes are the forms of communication most used among horses at liberty, though smell is also important. The silent language of horses does not seem to vary among the equines I have observed, whether they be the horses of the Camargue or zebra on the Kenyan plains.

Voice is a much less used form of horse communication. I was once told by a Californian that his mares and geldings have vocabularies of twelve sounds, clearly understandable to him; an Englishman has written that his horses use some thirty vocal expressions, ranging from "I want my bloody breakfast" to "Let's get the hell out of here!" These horse vocabularies are highly sophisticated in comparison to the seven basic vocalizations that I have heard used by free-running horses in western America, Andalusia and in the Camargue.

Marking is another fascinating subject that will take much more time to properly define. Herd stallions, rarely mares, mark the excrement of other horses with their own urine or dung. Years ago, when I first began photographing equines, I assumed that marking, as with the Grevy's zebra and the African ass, was related to territorial claims, and that even though this was an atavism it showed the modern stallion's concern with establishing physical boundaries. However, later observations made me think that marking, so important in the lives of male horses, has nothing to do with territory. If it were a behavior pattern on its way out, it would not be done with the intensity and concern that stallions put into this activity.

Almost all defecation and urination by adult stallions is in reaction to that of other horses; the excreta of other stallions is marked with dung and the excrement of mares with urine. What, I had wondered, could be the purpose of marking? When the stallions that I watched marked mare urine, they were very particular about whose they marked. Family males paid little attention to unclaimed mares who were urinating or defecating, but they seemed to watch with great interest harem members. Marking of mare urine was more frequent during the breeding season, and was directed mainly at the urine of older mares who were in heat or coming into heat.

I concluded that there were two reasons for the stallion's strong preoccupation with covering only the urine of certain mares with his own urine. First, since horses have such a keen sense of smell, and since excreta is a means of communication among equines, a dominant stallion might cover a mare's urine to identify her to other males as "personal property." But far more likely, since the urine of mares in estrus or shortly before estrus contains large quantities of estrogen, the stallion, by diluting the female urine with his own, I'm convinced, is attempting to erase the "I'm in heat" message left by the mare which would attract other stallions and lead to possible conflict. Once in the Camargue, I watched a very in-estrus mare urinate as her harem stallion came immediately to the spot. As soon as she had finished, the stallion sniffed at the wet grass, raised his head and did a flehmen to test the estrogen content of the urine. Then, with his own urine he marked the mare's urine. Immediately thereafter, a colt member of that family group, approached and sniffed the same spot, did a flehmen, then marked the grass where the mare and the lead stallion had moments before urinated. As soon as that horse left this becoming-wetter-by-the-moment spot of grass, another colt approached it, sniffed the puddle of urine, lifted his head and did a flehmen. Presumably because the estrogen content of the mare's urine had been so diluted by the marking of the other two male horses, this colt did not mark the ground. The "I'm in heat" message had been erased.

These and a dozen other phases of equine social behavior continue to be the subject of the study that I began more than fifteen years ago. To be able to continue scrutinizing the behavior of horses in Andalusia, of Przewalski horses in captive herd situations, of the horses of the Camargue, and of both Common and Grevy's zebra in Africa is a privilege that in the future will be possible because of the generous patronage of the owners of the horses that are distinguished in this book. Because of them I will be able to prolong this study which in three or four years will be distilled in another book. Hopefully those published findings will result in better treatment of captive equines.

During the past fifteen years I have thought little of

49

standing firm in the wild when being charged by a threatening stallion, or of hanging by my legs from a slim eucalyptus branch, camera in hand, as almost two hundred horses stampeded beneath me; or of being hidden in tall grass in the Kenya highlands, watching zebra that may have been, at that moment, stalked by a lion that could have also had his eye on me. But not until Joan Embery and her husband Duane visited Cañada Grande, my ranch in southern Spain, did I ever feel comfortable on the back of a horse. At that time I had an Andalusian stallion called simply Blanco because of his whiteness, and during Joan's stay she rode him several times. "You should ride this horse, Robert," she would scold me. "He'd be perfect for you. He goes well and he's so well mannered."

After Joan and Duane left Cañada Grande, one afternoon instead of doing my daily jog around the ranch, I saddled up Blanco. The only way I can explain his patience and cooperation is that he must have thought: "Well, you've always tried to do good things for horses, so I'll give you a break."

In the days that followed, Blanco, in a very basic way, taught me to ride, but more important, he taught me that I could feel comfortable on a horse. Not only at last did I feel at ease on Blanco but, by joining with him, I could enjoy nature from a different vantage point, one I had never before known. The extent of the confidence he gave me can be measured with an African adventure that happened years later. In 1989, I took two mares and five former Maasai warriors and set up a camp in the Kenyan highlands where I wouldn't see another white face for five weeks. Those mares, Katie and Narok, provided me with an experience that few modern white men have enjoyed. As I recently wrote: "How could anyone, Hemingway and Blixen included, be disappointed with the view from the tent which Sekerot had provided me? To this setting, the mares Katie and Narok arrived like half expected lottery prizes. Bill Wheeler had purchased the gaunt Thoroughbreds near Lake Naivasha. From there he and Sekerot had ridden them down the Rift Valley and back across into the Loita Hills, where, had it not been for the veterinary supplies they carried, both animals, relentlessly bitten by tsetse flies, would have perished. Months later when they trotted into our camp, their bodies were still pebbled with welts.

"The company of animals, not people, was what we desired around camp, so the mares were welcome companions. Grazing in tall grass before the tent or on the other side of the stream, they were watched over, whispered and sung to by Moseka, a quietly handsome Tanzanian Maasai. In his care they seemed as unaware of danger from lions and leopards, whose pug marks tres-

passed their hoofprints, as if they had been pastured in some Sussex meadow. Elephants, however, did make the mares anxious. When an adolescent bull crashed and pulled branches, browsing across the stream from the corral, they fidgeted and snorted even under the quiet reassurance from Moseka, for whom they seemed to feel special trust and affection. Horse odors, neighs and nickers added another perspective to the camp, and I found fraternity and peace in their presence, as I have in the company of equines everywhere.

"On horseback, Sekerot and I explored the hills around camp, Moseka or Morkau leading on foot, spear-cutting the air, entrusted with detecting lion, elephant, or Cape buffalo in the thick cover through which we often passed. None of the Maasai who crossed our path had ever seen a horse. Most of the women and children ran away from our 'strange' beasts to gaze back in both wonderment and apprehension. More impressive was an entry into a Maasai settlement, people fleeing before the mares' approach, as the Aztecs surely scattered in the path of Cortez."

Of course it was dangerous to now and then leave my Maasai escort behind and dash across the savannah in company of the animals whose privacy I had invaded. Obviously a hungry lion would hardly distinguish between a fleeing zebra or a running horse, even with a man on its back. But the thrill that came from the experience was irresistible: "Sekerot saddled the mares and we set off at a trot, the hunter, spear in hand, in the lead and Morkau just behind the horses' tails. Once free of the stream's saplings and tangles, my heels touched the black mare into a canter. Zebra galloped off, angling to gaze back not only at the unfamiliar equines but at the men on their backs. Impala fled in soaring leaps. Topi stampeded by, rouge-slate flashes through a lattice of thorn, and ahead, giraffe loped from the horizon more as if to escape the rising sun than us."

The mares, especially Narok, offered the kind of company which at that time no human could have provided. Once, Sekerot and I took the horses, Morkau, and a one-man-tent, and rode to a salt-lick where we spent the night with the expectation of finding Cape buffalo in the morning. Of that experience I wrote: "With the approach of evening, a fine drizzle forced us inside the confines of the tent and almost extinguished our fire, which sparkled weakly in the horses' eyes. They would not spend tonight in the security of the corral, but in the open, where only Morkau's spears and torch could protect them from whatever lurked in the damp darkness. Hooded in a soggy blanket, Morkau stood guard, while Sekerot and I half slept. At five in the morning, I unzipped the tent flap and crawled out into the foggy pitch.

The rain had stopped, and to warm myself I half hung against the black mare's side, listening to her steady respiration while myself breathing the sweetness of horses nourished on fresh grass. When first light showed the way, I walked along a hill above the marsh and, with the binoculars, searched the high reeds for Cape buffalo."

Lions, however, were not only a threat on our rides, they also came into camp attracted by the smell of the horses: "'Sekerot,' I whispered. 'Sekerot.' He stirred as I raised my voice.' 'Lions. Lions.' Torch in one hand, the other unzipping the mosquito-netted door flap, my friend disappeared in a second to become no more than a faint shadow through the canvas of the tent. He and Moseka threatened the lions first with shouts, and then more strongly with beams of light, which generally are enough to frighten away lions in the night.

"The roaring ceased, and not until we were back in bed did a single call come from upstream, where the lions later killed a cow. Now calm, the horses, Katie and Narok, nickered softly from the corral, quieted by Moseka's Loita lullaby. Poor Narok. Little time would pass before lions would return, though now unannounced as Moseka slept, wrapped in a blanket, at the entrance to the prickly-thorn enclosure. A scruffy-maned male was the first to crash through the woven acacia branches, and before Sicona could spear it in the side, my favorite mare lay dead with her black neck broken."

Blanco may be thanked for embarking me on that African adventure with horses. If it hadn't been for the confidence that he instilled in me, I would have traveled only on foot and never on horseback through those glorious Kenyan highlands. However Blanco did not arouse in me the deep feelings that came from knowing another Andalusian, Majestad. As I loved Majestad, I have never loved another horse. For months after his death, I couldn't speak his name without becoming choked up. Majestad touched, as deeply as he did me, everyone who had the good fortune to know him. In the film, *The Last Remake of Beau Geste* he was ridden by the fine American actor James Earl Jones, who in several letters to John Fulton (the stallion's owner) expressed his desire to buy the horse and to take him to America, saying that never in his life had he been so moved by any living creature. It was at this time that Peter Ustinov became acquainted with Majestad and later wrote about him in my book *Stallion of a Dream*. Every year in the Sevilla Fair, when John rode his white stallion among thousands of other equestrians mounted on the finest Andalusian horses, it was Majestad who attracted the most attention.

Well past his prime when I photographed him for the books *Equus* and *Stallion of a Dream*, Majestad was in fine condition and had a youthful spirit. Some Spanish breeders felt that his head was too long for the modern Andalusian; however, it was that very length of head which, combined with his noble eye, made him even more appealing and romantic, reminiscent of the medieval horses that prance in the paintings of Madrid's Prado Museum. It is unfortunate that the reader could not have seen Majestad in movement, for he had such a high lift to his forelegs that he appeared to have been trained to walk in that manner.

In part it was Majestad who was responsible for my enthusiasm for doing the book *Equus*. He was the stallion that I used on the book's cover. It might be said that he was born for art and that he died for art. In the fall of 1977 I had taken him to an area just south of Sevilla for another shooting session, and it was there that he suffered a bad fall. Ten days later he was dead. The sadness of those of us who were close to him was in a way soothed by the knowledge that Majestad would continue to give joy to people all over the world. Happily, many persons have been thrilled, as I had been, by the sight of that white stallion in his field of red poppies. That picture has appeared in books and magazines, advertisements, and on postcards, greeting cards, note paper, calendars, posters, puzzles, and as limited-edition gallery prints. For as long as I could remember, his field each spring had been a mass of red blossoms. Since Majestad's death, not a single poppy has sprouted there.

As Majestad, Blanco and Narok continue to live in the pages of this book, so will the other horses whose stories are told here and whose images, interpreted by John Fulton, will continue to give horse lovers pleasure. The horses here are as special in different ways to their owners as those two white Spanish stallions and that black mare of Africa were to me. They represent twenty-three breeds. Some are living legends, others are champions, acclaimed for their beauty or athletic ability in the show ring. Others are horses of the heart. Each of them is special and for that reason it has been a pleasure to distinguish them. It thrills me to think that some child who read *Black Beauty* or the *Black Stallion*, will now, as an adult, be able to turn these pages and find his or her own horse a part of equine literature.

THE AMERICAN SADDLEBRED

All breeds have their enthusiasts, but American Saddlebreds seem to have some of the most impassioned followers. One look at the object of their affections and one can understand why.

Easily identified by its conformation and style, the American Saddlebred is considered one of the most beautiful horses existing in the world today. The high-stepping peacock of the show ring with long, arched neck blending into a deep, sloping shoulder, expressive eye and flaring nostrils offers action, intelligence, beauty, endurance, and a personality that endears it to owners and spectators.

Saddlebreds are known for their strong limbs, powerful hindquarters, and sloping pasterns, which make for a comfortable ride. They are intelligent, curious and alert horses, and have great presence, which contributes to their show image. They come in all colors.

America's oldest native breed dates back to the 1600s when British colonists brought in Galloway and Hobby Horses, small, hardy animals which were natural-gaited and comfortable to ride. Through selective breeding and crossing them to large, heavier-boned Dutch and French-Canadian horses, a superior animal called the Narragansett Pacer was developed in the colonies of Rhode Island and Virginia. Later, Thoroughbred blood was added for size and beauty. By 1776, an all-purpose riding horse, commonly called the American Horse, was recognized as a definite type.

Pioneers following Daniel Boone through the Cumberland Gap into Kentucky were mounted on these easy-gaited horses, and they played a major role in the settling of the Upper Ohio Valley. When the Civil War broke out, good saddle horses were highly sought after as military mounts by cavalrymen and officers of both armies. Saddlebreds served as the mounts of many famous generals.

In April, 1891, the American Saddlebred Horse Association was established in Louisville, Kentucky, the first publicly-held association established for an American breed of horse. Early emphasis in the registry remained on the easy gaits, the rack, slow-gait, running walk and fox trot. These easy gaits, inherited from the Narragansett Pacer, have given some Saddlebreds the ability to perform the rack, a quick, flashy gait in which each foot hits the ground separately, and the slow gait, similar to the rack, but not as fast. Although not all Saddlebreds are five-gaited, it is the performance of these two extra gaits that has given the Saddlebred its modern show horse image.

Most Saddlebreds trace to great horses of the past. Gaines Denmark, son of Denmark, a Thoroughbred foaled in 1839, established the noted Denmark family. Rex McDonald, a coal black stallion of Denmark breeding was foaled in 1890, and was such a sensation in the show ring that he was visited by United States Presidents and was one of the first Saddlebred horses admired by the general public. Bourbon King, of predominantly trotting blood, was a sensation as a five-gaited show stallion, winning the Grand Championship at the Louisville Show as a three-year-old. Bourbon King was the great progenitor of the Chief family.

Today there are an estimated 78,000 living Saddlebreds in the fifty States, Canada, and in many foreign countries. More than 1,000 horse shows in the U.S. and Canada offer classes for American Saddlebred show horses. Aside from the premiums paid out at these horse shows, added money programs of over $1 million dollars serve as an incentive to exhibitors.

Some of the most famous American Saddle show horses were Wing Commander, six times World's Grand Champion; My-My, also six times World's Five-Gaited Grand Champion; Bellisima, three times Three-Gaited World's Grand Champion; Sultan's Starina, five times Three-Gaited World's Grand Champion; The Lemon Drop Kid, four times Fine Harness World's Grand Champion; and Colonel Boyle, five times Fine Harness World's Grand Champion.

World Grand Champion Will Shriver wrote new horse show history during a four-year period when he defeated every horse he had shown against. He captured the Five-Gaited Stallion division and Grand Championship Stake at every major show in the United States and retired in 1976 to go into an even greater career as a breeding stallion.

Saddlebreds make excellent jumpers and endurance horses, superior carriage horses, and can even herd cattle. They were the first dressage horses in the United States, competing in "high school" classes in early horse shows, and their powerful implusion and elevated action still make them striking dressage horses. There are even classes for Saddlebred hunters. Saddlebreds' people-oriented attitude and intelligence make them wonderful pleasure mounts. My friend, actor William Shatner, has created a popular western country pleasure class for Saddlebreds.

The creation of man and nature in concert, the American Saddlebred is truly the horse that sprang from America's own soil.

Will Shriver

One of the good things that came about from this book was meeting people like Betty Weldon. Our friendship will be a lasting one. Quick-minded, determined, and with a strong sense of curiosity, she shares the two passions in my life, Africa and horses.

"I just love horses, and one in particular," she told me. "When Will Shriver won the Five-gaited World Championship in 1976, the most exciting night possible, horse people thought me literally crazy to move him from Kentucky and not stand him to the public. But Will was my most special friend. I wanted him with me. There is no way I can possibly explain the happiness that horses, Will Shriver, in particular, have given me."

Though still grieving six months after the loss of Will Shriver in August, 1991, it is the happiness and the excitement he brought her and the horse world at large that Betty Weldon remembers most.

Will Shriver leaves an exquisite image of kinetic perfection engraved on the minds of all who ever saw him. He thrilled audiences with his extreme, effortless motion, his true precise gaits, his exhilarating speed.

Called "a living legend that represents the ultimate ideals and standards of the Saddle Horse breed," he was foaled May 3, 1966 on the Weldon's farm, Callaway Hills Stables, near Jefferson City, Missouri. His sire was Johnny Gillen, son of the renowned Wing Commander; his dam, Fourth Estate, Mrs. Weldon's first show horse

Famed trainer Redd Crabtree of Crabtree Farms in Simpsonville, Kentucky, took charge of Will Shriver's training during the spring of 1972. They took to each other immediately, and with Crabtree's confidence in his greatness, Will Shriver at one time or another defeated every horse he ever showed against. He was an invincible force as he captured the Five-Gaited Stallion Division and Grand Championship Stake at every major show in the United States. He first became the World Champion Stallion in 1974 and repeated this victory the next two successive years. During an undefeated season in 1976, he proved his complete superiority over all five-gaited challengers.

Will Shriver was retired because there was really nothing left for him to win in the show arena. As the reigning World Five-Gaited Grand Champion, he was retired in a special ceremony at the American Royal Horse Show on November 20, 1976, marking the beginning of an even greater career as a breeding stallion. From 1984 on, he was the leading sire of five-gaited horses.

Will Shriver died on August 22, 1991 at the University of Missouri Equine Clinic at Columbia, after undergoing three surgeries in a three-month battle with colic.

"Will was not just a champion horse but so much more. He brought good to so many he touched, so many, many lives," Betty says.

In September, 1989, Will became the first horse to be inducted into the St. Louis National Charity Horse Show Hall of Fame, this at the same time his distinguished owner was inducted.

A special ceremony was held during the American Royal, on November 18, 1991, to honor his memory, and to celebrate the centennial of the American Saddlebred Horse.

Somehow, watching a videotape of the ceremony, the two occasions merge as one. Representing the Saddlebred breed at the American Royal Saddlebred Centennial ceremony were four World Champion Stallions, all sons of Will Shriver: Show Me Too, Callaway's Ghost Writer, Callaway's Blue Norther and Caramac. Fans were treated to a parade of more than twenty Saddlebred horses, all sired by Will Shriver, all competing in various divisions of the show.

Will's son, Callaway's New Look is the current Five-Gaited World's Grand Champion. He won this highest honor only two days after the death of Will Shriver.

Another honor occured in March, 1992, when David L. Howard, the publisher of *Who's Who In American Saddlebreds*, dedicated that year's edition of the 1986-1991 volume to CH Will Shriver. Because this honor is a reflection of the esteem in which Will is held by the industry's peers, it was very pleasing to Betty Weldon.

"I still have a dream with Will—that his offspring win all three divisions of the World Championship the same year. I don't think it ever hurts to dream," says the great lady who was the lamp to Will's brilliant light.

Fourth Estate

Fourth Estate's destiny was to be the first show horse of a great lady of the American Saddlebred Horse world, as well as the foundation mare of a modern Saddlebred dynasty.

Her owner, Mrs. William H. Weldon, then Betty Goshorn, saw her first real horse show when her riding instructor took a group to New York's Madison Square Garden.

Mrs. Weldon had gone on Virginia and Maryland hunts while in boarding school in Washington, D.C., where the stables were filled with Saddlebreds to be used by the students for recreation. "But this was different," she says. "My dreams got bigger and bigger. More than ever, I wanted an American Saddlebred show horse. The war came. I hurried through college in three years and for graduation from Mount Holyoke I asked Dad (Robert Charles Goshorn, owner of the Jefferson City newspapers and KWOS Radio), for enough money to buy a show horse.

Mrs. Weldon didn't pursue her dream until one year after graduating from college in 1944.

When she learned of the Kalarama Farm dispersal sale, held after the famous American Saddlebred sire, Kalarama Rex, died, Betty saved enough gas coupons – gas was rationed during the war – asked her mother and

a friend to accompany her, and set off for Kentucky.

"There was a broodmare I wanted – Pennypacker's Pride. She turned out to be dam of the dam of Yorktown, a renowned World Champion," Betty says.

Perhaps that was a portent foretelling the future, for Mrs. Weldon would become what she facetiously calls a "broodmareaholic." In time, she and her husband would own Callaway Hills Farm, one of the nation's major Saddlebred breeding operations.

But that particular gorgeous bluegrass day in 1944 ended with Betty's money still in her purse. The auction was very exciting, "but with all those men bidding, I was lost," she says.

Someone noticed Betty was a little dismayed and, when told why, suggested she visit George Gwinn's farm. "George is unquestionably the premier Saddlehorse salesman of all times," says Betty. "Once again, I was totally out of place with so many important people. George, always the true southern gentleman (n.y mother said he could out-Rhett Rhett Butler), treated me as though I were Mrs. Astor. I saw a beautiful deep seal brown yearling filly, Kalarama Khaki Kaper. I knew I must have her. She was the answer to my dream. Her price, $3,000, was all I had to spend. Later I learned it was something to dicker George down, which I did, to $2,500. I renamed the filly Fourth Estate." (The name was chosen in honor of the public press; Mr. and Mrs. William Weldon own the News Tribune Company and KRCG television in Jefferson City, Missouri.)

Foaled on June 6, 1943, Fourth Estate would live to 1960. Her bloodlines were those of some of the greatest. Both her sire, Kalarama Rex and her dam Lauradell, go back four times in four generations to Rex McDonald, the great black Saddlebred foundation sire.

"After Bill and I were married, we bred Fourth Estate and Kate Shriver (a mare my father had purchased) to the world-renowned CH Wing Commander. Kate did not get in foal, but Fourth Estate did, and presented us with a colt, Callaway's Johnny Gillen," Betty recounts.

Johnny, a spectacular five-gaited horse and considered one of the best sons of CH Wing Commander, was eventually bred to Kate. They had two World Champions, the first a gelding named after Mrs. Weldon's father, Rob Shriver. The second, foaled in 1966, was named Will Shriver. He would become one of the greatest Saddlebred show horses the show ring would ever see.

Fourth Estate did have her own show career as an outstanding walk-trot or three-gaited horse, shown by professional trainer, Garland Bradshaw. "She was a gutsy mare. Always ready to show at any time, always winning a ribbon," says Betty. "Probably Will Shriver inherited much of his courage from her. She was so special."

Kate Shriver

The second great show horse in Mrs. William H. Weldon's life was Kate Shriver. Despite her own outstanding record in the ring, Kate will be best remembered in history as the dam of the legendary five-gaited World's Grand Champion Stallion, Will Shriver.

The bright chestnut mare, foaled May 29, 1945, was a daughter of Anacacho Denmark and Reverie's Desdemona.

Writing about Anacacho Denmark in his article, "Great Show Horses of the Past," Lance Phillips said, "Certainly one of the greatest mares to ever wear fine harness was his daughter, Kate Shriver."

Kate was sold, over the phone, by George Gwinn, the premier American Saddlebred salesman, to Betty Weldon's father, Robert Charles Goshorn, who named the filly after his mother.

Kate was precocious, winning her first World Championship in fine harness as a two-year-old, in 1947. She won the Junior World's Championship the following year as a three-year-old, a title usually won by four-year-olds.

After Kate entered the show ring for the first time and made her impact, her younger full brothers, Oman's Desdemona Denmark, Clarma, and Ridgefield Denmark were not shown, but put to stud, says Betty Weldon.

Kate also won the Fine Harness Stake at the Kentucky State Fair in 1949 as a four-year-old, and then went on to become the Fine Harness World's Grand Champion, with Garland Bradshaw showing.

Garland Bradshaw, in fact, showed Kate to all her wins, though several times Betty drove her at his farm. "I never wanted to show her myself, as I knew I couldn't be good enough, and I wanted top show horses," explains Betty who says she can't come up with a formula for her success, "But, oh my, I've had my dreams and most of them have been about horses—American Saddlebreds.

"I don't remember when I didn't want a horse," she says. "Finally, when I was ten years old, my father bought me a registered Saddlebred from an old trainer in California, Missouri. I was so excited! And to top it off, she was going to have a baby—wonder of wonders! When the great day arrived and Astral Pat had her foal, guess what he was—a good Missouri mule! The seller, of course, wanted it back and knew all along that mules were more valuable than horses. We had lots of fun together, Pat and I, riding everywhere, but I still had dreams of a real show horse. How I even started to dream such dreams, I have no idea. The only horse show I can remember was one in a circular ring, I believe in Jefferson City, long before I got Pat."

Kate seemed the stairway to those dreams, but was only the prologue to the main event, and her brilliant

show career ended when she foundered.

Rob Shriver, Kate's first foal by Johnny Gillen, was a World Champion. Her second foal, a full sibling, was the great Will Shriver.

Kate was a very aloof mare, Betty recalls, not the friendliest, but very beautiful and very sensitive.

One of Betty's favorite anecdotes concerns Kate. "I had another mare at this time," she says. "I bought her myself, the same way Dad bought Kate. Her name was Star Final (a newspaper term, referring to a special edition), and when she won the Two-Year-Old Kentucky Futurity, the judge, Jack Thompson, said to me, 'She's almost as pretty as you are, Betty.' However, when Kate won championships, Jack teased, 'You're not as pretty as she is.'"

Kate lived to age thirty. She died in 1975, the week following an exciting win by Will Shriver at the American Royal Horse Show in Kansas City. At that time, the Weldons were living most of the time in Virginia, and Betty has always regretted not being at Callaway Hills Farm with Kate during her last days.

"So different from Will's last days," she reminisces. "There were never any regrets at any time about Will."

Callaway's Johnny Gillen

From about 1950 until 1974, Mrs. William H. Weldon was out of the horse business for a number of reasons. Among them, she was setting up her television station in Jefferson City, Missouri, getting married, and starting a family. She even sold a World Champion Five-Gaited gelding, Garrymoore, to buy a camera for her television station. But she kept the two mares, Fourth Estate and Kate Shriver.

She bred them both to CH Wing Commander, one of the greatest of five-gaited champions, and a true crowd-thriller belonging to Dodge Stables. Kate did not catch, but Fourth Estate did.

On May 18, 1959, Fourth Estate produced a dark chestnut colt.

Betty's husband remarked to her that the colt should be worth a lot of money. "Heaven forbid!" thought

Betty, who did not want to sell. Thinking quickly, she named the colt after her husband's best friend who had just died–Johnny Gillen. "What better name for the colt," she asks. The colt, of course, remained at Callaway Hills.

Callaway's Johnny Gillen was considered one of the better sons of Wing Commander. He was a spectacular five-gaited horse for trainer Dale Pugh, but was shown close to home. He won the five-gaited stake at the Iowa State Fair in 1967 and the stallion stake at the Illinois State Fair the same year, beating the reigning World's Champion Stallion, Young America.

Johnny Gillen was not extensively patronized and sired only sixty-seven registered foals, which must make him one of the highest percentage Saddlehorse sires ever.

His first foal arrived in 1963, CH Rob Shriver, out of Kate Shriver. Bred to Johnny Gillen again, Kate produced a colt that was to become one of the greatest sires of five-gaited horses of all time–Will Shriver, foaled May 3, 1966.

Will Shriver sired the ASHA Champions CH Coming Up Big and CH April Hill's Red Gold; his daughter, Ballerina's Wingover was the dam of CH Admiral's Mark, and another daughter, Gillen's Fairy Gold, produced CH City Glitter. Other show horses by Johnny Gillen are Jeannie Gillen, Gillen's Bewitched, The Peanut Vendor, Captain Gillen, and Palmer's Johnny Stonewall.

Callaway's Johnny Gillen did leave his own unique mark on the world, as the model for the Saddlebred stamp in the postal series issued in 1985. The series was Betty Weldon's idea. "At least I came up with the idea for the Quarter Horse, the Saddlebred and the Morgan," she says. "Roy Andersen, the artist, had a very difficult time getting the Saddlebred to look the way we thought a Saddlebred should look, and believe it or not, they even destroyed a plate to start over. The stamps were at that time, and I think still are, the most popular stamps ever printed.

"Johnny Gillen was never as well-known as his son but he will never be forgotten as the sire of Will Shriver," says Betty.

Looking back on all the various influences in her life, she says, "They have been first, my faith; next my family, in particular my Dad, Mom and my husband, Bill; then my interest and enthusiasm for the media, particularly the printed daily; my love of animals; and last, but not least, my education. None of whatever success I have had would have been likely without my education." Her advice to others includes the admonition: "Don't forget to dream–dreams do come true. Reach for the stars, and you may reach the moon." Which could be a metaphor for what she achieved in breeding horses–first Johnny Gillen and then Will Shriver.

Callaway's Blue Norther

Mrs. William Weldon has many outstanding horses, but Callaway's Blue Norther is one of her special favorites. The five-gaited chestnut stallion was named by the Weldon's daughter, Lenore, after a Texas storm.

"Callaway's Blue Norther is a prominent son and the prime representative of Will Shriver, along with other well-known sons, Caramac and Show Me Too," says Betty Weldon. Caramac, says Betty Weldon, "is more Will's color, dark liver chestnut. But Blue is most like him."

During the final three years of Will Shriver's life, "Blue" was his "roommate," stalled opposite him in the two-stall barn where Will lived for twelve years.

"Before Blue moved into Will's barn, various horses were placed opposite Will," says Betty Weldon recalling an incident that testifies to their singular relationship and Will's character. "At one point there was another stallion and one morning, a groom somehow released them both at the same time. Of course a fight started. I'm sure not by Will. Fortunately I was there and heard everyone yelling for me. I ran calling, 'Will, come to me this instant!' He did and I held on to him while the other horse was caught."

Blue Norther won the 1984 Five-Gaited World Championship as a three-year-old at the Kentucky State Fair World Championship Horse Show held in Louisville, Kentucky, and the American Saddlebred Three-Year-Old Sweepstakes in Charleston, West Virginia. As a four-year-old, he won the Junior Five-Gaited World Championship at the World Championship Horse Show in Louisville, Kentucky.

"Blue is the first of Will's sons to have had a colt that broke all sales records," Mrs. Weldon notes. Blue Norther's son, Callaway's Blue Moon, broke all of the records for a yearling sold at public auction, when he sold for $49,000 at the Tattersalls Summer Sale in July, 1989.

"Will's get broke all sales records at all major saddle horse sales. So far these records have not been broken," she adds.

"Caramac and Show Me Too are also following in their sire's footsteps as they each have sired horses who were World Champions at the 1991 World Championship Horse Show. Caramac sired Callaway's Carnelian, two-year-old Fine Harness World Champion, and Caramen Miranda, Junior Fine Harness World Champion. Show Me Too sired Show Me The Best, Ladies' Three-Gaited World Champion."

Two prospective champions by Will Shriver, Callaway's Gold Rush and Callaway's Capital News, are currently in training with the renowned Redd Crabtree in Kentucky.

"We are standing Will's sons to the public but Will never was (offered to the public)," says Mrs. Weldon.

"Will was bred only to Callaway Hills Stables mares — unique in our business. "One might say I became a 'broodmareaholic.' I purchased mares based on old time breeding — what I knew when I first started in the 1940s."

Standing at stud at Callaway Hills Stables, the largest breeding farm of American Saddlebred Horses in the nation, located north of Jefferson City, Missouri are the stallions Blue Norther, Caramac, Show Me Too, Ghost Writer, and Non Pareil, all sired by Will.

"We are looking to a future filled with many more champions that are either sons and daughters of Will Shriver, or sired by sons of Will Shriver," says Mrs. Weldon.

Callaway's New Look

Judy Shepherd of Hollywood, California told me she has been actively and successfully involved in the showing of American Saddlebreds since she was a small child. However, it was not until August, 1991, that her greatest dream – and what a dream! – became a reality, when her horse, CH Callaway's New Look was awarded the breed's most prestigious honor, World's Grand Champion Five-Gaited Horse at the World Championship Horse Show in Louisville, Kentucky.

That event took place only one month after Judy became New Look's owner. To make the story even more remarkable, the horse was showing in the five-gaited division for the first time. Ridden by professional trainer, Bob Gatlin, that fateful night, New Look challenged a tough field of thirteen horses in one of the largest five-gaited stakes in history.

With the absence of the two-time champion, Man On The Town, the Championship was wide open.

In a grueling three-horse work-off with Santana Lass and Unattached, the bright chestnut gelding with the big white blaze exhibited true show horse qualities which well warranted the title bestowed upon him. He emerged the victor, his amazing stamina and game attitude carrying him to the top, where he may well stay for some time to come.

New Look finished the 1991 season in the open division with the Grand Champion title at the National Horse Show at Meadowlands.

Foaled April 9, 1985, this horse is definitely a credit to his breeding. His sire was the great 1976 Five-Gaited World Grand Champion Will Shriver. Will's grandsire, and New Look's great grandsire, was the immortal Wing Commander who reigned supreme from 1948 through 1953, and was one of the most prolific sires of show ring champions.

New Look's dam was Look of Love, a gifted daughter of World Champion Fine Harness horse Colonel Boyle, a winner for the Arthur Simmons Stables for many seasons and, after retirement, a sire of a number of fine show horses.

"This breeding produced beauty, talent and attitude and remarkable show horse ways," says Judy.

Bred at Callaway Hills in Missouri, "New Look was shown extremely well in the young horse division," she adds.

In May, 1989, he was sold to the Asphalt Driveway Company of St. Paul, Minnesota. His owner/rider, Scott Smith, showed him successfully to a multitude of championship ribbons in the five-gaited amateur division. With his expressive eye and extravagant motion, New Look became a crowd-pleaser in numerous show rings around the country.

Judy had been absent from the horse world for twelve years, returning several years ago with renewed enthusiasm. Under the guidance of trainer Donna Moore, she purchased a number of promising young horses, the most recent of which was the six-year old New Look.

Now at home at Belle Reve Farm in Versailles, Kentucky, New Look and Judy are being prepared by Donna Moore as an amateur team to debut in the spring of 1992.

"Having ridden gaited horses most of my life, never before have I experienced the power, exhilaration, and excitement that this truly talented and remarkable horse so possesses," says Judy. "His wonderfully kind and loving disposition is as apparent under saddle as it is in his stall when he is boisterously begging for a peppermint.

"It is every horseman's dream to own a great horse. I am blessed to have one," she adds, and there's not much more one can add to that amen.

CH Santana Lass

"The most exciting horse I have ever ridden," Mary Gaylord of Golden Creek Farm in Simpsonville, Kentucky says of CH Santana Lass. This singularly talented and popular five-gaited American Saddlebred mare is a ten-year-old liver chestnut with a star. Probably the prettiest mare showing today, a real crowd-pleaser. "Everyone likes her," says Mary, one of America's most outstanding amateur exhibitors of both Saddlebreds and Hackney ponies.

CH Santana Lass has won nine World Championships and has been the Reserve World's Grand Champion the past two years. The combination of her brilliance and beauty have made her the queen of the ladies-to-ride division, where the judging is based on performance, manners and quality.

"Redd Crabtree, my trainer, showed her when she was three and four," Mary says. "I showed her in ladies' competition until 1990, then I showed her myself in open competition, against professional trainers." CH Santana Lass' sensational speed, thrusting trot and powerful rack, made her a legitimate contender in the tough open championship competition.

Sired by Sultan's Santana, 1981 World's Grand Champion Fine Harness, CH Santana Lass was foaled in 1982. She is out of Miss Blarney, who was sired by CH Irish American, the 1973 World's Champion Five-Gaited Stallion. Both sire and dam trace closely to Genius Bourbon King, a stallion noted for his great beauty.

CH Santana Lass was bred and raised by Thomas Galbreath at Castle Hills Farm in Versailles, Kentucky. She was initially trained by Steve Joyce who showed her for the first time at the River Ridge Horse Show in Columbus, Ohio, where she won her three-year-old five-gaited class with a spectacular performance.

"CH Santana Lass was always special," recalls Galbreath. "She knew she was different from the others, and she was always game in her training, as well as intelligent and cooperative."

The renowned Redd Crabtree of Simpsonville, Kentucky, purchased CH Santana Lass for Mary, as his client, shortly after that spectacular show debut as a three-year-old. Under Redd's direction, the mare has left a trail of glory and blue ribbons wherever she goes.

In her three-year-old year, CH Santana Lass won the junior five-gaited mare class at the Lexington Junior League Horse Show, and the World's Championship at the Kentucky State Fair for three-year-old five-gaited mares, plus the National Sweepstakes. She was shown by Mary for the first time that year at the Pin Oak Charity Horse Show in Houston, Texas, where they won the novice five-gaited class.

As a four-year-old, CH Santana Lass was a winner at Lexington, Louisville, and the American Royal in Kansas City, and then topped the National Sweepstakes with her total winnings of nearly $30,000.

The next year, CH Santana Lass was shown exclusively by Mary in ladies' classes, winning eight blue ribbons at the nation's largest, most competitive shows and ultimately crowned World's Champion Ladies Five-Gaited Mare.

By 1991, CH Santana Lass and Mary were seasoned and formidable contenders in open five-gaited competition. They were unbeaten in mare classes and championships at the Oklahoma Centennial, Midwest Charity, American Royal and Indiana State Fair shows. They topped the mare stake at Louisville to win the World's Champion Five-Gaited Mare title, and were again Reserve in the World's Grand Championship.

Mary Gaylord is a native of Oklahoma City, Oklahoma, and grew up showing Saddlebreds on the Southwest Circuit. It is no surprise Mary can hold her own against the pros, as at the age of thirty-six she has been showing for thirty years.

Whatever the future holds, Mary's dedication and perseverance and CH Santana Lass' beauty and brilliance make them a pair to remember in American Saddlebred show history.

The Groomsman

It all began as a lark on a cold, damp and dreary winter's day in Kentucky. World-famous trainer Don Harris was showing Heather Greenbaum and her daughter Julie some of his horses, when he half-jokingly asked them, "Would you like to see the next Junior Three-Gaited World Champion?"

Well, what would you say to a question like that? Heather, of course, responded yes. "From that moment, Julie and I were so taken with him that we had eyes for no other horse," Heather recalls. "All the way home, he was the only horse we could think and talk about. He truly had the poise, elegance, and most of all, the talent of a World Champion. He was by far the most incredible horse we had ever seen."

The 16-hand bay four-year-old gelding was named The Groomsman, and is known as "Mr. G." to his friends. (Another nickname is "The Hackney" because of his superb action.)

Mr. G. was foaled June 16, 1987, sired by the multi-champion Harlem Globetrotter and out of the mare Belle Supreme, a winning combination, as he has World Champion siblings.

"Don Harris had just purchased the horse and was

not at all anxious to sell him, because he had such confidence he WOULD be the next World Champion," says Heather.

Forty-eight hours later the Greenbaums made Don an offer on the horse, and he reluctantly accepted on one condition – that Mr. G. stay in his barn so he could show him at the World Championship Show in Louisville in August.

At River Ridge, Mr. G.'s first show prior to the World Championship, he was a show stopper. He took home the blue ribbon and was written up in all the magazines as the "awesome new three-gaited horse," an auspicious start.

At Louisville, he won the Open 15.2 and Over Junior Three-Gaited Class, then came back four days later and won the Junior Three-Gaited World Championship in a nerve-tingling four-horse work-off.

"From that moment on, my daughter and I decided that owning horses of that quality was in our blood. World Champion stock was the way we were going to go," says Heather.

Mr. G. is now at the Greenbaum's Emerald Hills Ranch in Scottsdale, Arizona, a training, breeding and boarding facility for American Saddlebreds and Hackney Ponies. The farm, founded in 1987, has increased Saddlebred awareness in Arizona, a state traditionally associated with Arabian horses.

Mr. G. is a showy animal in the ring – one of his distinguishing characteristics is a long beautiful neck sharply delineated by his mane roached in three-gaited style. "He sets his neck back so it looks as though it is in the rider's lap," says Heather.

Yet, he is as gentle as a lamb in his stall. "He loves to put his head on your lap if you catch him lying down, and he sticks his head through the opening in his door, hoping to catch kisses or treats," she says.

"Mr. G. has gone above and beyond all of our equine dreams," adds Heather. I've been in love with horses forever." On every childhood occasion, when she was asked what she wanted for a present, the answer was always the same: "A horse!" So her parents gave her a whole herd of them, plastic, wooden, stuffed or metal, but never the flesh and snorts kind.

"They claimed they could afford the horse, but not to feed it," she says. "It wasn't until I was thirty-five years old that my husband surprised me with my first horse, a five-gaited chestnut American Saddlebred. She was the start of my equine career.

"Horses have been and always will be a major part of my life," she says, "but Mr. G. will always have a special place in my heart as our first World Champion. Through Mr. G. I learned that going with your initial 'gut instinct' is usually correct," concludes Heather.

Kiwi

Bill Field was judging the St. Louis National Horse Show the first time he saw Kiwi. The bay American Saddlebred gelding was entered in the Newmarket Two-Year-Old Division. (Yearlings purchased in a select sale are eligible for the Newmarket.)

"I thought," and most of the judges agreed, "that he was the most outstanding horse in that division," continues Bill. "However, his mistakes made it impossible to tie him first, so he was placed second."

"The next time I was aware of Kiwi was when a client brought me a videotape of another American Saddlebred he was showing in the Lexington Junior League Horse Show," Bill recalls. "While viewing the video, I kept catching glimpses of Kiwi on the tape. He looked sensational; however, he was still making the mistakes that had defeated him as a two-year-old. The third time I saw Kiwi was at the American Royal Horse Show in Kansas City that same year. In the Three-Year-Old UPHA Five-Gaited Classic finals, he made the kind of show it would take to win but again, mistakes kept him from winning. At that time my father, John Field, said he thought Kiwi was worth all of the other horses in the ring."

In 1988, Field, who trains for Dr. and Mrs. Donald Petit of Arrowcrest Farm in Aurora, Oregon, lost a grand horse, Bluegrass Attraction, due to an unfortunate accident.

"Betty Petit asked me to find a replacement horse," he says. "I had no idea where to look for such a horse. But while in Minnesota judging a show I saw a horse that reminded me of Kiwi.

"After the show, I arranged to fly to Kentucky to see Kiwi. Trainer Ed Teater, and his son, Martin, had Kiwi in grand order when I arrived. As Ed stepped on Kiwi, I knew from the first step that this was the horse Betty Petit and I had been looking for. I called Mrs. Petit to tell her about Kiwi, and she and I flew to Kentucky that same week to look at the horse. Her response was the same as mine – love at first sight. As we got in the car to return to the airport, Betty turned to me and said, 'This is the horse I want.' I turned the car around, we went back to the barn, and we purchased Kiwi that day."

Kiwi was shipped to California in late August to prepare him for the California Saddlebred Futurity Horse Show in September. Although Kiwi was just four years old, Field decided to show him out of his age group, feeling that he would not be challenged in the junior class. Kiwi won the Five-Gaited Stallion or Gelding Stake.

"Rob Tanner, a California trainer, told me later that he thought I had lost my mind when I bought Kiwi," says Bill. "He had looked at Kiwi several times, but thought he would never be consistent enough to make the kind of show he had just witnessed."

Since that first outing with Bill, Kiwi has won five-gaited championships at CARES, the Hollywood Horse Show, Monterey Springfest, Del Mar National, Santa Barbara Horse Show, California Saddlebred Futurity, Cow Palace, and Winterfest, along with wins in Oregon, Washington and Indiana. He is now an ASHA Champion, a rating based on a point system.

Kiwi's greatest accomplishment, however, was at the Charity Fair Horse Show in 1988 when Betty Petit qualified him in the amateur five-gaited class.

"Because we were also showing Warrick Warrior, who had won that event, we saw no reason to show both horses in the amateur stake," says Bill. Without anyone's knowledge, I entered Kiwi in the Championship Stake with Mrs. Petit riding. We felt that this was probably going to be one of the best championship classes the West Coast had seen in a long time, and we believed that Kiwi would create his own destiny. Three World Champions were in the ring, and Mrs. Petit was riding against some of the best professional horse trainers in the business.

"From the time Kiwi and Betty stepped into the ring, it was obvious they were in a class of their own. Betty and Kiwi captured the championship that night," says Bill Field. "That win will always be one of my fondest memories."

Commander's Cadence

"To know him is to love him!" says Shirley S. Hoffman of Commander's Cadence, her five-gaited American Saddlebred stallion, describing the high every horseperson feels when they experience their horse as beauty in motion.

"When turned out at liberty, without restraints, he is 'The Showman.' He moves through the air like he was suspended – jumping and diving as if he were on strings like a marionette, trotting several inches above ground level and then coming to an abrupt stop, perhaps only two feet in front of his observer, setting his body in the traditional Saddlehorse 'park' stand and snorting at the viewer as if to say 'Here I am. Look at me!!!' Then almost immediately, taking off again, trotting as if floating on a

cloud, around the arena again to repeat his presentation, over and over and over, as long as you are willing to watch him. Everytime he is presented, no matter what the situation, he shows like no other horse can show," says Shirley.

He comes by it naturally. Foaled April 8, 1978, he is sired by Uptown Commander, a Wing Commander son, twice number one on the Saddle & Bridle Futurity Sire Rating list, and out of Lady Elsinore, a Supreme Sultan daughter. Commander's Cadence had the special distinction of being number six on the Saddle & Bridle Sire Rating list himself in 1989, out of 350 sires showing futurity get.

As a weanling and two-year-old, he was a champion in Iowa, Minnesota, and Illinois, showing against some of the very best. He holds the distinction of being the only two-year-old in the nation to have won all three divisions – fine harness, walk-trot, and halter – in the 1980 Iowa State Fair. In 1984, he was the National Champion "In Hand" Stallion at the American Royal Horse Show in Kansas City. All in all, through his career he has accumulated over sixty blue ribbons and championships.

"Cadence became the 'crowd-pleaser.' When he entered the ring, the crowd delighted in seeing him because they grew to know him as the ultimate champion he is. We reveled in his victories for years," says Shirley, who bought him in 1990.

Cadence's offspring, over one hundred to date, "are winners and winners and winners," she says. "Their biggest successes have been in halter. Generally he has at least one or two champions each year in the Colorado National Show Horse, Half-Arab and Saddlebred halter futurity classes, in itself quite a record. He was one of the first American Saddlebred sires to be nominated as a National Show Horse Sire and one of the first to be nominated to the American Saddlebred Grand National, the Saddlebred incentive program.

"Most importantly, Cadence is a model of excellence!" says Shirley. "He has taught so many people what the breed is all about. He shows himself in a way no human could show him, racing and diving and moving with the wind as he lets you know that he is The Best. He passes all this on to his young ones, plus lots of heart, as well as a strong, confident attitude."

Today, he relaxes in his own outdoor paddock at HiView Acres in Longmont, Colorado, awaiting the next visitors so that he can strut his stuff.

"We are lucky to have this great gentleman in our presence and we are proud to have the opportunity to show him and his youngsters to the world as some of the finest examples of the American Saddlebred breed. He is a true showman in every sense of the word," concludes Shirley.

Commander O'Lee

Commander O'Lee's sad, untimely death may lead to a new chance at life for others.

He was "a horse of a different kind," says Shirley Hoffman of HiView Acres in Longmont, Colorado. "Affectionate, sensitive, a friend, a companion, important to our lives, he left us with a special memory of a horse that came to us unhappy and left us with a legacy."

Commander O'Lee had the breeding which usually leads to a stellar show ring career. Foaled May 14, 1977 on the Missouri farm of Jess and Marjorie Bain, he was a grandson of Wing Commander, one of America's greatest show horses and one of the important contributors to the bloodlines most revered in the American Saddlebred breed. His sire was the Bains' stallion, Bainridge Commander; and his dam, Jubilee's Princess.

A lovely liver chestnut, on the black side of brown, with an elegant silver and gold mane and a tail that swept the ground, he had the look and the stance of the immortal Wing Commander.

He was left a stallion until he was four years old, then gelded and put through a big Saddlebred sale in the Midwest. "And so he came to us lonely and lost and wondering," says Shirley. "Barely broken,...with a deep frown of wrinkles on his forehead, he was very concerned about life – his life in particular. But as he and my daughter Sherri (Cooper) became important friends, he learned to trust and be trusted and to have friends, too."

His first year at HiView was "disastrous" for both Sherri and O'Lee. "He tried, and she tried, and they just couldn't get it together. But their friendship deepened through those difficult times and that friendship is the most precious thing that has survived."

O'Lee finally became settled in, and he and Sherri went in and out of the show ring, exploring different avenues, divisions, and classes, but he never quite found himself.

"At the time that O'Lee and Sherri were showing, the Saddlebred shows did not include the Country Pleasure Division, which is where he would have been best suited to perform," says Shirley.

On the other hand, he did excel in the "family pet division."

"He loved little children and so had lots of opportunity to have 'little people' on his back, in between his legs and on the ground under him!!" says Shirley. "He was patient and loving and my grandson, Brady, referred to him as 'his horse.' But he really and truly was EVERY child's horse."

All this was cut short when O'Lee died "in a tragic training accident, leaving behind lots and lots of sorrow." Shirley and her family would never have healed that wound, except for sublimating the pain in something positive. Out of their love for him and his special memory, they created the non-profit Large Animal Assistance Foundation to assist large animal veterinary teaching facilities in obtaining supplemental equipment that they could not otherwise afford.

"At the time of his illness and death, it would have helped us tremendously if we could have scanned his brain to see what was really going on inside," says Shirley, but the means was not available.

The Hoffmans' devoted veterinarian, Dr. Rick LeCouteur of Australia, on service at the Colorado State University Veterinary Teaching Hospital diagnosed O'Lee as having a brain anomaly which caused dementia and ultimately his death. Through this experience, they learned of the desperate need in veterinary teaching schools for special equipment.

Through O'Lee, Shirley and her family also learned something about horses as individuals. "O'Lee taught us that there are many facets to the American Saddlebred horse. He taught us that there are pleasure horses and show horses and children's horses and special pets and loved ones in our animal world, as well as our human world. O'Lee gave us so much that we feel we need to return that love and devotion by doing for other deserving large animals," says Shirley.

O'Lee also has a brick in his memory in Phase I of the sidewalk at the American Saddlebred Horse Association, in the Kentucky Horse Park at Lexington, Kentucky.

Sultan's Santana

When Mrs. Martha Siekman bought a weanling son of Supreme Sultan in 1970, her daughter Faffie asked that the striking red chestnut colt be re-named Sultan's Santana, after a popular music group of the time.

And so began a relationship which, like a favorite, never-forgotten song, survived the silence of a long separation and now plays on in Faffie's life.

Sultan's Santana had won a World's Championship in Fine Harness as a three-year-old in 1973 and was already on the way up in the National Horseman and Saddle & Bridle Futurity Sire Ratings, when the need to reflect a profit for taxes dictated his sale.

Santana would pick up the World Grand Championship in Fine Harness in 1981 for his new owner, Tom Galbreath, and establish frequent residence in the upper registers of the Futurity and Performance ratings. The following year he became the first American Saddlebred stallion to sell for more than $1 million.

When Martha Siekman died prematurely in 1980, Faffie was married to Juan Carlos Romero, an accomplished university professor in Guanajuato, Mexico,

where they had begun to raise a large family. "I'm not me if I don't have a horse in my life," Faffie has said, and she took up where her mother had left off, selectively combing the remaining herd to fine-tune her own breeding program. She incorporated the Siekman stallions Good Spirits, Lunar Fire GS, and Sultan's Magician, but through the years she remembered Santana.

Faffie often recalled her best moments with Santana—at the Lexington Horse Show and the World Championships at Louisville, when he became a champion as a young horse.

One day on a walk in the hills near her home, she came upon a picturesque village. Learning that its name was Santana, she had a premonition that she would once again own her favorite stallion, even though there was no reason to believe he would ever be available to her. Then in 1989, Santana was offered for sale, and he came home.

He is now owned by Rancho Romero of Appleton, Wisconsin and Guanajuato, Mexico. Because of his popularity, Faffie elected to leave him at Stallion Avenue in Shelbyville, Kentucky under the direction of George Haydon. There, this gorgeous peacock of a stallion, who embodies the striking beauty of his breed, has his own personal rooster named Juan Carlos after Mrs. Romero's husband. Santana shares his feed and water buckets with his feathered friend.

Sultan's Santana has proven himself equal to the dream. One of those rare stallions that reach the top in the show ring and then pass on their capabilities to their offspring, his most lasting reputation is in his consistent siring of world class show horses.

Ranked No. 1 Sire on the Saddle & Bridle Performance Rating in 1983, 1987 and 1988, and No. 2 in 1989, Sultan's Santana was also the No. 1 Sire of World's Champions in 1989 and 1990. Among his World's Champion get in 1990 and 1991 are Reserve World Grand Champion and World Champion Santana Lass; World Champion CH Moses, World Champion Santana's Charm, World Champion Cocoamotion, World Champion Stoneview's Sensation, World Champion Santana's Flair, World Champion Spanish Santana, World Champion Take Heart, Reserve World Champion Revival, World Champion Santana Sweetheart, and Mystical Mood, the 1991 World's Champion in Two-Year-Old Fine Harness.

Sultan's Santana's stakings include the Kentucky Futurity, the National Three-Year-Old Futurity, the American Saddlebred Grand National and the Breeders Jackpot. As a final testimony to his excellence, more than a few of his sons are establishing themselves as sires of outstanding show horses.

As a champion and a sire, Sultan's Santana is at the top of the charts.

Sultan's Great Day

When Bill Shatner first saw Sultan's Great Day at Donna Moore's stable in Lexington, he was aware that he was looking at a once-in-a-lifetime horse.

"I saw him in a twelve-by-twelve stall," he says. "He was looking through the bars, black as pitch, his eyes bright with excitement, and he neighed. I knew that if it was at all earthly possible, I wanted that horse to be mine."

Not long after that, Sultan's Great Day became the leading horse at Belle Reve, Bill and Marcy Shatner's burgeoning Lexington farm. The black stallion was first shown in competition at age two, winning his Two-Year-Old and Three-Year-Old World Championships in quick succession. During this time, Bill had the "privilege" of putting his hands on the reins and guiding his new stallion a few turns here and there in the cart, but no one had ridden the horse. The Shatners then took Sultan's Great Day out of the show ring and put him in the breeding shed.

"He became the fountainhead of all the beautiful colts and fillies that emerged from Belle Reve," says Bill. "But my love for him has nothing to do with his ability to put his stamp on every one of his foals, so that they emerged with his eyes, neck, head, forefront, hock action, and overall balance. No, it had more to do with the horse than that. It had to do with the feeling of awe at his regal spirit – the caged monarch. You see, I've always been torn between the extraordinary wildness, strength, and freedom that a horse has and the necessity of putting him in a stall and of restraining him with reins, bridles, saddles and carts. I have to ask myself, 'Where else would he have gone? What else would he have been?'

"The romantic notion of turning him out into the world so that he could stand at the crest of a mountain, backlit by the sun, with his mane blowing in the wind is just that, a romance. In reality, I know he would never survive.

"So it is with dual nature that I look at this magnificent king when I see him in Kentucky, penned up, restrained, shrouded. This noblest of all horses stays in his palace without being able to really move until he is taken out to be worked or bred, and then the magic of Great Day is apparent. In those brief moments each morning, Great Day comes out of his stall like a king emerging from a castle and he is monarch of all that he sees. His neck is proud, his head high, his eyes flashing."

Bill now occasionally rides Sultan's Great Day in the indoor arena, as well as on an outdoor track. However, one of his most thrilling moments with his black stallion was the day he took him for a ride into the woods. "He and I together," says Bill. "I, fearful and apprehensive

that he might do something that a stallion would find natural, and he, apprehensive of rocks, bushes and streams, things that he had rarely, if ever, seen. But between us, there was an understanding, and between us, there IS an understanding. I cannot imagine my love affair with horses going on without my relationship with Sultan's Great Day."

And I cannot imagine my own life without knowing horses like that magnificent black stallion, or without the people who own and love them, like Bill and Marcy Shatner, for my friends.

Winter Sultan

Winter Sultan is everything for which the American Saddlebred is so well-known: flashy, talented, a real showoff, smooth as silk to ride and very kind in temperament. Added to this classic breed charisma is his striking two-tone coat of dark liver chestnut and white, for Winter Sultan is a tobiano pinto.

"Spotted" has become the color of success for Winter Sultan and his owner, Nancy Sachs of Summertime Farm in Rosamond, California.

Nancy's farm was founded in April, 1976 out of her love of spotted horses, a love that goes back to childhood days and a black and white pinto Shetland Pony that thought it the best of fun to scrape her off his back on low-hanging tree branches. Nancy became involved

with American Saddlebreds' at the closest riding stable to her home.

"Arabians were popular in our area, and offered a greater opportunity for showing, so I soon became involved with Half-Arabian Pintos," Nancy explains. "When the National Show Horse Registry was formed in 1982 to create a new breed based on Arabian and Saddlebred blood, it only made sense that the other half of our Half-Arabian Pintos would be American Saddlebred."

The purchase of Winter Sultan ended Nancy's two-year-long search for the right Saddlebred stallion to cross with Summertime Farm's purebred Arabian mares. Winter Sultan's sire, Winter Carnival, one of only two pinto stallions sired by the immortal World Champion Saddlebred Supreme Sultan, was bred by the famous Scripps Miramar Ranch in San Diego, California. Somehow, Winter Sultan ended up in Wisconsin, and Nancy purchased him sight unseen, except for a glimpse on a two-minute videotape.

Winter Sultan arrived in California early in this third year and became an instant had-to-see horse. Mares attracted to his court that first year included some of the breed's finest, and the resulting foals included his first three champions. Winter Sultress, a fiery red filly, and Winter Heiress, a fancy marked pinto filly, were Champion NSH filly and Reserve Champion NSH filly at their first show. Twelfth Of Never was next.

Winter went on to sire eighteen champions before his seventh birthday, including Ebony En Ivory, Wintress, Winter White Chocolate, Winter Scandal, and the undefeated pinto look-a-like son, Art Deco.

Winter Sultan was shown very successfully as a youngster, but has been content to let his offspring do the showing for him in his adult years. He loves to dance and show off for visitors at the farm, but when he thinks no one is looking he takes long sunbaths in a sand arena. He also enjoys a pleasant ride through the desert, and is always the first horse Nancy reaches for when children want a ride on one of her pintos. "He definitely blows the wild stallion image to pieces," she says.

Winter is now something of a media star, as he has been featured on the cover of several breed magazines. Winter and eleven of his foals are featured in their own calendar and the walls of Nancy's living room are covered with numerous portraits of Winter in oil, watercolor and pastels contributed by his artistic admirers.

"Winter Sultan is a rewarding element in our lives," says Nancy. "He makes the hard work of running a breeding farm very fulfilling. We are now starting to cross Winter on some of his own kind, and a few Saddlebred foals are starting to arrive. His first has already been named a state champion two-year-old, and we look forward to a little spotted Saddlebred colt to follow in Winter's footsteps."

Sally Lightfoot

The odds against a small breeder, amateur owner/ trainer winning in a prestigious Futurity like the 1990 Santa Barbara loomed pretty large, says Julia Roseborough of Tucson, Arizona. She entered her 1989 chestnut American Saddlebred filly, Sally Lightfoot, anyway. The filly had not been shown at all as a foal, says Julia, because she just doesn't believe in putting a foal a few months old under that kind of stress.

So when Sally won Champion Yearling Filly and Grand Champion Yearling against very stiff competition – ten fillies and twelve colts in numbers alone – it seemed like the impossible dream come true.

"I was acutely aware at the moment the announcement was made of Sally's wins that this was the highlight of my whole life. This is the zenith! I found myself thinking at that time. That peak will never be reached again. It was extraordinary," says Julia, an Australian who learned to ride hunt seat during the six years she lived in England. Though Sally's wins might seem modest in comparison to the accomplishments of others, Julia says, "This was only the second horse I had bred and the first I had presented in a futurity."

The filly receiving these honors was sired by a California stallion, Johnny Three, by Indiana Peavine, out of Kathryn Manion; her dam is Starheart's Glory Be, by Starheart Peavine out of Headed for Glory by Heart of Glory, all of which makes for "an interesting and star-studded pedigree with numerous crosses to Beau Peavine, Black Squirrel, Montrose, and other famous horses," says Julia.

"I own her dam," Julia explains, "and I had a photograph of a futurity winner by Johnny Three which I thought was of the same quality I'd get from this mare. In fact, the filly is the second foal from the cross. Sally has an older brother, a gaited pleasure horse, Greatrex Johnson."

"Starheart's Glory Be was boarded at the time she foaled, so we missed Sally's arrival, as usually happens," Julia says. "She produced a very beautiful filly, big and strong, really upright, from the beginning. She was so beautiful that when I first saw her at a few hours old I rushed out and bought a lovely pink foal halter. She didn't wear it for some time, as she was so difficult to catch."

Julia's farm, Buena Vista Saddlebreds, where she breeds on a small but high quality scale, was begun in 1989. "I sort of do things on my own in Tucson where there is less of a Saddlehorse following than in Phoenix," Julia notes.

As for future plans for Sally, Julia says, "You sort of have to wait till they tell YOU what they want to be. You have to wait to put them in leather to know what you have. She is very nice to drive in harness, though she doesn't like to stand long enough to be hitched."

Nor did she first care much for the jog cart. "I had to put her back on dry ice," says Julia. "I took off her shoes and turned her out for a while. Just recently, I put her back under saddle. She is enjoying going to school and being ridden up and down the road at a high, collected trot. She is becoming really exciting.

"As a breeder of any scale, to win in futurities is an important, though by no means the sole pathway to success," Julia adds. "Since the American Saddlebred is a performance horse, it must prove its worth under saddle or in harness. It's still too soon to tell what Sally's niche will be, but she has the qualities that make a show horse."

Man On The Town

In the history of the American Saddlebred, only Man On The Town can boast of a lineage in which three successive generations have been World's Grand Champion Five-Gaited Horse.

Man On The Town, trained and shown by George Knight and bred and raised by Jean McLean Davis of Oak Hill Farm in Harrodsburg, Kentucky, won the title in 1989 and 1990. His sire, Yorktown was the World's Grand Champion Five-Gaited Horse in 1970, 1971 and 1972. Yorktown's sire, Wing Commander, was the legendary six-time World's Grand Champion Five-Gaited Horse from 1948 to 1953.

Man On The Town, foaled in 1984, is obviously a product of greatness, says Jamie Davis Crabtree, Jean Davis' daughter, though he set his own mark on Saddlebred history. The solid chestnut stallion "is powerful, fine and athletic," Jamie says. "Stallions can become coarse with age, but he has kept his refined beauty, and still looks like a refined version of his dam, Chantilly Rose," says Jamie.

"We raised 'Man' and it was immediately obvious that he was going to be special. His sire and dam had produced other top horses when they were crossed, but this one was exceptional and reminded us so much of his dam and her sire, Denmark's Bourbon Genius. This horse is special to all of us--my mother, myself and my children," she says.

"He did turn our lives around by fulfilling the belief that Yorktown would sire offspring that were as talented, if not more so than he had been. Man has accomplished this in spades.

"My mother's relationship with Man is extremely special," Jamie continues. "For her he fulfilled a life-long dream to raise the reigning Five-Gaited World's Champion. But her devotion is to the horse, not to the victories."

Man was undefeated as a five-gaited horse from the moment he first entered the ring as a three-year-old. But the family most remembers that night in 1989 when he first won the World's Grand Championship. "My grandmother had passed away the night before and it was a very hard time for the family," says Jamie. "We weren't going to show that night due to my grandmother's passing, but were convinced that she would like to have us stay to try to fulfill the dream. She would have been so pleased and proud of her daughter and her remarkable horse. It was through my grandfather's foresight that my mother purchased Yorktown and began her breeding program, and neither he nor my grandmother lived to see the destinies of his brilliant offspring. We felt that somehow they knew and were smiling," says Jamie.

Man was brilliant as he won the class. He closed the Monday evening performance of the 1989 World's Championship Horse Show by becoming the World's Champion Five-Gaited Stallion, and then set his sights on the trophy that was his by birthright. When the shavings had settled in Freedom Hall in Louisville on that following Saturday night, Man On The Town emerged proudly wearing the tricolor ribbon and blanket of red roses reserved for the World's Grand Champion.

"It was truly a night to remember, one that can rarely if ever be repeated," says Jamie, though the victories were understandably bittersweet. "I only wish my grandmother could have been there to share those victories.

"Our family has had horses for pleasure, but it has become a business over the years in that we have our own farm and breeding program," she adds. "Mother has completely dedicated her life to the American Saddlebred, a love that began for her in childhood. Oak Hill Farm was founded in 1964 in Harrodsburg, Kentucky after we moved from Virginia. She wished to move to Kentucky since it was the hub of the American Saddlebred industry and because she loved the state."

"Man was retired to stud in June, 1991 and the family is waiting none too patiently for the arrival of his first foals this spring and summer. We firmly believe in his ability to pass on his heritage as did his sire and grandsire before him," says Jamie.

CH Captive Spirit

Although there have been many outstanding moments in the life of five-times World Champion American Saddlebred stallion CH Captive Spirit, owner J.D. Vanier's most vivid memory is when he first saw him and knew that he was meant to own the black colt.

Mr. Vanier had long dreamed of personally selecting a superior show horse and CH Captive Spirit was that horse.

Vanier used only his own judgment, rather than relying on the advice of experts, in selecting "Spirit" and he has turned out to be the most successful of all the Vanier horses, Arabian or Saddlebred.

Mr. Vanier, distinguished as an owner of both those breeds of horses, noticed an advertisement for a black weanling colt, CH Captive Spirit, on the back cover of *Saddle & Bridle* in 1983. The colt had already been named World Champion Weanling, showing for his breeder, North Ridge Farm in Wayzata, Minnesota.

Mr. Vanier flew to Minnesota to look at the black colt, and on his own evaluation, purchased him.

The colt was naturally gifted from the earliest age and was cared for, trained and shown with utmost respect for that talent.

In the show ring Spirit radiates power, and with it, ability, strength and charisma. An extremely striking horse, he is coal-black, 17-hands tall, and athletically built.

Since most of Spirit's career was as a fine harness horse, he customarily has worn his mane and tail long and full. When he trots, he has a fluid, graceful motion that serves as counterpoint to his great physical presence and power.

A favorite family tale about Spirit recalls Spirit's first time competing for the World's Grand Championship in Fine Harness as a four-year-old. Just days before, he had won the World's Championship for Junior Fine Harness Horses. When he was walked to the warm-up ring, prior to the Grand Championship, he paused at the entry gate, raised his head and trumpeted his arrival to the ring full of people and horses. Everyone, including the reigning World's Grand Champion, turned to see what was going on, and stared at the tall, black stallion announcing his presence and his challenge.

That August night Spirit was named Reserve World's Grand Champion, and a year later he won the Grand Championship.

Spirit was a World's Champion or World's Grand Champion every year he was shown. Throughout his performance career, he was trained and shown by Tom Moore, one of the most respected trainers in the Saddlebred world. While most of his success was achieved as a fine harness horse, during his last season in the show ring, he was the Three-Gaited Reserve World's Grand Champion.

Under saddle, Spirit is described as "a controlled explosion, like sitting on the wind." His smoothness of gait is combined with propulsion appropriate to his size and strength.

More than any other individual horse, Spirit gave Vanier Farm, a premiere breeding and marketing facility with locations in Salina, Kansas, and Scottsdale, Arizona, the high level of credibility it was seeking in the Saddlebred industry. Vanier Farm particularly benefitted from Spirit in that Mr. Vanier had selected him before the stallion ever entered the performance ring.

Mr. Vanier is always able to rely on Captive Spirit. He answered all challenges in the show ring and promises to be a sire of outstanding merit. Spirit has been, and is, a source of joy for J.D. Vanier.

THE ANDALUSIAN

Emperors and kings prized him, and great conquerors from before the time of Christ chose to ride him as a reflection of their personal glory. Artists immortalized him in bronze. Poets fashioned their best phrases around his deeds in war. Painters enthroned their noble subjects on his back.

The horse of Spain is one of the greatest masterpieces of art that man and nature together have conspired to create.

One of the most impressive facts about this extraordinary breed is that the qualities so much admired in it today are unchanged from those of the Iberian horse of centuries ago. The Iberian horse was handled and ridden by men at a much earlier date than any other, and is probably the world's earliest riding horse. By the time of the Roman occupation of the Iberian Peninsula, the Spanish horse of that time was entirely recognizable as the purebred horse of Spain today. The sub-convex facial profile, the strong arched neck, rounded powerful body, and marked elevation in movement are quite clearly shown in horses depicted on Roman coinage and pottery of the period. The famous statue of the Roman Emperor Marcus Aurelius shows him astride a horse that could be an Andalusian of today.

The Spanish or Iberian horse was popular in the ancient world as a superior warhorse due to its strength and agility. Alexander the Great's Bucephalus is said to have been of Iberian origins. Julius Caesar wrote of the noble steeds of Hispania in *Del Bello Gallico*. Hannibal used Spanish horses in his invasion of Italy.

The Andalusian head is quite distinct, larger than that of the Arabian with a straight or slightly convex profile. The forehead is very wide with the eyes dark and kind. The ears are of a proportionate length and well-set. The nostrils are very large to allow tremendous air intake, and the muzzle is large enough to accommodate the large air passages. The neck is of proportionate length, well tied-in, and heavier than that of the Arab and Thoroughbred, yet elegant. In stallions, the crest is well-developed. The mane and tail are very long and thick; the shoulders, long and sloping with good muscle. Hindquarters are strong and lean with a rounded croup, and the tail is low set. The chest is strong and broad with well-developed muscles; the back, strong and short coupled. The legs of the Andalusian are usually sturdy (yet not coarse) clean-cut and elegant. As for color, most are greys, ranging from steel grey to pure white. Bays and blacks are occasionally found.

The Spanish stallions are unique in that they seem to be fiery and proud while remaining docile and extremely tractable. This seeming contradiction stems from the edict of King Ferdinand of Spain who enforced the old law that gentlemen must ride only stallions. This edict must have resulted in quite a few Spanish grandees being dumped by the roadside. Breeders began to breed for good temperament.

Because of its strength and agility, the Andalusian became the premier warhorse of Europe and was used in Spain's successful conquests. When the Spanish conquerors came to the New World, the Spanish horse carried them along. The breed has often been called "The Great Colonizer." Spain established stock farms in the Caribbean and supplied horses to all colonizing countries. For hundreds of years, the Spanish horse was the representative of its kind in the Americas, and all New World breeds carry its blood.

In order to conserve the best horses for breeding, the government of Spain placed an embargo on their export. For over 100 years, the Andalusian was virtually unseen by the rest of the world. Then in the 1960s the export ban was lifted. Now the popularity of the Andalusian horse is once again on the rise. Horsemen have rediscovered the traits that made this the most sought-after horse in the world – the strength, agility, beauty, pride and docility.

The Andalusian today excels in the dressage arena and as a western riding horse. When it comes to agility and the ability to work cattle, it is unexcelled. The Andalusian's strength and boldness make it a good hunter and jumper; its endurance is ideal for trail riding. As a show and parade horse the Andalusian's way of going combined with its appearance and long, luxurious mane and tail make it extremely striking as it moves with all the pride of its ancestors who carried Caesars and kings in their days of triumph.

El Cordobes

I have written about El Cordobes in my book *Vavra's Horses* and described how I first saw this marvelously handsome bay Andalusian stallion in Spain as a foal in January 1981.

As I sat on the stone bench that forms part of the wall surrounding the house and stables at Lerena Andalusian breeding farm near Seville, Spain, I looked over fields of poppies and daisies so vibrant and brilliant, not even the greatest of painters could have approximated the poetic impact of the scene. In a nearby pasture, a newborn foal galloped around his dam and then started pronking, duplicating the attitudes I have seen antelope assume in East Africa.

"What foal is that?" I questioned Lerena's owner, my friend Paco Lazo, who sat next to me, his eyes also fixed on the field and the horses.

"El Cordobes," he answered.

"Well, when he grows up, we'll never see him galloping free in a setting as beautiful as this," I commented.

As fate would have it, some seven years later El Cordobes and I would meet again, this time in the equally stunning landscape of Tennessee, one which burned with fall colors of auburn, maroon, burnished bronze, copper and gold. So stunning was the photograph I took of this now physically mature 15.2 stallion with luxuriant black mane and tail, it was used on the cover of my book, and remains one of my favorites.

Today, El Cordobes lives in Swansea, South Carolina, at Poole Training Center where he is in training with Blanchard and Debbie Poole.

His present owners, Jim and Eddie Lynne Carr of Florence, South Carolina, had admired Cordobes for some time. When the stallion became available for purchase, a dream came true for them to own and enjoy such a unique horse of such special bloodlines. His sire Poseido V is from the famous Terry line, and his dam Cordobesa XII from a well-known line of producers.

Jim and Eddie Lynne did not have the time or facility to promote and train a stallion such as Cordobes, so in August 1990 they sent him to Poole Training Center, where he has won many a new fan over to the Andalusian horse.

Cordobes's training has continued in dressage, driving and saddle seat English pleasure. He has won numerous classes and was named 1991 American Andalusian Horse Association (AAHA) National Champion Driving Horse.

Cordobes is now siring offspring with his same athletic ability, sweet nature, and willingness to please. His daughter, BW Marquesa, went AAHA Reserve National Champion Halter mare in 1991 as a two-year-old.

The Carrs and their two young sons, Ross and Clay, come to visit Cordobes as often as possible and whether they take him out on the trails or sit in the cart behind him, they always have a wonderful time.

"Many other adults and children have been given the thrill of riding this internationally-known stallion with his high, flashy smooth-as-silk trot and his rolling canter that makes one feel on top of the world. Each rider has walked away having fallen hopelessly in love with him," says Debbie Poole.

She and Blanchard have been serving the horse public since 1961 and have trained hundreds of champions of all breeds for their clients over the years. "While we'd had as many as thirty horses in training, no other horse offers more enjoyment and pleasure to train than Cordobes," says Debbie.

"Cordobes projects himself majestically but is a sweet, gentle spirit who even enjoys a lick on the nose from the barn dog, Cody. We have only known Cordobes for a very short one and a half years, but we all look forward to many more memorable and happy times to come with him, as well as his sons and daughters," Debbie continues. "Cordobes may be owned by Jim and Eddie Lynn Carr, but he has become a part of every life he has touched. People come from hundreds of miles away just to see and touch him."

I, for one, am glad I was one of the very first to observe and enjoy his presence on this earth.

Caribe

Caribe, the dark bay-black Spanish stallion belonging to Mary Ann Austin, has a lot of Latin *alegria* to his character. Mary Ann describes him as "quite impy. Everything is one big joke to him. He's just a barrel of fun, full of tricks! The things he can get into!"

Jokester that he is, Caribe, now five and a half years old, is quite serious about one thing – romance. "He will not breed unless he likes the mare, and he is very, very picky," says Mary Ann, a third-grade teacher in Canada.

"We don't know what it is," she replies, when asked what turns him on or off. "He either likes a mare a lot or he just doesn't. It's probably the most hilarious thing about him."

Caribe, 15.1 and without any special markings other than a "very lush" mane and tail, is a Canadian horse now, but came from the tropical Caribbean.

Mary Ann and her husband John brought Caribe, after seeing a video of him, from Sr. Don Tomás Batalla Esquivel in Costa Rica.

Mary Ann says they learned a very hard lesson, one they would like to share with others: "Never import a horse from a southern climate in the wintertime." A shivering Caribe arrived in Canada on January 6, 1990. Ear-

lier, in order to fulfill Canadian importation regulations, he spent two months in New York State where at times the thermometer plunged to forty-nine degrees below zero. "His first winter was the hardest for him. He had to wear two blankets all the time. Through inexperience, we could have lost him," Mary Ann says.

Finding Caribe culminated the Austins' long search throughout the United States for a dark bay-black horse of *pura raza española.* "It was strictly ego. We knew the color was a rarity and we decided to go for it," Mary Ann explains their quest.

They could find only Andalusian/Lusitano crosses here. "We wrote to Mexican breeders, but they did not answer their mail," she adds. Then through a contact in Montreal they learned of Don Tomás Batalla Esquivel, through whom they acquired Caribe for their El Caballo Andalusians in Little Britain, Ontario.

Their plans for Caribe include introducing him to the reining world. "We have quite a lot of reining horse activity in Quebec. The Andalusian is very versatile, very flexible, and as a reiner I think he would be quite attractive," Mary Ann notes.

The Austins got into Andalusians by a circuitous route. "I'm of Czechoslovakian descent and I wanted a Lipizzan for a long time," Mary Ann explains. "If I were born in the Old Country, there is no way I could have a Lipizzan. One would have to be nobility.

"We had paid off a few bills," Mary Ann remembers, "and I said, 'John, wouldn't it be nice to have a horse?'" They answered an ad in the *Toronto Star* for a Lipizzan, but it had been sold. The same seller also had an Arabian mare for sale, and Mary Ann bought her without determining if she were rideable. "I had to have a horse, you see." Then of course she had to buy a horse for her husband, one which also turned out to be unrideable. That one was followed by a Quarter Horse mare "guaranteed rideable" that turned out to be what Mary Ann humorously calls a "feral race dropout." The mare spent two years in training, trying to learn to be a socialized horse, but it never worked out. Next came a Northern Dancer Thoroughbred, "because I wanted to have nobility in the barn," says Mary Ann.

By this time the Austins had four horses and still not one to ride. Then, at the barn where all their horses were being trained, some newly imported Andalusians arrived. Adding two Andalusians to their collection, the Austins finally found what they had been seeking all along. They now have ten Andalusians.

"When you get to middle age, you are supposed to be thinking of your health, your future, things like that," says Mary Ann. "The horses are keeping us young and it's opened an entirely new world for us, a new education and a new reason for being."

Destinado V

"Nothing prepared me for the lightning bolt that hit me when I first laid eyes on Destinado V," says Penelope Burley of Studio City, California. "Suddenly, in my heart, I knew that this was the horse of my dreams! Talk about a gut reaction! This magnificent horse was just standing in his stall. I hadn't even seen him move, but I knew this was the right horse for me. I just had a sense of knowing that this horse and I were meant to be together. An hour later, after he had been put through his paces, my heart pounded as I scribbled out a deposit check for him. I raced home to beg, bargain, plead or steal the balance from my husband.

"As luck would have it," adds Penny, "a couple of days later I received a long distance telephone call informing me I was about to receive a surprise inheritance from my late mother. Coincidentally, it was almost the exact amount of Destinado's asking price. I felt as if this was destiny at its best."

"Dusty," as Penny calls him, looks as though he stepped from an old oil painting of the Iberian horse. The exceptionally well-proportioned Andalusian gelding was foaled at the Garrison Ranch on March 29, 1981; his sire is Temerario V; and his dam, Lucena II.

"When I bought him in March 1988, he was rocking horse, polka-dot dapple grey, 16 hands, with three black feet and one white. His tail is long, thick and wavy and he has a pink snip on his upper lip, in the shape of an upside down heart," Penny describes his striking looks.

"This horse has definitely turned my life around," adds Penny, a pleasure horse owner. "He has given me focus, he has taught me so much – about horses, about myself, about winning, about losing, about trying. I started to take riding more seriously when I got Dusty as I did not want to embarrass him.

"He is very athletic, and genetically knows things like the levade and passage. His extended trot is like floating on air. There is a lot of 'air under his feet' and his gallop is so powerful it takes my breath away."

His athleticism is reflected in his impressive show record. Or as Penny puts it, "I do not intend to boast, but we have a thirty-two gallon container full of Dusty's ribbons."

The ribbons are from years 1988 through 1991, with 1989 his best, when he won Overall High Point Performance Champion, High Point English Horse, High Point Amateur Rider, and, ridden by a nine-year-old girl named Amanda Latta, the 1989 High Point Junior Exhibitor Award on the International Andalusian Horse Association circuit.

Best of all, however, is the way Dusty performs as a companion animal.

"He knows what I'm thinking and what kind of mood I'm in," says Penny. "He's very intelligent, curious, inquisitive and communicative. He loves any edible treat: bananas, potato chips, champagne, Seven-up. If he sees me eating, he'll say 'Please' by extending his neck and tilting his head to one side until I give him a bit.

"There are too many special moments to list them all," she adds. "Once we crossed a raging river, the banks swelled by a downfall. We were both scared, but he carried me to safety. Once, when he didn't feel well after a vaccination, he stood beside me resting his head on my shoulder, groaning quietly to elicit my sympathy. Another time, he bucked me off in a class at a horse show and then ran back to me and stood patiently for me to get back on.

"My horse has fulfilled so many of my dreams, even dreams I didn't know I had. He fulfilled my dreams of competing in the show ring and he superceded all of my dreams with his accomplishments. In fact, my dreams are realized every day when I walk up to his stall. He keeps me sane, he keeps me fit, he keeps me honest, and we have fun together. I've never been happier," she says. "I feel a deep and enduring love for this horse that is unique in its intensity."

Reina GF

"There she was with her mother's milk dripping off her muzzle," says Connie Connelly, describing the first sight of the rare black Andalusian filly she and her husband Michael had no intention of buying.

They had seen their first Andalusian in their hometown of Kansas City, Missouri in 1984. "Our children were old enough we felt to enjoy having horses," says Connie. "We wanted a different, unusual breed. We started watching the classified ads in the newspaper and found a Half-Andalusian gelding for sale."

The Connellys called and asked, "What is an Andalusian?" They were sent to see the gelding's sire, Helenico T, owned by Pam Schmiedeke. "He is a 17-hand stallion, pure white and magnificent in every way. We decided we HAD to have purebred Andalusians. It would be six years before we realized this dream," Connie says.

"Finally in April of 1990, we went to California on a buying excursion. During this trip we intended to buy two breeding-age mares." First the Connellys visited Ira and Andy Dack of Rainbow Farm and talked them into parting with a three-year-old mare, Daniella. Their next stop was Gremlan Farms of Bakersfield, California. There

they met Lanys Kaye-Eddie and the extraordinary 16.1-hand black mare Ladina with the ten-day-old filly, Reina, by her side.

The Connellys learned that Lanys had been captivated by this special black mare when she went to Spain in 1986. Ladina was sired by the majestic Ganador VI who was bred by Don Francisco Lazo Diaz from original Terry stock. Her dam was Cubana VII; her aristocratic grandam, Valenciana XVII. Ladina's exciting height, exceptional conformation and shiny black color impressed the judges in four trips to the show ring in 1988. In 1989 she overwhelmed the competition and became the IAHA National Champion Mare, by unanimous choice of three judges.

They learned that after Ladina's dam, Cubana VII, died tragically early in 1987, Ladina had become even more precious as the last of a line that represents 200 years of knowledgeable and dedicated breeding.

They also learned that Reina's sire, Teodoro, was the only Andalusian to date to win the National Champion Stallion title with both the American Andalusian Horse Association and the International Andalusian Horse Association in 1989 and 1990 respectively; and that he himself is by Xenophon USA, a well-known high school horse on the East Coast.

But because the Connellys wanted a breeding-age mare, they decided to continue on their way. "We were literally backing out of the drive to leave when the feeling came over us to talk to Lanys about selling Ladina's filly. Luckily, Lanys agreed to sell her. We have enjoyed her every day of her life since," says Connie.

Reina will figure prominently in the Connellys' breeding program, she says, "We were so impressed with her development that we contracted for Ladina's 1991 foal by Teodoro, a beautiful black colt named Navarre GF. Currently we are purchasing breeding stock and hope to become major Midwestern breeders of purebred Andalusians," says Connie.

Reina is Spanish for "queen." "Even without knowing this," continues Connie, "her trainer gave her the barn name of 'Queenie' due to her regal, arrogant attitude as a weanling. One of her less-than-regal traits? She loves peanut butter cheese crackers."

Reina was shown as a weanling in 1990 in the IAHA Futurity where she placed in the Top Five nationally, shown by a prominent California trainer, Vaughn Smith of Collins Country Farms. The latter will campaign her at the 1992 California shows and, once she qualifies, the IAHA National in Abilene, Texas. She will compete in junior halter and junior driving.

"Reina's breeder, Lanys Kaye-Eddie said, 'Ladina is a once-in-a-lifetime mare.' We feel the same about Reina," says Connie.

Granadino XI

"The good ones find you," top trainers say of the serendipity factor in horse-hunting, and the story of Granadino XI once again proves the adage.

The first time Beverly Denham saw Granadino, she was not looking for a stallion. It was 1984, and she was in Spain searching for mares for her breeding operation, Denham Ranch, in Grandview, Texas.

Her quest had taken her to a small ranch belonging to Francisco Olivera in the village of Alcala de Guadaira, just outside of Sevilla, Spain.

"Francisco was so proud of Granadino," she told me, "he could not let us leave before seeing him. I was expecting to see another nice, white Andalusian, not a horse with so much fire and presence," says Beverly.

"Granadino had so much action, chills ran down my back. At first I thought he was too much horse for any amateur to handle. Not knowing how gentle he really was, I continued my search for mares."

But the 16.2 pearl-white stallion with shades of silver running through his mane and tail – platinum poetry of motion under the gas-jet blue Spanish sky – had burned an indelible impression in her memory. Two years later she was drawn back to the small village to see Granadino again.

"I wanted to get to know him better, to see what he was really like," she says.

She learned more about him. The stallion was foaled in Jerez de la Frontera, Spain on February 24, 1978, sired by the great Leviton, known for siring champion offspring; his dam is Granadina VII by Adentro out of Tomatera III.

"After spending some time with Granadino, I realized why he was so special to Francisco Olivera," Beverly continues. "Having owned horses all my life, I could see there was something different about Granadino. He was proud and in his pride, he carried the true presence of Spain."

Once knowing him, Beverly could not part with him. Granadino came home with four mares and a weanling colt. The journey took three weeks in all, by surface roads from Sevilla, Spain to France, where the horses boarded a 747 flight to New York, then continued on by horse trailer to their destination of Dallas, Texas.

By the time Granadino was imported to the U.S., Denham Ranch had already established its breeding program, with mares imported in foal in Spanish stallions.

It wasn't until the following year that Granadino was used as a breeding stallion.

By 1991, he had sired twenty-four foals on the ranch. "He not only proved himself in both performance and halter divisions, but more importantly as a breeding stallion. With his typical head, strong neck, short back and long legs, he has often been called, 'very Spanish' by visiting Spaniards," Beverly says.

In 1990 Beverly returned to Spain once again, to visit Francisco Olivera and show him photos of Granadino and his offspring. She in turn saw Francisco's five-year-old mares and stallions sired by Granadino. "Francisco was delighted to see me and very sentimental when we talked about Granadino," Beverly says. "With a tear in his eye, he told me he was truly sorry he had sold him."

Of course, Beverly felt just the opposite.

The passing of time, she tells me, has not quenched the fire Granadino possessed in Spain, and he has thrilled many people in the parades, exhibitions and special clinics in which he has participated, all promoting the Andalusian breed.

"As spirited as he seems," Beverly says, "Granadino can be an exceptional children's horse, totally relaxing and making all the children who have ridden him fall in love with him. On the other hand, he can be everything the most experienced rider could ever want in a horse. He's able to perform a Spanish walk, piaffer and passage that visitors to the ranch never forget.

"At shows, he draws people to him, regardless of where he is stalled," she adds. "With his kind eye and gentle disposition, people often say he is the type of horse they have always wished to own" – this stallion that was the "silent" wish of Beverly's own heart come true.

Mariah

Having owned Quarter Horses, Appaloosas, Saddlebreds and Morgans, Dr. Linda Ehlers of Palos Hills, Illinois decided to look at the rare Andalusian breed. She noted a magazine ad for a prominent ranch in California, called the number and explained to the breeder her tale of woe as a show horse owner, she says. "Burnt out on the high-stepping, high-pressure show world, I wanted a horse that I could enjoy as well as one that I would be proud to own. A horse that had a mind, heart and a sense of reality unspoiled by whips, chains and firecrackers."

Linda was sent photographs of a three-year-old filly just bred to 1983 World Champion Castablanco. The breeder told her that this mare's full-blooded sister had been bought by a woman with similar needs to hers, and that the woman had called a year later to wax melodic about how sweet and gentle her horse was.

"I had the pictures for weeks and kept going back to them," says Linda, who discussed the filly with her horseowning friends, all of whom thought she was crazy to even think about buying an unbroken horse sight unseen.

"Yet I had a feeling that this was the horse for me," she says, and Mariah arrived in Illinois in June, 1990.

"When the driver unloaded Mariah, he told me he wished he had a truck full of her type to haul," says

Linda. "She'd loaded like a dream, traveled quietly, and handled without upset, in spite of the fact that this was the first time she'd been trailered. I felt like my intuition had been confirmed."

After a week or so, Linda put Mariah into training. "It was fun to hear the Quarter Horse trainer speak in glowing terms about the ease with which Mariah took to a saddle. She was in training for about four months and then put out to pasture to await her foal, born in January, 1991. Later that spring, Mariah was introduced to the miles of trails in my area as well as to more basics of English riding. She developed a reputation as the young horse that calmed older horses when she was on the trails."

All seemed well, but, Linda says, "Like many young horses, late last year she went into a period where she got skittish and a little flighty. These bouts were unexpected and unprovoked," she says.

On a cool, damp day in October, 1991, Linda decided to take her to the outdoor arena and do a little work there. "While I can't relate what happened from that point on due to retrograde amnesia, I can tell you that when I woke up in the ambulance, my head hurt a lot. As a matter of fact, everything hurt a lot. After three hours in the emergency room I was allowed to go home with admonitions about resting and wearing a helmet the next time I ride.

"Along with a concussion, I'd received a whiplash injury to my neck and sprained most of the muscles in my lower back," she says. "It took a week before I could go back to work and six weeks before I could handle a full schedule of patients without the struggle of thinking this is part of a post-concussion syndrome.'"

The struggle to overcome anxiety kept Linda from riding consistently. Then in February, 1991, during a lesson, Linda had another mishap with Mariah, this time bumping her head lightly on the arena wall, fortunately on the side opposite her concussion.

"At this point, I am learning a new meaning to confronting one's fears," says Linda. "Mariah has forced me to examine all my years of daydreaming about horses and my own capabilities as an athletic woman... and it is hard to control the anxiety and fear about riding that often creeps into the pit of my stomach, sometimes when I am just standing near her."

"To me, horses have always symbolized a type of freedom that words fail to describe. They have been an escape from a frantic-paced life and a world that is too often cruel, vicious, and without reason. The smell and dust and sights in a barn remind me that life can still be lived in human terms. Recovering from the head injury has meant asking whether the escape is worth the price. I don't know for sure yet. I do know that I'm still going to the barn as often as possible."

Flamenca De La Parra

After I met Moira Dills at a horse show, this charming young Englishwoman showed me her paintings of horses, done in a bold style and vibrant colors that reminded me of the great French painter Gaugin. Though she's not American by birth, her paintings capture the vital, earthy feeling of the American West, which she now makes her home.

Moira told me that when she began to paint in 1989, she endeavored to find the most beautiful horses possible to put on canvas. "I searched pastures and pictures," she said, "but always the horses seemed to fall short of my expectations." Her frustrations as an artist ran parallel to those she experienced as an equestrian.

"Over the past ten years I had bought and sold eight horses looking for something that did not seem to exist. A perfectionist at heart, I longed to find the breed and style of riding that was right for me, but what was it?

"Then I discovered the Andalusian! The magnificent Spanish warhorse, immortalized by the Renaissance artists of Europe, bred for kind and noble temperament, along with marvelous movement."

Moira visited the breeding farm, Andalusians de la Parra in San Antonio, Texas, belonging to Rafael and Maritza Parra, whose name is synonymous with the finest horses. Moira rode their beautiful stallion, Primoroso "and I knew then I had finally come face to face with my destiny with horses," she says.

In May, 1991 she attended the First Annual Festival of Spanish horses, and saw the stallion Boticario de la Parra perform. He took the Regional Championships as well as Moira's heart. She learned that the Parras had a two-year-old filly by him for sale.

She was anxious to see her, for her quest was not an ordinary one.

"I wasn't just looking for a halter or performance horse; I wanted something that was also aesthetically pleasing to me an an artist, as she would be gracing many of my future canvases," Moira says. "As the handler brought her out of the barn, I saw her from a distance and knew that I wanted her. Her beautiful head with graceful neck impressed me as she glided daintily toward me for closer inspection. She had the presence of her sire, and her dam was a beautiful bay mare, Colombiana de la Parra, sired by the magnificent black stallion, Dejado, featured in the book, *Vavra's Horses*."

Flamenca de la Parra was delivered to Moira's ranch in Granbury, Texas a few weeks later. Last November at the Fort Worth Nationals, Moira had the pleasure of seeing Flamenca's sire, Boticario de la Parra, become National Champion. It was on that occasion that I had the pleasure of meeting her. It was a good day for all.

"Not only had I found my desire, the impassioned Iberian horse of the Spanish bullfighter, but along with

it, the levade, courbette, passage and piaffer, all performed by these wonderful horse with grace and ease," she says. She now studies classical dressage under Charles Osborne of Fort Worth, a former student and friend of the great Portuguese master, Nuno Oliveira.

"Flamenca is all that I was promised an Andalusian should be and even though I am not riding her yet, watching her in the pasture with my other horses against a Texas sunset is an artist's dream come true," says Moira.

Laponio VI

One fateful evening, Alayne B. Fairbanks and her family went to attend the Royal Lipizzan Show in Ogden, Utah, simply to see the beauty of the trained horses. It was an outing which would lead to their owning a very special animal.

Several Andalusian stallions performed in one segment of the show. The curtain opened, stirring Spanish music played, and Alayne saw before her eyes the most beautiful horse she had ever seen. He was dapple-grey with black legs and had one of the most spectacular manes in existence, a shoulder-length "scarf" of silver sheen.

"When I remembered to breathe again, I jokingly asked my father to buy this horse for me," says Alayne. Much to their surprise, as if he'd overheard her, the announcer said some of the horses in the show were for sale; anyone interested could meet with the show director after the performance.

They went backstage, though Alayne's father had no real intention of buying the horse; it simply was a way to see an Andalusian stallion up close.

Alayne learned that Laponio VI was a registered Andalusian foaled February 14, 1980, bred by the Garrison Ranch in California. His sire was Leopardo II and his grandsire Legionario III, both famous Andalusian stallions. His dam was Lanca IV, known for producing classic foals.

When the Royal Lipizzan Show moved on to the fairgrounds in Salt Lake City for a week and a half, Alayne followed it there, and had the opportunity to ride Laponio VI herself.

On one occasion after riding him, the weather turned and became cold and windy. Alayne was coatless, so as she stood there, listening to what the head trainer had to say about Andalusians, she wrapped Laponio's long mane around her shoulders and arms to keep warm. "He stood there so patiently with me soaking up his warmth under his mane, that I found out then and there what the Andalusian temperament is like," recalls Alayne, who had lost her heart to Laponio. Much to her disbelief, her father called the owner of the show, Gary Lashinsky, and was able to purchase the stallion before he left Salt Lake City.

At the time the Fairbanks bought Laponio, in 1985, there were no registered Andalusians in the state of Utah. Purchasing Laponio gave Alayne the opportunity to be a pioneer in introducing this breed into the State. In 1988, the Fairbanks began breeding with him, purchasing purebred mares and naming their business in Ogden, Utah, Mountain West Andalusians. In addition to breeding their own purebreds, they cross-breed to Quarter Horses to produce Aztecas, to Arabs to produce Aralusians, and to Thoroughbreds to produce Iberian Warmbloods, all of which have their own registries.

"Laponio has sired magnificent purebred and crossbred fillies and colts, which are a tremendous credit to his capabilities as a sire," says Alayne.

Because of Laponio's exceptional appearance and his regal way of moving, he is the immediate center of attention wherever he goes. He appeared at the Equifest Celebration at Santa Anita Racetrack for two years as the representative of his breed. He also briefly rejoined the cast of the Royal Lipizzan show when it returned to Salt Lake City in 1988.

He's won many ribbons and trophies, including the 1989 National Championship for Versatility from English to Western. He loves to be in parades and has appeared in the Tournament of Roses Parade in Pasadena, California and also in the Utah All-Horse Parade in Salt Lake City, winning ribbons in both.

Laponio is currently in Los Angeles being trained by Dianne Olds Rossi for exhibition work.

Alayne says being able to own Laponio, to form a business around him, and to perpetuate his bloodline have all been gratifying experiences. "We look forward to the future with great expectations. He has brought the family so much joy in watching him and being a part of his progress and has earned us so much attention. He is like a member of the family and we love him dearly."

Revoltoso

Felix Garmendia is a friend I met long ago. His daughter once did me the favor of hand-delivering to me in Spain one of my favorite Basenji puppies from California.

Felix knows that you can go your whole life and not find the horse that is right for you. Until a couple of years ago, that was the case with this colorful gentleman, an industrial engineer by profession and a breeder and importer of purebred Spanish Andalusian horses by avocation.

Felix has brought in some very famous Spanish horses to his El Cortijo del Sol Ranch in Santa Clarita, California. He brought in the Spanish Champion Stallions Juguetón and Brioso VII, Unico VII from the Terry farm, plus wonderful mares like Obelisk and Presumida. And he sold them all.

"Not the perfect mount for me," he says as he explains why he sold first this one and then that one. "You can go your whole life without finding the perfect mount. Your temper does not match with the horse's temper. It is very hard to match a horse with a man.

"My latest acquisition is Revoltoso. This one is going to die with me or my family. He's a son of a gun, like me. We get along fine," says Felix, who grew up on a farm in northern Spain with work horses and big mules. He came to the United States "thirty-five years ago, for freedom and for better living conditions." There followed years of hard work to establish himself financially before he could afford to buy his first purebred Spanish horse from Allen Parkinson in Scottsdale, Arizona.

From his many visits to Seville and the farm of El Conde de Odiel, Felix knew the bloodlines of the bay stallion Revoltoso before he had ever seen him. He'd had a preview through seeing several siblings. Foaled on February 12, 1977, Revoltoso was sold to Costa Rica, where Felix went to see him.

"I was very humble and very nice when I approached the owner. It was like a miracle. I couldn't believe I could own the horse, but I bought him in five seconds. The owner had paid $150,000 for him a few years ago, but he had already bred all his mares to him. He said to me, 'If you like him, I sell you the horse for so much.' I went over there, I look at the horse in his stall and I said yes. The owner said, 'You didn't even see him move.' 'I don't have to, I don't need to,' I said, and buying Revoltoso is the best decision I ever made in my life.

"What a pleasure it is to have a horse that understands you. This is why I sell those other horses," he explains. "The chemistry has to be there.

"Revoltoso and I are two sons of guns who understand each other. I can drive a truck or a Jeep or a Mercedes and as soon as I come to the gate of the farm, he knows who it is. He is dancing in the barn. I go nuts. I love this guy to death, believe me. Then I have to put the

chain over his nose, because he is very powerful. You can see the fire in his eyes. He's happy. So full of energy, he's turned out a couple of times a day. When I sit on him, I never see such a high action. You see pretty horses but you never see horses that move like this." Revoltoso is fully trained in high school gaits and does the *piaffer*, *passage*, and Spanish walk. "The whole enchilada," says Felix. "He was trained by Antonio Ojeda from Morón de la Frontera, probably the best trainer I ever came across.

"I breed horses for pleasure, as a hobby," Felix adds. He has nine of them at his twenty-acre El Cortijo del Sol in Canyon Country, including good mares from Manuel de la Calle in Jerez and Válido, the son of Juguetón. "I didn't start a farm to make money. Everybody wants to make a fortune with horses." "Horses are for love, not money," says this man who has lived his philosophy.

Pregonero CGB

The pure Andalusian stallion Pregonero is good medicine for Dr. Jorge Gomez, diplomate of the American Board of Surgery and the American Board of Plastic Surgery. "This is the horse of my dreams. I don't think that I can ever replace this horse," is his diagnosis of the situation.

One of the special things Dr. Gomez says he has learned from his relationship with Pregonero is "that sharing a few moments of the day with this animal brings me a certain kind of peace and renewed energy."

Pregonero is Dr. Gomez' personal dressage mount, shown both in exhibitions and recognized United States

Dressage Federation competitions. Pregonero has been showing fourth level, and in 1992 moves up to Prix St. Georges. Dr. Gomez and Pregonero work with Rosalind Kinstler, a popular Michigan instructor.

The stallion, 16.1 hands high, and at present a silvery white in color, with a single black spot on his right hind fetlock, is far from an amateur's horse. "This is a horse that should only be handled by experienced people", says Dr. Gomez. "His personality is unique, but I could not call him a familiar horse. Although when I am away for a period of time, I'm told that he acts differently and looks like he is missing me. Our relationship is a mixture of love and respect."

Asked if there have been any special moments, he replies, "Perhaps the time it took for us to adjust to each other. It took me one year to be able to have the horse understand me and for me to understand him," he says. "We had to learn to trust each other and go through the process of correcting mistakes with care.

"He loves to be outdoors and when he is turned out, it is a joy to see him galloping, jumping, rearing. He is a truly athletic horse and, on the other hand, when he is ridden, he is the most kind, gentle, extremely obedient and sensitive horse. Minimal aids have to be used to ride this horse. He is a perfect horse for dressage. His extensions are beautiful. His *passage* is near to perfection."

Foaled April 19, 1978, Pregonero is the son of Pregonero IV and is out of Gachona. Spanish-bred, he was imported to the United States in 1984, and was purchased by Dr. Gomez from the California farm of Fernando Gonzalez.

Pregonero is the mainstay of GG Andalusian Farms in East Lansing Michigan, the breeding farm owned by Dr. Gomez's wife, Ginette. Purebred Andalusian horses are bred, along with a cross with a Czechoslovakian Warmblood breed called the Kladruber. These crossbred horses are bred with the exclusive purpose in mind of developing a competitive dressage horse.

Pregonero has a stunning physical presence. "His stance is majestic, his mane and tail are full, and his coat takes on a silvery shine. He commands attention whenever he is performing," says Dr. Gomez.

One of Dr. Gomez' favorite anecdotes is that after Pregonero appeared at a certain barn, the owner of another Andalusian stallion quickly moved to another place "because until he saw Pregonero he thought his horse was the most beautiful.

"Pregonero certainly made an impact on my life," adds Dr. Gomez. "He commands my special attention and is the source of pleasure and relaxation. Horses offer an outlet for relaxation from the pressure of daily life," he adds. "Riding is the preferred sport for my family and me."

Aida

My friend, Tita Grey (Marcella Grey de Martinez), has been a breeder for 25 years, not only of Andalusians, but of many other breeds, and says, "Never have I bred an animal that has given me so many satisfactions, either under saddle or showing in public than the black Andalusian mare, Aida.

"She has a tremendous power in her body, yet a child can ride her and she can be as gentle as a puppy," says Tita, whose ranch in McAllen, Texas is called Meson Doña Macaria.

Aida's tale begins with nearly as much drama as the story of the operatic heroine for whom she is named.

Black Andalusians are quite rare. Tita, however, came across two of them, as if arranged by fate, while on a trip to Seville, Spain in 1984.

First she found a beautiful mare which she says, "I knew had to be mine the moment I laid my eyes on her. After several days and visits to the farm, I finally convinced her owner to sell her to me."

The mare, Estudianta XIV, due to foal, delivered but accidentally stepped on her foal. Although all attempts were made to save him, he did not live long. "Filled with all the disappointment in the world," Tita visited another farm, where she saw Calesero III, "the most spectacular black stallion I'd ever laid eyes on.

"That was when the idea to breed my beautiful mare to this magnificent black stallion was conceived," she says. "The liaison took place and eleven months later, on October 1, 1985, the idea took form in a beautiful black filly who had the magnificent sternness and at the same time the sweet melody of an opera; hence her name, Aida."

Aida nearly did not make it to birth; her in-utero life came close to ending in tragedy. Her mother, while in foal, was shipped from Seville to Mexico on an almost-disastrous air freight flight.

"Assigned to a run-down plane by an unscrupulous air freight broker, forty-three horses were loaded, and shortly after the plane took off, one of the motors burned," Tita says. "Only by God's grace did the plane make it to the Bermudas, where it landed with great difficulty. The plane had lost so much altitude it was flying at 3,000 feet."

All this stress affected the mare so that Aida was foaled slightly underweight. Today, however, she is 15.3 hands tall, strong, with beautiful conformation, and she is an apt pupil for training.

Like many breeders in Spain, Tita does not do much with her mares other than break them to learn what type of temperament they have. "But Aida was so spectacular with her naturally elevated movement that it was very obvious she had to go all the way in her training till she perfected her high school," she says.

"Ever since, when she has been shown in competitions and exhibitions, she has always been admired. And, most gratifying to me," says Tita, "when she has competed, she has always come out victorious with a championship ribbon. Her performances are very close to perfection. She comes out trotting like she wants to eat up the whole world.

"My trainer for twenty-nine years, Rafael Ramirez, has trained many horses in all those years, not only mine, but horses for *rejoneadores*, dressage riders, show and pleasure people. He says Aida is the second most intelligent and spirited animal he has ever ridden," she adds.

In February, 1992, Tita sold Aida to a new owner who had become deeply enamored of her, but who vowed to always leave the mare with the breeder and her trainer, since they had made her what she was. A fitting, fairy-tale ending for a storybook-beautiful mare.

Embajador IX

From his almost humanly expressive eye to the tip of his dark silken muzzle, Embajador IX's head has an extra dimension of length to it. That characteristic, linked to his long-ago Barb ancestors, makes him look as though he descended from an oil painting by Diego Velasquez hanging at the Prado Museum in Madrid, just as much as from his biological parents, Hosco II and Embajadora.

The ancestral look of this shimmery white Terry stallion is explained by the fact he is of the purest Carthusian strain, a grandson of Nevado III, who is considered one of the most important stallions in twentieth century Andalusian breeding.

Embajador was trained in dressage to fourth level by Dr. H.L.M. Van Shaik, and is said to have been his favorite mount, an impressive imprimatur as Dr. Van Shaik was a highly respected dressage master and author.

In 1983 Linda and Allan Hamid of Woodbury, Connecticut purchased Embajador from Dr. Van Shaik of Vermont after falling in love with the horse at first sight.

Until then the Hamids had admired Andalusians from afar. Linda Osterman Hamid had spent her junior year at the University of Madrid, which made her an ardent *aficionada* of Spain and its magnificent horses; later she became a Spanish teacher. Allan Hamid, a history teacher at Fox Lane High School in Bedford, New York, had always been intrigued with the Middle Ages. He too became enamored with Andalusians during their many trips to Spain, where they attended the Jerez Horse Fair and saw the spectacular performance at the Royal Andalusian School of Equestrian Art.

In 1984 they began their breeding program when they purchased the lovely Andalusian mare, Bandolera, from Ambassador Alejandro Orfila of Middlebury, Virginia.

As Embajador proved himself as a sire, Allan began researching the breed's history and learned that the Andalusian had contributed to the development of the French Norman Horse.

Allan, a rider who appreciates a beautiful athletic mount with substance and size, decided to bring back the war horse of the ages as the sport horse of today by blending the genes of the Andalusian and the Percheron to recreate the phenotype of the medieval knight's charger.

He launched his crusade in 1987 when he purchased several Percheron mares and began breeding them to Embajador. His focus was to produce as many good riding horses as possible.

"This is a recreation – breeding that has not really existed for several hundred years," Allan says. He points out that in the past Spanish blood contributed to the foundation of many other breeds, such as the Lipizzan, Friesian, the Cleveland Bay, Oldenburger and the Kladruber.

Year after year, the Hamids have bred foals of consistent type – foals that embody the best characteristics of both breeds: boldness, natural collection, elegant, long necks, noble heads, a well-angled shoulder, a short back connected to powerful hindquarters, and a proud character combined with a docile nature.

In 1990, with their goal to recognize and preserve and perpetuate the Spanish Norman horse, the Hamids established the Spanish Norman Horse Registry, Inc., with Allan as president, and Linda as registrar.

According to the Hamids, their desire is to make an important contribution to the horse world by offering horsemen an exceptional but affordable American sport horse.

Embajador, whose name means ambassador in Spanish, is living up to his name in a unique way – in a modern role which recreates a medieval Spanish breeding tradition.

Excalibur

"When you see Excalibur at home, you know he's king of the hill," says Donna Hecht, who with husband, Jay owns Jdon Farms, located in a little pocket of the Angeles National Forest known as Canyon Country, California. "He stands up on top of his mountain and watches over us all. Even the times he's left the ranch on one of his unauthorized solo jaunts, he only goes higher up so that he can watch us all better. We don't own him; he owns us."

Excalibur is a dark-grey-turning-white Andalusian stallion foaled in January, 1989. At 16.3-hands, he is taller than most Spanish horses, and definitely promises to contribute size to the breed. Although he is very friendly, and everyone who sees him falls in love with him, he can at first be somewhat intimidating because of his sheer size.

"We are awed by the powerful beauty and the nobleness with which nature has endowed this particular Andalusian," says Donna. "He has fulfilled our goal of raising big, beautiful, healthy horses that make your heart sing. We are proud to proclaim 'Excaliber – bred by, owned by and standing for Jdon Farms!'"

Donna started out with one mare, Lucenda V, and her foal, Brazos, now a gelding, and "went on from there," as the saying goes. She now has seventeen horses at Jdon, with three more on the way.

Lucy was Excalibur's dam. His sire was Bizarro X.

Donna reports that Excalibur spent his yearling year at the farm pushing his soccer ball up and down the hills. He had a habit of jumping out of his five-foot-high pasture fence for, as is the case with most intelligent horses, he was always curious to know "what's on the other side. In circumstances where most horses would spook, Excalibur is thrilled to find something to investigate," Donna notes.

"The year 1992 will be the first year he will be bred, and we are really looking forward to the 1993 foal crop," says Donna. "Our whole ranch was bought with this in mind...we started our breeding program because Excalibur is so wonderful.

"Jdon Farms is close enough to the city of Los Angeles for fun," Donna says, "but far out enough to be heaven for horses. The exciting young stock being bred at Jdon Farms excels in both halter and performance, and everyone shown comes home with the blue or the championship. Each and every one of these beautiful, strong, healthy horses is a living work of art and each one personifies its Spanish heritage.

"Excalibur, commanding in both size and presence, is a wonderful example of the breeding at Jdon Farms," Donna continues. "In October of the year he was foaled he won his first blue ribbon in the weanling class at the Burbank Fall Classic. In 1991, he dominated the junior stallion division of the International Andalusian Horse Association (IAHA) and at the end of the year he took home the National Junior Champion title. In 1992, he started his performance career by winning every class he entered in the hunt seat division at his first show," she says.

Of all the horses at Jdon, Excalibur is Jay Hecht's favorite. He has expected great things from the stallion who has come through with flying colors. Excalibur's show record is outstanding. Some of the other highlights are: in October, 1989, Top Five Futurity Weanling, IAHA National Show in Burbank; in June, 1991, First Place Two-Year-Old Colt and Reserve Junior Champion, Two Years and Under, Del Mar Charity Fair; in August, 1991, First Place Two-Year-Old Colt, Ventura County Fair; in March, 1992, Hollywood Charity Show Halter Champion; and in April, 1992, Reserve Champion, Albuquerque.

Ofendido VII

"This is going to be MY horse," declared Karen Jenkins when she bought the Andalusian stallion, Ofendido VII in 1986. Karen, whom I met at a dog show, is one of the rare people I've known who shares my love for both Spanish horses and Basenji dogs. She told me she had grown tired of the show ring and having to give her best horses (then Tennessee Walkers and Saddlebreds) to trainers to ride, while she was restricted to riding the second string. With Ofendido it was going to be different, she vowed.

Ofendido, a grey 15.3½-hand stallion was foaled in 1975, and imported from Spain by Pedro Salas of La Lomita ranch in San Luis Obispo, California in the early 1980s. He was bred by Romero Benitez, and sired by Jenson, a well-known stallion at the military stud in Spain. He stood at stud at La Lomita for a number of years and sired a National Champion Mare, Elegancia T, and a champion performance horse, Karo T.

"When Pedro decided to return to Spain in 1986 and was dispersing all the horses he had brought to this country, I was able to lease/purchase the stallion," says Karen. "Pedro was going to take him back to Spain and I

talked him into letting me keep him in this country." She has been breeding since 1984 at her Music City Andalusians in Nashville, Tennessee.

"I had several friends who had Andalusians years ago. I had seen them back in the mid-1960s at an exhibition in Florida, and I was fascinated with them." When the time came that Karen changed what she desired from the horse world, she wanted a personal, special kind of horse and she remembered the horses she'd seen in Florida. "I went to California and spent two weeks there looking at various ranches in the fall of 1984. That's when I got started with Spanish horses," she says.

Today Karen has some twenty on her farm. "A small operation," she says, "with Ofendido as the head sire, the main boy."

He has the rare gene for siring black, she says, and already has sired a black daughter, Alana; a black two-year-old colt, Estrellado; and a new black foal.

Under saddle, Ofendido "is an all-around kind of guy," says Karen. She's shown him in dressage and western pleasure, and has won several driving and western pleasure championships.

"Last year at the Nationals in Fort Worth, Ofendido won the dressage suitability class at age seventeen," adds Karen. "He learned to drive at the age of fifteen. He's a wonderful driving horse and I ride him sidesaddle." Karen has shown Ofendido in Spanish Heritage costume classes, in which he looks especially stunning as he is "very silver," at this point.

As for personality, "Well, he's a love. He likes to show off. When you take him out to show him to people, he hams it up, acts like he's going to be wild, does his stallion thing, looks out across the distance, snorts and tosses his mane," Karen laughs.

"Ofendido is very sure of his number one position. If I don't come to him first in the barn, he turns his back on me. He's definitely my horse. Anybody can handle him, but I've had World Champion Saddlehorses and Walking Horses and a Quarter Horse Champion Mare. I've shown horses for thirty years and these horses, the Andalusians, are different, special, and very smart. Ofendido is very sensitive to his environment and he senses what you want from him."

As a breeder, Karen says, her interest in Andalusians is "to produce a horse that has athletic ability, correct conformation for dressage, and good temperament. Ofendido has all these things.

"Most people who come to Ofendido (with their mares) are looking for his well-known temperament. He represents the type of horse I like to breed – a horse that people can take home and it will become their friend, companion and athletic partner."

Oriana S

Oriana S was the first Andalusian that Karen Jenkins bought, although she had previously been involved with and owned horses of several other breeds. She and a friend went to at least ten different ranches in California without Karen seeing what she wanted. "I was looking for something to hit me in the face. When we got to La Lomita, owned by Pedro Salas, it was the last place we were going to look," says Karen.

The horses at La Lomita were called by shaking a feed can. They were coming down a hill, when Karen caught sight of "a very dark grey, gorgeous mare. She just stood away by herself with a look on her face that said 'You aren't going to sucker me with that routine.' She wasn't unfriendly, just aloof," adds Karen. "Then she started doing show poses in the pasture."

Later Karen would learn that this was the 1983 National Champion Mare. She was heavy in foal at the time, but as Karen walked around her, she struck a pose and let Karen admire her beautiful head and neck and conformation. "There was an aura about her," says Karen. "I said, that's what I want! Unfortunately, she wasn't for sale. I told Warren Mather, the trainer, 'When Mr. Salas changes his mind, let me know.' That was in October 1984. Warren called the first part of December to say that Pedro would sell the mare under the condition I would leave her in California for a couple of years. That was fine with me." Karen bought Oriana, plus a yearling filly, Gracia T and a gelding, Jaro T and took the latter two home with her to Nashville, Tennessee while Oriana stayed behind. "Oriana was a very special mare," Karen says in explaining Mr. Salas' concern. "She was imported by him and was by the stallion, Jecomias out of Orotava, a very, very famous mare who is a legend in the breed.

"Her temperament was very much like that of Orotava, very sweet, very loving, a delight to be around. Visitors' eyes could focus only on her, she was so exquisite."

The following February after Karen bought her, Oriana produced Oro T, who became 1985 Weanling Futurity Champion. Her next foal, by the same sire, Caprichoso S, was a filly named Airoso, who was sold. She became National Champion Junior Mare and Champion Mare in several shows. By the time Oriana's third colt by Caprichoso S was foaled, she had come home to Nashville. That colt's name is Apasionado, and he was champion of two shows as a three-year-old. Next Oriana had a foal by Ofendido named Sereno, and in 1989 another named Oriano.

"In the fall of 1989 Oriana became suddenly very ill with colitis X and died within six hours," says Karen, explaining that disease is an enteritis that quickly builds up toxins in the body. Oriana had had a bout with it the preceding June, but after treatment, which included administering thirty-two liters of fluid, Oriana quickly recovered. In November, however, it struck again and she did not recover.

"It was a very tragic loss," says Karen. "She was only nine years old. She came from a line that had produced dynasties and she would have produced her own if her life had not been cut short. Her dam, Orotava, had been bred to many stallions, always producing something unique, including two National Champion mares, Kiva S and Oriana S.

"Since I had sold Oriana's only filly, I was left without a daughter," says Karen, "but I still have two of her sons, Apasionado and Oriano.

"Oriana S was that special horse I had searched for," says Karen. "I always have that picture in my mind of her coming down that hill with that expressive look which said, 'Look at me, I don't belong with that group down there, I'm special!' She always knew she was." Karen will keep her so forevermore in her memory.

El Sol De Regalado

Growing up, Kathryn Just of Alpine, California, only knew and admired horses from afar. "Their circus performances and parade participation always left me dreaming, but owning one was not a reality," she says. As time went on, Kathryn traveled the world, created her own business, and married. One day over brunch, she and her husband decided to move out of the city and find a ranch in the country. "I am somewhat spontaneous and never seem to have enough time to think things over. I know what I want, I see it and buy it," Kathryn notes.

"It was only appropriate to now look into purchasing a riding horse, since our area had excellent riding trails," Kathryn adds. "Since my main exposure was to the large white ballet horses seen in circuses, which I found were often Andalusians, I looked into the breed. They are not common in my area and it was difficult to find one to look at."

One day a friend called to let Kathryn know a seven-months-old colt by Regalado II and out of Atrevida was available. "My friend said she saw the colt and that it looked sound. Without seeing the colt I bought him," says Kathryn, reasoning, "If I saw him, I wouldn't know what to look for, so I took a chance."

Most of the horse people that Kathryn knew of course thought she was a bit of a fool to take on a valuable colt when she had so little knowledge about horses. "They all told me of horrible things that colts and stallions can do, but I knew I would have him in professional hands for two to three years. Although he would be quite an investment, I felt he was worth the chance. Sure, it would be a long time before I would be able to ride him, but I needed the time to learn how to ride properly anyway," Kathryn remembers. Most important, her dream of owning an Andalusian was coming true!

Filled with excitement and anticipation, Kathryn tried to select the perfect name. It had to speak of fire, strength, brilliance, beauty, excitement, thunder, and kindness. And she found it – El Sol (the sun) De Regalado (for his sire, Regalado II).

After his arrival, Kathryn showed the colt love and kindness, but as he soon grew to 16 hands, he was too tall for her to reach and he was getting a little too playful. "Before anything happened to him or me, I sent him to a training facility. He was never aggressive, but I did not know how to correct him if he did something wrong," she says.

"I put him in what I consider private school for about two years, in training for halter performance. He did well and won ribbons at the shows he entered," Kathryn says. More recently, she brought him closer to home and is preparing him for dressage training. "I am learning dressage riding at the same facility, so hopefully one day I will be good enough to ride him," she says. "We have at least another year before we start him under saddle, so I have some time to learn.

"I am thirty-two years old, and have only been around horses for three years, but I feel as though I've started life again," says Kathryn. "Learning to groom, balance, walk, trot and run is a wonderful discovery for me, and I'm so grateful that 'The Horse' has touched my life. It's no wonder so many books, songs, photos, paintings and movies, are based on horses. It's no wonder they are cherished and loved as much as they are. My eyes are opened to a new wonder, and I wish every animal person could know a fine horse at least once in his or her life," says Kathryn, a neophyte who is making good on her risk-taking.

Bravo

Bravo, son of the legendary Legionario III, Grand Champion of Spain in 1965, has a three-fold job description at Rancho Vistoso in Santa Fe, New Mexico.

First of all, he is a breeding stallion and secondly, he is a public relations horse, helping to promote his breed in the state of New Mexico. Third, he is owner Edward Klopfer's special friend and teacher.

"Bravo is a horse that comes along once in a lifetime," says Edward. "He has a real presence and when in the ring or in a parade demands the attention of everyone. He is intelligent, mischievous, graceful, extremely athletic, loves to show off, and sometimes has a mind of his own. Riding him is always fun and often a challenge," adds Edward, who began riding at the age of nine, when his mother bought him a Christmas present of twenty-five rides at a local riding stable. College and the U.S. Navy interrupted Edward's riding activities, but they resumed in 1977 when he and his wife Donna moved to Santa Fe.

"The West got me riding again," he says. In 1986 he began to reduce his engineering practice and he and Donna started their small Andalusian breeding operation, Rancho Vistoso Andalusians. With the help of California trainer, Art Gaytan, two females – Lanca III from Garrison Ranch and Dax Aploma, a three-year-old filly from Rainbow Farms, a Reserve National Champion in 1987 – were purchased.

Two years later, the Klopfers decided to purchase a quality stallion, and through Art Gaytan obtained Bravo.

"The gamble proved to be in our favor, as his libido, fertility and the offspring he has sired have been most impressive," says Edward.

To date, Bravo and Lanca III have produced two magnificent colts, Relampago, foaled in 1989, and Trueno, foaled in 1990. (Lightning followed by Thunder.) Both colts are intelligent and easy to handle, even by Donna, who is completely new to the horse world.

The aptly-named Bravo also is a star performer. When purchased, he had been trained to fourth level in dressage, in California. The Klopfers retained dressage rider Tosha Zubrisky to show Bravo. Even competing against the massive Warmbloods who dominate dressage today, the pair scored well enough to be invited to the USDF Nationals.

Bravo's handsome appearance and his movements have always created a stir in the show ring, says Edward. "No one who sees Bravo ever forgets him.

"Bravo's training and ability prompted me to begin dressage lessons with April Maybee in Santa Fe, and Charles de Kunffy who comes to her stable for clinics. My riding skills have improved considerably, and I owe this to Bravo," Ed adds.

One of his most special times with Bravo was riding him in the Tournament of Roses Parade in 1988. "How he loved the attention and excitement," says Ed.

In the future, Ed and Bravo will focus on freestyle riding to music at shows. "He is at his best when he is allowed to 'ham it up' with flying changes, half-passes, and passage," says Ed. "He can give an electric performance which people do not forget, because he is so athletic and agile.

"Bravo is my pal and my teacher. A person could not want more in a horse!"

Celoso VI

"Celoso" means "jealous" in Spanish. And jealous, envious, is exactly how Pamela Kelley felt the first time she laid eyes on the four-year-old almost-black Andalusian stallion as he stepped off the horse van in the mist of a dark November night in 1985. Even in the dim light she could see that he was beautiful, short-coupled, long-legged, with a flowing mane and tail. He was amazingly calm, too, considering he was being delivered on a cold, foggy night to a strange place. "It seemed as though he belonged there, with me, for good," remembers Pamela.

Son of the legendary Temerario V, twice National Champion Stallion and grandson of the International Champion Legionario III, no wonder Celoso VI had presence.

Pamela had just spent a year's study in England with Danny Pevsner (who had trained at the Spanish Riding School of Vienna) and Celoso's owner asked her to take charge of Celoso's dressage training at her farm in Southern California.

"I felt excited and, truthfully, a little nervous, about

using all the knowledge Danny had given me on Celoso," says Pamela.

The stallion settled into her barn almost immediately. Pamela had several Andalusians of her own, including Grand National Champion Garbosa XII and Reserve National Champion Sonrisa. Celoso was in horse heaven whistling at those gorgeous girls across the aisle. The only horse he didn't take to was the other stallion in the barn, a Lusitano named Rapaz. "But I guess that's why his name was Jealous," says Pamela.

"The time came to ride this boy. He had been started very nicely at his previous stable. He had brilliant manners and was so absolutely accurate that one dare not be incorrect with him. I told my husband Richard that it was a bit like having lunch with Prince Charles and always having to be careful to use the right fork. The more I worked with this horse, the more I fell in love with him. And the more I wanted him to be mine."

The fates, heeding Pamela's longing, devised a way. In 1988 her husband was promoted and had the opportunity to move the headquarters of his company. He and Pamela flew East to see for themselves what living there might be like. Just a few days into their trip they found their present home, Hardscrabble Farm in North Salem, New York, one of the horsey capitals of that area. They talked excitedly on the plane back to Los Angeles. Needless to say, the conversation turned to the transportation of their horses and inevitably to the question of Celoso, the one horse in their barn they didn't own, and the one horse Pamela least wanted to leave behind.

Celoso's owner came out and, seeing how happy the horse was and how much Pamela loved him, was persuaded to make a deal. Celoso was now hers.

Off they went to North Salem: Celoso, his girls, and even his arch rival, Rapaz. The warmth of spring baking the earth and the soft smells of fresh grass made all the girls dream of motherhood. That suited Celoso, too. By the following spring, four foals, all with his stamp of elegance, were on the ground. Eventually they went to farms from California to Connecticut.

It was now high time to get back to work; Pamela felt the need to take her riding to a higher level and began working with Lucy Niewisch who had studied in Germany and had run the training and breeding facility of the Rockefeller family for twenty-five years.

With Lucy's help, Celoso's stride was dramatically changed and improved. His movement became very forward, and he learned self-carriage.

"We now feel Celoso has come into his own. He's in his prime. And it's hard to believe that over seven years have passed from the moment I first laid eyes on him," says Pamela. "Where do we go from here? I'll have to ask Celoso!"

Banbury Elsa

Banbury Elsa is a very proud and regal purebred Andalusian broodmare who asks for very little attention from her owners or her foals, but gives greatly of herself. She brings something special into the lives of everyone she touches just by being who she is.

"The joy Banbury Elsa brings to the Kennedy family comes simply from having her and her offspring at our small farm," says John P. Kennedy of Lee's Hill Farm in New Vernon, New Jersey.

"Elsa always provides ample nourishment for her foals and exhibits great patience from the time they first stand until the time they are weaned. She is always protective and sees that her youngsters are first into the loafing shed in high winds or thunderstorms. If the space is limited, she will remain out in the weather, as if on guard," says John.

"From a business standpoint, having just Elsa and her youngsters to care for is a minimalist approach," he adds. "The Kennedys prefer to bring Elsa to fine purebred stallions and keep her offspring as young, matured fillies and colts. In this way they can see them grow to the age of four or five before selling them, preferably to buyers in the local area. This serves the desires of most of the buyers who prefer a horse ready to be enjoyed as a pleasure horse or ready to be started in training for eventing or dressage. Since Andalusians are slow in maturing, the Kennedys benefit from having Elsa's offspring at the farm well beyond the weanling stage."

Banbury Elsa was bred by Sally Cleaver, a prominent breeder of Spanish horses, and foaled on May 16, 1976. She was sired by Octobre, out of Eslava, who in turn was sired by the famous Terry stallion Honroso II. Elsa's dam's dam was the eminent Orotava, sired by Leopardo, one of the leading stallions of the Spanish Military Stud, and a sire used by the Peralta brothers in their program for breeding bullfighting horses. Orotava was foaled in 1960 at the Tabajete stud farm near Jerez de la Frontera; her family has had tremendous importance all over the world.

Eslava has been nearly as successful as a broodmare as her famous dam, Orotava. Eslava's filly Banbury Eureka was sold to Maritza Parra of San Antonio, and Banbury Estella went to the stud of J. Miller in Australia.

The Kennedys first became familiar with the Andalusian breed while vacationing in the south of Spain in the early 1970s. Many years later, in 1986, the Kennedys purchased Banbury Elsa from Mrs. Cleaver, with whom they have been friends since Banbury Cross Farm was established in Goshen, New York.

Elsa was brought from Banbury Cross Farm in Colorado to Lee's Hill Farm in foal to Banbury Coronel, one of that farm's leading stallions. Her foal, Banbury Juan Pablo, was recently sold as a four-year-old to Cathy Stephanowicz of Hainesport, New Jersey, as a dressage prospect. Banbury Elsa was later bred to Banbury Sampson. That foal, Banbury Elena, has remained with the Kennedys.

At the present time, Banbury Elsa is in foal to Celoso IV, who is owned by another prominent Andalusian breeder, Pamela Kelley of Hardscrabble Farm in North Salem, New York.

"Elsa is, beyond everything else, a wonderful mother possessing all the wonderful characteristics of the Andalusian breed, notably great intelligence and character. She passes on her tractable disposition along with the good bone and strong conformation that are the signature of the breed," the Kennedys say in tribute to this devoted mother mare.

Falicia

From their front porch on their new horse farm, Cahaba Valley Andalusians, just south of Birmingham, Alabama, Judy Thompson and Bill Killingsworth can sit in their rocking chairs and gaze at a wonderful sight.

Their pastures are similar to those of the blue grass area of Kentucky in that they lie over limestone rock, are deep green and bordered by stands of stately oaks and cedars, and are filled with horses whose beauty matches, even exceeds, the natural loveliness of their farm.

Ten exquisite horses of Iberian blood graze in these pastures, the only Andalusians in the Deep South states of Alabama and Mississippi, say Judy and Bill. They take great pride in introducing their neighbors to their horses and seeing the excitement in people's eyes when they see this magnificent breed for the first time. They recall experiencing the same uncommon excitement five years ago when they themselves saw their first Andalusians.

Judy recalls it was October, 1987. They were living in Santa Ynez, California, and had gone to visit Bruce Howard, a noted Southern California horse trainer. He recommended the Andalusian breed to them and showed them the young stallion Castiblanco III, the 1983 National Champion Stallion, a grandson of Legionario III, National Champion of Spain and the first Andalusian imported into this country by the Garrison Ranch.

"He was easily the most spectacular horse either of us had ever seen; our love affair with Andalusians began," says Judy.

Through their neighbors, John and Bo Derek, who owned and bred Andalusians, the gelding Caprichoso S III, became "our first Andalusian and my best friend," says Bill.

Soon after, Judy purchased Bilbaino V, a five-year-old gelding, for her pleasure horse. That same year, 1988, Bilbaino V was named the IAHA National Champion Gelding. "Needless to say, after that we were hooked and in a very big way," says Judy. "We now have ten Andalusians, and love them all, but our stars are Falicia and Zafiro."

Remembering Castiblanco's looks, movement, and breeding, Judy and Bill wanted to own one of his offspring. They first saw his three-year-old daughter, Falicia, in 1989, as she began her show career. An immediate superstar, in her first year of showing, she was National Reserve Champion Mare, and in 1990, she was selected National Champion Mare. Judy and Bill bought her in 1991. The dappled grey, who stands a magnificent 16.2 hands, is now the premier mare of Cahaba Valley Andalusians.

Bill enjoys driving Falicia, which he says is like "driving a V-12 Jaguar. You have beauty and refined elegance, but power that commands utter attention and respect."

Judy and Bill plan to show Falicia throughout the Southeastern United States in 1992 and then will cross her with their star stallion, Zafiro, hoping to share with others their goal of breeding Andalusians that have the substance, strength, style, personality and athletic ability that distinguish the very best of the breed.

Zafiro

Judy Thompson and William Killingsworth recall seeing Zafiro, now the star stallion on their Cahaba Valley Andalusian horse farm in Alabama, for the first time in 1988 as a four-year-old in training.

"We thought he was the most sensational-looking and spectacular-moving horse that we had ever seen," says Judy.

"Zafiro has a marvelously refined and chiseled face with the classic Andalusian forelock cascading over his alert and intelligent eyes. He is now a beautiful silver dapple grey standing 16.1 hands, but his arched neck, proud upright carriage and lush abundant mane make him appear to be much larger," she says.

"We were, and continue to be, unabashedly starstuck by this very special creature," says Bill, who adds that a close friend of theirs describes Zafiro as "the most gorgeous living thing he has ever seen."

"We loved him and wanted him from the first time we saw him, but his breeder, the Garrison Ranch, did not seem to want to sell him," adds Judy. "When we returned from our wedding trip in February, 1990, we were thrilled to learn that the Garrisons had miraculously included Zafiro on their annual sales list. We decided that he would be the perfect wedding gift to ourselves," she says.

The couple called immediately to close the deal, and luckily so, as several other admirers were interested.

"By the time we purchased him, Zafiro had earned literally dozens of show championships in saddle seat and pleasure driving," says Judy.

"Bill decided to learn to drive and during 1990, Bill and Zafiro made a spectacular pair at many Andalusian shows."

Their trainer, Bruce Howard, showed Zafiro for the 1991 show season, during which Zafiro earned awards as the 1991 International Andalusian Horse Association High Point Pleasure Driving Horse and National Pleasure Driving Champion.

After Zafiro is campaigned in 1992, Judy plans a possible new career for him.

"Zafiro is a dynamo to ride saddle seat," she says, "but I dream of having him trained in *haute ecole*. His high, round action, controlled energy and mental quickness make him a natural to master the movements. His extraordinary beauty and quality should make him a superior and awe-inspiring exhibition horse."

Zafiro, who comes from a family of champions, and is a champion himself, is now the sire of champions.

His first foal crop was born in 1988. Two fillies, Zafira and Zinnia both have been successful in the show ring. Zafira was the 1990 IAHA National Champion Junior Mare and Zinnia was 1991 IAHA National Reserve Champion Mare. During the 1991 show season, Zinnia also won several Pleasure Driving Championships. Zafiro had sired five more foals, all fillies, one of which, Maresa, belongs to Judy and Bill.

As breeders, Judy and Bill are aiming for the animated front-end action coupled with the powerful impulsion off the hocks, which characterizes the very best performance horses both in the show and dressage rings. They are combining outstanding physical beauty with the kind of movement that makes the Andalusian four-legged poetry in motion.

Infante T

"This horse has more heart than I have ever seen," says Nancy Lindquist of her Andalusian stallion, Infante T, whom she shares with her husband, Buck, at their Danza Del Sol Andalusians in Gregory, Michigan.

"Personality-wise, Infante T is the most incredible horse I have ever encountered! He is very intelligent, and perhaps even more important, he has a desire to please! Oh, Infante has his moments where he would rather just fool around. All stallions do, but on the whole, Infante will try very hard to do what you ask," says Nancy, who helps her veterinarian husband with his large and small animal practice.

The following is just one example of what Infante does for the Lindquists: In 1990 when the stallion was five, Buck and Nancy left Michigan with him, two mares and a gelding in a large, four-horse trailer for an Andalusian show in Tennessee. About 11 p.m., moving along on the expressway, two tires blew out. They crawled off the expressway to a large truck stop and tried to find someone to fix the tires. Impossible at that time of night, they were told. While Buck and Nancy were trying to make arrangements, Infante and their other Andalusians stood quietly and patiently in the trailer. Huge semi-trucks rolled in and out too near them all night, precluding any chance of letting them out for a stretch.

The next morning, Buck went into the nearest town to buy tires, replaced them, and got back on the road.

They pulled into the show grounds that afternoon, only to find that the stallion halter class in which Infante was entered was being held for them. At this point Infante had been in the trailer for twenty-eight hours straight.

Buck and Nancy looked at each other, took deep breaths and got Infante out of the trailer. She changed clothes while Buck put Infante's show halter on. Nancy ran with him to the show ring to find their class ready to go into the ring. Infante was brushed but didn't have his usual "spit and polish."

"I looked around at all the other Andalusian stallions who were shining clean and rested and wondered what I was doing to Infante by asking him to show after all he had been through," says Nancy. "As the stallions went into the ring, I apologized to Infante and asked him to just do his best; I loved him no matter where we placed."

But Infante reached down into his heart, pulled out some inner *brio*, and actually went strutting into that ring. He put on a real show for the judge.

"I was so proud of him, I didn't care if we came in last," says Nancy. "When it was all said and done, the judge placed Infante second. He had beaten all but one of his competitors."

Infante, which in Spanish means "heir to the throne," has done quite well since in the show ring. In 1991, in only three shows, he went up against some of the best Andalusians in the country and took Champion Halter Stallion once, Reserve Champion twice, Get-of-Sire class twice, and Dressage Suitability at all three shows.

But the second place they won in Tennessee "means more than all the other firsts, reserve championships, and championships Infante has since gone on to win!" says Nancy.

The Lindquists found their Spanish treasure in 1986 at a sale in California, and broke him themselves when he was three. When he was four they enlisted the help of Julie Doll, a dressage trainer, who has become his admirer and second horse "mom."

Performance star, halter hero, sire of substance, great companion animal, there's only one area where Infante's genetic ancestry hasn't quite kicked in yet.

Trainer Julie took Infante on his first trail ride. "Our first encounter with cows was quite something," she recalls. "They were pretty scary standing still, but when they ran at him and started mooing, I thought we were going to lose him. He didn't run, he turned into a rock—well, a quivering rock. His heart was pounding so hard, I could feel its pulse under my leg."

So much for a bullfighting career!

Del-More's Danzante

The Spanish stallion, Del-More's Danzante, alias "Z," made the front page of the local newspapers after being picked up on a "vagrancy" charge in his hometown of Summerville, South Carolina, just north of historic Charleston.

Z had somehow, through the grace of God and his own good sense, survived Hurricane Hugo, the most devastating storm ever to hit the continental United States, on September 22, 1989. His owner, Thomas E. Mavrikes, made the decision not to lock Z in his stall, as he would stand a better chance of surviving by running free. The 135 m.p.h. winds hit full force at ten p.m. and continued until midnight.

When dawn broke, Thomas did not know what to expect. Making his way to the paddock, he found Z surrounded by fallen trees and limbs that had boxed him in so that he could not move forward or backward or even side to side. At his feet stood his two companion goats, all spattered with mud, which at first Thomas thought was blood. After he managed to free Z, he found there was not a scratch on him, or the goats.

So much damage had been done by Hugo that a lot of quick fence-mending had to be done. Early one morning a short time later, Thomas received a phone call from the Summerville Police Department, saying there were reports that a white stallion was walking down Main Street, through the center of town.

Thomas had undergone oral surgery the day before, and had been heavily sedated. However, this news awoke him enough to check to find Z was missing. "I was extremely stressed out," he says.

A policewoman finally found Z standing under a lamp post on a side street. She quietly walked up to him and slipped a rope around his neck. Thomas, asked to come and get him, haltered Z and walked him back home.

"Again, this behavior pays tribute to the good sense of this fine stallion," says Thomas. "Since this was the first time in ten years that Z had gotten out of his large paddock area on his own, I certainly couldn't fault him for finding his way out of a place that wasn't well-repaired after Hurricane Hugo. He just decided that he wanted to take a walk."

Thomas had found Z through a breeder's ad in a magazine, a magazine which he was leafing through while recuperating from a compound fractured skull with multiple brain bruises. He had landed on his head "jumping ship" from a runaway gelding on the twenty-ninth day of a month's lease. "I thought surely there must be another breed of horse that would be easier to handle," he says.

His eyes kept returning to a portrait of a purebred Spanish horse, prized for its symmetry, its beauty.

He flew to Dayton, Ohio, and met Z (sired by Recluta II out of Banbury Chata), when he was only three months old. Z came home to Summerville in January, 1982. As a first-time horse owner, Thomas is proud of raising his young colt on his own. He has many memories of their "firsts" together – first bath, the first time Z wore a blanket, first walks around the neighborhood showing him off.

"Z took it all in stride and never gave me a bit of trouble," says Thomas. He was inspired to take an interest in breeding, adding two purebred mares to the small operation he called El Greco Andalusians in honor of his Greek-American ethnic background.

"My acquisition of this Andalusian stallion has meant not only gaining a great pal and companion, but through him I have also met and become involved with so many fine people interested in the breed," says Thomas.

"My horse, Del-More's Danzante, has given me tremendous pleasure over the years, and has added immeasurably to the quality of my life. He has taught me the art of giving."

Majorio

Majorio once stole the day from a bride when he became the star of her wedding. The white Andalusian stallion with a nose-tip forelock proudly carried the princess-dressed bride "down the aisle" through a rose garden. Stopping to bow elegantly before a string quartet playing the theme from *Romeo and Juliet*, he allowed the bride to slip from the saddle and meet her waiting bridegroom. The scene was straight from a storybook, and the bride didn't seem to mind that Majorio stole the show!

Majorio was always into show biz. Edith Evans-Williams, who owned the former "Kingdom of the Dancing Stallions" and was an accomplished *rejoneadora* or bullfighter on horseback, had taught him a repetoire of exhibition moves, such as bowing and the Spanish walk. Before the stallion was purchased by Richard and Marcia Moquin of Placerville, California, he worked with a dressage rider who rode with Olympian and Pan American Games medalist, Hilda Gurney.

The Moquins purchased Majorio, now twenty, as a six-year-old from The Garrison Ranch, after seeing a television Christmas special featuring Andalusians. They were fortunate to relive some of his early years through

pictures and stories provided by his breeder, Pat Garrison.

"He was a beautiful example of a horse of any breed, but was almost mystical with his luxuriously flowing mane and tail," recalls Marcia.

After purchasing Majorio, the Moquins' lives took on a whole new dimension and a direction revolving around horses. They soon found themselves learning to ride a horse trained far beyond their casual expertise. Both the Moquins had ridden solely for pleasure before they bought Majorio. They found he had many "buttons" they didn't quite understand. "Therefore when we rode him, he did many unexpected things. A tight rein and a sloppy leg might result in a piaffer," says Marcia. "After some time, with the help of trainers, we learned where the buttons were, much to Majorio's relief. He never really lost his patience, but often you could sense that he was quite perturbed at the ignorance of his new and inept riders. Fortunately, his wonderful temperament and the fact that he had been expertly handled as a young horse made him an easy lesson."

The Moquins also had to learn the ropes of showing and establishing a breeding program, while becoming actively involved in the beginnings of the International Andalusian Horse Association.

"The writing of that one check was the beginning of a whole new way of life for us, and the start of what now numbers a herd of twelve at our Grandalusian Ranch," says Marcia.

The unique name for their farm, founded soon after their purchase of Majorio, came about when a teenage friend fell in love with the stallion and began referring to him as "the grand illusion Andalusian."

"We liked the label and took the name for our ranch," says Marcia.

Majorio has become a very dear member of the Moquin family. "He was our first 'child,' soon to be followed by a daughter and son of the two-legged variety," says Marcia. Majorio became Richard's western pleasure mount while Marcia was pregnant, winning numerous amateur owner and open western pleasure championships.

"Our children have grown up around the horses and it is amazing to watch a special relationship develop between horse and child. Majorio seems to sense something special about children and always shows a sensitivity and gentleness around them," she says.

Majorio, well known in the Andalusian world for the refinement of his head, has been featured in many Spanish riding exhibitions and has participated in twelve Tournament of Roses Parades in Pasadena, California. Even as a twenty-year- old, he has lots of zest and thoroughly enjoys life and the audience's response when in a parade, exhibition, or the odd wedding.

Almirante

Almirante was one of the first Andalusians to be seen in the state of Texas. And the first Andalusian Patty Mitchell owned.

"The Parras (Rafael and Maritza) and I were the only two to introduce the breed to this area of the country," says Patty.

Patty had no idea what an Andalusian was or looked like when her father came home from a trip to Mexico City and a visit to the ranch of a friend, Gabriel Alarcon, Jr., and said, "Would you like to have one? They're white."

"He called them Spanish horses," says Patty. "He thought it was the way to go. It was something novel for the time, about sixteen years ago. It's grown since then," she says of Andalusian horse *afición*.

She saw Almirante in a photo. He came from the ranch of Alarcón in Mexico City, but she bought him through a man in California, whom she knew and trusted. "My first reaction when I saw Almirante was 'I don't believe I have my first Andalusian. I have something nobody else has.' I was in hog heaven."

Then the snake appeared in her Eden. "When I went to get Almirante's papers, he was registered as a half-Andalusian. The seller said, 'Well, we'll take him back.' I couldn't; I was in love with him by then. He was too good, too wonderful, to give him up." Spectacular to look at, he was solid white, his mane falling past his shoulder.

Later, Patty says, "Anyone who ever saw him who knew Andalusians said, 'There's no way he could be half—he's pure.' It turned out his great-grandam's papers were messed up and couldn't be fixed."

Almirante turned out to be as special to work with as to look at. Patty had only worked with one or two stallions of other breeds, "but Almirante kind of blew my mind. He was such a gentleman, even at age three."

Eventually, Patty bought another Andalusian stallion and three mares and began breeding, calling her place Doñana Farm (in Tomball, Texas). "I had fifty of them at one point," she sighs. "Mostly stallions. It was craziness, but absolutely wonderful."

Patty broke Almirante and trained him herself. "I took him all the way. We got up to almost fourth level in dressage. He taught me a lot. I taught him a lot. He was one fantastic animal.

His foals were registered as half-Andalusians. Two of them are working in circuses, doing dressage work.

"He was ten when he died. He colicked. I was out of town. They sent him straight up to Texas A & M where they pulled about fifteen gallons of fluid out of his belly; it was sand colic. I brought him home and he was nothing but bone. He made it another five months. Then I had to take a trip to Louisiana to get my owner's license for Quarter Horse racing, and he died the morning I left. He had thrashed himself to pieces. I'm glad I didn't see it. It was very devastating. I never thought he'd die, so I never took any pictures of him..."

In his memory Patty had a plaque made by a friend who did wood carving. "I used some words I found in *Equus*," says Patty:

"'And God took a handful of southerly wind. Blew his breath over it and created the horse. Through his mane and tail the high wind sings. Fanning the hairs who wave like feathered wings.' I keep the plaque in the barn hanging on the wall where everybody can see it. It has Almirante's name at the top...

"We were really a pair. I've never had another one since. Oh, I've had other horses...but not one can take his place..."

Amiga

It is seldom that an author has the fulfillment of knowing that his work has been instrumental in bringing great beauty into someone else's life.

That was the welcome surprise for me when I read Gisela Mueller's account of her "greatest love affair ever," which she says began on Christmas, 1985, when she received two of my books – *Equus* and *Such Is the Real Nature of Horses*.

"The cover of *Equus* with the majestic snow-white Andalusian stallion in a field of wild poppies fascinated me beyond what any words can describe," says Gisela, of Haddam, Connecticut.

"This was the horse I wanted. His name was Majestad; how befitting!"

Needless to say, she could not have him in the flesh, but if horses have a collective soul as some philosophers believe, then she found a feminine version of him in her grey Andalusian mare, Amiga.

Gisela found Amiga, sired by Arrogante, and foaled May 25, 1980, in California. "It was a wonderful relationship from the very start," says Gisela. "Amiga is beautiful, intelligent, very spirited and yet so gentle. There is trust and great understanding and also respect between us. Amiga is my best friend and I am hers. I can see it in her beautiful, big, brown, velvety eyes that can express any emotion or feeling so well."

Gisela wasn't happy with boarding Amiga for the first two years, so she bought her own place where Amiga could be queen. "To see her gallop through the green pastures, her long silky mane flowing in the wind, is a picture to behold!" she says. "What power, agility, and grace. I wish I could give her thousands of acres to run in, but a little less than nine acres will have to do, and I think she is happy."

In 1987 Gisela bred Amiga to the outstanding stallion, Caprichoso S. When Amiga went through motherhood, so did Gisela in an empathetic way.

"I think that during that time we became even closer. As her time came nearer, I started to worry," says Gisela. "Everybody gave me advice that made a total wreck out of me. My greatest concern was: What if something goes wrong and I lose Amiga? The last several nights of her pregnancy I got up every two hours to go in the barn to check on her. I wasn't about to trust the monitor attached to her stall.

"Finally, one evening, I was so nervous, that I did not wait the two hours to check. I felt that she needed me. As I came in the barn, she looked at me, laid down, and the miracle of birth began. I know in my heart that she had waited for me to be there by her side. Her big brown eyes constantly looked at me."

Luckily, Amiga didn't really need help. Everything went well and she had a colt.

"The only name I wanted was Majestad," says Gisela. "Wasn't it THE Majestad that made me fall in love with the most aristocratic, noble and beautiful horse in the world – the Andalusian?"

For five months, it was "a heavenly time" for all, Amiga trusting Gisela with handling her foal in any way.

But the inevitable sad parting came when Majestad left for what Gisela calls "kindergarten." He went to another farm where he could be in a pasture socializing with playmates his age. It was traumatic for all, but time has helped heal the pain.

Living on the northeast coast of the United States as they do, Gisela and Amiga have to contend with harsh weather conditions, including below-freezing temperatures during winter. "Every year we can't wait for spring to arrive," says Gisela. "Soon the pastures become green and the flowers bloom, especially the wild poppies that we seeded. It is like a little bit of heaven. To ride Amiga through the green meadows with poppies dancing in the breeze makes me feel like stepping out of a page of Robert Vavra's book. I feel it is a privilege and an honor to know and live with a horse of a unique and noble breed. This I solemnly vow: to cherish and protect this rare, magnificent creature – the Andalusian horse of Spain."

May the fates protect and cherish all those who feel the same way.

Caprichoso S II

Caprichoso S II is a show-stopper as a *haute ecole* exhibition horse, a real credit to his trainer, Glen Randall of Newhall, California, famous for training many well-known movie horses, including Cass Olé of *Black Stallion* fame.

While Caprichoso hasn't hit the movie screens, he is a wonderful public relations horse for both the Iberian breed and his owner, Ann B. Ohrel of Rancho El Canto in Tumacacori, Arizona, professional breeder of both pure Spanish and Portuguese horses, the Spanish/Portuguese cross and the Azteca, an Iberian/Quarter Horse cross.

"Caprichoso's beauty and the high quality of his get have attracted people to the Andalusian breed and helped to promote our ranch," says his owner.

Ann had been exposed to other breeds, since she started riding at five-years-old, showing in saddleseat equitation and in five-gaited classes.

After she married, Ann got into Tennessee Walking Horses and eventually had horses that won seven World Championships at the National Celebration in Shelbyville, Tennessee.

But nothing quite made the impact on her that the Iberian horse did.

"In 1959 I went to a *corrida* in Ciudad Juarez, Mexico, to see a Portuguese friend taking part in it," Ann recalls. "As a bonus, a *rejoneador* performed on an Andalusian horse. I had never seen a horse as athletic and beautiful, and I started looking for one. At that time there were very few in this country, and after searching for nine years, I bought Lusitano in 1968 from *rejoneadora* Edith Evans, who had used him for *rejoneo*. After that I bought two purebred Spanish mares and then Caprichoso, who has fulfilled my dream of breeding the world's most beautiful horses and introduced me to Spanish and Portuguese culture, music and history, as well as many new friends."

Caprichoso is a brown-flecked grey, has a very long, thick mane and tail and a beautiful classic head which Ann says "make him look like a dream horse."

Caprichoso was foaled February 19, 1976 at Palma de Mallorca, bred of 100 percent Terry bloodlines, by Pedro Salas. He was imported by Don Pedro to his ranch, La Lomita, at San Luis Obispo, California.

"My husband and I were looking for a stallion to use on the daughters of Lusitano and visited several of the best breeding farms on the West Coast. We kept returning to La Lomita again and again to see Caprichoso. "Even at two years of age, he seemed to have the conformation and presence which would complement the qualities of our mares," says Ann.

"As a three-year-old, Caprichoso was sent to Glen Randall, and his training changed my focus from just pleasure riding to dressage and high school exhibition work," says Ann. "Spectators are as impressed by his bows as they are by his passage and piaffer.

She describes Caprichoso, whose name means "full of caprices or whims," as just that. "He is highly intelligent and seems to anticipate what you will ask him to do. If he doesn't feel like doing it, he will substitute what he wants to do. That is, if you ask for the passage, he may give you the Spanish walk. If he has a strong, self-confident rider—one he feels won't let him get away with his antics—then he gives up and behaves."

Caprichoso has a son, Conquistador, who was the Reserve All-Around Champion at the 1990 IAHA Nationals. He has several daughters who are doing well in open dressage competition and combined driving.

"Horses have always been of utmost importance in my life, so much so that most of my friends are horse people and almost all my vacations are horse-oriented," says Ann. "I can't imagine life without horses."

Dejado

Dejado and I first became acquainted in Sevilla, Spain, the same place where years before I had met his American owners, Rafael and Maritza Parra.

Dejado was foaled on the farm of another friend, the late Manilo Novales, respected breeder of Andalusians. So when I think of Dejado and his ebony beauty, I think of the most brilliant fields of red wildflowers that in the springtime surrounded his existence, and the ochre summer pastures where as a foal he spent his youth.

The Parras had also seen Dejado when he was very young and kept an eye on his progress.

His bloodlines were brilliant. His sire was a very famous stallion, Ganador VI, from the Escalera line, and his dam was Dejada II.

He was also "a very, very unusual color," says Maritza Parra, one of the most charming of horse-loving friends ever to enter my life.

Andalusians are generally born black or dark brown, but usually change to grey, white, or bay in maturity. Photographing Dejado (he was in my book *Vavra's Horses* as one of the ten most beautiful stallions in the world) proved that "negro" is not simply negro. His color depended upon the time of day he was photographed. The ever-changing light highlighted his ebony coat with shades of blue, green, silver and red. No better example than he could be used to illustrate that "black is beautiful."

"We first saw Dejado when he was one year old," says Maritza. "We went back to see him when he was two and we went back again to actually purchase him when he was three. By that time, he had passed his stallion inspection in Spain, a process by which he was evaluated by three officials of the military stud."

Dejado is now eleven and is sovereign stallion at Andalusians de la Parra in San Antonio, Texas.

Trained in classical dressage, he is used in exhibitions as well as for breeding.

"I consider Dejado one of the star Andalusian stallions anywhere," says Maritza. "I love, and my family loves, all our stallions...but my husband, Rafael, has a weak spot in his heart for Dejado," admits Maritza.

"I think it is his gentleness and his fire. He can be so quiet and then two minutes later he's performing and he has all this energy. He has this pride and the look in his eye that says, 'I'm the best in the world.'"

Dr. Parra, a highly respected neurosurgeon, has traveled many times to Spain in search of a new stallion or mare to add to the already outstanding bloodstock at his breeding farm. He and his family have done more to promote the Andalusian breed in this country than any other breeder.

At the 1988 Horse Fair at Belmont Racetrack in New York, 250,000 people were captivated by the spectacular demonstration of the Andalusians de la Parra. Another performance in Illinois at the largest horse exposition in the United States followed. As goodwill ambassadors, this outstanding family and its stallions have traveled to Oklahoma, Nevada, California and throughout Texas to offer exhibitions for charity events while promoting the Andalusian horse.

In these exhibitions, Dejado is sometimes ridden by the Parra's lovely daughter Maritza, and sometimes by their son, Rafael Alberto, who show the stallions in authentic Spanish and Portuguese saddles, bridles and costumes.

The Parras have taken the care to hire the world's top trainers – trainers with intimate knowledge of the breed's mentality and athleticism.

For many years, a guest trainer at Andalusians de la Parra was the immortal Nuno Oliveira of Portugal, considered one of the last of the classicists. Since his recent passing, Nuno's son, Joao, comes to San Antonio to spend an entire month overseeing the training of the Parra horses and polishing their performances.

The Parras continue to live by the feeling that the very nobility, rarity and majesty of their horses demands nothing less than the best they can provide.

Banbury Rebuscada

Purebred Spanish horses were reintroduced to the United States in 1964 when Glenn O. Smith of New Mexico imported the Marquis de Paradas mare, Rebuscada.

Years later, Smith told breeder Sally Cleaver, owner of Banbury Cross Farms, that she must one day name "a good one" in honor of the first Spanish horse to set hooves on American soil since the days of the Conquistadors.

Banbury Rebuscada was foaled in New York in the summer of 1979, sired by Banbury Cross Farm's major breeding stallion, Octobre, himself a son of the famous Capitan XIII, and out of the Banbury mare Celosa, by Embajador IX, a Carthusian stallion. "She was pretty spectacular-looking," says her present owner, Margot Reynolds. "Big black eye, dappled grey, and Sally thought she was the proper candidate for fulfilling her promise to Smith."

Six years later, in the spring of 1985, Margot bought the "sweet, expressive" Banbury Rebuscada.

"It was quite literally a dream come true, a dream that had its beginnings seven years earlier in the town of Puerto de Santa Maria in the heart of Andalucia," Margot says.

In the spring of 1978, Margot accompanied Naval Officer husband, Mike, to his new duty station at the base in Rota, Spain. "I promptly fell in love with almost everything Spanish, but most of all with the aristocratic Spanish horses," she says. She had owned horses in the United States and as a budding dressage rider asked the advice of her landlord, Eustacio Torrecillas, where to find a suitable horse and where to take instruction.

An entire set of fateful circumstances seemed to fall in place. Sr. Torrecillas was later the director of Rumasa S.A., a group which would take over the famous Terry winery and stable of Carthusian horses. He gave her recommendations which led to her finding and purchasing the fabulous Lapiz, a bay Lusitano beautifully trained to high school by the Portuguese *rejoneador*, Lupi, and to spending four years riding the stallions of the *Escuela Andaluza del Arte Ecuestre* in nearby Jerez de la Frontera, studying under head rider Luis Ramos Paul.

Besides twice-a-week lessons and training sessions at the Escuela, Margot spent countless pleasurable hours riding around the vineyards and roads in El Puerto. While she had the fabulous experience of riding several of the most famous performing stallions of the Ecuela, "it was Lapiz, above all other horses, who taught me to ride and showed me how very subtle the level of communication can be between horse and rider," Margot says. Lapiz could walk in a circle on his knees, per-

form the *terre a terre* (an animated canter in place), the Spanish walk and many other movements which Margot kept discovering as if they were treasures in a genie's lamp.

"Dear Lapiz, he forever cemented in my heart a passion for the style, grace and gentle nature of the Iberian horse," she says.

Unfortunately, Margot had to leave Lapiz behind when she left Spain. "Today, in order to ensure that I may always have these remarkable animals in my life, we breed them on a small scale," says Margot, now of Watsonville, California.

"Cheery, bossy, and filled with personality, Rebuscada is the matriarch of our little band of Spanish treasures. She is an energetic, high-powered, showy mare who never fails to elicit favorable comment," Margot says. "Rebuscada had some initial training by French dressage master Dominique Barbier. But because she has produced such outstanding offspring, she is only occasionally ridden and seems delighted with her role as head broodmare.

"We have always felt pride and joy in our relationship with this beautiful example of the Andalusian breed. After our upcoming retirement to Texas, I plan to continue riding dressage and breeding athletic horses suited to the sport."

Caprichoso E III

When I met Katana Dembicki-Rubenstein at an Andalusian show in Fort Worth, Texas, I found this young woman to be an enchanting romantic.

"Live the Fantasy," says the legend on the flyer advertising Shadowfax Farm in Erieville, New York, this above a photo of long, blonde-haired Katana dressed in a gossamer and lace white summer frock, leading one of her Andalusians over a tall-grassed hill by his flower-laced mane.

Therefore I found it rather fitting that one of her favorite horses, her Andalusian stallion, Caprichoso E III, is very much a Romeo, with equine romance eternally on his mind.

Unlike Starwood Heritage and Argentino, Caprichoso E III has no sadness in his story. "He came from a wonderful farm, he's a happy fellow and has had a happy life," says Katana. "and he has plenty of mares to look out for."

Katana and her husband found the striking, robust young grey stallion, foaled February 16, 1984, while they were vacationing in Arizona. They looked at other horses but their thoughts kept drifting back to him. "We just happened to be there when 'Cappi' was being worked. He was very green, but a real pleasure to watch," she says.

Three months later he arrived at her farm, full of enthusiasm for his new life. Katana remembers him as coming off the trailer standing on his hind legs and remaining excited for nearly six months.

"He was not uncontrollable or nasty; he was simply focused on one thing and one thing alone – mares."

For Cappi, it was always spring, and he was like the adolescent boy who has just discovered the opposite sex and hangs around the schoolyard corner trying to impress young girls as they go by, sometimes over-reacting in the process.

"For months, every time I brought Cappi into the arena, he would try to romance his own image in the mirrors," Katana says. He was so ardent that Katana had to devise an equestrian version of a cold shower. "I would have someone stand in the arena with a water hose to spray him when he became aroused. Or if I was alone, I would place filled water buckets around the ring, so that I could ride by, pick up a scoop and dump water on him when he got out of hand. He must have gotten tired of having cold water thrown on his ardor, because he finally developed some self-control."

Fortunately he has calmed down and allowed his "very sweet, affectionate personality" to show, though he is still very possessive of Katana and very jealous of any other animal that attracts her attention.

With his new-found maturity, Cappi is developing into a spectacular dressage horse, says Katana. Since he is more excitable and more exuberant in his movements than her other Andalusian stallion, Argentino, Katana believes he will make a better exhibition horse than a competition horse.

"He is amazingly quick to learn," she says, and the demanding high school movements of passage, piaffer and canter pirouettes come naturally to him. Cappi has plenty of "scope" – an ability to canter in place one minute, then extend his stride so that he is across the diagonal and on the other side of the ring in the blink of an eye.

"Riding Cappi is like riding the wind," says Katana. "He is so powerful but so light. When he gallops, with his mane and my hair flowing, reality disappears and fantasy begins. We are no longer earth-bound creatures. We become part of the sun and the wind. Cappi, like so many of my other horses, possesses the spirit and the fire that bring excitement to my life."

Argentino

The "Black Beauty" in Katana Dembicki-Rubenstein's life is actually a grey Andalusian stallion named Argentino.

Katana found Argentino at a very low point in his life and rehabilitated him, providing the "green pastures" of peace and restoration for him.

He's a very special horse to her, because of what they have in common.

"I guess it sounds silly, but I also got Argentino at a really low point in my life. I had been extremely ill and both of us are trying to make a comeback," she says. Is it working? "I hope so," this pretty, romantic blonde says with lilting laughter.

Certainly they seemed destined for one another. "A few years ago, Argentino had been advertised for sale in one of the Andalusian magazines," says Katana. "When I called his owner, she was quite sure that he was too much horse for me and that I would never be able to handle him. So I did not pursue him further. Instead I purchased a young Andalusian stallion, Caprichoso E III."

Time passed, and in May of 1990, Argentino's owner called Katana to see if she was still interested in him. Katana replied no, that she already had a stallion, but she might be interested in a mare that was also for sale. When she went to see the mare, the owner told her that Argentino, who had competed at Fourth/Prix St. Georges Level in the Young Riders Championships at Tempel Farms in Wadsworth, Illinois with rider Todd Flettrich, had been injured during Grand Prix training. He was recovering in a stable in Pennsylvania. "And since I lived in New York State, couldn't I stop in and check on him? Even though the stable was more than an eight-hour drive from my home, I went. What I saw was a very regal stallion, still very lame; some ten months after his injury, his leg was still hot and swollen," she says.

Katana's heart went out to Argentino. "Although I did not need another stallion, and even though the veterinarian could not or would not speculate as to whether he would ever be sound again, I bought him."

Argentino "came home" to Shadowfax Farm in Erieville, New York. With help from a combination of the farrier, the veterinarian, and Mother Nature, Argentino's leg healed.

But it seemed that Katana's love and empathy was the real magical medication and restorative.

Katana gave Argentino a large, light, airy stall so he can hang his head over his door to see the other horses and he has acres of pasture to kick up his heels. He even has plenty of mud to roll in, one of his favorite things.

She's riding him again, and finds him "a treat." Argentino is an extremely powerful horse. He can gracefully change from an overpowering extension to a feather-light collection.

"Right now I clinic whenever I can with Max Gahwyler and Frank Greylo, both dressage trainers. Argentino and I are still working hard to figure each other out, trying to coordinate our bodies to create an ideal picture to present in the competition ring. We may never reach Grand Prix level, but we hope to create a great impression in people's minds.

"As Starwood Heritage (Taj) was a major force in my life while I recovered from a car accident, Argentino came into my life when I was recovering from a serious illness. I guess that my believing in my horses and seeing them overcome their problems has helped me deal with my own," says Katana.

"These horses, actually all of my animals, the dogs, cats, sheep and goat, are my life. They are my friends, my work, my entertainment, and my dreams. They give back to me as much as they get."

Majorio IV

"Zorro," as the grey Andalusian gelding Majorio IV is known among friends, is a horse with a great sense of humor. "He has been known to fill his mouth with water, casually stride up to the front of his stall where someone is sitting and, leaning back against the stall door, open his mouth and let the water spill down the backside of his victim," says his owner, Deletta Saar of Los Angeles, California. "When turned out in his paddock, he races around at a full gallop, carrying a huge cone in his mouth. When he sees anyone approaching, he runs to get the cone and tosses it over the fence, then cavorts and snorts till you toss it back or have a game of tug of war with him. He also plays with a fifty-gallon plastic water tub by putting his head inside and running it around the fence till he crashes," adds Deletta.

She describes Zorro as "a very Spanish-looking Andalusian, typical in height and stature of the textbook description of the breed. What attracted me first to my horse is his beautiful head," she adds. "He has a straight profile and a sweet kind eye. He also has an incredibly

luxuriant mane and tail which embellish his overall showy and elegant presence. I once had a judge tell me, 'I haven't seen this fancy a horse in a long time.'

"Zorro's preference for human companionship takes precedence over even his beloved feed bin. He knows the sight of my car coming up the road, and by the time I shut the gate and park, he is clamoring to get out and be with me. If I have to do anything before I take him out of his stall, he sets up a litany of protests till I come back for him."

Zorro was eighteen months old when Deletta bought him and hadn't been handled much. "It's not easy waiting for your horse to grow up while everyone else is riding the trails or winning ribbons at horse shows," says Deletta. "But each week for the next year or so was always an adventure. I guess I, like a parent watching a child grow, experienced that same sort of wonder at all the new things my colt learned and the way he always expressed his individuality."

While Zorro prospered under Deletta's constant affection and reassurance, he had certain idiosyncracies, such as always moving so he could see the handler while in halter classes. "It was two years after I got him that we discovered something was really wrong, and so many different behavior quirks started to make sense," she says. She learned Zorro is almost completely blind in the left eye due to an unknown injury which detached the retina. "We started to adjust our treatment of him, never punishing him for behavior due to the blindness (formerly interpreted as mischief).

"My horse is incredibly trusting, affectionate and willing to please, despite his handicap. He will go anywhere I lead or ride him. With the urging of my voice, he will move ahead when, because of his impaired sight, he is frightened of something new or obstacles that are threatening to him," Deletta adds.

"Zorro and I have grown up together. We have learned to trust each other and somehow were meant to care and watch out for one another," says Deletta, who picked the colt because he seemed to need mothering. "I have tried to provide him with an environment where he will thrive and be excused for his shortcomings such as his impaired sight and behaviorial annoyances." Before she had the five-year-old gelded, he would get overexcited around other horses, but now has calmed down considerably.

"He has always been kind to me and provided me with the opportunity to be elevated to a level of riding I would not otherwise be motivated to achieve. We really are on the brink of what will probably be our best time together," says Deletta. She had waited a long time to fulfill what she calls "that undefinable compulsion to find that special horse who leaves an imprint on your life forever."

Lisonjerio II

The story of Lisonjerio II is one of a horse with incredible heart, and an owner with the determination and devotion to match.

Barbara Smith, of Spanish Oaks Ranch in Albuquerque, was living in Connecticut at the time she flew to see a colt bred from imported stock in 1976 on a ranch in Silver City, New Mexico.

She had been looking for a Andalusian dressage prospect that was straight-moving and at least 16.2 hands. Trainer Dianne Olds Rossi recommended Lisonjerio II.

Six weeks after she bought Lisonjerio, Barbara got a call from the shipping company that "Las" was on his way to Connecticut. "I very happily got ready for his arrival," she says. Then the unthinkable occurred. The shippers had lost the colt and couldn't find him.

"Two months later I got a call from the shipping company saying my horse would arrive in a few hours and I had better have the vet standing by. The poor horse was severely dehydrated, had a bad case of shipping fever and could hardly stand," due to the contracted tendons he had developed, says Barbara. The vet advised her to send the horse back.

But Barbara was determined to do her best for him. As soon as he had recovered somewhat, she sent him to the University of Pennsylvania's renowned equine veterinary center at New Bolton.

There surgery on both of the colt's front legs had good results. Barbara was told the horse would have, at best, six years of use before crippling arthritis set in.

"If he has but six years, he had to make the most of every moment," she decided.

And so he did. Six weeks after he was first ridden, Las was entered in training level classes at the prestigious Westchester/Fairfield Dressage Association Show against outstanding competition.

It was then Barbara learned what a tremendous show horse Las was. He won every class he was in, nine trophies in all, including overall high point trophy in the show. Out of nearly 700 rides, he had the highest score — in the mid-70s.

One story in particular stands out about Las. One spring Sunday, Barbara decided to go for a ride in the indoor arena. Her children, who knew riding Las always put their mother in a good mood, came along in the hope she'd take them to dinner and a movie afterward.

"Las and I were enjoying our ride with no one else in the usually-crowded arena," Barbara recalls. "I decided to let him run a little and had completed a few turns around the arena, when Las came to a stop so sudden I ended up on his ears. I kicked him hard to get him going again, but Las didn't move a muscle. It was then I heard a little voice say, 'Mommy, up!' I looked down to see my fourteen-month-old son Kurt, standing underneath the horse with his arms reaching up, as children do when they want to be picked up. Las stood perfectly still while I dropped the reins and bent over to pick up Kurt. As soon as Kurt was secure in the saddle with me, Las walked quietly over to the corner of the arena where Kurt's terrified babysitter was standing. The horse's good sense proved to be greater than that of the two humans involved."

Las reached fourth level before arthritis forced his retirement. His offspring are now carrying on for him in the show ring. His first purebred foal, Windhill Amada, won National Champion Mare of the AAHA in 1986. At the 1991 Feria de los Caballos in Albuquerque, another filly, Encantada, won the Hunter Championship and carried an eleven-year-old girl to a blue ribbon in English Pleasure, Junior Exhibitor.

For Barbara, Las is "an amazing example of bravery and self-control. It has been said that every horseman will have one good horse in his or her lifetime, and Las fits the bill for me."

103

Bravio

Although they believed they didn't stand a chance of placing in the event, Suzan Sommer of Sommer Ranch Andalusians in Sylmar, California, and her friend Marge Booth decided to enter the young stallion Bravio in a trail trial competition in June, 1991. It would be good experience for all of them, they thought.

A green-broke stallion who had been ridden outside his backyard training arena on only five occasions, Bravio would be facing a field of forty-eight competitors, mostly Quarter Horses and Arabians.

To top it off, this was also a first for his rider, Marge, who had never participated in a trail trial before.

For those not familiar with the term, a trail trial is a cross-country course complete with both manmade and natural obstacles. A horse and rider may be asked to do anything from swimming a deep-water crossing to negotiating a variety of gates in a proper and safe manner. All kinds of "obstacles" may be presented to horse and rider, including motorcycles and joggers, or a bag lady complete with shopping cart and trash bags filled with rattling soda cans.

Bravio's first competition took just a little over two hours and included many of the obstacles described above. Much to Suzan and Marge's surprise, when the final rider crossed the finish line and scores were tallied,

Bravio was proclaimed the victor with the least amount of faults. He had accumulated only four out of a possible 100 faults.

After this victory, Suzan decided to try her hand at trail class competition herself, and she signed up for the Championship Trail class offered at the Equestrian Trails, Inc. Three-Day Convention Show in Southern California. It was again a first time for both, and they were up against some very serious and seasoned competitors.

When Suzan examined the posted course, she panicked! It required things she had never asked Bravio for before – crossing a teeter-totter bridge, backing through three barrels placed the width of the horse apart, sidepassing to a trash bag of soda cans picking them up and moving back to a trash can to dump them, just for starters. She wanted to withdraw but Marge wouldn't let her quit.

"When it was over, I knew we had done far better than I had ever expected, but it was still the shock of my lifetime to be announced the Championship Winner!" says Suzan.

The year wasn't over. At the Fall Classic in Burbank, California, Bravio also proved himself to be a Halter Champion, placing first in the Four-Year-Old Stallion Division, and then took the Reserve Senior Show Champion Stallion title under Spanish Judge Salvador Sanchez Barbudo.

Bravio's many accomplishments in his first year under saddle are a testament to the breed's athletic abilities and willingness to please, as well as Suzan's eye for a horse.

She searched for a year for just the right horse to start her breeding operation, traveling across the United States and even into Mexico. It wasn't until she came across Bravio in Texas that her search ended. He was two and a half years old, unbroken and shy, but had the conformation and movement for which Suzan was looking. "I knew that all he needed was a little patience and a lot of love," she says.

Bravio made the long trailer ride from Texas to California without incident, arriving at Sommer Ranch in July, 1990. Suzan slowly began working with him, even reading to him for hours in his stall to gain his trust, while introducing him to clippers, bridle, and saddle.

"No matter how scared Bravio was, he never pinned his ears back or made an aggressive move towards me. It wasn't long till he followed me around like a puppy dog eagerly seeking my company," Suzan says.

"I look forward to producing more little Bravios in the future," Suzan adds. "I am sold on this breed that comprises such a complete package of beauty, brains, athletic ability and an unequaled gentle nature."

Ceaser

"Getting a young horse and watching him grow into a magnificent obedient stallion that a very young child can handle is certainly something we are very proud of," says Susan E.R. Starks of Southernly Winds Andalusians in Kahuku, Hawaii.

"My 16.3-hand honey-grey Andalusian stallion Ceaser has given us the chance to continue the legacy and to protect the tradition and very rich cultural heritage with which I was blessed to be born," she adds.

Ceaser, foaled April 5, 1988, was sired by Temerario V and is out of the mare, Rubi, both of the Garrison Ranch in California.

"Ceaser came into my life because my husband, Tommy, wanted very much to get involved in my family's lifestyle, which, of course, is raising Spanish horses," Susan notes. "Many members of my family have dedicated their lives to understanding, teaching and training these magnificent Spanish horses. I don't want to call horses a profession, but rather a way of life and a very real philosophy of life applied to everyday living. Southernly Winds Andalusians is a small extension of the ranch of my father and his father before him, dedicated to the preservation and protocol of the great Spanish horse."

Tommy did his homework, found Ceaser, purchased him as a weanling colt and presented him to Susan as a gift.

"Ceaser did not necessarily change MY life, but definitely my husband's," Susan adds. "Tommy has always had cattle and horses, but Ceaser got him very interested in becoming involved with a tradition and providing a legacy for our daughter Paloma. Paloma is being groomed to be Ceaser's rider and master."

Susan describes Ceaser's looks as resembling a work of classical art: "Very defined, chiseled features in the face, and extraoradinary muscle formation throughout his body. Though a very big horse, Ceaser is so gentle and kind, you can see his soul if you look deep into his eyes – an experience which humbles one to the greatest degree.

"Ceaser loves everyone and everything," she adds. "I attribute this to the very special upbringing he has had. He plays with our goat and our dog, and to see him play with the kittens is our greatest joy.

"When he was a foal, I would make my rounds to the barn after everyone had gone to sleep and quietly walk into Ceaser's stall. He would be all curled on the bedding and would let me sit next to him for the longest time, occasionally opening his eyes to let me know, 'It's okay, Mom.'

"I feel the special relationship I have for Ceaser is a lasting bond. He will always be a part of my family, with every consideration made for his well-being – never to be taken for granted."

Ceaser is currently being schooled in classical dressage by Master Colonel Roberto Perea. "Riding him is a dream come true," says Susan. "It is incredible to feel the precision of each and every step; he glides, he obeys, he anticipates my every thought. It's magic."

After his formal training is completed, Ceaser will continue the heritage of bull-turning and bull-herding. Unlike bull-fighting, no animals are abused.

"Ceaser's coming into our lives has enriched us to an extent beyond belief," Susan says. "I have learned, and continue to be reminded every single day, how precious and wonderful my life is because of all my horses."

"Horses have been our family's lifestyle, and my parents always gave me the greatest encouragement to continue that lifestyle. Horses give me my greatest pleasures in life. With everything I feel for them, I wish to pass my feelings and beliefs on to anyone and everyone with whom I come into contact, and especially to my daughter, Paloma."

Don Marco

"As a child, I had visions of a beautiful white horse with black mane and tail who would sprout wings and carry me to wondrous places," says Bonnie Tanner of Dragonwood Farm in Lincoln, California. "As I grew up, I never lost that vision and while I continued to be involved with horses I never found that Pegasus horse."

Then one day she saw that horse looking out at her from the pages of a magazine – "a gorgeous dapple grey stallion with shimmering mane and tail and a powerful demeanor that made simple English pleasure look like flying." Pegasus's earthly name was Leopardo II, and he was the sire of multiple national champions. He was sired by Legionario III, 1969 Champion of Champions in Spain and the foundation sire of the Garrison Ranch.

For five years, Bonnie searched for a horse that could match her dreams. By 1989, Bonnie had tracked down Helen Pastorini, an Andalusian breeder in northern California, who with Mark Richards, owns Inquieto Ranch in the Los Gatos Hills. Here Bonnie found a precocious dark brown yearling colt with the Leopardo topline, strong short back, beautifully arched neck, long legs, and a wealth of mane and tail. "His name was Don

Marco and I knew he was the one! Pegasus was finally mine," Bonnie remembers.

Don Marco grew from a gangly brown yearling to a breathtakingly beautiful dark dapple grey stallion with a gorgeous head, large lively eyes, arched neck, powerful shoulders, and strong, muscular hindquarters. "It is easy to imagine a horse like Don Marco doing the levade under a medieval knight in full battle armor," says Bonnie. "In fact, it is these visions of medieval glory and romance – dragons, knights in shining armor, rich tapestries of forests and unicorns – which the Andalusian conjures in the mind that has resulted in our farm name, Dragonwood."

A medieval wizard couldn't have conjured up a spell with a more thrilling outcome than that of Don Marco's first show ring appearance – he was named Ventura County IAHA (International Andalusian Horse Association) Show Champion Colt. "We have a very interesting video that my husband Bud took of this show," says Bonnie. "When Don Marco's name was announced as the champion, the camera goes up to the sky, with a nice shot of the tops of palm trees, and then down to the ground. Contrary to the way he felt, Bud's feet were still on the ground. In Don Marco's second show, at the age of two, he went on to be named Reserve National Champion Colt by the IAHA show committee, and as a three-year-old, was 1991 Champion Stallion at the annual IAHA show in Orange County."

In 1991, Leopardo II passed away, making Don Marco's bloodline even more precious. "We believe Don Marco is a credit to the breed and in passing his qualities on to his foals he is sure to make his mark as a sire in his own right," says Bonnie.

"At home, he is so smart that if I'm not careful, he can get ahead of me and I always need to have a keen mind around him! One of the 'cute' things he does is open the gate for me. I will lead him to the arena gate and he'll push it open with his nose, back up a step and push it over to open it all the way. He'll do this with me on his back, too. Wouldn't it be fun to enter a trail class and negotiate the gate obstacle in our unorthodox way?" Bonnie asks.

"Owning Don Marco has truly fulfilled my dream to ride Pegasus. All the stresses of life melt away when I walk out to the barn and hear him whinny in greeting. Watching him grow and change into the commanding stallion he has become, while also developing a mutually respectful friendship with him, has been a rewarding experience which I hope to be able to pass on to others as we place his foals in loving homes," says Bonnie. "The Andalusian is truly a noble breed with a history of conquering nations; Don Marco and the Andalusian breed have a future of conquering hearts."

Sultano

"Sultano is a very unusual and popular stallion to all who come to know him," says the charming owner of this thirteen-year-old Andalusian, Shelley S. Tulloch of Clear Lake Equestrian in League City, Texas.

"His behavior around our colts best exemplifies his wonderful personality," adds Shelley. "Instead of being bossy and mean as many stallions can be with other horses, Sultano is gentle, sweet and loving to every foal.

"We have one colt, Tejas, who is a real character," continues Shelley. "At age one year, he learned how to open the barn door. One day he let Sultano out into the paddock with four colts, much to our shock. We freaked! We thought 'Oh, God, he's going to kill them!' We expected the absolute worse!" Instead, Sultano played with the four youngsters as if he were still a colt himself.

"Sultano reminds me that horses are like people in that the best ones always remain a child at heart," says Shelley, a busy lady with three children under five and her own computer consulting firm.

Shelley bought the pure white 15.1 stallion with an extra thick mane and tail, beautiful head and movement three years ago from another Andalusian breeder who was financing a new business.

Shelley had answered an ad in the *Houston Chronicle* "tacky as that sounds," she says, for a beautiful mare, Cubanita.

"Shortly after I purchased the mare, the breeder really needed capital, and called to say that he had to part with the stallion Sultano too, and that there was no one else he'd want to own the horse.

"I was thrilled and just said, 'I'll take him,'" Shelley explains. The ex-owner still keeps in touch with her about Sultano and came to see him at a horse show.

"Sultano has been a broadening experience in learning how wonderful Andalusian stallions are, Shelley says.

"I got into breeding Andalusians in 1989," she adds. "Prior to that I owned a wide variety of breeds – Thoroughbreds, Appaloosas, Quarter Horses. You name it, I had it," she jokes.

Shelley held a semi-dispersal sale of her own after buying her first Andalusian. Reasons she likes them? "They are more docile, more people-oriented, much easier to train, much more eager to please. They really maximize your pleasure in owning a horse," she says.

"Currently I have nine horses," she adds. "I do have one non-Andalusian, a Miniature Horse for my two-year-old daughter, Tegan." But even Tegan seems to lean toward Andalusians.

"Of all my horses, Sultano is Tegan's favorite. She always asks to see him first and loves to feed him a carrot, sit on his back and love him," says Shelley.

Sultano, foaled October 14, 1978, is currently in dressage training with Jean-Philippe Giacomini. "We've shown Sultano just a bit," says Shelley.

She rode him herself in a musical freestyle, which is his forte. "He really gets into the music," says Shelley, who chose a song from The Doors, called "Spanish Caravan," for their ride. "Just a perfect choice," she says.

Sultano has won three Reserve Grand Championships in English Hunt Seat classes, and won a lead line class. "He was a perfect gentleman with my four-year-old son, TJ, riding," says Shelley.

"I've loved horses all my life, as far back as I can remember," she recalls. "For years, as a child, I regularly begged my parents to get me a horse, but to no avail. The monumental moment came when I was a teenager and a close friend bought me my first horse, a gorgeous Palomino gelding.

"It is almost a spiritual thing with me," she says of her love for horses. "After my first horse, there was a period of about two years when I did not own a horse and I really felt an emptiness during that time. I know they have a very strong ESP – a feeling of an unspoken communication with them that I really love, especially with Sultano."

Catherino

"As the great Mestre Nuno Oliveira once said, 'Where force begins, art ends,' and Catherino was forced beyond his mental and physical capabilities in his early years," says Holly Van Borst, the rider and friend of this Andalusian stallion.

Catherino's story begins in Perth, Australia, where he was foaled in September, 1979. His sire, Escribiente VI was of pure Terry breeding, and his dam, Catherina, was by the famous Bodeguero, whose mother, Orotava, was well-known throughout Spain as one of the premier mares of the breed. Catherino was bred by Ray Williams, a kind of visionary man who decided in the late 1960s to import the finest breeding stock available in Spain to his ranch, the Bodeguero Stud.

His idea was to create "The Kingdom of the Dancing White Stallions," a dinner theatre where people could watch displays of classical horsemanship as the evening's entertainment, while enjoying a fine meal.

Catherino was only two years old when Mr. Williams decided to move his entire operation to California. "It was during this period the training of the horses became inconsistent and unbalanced," says Holly. "To say that Catherino's introduction to training was at man's hard and unthinking hand, and that he was subjected to the egotistic and uncaring demands of an 'instant mastery' training philosophy, is an understate-

ment. It is ironic that this breed, purposely bred for its heart and stamina, could be subjected to man's self-defeating ignorance and ill-will. Through no deliberate effort on the part of his breeder, Catherino became the object of just such treachery and deceit in his first year's training."

By the time Catherino had been sold to his third home at the age of five, he had earned a reputation for being an untrustworthy, ill-tempered stallion. At this point in his life, the physical abuse stopped and the starvation began. During the winter of 1985 and through the spring of 1986, Catherino, along with all the other horses at this ranch, were living off very little food and almost no care. In June, 1986, Hector Alcalde of Takaro Farm in Middleburg, Virginia, found Catherino in his state of deprivation and, as much out of pity as hope for his future, purchased the then six-year-old stallion, along with an older one in equally appalling condition.

Catherino and his stablemate, Andaluz, departed their equine version of Auschwitz in July, 1986. They arrived safely, even in their starved, dehydrated condition, at Takaro Farm. Catherino had just begun to gain weight when in August he became sick with an upper respiratory infection, his fever spiking at one point to nearly 106 degrees.

At that point Holly was eight months pregnant with her son, Pieter, born the following month. "Looking back on the photos of me hand-walking 'Cat-Man,' as I affectionately came to call Catherino, must have presented onlookers with a comical sight," says Holly. "Fortunately, both of our conditions were temporary!"

Catherino returned to his intended magnificent, noble state, both physically and mentally. He probably never reached the level of excellence he might have through correct, humane schooling, but he did go on to win many conformation and performance awards within the Andalusian breed. He also introduced thousands of people to the sculpted beauty and grace of his breed through exhibitions given throughout Virginia and bordering states. He also proved to be a worthy, trusted friend to Holly. "The very fact that this beautiful stallion was of such a magnanimous nature that he allowed me to connect with him by trusting me was in my mind nothing short of a miracle," she says. "He taught me more than any other horse about the value of adhering to the principles of classical horsemanship.

"Even though Catherino does not belong to me in the legal sense, I will forever belong to him," says Holly, "and hopefully watch over his care from a distance to protect his spirit and soul. Through his offspring, who all carry his unmistakable presence and character, he will continue to educate people about the 'Horse of Kings.'"

Destinado/Dacio IV

"Destinado's name implies what he has brought to me," says Tina Cristiani Veder, a seventh-generation member of the world-famous Cristianis, regarded by *aficionados* as the premier equestrian family of the circus.

"All the circumstances that surround Destinado and his life and his coming to me, are, in my mind, destiny for both of us. He opened the door to the dreams that I have nurtured deep within my heart since I was a child," Tina told me.

Tina has always been familiar with Andalusian and Lusitano horses as her family had used Andalusians for high school, long line and liberty displays while performing with circuses all over Europe and in America.

As a child, she watched some of the great trainers of this century working their horses in high school movements and wondered if someday she would have a magnificent stallion dancing together with her in such perfect harmony.

Many years passed. Tina pursued all the creative interests that captivated her, but never her first true love, horses.

"Because of this, I always felt as though there was a piece of me missing and, of course, there was. Like the prodigal son in the Bible who left his father and home, I had left my first love and had not been true to my dream. Finally, my awakening came, and I realized that I needed this dream to feed my soul. I started by buying young stock to form a foundation breeding program, but my youngsters gave me only one part of my dream."

She felt she needed a figurehead to represent Caballos de los Cristiani, her farm in Bolton Landing, New York.

As if in answer to a prayer, Destinado came into her life through an unexpected phone call from Evelyn Westmoreland, who offered to pass Destinado on to Tina so that his training would not be wasted. "As I watched the video Evelyn sent me, I knew that Destinado possessed the drama and presence I wanted in my exhibition stallion," says Tina.

"Since he has come to me, we have worked together with my friend Alex Konyot, world-renowned trainer and rider, and have been doing exhibitions in the Northeast.

"For many, he is the first Andalusian they have ever seen," adds Tina. "Destinado epitomizes the beauty and majesty that the 'Horse of Kings' was named for. He is a stallion full of fire and, because of this, he exudes a masculine presence that is awe-inspiring. When he enters the arena, his magnetism draws everyone's attention and holds it captive until he exits. This makes him the ideal exhibition stallion as well as the perfect ambassador for my farm as well as his breed."

Yet her favorite story about Destinado relates to a personal moment, when she was giving a riding lesson on him to her ten-year-old daughter Rivka. "After she was on board and trotting around the ring, I recalled that we were expecting two mares to arrive shortly for breeding," she says. The 16-hand Destinado always let everyone know in no uncertain terms that he was "king of the mountain," usually in the way of a big vocal welcome to the young ladies, with a piaffer or passage thrown in to dazzle the newcomers.

Tina was concerned that Rivka would become frightened by his stallion antics. But before she could end the lesson, the two mares arrived. All the other horses began greeting one another.

"I could see that Destinado was dying to answer back, but he behaved as though he was carrying fragile eggs on his back. Never once did he do anything that would cause my daughter the slightest anxiety. He put this child who loved him and was kind to him above his most powerful drive. As I witnessed the nobility and loyalty of this magnificent horse, I was filled with such admiration, respect and love that it was hard to hold back the tears," says Tina. "I view Destinado as my teacher, my companion, my teammate, my pet and my dreammaker."

Danzar K

Sherry E. Tingley-Ward bought Danzar K, a grey colt sired by Majorio by Capitan XIII and out of Alegria by Legionario II, in 1991, as a yearling. Since then, she's had the delight of watching him develop from an awkward colt into a beautiful stallion.

"Danzar was magically transformed into a dream horse," Sherry says, "one with an exceptional head, dished face, beautifully tipped ears and large, expressive eyes."

Since Sherry was not experienced with green colts, she was a little intimidated by Danzar when she brought him home. "I wasn't sure if I could handle him, and I didn't want to break his spirit, but I didn't want him to get away with anything, either," she says.

"Danzar has always been easy to handle because he has a good mind, but he can be a little tornado when he wants to. But when I go into the corral or box stall to catch him, he calms down immediately, walks over to me and drops his head into the halter. He is gentle with me, yet there is a wild side to him. I hope to control that wild side, but never to destroy it.

"My trainer, George Liblin, decided it would be a good idea, since Danzar is a stallion, to start his training as soon as possible, so I won't get hurt as he matures. I was concerned how starting at such a young age would affect his mind.

"Liblin rides him one day, then drives him the next," she says. Liblin reports that under western saddle Danzar has a good disposition and is very smooth to ride.

"My trainer doesn't care much for colts, says they should all be gelded!" says Sherry. "But Danzar has proven him wrong! Danzar has exhibited one of the finest minds you could ask for, and already does his flying lead changes like a real pro.

"Danzar's male hormones are now kicking in at high speed and by getting him under saddle he is easier to handle," adds Sherry. "The colt also took very well to the work harness. He really 'gets into the collar' and pulls without giving up. Eventually Danzar will be harnessed to a vis-a-vis carriage. Danzar's training has included exposure to flying plastic bags, mailboxes, trash cans, baby strollers, firecrackers, water, cars, dogs – all things you may encounter while out riding and driving."

Sherry owns Ward Farms in Ontario, California, founded in 1985 when she bought her first Andalusian, a gelding named Zarado. Two years later, she bought the filly Asombrosa.

"My dream is to have all three of my Andalusians harnessed together – two in the back, one in the front – in a 'unicorn hitch.' Wouldn't they be stunning going down the street? Eventually when Danzar is a finished carriage horse, we will do weddings with him," Sherry says. "I can think of nothing nicer than an Andalusian trotting up the road to pick up the bride and groom."

Danzar is also a ham who loves to do his "Mr. Ed" act for visitors. "He sticks his head out of the feed window of his box stall, rolls his eyes all around, sticks out his tongue and rolls his lip back and chews at the air as though he is trying to talk. At the same time, he twirls his head around. These antics may go on for fifteen minutes," says Sherry.

"I feel so proud to own such an awesome creature, it almost brings tears to my eyes. I am very lucky that Andalusians are so willing to learn and have such good attitudes. Not one of my Andalusians has ever reared, kicked or bucked while in harness or under saddle. Danzar's sire, Majorio, is in the Tournament of Roses Parade every year. Some year, I'd love to ride beside him," Sherry says.

"I have had some problems throughout life and my horses provide excellent therapy for me. When things look bleak, I go to my horses and just stroking their glossy hides makes all my cares seem to vanish. Andalusians are very people-oriented. They will leave their food and come over and stand near you if they sense you want their company. They will take time out of their day for you, just like a good friend will."

Centella VI

The ten-year-old Andalusian stallion, Centella VI has lived in far-flung parts of the world, but he seems to have found a permanent home in Texas.

Centella VI stands at stud at the G Ranch in Hungiford, Texas, operated by Roy L. Wyatt. "The G Ranch," says Roy, the owner of Centella VI, "consists of 1,153 acres of good, well-watered land and is located approximately fifty-eight miles southwest of Houston on U. S. Highway 59. Centella VI will be there from now on," declares Roy, "as he is too good to let go or get away."

Roy Wyatt has had a fascinating life as an importer/exporter of cattle and horses. He was born and raised on a "cow-and-horse outfit," as he describes his first home. His father crossed Percheron mares with burros to produce mules, and Roy rode a horse to school his first and second years of education. An ex-U. S. Marine Corps officer with eight years of active service, mostly in the Pacific area, Roy has owned and operated a large ranch in Nicaragua for the past twenty-four years. He also has four expansive ranches in the Pucalpa, Peru area, where he runs nelore (Brahman) cattle, plus sixteen head of purebred Andalusian horses. "I breed pure Andalusian stallions to native mares," says Roy. "The results are large, stout, smart and durable horses good for working cows on a cattle ranch. Centella V has some offspring in the operation."

It was during one of his business trips to Peru that Roy saw Centella VI at La Parada, on the beach south of Lima. "I sure did like him," says Roy. "It took a while, about a year, feeling the owner out to see if he'd sell him." Roy was able to finalize the sale in 1991.

Roy had seen Centella VI's sire, Centella V, in Spain at horse shows and at the ranch of breeder, Don Salvador Guardiola Fantoni in Los Palacios, Seville. In 1984, Centella V (by Centella IV) was the champion of the breed in Spain. Seeing the magnificent stallion "planted the seed," says Roy, of wanting to own a similar horse.

Centella VI was foaled February 22, 1982 on the Guardiola ranch, which is as famous for the *toros de lidia* (fighting bulls) that it raises, as it is for breeding fine horses. (My own stallion, Blanco, bore the Guardiola brand.) In November, 1991, at the national championships of Andalucía in Sevilla, the heirs of Don Salvador Guardiola Fantoni won the special prize for the greatest number of winners in the show.

Centella VI himself was the champion of Spain as a two-year-old in the national show of 1984. He bred many mares in Spain before he was shipped to Peru three years ago. Roy reports that Centella has many offspring in Peru as well as in the United States. "So he now has offspring on three continents," he notes.

"Like a ballet dancer, Centella is very well-schooled," continues Roy. "He's had approximately seven years' schooling, mainly by Jaime Guardiola in Spain and he is able to do all the high school movements. He's wonderful to ride, gentle and very well-mannered." Originally a dark grey, Centella is progressively turning white.

Roy does not have a rider that can show Centella properly, but hopes to bring one from Argentina. Roy once raised Quarter Horses and has only been involved in Andalusians for the past few years. By Texas standards, he says he was never considered a big breeder of Quarter Horses, "owning only fifty-five of them." He also bred mules on his ranch in Nicaragua, crossing horse mares with jacks, producing pack animals sold to the coffee plantations to bring the coffee out of the mountains.

Centella VI is now Ray's new focus. "He definitely is a horse fit for a king. He is so gentle, and he is also gentle with the mares that he breeds," says Roy.

THE APPALOOSA

The knowledge that the Appaloosa is a horse with a long and important history in the ancient world and is not just "an Indian pony" may surprise some fans of this most dramatically-marked of all equines.

The spotted horse has been known to man for 20,000 years or more, and has been used for 5,000 years in many different countries. From cave walls in France, created approximately 20,000 years ago, to Egyptian drawings and Greek pottery in 1400 B.C. and Chinese scrolls in the seventh century A.D., the spotted horse has been celebrated by artists through time.

The Nez Perce continued raising their prized horses until the late 1880s when rich placer diggings on the Nez Perce reservation brought thousands of settlers who took over most of the tribal lands.

The Nez Perce Indians of Washington and Idaho became especially sophisticated in producing mounts that were prized and envied by all. The Nez Perce allowed only the best animals to reproduce. They carefully selected and cultivated horses with specific desirable characteristics. The result was a group of strong, swift horses capable of traveling long distances across rugged terrain.

Local tradition recalls that the Nez Perce living along the lower part of the Pelouse (or Palouse) River in northern Idaho owned a large herd of spotted horses. The wheat farmers homesteading the land along this stream called these horses "Palouse" or "Palousey" horses.

The Nez Perce continued raising their prized horses until the late 1880s. Rich placer diggings on the Nez Perce reservation brought thousands of settlers who took over most of the tribal lands.

The numbers were gradually reduced and by the 1930s, the Appaloosa (as the horse had become known) was nearly lost as a breed. Then in 1938, a small group of dedicated horsemen banded together to form the Appaloosa Horse Club to preserve, improve and standardize the Appaloosa breed.

Today, the Appaloosa Horse Club is one of the outstanding international breed registries in the world, with more than a half million Appaloosas registered through headquarters in Moscow, Idaho. It remains dedicated to protecting and promoting the distinctive horse known as the Appaloosa.

Perhaps this is as good a place as any to say that not all spotted horses are Appaloosas. Certain well-defined characteristics mark the breed. The modern Appaloosa horse bred in the United States is most frequently identified by the unique markings on the rump, seen as a blanket of white on which there may be spots or smaller flecks of one or more colors. Some Appaloosas carry the spotting all over the body, but it is usually most dominant over the hips.

Others show white over the hips without spots, and still others appear mottled all over the body or show white specks or spots with dark background.

Other important characteristics which must accompany the coat color and pattern are the white sclera encircling the eye and parti-colored skin, especially noticeable about the nostrils. While the Appaloosa may lose much of its color with age, the spots remain on the skin and may be readily seen under the hair. Hoofs are parti-colored or striated vertically.

General conformation is that of a close-coupled stock horse, standing 14.2 to 15.2 in height and weighing 950 to 1,100 lbs. when mature.

K-Bar Khan

This Appaloosa stallion with a black and white blanket is not only a top performer in many disciplines and a proven sire, but he's a successful matchmaker as well!

"I'll always remember that because of Khan, I met my husband and partner in life, Dick," says Diana Beaufils. "Both of us have a very tender heart for one wonderful black and white stallion, as he gave us the rest of our lives. Dreams really do come true." She and Dick own Liberty Bell Ranch in Tucson, Arizona.

The romantic tale goes back to the time when Diana lived in Elizabeth, Colorado and commuted to work in Denver. One day she ran out of gas and pulled into a small ranch near Parker to use the phone. While waiting for assistance, she asked if she might go to the barn and look at the horses. In the very first stall was a magnificent two-year-old black and white colt, K-Bar Khan. Diana learned he was a son of K-Bar's Sugar Leo, whom Diana had admired at the National Western Stock Show in Denver years before as the most striking horse she'd ever seen.

Three months later, she received a booklet in the mail advertising a dispersal sale at that Parker ranch. All the horses were for sale, including K-Bar Khan.

Diana went to the sale to watch her favorite horse pass into someone else's hands, as she felt she could not afford him herself. "With much sadness, I sat there as the final gavel came down," she recalls.

But weeks later information reached Diana that Khan had not left for his presumed new home. The sale transaction had been cancelled and the people at Parker were happy to work out a new arrangement. A few hours later, Diana says, "I became the happy owner of one beautiful Appaloosa!"

Diana selected a trainer to show Khan and handle the breeding. After going to only a few shows, quite a few mares were booked to him.

"It was at one of those shows that I met my husband, Dick," she says. "He had raised and shown Appaloosas for many years and owned a stallion and a breeding farm. He asked me why I had a trainer ride my horse, when he was sure I could do a much better job." After discussing what might be accomplished with Khan, Diana moved the stallion to Dick's farm.

"We bred Khan to a lot of mares. I learned a lot about breeding and genetics. And best of all, I learned to ride and show Khan and to win. My most prideful achievements with him were the numerous successes of those years. The compliments Khan got at every show and the way he always made heads turn made for proud and wonderful show days," says Diana.

Khan has performed in western pleasure, English pleasure, trail, endurance, hunter hack, dressage, and has even competed working cattle. As one might expect from such a versatile performer, "He has the most wonderful disposition and has always been a willing partner," Diana says.

Today, new career directions give Diana less time to spend doing what she loves best--riding and showing Khan. "But Dick and I still stand him to a select group of mares every year, still breed beautiful black and white foals, and still bring dreams and hopes to many new horse owners," she says.

THE ARABIAN

The origins of the Arabian horse, unrivaled in beauty, stamina and intelligence, are controversial, and many writers to avoid argument say those origins are "shrouded in mystery" or "uncertainty."

Evolution, however, suggests the breed descended from a type of wild horse indigenous to the Arabian Peninsula as far back in prehistoric times as the last Ice Age.

As with all widely-dispersed animals, various geographical subspecies emerged. The subspecies which adapted itself to the arid steppes and desert regions around Mesopotamia (modern Iraq), along the Euphrates and then down to Egypt, already possessed the physical characteristics of the Arabian horse of today.

As with other grazing animals of this habitat, when danger threatened this horse, there was nowhere to hide. Flight was the only escape. Thus a slender animal evolved, reactive and swift as a gazelle, always on the alert, with muscular hindquarters capable of powerful takeoff thrust, and a high set neck. The head was refined and exquisitely beautiful, with large expressive eyes and wide nostrils. The trunk was light, limbs muscular, tail carried high.

This Near Eastern native horse presumably had been domesticated and bred by man much longer than other types. Already endowed with a superior heritage, this horse, which was dependent on man like no other breed for its survival, was developed by the Bedouin in the wild Arabian highlands into a beast of unequalled beauty and brilliance.

The combination of cruel climate, the pitiless elimination of inferior specimens, and the willingness of the Bedouin to fanatically pursue purity (taking long journeys to find the best stallions for their mares) resulted in the production of horses of incomparable quality. These horses would emigrate from their arid home of origin to exercise an unequaled influence on horse breeding worldwide. Scarcely a single breed exists today which has not at some time or another been improved by an infusion of Arab blood.

No matter where it has gone, and no matter how much time has passed, the Arabian horse has retained from its desertbred ancestors the qualities which make it so cherished today: faithfulness to type, genetic potency, health, refinement, longevity and fertility, beauty, harmonious proportions and physical perfection, intelligence, friendliness and good temper combined with a fiery spirit, adaptability and readiness to learn, stamina and power of recovery after great effort.

The Arabian horse first came to America in connection with Thoroughbred breeding. Early importations of Arabs, Barbs and Turks were registered by the Jockey Club, no registry for Arabians being available until 1908, when the Arabian Horse Club of America (now known as the Arabian Horse Registry of America) was founded. These early Oriental horses were either incorporated into the American Thoroughbred or used to improve local stock.

In the mid-nineteenth century, A. Keene Richards, a Kentucky Thoroughbred breeder, made the largest single group importation of purebred Arabians, selecting the horses himself on two trips to the Arabian Peninsula. Richard's program of crossing the desertbred stallions with his mares was lost in the Civil War.

In 1879, two stallions were presented to General Ulysses S. Grant by the Sultan of Turkey. One of them, *Leopard, sired the first American-bred Arabian, foaled in 1890. The Arabians brought here for the Chicago World's Fair in 1893 were mostly lost in a disastrous fire. Of those that survived, the most notable mare of the group was *Nejdme, later honored with the "Number 1" registration in the Arabian Horse Club of America's studbook. The exhibit awakened American interest in the Arabian breed. The next importation that received worldwide publicity was that of Homer Davenport in 1906. (Davenport was one of many Americans influenced by the Chicago World's Fair horses). Davenport's book, *My Quest of the Arab Horse*, added further fame to the twenty-seven horses he selected in the desert.

Importations became more common after that, and for those who wish to study them and follow the history of the foundation of Arabian horse dynasties here through the decades, they have been chronicled in better style and detail by other writers, such as Gladys Brown Edwards and Mary Jane Parkinson. The latter is a popular and able writer for *Arabian Horse World* magazine, the largest of the Arabian horse periodicals.

Obviously, the descendants of that Near Eastern subspecies so dependent on man for survival thrive in their latest geographical home, America. The profiles in the Arabian section of this book are of some of the greatest horses of the breed of this century. Their individual stories combine to form the latest chapter in the history of this animal, one of the most glorious the world has ever known.

Negatraz

Can anyone imagine a more unique and memorable Christmas present to end all Christmas presents than the one Jack McMillan (president of Nordstrom, the Seattle-based group of department stores) gave his wife, Loyal in 1989? Under the tree, figuratively at least, was Negatraz, one of the most outstanding sons of *Bask++ and one of the few stallions known as sires of breeding stallions as well as top-producing broodmares. A goodly number of today's most popular stallions can claim Negatraz as their sire or grandsire, among them Medalion and Monogramm.

Since Christmas of 1989, Negatraz has been at Meadow Wood Farms in Snohomish, Washington, just north of Seattle, one of the major Arabian breeding farms in the nation. As senior sire of one of the finest herds of pure Polish Arabians in the United States, he continues his career there as a breeding stallion under new and fresh direction, says Gail Deuel, manager of Meadow Wood.

At age twenty-one, he looks and acts like a horse half his age, Gail reports. "The few years that he's been at Meadow Wood Farms have seen some wonderful foals produced, with much thought and care going into choosing the mares for him.

"He's a very easy horse to work with," Gail continues, "especially for a stallion. "He loves showing off for guests, often not allowing himself to be caught until he's sure that everyone has had a good look!"

Negatraz has always made the world look, and keep on looking, since he was foaled February 2, 1971 on the Ohio farm of Dick and Kay Patterson. The bay colt, marked almost exactly like *Bask++, was the result of long and careful planning. After the Patterson mare *Negotka was Reserve Champion Mare at Scottsdale in 1970, she was booked to *Bask++, then already well on his way to becoming one of the most influential Arabian stallions in modern history.

*Bask++ had already won U.S. National Champion Stallion in 1964, U.S. National Champion Park in 1965, and U.S. National Reserve Champion Formal Driving and Formal Combination in 1967.

This son of his, who would add much to his already evident significance as a breeding stallion, was bold and showy and full of himself as soon as he could stand. Named after his eminent grandsires Negatiw and Witraz, he was quite a challenge for a young mare raising her first foal. His self-confidence, however, helped him win the Ohio State Futurity as a yearling. The following year, 1971, Negatraz made the trek with the rest of the Patterson horses to their new home in Sisters, Oregon, where he would begin his career as a breeding animal. The Pattersons showed him only as a youngster, figuring he was much too valuable as a potential breeding stallion to take the risk of removing him from the farm. He did his share of winning though when he did, counting among his victories the Ohio Two-Year-Old Futurity.

Of the over 450 foals he has sired since then, many have been Class A, Regional, and National winners in numerous disciplines.

More than half of Negatraz's foals are bay, reflecting the strength of his sire line. They are consistently stamped with his type, and most mature to a greater size than their sire, who stands 14.3 hands. He is also strong in siring a great deal of beauty, particularly about the eyes and ears, and he gives good toplines, along with his wonderful disposition. Trainers from around the country report they love working with Negatraz offspring for their good attitudes.

Beyond all his achievements as a superstar of the breed, Negatraz is a very special companion animal to Jack and Loyal McMillan. "He came from such a loving home and is very affectionate," says Loyal. "He responds so much to our caring, and that's important to us. Even if he weren't beautiful and a superb sire, we would still love him." Happily he is all that and more, a gift to anyone who loves the extraordinary.

*Probat

Jack and Loyal McMillan, breeders of pure Polish Arabians, purchased their beautiful 600-acre farm, Meadow Wood, about five years ago. "We initially purchased a couple of horses for pleasure," says Loyal. "From there, things certainly progressed. After reading the *Arabian Horse World* and studying pedigrees, we made several trips to Poland with other well-known and established breeders. We learned from the Poles and from our fellow breeders and tried to pattern our program after theirs by acquiring the best Polish mares to breed to our stallions. The results have been rewarding."

Since February, 1988, the stallion roster at Meadow Wood has been headed by a magnificent bay named *Probat. He was part of the package when Jack and Loyal McMillan acquired the entire Lasma stallion herd, including various shareholder interests in many of the nation's leading pure Polish stallions as well as outright ownership of several, including *Probat.

A stallion who has never been shown, but is the sire of international champions as well as racing champions, *Probat has an unusual story in that he was "borrowed" by the Poles from Sweden. When the stallion Comet died at a young age, Poland was left without a son as his successor. A little detective work revealed that one of the best Comet sons was Pohaniec (out of Planeta by *Naborr), who had been sold to Sweden's Blommerod

Stud as a five-year-old, right off the track. Pohaniec was siring very well at Blommerod when, in 1979, Adam Sosnowski, manager of the Polish Department of Agriculture, paid a visit. He gave particular attention to *Probat, a handsome, bay four-year-old Pohaniec son out of Borexia, who had bred seven mares that season, primarily daughters of *Exelsjor, Negatiw, and Dardir.

Mr. Sosnowski negotiated a two-year lease of *Probat, in exchagne for Poland's Celebes son, Algomej. "So, *Probat came to Michalow State Stud in Poland," Loyal continues the story. "It was a real poker game, but the very first year, a royal flush! The offspring were beautiful. From that very first foal crop came five chief sires, one Polish National Champion. Very unusual.

"*Probat's son, *Fawor, was Polish Junior Champion, European and World Junior Champion at age two. Then he went right to the track where he was a stakes winner and won the Animex Cup."

The Poles were so pleased by their *Probat get that they extended the lease for an additional two years. The stallion stood at Janow-Podlaski State Stud for the 1982 and 1983 seasons, where he again benefitted by having a second group of Poland's choicest broodmares at his court. As he had done at Michalow, *Probat again distinguished himself by siring foals of unusual quality and talent.

At the close of 1983, *Probat returned to Blommerod, where in December, 1984, another distinguished horseman came to take a look at him. Dr. Eugene LaCroix began negotiations to purchase him. *Probat came to America in 1985, then returned to Poland, where he stood the 1986 season at Michalow, and the 1987 season at Janow-Podlaski. On April 1, 1987, he was returned permanently to the United States, where he stood the remainder of the season at Lasma East in Kentucky. Shortly thereafter he was purchased by the McMillans.

Of all her stallions, Loyal finds *Probat indeed is special in his looks. He has a gorgeous head with beautiful eyes, a long neck, high tail carriage and a presence unmistakably Arabian.

"*Probat also has a very good temperament. He is very sweet, calm and friendly to people and his foals exhibit those traits as well," says Loyal "The *Probat line is very successful because of his own individual excellence, and because his pedigree is the strongest: Kuhailan on the top and Kuhailan on the bottom, with a touch of Seglawi through *Naborr and Aquinor.

*Probat has certainly fulfilled many special dreams for us," continues Loyal. "His foals are magnificent and they alone are a dream come true. As they grow and are shown or have foals themselves, future dreams will unfold."

*Enrilo

Meadow Wood Farm, a kind of Noah's Ark on terra firma along the Skykomish River thirty minutes from Seattle, Washington, is light-heartedly referred to within the McMillan family as "Loyal's Empty Nest Project," all five children of Jack and Loyal McMillan having grown and flown the coop.

Along about July, 1985, Loyal McMillan began filling the 600-acre "nest" with all kinds of animals in pairs, starting with chickens and escalating to pigs, goats, lambs, cows, and llamas. An Arabian mare in foal followed. Then a Polish Arabian mare in foal, and the next thing you knew...

Meadow Wood had evolved into one of the major Arabian breeding farms in the nation, standing great Polish stallions such as *Probat and his son *Enrilo.

"A handsome chestnut marked with white, one of the most outstanding characteristics of *Enrilo is that he possesses extreme Arabian type. His head is one of the most exquisite in the breed. He also exhibits exceptional ability as a beautiful mover," says Loyal. "These qualities are attributed to the double Comet in his pedigree, the great Polish stallion Comet appearing as his great grandsire on both his sire and dam side."

*Enrilo was foaled in February of 1981 at Michalow State Stud in Poland and was used as a breeding stallion there, bringing rave reviews from the Poles.

"I used *Enrilo for three reasons," said Ignacy Jaworowski, head of the Michalow Stud. "One, he is from one of the best female lines in Poland. (His dam is Emisja, Polish National Champion mare.) Two, he is linebred Comet. And three, he represents what Polish breeders expect in the Arabian horse."

"The most beautiful son of *Probat!" Polish horse inspector Izabella Zawadska called *Enrilo.

"*Enrilo stood second behind his paternal half-brother *Fawor as Polish Reserve Junior Champion Stallion. In turn, several young *Enrilo sons did very well at halter in Poland in 1988, winning the Two-Year-Old Colt class at the Polish Nationals and standing Reserve Junior Champion," says Loyal.

*Enrilo was imported in October, 1986 by Lasma Arabians Ltd. of Scottsdale, Arizona. Early in 1988, the McMillans acquired both *Probat and *Enrilo for Meadow Wood when they purchased the entire stallion holdings of Lasma Arabians (which included full ownership of ten top pure Polish stallions and interests in ten more pure Polish stallions).

"*Enrilo has already sired many champions in the United States, as he did when he was in Europe. Not only are his foals beautiful, but they inherit his extraordinarily kind disposition," says Loyal.

"*Enrilo represents the strongest amalgam, or combination of different elements, of a Polish pedigree — Kuhailan on the top and bottom with just a touch of Seglawi in the dam line. His dam, Emisja, a daughter of *Carycyn (Comet x Cerekiew, by Wielki Szlem) and the mare Espada (Aquinor x Eskapada by *Naborr) making *Enrilo double Comet, double Aquinor and double *Naborr, with multiple crosses to the great Amurath Sahib," she adds.

"*Enrilo and his sire are next-door neighbors in the barn. They get along very well and seem to enjoy each other's company," she reports. "Although he has not bred as many mares as his sire, all of *Enrilo's foals have his lovely head and even at an early age they exhibit good motion."

For Loyal, building and sustaining a beautiful home for these horses which are nature's work of art is her own special form of creativity.

*Etiologia

In February, 1991, Roman Pankiewicz, writer, authority on Polish bloodlines, the former director of the Albigowa State Stud where he bred the immortal *Bask, came to the United States for a visit. He came to visit Jack and Loyal McMillan's Meadow Wood Farm in Snohomish, Washington, for a singular purpose. To see *Etiologia. There are approximately two hundred horses on Meadow Wood pastures, but Mr. Pankiewicz wanted only to see the one. In his hand he carried some carrots wrapped in a paper towel. He spoke no English at all, and when he went into the stall with the seventeen-year-old bay mare, whom he had last seen as a yearling in Poland, he fed her the carrots, and put his arms around her neck, with tears in his eyes.

That's how special this exquisite creature was.

*Etiologia, foaled January 10, 1974, sired by Celebes out of Etna, was a special horse even in the way she was chosen to come to the United States. American breeders

Richard and Kay Patterson were on one of their many trips to Poland.

One evening they were waiting for Dr. Eugene La-Croix, who was in a closed meeting with the Poles going over the details of the leasing of the stallion *El Paso to the United States.

Richard and Kay had been told by the Poles that they could purchase their choice of two of the yearling filly crop. So the Pattersons decided to spend their time looking over prospects and went into the dimly-lit barn at Janow-Podlaski State Stud that evening. Two of the yearlings caught their eye right away. They gave the Poles the two brand numbers of the fillies they had chosen, not even knowing their sires or dams. The fillies turned out to be *Etiologia and *Alpaga, easily two of the best daughters Celebes ever sired.

*Etiologia was imported on October 25, 1975. During her life at Patterson Arabians, she produced excellent foals by *Dar, Meridian, *Deficyt and Negatraz.

She was a wonderful mother, and always easy to breed.

In 1987, she was purchased, with a Negatraz filly by her side, by Loyal and Jack McMillian, of the Seattle-based Nordstrom department stores, for $300,000 at the Polish Collection II Sale at Scottsdale.

"Her price was high, but well worth it," says Loyal.

While she was owned by Meadow Wood, *Etiologia produced foals by Negatraz and *Probat.

During the last two years of her life, *Etiologia unfortunately was ill with hepatitis. Then she foundered. She gradually grew worse, though she had good days and bad. In 1991, she was pregnant with a *Probat foal, and due to her illness, there was great concern for the welfare of both mare and foal.

Even in her condition, she delivered a healthy filly. Though she spent the better part of her days lying down in her stall, she was, as always, "an excellent mother," says Loyal. "She simply nursed the baby lying down!" As her condition worsened, it became necessary to wean the filly early.

"On Christmas Eve, 1991, *Etiologia had to be euthanized. It seemed fitting that such a wonderful horse should be at peace and free of pain on such a holy day," Loyal notes. And it seems fitting that *Etiologia, being so special, spent the final years of her life at a place as beautiful and wonderful as Meadow Wood.

"*Etiologia is very much missed, but we are reminded of her every day through her wonderful daughters Etamia (by Negatraz), Etolia (by *Probat), and Etiologiaa (by *Probat). We are excited to see her embryo transfer foal, by *Probat, due in August, 1992," says Loyal. "We also have a two-year old colt out of her, MWF Etan, by *Probat.

"Through her offspring, *Etiologia remains with us."

*Bufa

Dam and grandam of numerous champions, *Bufa is unquestionably one of the great pure Polish mares of all time. Her long, colorful and productive life began in Poland, her native land.

During the late 1960s, Toik Halberg of Iron, Minnesota visited Polish Arabians in their native habitat, the state studs and the racetracks of Poland. On his second trip, Toik saw a grey mare being unloaded from a truck as she was being returned to Janow-Podlaski State Stud from the track. The 15-hand mare, foaled April 14, 1964, was *Bufa (by Negatiw), and she had all the qualities Toik had learned to expect from Negatiw offspring.

"I liked her trot and her long neck and the pleasant head, not extreme, but pleasant," he says, and so he bought *Bufa, who was in foal to *Eleuzis (Aquinor x Ellenai).

The following May, *Bufa foaled a big, strong bay colt, *Hal Gazal. The latter grew up to be a real beauty, a Top Ten Stallion at the 1977 U.S. Nationals (he was third in points), a win he repeated at the 1978 U.S. Nationals (fourth in points). *Hal Gazal was eventually the sire of twenty champions himself, and was syndicated in 1983 for an aggregate value of $1,225,000.

Ken White, who bought *Hal Gazal from Toik Halberg, pays tribute to her contribution by saying, "If you look at *Bufa, if you look at the dam line of *Hal Gazal, you have the perfect example of the valued Polish tail-female line. If you want to see what Hal is, look at his grandam *Busznica. He looks so much like her, it's incredible."

Mike Nichols' appreciation of *Bufa began while he was visiting the Polish State Studs in 1969, following the same "trail" as Toik Halberg. He tracked the mare to the Halberg farm in Minnesota and offered to buy her. Toik said no. Over and over. It took a six-year campaign of persuasion on the part of Nichols until finally Toik weakened, and *Bufa joined the highly esteemed Nichols-DeLongpré broodmare band. She was successively bred to NDL's double National Champion Stallion *Elkin, then to *Eter, to Barbary and to *Pesniar.

In a touching tribute to her specialness, when *Bufa was presented as Lot 1 of the 1982 Nichols-DeLongpré Sale III in September, 1982 at Santa Barbara, the pre-bidding announcements were halted as Dick and Lollie Ames of Cedar Ridge Arabians stepped out of the wings. They presented a garland of red roses for the lovely *Bufa in the name of her son *Hal Gazal, whom they owned at that time. "Just gorgeous. That's the only word for her," Lollie remembers *Bufa. Then the bidding opened on "one of the greatest Polish mares of all time," and *Bufa, at age 18, topped the sale at $550,000.

Today she lives at Meadow Wood Farms, in Snohomish, Washington, owned by Jack and Loyal McMillan. Even at the age of twenty-eight, *Bufa pos-

sesses all the most sought-after Arabian characteristics.

"Here at Meadow Wood," says Gail Deuel, farm manager, "we have open houses during the summertime in which we have a presentation of some of our most special horses. The horses are allowed to trot freely to a musical accompaniment, and *Bufa is always the 'grand finale.' She enters the ring with her tail over her back, trots around and snorts at the audience. Her song is 'A Long and Lasting Love,' and everyone is so touched by her unique beauty that they have tears in their eyes. She is truly a treasure, and we are privileged to know her."

Top Contender

An innate show horse, with echoes of his grandsire Khemosabi and his great-great grandsire Fadjur, Top Contender is a horse who has never failed to excite an audience.

As a three-year old colt he was a National Champion, the judges' unanimous choice for National Champion Futurity Colt, an incredible feat for a horse that has shown at only ten shows in his entire life.

From the first time he stepped in the ring as a yet unnamed foal, he's had that kind of impact. At his first show, the Sun Country Classic in Albuquerque on June 11, 1980, veteran trainer and handler Chuck Kibler, who hadn't seen the foal until five minutes before the class, led him into the ring. The judge pinned the colt Junior Champion Stallion, an amazing feat for a three-month-old foal.

In 1985 he was U.S. National Reserve Champion Stallion and in 1987 U.S. Top Ten Stallion. Since then, Top Contender was declared Grand Champion Stallion at the Buckeye and Scottsdale Shows, the two largest Arabian shows with the exception of the Nationals, as well as Canadian National Champion Stallion. He is also a champion driving horse many times over.

Owner Bud Adams of Adams' Arabians in Scottsdale, has always believed in his colt, yet he has never seen him show. "I bred that horse, foaled him out, did all the training and conditioning on him for three years. No one else even touched him with a brush until he was U.S. National Champion Futurity Colt. I think so much of that horse, I'd rather people criticize me than him. I just don't watch."

His emotional involvement with TC (what most of the people working on the farm call him) began pre-foaling.

In the spring of 1980, the Adamses were in the process of relocating their ranch to Scottsdale, although some of their horses, among them Bud's favorite mare Rho-Sabba, a daughter of the double National Champion Khemosabi, were still at Bosque Farms near Albuquerque. When Rho-Sabba, bred to *AN Malik, began waxing, Bud hopped a plane and was on his way to deliver her. Bud could see even in the earliest hours of the strapping colt's life that it was very special – bold, bay, brash and beautiful.

Bud was certain his colt was destined for National titles and so began training and grooming him toward that ambition.

Top Contender's appeal to the judges and spectators is the combination of his explosive nature, his very solid and correct conformation, and his abundance of true Arabian presence.

"He just revels in that show ring," says Kibler, "and he loves to jump around and play, but he's totally controllable. I love him, because he is so easy to show. When you put your hand or whip up, he stands and shows and he'd do that for three hours if you could keep your hand up that long."

Part of the master breeding plan at Adams' Arabians is Top Contender on Bask Flame daughters, already proving an excellent cross. "He passes on to his foals his incredible length of croup and neck, plus his elegance, refinement, and charisma," Bud says, while his wife Lou adds "ease of handling and a show attitude."

"TC with his wins in both halter and performance, is the kind of horse we want to raise and have always tried to raise," says Bud.

Top Contender became just what his name implies – a tough horse to beat at any level of competition.

Bask Flame

Bask Flame's public appearances have been rare, his show career minimal, his promotional campaign nonexistent. His stablemate, Top Contender, is much more of a celebrity. Yet by staying at home and quietly getting the job done, Bask Flame has earned his place as an *Arabian Horse World* Sire of Significance.

Folks who breed their mares to him and those who have bought his foals all recognize the star quality of this stay-at-home stallion.

Bud Adams is certainly glad his wife Lou disregarded his advice as she left for the 1978 Scottsdale show: "Don't buy any more horses; we have enough."

Lou bought Bask Flame when he was still a small spark, in utero, along with his mother Mudira, for $40,000. The mare was the most expensive horse they'd ever purchased, because they had always raised their own, but the investment has paid off famously.

An *El Mudir daughter, Mudira had been bred to *Bask, Number One on just about everyone's top sire list. Bask Flame is in fact double *Bask. Mudira's dam Basquine, is also by *Bask.

The bright chestnut foal's early days were spent peacefully in a New Mexico pasture with his dam. At the time of Mudira's purchase the Adamses were living at their Bosque Farms near Albuquerque, New Mexico, and planning their retirement from school teaching careers. They had been involved with Arabian horses since the early 1950s when a neighbor, the colorful Carl Raswan, had shown them his horses.

When the Adamses bought a new property in Scottsdale for Adams' Arabians, Chuck Kibler went to work for them, attributing his decision directly to Bask Flame: "As soon as I laid eyes on him, I thought, 'Well, that's as good a horse as I've ever seen.'"

Flame was brought to Scottsdale as a two-year-old and bred to twelve purebred mares and one Half-Arab. The arrival of his first foal crop in 1981 was convincing proof of his potential in the breeding shed. "When I saw those foals, I knew right then he was a great breeding horse," says Chuck. "At least four of them were excellent halter horses and they've become great performance horses as well."

That same year Bask Flame was shown in Scottsdale where he was second to Arn-Ett Perlane in the class for three-year-old colts. That year he bred about forty-eight mares. The quality of his foals continued to attract an increasing number of mares, so his performance career was placed on the back burner.

The highest number of mares bred to Bask Flame in a single year was 120, most of them outside mares. The Adamses breed only five of their own mares a year, some to Flame and some to Top Contender.

Nevertheless, Flame's contribution to Adams' Arabians has been remarkable in dollars and cents.

Just staying put, Bask Flame elevated the Adams operation to a major breeding farm. Bud says, "Flame built the whole place. Our arena alone, where we hold our big do's cost almost an even million dollars and Flame did that all on his own."

Flame has been well represented as a sire at Scottsdale each year since his foals were first shown there in 1983.

"The best of Bask Flame's offspring are truly outstanding," says Dr. Robert Baker of HRB Arabians in Tucson, Arizona, an Arabian breeder for 25 years.

Flame himself was shown again in the late 1980s by Kibler and went Top Five at the regionals in Reno. Having been down on the farm all his life, he just liked to stand in the middle of the ring and look around.

But showing or staying at home, Bask Flame just may be, as Kibler says, "one of the best horses in the world!"

Khaffire

Khaffire is "imperious, sensitive and playful," say his owners, a description befitting a horse with a regal pedigree. He is a *Bask grandson on the sire's side, and a Khemosabi great grandson on the dam's side.

Foaled March 16, 1986, the 15.3 bay stallion is owned by Dr. Mario and Antonia Arroyo, who first saw him at an Arabian show at Griffith Park, California, in 1987. Khaffire was shown in the yearling colt class and won the Junior Champion Colt title.

"This show was a very thilling moment for us, because Khaffire became ours and started us on a new adventure," says Dr. Arroyo.

The Arroyos had never before seen a colt like him: beautiful, charismatic, and athletic. They could hardly take their eyes off him. His owner, when approached, was at first a little reluctant to sell. But after some negotiation, Khaffire became a member of the Arroyo family of Arabian horses.

The Arroyos own and operate AYM Arroyo Arabians, a breeding and training facility for Arabians, Half-Arabians, and National Show Horses, on a ten-acre ranch in the beautiful Santa Ynez Valley of California. When the Arroyos founded the facility in 1986, they owned three Arabians and had no idea of what was in store for them in the horse industry. With the purchase of Khaffire, their involvement took off in several new directions, including breeding and showing.

Khaffire has a long upright neck, an aristocratic presence and carriage, vitality and a self-contained look. "He gives us goosebumps as he enters the show arena. Our emotional involvement is so very intense. He captures the attention of people right away with his presence," says Dr. Arroyo. Under saddle, he adds, "Khaffire is powerful, charismatic, elegant, harmonious and picturesque."

Khaffire's talents caused him to be chosen by the premier Arabian trainer, Ray LaCroix, for both halter and performance competition. Ray showed Khaffire to a first in Stallions of 1986 at the prestigious Buckeye Show in 1990, as well as Top Ten English Pleasure at the highly competitive Scottsdale Show in February, 1991.

To date, Khaffire's outstanding show record also includes Champion Stallion 29th Annual Spring Show, Louisiana in 1990; Reserve Champion Stallions Three and Four Years Old, Oklahoma Centennial in 1990; U.S. National Reserve Champion Futurity Colt in 1989; Reserve Champion Three-Year-Old Colt at the Cal-Bred Futurity in 1989.

"Khaffire has fulfilled all of our dreams and desires as a performance horse and now as a breeding sire," says Dr. Arroyo. "His foals possess the presence and disposition of their sire as well as his elegance and athletic ability. His offspring are winning in halter, having inherited Khaffire's charismatic attitude. The future is bright for them to be National quality performance contenders for they have all the necessary ingredients."

Dr. Arroyo has been attracted to horses since his boyhood in Ecuador, and his wife Antonia dreamed of owning an Arabian stallion someday. "She had a mare named 'Dorada' as a child in Cuba, which helped her develop her love for horses," says her husband. "Anyone who loves horses understands that you love all horses, but that there is always that special one that stands out. When I first saw an Arabian horse, I said, 'That is my favorite breed of horse.' Khaffire combines all the beautiful qualities that an Arabian horse can have.

"Life with this Arabian stallion is thrilling, and more dreams are on the way."

Gdansks Destiny

"Ugly duckling" stories are always a pleasure to write and read, and certainly Gdansks Destiny's tale is the classic equine version.

The black/grey Arabian stallion was foaled February 6, 1986, sired by the famous *Bask+ son and park horse champion, Gdansk+, and purchased as a yearling colt by Ray and Lucy Delfino of Delfino's Arabians in Hayward, California. Ray asked Arabian trainer Roger White, owner of Bayview Training Center in Hayward, to evaluate the new colt.

"He was tall, gangly and black with nothing in proportion," recalls Roger. "His legs were much too long for the rest of him and he moved like he had no idea what to do with all those legs hanging off of him. He reminded me of a very large and clumsy spider. However, there was a very special quality about this colt. He had a bright and inquiring personality that immediately made me like him. Given time to grow and proper work, I knew this could be an outstanding horse. Plus his pedigree indicated to me that he would be a long time in maturing, as many of the Gdansk+ offspring are."

About this time, Sandi Schmuck, a partner in the trucking company Boyd Special Commodities Inc. located in Fremont, California, had a Quarter Horse mare named Amber boarded at Delfino's Arabians, in the stall next to the yearling colt.

"When I would bring carrots up for Amber, I started sharing them with Gdansks Destiny," says Sandi. "I was really starting to fall in love with him. When turned out to play, his favorite toy was an orange work cone. He would play with that thing like a young child, getting down on his knees to pick it up and throwing it out of the arena much like a child would throw a ball. I would stand there in amazement, wondering what it would be like to own a horse of his stature. Well, that dream came true and was the beginning of a wonderful adventure."

Shortly thereafter she put the colt in training with Roger White.

"As I started working with him, he reminded me more and more of a long-legged gangly teenager that I had known in the past whose nickname was 'Bubba.' That became his barn name," says Roger.

Late in 1987, Roger decided Bubba should begin his halter career to gain some ring experience. He didn't win much because he wasn't as balanced and filled-in as some of the other colts.

Then tragedy was narrowly averted at the start of the 1988 show season. Bubba caught a hind leg in the bars of his stall and exposed the entire cannon bone on the inside of his leg. It took three months, but he healed perfectly.

Shown again, he had a little more success than the previous year, but was still not as "together" as many of the other youngsters.

Sandi and Roger were both told on many occasions that he should be gelded because he would not amount to much.

Somehow, though, they never lost their faith in the ugly duckling. He began coming into his own by the spring of 1990. He had grown to 15.3 and was greying out, his mane and tail turning glistening silver.

He began winning classes and show championships and qualified for the Region 3 (Northern California) Championship Show in Reno, Nevada.

"It was going to be some of the toughest competition we had been up against with him, thirty of the best stallions I think I'd ever seen in the show ring at one time...but Bubba was really on," says Roger.

When they called Bubba's name as one of the Top Five, Sandi and Roger were on Cloud Nine. "He had finally shown a lot of people that they had been wrong," says Roger.

Gdansks Destiny has slowed down his show career these days, and is paying more attention to breeding mares. As befits a "swan," Bubba "spends a lot more time being spoiled these days," says Sandi. "Even his taste for treats is regally exotic. His favorites are grapes, which he pulls off the bunch one at a time, and strawberries by the basketful.

Once an awkward misfit, today "Gdansks Destiny symbolizes grace, beauty and poise. He is my best friend and no one could love their horse more," says Sandi.

Monogramm

While Bill and Meredith Bishop owned horses for most of their adult lives, in support of their children's interests and because of the relaxation they afforded at the end of a long, strenuous day, none changed their lives as dramatically as their beautiful chestnut stallion, Monogramm.

The Bishops had been living in Woodside, on the San Francisco Peninsula, on three acres of land with a three-stall barn, a small riding arena and one turnout paddock arena, when they began hearing about Monogramm.

Serious breeders and admirers of Polish and Russian Arabians, they, in fact, started hearing about Monogramm right after he was foaled in 1985. "Lots of us went to see him in remote Sisters, Oregon," says Bill.

"We'd heard about him from people who aren't easily impressed. And we knew the quality of his dam." She's the extraordinary mare, *Monogramma, who'd set a race record in Moscow, Russia, that still stands after twenty-five years. Monogramm's sire, Negatraz, son of the immortal *Bask, is himself distinguished as the sire of at least fifty-four champions with twelve National winners.

The Bishops found Monogramm was exquisitely typey, with the color and athletic ability he inherited from his dam's side. "Everything looked like he had the right genes to sire the beautiful athlete," says Bill, and so they bought him in the spring of 1986.

But Bill and Meredith were not quite prepared for what owning a stallion of this quality came to mean. They learned that with him came an obligation to him and to the breed. They had to provide him with the right trainers, the right show opportunities, the right mares, advertising and promotion. Their sense of obligation mandated that they had to do it right or not at all.

And so they founded Bishop Lane Farm in 1986. Now they live on fifty acres in Sebastopol, north of San Francisco, where Monogramm stands with his mares at a facility of forty-five stalls, twenty pastures, five employees and seventy horses. Another one-hundred-acre training facility is in Santa Rosa.

"I'll say our lives have changed!" comments Bill. Their goal has become "to breed our ideal Arabian, an extremely athletic horse with exotic Arabian type." They are on their third foal crop now and already have a few individuals of the quality for which they are searching.

Monogramm, in fact, won the prestigious get of sire award at the 1991 Scottsdale All Arabian Horse Show, the largest Class A Show in North America. He also won the 1991 get of sire award at the fall Santa Barbara show. In 1990 he was among the Top Ten stallions in the U.S. National Championships.

But the greatest rewards for the Bishops are the private ones.

"It may be possible for us to own his flesh and the fancy foil-stamped papers from the registry, but no one will ever own Monogramm's soul," says Meredith. "He makes his own choices. About virtually everything."

Even as to where his turnout paddock is. He likes being turned out in a paddock from which he supervises everything and everyone, including the cars and people which pass by. Unless of course, you have the audacity to turn out another stallion. Then he only supervises him. And pumps himself up to about seventeen hands to do it.

"There are times at home when he'll strike a pose which will remind you of all the beautiful images of horses you've ever seen. And every spring, every time a foal is born, is special", adds Meredith.

Shaikh Al Badi

Now in his twenties, Shaikh Al Badi, whose name means "sheikh of the desert," is the leading living straight Egyptian sire of National winners, with fourteen to his credit. He has sired a total of seventy-eight known champions to date. One of the last living sons of *Morafic, Shaikh is a living treasure both for his pedigree and in the breeding shed. Both his sire and his dam, *Bint Maisa El Saghira++, are by the great Nazeer.

Foaled January 17, 1969, the 15.1-hand grey stallion is owned by the Shaikh Al Badi Syndicate and stands at Bittersweet Arabians, Inc. at LaGrange, Kentucky. Bittersweet is a breeding farm with a number of prominent Polish and Egyptian mares and stallions, plus complete training facilities for clients' horses.

"The first time I saw Shaikh Al Badi was at an Egyptian Event in the early 1980s at Lexington, Kentucky," says Jenny Bizzack, who with husband John has controlling interest in the horse. "Shown in halter in the outdoor arena, this great grey stallion made a deep impression on me that day and I never forgot him. I didn't see Shaikh Al Badi again until the day he came to live at Bittersweet Arabians in 1985. He has been a big part of our lives ever since.

"Many people come to Bittersweet Arabians to see Shaikh Al Badi and perhaps have their picture taken with him. On those occasions, says Jenny, "he stands very alert and very majestic, enjoying the attention. The stallion barn where he lives also houses other noted stallions, but Shaikh Al Badi is always the one visitors know and seek out.

"Shaikh Al Badi loves the attention he invariably receives from visitors when they stop by his stall. He comes to the front of his stall, sticks out his tongue and slides it up the iron bars. Then he stands there with his tongue hanging out of the side of his mouth, hoping someone will scratch it," says Jenny.

"When the stallion is led from his stall for pictures, to be presented to visitors, or just for a walk, his whole appearance changes to the fine specimen of an Arabian stallion. Though he is a senior citizen, his attitude and beauty are still outstanding."

Shaikh Al Badi has founded one of the top Egyptian sire lines today though his sons, one of which is Ruminaja Ali, U.S. National Reserve Champion Stallion, and sire of U.S. and Canadian National Champion Stallion Ali Jamaal.

Shaikh Al Badi was named 1972 U.S. National Reserve Champion Futurity Colt, and he has sired fourteen U.S. and Canadian National winners. National stars include Our Cleopatra, 1983 Canadian National Champion Western Pleasure AOTR, 1983 U.S. National Reserve Champion Western Pleasure AOTR, and 1983 U.S. National Champion Western Pleasure; Ruminaja Ali, 1979 U.S. National Champion Futurity Colt and, as mentioned, 1983 U.S. National Reserve Champion Stallion.

One of Shaikh Al Badi's sons, Shaikh Al Kuran, a straight Egyptian stallion, stands at Bittersweet Arabians. Shaikh Al Kuran is a multi-champion in halter who placed in the Top Ten in his age group at the 1991 Egyptian Event.

"Having controlling interest in Shaikh Al Badi and having him live at Bittersweet Arabians is an interesting experience. We hope we can enjoy him for a long time to come," says Jenny.

*Bint Amal

While many other horses have come and gone at their farm, Royal Arabian Stud in Mountain Center, California, "Our star is *Bint Amal," says Robert Brunson, who with his wife Erika, has been an Arabian horse enthusiast for over thirty years.

"To write about such a young individual when we've had so many other horses, many for a longer period of time, might seem odd," explains Robert. "But we know this one ranks among those that are different."

It all began with two stallions criss-crossing the Atlantic.

Don and Judi Forbis of Ansata Arabian Stud in Mena, Arkansas, and Dr. Hans Nagel of Katharinenhof Stud in Bremen, Germany, decided to exchange stallions for a couple of years. Ansata Halim Shah, 1983 U.S. Top Ten Futurity Colt, and later Reserve Junior World Champion at the 1983 Salon du Cheval in Paris, went to Germany.

Dr. Nagel's *Jamilll traveled westward, and became 1983 U.S. Top Ten Stallion during his short stay in America.

Thus a straight Egyptian filly was born in Germany in 1985, sired by Ansata Halim Shah out of Amal, a half sister to *Jamilll. Born a bay, the filly would turn grey as years passed.

The Forbises, who first saw her in 1986, imported her as a yearling and then contacted the Brunsons, whom they knew were looking for an outstanding filly to show and use later in their breeding program.

The Brunsons immediately responded to *Bint Amal's extreme refinement, a trademark of her sire's get, and to her beauty. Both were determining factors in their desire to acquire her and show her to her maximum potential.

The Brunsons wasted no time in getting their new filly into the show ring, where she had a very successful career with the following accomplishments: Egyptian Event Top Ten 1986 and 1987; Texas Shootout Junior Champion Filly, 1987; Lufkin Fall Festival Junior Champion Filly, Grand Champion Mare and Supreme Show Champion, 1987; Pyramid Society (California) Classic Champion Extended Futurity, Reserve Senior Champion Mare, and Reserve Champion, February, 1989; Egyptian Event Champion, Extended Specialty Futurity, June, 1989; and Reserve Champion Mare, 1990, at a Class A Show.

Robert says Amal's success is due to several factors. "In addition to her feminine beauty, free floating movement, and intelligence, she has that special look, a star quality, tempered with a delightful and pleasant personality.

"Everyone loves her: trainers, grooms and fans from coast to coast. One cannot help but notice there is a sweetness about this mare that is reflected in her actions. The way she greets you with her gaze and kind eye and soft arch of her neck as she reaches with her nose, hoping for an equally soothing touch from whomever is there."

While this book is all about horses who have fulfilled their humans' dreams, here's one who may be the reverse of that.

Since Amal is always a good sport with whatever is asked of her, the Brunsons hope that someday they will be able to fulfill HER dream.

Nancy Realmuto, parapsychologist and psychic, gave Amal a reading at Ansata. Amal told Nancy she would like to be a dancing horse like the famous dancing horses of Egypt with their lovely, beautiful movements.

But for the moment, Amal is taking a break from her first four years on the show circuit and enjoying motherhood. "We look forward to her future," say the Brunsons.

WM About Time

WM About Time demonstrates what a horse can do when its natural talents and preferences are acknowledged and respected, says Dr. Joanne E. Callan, a psychologist.

About Time, a very feminine, purebred bay Arabian mare with a small diamond on her forehead, was initially earmarked as having high potential in English pleasure competition.

"'Abby' soon let us know that she had other talents," says Joanne, whose small Arabian horse business in Solana Beach, California, is called Calarab. "We decided to try her one day as a western horse and she immediately made it clear that she was happier."

Initially this was disappointing to her primary rider, Megan Callan, who had to consider giving up English pleasure performances. However, as soon as Megan watched Abby move in both western and hunt seat, there was no doubt as to her talent and her own enjoyment in these divisions.

Abby's subsequent change of training and a Sweepstakes nomination through the International Arabian Horse Association proved to be wise decisions as Abby has gone on to win the following titles: 1991 U.S. Top Ten Hunter Pleasure Amateur Owner to Ride, Region 2 Top Five Hunter Pleasure AOTR, Region 3 Top Five Western Pleasure JOTR and Hunter Pleasure AOTR, Scottsdale Top Ten Western Pleasure JOTR, plus many Class A Championship and Reserve Championship ribbons.

"To perform so well in these new classes, Abby had to work hard in her training. She made remarkable progress from her earlier playfulness, and became quite calm and cool, even disciplined in competition. She made an impressive transition from her earlier English to western riding," says Joanne.

The Callans found Abby after looking for several years for an Arabian mare of Spanish bloodlines that had potential both as a performer and as a broodmare. Abby had placed Top Ten in the English Pleasure Futurity at the Santa Barbara show. "She was just what we had been looking for: beautiful, friendly, and athletic, although still feminine and delicate in appearance," says Dr. Callan. "Beyond her exceptional conformation, she showed the promise of being versatile and consistent in competition, and she seemed to have a sense of playfulness about her which would make it fun and rewarding to work with her."

Foaled on April 4, 1983, About Time was sired by *Barich De Washoe, a stallion bred in Spain. Her registered name was given to her because her breeders, Bill and Mary Ann Hughes of Wil Mar Arabians in Chino Hills, California were hoping for a filly out of her dam, Bint Saphira. When Abby finally arrived, after they had gotten five colts in a row from their other mares, Mrs. Hughes exclaimed, "Well, it's about time!"

"As much as we love this story about her arrival and how she was named, we call her Abby," says her owner.

As a psychologist, Dr. Callan adds her own insight to Abby's training: "Abby is a reserved mare under saddle and calls for a sensitive rider and trainer, both on and off her back. Because she wants to please, we have to be certain that when she is learning she does not feel that she is being punished when she is asked to do more. We have to be careful how we ask her to do things, so that she doesn't get her feelings hurt."

"She has a special kind of magnetism about her," adds Dr. Callan. "People are immediately attracted to her. Much of her appeal comes from her big, soft eyes. She looks at you as if she understands what you are saying and moreover seems to say that you are on the same wavelength with her—that you and she are kindred spirits in this world of people and horses.

"Our relationship with Abby has been one of special joy and privilege and we look forward to her continuing performances and to the wonderful offspring she will produce," concludes Dr. Callan.

TW Forteyna

TW Forteyna, one of the Arabian breed's legendary broodmares, has established a royal dynasty of wonderful offspring. Because of her, Blackhawk Valley Arabians of Pleasanton, California, has become a major breeding farm, noted for producing outstanding show horses.

Foaled February 8, 1974, the 15-hand dark bay mare by *Fortel and out of Tapiola, was seven years old at the time Cory Soltau and Ralph Sessa, Jr. purchased her for Blackhawk Valley Arabians. She has been bred to Bey Shah+ every year since 1981 and has produced seven fillies and two colts by him. The six offspring shown from that cross have all been champions. (Forteyna's lifetime total of foals is twelve—nine fillies and three colts).

A charming magazine ad for Bey Shah+ (bound to make other mares, or at least their owners, jealous) is a Valentine from the stallion to his long-time mate. It reads "To TW Forteyna, with love from Bey Shah+. Ours

has been a fine romance and we have the kids to prove it" And it lists a few of the progeny.

TW Forteyna was actually chosen as a potential mate for Bey Shah+ by Cory Soltau, a large-animal veterinarian. In his practice, Cory kept his eyes open for a mare that would complement Bey Shah+. At the ranch of George and Patsy Gerling, he found Forteyna and leased her for a year.

Forteyna was bred by Carl and Pat Hendershot of Trade Wind Arabians of Tracy, California, and was "gorgeous" with unusually large eyes, big nostrils and large feet. (Cory is an endurance rider, so large excellent feet are important to him).

Early in March, 1982, Forteyna had her first Bey Shah+ foal. For Cory and Ralph, it was and is the most special moment they can remember with this mare. Forteyna foaled in a pasture of knee-high spring grass stippled with the pale yellow of wild mustard. It was a suitable reception for the big, gangly black filly they named Shahteyna, who was destined for stardom. Five years later Shahteyna would become the U. S. National Champion Mare.

Shahteyna's quality convinced Cory and Ralph to purchase Forteyna and to breed her back to Bey Shah+ immediately. This second rendezvous produced Bey Sonya in 1983. Bey Sonya began showing in 1983, winning Cal-Bred Futurity and Nor-Cal Reserve Champion Three-Year-Old Filly. In 1987 at Scottsdale, Bey Sonya won Top Ten Mares of 1983. Since then, endurance rider Teresa Cross rode Bey Sonya in the Tevis 100-Mile Ride of July, 1991; Bey Sonya finished forty-second in a field of 229 starters. In the same ride, Cory rode his Half-Arabian gelding, Master Charge, who crossed the finish line with Bey Sonya. Cory plans to ride Bey Sonya in the 1992 Tevis and to win his 1000-mile buckle.

Forteyna's 1985 bay colt Sensational Bey was purchased by Jim Maroney of Ennistymon at Oswego, New York and Bob Chengarian of Ararat Arabians, and has a number of winning offspring on the East Coast. Bey Teyna was 1992 Scottsdale Reserve Champion mare. PS Tatiana is dam of the Scottsdale Reserve Junior Champion colt, RHA Khnight Ryder; Bey Prost and Shahdorable are other offspring of which their parents can be proud.

Today Forteyna reigns as Queen of Blackhawk Valley. "She is extremely independent," says Cory. "Forteyna truly likes Ralph and me, but she is happiest when she is left alone." She is most content as a mother. Cory feels her strong character—she even prefers to foal on her own—is perhaps due to her Polish heritage.

And as far as that romance with Bey Shah+ goes, Ralph and Cory say they have no intention of breaking up a good thing.

Sensational Bey

Sensational Bey means different things to his two owners, Jim Maroney and Bob Chengerian.

"To me, who cares for him daily and functions as soul-mate," says Jim, "'Bey' is majestic and awesome and very kind and easy to handle and 'funny,' with his peek-a-boo antics. He loves to scare himself and will hide behind trees or other individuals and peek around them if I so much as crinkle a candy wrapper. He'll keep snorting and hold his tail ramrod straight, and then, as soon as I call to him, he will come immediately, expecting and, more often than not, receiving the carrot his performance so justly deserves.

"To Bob," continues Jim, "who weekends with Bey, the horse is an idol, a hero, a never-failing sire who passes on his desirable qualities, a very rewarding investment and The Champion."

The last reference is to the fact that Sensational Bey was New York State Breeders Association Champion Stallion and Region 16 Top Five Stallion, both in 1988. But he soon gave up his show career to be full-time breeding stallion.

"What comes through loud and clear in the Bey foals is the snort-and-blow quality. Everytime," says Jim. "We don't have any that don't turn on. We consistently see the correct, athletic conformation and the exotic type in the foals. Bodies may vary, but always the tail carriage, the upright necks, good length from point of croup to point of hip, long shoulders, long legs, short backs, and fine throatlatches come through."

Sensational Bey is out of TW Forteyna (*Fortel x Tapiola by Sur-Grande), *Arabian Horse World* Aristocrat and Bey Shah's most notable mate. Forteyna is the dam of Shahteyna, the 1987 U.S. National Champion Mare by Bey Shah and of six more Bey Shah National, Regional, and Futurity Champions.

Because of their admiration for Shahteyna, when Jim and Bob went colt-shopping in 1987, they went to Blackhawk Valley Arabians in Pleasanton, California, home of TW Forteyna. Owners Cory Soltau and Ralph Sessa, Jr. trotted out all the Bey Shah/Forteyna colts for their consideration.

"When they brought the two-year-old Sensational Bey out of his stall, my response was electric," Jim remembers. "He was regal and loaded with presence. Instantly I knew this horse had all the right parts and the right charisma, and that he needed to be out East."

Bey came to Jim Maroney's Ennistymon (named after the lovely Irish town from which his grandfather emigrated) at Oswego, New York, near Lake Ontario in late June, 1987.

"Sensational Bey was unique in that we don't have a lot of horses like Bey Shah in this neck of the woods, horses that have size and substance and still consis-

tently sire type and beauty and athletic ability," says Jim, who has served as president of the Empire State Arabian Horse Association.

Two Sensational Bey offspring, Satin Sensation, out of Silk N Saten by Bakkarat, and Sensashahnel, out of Aangelique by Sey Magnifique, are now in the show ring and racking up the wins. Satin Sensation was Junior Champion Filly at ten months of age. Sensashahnel was Grand Champion Mare and Region 16 Top Five Futurity in 1991.

Eleven Sensational Bey sons and daughters are already show winners. In Regions 16 and 17 they have brought in a Sweepstakes Reserve Championship and several Top Tens, a Top Five, and Futurity ribbons.

"Sensational Bey is beyond anything Bob and I ever expected of him as a breeding stallion and he's made every mare owner happy. For the future we anticipate only making him the happiest camper in the world," says Jim.

*Estopa

The exquisite pure Spanish Arabian mare *Estopa and her owner, Sigi Constanti, have been together for over twenty-two years, in one of the closest, most devoted relationships I have ever learned of.

During that time, *Estopa has been a powerful influence on Sigi's life, as well as an overwhelming influence on Arabian horse breeding programs around the world.

As a result of *Estopa's influence, Sigi sold her family business and concentrated completely on the breeding of Arabian horses and developed a breeding program based on *Estopa's progeny. Over the past twenty years, *Estopa's family has produced more National, International, and World Champions than any other family of Arabian horses in the world. Her name appears in the pedigrees of Arabian horses in nearly every country where Arabians are bred.

Among *Estopa's most famous offspring are the International Champion and prepotent sire of champions, *El Shaklan, and World Champion and sire extraordinaire, *Ibn Estopa.

*Estopa's beauty, charisma and success have helped to establish the reputation Spanish-bred Arabian horses enjoy today.

"After her National Championship in 1978 in Germany, many breeders went to Spain to purchase their Arabian horses," says Sigi.

*Estopa, who was also European Champion Mare in 1979, was sired by Tabal out of Uyaima.

Sigi first saw and fell in love with the 15.1 white mare during a 1970 trip to Spain, at the farm of prominent breeder, Don Miguel Osuna in Ecija.

One glance and one can understand why. *Estopa has an absolutely unforgettable head, very chiseled with large, expressive black eyes. Her movements are powerful but graceful. "She reminds me of horses on the canvases of Adams, Vernet and Schreyer," says Sigi.

"*Estopa was five years old when she came into my life. She always radiated a special aura that set her apart from the others."

*Estopa has been with her, through thick and thin, ever since. Sigi took her back with her to her farm in Germany that year, and she moved with Sigi to Santa Ynez, California in 1984, where Sigi and husband Jay Constanti are owners of Om El Arab International.

Above all else, *Estopa is an emotional experience for Sigi. "I come to spend time with her every day, and she leaves her food or grain to be close to me. I groom her with my hands, and she often puts her head on my shoulder and we both relax peacefully. We hold conversations only we can understand and have secret agreements that are kept between the two of us."

In heart-stopping drama, Sigi almost lost her great love when her former husband became determined to sell *Estopa, who had become "community property" in California, when they parted ways. Following intense litigation, Sigi won the right to provide her with a home for life on her own farm where she can spend her older days in the mild weather of the Santa Ynez Valley.

"*Estopa enriches my life and fills my heart with joy. I credit her with being singularly responsible for the successes of the Om El Arab breeding program. We refer to our farm as *Estopa's farm. She has fulfilled all of my dreams and more," says Sigi.

"Quite simply, through her, I have learned that just one does make a difference. She has influenced breeders everywhere. Similarly one person with something special to offer can likewise make a difference in the hectic confusion of today's world."

R H Desert Finesse

RH Desert Finesse was born on Valentine's Day, February 14, 1977, perhaps as a promise of all the love the grey Arabian mare would bring into the lives of Baron and Judith Clements.

The Clements have a breeding farm, Luxor Arabian Farm, in Bleiblerville, Texas, which is home to a variety of mares, geldings, colts, and a stallion.

But Judy says she chose Nesse to pay tribute to in this book "because she is such a wonderful, gentle mare. In making the decision, I went down the aisleway of the barn, and each horse tugged at my heart. Even the two that we've lost seemed to be in the barn that evening. But when I got to Nesse's stall and she looked at me with those soft, fluid eyes, I said aloud, 'Let's honor you, Nesse. You never demand anything of me, not even a hug when I forget to give you one.' And then I looked around at all our 'squeaky wheels' and I had to laugh. All so different and all so loving."

The Clements' breeding business all started with a loving gesture on the part of Judy's husband in 1983, when he asked, "What would you like for Christmas?"

"I think I'd like to have a horse again," was Judy's answer. "Off and on all my adult life, this thought would drift in and I'd resist. Who had time these days? As a teenager, when I owned my first horse, it seemed I had all the time in the world. Drop my school books, change my clothes and head for the stables. This time, I decided I'd make time."

Through a newspaper ad, Judy found and bought Finali, a chestnut with flaxen mane and tail at the farm of Judy Guess. The women became friends.

By the time the Clements' horse family had grown to three, Guess asked Judy if she would be interested in buying Desert Finesse, the most quiet, dignified mare Judy had ever met. After some "fancy footwork" she got Baron to agree.

"The lights in the barn cast a mystical glow and as she stepped out of the trailer, all Baron could say was, 'She's beautiful, she's really beautiful,'" she says. But she noticed that Baron would kind of keep his distance with Nesse. When she asked him if he liked her, his answer was, "I really like her, but she doesn't like me."

She explained that Nesse was a very reserved, quiet mare, and felt badly for the both of them that they couldn't get together.

Not too long after that conversation, Judy was driving up to the barn upon her return from a horse show when she noticed the vet's truck.

Nesse was in foal, her baby had gotten into a position that was uncomfortable and she had decided to lie down right after dinner. Everything was fine now but, the vet added, she might want to check on her husband. There he was in the barn, with Nesse resting her head on his lap. "Talk about bonding," says Judy, who remembers this as one of her happiest moments.

Nesse had a beautiful filly and was bred again, setting off a baby boom and another long search for the right farm.

"From one horse for Christmas to the responsibility of propagating and improving the breed. This is the most profound undertaking I've so far experienced," says Judy. "I mentioned time at the beginning. If having horses has taught me anything, I'd have to say the most important is that all things come 'in time.' By being so steady, Nesse has helped me keep the perspective of 'for everything there is a season.' I've learned that time is a human invention, and if you are willing to wait, life unfolds."

*Moment

While at the 1991 Arabian Nationals in Albuquerque, New Mexico, I had dinner with Sharon and Bob Davis, an enjoyable event in itself made memorable by the tale Bob told me of their magnificent stallion, *Moment.

A story so filled with foreign intrigue it could have come from the word processor of a spy thriller novelist, it opens behind the Iron Curtain in 1969, when the grey stallion *Moment was foaled at the Tersk Stud in the USSR.

*Moment, a full brother to U.S. National Champion *Muscat (by *Salon out of Malpia by Priboj) was sent to Bulgaria when he was three-years-old, then returned to Tersk in 1977 when *Muscat left Tersk to come to the United States, then disappeared back into Bulgaria again. Howard Kale, Jr. made a famous 200-mile taxi ride in Bulgaria to try to see *Moment in 1977, only to be told that the stallion was not for sale. Peter Clausen of Valhalla Arabians at Spokane, Washington was ultimately luckier, though it took four visits, and many more miles by ancient taxis and trains, before he convinced the suspicious Bulgarians to sell *Moment to him in 1983.

The Davises, owners of Morning Glory Arabians in West Palm Beach, Florida, acquired *Moment only recently, at the age of twenty-one, after Peter Clausen sold him to a neighbor. Pat Mooney, the manager of RA Aloha Arabians in Spokane, Washington, to whom Clausen had sold *Moment in 1990, called Sharon and informed her that *Moment was for sale.

"I have always wanted him, and we do need him for our Russian breeding program," Sharon told her husband. "What about our other two Russian stallions, *Tamerlan and *Monokl?" asked Bob. "They are Arax horses and *Moment is from the Naseem line," Sharon replied. "Well, it would be nice, but I don't think we need another stallion," said Bob. "I remember reading a story about him several years ago. Someone told me that Peter Clausen took a suitcase full of cash to Bulgaria to buy *Moment. I wonder how much they want for him now? Let's don't get carried away."

Next scene, Sharon is driving Bob to the West Palm Beach airport so he can fly off to take a look at *Moment. The scene after that, he is calling Sharon to tell her, "You are now the proud owner of one of the most beautiful grey Arabian stallions in the United States."

"Gentle and undemanding, from the very first, *Moment showed an affinity for Nutter Butter cookies," says Bob. A regal stallion with large black eyes, he was at home immediately, and could often be seen looking soulfully from his stall, out over the many mares and foals frolicking in the mild Florida weather. The Davises planned his future breeding career carefully, setting aside their special mares with whom the Naseem/*Salon cross could be utilized to best advantage. With *Moment home at last and at peace, it would seem that the story should end happily. But as the first breeding season approached, *Moment began showing symptoms of a serious equine malady, Equine Protozoan Myelitis (EPM).

"It isn't infectious. It's a parasite that works its way to the brain, causing a slow and steady loss of equilibrium. *Moment will eventually not be able to stand," the vet told them. The Davises looked at each other in utter dismay and asked what they could do. "There is a treatment that works sometimes, but I must tell you the chances are not good," said the vet. "It shouldn't end like this," Sharon lamented. "None of our mares are bred to him. Maybe it isn't meant to be."

*Moment responded well to treatment and made a complete recovery. The Davises knew he was feeling fine when they led their mare Poetry past his stall and it appeared that *Moment was trying to open the door to join her. The Davises decided Poetry was a great choice for *Moment. A colt was foaled, one which looks just like *Moment except he is bay. The Davises knew this colt would be the heir apparent to *Moment and named him "Bay Moment."

"They are both at Morning Glory Arabians, father and son, *Moment and Bay Moment. They are the past, present and future," says Bob. "*Moment is a million dollars and a million miles away from his birthplace, but now he is content and settled for life, overseeing his band of broodmares and watching his heir grow to maturity." A happy ending at last.

Redwinds Chaparral ++

Of all the many horses in the country area where Carol Di Maggio lived as a child, then the proud owner of a pinto mare named Comanche, "Not one was a purebred Arabian or even a partbred for that matter," she says. "We only read about them in magazines. Back then I don't think that I thought I would ever see or ever own one," she adds. "I read Walter Farley's Black Stallion books and remember thinking, 'If ONLY!'

"Well, Redwinds Chaparral++ isn't black, but it really doesn't matter. He has fulfilled my wildest dreams," says Carol of the dark mahogany bay stallion she and her husband Dr. Vincent Di Maggio purchased in November, 1990, for their Bright Future Farms in Walnut Creek, California.

There are now all of thirteen purebred Arabians, as well as one Thoroughbred, and one Shetland Pony at Bright Future Farms, but it is Chaparral who embodies its name.

"I have great expectations that Chaparral will put Bright Future Farms on the map," says Carol. "He has bred some very nice mares, so we have high hopes for some good foals."

Chaparral was foaled on May 26, 1978, a son of Ga Gajala Song, a Gainey-bred halter champion and sire of halter and performance champions. His dam, Amurath Roxana was Pacific Slope and Region 1 Champion Mare.

He is one of 1,500 Arabians out of almost 500,000 horses registered that have achieved the Legion of Merit Award, devised for horses who have successfully competed and accumulated enough points in halter and performance, which accounts for the two pluses after his name.

"We are extremely proud of this horse," adds Carol. "Not only does he have the ability to perform, but he has beauty as well as a wonderful disposition and mind. What more could one want in a horse and companion?"

She had first seen him on August, 1988 at a local horse show where he was judged the Champion Stallion.

Later a friend suggested that she take a look at Redwinds Chaparral when Carol was selecting a stallion to breed to a mare. She learned he had been in Ohio for several years and had been shown there, and that he had sired fourteen foals, one of which was a futurity winner and one a Western Pleasure Champion, a bay mare named SF Ceara Wind, still being shown. He had won a Top Five title at the Region 3 Championships, and went on to Scottsdale in 1989 and 1990 where competition is as tough as it gets and was chosen Top Ten both years.

"But the 'jewel' in his crown," says Carol, "is a 1989 U.S. National title at halter, won competing against horses that are household names (in Arabian-owning households, of course).

"I will never forget seeing him come trotting into that arena that day. He wasn't my horse at that time, but I was his greatest fan and still am," she says of this free spirit she feels no one could ever really own.

"I know people probably feel, what a corny name for a horse ranch, 'Bright Future Farms,' but I feel it is appropriate, especially now that we have Chaparral. I hope others will have the opportunity to know what one will do and say for the love of a horse."

*Ralvon Elijah

I first saw *Ralvon Elijah at the Scottsdale Arabian Show, an unforgettable flash of copper and gold under the desert sun. The toast of Europe and Great Britain, his name, bloodlines and looks made him a sensation.

Inquiring about him, I found *Ralvon Elijah is considered by some to be one of the most distinguished internationally-winning stallions in history. And that his reputation had preceded him here. He was British National Champion in both 1984 and 1985, winner of the All Nations Cup in 1985, and winner of the Lloyd's Bank All Breed Championship at the Royal Agricultural Show in England, the first time in history the honor had gone to an Arabian.

When the robust, iridescent copper stallion with the extraordinarily long, high-set neck trotted brilliantly into the show ring in Scottsdale in February 1988, the audience collectively applauded.

Bred in Australia by Ron and Val Males of the Ralvon Arabian Stud in New South Wales, Australia, *Ralvon Elijah was sired by Ralvon Nazarene, Australia's National Champion Stallion in 1984 and 1985.

He was purchased in 1978 by Michael Pitt-Rivers, owner of the Tollard Park Stud in England, and imported to England as a yearling. He was kept under wraps until he was five years old, after which, under Pitt-Rivers' ownership, *Ralvon Elijah achieved his greatest show ring triumphs.

In 1986 *Elijah was acquired by American interests and is currently principally owned by Don and Jo Ann Holson of CAVU Arabians of Sanger, Texas.

"We first saw *Elijah in 1986. We had learned enough to know when we saw him that *Elijah was truly special, the embodiment of our concept of the perfect Arabian. That's just what he is to us," says Jo Ann Holson.

"Although we are very pleased at what he has sired, we hope the best is yet to come. We tried to incorporate that same attitude into our farm name, CAVU Arabians," she told me. "We wanted something that would be apropos to the two of us and also depict something of our outlook and attitude. Don, a retired pilot, came up with an aeronautical term that seems perfect, aviation being a large part of both of our lives," says Jo Ann, a flight attendant with American Airlines. "CAVU stands for ceiling and visibility unlimited – to a pilot that means that you can go as high and as far as you can see. And with luck, we think we can."

So far they are flying high. In England, *Elijah's offspring continue to win. In America, the Holsons produced *Elijah's first U.S.-born foal, CAVU Eligenesis, as well as *Elijah's first USA Supreme Show Champion, CAVU Elijana.

Of the four CAVU offspring he sired in 1988, so far three have been in the ring and have all won firsts, Reserve Junior Championships, Junior Championships or Supreme Show Championships. Of the four 1989 foals, two are now in the ring and are following the same pattern.

"*Elijah is a dream come true to us," says Jo Ann, "but he is also special to many people, and more importantly he is special to the Arabian breed."

Canadian Love

"We knew he had the ability to make it to the top," Joanne Justik says of her fourteen-year-old Arabian stallion, Canadian Love. Justik, owner of Pine Valley Arabians in LaGrange, Kentucky, bought the chestnut with a white star as an unshown four-year-old, from Shiloh Arabians in 1982. "They turned him out and we knew he was special right away. He had a free-flowing motion, even in the pasture," she says.

But as can sometimes happen with a talented young horse, bad luck in getting the wrong trainer nearly ruined him.

"We had a trainer at our barn who was very young and not very professional. He didn't condition Canadian Love enough and he hurt his tendons; the trainer said the horse was no longer able to perform in the ring," says Joanne.

Justik could have given up on the horse, considering the negative advice she received from the trainer and a veterinarian. "We weren't sure what we were doing at the time," she recalls. "We had just gotten into the competitive part and we didn't know a whole lot about legs. We were feeling our way. We were all concerned and wanted the horse to get back to where he was."

Joanne bought a "freeze machine," which ices legs, and her son, Victor, nursed Canadian Love's legs back to soundness by putting him on the machine every day for an hour for six months.

The veterinarian took x-rays after six months and while the horse had improved, the veterinarian said he couldn't guarantee the horse would ever really be himself again.

"We looked around for a trainer and settled on Dick Kiesner of Texas. We sent the horse there and with the guidance of veterinarians, they brought him back slowly and he did come back stronger than ever, but it took time and work on everybody's part," Joanne says.

Canadian Love recovered well enough to go to renowned trainer John Rannenberg at Rohara Arabians in Florida. "He seemed to click with Canadian Love," says Joanne.

The stallion had many wins, both with Dick Kiesner (in 1985) and with Rannenberg for the rest of his career. In 1985, Canadian Love was United States National Reserve Champion Pleasure Driving; in 1987, Region 12 Champion English Pleasure Champion (by unanimous decision), Scottsdale Champion English Pleasure (a unanimous decision), and Buckeye Champion English Pleasure (a unanimous decision); in 1988, he went U.S. National Champion English Pleasure by unanimous decision; in 1989, he was Canadian National Champion Informal Combination (riding and driving); and in 1989, U.S. National Reserve Champion Informal Combination. "He's had many Top Tens in between," says Joanne.

Part of the credit for his victories goes to Joanne for the support she gave her horse. "He was away from home being trained and being shown, but my devotion was always there," she says. "I went to every show he was in. I made sure he had proper care."

That care included taking x-rays every six months as he began to recover, and continuing to take them thereafter. "At the beginning of every year when he was showing, we took x-rays to make sure he was all right," she says.

"He's one special stallion, in his character, his attitude. He's got a lot of heart," Joanne adds. "You can quote John Rannenberg who told me, 'He gave all he could, with no problems.'"

Canadian Love is now retired and stands at stud at Lasma East International Centre, just down the road from Joanne's farm.

"His offspring all inherit his attitude, his looks, his big, pretty eye," she says. "A colt, Canadian Red, out of a mare named Bey Basquell is three weeks old and looks just like his daddy.

"I will not sell him," Joanne says of Canadian Love. "He will be mine forever." She's gotten as much as she's given the horse, she feels. "If it weren't for him, I don't think I'd be in the business at all. He's given me the incentive to stay."

Little Liza Fame

Virginia W. Wood, owner of Gold Wood Farm in Scottsdale, Arizona, has always had a natural eye for a great horse, and proved it beyond doubt with Little Liza Fame.

Virginia, better known in the Arabian horse world as "Pidge," saw a photo of Liza in the *Arabian Horse World* magazine. She immediately flew to Savannah Farms in Gilroy, California to see the filly, a bay with a small perfect white diamond centered on her forehead, and purchased her. Already the owner of a double National Champion Futurity Filly, Pidge knew she had just bought her next National Champion.

Little Liza Fame did not disappoint her.

Foaled May 27, 1987, sired by U.S. National Champion Stallion Fame VF and out of the mare Katahza, a daughter of Canadian National and U.S. National Reserve Champion Stallion Aza Destiny, her incredible show record includes many show and regional halter championships, including 1990 Cal-Bred Futurity Three-Year-Old Filly Champion, 1990 Canadian National Champion Futurity Filly, and 1990 U.S. Top Ten Futurity Filly.

Liza did not stop there.

In 1991, Pidge and Liza's trainer, Dick Adams, of Savannah Farms, decided it was high time to try her out under saddle with talented trainer, Bill Melendez. After an amazingly short amount of time and only a few outings in the show ring, Liza was the Region 2 Champion Western Pleasure Junior Horse by the judges' unanimous decision. A few weeks later, Liza was Canadian Top Ten Western Pleasure Junior Horse. Within one month of THAT win, Liza was named Champion in the very prestigious Southern California Western Pleasure Futurity/Maturity.

After only four and a half months under saddle, Liza and Bill took United States National Reserve Champion Western Pleasure Junior Horse.

Time out was taken to breed Liza for her first foal, due in April, 1992. She was bred to U.S. National Reserve Champion English Pleasure Huckleberry Bey, who carries the same sire line as Bey Shah, sire of Fame VF. Pidge has decided that the blood of Bey Shah will be the focus with her mares.

After Liza's foal is weaned, she will return to the show ring to focus on becoming an open western horse, with all sights set on the 1993 U.S. Nationals competition.

Little Liza Fame is the ideal Arabian horse both in looks and temperament: large, dark eyes, teacup muzzle, dished head, sculptured ears, long neck, slim throatlatch, and tabletop croup with a high-set, free-flowing tail. She also is a natural athlete, has an intelligent mind, and a sweet disposition. Little Liza Fame has meant a lot to the Gold Wood Farm name and reputation.

"Liza is always pleasant whether in the show ring or in the paddock being a 'regular horse,' adds Pidge. Her favorite treats are red and white peppermint candies and she will practically climb into Pidge's pocket or purse looking for them.

"These are all the qualities it takes to set the National Champion apart," says Pidge. "She has kept Gold Wood Farm at the top in the show ring. I know she will continue to do so. Liza will produce foals that will improve the Arabian breed and she will willingly enter the show ring anytime we ask her and bring home more ribbons. She is the one horse that I have really allowed myself to become emotionally involved with. When I am alone with her, feeding her treats, petting and scratching her, she loves me back and I can feel it. It's not often that horses return affection, but those that do are the special ones you have to keep. Liza is the one."

Fame VF+

When Fame VF+ was a yearling, his breeders, Pat and Bob Radmacher, and his trainer, Dick Adams, turned him out in a low-railed arena for a mutual friend to admire. He immediately put on a spectacular show, trotting from the far end of the arena to the near end where they were standing. Then without hesitating, he jumped the arena rail and raced away through a neighboring unfenced field. "No one said a word or moved a muscle," recalls Pat. "It was as if we were stunned as we watched our dream literally disappearing. He raced straight away for about half a mile, pulled up, let out what might have been a laugh, and then turned and trotted back to us of his own will. If I have not officially thanked You, 'THANK YOU, GOD!!!'"

That's because Fame, the runaway yearling, has since made their fortune. Show after show, he has taken his place in history. In February, 1991, at the Scottsdale show, fifteen of his get exited the ring with Top Ten ribbons or better, making the 1987 United States National Champion Stallion the 1991 Scottsdale leading sire of halter winners.

Later, Bob Radmacher led Fame VF+, every inch a king, through the huge audiences of Scottsdale spectators for their personal inspection. Then, when Fame VF+ was presented individually to twenty of his champion offspring, it was clearly obvious that this magnificent animal was a regal and magical creation.

I have, in fact, always enjoyed looking at Fame VF+, even in pictures, as he is very photogenic. The most distinguishing things about him are his intelligent and expressive look and his majestic attitude.

Sired by Bey Shah and out of the great Raffon daughter Raffoleta Rose, Fame VF+ was foaled at Bob and Pat Radmacher's Valhaven Farm in San Juan Bautista, California, on March 28, 1982. He is owned by the Fame VF+ Partnership, which includes Bob and Pat Radmacher, Dick and Sue Adams of Savannah Farms in Gilroy, California (where Fame stands), and Rob Salomon.

The night Fame was foaled, Pat Radmacher was so disappointed that he was a colt that she went into the house to bed, not staying to admire the new arrival. The next morning she took a good look at him. "I knew right then that he was special," she says. "When Dick Adams came over to see him the next day, he predicted that the colt would be a National Champion by the time he was a five-year-old. That, of course, is exactly what happened."

The Radmachers are small backyard breeders who bought their first purebred mare in 1972. At the time Fame VF+ was being campaigned, there was a widespread belief that a small backyard breeder and a relatively unknown trainer could not join in a team effort to produce a National Champion, the most coveted and economically valuable award within the Arabian breed.

The experience with Fame VF+ proved that prejudice unwarranted.

"Because of Fame VF+'s exceptional quality and our strong determination, we achieved our goal," Pat says.

"We rose to the top together, enduring the bad and rejoicing with the good," she says of Fame VF+. She adds that he is a very "people-oriented horse. He is especially kind and gentle with children and persons who are unaware of his tremendous strength and power."

Although trained as an English pleasure mount, he has only been shown in Arabian halter classes. In 1994, he will return to Valhaven Farm for the many years remaining in his breeding career.

To date he has sired over seventy Class A Champions. He has sired two National Champions, two National Reserve Champions and many Top Tens, in both halter and performance.

"Because of his tremendous success as a show horse and as a breeding stallion," says Pat, "Fame VF+ has allowed us to remain in a very respectable position within the equine world. He and we are respected worldwide. He's given us much excitement and the economic means to continue forward. He's taught us to persevere and to campaign with determined patience."

*Penitent

Whenever I've seen the grey Arabian stallion *Penitent, I think of unicorns made of moonbeams in magical glens; his ethereal beauty is so distilled it seems unreal, as if he belongs to another plane of existence.

He is without doubt one of the most beautiful and charismatic horses I have ever seen.

Audrey and Arnold Fisher of Dunromin' Arabians, which lies on two hundred eighty-six rolling acres one hundred miles north of New York City, in Pine Plains, felt the same way when they first saw him, judging by their memories of the occasion.

During their first visit to Poland in 1987, they went the rounds, attending the Polish National Horse Show and the annual Polish Prestige Sale. Audrey, who is involved in the daily management of the farm, and Arnold, who is a member of a family-owned real estate development company in New York, toured some of the major stud farms, including Michalow State Stud, where a full presentation of the stud's mare families and stallions was made for them.

"The chief herd sire was brought out, a horse who had extreme type, good size, incredibly animated motion and unparalleled presence," says Audrey. "The sun shone on his beautiful fine coat and before us he appeared like a moving oil painting. We could not help but fall in love with him, and we are sure that every one of the several hundred visitors witnessing his presentation was in awe of his beauty."

In the spring of the following year, Dunromin' Arabians imported *Penitent.

"On the very day he stepped on our farm, we knew that we had acquired one of Poland's national treasures, and a treasure to the Arabian breed in general," says Audrey.

"*Penitent brought to our farm a new dimension of more extreme type and beauty for our Polish breeding program, a program which has been well received in the show ring and by other breeders," says Audrey.

"Among his offspring, two of his U.S. fillies have become champions. His son *Eldon was named European Supreme Champion Stallion in 1991."

*Penitent, foaled April 23, 1979, a 15.2 hand grey who has turned pure white, was bred by Janow-Podlaski State Stud Farm in Poland. His sire is Partner, a Polish National Reserve Champion Stallion and European Supreme Champion Stallion.

His dam is Penza, a successful racehorse and producer of winners on the track.

As is the case with most Arabians in Poland, *Penitent was trained to race as a three-year-old and ran two years on the track.

*Penitent was also shown in hand in Poland and became its National Champion Stallion in 1985. In 1987, he represented that country at the European Nationals in Belgium and became European Supreme Champion Stallion.

*Penitent has not competed in the U.S., but for conditioning purposes trainer Larry Jones has trained him to drive.

But he is still a walking work of art to the Fishers. "He is unmistakably the epitome of the Arabian stallion," says Audrey. "We are convinced that he is way above average in intelligence for a horse. He is very much aware of his surroundings, but at the same time, visual happenings way off in the distance will get his attention and cause him to stand and gaze for a long, long time. While he is gazing, we gaze into his large black eyes. It appears that there are hundreds of years of experiences and knowledge catalogued in his beautiful head, and whatever he is focusing on at that particular time must be new information for his memory, or triggers some memory from the past. His personality is consistent with his looks. He is spirited and yet a loving stallion," she says.

"Penitent is a major reason for us to be totally content with our lives as breeders."

Moonstone Bey V

Moonstone Bey V is a "good citizen," and a horse of many firsts for Arnold and Audrey Fisher of Dunromin' Arabians in Pine Plains, New York.

"In our early days of breeding, he was the first stallion we handled in natural breeding to some of our mares and to clients' mares," says Audrey. "He seemed to know what to do, was gentlemanly about it, and allowed us to learn with him in a correct manner.

"For our trainer, Larry Jones, Moonstone Bey V (the V is for Varian) was the first horse he led into the National show ring; in 1990, at the U.S. Nationals, Moonstone became a U.S. Top Ten Stallion."

That performance was the Fishers' most memorable moment with the rich bay-colored stallion.

"As owners of Moonstone Bey V, we were complimented numerous times on the superb performance of Larry and Moonstone. It was evident to all that they had a very special relationship," says Audrey.

In halter competition, Moonstone was a Top Ten Yearling Colt in 1983, and was in the top ribbons in every class he has ever competed in, with most placements first or reserve. Another major placing was 1985 Canadian National Reserve Champion Stallion.

"Under saddle, his forte is western pleasure, which is very indicative of his personality – soft, gentle, mannerly, and under self-control," says Audrey.

Moonstone, foaled on March 12, 1982, stands at 15.2 hands. Sired by National Champion Bay-El-Bey++, his dam is Moska, one of the most important mares of Varian Arabians' breeding program.

"In the early days of Dunromin' Arabians, one of the first farms we visited for educational and horse-seeking purposes was Varian Arabians," says Audrey. "Moonstone was a yearling at the time and we were immediately attracted to him. He was, and is, all stallion in appearance with refinement and beauty thrown in."

"Through both the sire and dam lines, Moonstone is a true product of Varian breeding and a fine representative of all that Sheila Varian has worked so hard to achieve in her thirty-plus years of breeding history," adds Audrey, who has one anecdote that tells it best:

"At the 1985 U.S. National Show in Albuquerque, Moonstone Bey V was named the U.S. National Reserve Champion Futurity Colt. His sire Bay-El-Bey++ was on the show grounds and we agreed with Sheila Varian that the spectators would enjoy seeing such a famous stallion and one of his best offspring together. The crowd at the stalls was in the hundreds. The stallions were brought out into the aisle and introduced by Sheila, who as always, brought tears to many people's eyes with her account of the history behind the two horses we were observing.

"Sheila told the spectators they were welcome to come closer to the stallions and touch them. A small group of children made their way up to Moonstone and stood by his shoulders and front legs, barely reaching above his forearms. Moonstone gently lowered his head as if to make it easier for the children to pet him. He remained as still as a statue while the children stroked his forearms and chest, as well as his beautiful head. It was a sight that we wish the whole world could have seen," says Audrey.

"As Moonstone was one of the first horses we acquired, he contributed greatly to our farm's history and future," she concludes. "He helped to create the love we have for the Arabian horse and the commitment we have made to caring for the ones who are members of our herd."

SS Follow Me

SS Follow Me is a "career girl" mare, one with conformation so perfect she was named U.S. National Champion Mare in 1990, when she was seven years old.

A chestnut Arabian mare with a fine blaze of white down her face, she is a horse whose qualities can be appreciated by horsemen of all breeds.

"SS Follow Me turned our lives around in that during those early days of our breeding farm, at which time we were virtually unknown in the Arabian industry, her spectacular appearance and success at the Scottsdale show helped to put us 'on the map,'" says Audrey Fisher, who with husband Arnold, owns and runs Dunromin' Arabians in Pine Plains, New York.

Within two weeks of owning her, the Fishers watched as the nine-month-old filly competed for the first time at Scottsdale, where she won the yearling filly class and was named Reserve Junior Champion Filly of the show.

SS Follow Me's show career covered a six-year period during which time her two most spectacular wins were at the United States National Show: United States National Champion Futurity Filly in 1986, and in 1990, United States National Champion Mare.

"She is the first in United States National history to be judged as such by unanimous votes, both times," says Audrey. "She is also the only United States National Champion daughter of her sire *Aladdinn, the 1979 U.S. National Champion Stallion. And Dunromin's first National Champion Mare, which makes her even more special.

"In addition, she is a multichampion halter filly/mare on a regional level. "She could be considered one of the greatest show mares in this country; certainly from the spectators' viewpoint, she has been one of the most popular," says Audrey.

Through the pedigree of her dam, Contessa-B, United States National Champion English Pleasure Horse and daughter of the immortal *Bask++, SS Follow Me has benefitted from the influence of Crabbet bloodlines which contributed to her flawless conformation, overall quality, and her color. These she seems to pass on.

SS Follow Me took two years out of her show career to carry and raise a beautiful bay filly, Follow the Moon, foaled in 1989, and sired by Dunromin's stallion, Moonstone Bey V. This filly has been a multichampion halter horse as a yearling and two-year-old.

Because she was a career girl most of her life, SS Follow Me has somewhat of an independent, self-sufficient attitude, her owners report. This has limited her attachment to particular people or horses, but has enabled her to be the professional she is.

"There is no doubt that a major contributing factor to the success of a show horse is that individual's ability to adjust from one 'life' to another, without the adverse effects of emotional and physical strain," says Audrey.

"She has always exhibited the emotional strength and stability that a horse requires to comfortably leave the horse farm, travel and train on the road, compete at shows across the country and, upon return to the farm, settle back into her life as a horse on the breeding farm with no difficulty," says Audrey.

Speaking for all those who have known Follow Me since her youth, including the Fishers and Larry Jones, her trainer, "Our relationship could be considered one of mutual respect," says Audrey. "She has given us tremendous joy and excitement in her show endeavors, and for that we are truly grateful to her. She has earned her right to choose the way she wishes to live amongst us, and we are happy to oblige her. She has been the banner carrier for our farm for many years."

Spinning Song

A beauty in jet black, Spinning Song taught the Fishers that the words *elegant, majestic, classy,* and *regal* were not adjectives reserved for human ladies. They were just as appropriate in describing this Arabian mare with large, black, deep, expressive eyes, and a personality that inspire awed love. Though "blowy," snorty, and spirited, Spinning Song was always in complete control of herself.

For Arnold Fisher, it was love at first sight when he first saw her in 1983. Arnold and his wife, Audrey, were visiting an Arabian breeding farm in Kentucky. The seven-year-old Spinning Song had been sent there to be bred and had by her side her 1983 black filly, by Huckleberry Bey++, Sweet Illusion V. Arnold inquired who owned the mare and, as those things go, within a few months the Fishers' Dunromin' Arabians was the new owner. "Or should we say, she owned us for nine years," says Audrey.

Spinning Song became Arnold's favorite mare.

"Spinning Song was the one horse on our farm who brought tears to the eyes of many people; from horse enthusiasts to Spinning Song followers to seasoned horsemen, nobody escaped the feeling of overwhelming speechlessness when this mare was presented at liberty to them.

"Her personality and looks created an aura that attracted people to her in real life as well as through her photos in magazines," says Audrey. Spinning Song even had her own fan club whose members followed her career and sent her fan mail.

Foaled on January 11, 1976, the 14.2 hand mare was jet black, with a small white mark on her forehead. Sired by the Polish stallion *Bask++, she was out of Moska, a daughter of the famous Khemosabi+++, and a treasured mare of Varian Arabians' breeding program.

From 1980 on, Spinning Song was a broodmare. However, in 1988 she was not carrying a foal and trainer Larry Jones felt she was a good candidate to drive, due to her steady nature and self-confidence.

Never shown in a performance class before, at the age of twelve, she was entered in a pleasure driving class at a Class A regional show.

She was on the show grounds several days before her class and during that time was exercised in harness in the warmup areas and hand-walked and grazed around the grounds several times daily.

"As she walked around the grounds, she was like E.F. Hutton," says Audrey. "Everybody stopped, watched and listened. Most of the people on the show grounds knew her by sight, but could not believe that it was really Spinning Song at a show. At our stalls, where we had other well-known show horses with us, including her maternal half-brother, Moonstone Bey V, we had never received so many visitors.

"When the time came, she entered the ring proudly, and the judge seemed to be immediately impressed by her. For us, however, to watch our beautiful black Spinning Song driving around a show ring with at least twelve other horses and buggies was a 'white knuckle experience.' The class seemed to go on for an eternity. We were proud and yet anxious for it to be over," recalls Audrey.

But Spinning Song executed her class perfectly and won the blue ribbon. This is one of the Fishers' most memorable moments with the mare, who is now sadly gone.

She leaves behind two famous offspring, both beautiful black daughters by the stallion Huckleberry Bey++, Sweet Inspiration V, and the now multi-champion halter horse, Sweet Illusion V.

"In our careers as breeders, Spinning Song has taught us that some things cannot be duplicated. She has wonderful offspring, but none can compare to her as an individual," says Audrey.

"We never dreamed we could know an animal who possessed such extraordinary characteristics, but had we dared to, then Spinning Song has fulfilled that dream 1000 percent."

Glorieta Salima

"Glorieta Salima beautifully reflects the characteristics that have made her bloodlines famous, particularly that 'look at me look' in her eye. She has presence – the essence of knowing who she is – and when she looks at you, she looks AT you with intensity. Furthermore, she is feminine, beautifully balanced, and, in type, is typical of the famed Dahma Shahwaniya strain which, according to Bedouin testimony, descends from the horses of Solomon. To me, she is the ideal Bedouin mare," says Judith Forbis, who bred this mare at Ansata Arabians in Mena, Arkansas.

"Glorieta Salima reflects the qualities of her very linebred star-studded pedigree," adds Judith. "Her sire, *Ansata Ibn Halima, was a U.S. Top Ten Arabian Stallion three times and was one of the very few Arabian stallions to sire a U.S. National Champion Stallion and a U.S. National Champion Mare. He appears in Glorieta Salima's pedigree three times. Her dam, Glorieta Sabdana, was a full sister to U.S. National Top Ten Futurity Filly, Ansata Sabrina, whose sire was 1971 U.S. National Champion Stallion, Ansata Ibn Sudan."

Although Jim Fleming and his family have owned the mare for just over a year, Glorieta Salima has already presented them with a gorgeous colt by Prince Fa Moniet and is currently being bred back to him, helping to fulfill a dream.

Jim, a great admirer of the Ansata breeding program attended the "Just Before Christmas" Ansata production sale in December, 1990, hoping to purchase an *Ansata Ibn Halima granddaughter. Through luck he acquired the flea-bitten grey Salima. He also bought an Ansata Shah Zaman granddaughter who was in foal to Ansata's elegant white stallion, Prince Fa Moniet.

"I immediately phoned my wife and told her of our good fortune and that at last we had our foundation mares!" Jim recalls, for their quest had taken a roundabout route.

The Flemings' interest in Arabian horses began in 1978 when the family attended their first Arabian show in Toronto. In 1979, as a start, they purchased two horses of mostly Egyptian blood. By 1983 they had accumulated twenty-eight Egyptian-related horses, but soon realized that because of their lack of knowledge and poor advice, they were at best average quality. Subsequently they sold or gave them away.

"During our initial years in the horse business, we became intrigued with the beauty and history of the straight Egyptian horse as defined by the Pyramid Society, a fraternal breed organization formed to preserve and perpetuate this particular nucleus of bloodlines," Jim says. "We decided we would select Ansata-bred horses, or mares which were suitable to breed to the Ansata stallions," he continues.

This year the Flemings have five mares being bred to Ansata stallions. "Glorieta Salima, affectionately known as Sally, is our favorite," says Jim. "The whole family is very involved in the horse operation. It provides us with something to do, something to love and something to hope for."

He and his wife, Mary have four children – one son, Jim, not at all taken with horses, and three daughters, Anne, Barbara, and Lynne, all interested in horses. Anne, the oldest daughter, is a veterinarian specializing in equine medicine. Lynne is a graduate in animal science. Recently Barbara and her husband, Eric, together with Jim and Mary, jointly purchased a farm close to Toronto. Barb will manage the farm and horse operation.

"For many years Jim Fleming has attended the annual Ansata seminars held at our ranch to educate people about the history of the Egyptian horses, as well as developing a planned breeding program," Judith Forbis says. "After a period of time, Jim determined he wanted to breed straight Egyptian Arabian horses of Ansata bloodlines and as a result of his perseverance he eventually achieved his goal." Now he and his family are part of the worldwide Ansata circle and are enjoying the development of their own straight Egyptian breeding program of which Glorieta Salima is the queen.

Ansata Halim Shah

Ansata Halim Shah is a most important link in the chain of stallions having consistent beauty, quality and type that have made Ansata Arabian Stud world-renowned. He was bred by Judi Forbis, a remarkable woman whom I know as wise and candid and direct, a very special horsewoman who has been a kind of "Indiana Jane" of the Arabian horse world.

"Every breeder looks for the ideal horse," says Judi who in 1957 signed on for a government job that took her to Ankara, Turkey. She rode with the Turkish cavalry, found an Arabian mare with which she won the jumping championship of Turkey, met and married Don Forbis, manager of Halliburton Company's Turkish oil field services, the following year. Since then this couple has pursued their mutual interest in the Arabian horse together. They continued to live for many adventurous years in the Middle East, finding their ideal in the straight Egyptian Arabian and importing three grey yearlings all sired by Nazeer as their foundation stock. Before they settled at their farm in Mena, Arkansas, Judi completed an important book, *The Classic Arabian Horse*.

"Ansata Arabian Stud has been blessed with more than its share of great ones," Judi says. "However, Ansata Halim Shah came along at a time that was crucial to the stud. His sire, *Ansata Ibn Halima, passed away when Halim Shah was only a year old, and it was critical that we have a super replacement for him. Ansata Halim Shah actually surpassed our expectations for he is such a remarkably prepotent stallion that he even exceeded his sire's reputation for consistency.

"Additionally he is the most exquisitely refined stallion we have ever bred. He is in many ways a dream horse because of his ethereal beauty, a vision in white. He is perfectly balanced, carries himself like a peacock, and has a head that is unusually dry and chiseled – like a porcelain statue. This overall exceptional beauty is a trait which he has passed on consistently to his get and which has earned him a worldwide reputation as a sire. By providing the genetic prepotency to pass on his valued characteristics to future generations, our dreams continue to be filled," says Judi.

"He is a rare individual and a rare breeding stallion, and special horses always have a very special place in one's heart. I love him because he has character and is very self-assured. He has what Mike Nichols called 'star quality.'

"I remember when he won the Reserve Junior World Championship in Paris, in December of 1983," Judi continues. "It had been a long trip for the young horse, but he traveled well and showed beautifully. The competition was very keen and while Ansata bloodlines had won championships at the Salon du Cheval before, this was the first opportunity we had to attend in person with a horse we owned. Another son of *Ansata Ibn Halima also participated this same year and won the World Championship title. Thus it was doubly meaningful to have two champions by our foundation stallion win at this show."

Halim Shah was not shown thereafter, as he had become too valuable at home and the Forbises did not want to risk him on the road.

At age twelve, Ansata Halim Shah has distinguished himself worldwide as a world-class champion sire. Get of this stallion have made names for themselves in the Arabian Gulf country of Qatar, Europe, the United States of America, South America and Australia. They have won championships in halter as well as in performance, including racing.

"Horses have been our life," concludes Judi. "We owned Arabian horses in the Middle East, studying them among the tribes as well in the stables of kings and princes. They have provided a most unique lifestyle and opened doors to many enjoyable acquaintances and friendships throughout the world. I cannot imagine what our life would have been without them." Nor can I imagine my life without horse lovers like Judi.

Good Thunder +/

Allen and Barbara Jarabek first saw their bay Arabian stallion, Good Thunder+/ on a small farm in Sarasota, Florida, where they earlier bought their first two horses. They had retired in Sarasota and thought they would enjoy riding. "We started going to horse shows and enjoyed it so much that we started buying more Arabian horses, breeding them and showing them," says Barbara Jarabek. "That was five years ago, and we haven't started riding yet!

"We saw a lot of Good Thunder on that small farm and liked him very much, but we really didn't realize how exceptional he was until his owners put him into training with a professional who started to show him in pleasure driving."

Foaled on April 10, 1983, Good Thunder was bred for performance. He was sired by Wisdom (by *Bask) out of the mare GL Americle, a daughter of Amerigo, a champion himself and sire of several National winners. Amerigo's National stars include Bantu Amerigo+ and four-times National Champion Khemosabi+++ (the breed's leading living sire of champions) virtually all of them, like Good Thunder, in performance.

"Our own trainer, John Rannenberg, and breeder, Roxann Hart of Rohara Arabians, saw Good Thunder at a show that we missed and liked him so much that they recommended that we buy him," Barbara says. "The owners, who were friends by this time, agreed to sell him to us. They entrusted him to our care because they knew that we would do whatever was necessary to train and promote Good Thunder and that we would always keep his best interests at heart."

Good Thunder has given the Jarabeks many special moments to remember. In 1990, he was named U.S. and Canadian National Champion Pleasure Driving and Region 14 Champion Pleasure Driving; in 1991, Canadian National Champion Informal Combination, U.S. National Reserve Champion Informal Combination, Scottsdale Champion Informal Combination, and Region 12 Champion English Pleasure; in 1992, Scottsdale Reserve Champion English Pleasure Stallions.

This remarkable horse has exhibited the style and natural athletic ability that in only two years have earned him the Legion of Supreme Honor Award denoted by the symbols +/ after his name, an award established by the International Arabian Horse Association to recognize those horses that have earned points by competing in shows throughout the United States and Canada. Only 534 horses had qualified for this award as of November, 1991.

"Good Thunder is a very proud horse and a real crowd pleaser," says Barbara. "When he arrives at a show he prances off the van with his long neck arched and he bellows to announce his arrival. He commands attention and goes through his paces with a 'look at me' attitude, his ears pointed forward and his tail held high. To quote John Rannenberg, 'This horse never lets me down. He is the most focused, reliable horse I have ever shown!'"

John has his own special relationship with the horse. Good Thunder nickers at him when he comes into the barn. "He actually puts his head over John's shoulder and hugs him!" says Barbara. "Needless to say, this horse has certainly added a new dimension to our lives. We have traveled all over this country and Canada to support him at the horse shows and have met many people through him. We are really excited about the next phase of Good Thunder's career, as a breeding stallion. We just could not be more pleased with Good Thunder!"

The Real McCoy

The foal watch in 1960 for the mare Fersara, Bint Sahara's first Ferseyn daughter, held a keen sense of anticipation. Frank McCoy, a name associated for nearly fifty years with the best in Arabian horses, had wanted a stallion in residence at his McCoy Arabians, and he believed in breeding his own stock. He had meticulously planned a mating to produce his future herd sire.

Frank's friend, Dr. Eugene LaCroix, had the *Raffles son, Aarief, at Lasma in Scottsdale. "Good one," Frank thought. Selection of the mare was easy. Fersara was the greatest show winner of her time, twice Pacific Coast Champion Mare, once Reserve.

A now-fabled desert breeding was arranged, one which at that time wasn't thought of as anything much out of the ordinary. Dr. LaCroix trailered Aarief to the California desert town of Indio, and the McCoys trailered Fersara there from their then home in Cudahy, and a rendezvous under a palm tree in the desert was accomplished. The result was Sara Lyn, a chestnut filly who became a top McCoy broodmare, but nevertheless was not the awaited future herd sire.

A second trailered tryst was arranged and turned up The Real McCoy. On May 7, Fersara delivered a colt. "That was it," said Frank. "The one I had been waiting for. Good-looking, bold, big eyes. I just liked him."

Frank and his wife Helen named the colt and registered him as Silky Rief. But as the months went by, he looked better and better to them. When Fersara died that same year, making impossible any more foals of that cross, Frank and Helen decided the colt should have the name he deserved and officially changed it to The Real McCoy, a phrase which in American usage means the certifiably genuine.

The colt would not only live up to his name, but realize a particular dream of Frank's, that of breeding a second generation of Arabians that met or exceeded his image of the ideal Arabian horse.

The Real McCoy brought home blue ribbons from his first show as a yearling, and won his first show championship as a two-year-old.

But Frank and Helen felt that if one were serious about standing a stallion, one kept him at home to take care of the mares, rather than have him out on the show circuit. So The Real McCoy was retired in 1967. His record: nine championships and seven reserves in halter, including 1965 Pacific Slope Reserve Champion Stallion.

Frank and Helen bred him to their Ferseyn daughters out of Bint Sahara and breeders brought mares by the droves to the new McCoy ranch in Chino, California, so that Frank was continuously kept as busy building stalls as The Real McCoy was settling mares. The year 1974 was one of his best. The Real McCoy had a record high of 54 foals.

He made the *Arabian Horse World* list of All-Time Top-Siring Stallions, and is noted as the sire of some forty champions, including eighteen National Champions, Reserves and Top Tens.

The mares kept arriving until January, 1983. The Real McCoy was being returned to the stables one day after his early morning exercise on the walker, as he had been doing every morning for twenty years. He slipped as he stepped into this stall, breaking his leg in a spot where it could not be pinned or cast, and the decision was made to put him down. He died just a few days before the World of Frank and Helen McCoy Sale at Scottsdale where two granddaughters, both sired by McCoy's Count, were the top-selling lots. Centerfold, a halter and performance champion, brought $205,000, and Cover Gal, three times U.S. Top Ten Mare and Scottsdale Champion Mare, brought $200,000.

Frank reminisced about The Real McCoy after he was gone: "I'll probably never have another horse that is as popular as McCoy was. He just came along at the right time – before there were very many imported horses – and he really had a chance to show what he could do as a sire. He didn't have to apologize for anything. You see so many horses and you think, that one's pretty good, but he's a little weak in the back, or somewhere. But that old horse, he had it all, every bit."

He was the real thing.

Andhra

"The best way to describe Andhra's personality," says her owner, Richard W. Freeman, Jr. "is that she is equally beautiful on the inside as she is on the outside. This type of mare is every handler's dream. Her disposition is so gentle, trusting and willing that anyone is able to handle her."

This angelic Arabian mare, the living reincarnation of those so beloved by the Bedouin that they lived with them under their tents as members of the family, also successfully passes on her loving disposition to her offspring, says her owner.

He describes her as having "a beautiful eye, lovely coat, long mane with a forelock which grows freely and falls well past her eyes."

The 14.3 bay mare with two left white legs and a small star was bred by Richard and Kay Patterson of Sisters, Oregon. "Richard Patterson was patient and kind as he showed me each horse in its stall," says Richard Freeman. "I carefully listened as he described the strong and weak points of each." Richard Freeman purchased Andhra at the Polish Collection II Sale at Scottsdale in February 1987, where she was consigned by the Patter-

sons. Andhra, foaled May 8, 1982, a daughter of the *Bask son, Negatraz, out of *Andorra, "became one of the most important horses in the auction for me," he adds, and he was able to acquire her.

The mare fulfilled every hope and promise he'd had for her. At the Fall Louisiana Arabian Horse Show in Baton Rouge, Louisiana, in September, 1991, she won the Three-and-Four-Year-Old Mare Class, was Senior Champion Mare, and Reserve Grand Champion Mare.

Today she is destined to be a "marvelous broodmare who consistently produces special horses," says her owner.

Richard finds "a growing recognition of the power of her breeding, which allows her to be a strong producer of the type of pretty, athletic horse I am trying to breed, using a variety of stallions."

His Freeman Arabians, located in a spectacular barn with splendid landscaping a few miles south of Folsom, Louisiana, is a breeding facility dedicated to the perpetuation of the centuries-old Arabian breeding program of Poland.

The main bloodlines represented by Freeman stock are through the stallions Celebes, *Pietuszok, Negatiw, Comet, and *Bask. Daughters of Meridian, Negatraz and *Deficyt play an important role in the breeding herd.

"We believe that the well-bred Arabian horse is characterized by noble spirit, athletic ability, tractability, stamina, soundness and beauty," says Richard. "We believe that the well-trained horse is characterized by an easy-to-handle nature, good manners, a willingness to please, and an intact spirit."

Richard became a horse owner rather serendipitously. In the mid-1980's he and his wife Pam traveled out of state to purchase a llama at what was then the largest llama breeding ranch in the country. It turned out that Polish Arabian horses were the major business of that ranch. And that there was a waiting list a year long for llamas. Unless the prospective llama buyer was willing to buy a couple of Arabian geldings at a bargain price...in which case they would move to the top of the llama waiting list. The two geldings along with several llamas went home with the Freemans to Louisiana.

Then, for Christmas of 1986, his wife Pam gave Richard a Polish Arabian mare named Aristakata. Struck by her great beauty and refinement, Richard became fascinated by Polish Arabians and set out to study the breed and to gradually build the Freeman herd to what it is today.

While Andhra symbolizes the epitome of the goals of his farm, she has also given Richard some personal gifts, including "confidence regarding my ability to make breeding choices, new friends, lots of learning about Arabian horses."

Monopolii

When Richard W. Freeman, Jr. first saw the young stallion Monopolii moving in the open in an arena, he says "The look of him changed forever the way I evaluate a horse."

Monopolii was a two-year-old then, owned by Carol Curran of Peach Creek Farm in Brenham, Texas. He had the "most impressive, solid athletic motion I had ever seen in a colt or stallion. He seemed to have unlimited potential as a special horse," Richard recalls.

Over a year later, Richard was visiting Peach Creek Farm again to purchase some mares, as that farm's activities were winding down. "What are your plans for the stallions?" he asked and learned they too were for sale.

He immediately made an offer for Monopolii, who was foaled August 14, 1986, sired by Negatraz, a *Bask son and the sire of nearly sixty champions and twelve National winners, and out of *Monogramma, a stakes-winning racehorse in Russia who set a track record that holds till this day.

"Monopolii turned the dream of breeding pretty, athletic Arabians into a reality," says Richard. "Our whole Freeman Arabians program relies heavily on his ability as an individual as well as his ability to pass it along to his foals," he says.

Monopolii's most immediate and obvious attribute is his presence. "People recognize it immediately and respond to Monopolii's charisma," says Richard. "He also loves to work. He's quickly bored if he's not working or turned out to oversee the whole landscape of the farm in Folsom, Louisiana."

Monopolii was shown in the Free Style Liberty Class at the Scottsdale All-Arabian Horse Show in February, 1991 and was the crowd's obvious favorite. Unfortunately, however, his handler failed to remove his halter, and Monopolii was disqualified from the judging.

Richard's current plans for him are as an exciting dressage prospect, a long-term training commitment, but certainly a perfect outlet for his "beauty in motion" qualities.

"This athletic ability has meant seeking ways to fulfill his potential as a breeding sire," explains Freeman. "The idea grew to cross him with top-level Warmblood stock talented in dressage and jumping. We now own Danish Warmblood mares and plan to breed them to him to blend his excitement with their own special grace of motion."

To date, Monopolii's daughters, Arpolia, and Salinia, have placed first and second respectively in the Louisiana Futurity, 1990 Fillies, held in the spring of 1991.

Richard feels that the purity of the Polish Arabian bloodlines makes these horses ideal for the horse lover with little previous breeding experience. "With Polish Arabians, it is easier to breed for more than one trait at a time than it is with other horses; consequently Polish Arabian breeding offers many unique challenges," he says.

With the assistance of breeding manager Bonny Burley and trainer Bill Evans, Richard has made his Freeman Arabians one of the leading breeding programs in the world. Marketing consultant Don MacBean has recently been able to foster a demand in Europe for Freeman Arabians, and with the star stallion Monopolii at home in the barn, the future seems bright indeed.

Maarji

"I want to say lap cat," says Lewis Huffstutter, struggling to pin down exactly a personality description of his beloved Arabian mare Maarji. "She was an incredible horse, an unforgettable kind of animal, warm, affectionate, people-oriented, the perfect match for me.

"I was just a teenager when she was foaled and had a burning love for horses, in particular Arabian horses. Having grown up on dreams fed by Walter Farley's 'Black Stallion' series, plus many more books far too numerous to list, I had and have to this day a passion for these wonderful horses," says Lewis.

But even beyond those book-fed dreams of his, he says, "Maarji was unique. Her individual beauty was always remarkable...a grey who turned to ivory white as she aged...with large expressive eyes, perfect head, a fine teacup muzzle.

"Her personality too was out of the ordinary. She became my lifelong friend and companion. She was the queen of the place, no matter how many horses I had. We literally grew up together. There was no master/animal relationship, for we were always two equals, friends. We learned to ride over the hills and through the wooded meadows of northern California and when she became a broodmare, we raised many of her offspring together.

"I chose her mates very carefully, much as one might seek a mate for a queen. Some of her mates were Ansata Ibn Sudan, Dalul, El Dayim, Hadaiya Eindafa, Enferno, Nafix and other fine stallions of note within the Arabian breed.

"In her lifetime, Maarji gave birth to fifteen foals, of which fourteen lived. I can remember each one of them as if it were just yesterday that they arrived, all bright and eager. Each one was of exceptional quality and type

and many went on to establish themselves as show horses and life companions to other people.

"Her foals were sold to people all over the U.S., one went to Mexico and there's a granddaughter in South America, one in Canada. Most have stayed with their original buyers." Lewis kept Maarji's first son, Naafaj, until he was four years old. "The well-known rider Erin McIndoo campaigned him and they were high point junior rider wherever they went. He gave her her start in horses," Lewis notes.

Maarji came to Lewis as the result of a carefully planned breeding. "I owned her dam, an older mare named Dur-Rah," he says. "Because of my father's work, he was away for two or three years at a time. For my eighth-grade graduation in the late summer of 1958, when I was fourteen years old, he returned from the Far East and bought Dur-Rah for me as my riding horse." Lewis showed Dur-Rah only once, as a yearling, and she came away a regional show champion.

In the spring of 1961, Lewis bred Dur-Rah to the "Fabulous Fadjur" who combined his genetic material with that of the lovely Dur-Rah to create something very special. Maarji was foaled on Easter Sunday, April 22, 1962, an Arabian of extreme type. "Maarji was to be Dur-Rah's only daughter and from the moment of birth she was a very special horse, having the personality of a people-lover from day one," Lewis recalls.

"Maarji is gone now. She died early in the spring of 1987 of complications of old age, but she is still somehow with me in spirit and in her daughters, Sanaah Bint Sudan, Chastitie, and Maarji's Dafadil," says Lewis. "I have continued with my love of horses by becoming a breeder and now have approximately eighteen horses, by far the majority directly descended from Maarji. Even so, she was one in a million—oh, so very special. What an honor it was to have known her."

Alada Baskin

After spending several years searching for a special colt to use in her breeding program, veterinarian Georgene Holasek found Alada Baskin quite by accident while working at a training stable. It was love at first sight. "He was just what I had been looking for, beautiful head, long neck, great shoulder, long legs, excellent long quarters and a lot of action at the trot, all with that extra charisma that only the great ones have.

"He fit exactly into my breeding program of *Bask-bred mares, adding the qualities that I wanted to strengthen in them," says Georgene.

Although she has owned representatives of many breeds, Georgene's Rock Isle Arabians in Waconia, Minnesota was started in 1964 with the purchase of her first purebred Arabian stallion. Her scenic, wooded, 200-acre farm has several barns, eighty box stalls, complete veterinary and artificial insemination facility, two indoor arenas and many pastures, all located next to several lakes and a 4,000-acre park.

It was to this new home that "Lad" came as a skittish yearling with incredible promise. "He went to Scottsdale, Arizona for his first show where he really excited the crowd with his spectacular entrance at the trot and his charisma," says Georgene. "After winning second place out of eighty-plus colts, he took the ribbon from the ribbon girl and held it in his mouth for his win photo, as much as to say, 'This is mine. I won this!'"

Lad was sired by *Aladdinn out of a *Bask-bred mare, foaled May 25, 1982. "Alada Baskin is one of the best Arabian stallions in the world today with an exceptionally typey head, superb conformation and as a bonus a lovely burnished golden color," says Georgene.

Lad has many wins, from Scottsdale to the Ohio Buckeye. The biggest are 1986 U.S. National Reserve Champion at four years of age and 1990 U.S. National Reserve Champion at eight years of age. The most special moment, however, was when he won Supreme Champion over all ages and sexes at the big Minnesota All-Arab Show when he was only two years old. "He was the first horse in the ring and as each one entered, he just snorted, pranced, and got higher and higher," says Georgene. "The judge couldn't take his eyes off him. His comment to us was, 'That horse is awesome!'"

Alada Baskin offspring are still fairly young but have won multiple championships including U.S. and Canadian National Top Tens in halter and performance, Class A and regional championships in halter, English, western, driving, and country English pleasure.

"Lad is such a good sire that I feel as if he and I are partners in a breeding program that has already produced so many good individuals and that he has already made a significant contribution to the Arabian breed as a whole. I like to feel as though I am a part of this contribution and feel honored just to own and handle this horse," says Georgene.

Georgene realized a delayed dream when, at age thirty-five and while raising two teenagers, she went back to college and got her degree in veterinary medicine. "Horses in general have supported me, including paying for my education as a veterinarian," she says.

"Horses have been my life. As a rider, breeder, exhibitor, equine veterinarian and now as a horse show judge, I have learned my best lessons from horses, the most fascinating creatures on earth. After thirty-five years of owning them, I am still learning how they think and communicate."

Gai Parada

When I asked Daniel J. Gainey just what the stallion Gai Parada meant to him personally and to the breeding program at Gainey Fountainhead Arabians, he answered: "Gai Parada to us exemplifies our Gainey breeding program – fifty years of creating beautiful athletic horses. Arabians that look like Arabians!

"Gai Parada also personifies for us the golden cross created by my father, Daniel C. Gainey, and James P. Dean. In him, one will find all the elements and characteristics cherished by two great breeders of extreme foresight."

Dan's father, Daniel C. Gainey, through passion and single-mindedness and with a natural instinct, had worked at creating a line of horses much as a sculptor works at creating a bronze. Like a fine artist, Daniel C. Gainey not only reproduced the image about which he had dreamed, but was able to repeat that image in successive "castings."

The latter were personified in two white stallions of the desert with large dark eyes and refined forms, Ferzon and his son Gai Parada.

"Gai Parada possesses a beautiful, typical Arab head, high tail carriage, athletic ability and beautiful movement, a wonderful level topline, long, arched neck and straight correct legs, as well as a wonderful disposition," says Daniel J. Gainey.

"He is the embodiment of everything we tried to achieve over the past five decades and he has proven himself a worthy sire through his sons and daughters who have gone on to receive National Championships in both halter and performance.

"He is one of only a very few National Champion Stallions to also have a National Champion title in performance.

"The most wonderful thing about designing a breeding program, adhering to it and watching the progress through the years," he continues, "is the satisfaction one gets from knowing the program is being successful when a horse like Gai Parada emerges – a champion in the show ring and a supreme sire of champion offspring. Proof that your breeding program works and that mere mortals have been able to affect a breed of horse so greatly as to create living art, beauty in motion – the Gainey Arabian."

This is one of the most outstanding achievements of Dan and his lovely wife Robin: Over the years, horses bearing the name of Gai Parada's sire, Ferzon, several times in their pedigrees have become known as "The Gainey Arabian." No other related group of Arabian horses bears a man's name. There is the Polish Arabian, the Egyptian Arabian, the Spanish Arabian, the Russian Arabian, and the Gainey Arabian. The latter name evokes a picture of extreme type and beauty.

"The Arabian horse is the expression of living art in its extreme beauty," says Daniel J. Gainey. "Although these animals are diverse in their ability to perform, they are equally thrilling to simply watch quietly grazing in pasture. This we feel is what sets the Arabian horse apart from the rest – this beauty, stamina, grace, ability and disposition combine to make them unique in the world of the horse."

Even though the sun will soon set in Gai Parada's life, the Arabian horse world will continue to be illuminated by the brilliance of the dynasty he will have left behind.

Ferzon

"To me the perfect Arabian horse is one that has a delightful disposition, is an excellent walker, has lots of action at the trot and has a sure-footed soft gallop," said Daniel C. Gainey. "My ideal must also have extreme refinement, very fine dry bone, perfect legs and greatly exciting overall desert type, with a superbly small, dry head and ears and big eyes. The only horse in the world that has true elegance is the Arabian, so his very special value is enhanced if he has the beauty you cannot resist."

Daniel C. Gainey, as fine a breeder of Arabian horses as the breed has known, and a one-man public relations force for the Arabian horse, bred first of all for beauty. Then because he believed that "a horse was made for man to ride," he wanted pleasing motion and other qualities that ensured a pleasant experience on that horse's back.

That was Gainey's vision of the ideal Arabian, and the grey stallion Ferzon solidified that vision. It was Ferzon's prepotency through several generations that helped to establish the expression "Gainey type."

Many breeders related to Gainey's concept of the ideal, and Ferzon-related horses became foundation stock for breeders nationwide, making his influence on the whole industry pervasive.

Ferzon was so famous he became a celebrated legend and visitors and tourists both foreign and domestic arrived by the busload for a close-up look at him and his descendants at the Gainey's ranch at Santa Ynez, California.

There Ferzon lived the life of the exalted patriarch. "First of all, he owned the joint," says Daniel J. Gainey, Daniel C.'s son. Ferzon was indulged. When visitors asked what an aged stallion does all day, the stock reply was, "Anything he wants to do." He got an apple a day, every single day.

Ferzon had been bred by another great name in Arabian breeding, Frank McCoy, who had crossed his prize-winning mare, Bint Sahara, to Ferseyn for a grey filly foaled in April, 1947, who became the famous Fersara. She racked up more championships than any other filly or mare in Southern California, and when it was time to breed this prize, Frank came up with Ferneyn, a Ferseyn son.

Frank and Helen McCoy chose the name Ferzon for the grey colt foaled by Fersara on February 26, 1952.

That summer, Daniel C. Gainey of Owatonna, Minnesota, came to Los Angeles on business. The itch to add something new to his breeding program brought Gainey to the McCoy pastures for a look at the famous Fersara with Ferzon at her side. A colt with three crosses to Skowronek offered the possibility of strengthening the Skowronek lines Gainey had already collected at Gainey Fountainhead Arabians at Owatonna, Minnesota. An offer was made and as quickly refused.

A year later, when Ferzon had already been Reserve Champion Stallion twice, Frank was asking $10,000 for him, an unheard of price for a yearling colt at that time. Gainey sent his manager, Preston Dyer, to see how the colt was looking. A few phone calls crossed the country, a check was in the mail and Gainey Arabians had a new stallion.

The special companionship and the pride of ownership of Ferzon lasted for twenty-six years for Daniel C. Gainey, ending when he died in April, 1979.

His son Daniel J., who took over the Gainey businesses and Gainey Arabians in 1976, says, "My father bred Arabian horses for the pure love and enjoyment of it, and Ferzon certainly contributed to that enjoyment."

Ferzon died, after only a few hours' illness, on July 19, 1982.

His foals total 227, ninety-two of them bred by Daniel C. Gainey. A tally of the wins of Ferzon offspring shows twenty-four U.S. and Canadian National winners.

Forty years after he was foaled, Ferzon is still today a pervading element in the breed. As they have for decades, breeders know that Ferzon blood can be counted on for "pretty" and for Arabian type.

Rohara Samurai++

"Rohara Samurai++ was an extremely inquisitive foal," says his owner, Roxann Hart. "His mother was constantly trying to keep up with him. Samurai would always carry things in his mouth—sticks, a towel or a ball."

As he grew up, it looked like he might be headed for a career in major league ball-playing.

"Sam, (his barn name) is a ham," says Roxann . "He puts on many exhibitions, playing with his hippity-hop ball. My son, before going off to college, played what almost looked like soccer with him. He would kick the ball and Sam would chase it and retrieve it. The more people clap, the harder he plays."

But that was just kid stuff. Sam grew up to be a Champion Stallion and the mutual favorite of Roxann and Karl Hart, owners of Rohara Arabians in Orange Lake, Florida.

"He has helped to enrich my life through his wonderful personality," says Roxann, into whose life this 15-hand grey stallion arrived serendipitously. At the Wayne Newton sale in Las Vegas in 1980, she purchased the mare Snow Goddess, a daughter of the double National Champion Stallion, *Aramus, a Polish import. "This colt, Rohara Samurai++, was in utero at the time," says Roxann. "His sire, *GG Samir, was imported from Spain by Jay Stream.

"Rohara Samurai++ contributed to the Rohara show string and when he was three, we were able to see his first foals. We felt that even from this limited foal crop he would be a sire of note," Roxann says.

Sam's looks are very special. "A very exotic head, extremely dished, wonderful top line and long, level croup," says Roxann. "But more than just a pretty head,

Sam is a very smooth-gaited western horse and a dedicated worker who is alert to his surroundings."

"I've become very fond of Samurai...he is an extremely beautiful horse, calm and a pleasure to ride," testifies Roxann's husband Karl, whose role at Rohara is in the overall planning for the farm.

"Samurai is a special horse in that he has accomplished so many aspects of what makes a successful show horse and sire," says Roxann, for whom "horses have, along with my family, literally become my life. In many cases, they have given me direction, dear friends and goals."

Shown by professionals Rick Moser, Alfredo Ortega and John Rannenberg, Rohara Samurai++ has won many championships in halter, western pleasure and most classic. He was Canadian National Top Ten Futurity Colt as well, and is the recipient of the International Arabian Horse Association's Legion of Merit Award.

A very special moment was Samurai's presentation in the stallion parade at the Ocala Extravaganza, where his offspring won so many titles. "It was a prestigious evening for Rohara and Rohara Samurai++," recalls Roxann.

Samurai has had many winning sons and daughters in both halter and western pleasure. Over twenty of his get have been exported to foreign countries and have competed successfully. They have also become foundation breeding stock in Ecuador, Colombia and Brazil.

"Samurai has been an economic contributor to Rohara through both his breeding fees and the sale of his foals," says Roxann. "He has the ability to draw visitors to the farm and has his own fan club of loyal supporters. He exemplifies the idea that beauty, form and function go hand in hand."

Ivanhoe Tsultan

Ivanhoe Tsultan made one of the most spectacular horse show entrances in history at a Des Moines, Iowa, show. "We were heading into that ring at full tilt, so full tilt that I didn't notice that the horse in front of me had stopped, and I knew we were going to crash into his rear end," says Gary Schneider, Tsultan's owner and handler at that time. Gary jerked down hard on Tsultan to try to stop him, and the bay stallion with the trademark long, snaky neck went down crossways right in front of Gary, who says, "In that split second, all I could do was hurdle over him, and just as I was flying over his back, he rolled over. When I hit the ground he jumped up and we took off again just as if we'd planned a grand entrance. The crowd gave us a standing ovation, and the judge was still snickering when he judged us."

Tsultan won that class, a victory symbolic of the way he has always rolled with the punches and come out on top. Ivanhoe Tsultan had to earn his recognition as a sire without the benefit of a famous foreign-born sire. His pedigree is an all-American "melting pot" one. (He is by Ivanhoe Tsatan out of Hillcrests Bint Imaraff.) He made the climb to the top strictly on the record of his offspring. Of his 560 foals (through Volume 63 of the stud book), 49 are champions.

The 14.3 stallion, foaled April 7, 1971, won twelve championships himself at halter and many get-of-sire classes. Over eighteen years ago, his last time in the show ring, he was U.S. National Top Ten Stallion; since then he has left the limelight to his sons and daughters.

The fates took a turn in his favor in 1981 when his lovely pure white, tall and elegant daughter, Rohara Tsultress+, became United States National Champion Mare.

"Tsully" belongs to Karl and Roxann Hart, who made the lucky purchase of her dam Emenee, with Tsultress in utero, at the 1976 International Arabian Horse Sale for a mere $8,200.

When Tsully was foaled January 30, 1977, she convinced Roxann that Tsultan should become an integral part of Rohara Arabians, her multi-purpose training and breeding facility now in Orange Lake, Florida.

She kept calling Gary Schneider (who had bought Tsultan from his breeder, Pearl Draves of Ivanhoe Arabians in Manhattan, Illinois) and kidding him about how much Tsultan would enjoy Florida sunshine. During one of the Midwest's worst winters, Gary weakened and leased Tsultan to Roxann in late 1979.

Tsultan stood at Rohara for two years before returning to Gary Schneider in 1982. Roxann then purchased a fifty percent interest in the stallion. Shortly thereafter, he was syndicated and came to live at Rohara permanently.

"Ivanhoe Tsultan literally put Rohara in the breeding business," says Roxann. "In 1980 he bred eighty mares and the following year he bred ninety mares. His foals were in demand and winning in show arenas. Ivanhoe Tsultan caused me to make the equine profession my life."

And Tsultan had circumvented another obstacle. "Ivanhoe Tsultan needed to prove that an American-bred stallion could breed predictably," says Roxann. He taught her to "go with the good horse; go with the individual.

"My relationship with Ivanhoe Tsultan is one of respect and awe," she says. "I travel all over the world looking at Arabian horses. I also attend multitudinous horse shows. No matter how many stallions I see, I feel there is no horse that has the look and power that he exudes.

"Tsultan has given me National Champions and Top Tens (in Mare Halter, Stallion Halter, English Pleasure, Pleasure Driving, Western Pleasure Junior Horse, Informal Combination, and Dressage), a firm foundation for my farm and the knowledge that I couldn't have achieved that without him. He has taught me life's many parables, both its struggles and its successes. This particular Arabian horse has greatly enriched my life. He has become my vocation and advocation."

Geym

One of the photos my friend Tish Hewitt submitted for this book was of her three small children sitting in a row on the bare back of Geym, the silver white stallion with big black eyes.

"That was essentially his personality," this fascinating, dynamic woman told me. "He has little people on him and he's a stallion." Tish knew the children were on a kind and loving horse.

"Geym's dam, Rageyma, is the only mare I know of that would leave her grazing down by the river and come running when she heard there were visitors on the farm, just to 'talk' to them. It's a kind line," adds Tish.

I met Tish Hewitt when she rented a *finca* in southern Spain a few years ago. We spent a memorable day together, sharing our love of fine horses, as I took her to visit some of the best Spanish horse farms, including that of the Conde de Odiel.

Tish told me that her own Friendship Farms in East Moline, Illinois was truly lucky in the timing of the acquisition of its bloodstock. Five years earlier, or five years later, the concentration of the individual horses she chose would not have been possible, either in such numbers or in such quality. "It required two years' study of studbooks and Arabian types before we were ready to acquire our first Arabians," she said. "During this time, we decided that in order to produce the classic type of Arab and not to sacrifice good substance and disposition, we were primarily interested in the blood of Skow-

ronek (through *Raffles and Naseem) and of *Mirage, superimposed on highly selective female lines. The female lines originally decided upon were those descended from the Jellabiet mare of Abbas Pasha known as the Jellabiet Ibn Feysul.

"In our study of the original combination of Jellabiet plus Skowronek and *Mirage, it became evident that the most direct source of this blood existed in only a few individuals. One of these was the grey stallion Geym who was ideally bred for our program," continues Tish. "At that time Geym was the senior stallion in the Selby Stud at Portsmouth, Ohio, and it seemed unlikely that he would be obtainable. We did, however, manage to buy or lease several of his daughters."

Then came that marvelous spring morning in 1959 when Tish's dream started to focus into reality. Tish and a friend happened to be in Ohio and decided to spend a day visiting the Selby Stud, founded by Roger Selby, a pioneer of the Arabian horse in America.

"Roger Selby left me speechless when he said he would be willing to sell Geym and all of his mares to me. You see, I was familiar with all of those bloodlines from the studies I had done. I knew that was exactly what I wanted. I accepted with alacrity and rejoicing," Tish recalls.

Geym, and the other Selby Stud horses were moved in a six-horse trailer caravan to Tish's Friendship Farms. "Some of those horses had never been loaded before," she recalls the transfer with some amusement. "But at least they all were friends.

"As far as I am concerned, acquiring this Selby stock has always been a responsibility of the highest order and represents the true beginning of Friendship Farms," Tish told me.

I learned from Tish that Geym's pedigree reads much like a who's who of celebrated stallions and distinguished mares. Geym, bred by the Selby Stud and foaled in 1942, is a Koheilan Jellabiet Feysul. His sire was the immortal *Raffles by Skowronek. His dam, the aforementioned Rageyma, was by *Mirage and out of *Kareyma, the latter by Naseem and out of Julnar. Julnar traces in direct line to the famed Jellabiet Feysul mare brought from the desert by Abbas Pasha (a nineteenth-century Egyptian breeder) and considered by many authorities as one of the very finest mares ever obtained from the desert.

After many years of making mare owners, Tish and her children happy, Geym was gently put down at the age of thirty-three, because of his arthritis.

Geym stood to many outside mares and sired a Canadian National Champion Stallion, Lea Baron, through whom Tish is now trying to retrieve Geym's bloodlines for her farms.

*Nizzam

Asked about *Nizzam's personality, Tish Hewitt replied, "Funny...he was very vain. He knew how good looking he was. He did it in Holland and he did it here – you'd lead him out and instead of rubbing his head against your arm, he would strike a pose and nobly look into the far distance. When he saw his image in the riding hall mirror, he would stand for hours looking at himself."

*Nizzam had good reason to be vain. An exceptionally beautiful bay stallion, he was foaled in 1943, bred by the distinguished Rt. Hon. Lady Wentworth of Crabbet Park in Sussex, England.

Sired by Rissam out of Nezma, and tracing back to Naseem (by Skowronek) through his son Raktha, he had been sold to a man who, after a time, decided to sell out and head for Africa. It was the initial intention of Lady Wentworth, who with her mother, Lady Anne Blunt, founded modern day Arabian horse breeding in England, to buy back this stallion. But after Lady Wentworth learned that *Nizzam had served in a circus, she did not want him in her Crabbet Stud. Because of Lady Wentworth's sensitivity in this matter, a Dutch surgeon, Dr. H.C.E.M. (Pieter) Houtappel had the opportunity to obtain a superb stallion for his Rodania Stud in Lauren, Holland.

While in Dr. Houtappel's ownership, an article about *Nizzam appeared in a German magazine. Patricia Hewitt read the story, liked the photo of one of *Nizzam's sons, and appeared at Dr. Houtappel's farm in Holland one day, intending to buy the son. The son was already sold, but Dr. Houtappel asked if she'd like to see his sire. He led out the deep dark bay with dappling under the coat.

"That was it!" says Mrs. Hewitt, the owner and founder of Friendship Farms in East Moline, Illinois (one of the top producers of Arabian horses in the United States) and one of the finest and most versatile horsewomen who has ever trained or ridden a horse. Tish is the great great granddaughter of John Deere; her husband, William A. Hewitt, served as Chairman of the Board of John Deere and Co. and, after his retirement, was appointed United States Ambassador to Jamaica.

None of this at the time was of any account to Dr. Houtappel. The surgeon/horse breeder and international judge said *Nizzam was simply not for sale when Tish Hewitt asked to buy him. *Nizzam was, in fact, the surgeon's favorite.

Tish Hewitt, however, was not so easily dissuaded. Many, many letters and calls followed, sometimes in the middle of the night. Dr. Houtappel finally capitulated enough to say yes to a two-year lease and sent *Nizzam to the United States with Rob Schols, his groom.

Once here, *Nizzam was rapidly booked up.

*Nizzam had already won several championships in Holland, and won several more in this country. His foals were in demand and brought a good price. So many people came to see the Dutch treat, Rob Schols claimed he was wearing out *Nizzam's shoes leading him in and out of the barn.

When Dr. Houtappel visited the United States to judge the 1960 National classes at Estes Park, he was invited to be a guest at Friendship Farms prior to the show. While there, Tish begged him on a daily basis to let her have *Nizzam forever. Dr. Houtappel kept saying no, but she kept changing tactics, one of them arguing that *Nizzam was already seventeen, too old to return to Europe.

As last he gave up, and Tish Hewitt bought *Nizzam in partnership with Jim Lewis of Lewisfield Stud at Charlottesville, Virginia. For Tish, acquiring *Nizzam was more than a personal whim, however. It made her feel deeply the responsibility of breeding him in such a way as to make an impact on American bloodlines.

*Nizzam was stationed at Friendship Farms and later on at Lewisfield, where the warmer climate was easier on him. *Nizzam died on April 1, 1971.

Today one of the stallions standing at Friendship Farms traces back on the bottom side of his pedigree to the famous *Nizzam. Get Smart, by Conquistador, a Raffles-bred stallion, is out of Gilead, a *Nizzam daughter. "The only thing I ever did to get smart was not to geld that horse," says Tish Hewitt. Get Smart's offspring are "fabulous" she says, part of the living legacy of his superb grandsire, *Nizzam.

Khemosabi +++

The leading living sire of champions, the leading living all-time sire, a double National Champion in halter and performance, at twenty-five, Khemosabi+++ is adored by the owners of his offspring, as well as by Arabian horse owners worldwide who simply pay homage to him as a great horse.

One word stands out when attempting to describe him – classic in every way.

Khemosabi is called the "All-American Hero" because his is a kind of Horatio Alger story of the Arabian horse world. He was the backyard foal that reaffirmed the American belief that small, knowledgeable breeders could achieve success, not only to the top, but to the level of legend.

When Khemosabi was foaled on Mother's Day, May 14, 1967, in Whittier, California, he was the entire foal crop that year for his breeders, Dr. Bert and Ruth Husband. No one loved him more than they did. It took months of discussion just to name him. Finally, Khemosabi, a name meaning "faithful friend," settled on him like a mantle.

A bay colt, with good body, straight legs, a very typey head, and irresistible personality, when he was foaled his markings of four white stockings and a blaze were not in vogue, but he brought them back into fashion, and they became his trademark.

A lover from the start, by the second day of his life, he showed a tendency that persists to this day – he prefers humans to horses. His dam, Jurneeka++, a good mother, tried to protect him from strangers, but he ran up to anyone he saw.

He ran around the Husbands' yard until he was almost two years old. In March of that year he was sent to Sheila Varian, where he bred several mares, beginning his breeding career. From 1977 to 1981 he stood at the Pereira Ranch at Santa Ynez, California, and it was during those years he proved himself as a sire.

Khemo did not have the appeal of an exotic, imported stallion or the appeal of a linebred or inbred pedigree, and he had to demonstrate his prepotency with a variety of mare lines. By the fall of 1981 he was syndicated. He now stands at DeLongpre' Arabians in Santa Ynez, California.

His breeding career, at twenty-five, is still going strong. He's in condition, and looks like a six-year-old. Only closeup will one see a few white hairs on his face.

For those interested in the statistics on him and his progeny, this *Guiness Book of Records*-breaker has been the subject of a major article every odd-numbered year since 1983 in the *Arabian Horse World* magazine.

But just off the top, to date he has 1,077 registered foals and at least another hundred should be on the ground by the time this book is out. He is the sire of more foals than any other Arabian stallion, living or dead. Two hundred forty-nine of his sons and daughters have won over 1,500 quality championships to date. He has established a sire line and has sired top-producing daughters. And he has established a legacy – Khemo grandget and great grandget are adding to his luster.

No one is quite sure why and how Khemosabi is so prepotent. "His pedigree is a total blend, other than the two lines to Fadheilan, and for some reason or other genes fell together properly. Although I planned the breeding very thoughtfully," Bert Husband says, "I can't take credit for that."

He believes twenty-five years from now Khemosabi+++ will be viewed "as a stallion who maintained the type, the refinement, beauty and presence of the Arabian breed, with offspring that are really wonderful companion animals, yet spirited and full of presence in the show ring." What more can the breed expect from a "faithful friend"?

Jurneeka++

Jurneeka++ was a mare with a destiny. And she seemed to know it. If her most famous son, Khemosabi, is a king among Arabian sires, then she was the *grande dame* of dams.

Dr. Bertram P. Husband first saw the then five-year-old bay Arabian mare, considered the truest daughter in type and charisma of the "Fabulous Fadjur," at Jeff Wonnell's training stable in La Puente, California. "Bert just stood and looked – sort of transfixed," says his wife Ruth. He asked the price on her, which was nearly the price the Husbands had paid for the purchase of their first home. This much to the shock and horror of Ruth, who nevertheless went to the bank and arranged for a loan, realizing this was Fate, not to be obstructed.

"My father loved Jurneeka++," says B. Paul Husband, Bert and Ruth's son. "For him, she was a dream fulfilled. As a poor farm boy in Saskatchewan, he had dreamed of owning a champion Arabian mare. She was it. My father was quite taken with her, particularly with her beauty. I was not impressed, I simply thought she was too fat." Twelve years old at the time, what could he know of love's vision?

A little Rubenesque or not, Jurneeka++ was a star and she knew it. Foaled April 24, 1958, she was not even-tempered, but volatile, strong-willed, flighty, fiery as the Spanish gypsy Carmen.

But unlike the heroine of Bizet's great opera, she returned Bert's love. "He attended all of her foalings. She would pace her stall nervously, but as soon as Bert stepped into the stall, she took a huge breath, heaved a sigh, laid down and foaled," Paul remembers.

Even her romantic encounters were the stuff of legend. A midnight rendezvous on a racetrack with the stallion Amerigo in the summer of 1966, after the last class of a horse show in Salem, Oregon, produced Khemosabi. Ruth Husband, seeing trainer Jeff Wonnell walk into the far end of the barn with Jurneeka and Amerigo, intuiting what had passed, remembers she thought: "Heavens, I hate for a daughter of mine to get married without flowers, so I grabbed some alfalfa hay and handed it to her and she promptly ate it."

"Jurneeka++ would turn around the life of my entire family by producing Khemosabi," says Paul. Although Carinosa+/ produced more champions than Jurneeka++ (who had eight foals), Jurneeka++ produced the one that outdid any other that was ever foaled at their farm, the four-time National Champion, and the Arabian breed's all-time most prolific sire, Khemosabi+++.

While he was the entire foal crop that year for the Husbands, backyard breeders in Whittier, California, Jurneeka++'s efforts ensured an illustrious place for them in Arabian horse breeding history.

Jurneeka++ adored the limelight and had a magnificent show career which earned her the coveted Legion of Merit Award. Among many championships, she was U.S. Top Ten Mare in 1963, National Reserve Champion English Pleasure in 1964, and U.S. National Reserve Champion Western Pleasure Horse that same year.

But one of her chief foibles was "she knew that she was 'a big time star,'" says Paul, "and the bigger the show, the more the noise, the more the applause, the better she would work. In the smaller shows she really did not work as well. She seemed to be saying: 'I'm the great Jurneeka++...Surely you don't expect me to work in this little show!' And she wouldn't."

Jurneeka++ had another facet to her, says Bert, now of Brea, California. He rode her several times in the Tournament of Roses Parade. "She loved the bands, floats and the applause and acclaim of the vast crowds," he says. "What a joy that experience was, what a companion animal! Everyone needs to be creative in life and art. Jurneeka++ created and expressed art in my life and created a successful equine business."

"I am sure that she thought that the crowd had turned out just to see her," comments Paul wryly on Jurneeka++'s Tournament of Roses promenades.

Paul knew Jurneeka++ as only a rider can: "There were times when she would set her head just so, and the bit was held so lightly in her mouth that it seemed as if there was simply a neuron path from her brain to my fingers with the reins, the bit and her mouth as the intermediaries. She was extraordinary, one of a kind."

Her great spirit regrettably left this earth in March, 1985, at the age of 27.

Carinosa+/

This lovely chestnut mare is a kind of super stage mother of the Arabian horse world. According to the noted statistician Arlene Magid, Carinosa+/ is the top producer of National winners. And what a showbill of stars!

Her daughter, the grey mare Caridina++, by Jurdino++, is a U.S. National Reserve Champion English Pleasure, Legion of Merit and dam of champions.

Her son, the bay stallion, Khari++, by Khemosabi, is Canadian National Champion Stallion, U.S. Top Ten Stallion, U.S. National Reserve Champion Futurity Colt, Legion of Supreme Merit, and sire of champions.

Her daughter, the bay mare Khara Mia+, by Khemosabi, is U.S. Top Ten English Pleasure, U.S. Top Ten Pleasure Driving, Legion of Honor, dam of champions.

Her son, the chestnut gelding Marqui by Tornado, is champion in English Pleasure, and Champion in Pleasure Driving.

Her son, the grey stallion Ibn Jurdino+, by Jurdino++, is U.S. National Champion Working Cow Horse, halter champion, Legion of Honor, and sire of champions.

Her son, the bay stallion Kharibe, by Khemosabi, is Canadian Top Ten Stallion, Region 1 Champion Stallion, sire of champions.

Daughter Kharinosa+ by Khemosabi, is U.S. Top Ten Western Pleasure, Canadian Top Ten Western Pleasure, and Legion of Supreme Honor.

Her son, the bay stallion Khardan, by Khemosabi, is a halter champion and holds many championships in western pleasure.

Daughter Khaliope, by Khemosabi, is champion mare, and U.S. Top Ten Western Pleasure Junior Horse.

Her son, the bay stallion KC, by Khemosabi, is a Champion Stallion.

Another son, the bay stallion Kharino, by Khemosabi, is Champion Hunter Pleasure, Champion Hunter Hack, Champion Regular Working Hunter, Champion Modified Grand Prix for Arabian Jumpers, and Qualified Field Hunter with the Los Altos Hunt.

This superb broodmare, foaled April 5, 1963, is owned by Dr. and Mrs. Bert Husband of Haifa Arabian Horses in Brea, California.

By the imported Crabbet-bred stallion *Serafix and out of the imported Polish mare *Caliope, she was purchased at the age of three months from John Rogers and delivered to the Husbands at the Southern California Show in Santa Barbara.

"I fell in love with her at first sight—she was mine!" says Ruth Husband, who adds that "Carrie grew like tall children everywhere, going through awkward stages, stumbling over leaves and butterflies, and never quite knowing where her long legs were taking her. She grew, developed, and at maturity fulfilled the promise of her heredity. The family teased me about my clumsy horse. They changed their tune when she put herself together and won classes."

At eighteen months Carinosa+/ went into training with Jeff Wonnell. Just past two years of age, she was winning driving classes. She was U.S. Top Ten English Pleasure and also earned the Legion of Supreme Honor Award.

Carrie had another uncommon talent. "Carrie loved to jump; in her pasture was a hill and an area where dirt had been removed," recalls Ruth. "All the other horses would run down the hill to the flat area. Carrie always ran half way down, and then jumped to the flat area, then raced to the top of the hill with her tail popped over her back. Since she had jumped, she always beat the other horses." (Perhaps that's where her son Kharino gets his talent.)

Ruth's husband Bert has also ridden Carinosa in native costume in the famous Tournament of Roses Parade in Pasadena on New Year's Day. "They had a good time," says Ruth, who sums up this supermother of champions: "Carinosa+/—a splendid show record, an honest horse, a producing delight, a treasure."

Gabriel's Fyre

Some people wait a long time for that special horse to come along; but with others, he leaps into their lives and says "Surprise!"

Such was the case with Gabriel's Fyre, foaled with what might be considered an especially good omen on May 14, 1990, the same birthday as his legendary sire, Khemosabi.

Even as a young colt, Gabriel's Fyre set the show ring on fire.

A bay with three white socks and a blaze, he entered the show ring for the first time at age twelve months. He was straight out of an outdoor pen where "Gabe" and his sister, Khemoniquel, spent their first winter as hairy, tail-chewing friends.

His fiery carriage, spirited trot, and "look at me" attitude made his owners, Donald and Elizabeth Fillpot, owners of Sterling Oak Arabians, in Fresno, California, realize Gabe was a potential champion. His carriage, head and neck set were exceptional, reminding one of a chess piece – the knight, says Elizabeth. "He had 'show horse' stamped all over him."

After his first win in Fresno, Gabe, already standing 14.2 as a yearling, went on to two bigger shows and, competing against older horses, became Reserve Champion in both.

The Fillpots say one of their most special moments with Gabe was the first time Steve Heathcott took him into the show ring and he demonstrated that magnetism and charisma that makes a horse a champion.

The Fillpots, neophytes in the horse world, marvel at their luck in acquiring a potential superstar.

"We were not involved in horses – didn't know what an Arabian horse was – when in the spring of 1989 we purchased property in the foothills outside of Fresno," explains Elizabeth. At that time, the height of their ambition was to have a family horse to ride through the foothills after they built their house and barn.

Then they happened to see an Egyptian Arabian filly turned loose in an arena at a sale barn and, struck by her beauty, Don made a successful bid on her.

"At that point we started in the Arabian horse business with no real knowledge of horses or even a ranch," Elizabeth adds. "We were able to board the filly at the sales facility where we purchased three other Arabians over the next year."

During that year, they studied Arabian bloodlines and decided they liked the beauty, correctness and attitude of Khemosabi horses. When a Khemo colt and filly, not yet one year, became available, the Fillpots purchased them, having seen the horses only in a homemade video.

"It is amazing to us how after less than two years in the horse business we have become so involved, and we

anticipate many wonderful times and championships with Gabe," says Elizabeth.

"We consider ourselves extremely fortunate in owning Gabe, a horse who carries the rare balance of refined beauty and substance."

Even as an emerging stallion he is gentle to be around, yet exudes high spirits in the show ring.

When he is lying down in his stall, the Fillpots go in and sit with him. He puts his head in their laps and loves to be loved.

And, as a horse raised among the vineyards of the fertile San Joaquin Valley, naturally Gabe's special treat is a bunch of ripe, juicy grapes.

"Gabriel's Fyre has an honesty and integrity, a willingness and generosity that bring such great joy to us," concludes Elizabeth. "We know he will be a magnificent champion and a wonderful sire."

Reign On

Here's a horse so successful he was able to "buy" some expensive electronic equipment for his owners.

Reign On is bred and owned by California State Polytechnic University in Pomona, California and the pride of ownership in him is campus-wide, for he has been Scottsdale Park Horse Champion twice (in 1986 and 1989), Canadian National Champion Park Horse, and Region 1 Champion Park Horse.

"Reign On is the greatest sire and modern-day performance horse bred, trained and shown by the W. K. Kellogg Arabian Horse Center," says its Director, Professor Norman K. Dunn. "He is Cal Poly's first National Champion, and we're naturally extremely proud that he was not only National Champion Park, but that he won by unanimous decision.

"Reign On's early success and breeding book enabled the Arabian Horse Center to purchase its first computer and copier and brought national and international attention to us," continues Mr. Dunn. "He has provided a great deal of favorable publicity for the University, the Arabian Horse Center, and all of us who have been involved with him.

"Reign On's 1986 Scottsdale Park Championship performance with trainer Allison Elwell will always be a

wonderful memory for all who viewed the class or the video tapes of the performance. I am sure Reign On was a special challenge to Allison, as this was her first great, great star to train and ride."

Norman Dunn calls Reign On "a great and true Arabian performance horse with one of the breed's finest and most balanced trots."

This stylish 15-hand stallion who carries himself tall and "trots off both ends" was foaled February 11, 1980. He had star quality even then in pasture with his dam. He is by the great sire, *Bask, (also a National Champion Park) who gave Reign On his superb hocks, his shapely neck and his brilliance. His dam is the English Pleasure Champion, Spring Rain.

The Arabian Horse Program at Cal Poly is the current effort representing more than sixty years of breeding Arabian horses at the site. W. K. Kellogg, cereal manufacturer of Battle Creek, Michigan, bought his first Arabian horses in 1925 and purchased land (now the University campus), and became one of California's pioneer breeders. The Kellogg Ranch horses and the Sunday shows were excellent promotional efforts for the breed for decades.

"Reign On's tail female line represents five generations of Kellogg breeding," says Dunn. "He was named in honor of his great sire, *Bask, and of Professor Byron Good of Michigan State University, a great horseman friend of the Kellogg Arabians. Professor Good and *Bask both died the year prior to Reign On's birth.

Reign On is a typical proud pure-white Arabian stallion. His groom and true caretaker for his entire life is Ann Clausen, a Cal Poly graduate and now a staff member.

The Arabian Horse Center produces from nine to fourteen foals per year and every Arabian raised on campus is trained by a staff member or one of the many students involved in the equine program. The current horses trace, especially on the dams' side, to many of W. K. Kellogg's purchases of the 1920s and 1930s.

"We have learned the challenge as well as the true satisfaction of breeding great horses that sire and produce well," says Dunn, a lifetime horse lover.

"Many times we have great dreams of success and notoriety for a program, a horse, or an idea — dreams that never come true. But the breeding of fine horses such as Reign On, the building of the W. K. Kellogg Arabian Horse Center and the experience of working with hundreds of wonderful students the past thirty-two years are dreams come true. We are certainly proud of our horses, but our most important mission is to contribute in some way to the many fine young people who share the same feeling of awe, love and respect for horses in general, and especially for the Arabian breed."

Padrons Psyche

For Steve Lengacher of Four Star Arabians, hearing the announcement of Padrons Psyche – a three-year-old Arabian stallion whose coat seems to contain all the rich russet glow of autumn – as the United States National Reserve Champion Stallion in 1991 at Albuquerque, New Mexico was an arrival. "Totally overwhelming," he says, "like being good enough to play with the Los Angeles Lakers."

"The win meant so much to me for a lot of reasons," added Steve. "I've always loved horses, but had some tough growing-up years until I was adopted by the Lengacher family. Four Star Arabians became financially possible as a family venture about four years ago. With the purchase of Psyche and others, we're serious."

Compounding the victory's sweetness, Steve and Lyle Bertsch of Zahara Arabian Stud, both of Fort Wayne, Indiana, had bought Psyche in partnership just a little over six months before. This was the first time Steve had ever had a horse at the Nationals, and in fact only the third time he'd attended the show. Lyle, on the other hand had been in the Arabian business only ninety days after buying Alimileegy in 1976, when he had a National Reserve Champion Western Pleasure. "The moral of the story is that if it doesn't happen quick, forget it," says Lyle.

This stallion on the fast track who is the star of this success story was judged United States National Reserve Champion stallion just nine years after his sire *Padron was named United States National Champion Stallion at the age of five years, relatively young to have made that achievement. Padrons Psyche, however, went him one better in the records book. He is one of only three three-year-olds to go United States National Reserve Champion Stallion since National Champion Stallions were first named in 1958.

Lyle Bertsch reacted to Psyche with the same un-equivocal reaction as the judges in Albuquerque: "You know, some horses just seem to draw you to them, call it charisma or whatever, and Psyche is such a horse. Brings goose bumps. Those horses are few. You might run into two or three in your lifetime. And that's what Psyche did to me." Steve, a long-time *Padron fan, was thinking the same way about Psyche and the two bought Psyche in partnership a few days after that first look.

Psyche's charisma is very much like that of his sire *Padron, who was bred in Holland, sired by the Tersk-bred stallion Patron, and out of *Odessa NSB, a mare bred in Belgium of almost all Crabbett bloodlines. With his wins, Psyche gave *Padron his thirty-first National winning offspring, and the first in Stallion Halter.

"Psyche has a lot of natural vitality, is a very 'up' horse and very bright. One who puts on quite a show in the ring," says Steve, who became the sole owner of Psyche shortly after the Nationals. But as far as he's concerned, Psyche doesn't have to be showing to be beautiful.

"Very few horses can stand in a stall with a hind leg cocked and look pretty. Psyche is one of those. He doesn't have to 'blossom' to be pretty, and that's just one of his appealing features."

Psyche bred twenty-some mares as a two-year-old and twenty-nine in 1991. "His foals look very much like *Padron, with a lot of type, a lot of size, a lot of presence," says Steve.

Years before the advent of Four Star Arabians (whose name comes from Star Builders and Star Realty, the family business interests), Steve dreamed of one day owning a National Champion Stallion. "Come what may with Psyche in 1992, I feel very fortunate to be a part of his life and I only wish everyone could experience and appreciate his kind of beauty," he says.

Flaming Tron Ku

"To be in the winner's circle with Flaming Tron Ku was such a thrill, one we've never experienced again with the same intensity," says Deborah Mihaloff Kirshner of her great grey Arabian stallion, raced with great success twenty-five times over three seasons.

Flaming Tron Ku had beat all others to the finish line seventeen times, came in second once, and third twice. He had won nine stakes races and set or equalled eight track records, four of them still held at Delaware Park.

"He was setting so many records; he always went for the lead and kept it," continues Deborah. "After he won, everybody would go to the track's back side to see him. It was not unusual to find him standing placidly, looking out of his stall, with lipstick all over his muzzle from the kisses women had given him. The last time I remember seeing him, I had gone to Florida for the Darley Awards and we drove up and found him gazing out his stall door onto the training track and expressway. This was his entertainment, watching the cars go by, or the horses in training. He seemed to be watching to see if any of the horses were good. I'm sure he called out to a few and

told them what to do. I'm sure he wished he was down on the track himself and wondered why he wasn't. He loved to gaze out with such a strong look, as if he saw things we didn't."

I know that look well, as I myself saw it when I photographed Flaming Tron Ku for my book, *Vavra's Horses*. The image I chose of him, as he galloped among trees hung with Spanish moss at Town & Country Farms in Florida, is one of the most beautiful in the book – a grey horse of the desert whose dappled coat is tinted softly with the wine of the Sahara's setting sun.

"He knew he was great and when he didn't win on those few occasions, and he did know because he didn't go into the winner's circle, you could tell he was disappointed. He wasn't the same when we went back to see how he was," recalls Deborah.

"Tron Ku's wins made it so easy to get completely committed to Arabian racing, so much so that my husband Alan would become vice chairman of the Arabian Jockey Club that he helped create."

The breeding program at the Kirshners' Cre-Run Farm in Montpelier, Virginia was totally changed with the thought of breeding Tron Ku to the Cre-Run mares. "We also purchased and raced other mares we thought would cross well with him," says Deborah who started breeding horses about fifteen years ago with showing in mind. "Then about ten years ago, I started to focus on racing. Fortunately, our original stock had a lot of the good characteristics a horse needs for racing."

"Both Alan and I are involved with the horses through another business insurance. I am the founder of Markel's Equine Insurance Program and a resident vice president," Deborah says. Alan is also the chairman of the Arabian Horse Trust.

Tron Ku's pedigree could be a "Who's Who in Arabian Racing." He is by Ibn Kontiki, whose own sire, Kontiki was considered a great race horse. Flaming Tron Ku's dam was Flaming Emotion, sired by *Mohacz and out of the wonderful Spanish mare *Rabadilla.

The Kirshners were visiting Town & Country Farms when they first saw Tron Ku. "We immediately thought 'Here is a horse that can run.' Town & Country wanted to sell him, but at the time we could not afford him by ourselves, so Town & Country remained partners with us until Tron Ku's untimely death," says Deborah.

"Tron Ku's foals will go into training in the fall of 1992, and will make their debut on the track in 1993. Through his son Tron Ku Tu, we will continue his great legacy," says Deborah. "Tron Ku taught us the beauty of racing – to watch a horse develop into an athletic machine, knowing he was giving his all and that there was no question as to who was the best on that given day."

*Kasanova

During a trip to London in 1980, Deborah Mihaloff Kirshner and her husband Alan visited Rodania Stud, the farm of Dr. Pieter Houtappel, the founder of the Dutch Arab Society, and an instrumental agent in the acceptance of the Spanish Registry by the World Arabian Horse Organization.

"Upon seeing Pieter's beautiful Spanish-bred horses, I knew we had to have one," Deb says. "Alan never does anything in a small way, and on this occasion he more than lived up to his modus operandi. He put together a partnership which acquired half-interest in twenty-three of Dr. Houtappel's Spanish-bred horses. They would be flown to the United States and would continue their lives here."

*Kasanova, a grey pure Spanish Arabian stallion standing 15.2 hands, foaled July 21, 1981, was just a yearling when Deborah saw him at Rodania Stud.

Bred by Dr. Houtappel, *Kasanova is by *Makorr and out of *Kadidja. "Both his sire and his dam are out of the supreme broodmatron of Spanish breeding, Chavali. *Kasanova's dam, *Kadidja, is a British National Champion Mare," says Deborah.

"I fell in love with *Kasanova, so when he was imported into the United States, he came directly to my farm in Michigan and was raised there," Deb adds.

Subsequently, the Kirshners purchased *Kasanova out of the partnership and showed him under their name. Shown successfully in halter by Connie Cole, he was a Regional Champion Stallion. "Unfortunately we did not see him shown when he went Champion," says Deborah. "I know it was a special moment for the handler, and we were very excited to hear that he had won."

*Kasanova was also shown in western pleasure by Connie Cole. "He was the complete, beautiful picture of a fine western pleasure horse," says Deborah.

*Kasanova also had a short-lived racing career. "We raced him on two occasions at Pompano, in Florida. Unfortunately, he thought he was in a show when he came around to the home stretch and broke into a western pleasure gallop under the lights, to the screams of the fans. He could not get the show ring out of his mind, so we had to discontinue his racing career," she adds.

"In looks, *Kasanova is your typical Arabian horse. When people come to the farm, he is the stallion that we show to the novices to help educate them on Arabian type. I would have to say he is the most beautiful stallion that I know of. He is pure white now with a dark mane and tail. He is good-sized and very angularly built. His conformation is very correct, and he has huge eyes and a tremendous jowl."

Deb wishes that all Arabian stallions could have this horse's personality, and says, "He is gentle, kind and loving. When people are around, he puts on a very ani-

mated show for them. He is a special individual and we enjoy having him. A child can handle him, even after he is bred. Dressage experts who have ridden him say he is very talented in dressage as well. He moves like a dream."

*Kasanova has been bred to a few mares, and will be bred more extensively as he ages. "The total pleasure horse, he will be bred to mares that need type," says Deborah.

One of Deb's most memorable moments with *Kasanova occurred the first time she showed him at her veterinarian's open house. "When they opened the doors and everyone saw him, you could hear all the gasps and intakes of breath and expressions of never having seen a more beautiful stallion. It made me so proud that I was handling him and that he was a part of my life," she adds.

"He IS a dream. To share your life with a creature that is so beautiful reminds you that life is beautiful."

Tron Ku Tu

Tron Ku Tu was destiny's gift to Alan Kirshner and Deborah Mihaloff Kirshner, a kind of peace offering from the fates that had taken so much away from them.

"His sire, Flaming Tron Ku, was our great racehorse and his dam, Dalsinay, whose dam, Dalya, has been our best producing mare, was from one of my foundation lines that traces in tail female line to the great stallion, Balance who still holds two race records in Egypt," says Deborah.

"When Tron Ku Tu was foaled we were in Scottsdale, Arizona at the Scottsdale All-Arabian Horse Show. His sire was already deceased, so it was very special for us to have this colt, as we had no other mares in foal to Flaming Tron Ku," adds Deborah.

"I remember seeing the colt for the first time. We had just flown in from the Scottsdale show. He was only a few days old, but already he was a lovely individual and his independence reminded me of his sire. He has a lovely combination of the conformation of both his sire and dam and this could be seen in him even though he was just days old. Just to watch this horse out in the pasture reminds me of the way his sire used to move."

Then tragedy struck again. "Tron Ku Tu's dam, Dalsinay, would die thirty days after foaling Tron Ku Tu," says Deborah. "To this day, we do not know why she had to be put down. She was crazed and out of control and we were advised for the safety of those around her and for herself that she be put down. We therefore requested a nurse mare for Tron Ku Tu, and he was raised by Rumors Flying, a Thoroughbred. So with both his dam and his sire dead, Tron Ku Tu is totally irreplaceable.

"His personality is just like his sire's. You can tell he loves people, like his sire. He comes when he is called and is not nippy, even though at this age you would expect he might be."

While Tron Ku Tu is one of four colts to carry on their sire's legacy on the track and in the breeding shed, Deborah believes he is the best example of Flaming Tron Ku's offspring.

"Tron Ku Tu is very sure of himself, yet he is quiet, even though he should be a rambunctious two-year-old," she adds. "He conserves his energy, which will be an asset for the track. He lives totally outdoors with his own loafing shed in his own pasture. This will enable him to develop his abilities and personality. His sire was raised under very much the same conditions.

"Our relationship with this horse is just beginning, but I believe there will be many special moments to remember with him. He has not yet been broken, but will go into basic training in a few short months. I am sure he will be lovely to ride. People are not yet aware of him but soon will be.

"I believe this horse is a reincarnation of his sire and you can tell that he wants to make us proud, just like his daddy did. I am sure he will fulfill all of our dreams.

"His very existence has turned our life around," Deborah continues. "He will continue to carry on his sire's legacy for our breeding program. We have purchased mares that will be bred to him in the future, after his racing career is finished.

"Having Tron Ku Tu means we can continue the great heritage of Flaming Tron Ku."

MHF Eclipse

The chestnut Arabian stallion MHF Eclipse seemed to take his time coming into this world. Eclipse's dam, Dalya, was purchased as a two-year-old as one of the foundation mares for the breeding program of Deborah Mihaloff Kirshner and her husband Alan. She was bred for the first time at the age of four. Unfortunately she contacted pseudomonas, a disease which rendered her infertile for five years. "It was an ongoing battle from then on to get a foal out of Dalya," says Deborah. "Due to Dalya's size and conformation I had always dreamed that I would be able to breed a three-day event horse from her. So when Dalya did come in foal again, obviously I was very excited and went to the farm where she was kept on my way to the Scottsdale show. We stayed and watched her, but she did not have the foal. Of course, when I arrived in Scottsdale, I learned that she had foaled. When the show ended I flew directly back to Maryland to see the foal. I arrived at one o'clock in the morning and no one was around.

I quietly walked into the barn where I found Dalya and her colt. The colt was standing behind his mother and I could not see him. I slowly and quietly went into the stall and sat in a corner just waiting till he would come into view. When he came around and I took my first look at him, he reminded me of the old English paintings of the Thoroughbred stallion, The Great Eclipse, also a chestnut. At that moment I knew the foal's name would be Eclipse. As foals usually do, he eventually made his way over to me. By this time I was crying so hard with joy that my sniffling frightened him. You could tell then that he would be a runner. Once the mare was rebred, she and Eclipse came home to Virginia. He was given the pasture at the back of our house so we could see him all the time. With just a loafing shed he developed into a wonderful specimen of a racehorse," says Deborah. "He does not look like your typical Arabian horse. He is not pretty per se. He is very much an athlete and looks the part."

When Eclipse was three years old, he made his debut on the track. Alan and Deborah went to Delaware to watch that first race. It was pouring down rain, but Eclipse won by ten lengths. "I had not been that happy since Flaming Tron Ku," says Deborah, referring to their great racehorse, now deceased.

"Had it not been for the trainer," says Deborah, "Eclipse would have continued an excellent racing career. Unfortunately, he was run in a second race while very sick with pneumonia. Brought back as a four-year-old, he bowed a tendon and could not race. After the bow was healed, he was raced a third time in which he finished third after leading the whole race. After a fourth race, in which he finished fifth, the bow was reinjured

and he was retired to stand at stud."

Now five years old, he will have a dozen or so foals on the ground in 1993. "He has been bred to some of the best mares in the country," says Deborah, "mares like AH Singularity, whose half-brother was Racehorse of the Year in 1992, and Hilary, also the dam of two Racehorses of the Year."

"When you raise a horse from a foal, and when he possesses so much athletic ability, you can't help but feel good all over," says Deborah. "Eclipse fulfilled a special dream, just by being born. He will continue his legacy with his many wonderful offspring."

"Prior to Eclipse's first race and win, we had had a very depressing time and the race brought back the joy and happiness that I had not felt for two years," she continues. "It made me believe that things could be good again and encouraged me not to give up on life, that there are still beautiful moments."

HHR Serenata

Another valued friendship resulting from this book is one I began with Mary Jane Parkinson at the Arabian Nationals.

Mary Jane is a distinguished writer on Arabian horses. Her in-depth articles on prominent horses (and their owners) are highly readable portraits of equine personalities, which over time form a mosaic of the modern history of the breed.

"Janey" chose her chestnut mare, HHR Serenata, to distinguish in this book, a book to which she made an important contribution through her knowledge and her enthusiasm for the breed.

"Serenata helps me to remember what's important to the readers of my stories, their concerns and ambitions for their Arabians, their sleepless nights during foaling season, their thoughtfulness in making breeding decisions, their anguish when a horse is ill or injured," Janey told me.

Horses to her are a passion, a livelihood, a family activity, and Serenata is also special in that she was the first purebred Arabian of which Janey was the official breeder.

"She helped achieve that state and compounded the joy of the moment by being a bright and pretty filly," says Janey who has a small ranch near San Diego.

"There is a brightness that is special, a look of quality through her fine skin and prominent veins, her dry, refined head, splendid, large eyes, and fine muzzle, active, nicely-shaped ears, lovely tail carriage," Janey describes her grown-up looks.

Foaled April 22, 1977, Serenata "exists only because of the kindness of others," her owner continues. "Her grandam was loaned by friends to provide a start with Arabian horses. Then her dam, HHR Polonaise, was bred to *Eter, the stallion of my rather extravagant taste for the time, this through the kindness of his owner, Don DeLongpré, who offered a reduced breeding fee to a horse-crazy girl somewhat grown up."

Serenata had a rough introduction into this world. At ten days old, she became quite ill with a throat infection and had to be injected with antibiotics twice a day for about ten days. "Somehow she still loved people after that experience," says her owner.

She was shown only a few times as a youngster. "Placed in a halter class," Janey told me, "but showing is not her thing, thank you. She has never been on intimate terms with a saddle, and her greatest all-time athletic feat was jumping out of her stall at a show as a youngster."

Her offspring, on the other hand, have been doing proud by their dam in their own careers. One son is a Western Pleasure Champion. One daughter is an accomplished stock horse and one of the very few Arabians in the area excelling in team penning, working in a halter and outmaneuvering horses of other breeds with great regularity. Another daughter shows great promise as a working horse. Two daughters are valued as producers. Her youngest, a son, is growing up, learning the ways of the world, and discovering how handily his good looks and pleasing manner win friends.

Unusual stable habits? Yes. Serenata does not nicker, whinny or chortle to encourage fast delivery of her meals. She snorts and blows! First at her manger door, then at the courtyard door, then at her pasture door. If hay is still not forthcoming, she repeats the cycle.

Serenata has no problem with self-esteem. She has "a worldliness, an imperious air," about her, says Janey. "This lady knows what she wants in life, and long ago decided that the humans she deals with are only here to satisfy her needs. However, about three weeks before she is due to foal, humans are more welcome in her life, as they deliver scratches on the neck, food treats, and tummy rubs."

She's found the perfect human companion in Janey, for Serenata on a close personal level to her means "someone to care for. I've made my vow to take care of her all her days, come what may."

BRA Quintara

"Believe me, there is no drug in the world that can make you feel this high, to be Medicare age with arthritis, which affects the hands, and be a National Champion. I am on top of the world!" was Joyce Wyman's reaction when she and her lovely grey Arabian mare, BRA Quintara, won (by unanimous decision of the judges) the United National Champion Pleasure Driving AOTD title at the 1989 United States Nationals in Albuquerque, New Mexico.

The winning streak for Joyce and Quintara began with the Champion Pleasure Driving AOTD (Amateur Owner To Drive) title at Santa Barbara. With that, "The bug had bitten and I was hooked on Quintara and pleasure driving," says Joyce.

For many years a horse show mom, Joyce had watched her trainer Kit Hall show Quintara in 1986 and 1987 from ringside. "I was intrigued with this pleasure driving," she says, and in 1988 she asked Kit to train a western pleasure mare she owned as a driving horse.

Kit's reply was, "Why train a western pleasure horse to drive when you already have a pleasure driving horse?" That August he called Joyce and asked her, "When are you coming down to learn to pleasure drive? I have you entered in the Santa Barbara Fall Show the first week in September."

"So I went to Chino and learned to pleasure drive and to really get to know my Quintara, who by this time had become my horse!" says Joyce.

In October, 1989 Quintara, with Joyce at the reins, became United States National Champion Pleasure Driving AOTD. By 1990 they had won two National Championships together. (And they would add Canadian National Champion Pleasure Driving AOTD in 1991).

Arthritis, however, had progressed to other parts of Joyce's body, and she began selling most of her horses. "My husband, Phillips Wyman, Jr., and I had already sold our beautiful Wyman Oaks in Salinas, California, and were no longer breeding. We were down to five show horses with Kit and my first mare in Stanwood, Washington, where our oldest grandchild was learning to ride western pleasure," Joyce recounts.

For 1991, Joyce decided Kit would show her horses. Quintara was shown in both English pleasure and pleasure driving by Kit Hall and was either Champion or Reserve Champion.

"We had moved to Green Valley, Arizona, for the winter and Mill Creek, Washington for the summer," says Joyce. "The arthritis seemed to be a bit better or at least not so painful, so I asked Kit if I could once again pleasure drive Quintara at the 'Royal Red' Canadian National Championship Show in August, in Regina, Saskatchewan, Canada. She placed Top Ten in the English Pleasure Championship and Champion in Pleasure Driving

and Pleasure Driving AOTD. Excitement reigned!," recalls Joyce.

Kit Hall's quote to the *Arabian Horse World* magazine was: "Quintara is the most exciting horse I have ever seen under saddle or in harness. She has an effortless ability to trot level yet still maintain steadiness in the bridle on a loose rein. She is the most fluid English pleasure horse I have ever ridden. It is always a thrill to show her, and always exciting to win with her." Kit has trained her exclusively and at one time co-owned her with the Wymans.

A setback in 1991 at the U.S. Nationals, when Quintara became desperately ill with an airborne viral pneumonia, was followed by a glorious comeback!

"Need I tell you, here it is, 1992, and at the Scottsdale show it was, by unanimous decision of the judges, Champion Pleasure Driving AOTD; by unanimous decision of the judges, First Place English Pleasure Mares; by unanimous decision of the judges, First Place Pleasure Driving Mares and Geldings; and by unanimous decision of the judges, Champion Pleasure Driving with Kit Hall," says Joyce.

After this show, I said to Kit, "Thank you for introducing this new dimension to my life...Quintara and pleasure driving. I have loved all my horses, and they have all been successful in the show ring, but Quintara is the superstar!"

*Aladdinn

As has often been remarked of *Aladdinn, his story is as romantic as anything out of the *Tales of the Arabian Nights*, though his magic was created by his genes rather than a genii.

Bred in Sweden of all-Polish bloodlines, *Aladdinn has unprecedented achievements as a sire. A United States National Champion Stallion himself, he has sired four United States National Champion stallions. Most stallions of any breed are lucky to sire one champion son in the same division in which they have won.

When the 15.1-hand robust, bright bay stallion was foaled on February 13, 1975 at Mollebacken Stud in Tomalilla, Sweden, his breeder, Erik Erlandsson, called out to his wife Gulle to come "take a look at the best horse in all the world," something he told her he would say only one time in his life.

Erlandsson was an enterprising character who obtained much of his Polish-bred stock as aging circus stallions, including the playful bay stallion named Nureddin.

Nureddin was bred to Lalage, daughter of the dainty (14.1) mare Lafirynda, who was rescued from a life of abuse, pulling a plow for Polish peasants, and the result of this blending of prized Kuhailan and Saklawi strains was *Aladdinn.

Imported as a three-year-old from Sweden, where he had been the National Champion, by Lasma Arabians in 1978, *Aladdinn was syndicated by Lasma in 1979 for an amount which was greater than the syndicated value of Thoroughbred Triple Crown winner, Secretariat. *Aladdinn took immediate charge of the National show arena. Shown by Gene LaCroix, *Aladdinn was named U.S. National Champion Stallion in 1979, the unanimous choice of three judges.

Persons who had bought into the syndicate earlier just nodded and smiled wisely as he quickly emerged as a dominant sire through his champion offspring. He quickly established his reputation for an ability to pass along his blue ribbon-winning conformation, athletic ability and presence to his get.

As early as 1980, two years after he was imported, Aladdinn's daughter *Gongala was named the Scottsdale Junior Champion Mare, followed the next year by the *Aladdinn daughter Ddinnerka, who was the 1981 and 1982 Scottsdale Junior Champion Mare and 1982 Reserve Show Champion Mare as a two-year-old. That same year, Ddinnerka's paternal half sister, SS Opening Night, won the yearling filly class.

By 1983 the pattern had clearly emerged, and *Aladdinn was on his way to becoming an Arabian horse world phenomenon. His son Strike was Scottsdale Junior Champion Stallion, Reserve Grand Champion Stallion, and the talk of the show that year.

In 1984 AAF Kaset was both the U.S. and Canadian National Champion; Strike was the 1985 U.S. Champion Stallion, Almaden took the title in 1988 and Exceladdinn was the 1986 Canadian National Champion Stallion and the 1989 United States National Champion Stallion.

*Aladdinn, a nominated sire of the IAHA Breeders Sweepstakes and of the Arabian Incentive Foundation, has in addition other get which have won literally hundreds of Championships, Reserves, and Top Ten placings, in Halter, Western, Park, English Pleasure and Driving classes in the U.S. and Canada. It would take several pages of this book for just a partial listing.

Though a glamorous equine celebrity, at home "Big Al" is a favorite with all who deal with him, according to stallion barn handler, Ruben Gaona. *Aladdinn is one of the friendliest of the Lasma East International Centre's stallions, presenting himself at the bars of his stall to have his chin scratched. When he is turned out for exercise, *Aladdinn can be counted on to be a gentleman and go up to the paddock gate when he sees Ruben ready to bring him back to his stall again.

A model of good spirits, he is always dignified, always seemingly contemplating the details of some far-reaching theory, perhaps his own legacy to the breed that approaches the legendary.

*Wilkolak

After a successful racing career in Poland, *Wilkolak was imported to the United States in 1988. Owned by Teisan Auto Co., Ltd., he stands at Lasma East International Centre, in LaGrange, Kentucky, where he has begun to sire foals that reflect his own heritage and individual qualities.

A light bay stallion with large dark eyes, standing 14 hands, *Wilkolak is very independent and serious in character, says Lasma stallion handler Ruben Gaona. "He is a very tranquil horse, perhaps because he is older and more mature," adds Ruben. No matter what happens in his surroundings, *Wilkolak holds his ground and does not spook. And when it's time to come in from his daily romp, *Wilkolak is obliging, waiting quietly at the door for Ruben.

*Wilkolak was foaled on February 18, 1976 at the Michalow State Stud Farm in Poland. His sire, *El Paso, is a United States National Champion Stallion and an important progenitor of the Kuhailan-Haifi sire line. *El Paso numbers among his progeny eleven sons and daughters that have won United States and Canadian National honors. His son, *Europejczyk, was the 1988 Polish National Champion Stallion.

The successes of *El Paso offspring in the show ring are well-documented, while their high-earning wins at the racetrack are more and more numerous, thus creating two ways for breeders to go with *El Paso bloodlines.

*Wilkolak's dam, Wadera, is counted among Poland's most classic mares. She is also the dam of *Wizja, a United States National Champion Mare, as well as of a Polish National Champion Mare.

Choosing *Wilkolak to join the other impressive stallions that make their home at Lasma East International Centre is a reflection of that facility's leadership in the Arabian breeding industry. Located thirty miles northeast of Louisville, Kentucky, L.E.I.C.'s magnificent 850-acre farm is a full-service breeding, training and marketing operation.

According to Kazu Ishikawa, L.E.I.C.'s vice president and general farm manager, its breeding department's state-of-the-art technology and expertise afford a range of equine breeding applications that include frozen and transported semen and embryo transplant.

L.E.I.C.'s training department prepares its clients' horses for the show ring with individually-designed programs that enhance each horse's capabilities.

L.E.I.C.-trained horses consistently finish in the ribbons in halter, western, and English classes. The farm hosts informal schooling shows and a series of educational seminars, conventions, and workshops that cover such areas as breeding, training, judging, stable management, and veterinary health care.

Another area of L.E.I.C.'s wide range of activities to which Mr. Ishikawa points with pride is the farm's growing involvement in competitive trail riding. The farm hosts competitive trail riding clinics, 15-mile mini-rides for novice distance horses and/or riders, a 25/50 mile endurance ride, as well as the IAHA International Competitive Trail Ride Championship in October.

*El Ghazi

"I think *El Ghazi is one of the most beautiful horses we have here at Lasma East International Centre," says Ruben Gaona, stallion handler for the illustrious Arabians who stand at stud there in luxurious surroundings.

He's also "a real individualist," according to Ruben. Unlike the other stallions, *El Ghazi can be "un poco asustón." He likes to pretend he's spooky and skittish, perhaps as a way of handling his own high energy levels. Or perhaps he's fantasizing a little, pretending it's the old days and he's back on the racetrack in Poland.

When it's time for the stallions to be brought in after a morning's paddock turn-out at Lasma East, *El Ghazi will treat Ruben's efforts to catch him as an invitation to play. Once he has been induced to come in, however, *El Ghazi is much more serene, says Ruben, and dotes on being handled. "He just has a lot of nervous energy," adds the handler. "Once he's gotten it out of his system, he's actually very quiet and enjoys his bath." *El Ghazi loves to roll and usually is well-coated with mud by the time he comes in.

This 15-hand, dark reddish bay stallion, with a white star on his forehead and three white feet, was bred at the Janow-Podlaski State Stud in Poland, where he was foaled on March 21, 1983.

The breeding of this pure Polish Arabian stallion is aristocratic. His sire, the bay stallion, *Aloes, was the 1982 Polish National Champion Stallion and a major progenitor of the Kuhailan-Haifi line. *Aloes was also bred at Janow-Podlaski State Stud and was sired by Celebes out of Algoa.

*Aloes and his daughters personify the qualities of the Kuhailan type. The latter were eagerly purchased by foreign buyers. *Aloes left behind him twenty daughters, of whom twelve mares are at the stud. He was for a time leased to Sweden but returned in the fall of 1986 and in 1987 again served mares at Janow.

One of *Aloes' daughters, Equitana, was the Polish National Junior Champion Mare as a two-year-old in 1982, and later took second place in the most difficult competition of all at Janow, the broodmare class.

*El Ghazi's dam, Elektra, is by *Bandos, whose dam is Bandola, styled "Queen of Poland" and a full sister to the legendary *Bask++.

*El Ghazi's initial triumphs were on the racetrack in Poland, where he ended his racing carer with an impressive victory in the 1988 Bandola Stakes.

Shortly after that victory, *El Ghazi was brought to the United States by Lasma East International Centre in LaGrange, Kentucky. A year later, in 1989, he added a show ring success, winning United States National Reserve Champion English Pleasure.

A nominated sire of the International Arabian Horse Association Breeders Sweepstakes, the Arabian Incentive Foundation and the National Show Horse Registry, *El Ghazi is presently owned by Teisan Auto Co., Ltd.

*Muscat

It took thirteen trips to Russia and two and a half years of frustrating negotiations before the lead shank of *Muscat was handed over to Howard Kale, Jr.

Howard, member of a family which has bred, imported and shown Arabians since the 1940s, wanted the big, red chestnut stallion with the distinguishing mark of a half crescent on his blaze from the first moment he saw him at Russia's Tersk stud.

"The first day I saw *Muscat, he did the same thing for me that he does for everyone, and the more knowledge people have, the more intense the experience is. He was, and is, inspiring," says Howard.

But the Russians said nyet, and nyet again. Not for sale! declared Alexander Ponomarev, the director of horse breeding at the Tersk Stud. *Muscat was his "fair-haired child."

Sired by *Salon, *Muscat was the heir apparent at Tersk. Even as a weanling, he was considered the future progenitor of the Naseem line, known for its exceptional type and beauty.

Muscat's dam, Malpia, is by Priboj, celebrated as both a racing stallion and sire of many offspring with athletic ability. Malpia was out of Mammona, considered to be the best daughter of Ofir, and founder of the most important and influential mare family at Tersk.

So *Muscat was the special one, representing the best of sire and dam lines, which is what made him so invaluable to the Russians. And so sought after by Howard, who was relentless in dealing with Russian bureaucracy, which made making a deal with the Devil himself seem a cinch by comparison.

Howard decided to try to figure out what the Russians would want more than they wanted *Muscat, which turned out to be two one-million dollar Standardbred stallions.

Finally holding *Muscat's lead shank in his hand on the Russian-Polish border was "one of those rare moments of fulfillment in life," he says.

*Muscat, imported to America in 1978, really ARRIVED in 1980, when he became the Arabian breed's first Triple Crown stallion, named Scottsdale Champion Stallion, Canadian National Champion Stallion, and United States National Champion Stallion all in one year.

His elegance and balanced motion and attitude of self-worth make him a thrilling presence in the show ring and won him successive standing ovations. Many who saw him said he is a living piece of art, the closest they had come to seeing a perfect horse.

Whatever the world said about him, Howard feels *Muscat is superior enough to speak for himself, especially in what he has to offer the next generation.

Owned by the *Muscat Syndicate and standing at Lasma East International Centre in LaGrange, Kentucky,

*Muscat's foals are an affirmation of his exceptional ability as a sire to pass on his remarkable traits and genetic potential.

A nominated sire of the Arabian Incentive Foundation and the IAHA Breeders Sweepstakes, he has sired more than one hundred champions, including National Champions, Reserves and Top Tens in Futurity, Halter and English and Western Pleasure classes.

Among these is the breathtaking, exquisitely feminine Amber Satin, 1988 United States National Champion Mare. Other National winners among his offspring are Mpulse, SH Muscanne, My Mavica, Musknitsa, Muscap.

Today, daily life at Lasma East is one of serenity and contentment for the horse that many feel will be considered one of the greatest sires of the century. According to his handler, Ruben Gaona, *Muscat is a delight to work around. He waits for Ruben to come into his stall and scratch his head between his ears, and he responds by nuzzling Ruben's hand. But he seems never to forget his aristocratic manners, as befits Russian royalty. A gentleman at the dinner table, *Muscat always waits patiently for Ruben to serve him his grain, almost as patiently as Howard Kale, Jr. waited for him.

Steens

On September 8, 1991, his first time out at the California Arabian Classic Horse Show in Pomona, Steens took the blue ribbon in the yearling purebred colt class and went on to win the Purebred Colt Junior Championship. Not bad for a colt born on Friday the 13th! A foal so tall and long-legged, it took nearly ten hours for him to find the "breakfast bar," it was so far below his line of vision!

Steens, named for the singularly beautiful Steens Mountain in Oregon's desert country, was immediately recognized by his breeders as a colt that stood out from all the rest.

His good looks were no accident, for his sire *Probat, a world-renowned Arabian stallion of Polish bloodlines, is noted for siring beautiful, athletic horses. *Probat was a popular sire in Europe, standing in both Sweden and Poland before he was imported to the United States—he has sired many champions here and abroad. Steens' dam, the lovely bay mare May Oui, is sired by Negatraz, son of the immortal *Bask. It was a cross that has produced some outstanding foals in the opinion of the nation's foremost Arabian horse breeders.

Robert Leone, a retired Los Angeles police officer, had long searched for such an outstanding colt. He'd had a dream reaching back into his boyhood, when he had made frequent trips to the local library where he indulged himself in all the great classic horse stories. Horses of powerful presence, nostrils flaring and manes flying in the wind, galloped right off the pages for him.

The visualization, born within him as a boy, resurfaced again in the grown man.

While Robert and his wife Betty, a physical therapist, have had horses for most of their adult life, it wasn't until they acquired a pretty yearling filly named Aquitaine that they really began to think about breeding and showing these magnificent animals at their A to Z Arabians in Yucca Valley, California.

Aquitaine had supplied the "A" and their first-born purebred colt, Zirrafix, supplied the "Z." But after attending several shows with Aquitaine they realized that a superior colt would have to be considered for her and their other purebred mares. So Zirrafix was gelded and the search for their future herd sire was begun.

"In my search for such an outstanding Arabian colt," says Robert, "I happened across an ad in an Arabian breed magazine." He recalls it still, "It was for a *Probat son out of a Negatraz daughter; a pure Polish 1990 colt; black bay, four white socks and a star; beautiful conformation and extreme head, lovely disposition."

This ad seemed to stand out from the very pages it was printed upon for Robert, just as the images from the great horse stories of the past had pranced off the pages of the books he'd read as a boy. From that ad, Steens leapt into their lives and has been making an impact ever since.

Robert says, "I have always felt that the words of G.W.E. Russell were so meaningful when he said, 'The outside of a horse is good for the inside of a man.' The enjoyment I have received from these wonderful animals is shared by the many who have discovered the inner excitement of life itself, in viewing the grand Arabian horse. Beauty IS its own excuse for being."

Bask Elect +/

There are champions in the show ring and champions in the arena of life, and Bask Elect+/ is both.

Sired by the immortal *Bask, the all-time leading sire of champions of the Arabian breed, Bask Elect+/ made his own marks in the horse show world in the first nine years of his life.

The chestnut stallion with a distinctive thick white stripe in the middle of his copper-colored tail was twenty-eight times champion and twenty-eight times first place winner. He'd won his ninety points toward his Legion of Honor, as well as many regional awards.

His then owner, Bill Henry, had turned down an offer of $125,000 for Bask Elect+/.

Then on March 3, 1985, a day that began like any other at Heritage Farms Showcase near Houston, Texas, a freak accident changed his life forever.

B.E., as Martha Murdock calls him, was always nervous about having his hind feet shod and that day he kept resisting every attempt to do so. In all-out protest, he reared high in the air, lost his balance and fell over backwards. His head hit the barn wall and he slipped down to the floor at a crazy angle, his head pinned partly beneath his body.

Martha, then B.E.'s trainer, jumped to his side, and though she thought he was dying, pulled the stallion's head free. She saw that he was bleeding heavily through his nostrils and freed them of the blood clots that were suffocating him.

Ten minutes later, by the time the veterinarian came, B.E. was on all four feet again. The blow to his head, however, had damaged his optic nerve and resulted in total blindness. Henry left the decision to Martha whether to put him down or not.

At first it took several people to lead the shaky unbalanced horse in or out of his stall. Murdock spent countless hours helping him regain his equilibrium. Three months after the accident, she saw he was badly out of shape and in need of exercise. One night when no one else was around, she took him out and rode him bareback. After two or three turns around the ring, "he was just like any other horse," says Martha, who now lives in Brenham, Texas.

One year after the accident, B.E. was presented with his Legion of Honor Award (for which he had already accumulated points) at the Azalea Classic, one of the largest Arabian shows in Texas.

In September, 1987, Martha tried showing B.E. at a Class A show in Houston for the first time since he had been blind. "It was the biggest thrill I ever had," she said. "The crowd went crazy over him," and he won the Open English Pleasure Championship.

In October 1987, using all the means available to her, Martha became B.E.'s owner. Since then, B.E. has won 15 Class A Championships, five Regional Championships, two Scottsdale Top Tens, and three National Championship titles, the last 1991 U.S. National Champion Ladies Side Saddle English.

"B.E. has never stopped doing things that totally amaze me," says Martha. "Riding B.E. gives you the feeling that you are part of a miracle. He basically performs following voice commands. I am constantly reminded by him that anything is possible if you want it enough to never give up!"

Not that she's ever wanted a sympathy vote for her horse. At one point she started turning down the many reporters' requests to do stories about him, "so that we could compete like other horses," she says.

All such stories should have a happy ending, and there's one for B.E. In the spring of 1988, Dr. Ralph Johnson, a Minnesota veterinarian specializing in equine acupuncture, offered to treat B.E. in hopes of restoring some of his vision. After only four treatments, B.E. suddenly shied at a tack trunk that had always been there. Now he distinguishes objects with his right eye. Treatment for his left has not been so successful.

Dr. Johnson says, "Horses are a lot like people. And there are great horses with big hearts and personalities, just like people. But I've never met a horse in my twenty-eight years of treating them with more heart than Bask Elect+/."

*Numaa++

"Numaa++, the senior sire at El Camino Ranch in Redlands, California, has made a name for the ranch by putting super-athletic, smooth-bodied, and pretty Arabians on the ground," says owner LaVesta Locklin. "They are show horses, but more than that, they are excellent 'people' horses, horses that love attention, and have their sire's terrific and easy disposition. They are puppy dogs with a big motor.

"*Numaa++," she adds, "is known as the big, bold, tall Arabian sire." She explains that the asterisk placed before his name indicates that he is imported, and the two pluses (++) after his name mean that he has received the coveted Legion of Merit award for the accumulation of points in shows sponsored by the International Arabian Horse Association. He is the only pure Spanish stallion to achieve this award in the United States," says LaVesta.

*Numaa++, a beautiful bay colt with splashes of white that gave him a very distinctive and striking look, was foaled on January 10, 1975 in Ecija, Spain at the

Osuna Stud. His dam, Estiba, a bay Tabal daughter, was owned by Miguel Osuna Escalera, who was also the breeder of Estiba's half-sister, *Estopa, the well-known dam of *El Shaklan. Mr. Osuna had bred Estiba the prior year to Jaguay (by Zancudo), one of his favorite stallions at the Yeguada Militar in nearby Jerez de la Frontera. At least seven of Jaguay's sons and daughters have been imported to the United States from Spain.

Estiba's colt was named *Numaa++ by Mr. Osuna. He was so sweet-tempered he became the family horse and the favorite of the children in the family. He was kept at the family compound in the city of Ecija, and when he was old enough, he was hitched to the cart for the weekly trip to the feed mill to purchase feed for all the horses.

"On several occasions when American Arabian enthusiasts visited Spain they tried to purchase *Numaa++, but to no avail. *Numaa++ was the kids' horse, they were told. Then in 1980, when *Numaa++ was five years old, a group of Americans visited the Osuna farm, and while they were being shown the Osuna horses, one of the party was in the office making a deal with Miguel Osuna. This person was 'Rocky' Ullom, who came back to America the proud owner of *Numaa++," LaVesta relates.

*Numaa++ began an outstanding show career, becoming known for his wins in Arabian halter classes. In September, 1985, *Numaa++ received his Legion of Merit, presented to him by the elder statesman of Arabian breeding, Frank McCoy.

Bill and LaVesta bought him in 1986. He was shown that year to a Reserve Championship in Pleasure Driving at the Region 2 Show and to a Top Five English Pleasure at the same show. He was shown only a few times after he moved to El Camino Ranch, as he soon became much too busy as a sire each spring.

"He is definitely the top guy at El Camino, and he knows it," says LaVesta. "He is the epitome of the perfect breeding sire. He is 15.3 hands, but several of his kids are over 16 hands. One of his sons, Paul Numaa, is very much like his dad in appearance, but he is 16.3 hands at four years of age."

The National Show Horses sired by *Numaa++ are fast becoming known as champions, both in Half-Arabian classes and in National Show Horse competition.

"We have learned that training is important in a horse," concludes LaVesta. "But most basic is the production of horses with tractable minds, good dispositions, and athletic bodies in their genetic make-up. *Numaa++ has those genetic qualities that have taken us from a little backyard ranch to the forefront as a top breeding facility of super-athletic horses with wonderful personalities."

*Oral

Foaled March 1, 1973, in Baleares, Spain, at the breeding farm of Pedro Salas, the Spanish Arabian mare *Oral came into the world like the blooming of a rare and unexpected black orchid.

Neither of her parents were the color they produced in her. Sired by Garbo, a beautiful white stallion, and out of Jacerina, a chestnut Tabal daughter, *Oral is as black as night.

"Her tiny star and bits of white on her three coronet bands of her feet only make her black coloring even more striking," says LaVesta Locklin, who with husband William owns El Camino Ranch in Redlands, California where they stand the stallion *Numaa++.

*Oral's dam line is very distinguished, going back to Betonica, a bay mare out of Saklauia Yadran, a desert-bred bay mare who was presented as a three-year-old to General Franco by King Abdullah of Jordan in 1949.

"Oral is one of the breed's typiest mares and has produced primarily stallion quality colts with extremely beautiful heads," says LaVesta. "Most of the colts have been shown and are sold as youngsters to Arabian enthusiasts who see the destiny of the colt as their herd sire. And they become much-loved stallions who sire wonderfully well for their owners."

William and LaVesta Locklin bought *Oral in 1988 and as the owners of *Numaa++ continued to breed these two. The same cross with previous owners had already produced four bay stallions and a chestnut colt that was gelded. "However, after a few more colts," says LaVesta, "we decided to breed to a different stallion in an effort to get a filly, since the mare is getting older, and we want a replacement for *Oral in the event she becomes unbreedable or dies. *Oral has chosen to continue producing colts for us. Perhaps she is telling us we don't need a replacement yet, and truly it would be difficult to produce a filly any prettier than this mare.

"Perhaps *Oral's role as the producer of colts is divine destiny to assure more of her line is retained in the breed, since a stallion will get more offspring in a given period than a mare," LaVesta adds.

"Each owner of *Oral has felt she was special. I know of no other Spanish horses that are black, and few that are as beautiful," says LaVesta. "In 1989, my husband and I went to Spain. I searched for a black Arabian. I was shown many nice horses, but none were black."

She adds that El Camino Ranch does not "breed for black," as the program "is not based on color but on quality.

"*Oral typifies the beauty we strive for in our breeding program for Arabians and National Show Horses," she says. "Because *Oral produces such nice purebreds we do not breed her for NSH, and her colts are in demand as pure Spanish herd sires.

"As a 'Mom,' *Oral is super," LaVesta adds. "She is wonderful with her foals and for us to handle. We just treat her like the Queen of El Camino, which she is. She likes visits from other people and will walk up to them and enjoy the praise and remarks about her beauty.

"People come to our ranch just to see *Oral. She has become the symbol of our breeding program, and has definitely helped our ranch become known for excellent Spanish breeding stock."

As a broodmare, *Oral produces excellent foals every year for El Camino. "Because she has a nice, short back, she gets about as wide as she is long every spring when she is close to foaling," says LaVesta.

"To our knowledge, *Oral was never shown. She was never trained to saddle, and from the beginning, it was the plan that she would be the perfect mare to reproduce the Spanish horse," she adds.

"*Oral's home forever is at El Camino Ranch. She will produce her gorgeous foals as long as she is able, and then she will be provided a loving, caring home the rest of her life."

Monarch AH

One of his jockeys thinks Monarch AH is the Secretariat of the Arabian racing world – he's that superior to anything he runs against. The bay stallion certainly had the style of a superhorse when he was named 1991 Darley Horse of the Year at a special awards presentation in Los Angeles the same evening he scored a fifteen-length victory in the California Arabian Cup at Los Alamitos Racetrack, breaking the track record.

Once you learn the real story behind this outstanding Arabian athlete, however, he seems more comparable to an equine Rocky Balboa.

Foaled in March, 1987 at Town & Country Farms in Micanopy, Florida, a son of *Wiking, Polish and U.S. stakes winner and two-time U.S. Racehorse of the Year, and *Sasanka, Polish Triple Crown winner and 1972 Polish Racehorse of the Year, Monarch had to start fighting for his life before he was foaled.

*Sasanka became very ill during her pregnancy and required several operations. She foaled three weeks early, and though her foal survived, she died three weeks later. The colt was put to a nurse mare and bottle-fed by the farm owner, Louise Courtelis (Town & Country Arabians) and stable personnel.

Still, he was cheerful and demonstrated a tremendous will to live. He got his name because as a little guy he bounced around like a Monarch butterfly, here, there and everywhere. (The initials AH stand for the late Dr. Armand Hammer, his breeder and original owner.)

Somehow, though, in the process of being bottle-fed and catered to for the first weeks of his life, "he sort of got the idea he was human," says Louise. People were his peers, so to speak.

It was evident that, for his own good, Monarch would have to be integrated with his own kind, and it was with a lump in everyone's throat that the orphan was sent out to join the other foals in pasture. For a few weeks he looked pitiful, covered with bite marks. But not long after, says Louise, when someone went out to check on him, he was beating up on everybody. "Then we knew he would be okay."

Monarch arrived at Delaware Park as a three-year-old in March, 1990. His trainer, Philip Saxer, Jr., immediately thought he was special and once he let him loose on the track he did not disappoint. In fact, Phil felt Monarch had it all – brains, power, and good looks.

But training a horse as bright and people-oriented as Monarch had its challenges, one of the most important of which was to get him fit. That was difficult, says Phil, "because he goofed around so much, looked around at things, slowed down." Not having one horse that could keep up with him, Phil used two. He knew as long as there was another horse ahead of him, Monarch would give it all he had. So Phil would break one horse with him to get him going and when Monarch hit the five-eighths marker, he would break a second horse fifteen lengths ahead of him. Monarch would pass the second horse before the finish line, everytime.

Phil's program worked. Monarch's first time out, on June 4, 1990, he won his race at Delaware Park by fifteen lengths. On September 3, 1990, he ran in the AJC Delaware Stakes for a $60,000 purse, and Dr. Armand Hammer showed up to watch him run, and win, by eighteen lengths. Dr. Hammer, then ninety-two years old, got so excited, he ran to the winner's circle to get ahead of the crowd there. While Dr. Hammer was no longer alive to see Monarch's next victory in October, 1991, Monarch won the Armand Hammer Classic, the premier Arabian race in the country, by seven lengths.

In late 1991, Dr. Hammer's Oxy Arabian herd, including Monarch AH, was sold to Bob and Sharon Magness, owners of Magness Arabians of Colorado and California and of the corporate giant, Telecommunications, Inc.

The Magnesses, who have always had a few horses in race training, were ecstatic about Monarch. "Forget his racing record, forget everything," says Sharon Magness. "We fell in love with him when we first saw him. We had to buy the whole herd, seventy-nine horses, just to get him. Plans are to stand him at stud in 1993, but no matter what he does, this horse has been such a joy to have."

*Gondolier

The whole thing got started when cable television magnate Bob Magness' son Gary said to him, "Dad, why don't you get a couple of Arab mares and breed riding horses of your own?"

Today Magness Arabians of Colorado and California has 650 of some of the world's best Arabian horses, with the chestnut stallion *Gondolier the king of the roost.

Bold-moving and powerful, athletic and well-built, the chief sire and senior stallion at Magness Arabians is a superb example of the traits that Bob and Sharon Magness value in the Arabian horse: extreme type and beauty, natural performance and siring ability.

*Gondolier has a little extra something besides. When he was foaled (February 16, 1974) at Janow-Podlaski State Stud, "he was different," says Tomasz Skotnicki, manager at Magness Arabians in Santa Ynez, California.

Along with the very athletic body of the Polish horse, he had the exotic head of the Egyptian Arabian. That was the fortuitous result of his breeding. He was sired by Palas, a grey stallion of strong Egyptian lines bred at the Tersk stud in the USSR, and out of Gonagra, a Polish-bred mare, a great beauty considered one of the best Negatiw daughters.

Tomasz, former assistant for six years to the Janow-Podlaski Stud director Andrzej Krzysztalowicz, and a lifelong friend and companion to *Gondolier, believes he is the best Palas colt bred in Poland.

In affirmation of that belief, *Gondolier was named 1980 Polish National Champion Stallion.

When *Gondolier was imported to the United States in 1981, Tomasz was asked to come with him and to manage the stallion's syndication, and he's been devoted to his equine friend ever since.

*Gondolier was imported by *Gondolier, Inc. of Scottsdale, in which corporation Bob and his late wife Betsy Magness became partners. The stallion stood at Scottsdale until February, 1987 when Bob Magness, by then sole owner, started his Santa Ynez Farm. *Gondolier became a resident of California where he already had some good PR going as Pacific Slope Champion Stallion and Santa Barbara Spring Show Champion Stallion in the early 1980's. In 1982, he won the title of World Champion Stallion at the prestigious Salon du Cheval in Paris, France, shown by Tomasz, and in 1984 he won Scottsdale Top Ten Stallions of 1978 and Older.

*Gondolier is recognized as the sire of two National winners: LJM Heaven Sent, 1986 Canadian Top Ten Futurity Filly, and Valdalier, 1990 U.S. Top Ten Country English Pleasure. In addition, he is the sire of *Czarnolas, 1986 Region 18 Reserve Champion Stallion and a winner at the Salon du Cheval.

In 1991, *Gondolier bred some fifty-five mares. Tomasz says he does especially well with *Bask and *Bandos lines. A special *Bandos daughter bred to him may very well one day produce *Gondolier's replacement.

*Gondolier's foals are easily picked out, the manager continues, as they are the most gentle at the farm. "They come to you right away, want to stick their muzzles in your pocket and they nibble on your sweater. Even in the pasture they come to you asking to be petted." And out of the 150 or so youngsters that are broken at the farm each year, says Tomasz, the *Gondoliers are gentle and easy.

*Gondolier is a very powerful mover, and trots with definite English action. This movement, which he passes on to his foals, Tomasz believes comes from Palas. "All the Palas horses have good motion," he says.

At Santa Ynez, *Gondolier leads the life his exalted kingly status merits. His paddock is a three-quarter acre grassy area where he can graze or gallop at liberty. Or he is occasionally ridden by his old friend Tomasz. "Just for fun we go on the trail or work in the arena," he says. "He's an easy ride and he enjoys those outings."

At eighteen, Tomasz says *Gondolier is still young and looks even better now than when he was the World Champion Stallion. Tomasz believes there are many more years of their mutual companionship ahead.

Hucklebey Berry+

"In 1988, we had come to a crossroads familiar to many in the breed," says Gerry Maddoux of Maddoux Way Arabians, Ltd., in Lubbock, Texas. "We loved the horses but like the fellow married to the trollop, we wondered, 'What price love?'" Gerry and Babs Maddoux had invested a lot of money in breeding stock and then watched the prices for those horses fall to levels one would only associate with a worldwide depression. They had serious thoughts about saying "Enough!" They had well-conformed, substantial mares of good pedigree, but needed beauty and action.

"We decided to stay in," Babs says. "Hucklebey Berry+ made the decision for us. We had discovered that the elements we wanted to produce were associated with pedigrees strong in Polish bloodlines, influenced by good old American lines. For that reason, we were impressed with the Varian Arabians product. And we saw Hucklebey Berry at Scottsdale."

HBB, as they call him, (by Huckleberry Bey x Miz Bask by *Bask) was four at the time, and had already earned major East Coast Stallion Championships and 1988 Scottsdale Reserve Champion English Pleasure Junior Horse.

"Sheila Varian kindly came to our farm and felt that HBB would complement our mares. The decision was immediate. We wanted him and we bought him," says Babs.

"During his stay at Maddoux Way, we learned to appreciate the HBB charisma and sensitivity," she adds. "This is a horse that makes you smile. He is a cheerful sort, like his sire, Huckleberry Bey, and he enjoys himself, no matter what the occasion. HBB does not fret, takes life as it comes."

Under Maddoux ownership, HBB's first major win was 1988 U.S. National Top Ten English Pleasure Junior Horse. Then what they had waited, prayed and hoped for: U.S. National Champion English Pleasure in 1989 and 1991, the first horse in the history of U.S. National English Pleasure Championships to repeat the National Champion title.

What made the victory even sweeter was that a near-disaster occurred between the two titles. In April, 1990, Babs put HBB on a van bound for Michigan – promised shipping time, 36 hours – so that he might stand at Shea Stables for the rest of the breeding season and prepare for the 1990 Nationals. Because of shipping delays he arrived seventy hours later, more dead than alive with pneumonia, pleurisy, and complications. It took a month in an equine intensive care unit to put him right, and a carefully monitored convalescence to bring him back. By August, Tim Shea was riding him again and gearing up for the National Championship. But at Louisville he caught the virus going around, and he went Reserve.

By 1991 however, the Maddouxes knew HBB was better than ever. He began the show season by repeating the 1989 Buckeye Championship, then won the National Championship by the unanimous choice of five judges, just as he was unanimous in 1989.

The trainer remembers the glory of that night. "Ever since I started in this business as a groom," says Tim Shea, "it has been my dream to ride a purebred on Saturday night at the Nationals, with all the meaning implicit in 'Saturday night classes,' the important performance classes. I've done it before, certainly, but this night was special because not only is HBB an excellent performer, but to me, he's the most beautiful English pleasure horse of all time."

At Maddoux Way, smiles are growing wider as each HBB foal hits the ground. The Maddouxes can see English pleasure motion in those foals right from the beginning.

For the Maddouxes, a look back at four years of HBB ownership makes them doubly pleased that in 1988 they decided not to throw in the towel, not to forfeit their years of investment, but to try their best to make a true contribution to the breed. Says Babs, "HBB has allowed us to create a phenomenon, a purpose and a direction."

Bey Shah+

In April of 1991, Montreal businessman Georges Forest took some time while on a trip to northern California to visit the grandsire of one of his newly acquired Arabian mares. Having learned that the stallion Bey Shah+ lived in the town of Sonoma, he casually dropped in at the ranch and asked if he might have a brief look, never suspecting his whole life was about to change.

"My very first impression of Bey Shah+, as for so many others, was one of charisma," Mr. Forest recalls. "When he was turned out and pranced around and snorted, I was completely taken...he leaves an imprint. You just don't forget him."

Bey Shah+ cavorted in his memory for three weeks, drawing him back to a return visit. The idea of ownership began to tantalize him. Forest had really never believed that such a stallion could be privately owned, he says, "but by the beginning of June, Bey Shah+ was mine. Alone."

Although he knew the stallion was an outstanding example of his breed, at that point, Forest adds, he really didn't realize HOW important he was. It was not until later that Mr. Forest realized that he had purchased one of the great sires of the breed. "And I didn't know everything that came with him, a whole new lifestyle, a whole new world, a world that is quite demanding sometimes," says Forest, who until he bought Bey Shah+ had planned on winding down to a more relaxed lifestyle.

What he acquired in 1991, was the sixteen-year-old leading living sire of United States and Canadian National halter winners and the fifth-ranked all-time leading sire of United States and Canadian National winners (after *Bask, Khemosabi++, *Naborr, and *Aladdinn).

Mr. Forest learned that Bey Shah+'s reputation was firmly established in an equine coup d'etat at the 1987 U.S. Nationals, when he was recognized as the sire of the National Champion Mare Shahteyna and the National Champion Stallion Fame VF, while another daughter, PS Bey Elation was named U.S. (and Canadian) National Champion Futurity filly.

Bey Shah+ himself had won several National titles including 1980 U.S. National Reserve Champion Stallion and twice Scottsdale Reserve Champion Stallion. He also won the Scottsdale Get of Sire class in 1984 and in 1992.

But it is Bey Shah+'s flamboyant personality which has also brought him a following. "The most unique personality I've ever been around," says Doug Leadley, the trainer who has been with this Arabian stallion in one capacity or another since 1986.

A major junk food addict, "a character," the stunning, nearly 16-hand bay bred by Lester and Jennie Walton, is the son of the Varian stallion Bay El Bey++ and the *Bask++ daughter Star Of Ofir.

Bey Shah+ is publicly most memorable for his free style liberty horse class performances from the West Coast to the Midwest, which have won him a following of groupies a rock star would trade his guitar for.

With his own special recorded music playing, Bey Shah+ would enter the ring with his tail over his back, looking spectacular, and give the kind of show few people had ever seen before in or out of a liberty class.

"He just stopped hearts," is the way one spectator remembers him.

He always worked with his ears sharply forward, his eyes intently scanning the crowd, like any great performer carefully measuring the effect his grandstanding was working on his worshippers.

For Georges Forest, the years ahead bring responsibility to Bey Shah+, knowing that he has earned his position as one of the crown jewels of the Arabian horse world. "Owning Bey Shah+, is not a power trip, and Bey Shah+ is not my new toy," he says. "The horse is the important one. He comes first. I plan to be instrumental in helping him to preserve and enlarge his status."

179

O'Serrano

"Well, I guess if I have to look back to the very beginning, I owe it to a cow named Marilyn," says Sharon M. Oline of Montesano, Washington.

Sharon had a visit from her new neighbor, Vicki, who had recently bought Marilyn, a cow that had run through a few fences, and Vicki thought it might possibly have gotten in with Sharon's herd. One thing led to another and Sharon and Vicki started talking horses.

"I mentioned that I had been looking for a nice Arabian to show," says Sharon. Vicki told me about a very good friend of hers named Margaret Freisz. I met Margaret and bought a 1990 colt, a bay sired by DWD Tabasco, out of Gai Serena, who was sired by Gai Parada.

"My life immediately took a spin for the better," says Sharon, who is an equine professional. As a young girl she did gaming at junior rodeos. She also buys and sells horses and ponies, all breeds, all sizes, colors and shapes. She says, "I've been told I can see a diamond in the rough. I take in horses if I can save them from slaughter. If they are kind, there is someone out there to love and care for them." She also has had broodmares, breeding for show or race.

Through the colt, O'Serrano, Sharon made wonderful new friends. "Margaret Freisz invited me to the Scottsdale Arabian Show in Arizona," she says. "If it's possible to become addicted at first sight to the magnificence of the Arabian, I did...

"When I returned home, I knew this is the way I wanted to spend the rest of my life," she continues. "My husband, Don Palmer, called home from his business in Tacoma one evening and I told him I had sold the herd of cattle and was going to build an arena and stable for my at-home business and would specialize in lay-ups, boarding, buying and selling. That was the start of Shar-Don Farms," says Sharon, who is grateful to her husband for his support.

O'Serrano is now two years old. Sharon reports he is the color of a polished bing cherry with a beautiful long black mane and tail, and promises to be a good-sized 15.1 or 15.2 by his third year.

Sharon put the colt in training with Rich and Meryle Gault at Destiny Farms, owned by Galen and Linda Holmly in Ray, Washington. "The Gaults are very nice people and they have conditioned my colt for show. They like him and treat him very well, and that is what's important to me. The end result for me is that I will have a beautiful, well-mannered riding horse, and that is something to be proud of," says Sharon.

"O'Serrano will be a western pleasure horse and we will continue our new adventure together. I love the saying, 'The eyes are the window to the soul,' for in this case, this colt has soul!"

That's not ALL he has. O'Serrano is currently being shown in halter and placed in his first show. "The excitement I experienced was something else," says Sharon. "I never dreamed I would sit there with all these ill feelings...my stomach was in knots. When they called out his number, the joy of being acknowledged in the ring and the fact that the judges liked my colt was like giving birth. The pain was gone and I gave a sigh of relief...until the next show. I loved it!! And I'm already thinking of my next 'fix'."

Sirah Bey

Sirah Bey is a petite chestnut Arabian mare, with three white stockings and a lightning strip down her face, who has brought "joy that is out of this world" to her owner, small breeder Joseph D. O'Neill of Sonoma, California.

Joseph attributes his success story to a simple formula.

"Seek the advice of an outstanding Arabian authority," he says, in this case, Sheila Varian. "Take her advice," he continues, "and breed to an outstanding but unproven stallion," in this case two-year-old Hucklebey Berry, who would later be twice U.S. National Champion English Pleasure.

Then ask one of the most respected trainers in the business, Tim Shea, to take the resultant filly in training. He will agree after seeing only a video of her frolicking in her pasture as a two-year-old. Then hang on tight to your hat and your heart!

It all began when Joseph sent a picture and pedigree of his mare, Kes Ara Rahdames, to Sheila Varian and asked if she could recommend a stallion that would match well. Sheila said the mare had good old-line Arabian breeding with three crosses to *Raseyn and recommended the two-year-old Hucklebey Berry (by Huckleberry Bey by Bay El Bey by Bay Abi), as a stallion "that should give us more leg and presence," says Joseph.

The resulting Sirah was nevertheless a surprise to Sheila when she first saw her in a halter class at Scottsdale. She remarked to her owner that the filly had the best hock action of any of the seventy-eight yearlings entering the ring that February morning.

Sirah's sire also competed for the first time at that show and was Reserve Champion English Pleasure Junior Horse, a feat Sirah herself would duplicate as a four-year old.

Later, during a Varian Open House, Joseph showed the video of Sirah to Tim Shea, one of the top trainers of English pleasure horses, who was so impressed with the filly's natural action he enthusiastically agreed to accept her in training at his Shea Stables, in St. Clair, Michigan.

Sirah Bey began her fourth year competing in the junior horse classification in an interesting and exciting situation. She competed in all shows with her paternal half-brother Aragon Bey, also shown by Shea Stables. Both were from their sire's first foal crop.

At Scottsdale in 1990, after winning the mares/geldings competition with Tim Shea in the saddle, she was named Scottsdale Reserve Champion English Pleasure Junior Horse under the capable ride of David Gamble, Shea Stables' assistant trainer.

But it was 1991 that held the most thrills. Sirah was shown in Toronto, Canada; twice in Detroit, Michigan;

Scottsdale, Arizona; Columbus, Ohio; Regina, Saskatchewan, Canada; Albuquerque, New Mexico, and finally at home in San Francisco.

At the end, she had won two prestigious Reserve Championships, Top Eight (where Aragon Bey was Reserve Champion), Canadian National Reserve Champion English Pleasure Junior Horse, and Top Ten at the 1991 U.S. Nationals as English Pleasure Junior Horse.

Just ten days after the Nationals and after having been shipped from Albuquerque to San Francisco, Sirah was shown by David Gamble at the Cow Palace's Grand National Rodeo, Horse Show and Livestock Exposition, where she won her first class in Open English Pleasure on Saturday morning, and came back Saturday evening to win the Championship before a sold-out Cow Palace audience.

"I hope that other Arabian owners and small breeders will be encouraged to know that it can be done," says Joseph, who adds that Sirah Bey is now enjoying a well-earned rest and will be bred in 1992 to a *Bask son "for an even better result," though one can hardly be imagined.

*Figaro PASB

To say what is special about Lisa Levasseur's relationship with her Arabian Stallion *Figaro PASB is difficult, she says, "since everything about this relationship is special.

"I have made a point of viewing many of the great Arabian stallions since I have been involved with horses," she continues. "None has impressed me like *Figaro. I am only one of his many fans who recognize he has something more."

*Figaro has been at home at Lisa's Excella Arabians farm in Stony Plain, Alberta, Canada, since November, 1989, but his outstanding athletic career began years ago and far away with a sensational racing career. Foaled January 26, 1971, he dominated the tracks in Poland from 1974 to 1978, says Lisa, and even had a Polish stakes race, the *Figaro Stake, named in his honor. He raced a total of thirty-three times in five seasons, placing first or second twenty-six times. "He holds the record," she says, "for carrying the most weight, 145-1/2 lbs., matched against horses half his age, over 2000 meters...

the Poles' real criteria for determination of excellence."

At the conclusion of his racing career, *Figaro was purchased by Dr. and Mrs. Gunnar Bolstrum of Sweden, where he was shown and began his breeding career.

The Bolstrums had been shown fifteen of Poland's top stallions, among them *Gondolier, later a World Champion Stallion. "It took only thirty seconds for both the Bolstrums and the expert they had advising them to decide *Figaro was the one. That's how clearly he stood out in comparison to these great stallions," says Lisa.

*Figaro's extraordinary looks include an extremely long fine neck, a well laid-back shoulder, huge black eyes, and an ultra-fine throatlatch. He is refined yet has very good bone structure. His attractive flea-bitten grey color is not that common. His regal carriage and powerful action make him breathtaking to watch," says Lisa. "His personality is confident, bold and spirited. He is always at the edge of his skin, animated and far younger than his years."

Randy Shockley, arranging to lease him, brought *Figaro to Baywood Park, Ltd., in California, in 1985. This was a farm where Lisa had been employed for several years. She became *Figaro's special handler and developed a close relationship with him. "He seemed untamed in some ways," she recalls. "It took time to earn his trust so that I could touch his head or pick up his feet. During this gentling process, some special bonding took place for both of us."

Before *Figaro's lease was up, Randy Shockley passed away; Baywood Park was no more. Lisa, who never thought she would have a chance to own *Figaro, made an offer, against that of other high profile breeders.

The Bolstrums did not want to ship him back to Europe at his age – and Lisa's dream came true.

Acquiring him intrigued Lisa with the Polish breeding that had resulted in such a remarkable horse.

She learned *Figaro was one of the last living sons of Negatiw, who left a legacy of some of the very finest breeding and show horses the Arabian breed has ever known, age-old Polish breeding that is otherwise no longer available. His grandam, Forta, founded a line of top racehorses.

*Figaro has made Excella Arabians and myself much better known in the business," says Lisa, but the unique relationship they enjoy supercedes that.

"Since I met *Figaro, he has become an inspiration to me. I learned to be honest and true to myself from him. My respect for his heart and his integrity as a horse makes me want to live up to these qualities," she says.

"Simply having *Figaro is the culmination of a dream to own a great stallion. If there were a dream beyond that, it would be to produce from him a stallion who could fully live up to his legacy."

Mmusket

The first time Marge Penfold saw the Russian-bred stallion *Muscat at the Scottsdale, Arizona show, she knew that she had to have a filly by him out of her Bask-Tez mare, Rok Ofirka. When the foal arrived in 1981, it was big, dark seal bay, four white socks, a blaze and too beautiful to be anything but a filly. But no, it was a colt! Ladd Penfold, Marge's husband, was ecstatic, certain the colt was destined to be a champion performance horse and a great breeding stallion. Mmusket, as he was named, is well on his way to proving he is both.

Marge Penfold had believed in Mmusket from the beginning but the direction in which he should go at first was unclear.

He was a top ten halter horse with Mike Villaseñor as a yearling. The plan after that was to make him an English pleasure horse, when again Marge Penfold saw something at a horse show that impressed her.

She saw trainer Gary Ferguson go Canadian National Champion Stock in 1988 on a seventeen-year-old Arabian gelding named Beshta, one of the three Arabians he had in his training barn. When Gary went U.S. National Champion Stock with Beshta in 1989, the Penfolds said, "This is the trainer we want to ride our Mmusket."

Gary has a smooth and easy hand and takes each horse as an individual, working toward the heighth of performance for each one. Gary accepted Mmusket into his training barn early in 1991, setting a plan to have him calmed, peaked and ready for the Canadian Nationals in August.

Gary had never taken Mmusket to any large shows and did not know how well he would hold up on the long haul from Chino, California to Regina, Saskatchewan. But when Mmusket arrived in Canada he was calm and confident. "He just looks like he should have a leather jacket on – he's TOO cool," Tami Ferguson, Gary's wife, describes Mmusket's attitude on showing. Mmusket gave the competition all he had, going National Champion by scoring six points more than the Reserve.

"People think reiners are horses that are ugly, but if you picked the prettiest horse in the pen, you'd pick Mmusket," says Tami. "His beauty and charisma make him a real crowd-pleaser."

What does it take to be a champion stock horse? "It takes a lot of different things," says Tami, "but Gary looks for attitude in the horse, and you want them to have hocks that are closer to the ground. Whenever you see the big stoppers, they almost look like they're stopping when they are standing. Mmusket is well-balanced all around."

The short-term goal for 1991 was to breed Mmusket for thirty days and then get him ready to bring home a U.S. Nationals win. Which he did: Top Ten Stock.

"He's gone back into the pen doing what he does best," says Tami. "He's real good-minded, real easy to be around."

The long-term goal of the Fergusons is to make Mmusket one of the top performance and reining sires of his time.

This year he was bred to twelve of Marge Penfold's mares, some of them *Bask daughters. "Mmusket throws a big-bodied pretty-headed horse," says Tami. "He has one daughter showing this year as a three-year-old in western pleasure junior horse. She's Musk Be Passion, another seal bay who looks like daddy with his broad shoulder and broad rear and a face to die for. Mmusket also has a seven-year-old son, Musket Smoke, making a name for himself in amateur reining."

The Penfolds were so happy that Mmusket won in Canada that they made Gary Ferguson an offer to come work for them full-time, which he did. "The Penfolds are just phenomenal people," says Tami. "Really dedicated to their horses. The Penfolds, Gary and I know that Mmusket is a dream come true. He has given us all many wonderful memories to fill our scrapbooks and we are all hoping that we will have to buy additional pages to add to it."

TBA Wadani

"Wadani" is Arabic for "the exclusive one," and Seana Willis' Arabian stallion with his unique antics definitely lives up to that name.

Seana first saw Wadani when she accompanied a friend who was seriously shopping for a stallion. While the friend was talking to the owners, Seana wandered around the ranch and started watching three foals in the pasture. They were racing around and playing, but she noticed the leader of the group, a bay with three white socks, was definitely controlling the direction of the game. He wasn't the fastest of the three, but he was obviously the leader. He eventually led the group down to the gate and undid the latch, and then proceeded to terrorize everyone and everything on the property. He knew how far he could go with the game and when real anger was expressed by his "victims" he stopped and let himself be caught. His impish sense of humor was exceeded only by his utter lack of fear.

Seana was not in the market for a horse, but when she observed this little bay colt and his antics, "I just knew he was for me," she says. "During his first two years, I just worked on his ground manners and let him be a horse and socialize with the herd."

A contingency of her purchase, however, was to enter Wadani in a two-year-old futurity. Out of twenty-three horses, he placed first. Seana was surprised since, bored by the tame proceedings, he had fallen asleep in the middle of the class, and he WAS competing against very prominent bloodlines—Khemosabi+++, Bey Shah and *Bask. His own bloodlines, however, are nothing to be ashamed of—a Crabbet/Polish cross, his lineage is replete with performance champions.

When it came time to break Wadani, Seana wanted to start him right. "I knew he was athletic and smart and special and that he had the talent to go as far as I was willing to take him." She chose trainer Heidi Watson, observing that her horses turn out obedient and responsive and truly enjoying what they do.

But when she brought him to the West Wind Arabians for his training, she was a little embarrassed, for Wadani was going through "a major case of the uglies." His mane had been chewed on, his feet needed some trimming. But Heidi never said a word about his uncouth appearance and began working with him. Not only did he learn quickly, but he gained a tremendous amount of confidence in his new nurturing environment. He grew four inches his first four months there.

After four months of training, Wadani entered his first dressage show, scoring a few sevens, with the judge very positive in her comments. After his first year of limited showing, he qualified for the regional finals in two regions in two disciplines in both amateur and open divisions.

"The best show experience was his second show," recalls Seana. "We came in, rode three dressage tests and won all three. It was one of the best feelings in the world. All the hard work and worrying were justified in that one spectacular morning."

Wadani hasn't grown dull and boring, however. He is still an accomplished Houdini. The latch to his pen has to be very intricate and is often changed, because he will figure it out just by watching people work it.

"He isn't afraid of anything and his curiosity is always the dominant force of his personality," says Seana. "He has to check out every new thing that he sees before we can get any work out of him. He will stand and watch any activity going on and if he gets a chance will go over and physically inspect the work that has been done. He loves to play with big rubber tubs and safety cones and always puts his toys away when he is finished with them. And even though he is a mature stallion, he continues his daily ritual of sprawling out in the sun for a nap every morning. Maybe this is the secret of his growth," says Seana, for Wadani stands a whopping 16.2!

Full of himself as he is, he is also extremely gentle and Seana says owning him is like "owning a big, overgrown teddy bear."

West Wind Gandolf+

West Wind Gandolf+ got his name from the wizard in *The Hobbit* and in *The Lord of the Rings*. Like that wizard, Gandolf+ has great talents as an escape artist—he kept disappearing from his pen and appearing someplace else.

His owner, Pat Roark of West Wind Arabians in Bonita, California, found the grey Arabian serendipitously. She had gone to breeder John E. Motheral's ranch in Idaho to buy a beautiful chestnut colt she had seen. She arrived in a snowstorm, and in between dashing indoors to thaw out, she'd go out to look at weanlings. One colt, difficult to see because he was the color of the falling snow, was always out in front and chasing the other colts away from Pat. Something about him kept her coming back to look at him.

"He was the boss, he wasn't afraid of me, and he didn't intend for me to touch him or the other colts," says Pat. "When I left San Diego it was to buy that flashy chestnut colt; when I came home it was the elusive grey that had captured my attention and my heart."

But the path of true love is sometimes convoluted, and when the six-month-old Gandolf+ arrived in sunny San Diego from snowy Idaho, he could only be caught if Pat roped him. "My roping ability was far exceeded by his ability to outfox me," she says. "Finally I put him in a box stall by himself and went in each day several times a day to try to get him to eat out of my hand and allow me to touch him. He would have nothing to do with this! He and I spent a week getting nowhere. If I could get a rope on him, he would lead, but getting near him was just about impossible."

One day Pat invaded his territory a little too far, and he kicked her. "He could just as easily have broken my leg, but the kick was just enough. As I leaned against the stall wall in pain, Gandolf+ stared at me. Something happened to him in those few seconds, his comprehension of me changed. He turned and came to me tentatively, but he came! From that moment on I could walk up and catch him no matter where he was or how frightened he might be. If I called, he would come running; from then on he watched me intently and with great intelligence, a practice he continues to this day. Walking around the ranch, if I feel someone watching me...it is Gandolf+," says Pat.

Gandolf+, foaled May 20, 1978, is now a 15-hand gleaming white Arabian stallion with the exquisite head of a horse that could prance out of a fairytale. He is the chief herd sire at West Wind Arabians "where horses are bred to be performance and pleasure horses, to have the disposition, the mind and the athletic ability to do everything, to be the perfect horse for the amateur," says Pat.

A blend of Polish, Egyptian and Crabbet lines, his pedigree reads like a who's who of renowned Arabian horse breeders: Ali Pasha Sherif, W.R. Brown, Gainey, Selby, Babson, Kellogg, Davenport, the Polish State Studs, the Crabbet Stud.

He carries ten leading sires of champions in his pedigree and two Living Legends (the immortal *Naborr and Azraff). There are eighteen English champions and seventeen western champions in his pedigree.

Gandolf+ himself has been extensively shown. He has a superb record of Class A wins and won his Legion of Honor, a national performance award, in 1990.

Since his initial fear of intimacy, Gandolf+ has become a super companion. "He has always done anything I have ever asked him to do," says Pat, "and in return I do the same for him. The best way to describe what Gandolf+ and I have is a loving relationship, rather than a human/animal, master/servant understanding.

"In seven years of working with Gandolf+ there has never once been an incident where this stallion has put me in jeopardy or where I have felt he was not putting my safety as the highest priority.

"Under saddle, Gandolf+ is exhilarating," Pat adds. "Think what you want and he does it. The power he generates along with his fantastic conditioning makes you feel he could go on forever. He is PERFECT!"

Avatar Obsidian

Foaled March 24, 1989, he is the firstborn of Champion Mare Summertime Blues, the finest mare the Sennekers feel they have produced. He is by the stallion Avatar Al Sufi, "the horse of a lifetime" as far as Jan is concerned, and her personal mount for many years.

Obsidian is linebred to the great brood matron Bint Buena Suerte, his grandam on both sides. She is the dam of the most successful purebred Arabian park horse to date, Oran's Adagio (seven times National Champion), and the grandam of the most successful Half-Arabian park horse to date, six times National Champion Sufi's Fancy Free, to whom Obsidian bears a startling resemblance in appearance, color, and action.

"So Obsidian carries the blood of our foundation mare and our two senior sires, and he epitomizes our goal of producing extreme Arabian type and beauty, brilliant action, smooth conformation and an intelligent and trainable disposition," says Jan. "Obsidian embodies all the finest Arabian characteristics and since he is closely bred from superb individuals we expect him to transmit these qualities consistently and to distinguish himself as a sire."

At present, Obsidian is busy with his breeding career, and will begin his education under saddle in the fall.

"He has the high, powerful, balanced and extravagant trot characteristic of his family and carries himself proudly with his tail held high. We look forward with great excitement to his show career and the opportunity to share him with the world," says Jan.

She has become deeply attached to Obsidian because his extreme beauty and vitality are coupled with a wonderful gentleness and sensitivity.

"I am drawn to him most of all by his beautiful spirit and kind, inquisitive nature. He is confident and serene beyond his years," she says. "Everything I do with and for him is a pleasure. We play tag to exercise him. Left to himself, he will play tag with his shadow on the wall of the arena.

"Nevertheless, he is a businesslike breeding stallion, responsive to a quiet word or a light pull on the shank, a gentleman with the mares."

There is also a remarkable communion between him and his sire. "They touch noses and converse at length, with a little bravado, but no hostility. I honestly believe that Sufi acknowledges his son and is proud of him," says Jan.

"We savor Obsidian's presence and enjoy his company every single day. It is a great honor and a great responsibility to be blessed with such a horse. We have been given the gift of stewardship, to be servants of the noble breed, preserve and nourish the flame and then pass the torch to others through Obsidian," she concludes.

The black Arabian possesses a certain mythic power, a special dramatic and romantic appeal to which we are all irresistibly drawn. All the magic of this ancient breed is there, along with something more, mysterious and elemental and impossible to analyze.

So does Avatar Obsidian, the Arabian stallion belonging to Jim and Jan Senneker of Avatar Arabians in Perry, Michigan, have compelling physical beauty made even more stunning by his rare, raven color.

Explaining his extraordinary name, Jan says, "Avatar is a Sanskrit word meaning incarnation. To me Obsidian is an avatar of the future, both of our breeding program and our breed. Obsidian is, of course, black volcanic glass." Nearly as shiny and jet dark as her horse's coat.

"We use the phrase 'timeless elegance born of fire' to describe Obsidian," adds Jan.

KRA Duel Standard

Joe and Jeanne Vielock of Karma Ridge Arabians in Plano, Texas, are small breeders who have produced champions in both regional and National competition. They started out in 1982, assembling show-winning mares both in performance and halter, to get the "performance with type" blend they wanted.

But it wasn't until five years later that their breeding program produced the first stallion they thought was outstanding enough not to geld – KRA Duel Standard, a Gdansk grandson.

When "Duelly" was foaled early on June 3, 1989, the welcome mat wasn't exactly out for him.

He was born, the Vielocks told me, "alone and to a maiden mare who did not want to nurse him. He was still wet, only a few hours old and was chasing her around the stall trying to pin her against the wall to nurse." This was the first sign of Duelly's maturity beyond his years, or as his owners describe it, of his "thirty-six-year-old mind in a two-year-old body. Nothing bothered him."

When they opened the door to his stall, he turned to look at them, six people in all, and the black colt with three white sox and a star came trotting right over.

Little did the Vielocks know that this was only the start of a remarkable relationship with a unique personality, the equine equivalent of a "quick study."

Happily, Duelly did manage to become a suckling. Always self-confident, never intimidated despite the circumstances, Duelly grew up in the company of all adult horses. He may have been the world's youngest demonstrator of herd sire traits, delighting in running the mares from one pasture to another.

The Vielocks' trainer, Blake Krohn, convinced his owners to show Duelly in halter at the age of nine months. Much to even Blake's surprise, Duelly was "standing up" like a grown horse in two days.

He went into his first class at his first show very confident and stood very quietly, though all the other weanlings were making a racket, whinnying and jumping around. He won his class and went on to win Junior Champion against the big guys.

After that, he was brought home again to allow him to grow up a little.

Duelly was stabled in a barn with all mares, but he always led down the aisle like a perfect gentleman, no matter what the temptations. At two years, he was used for the first time as a breeding stallion, and again, once he figured out what it was all about, he was suave and cool as a senior stallion, to the general disbelief of the Vielocks' vet.

In December, 1991, the Vielocks sent Duelly back to their trainer to start to break and drive him, expecting he would be ready in six to nine months.

Well, it was the same old story again. Blake had him in the long lines only five times and he was so perfect, the trainer decided to put his young assistant up on him to see what he would do. "Duelly walked off like he was doing this all his life. By the second day, he was up in the bridle, riding like a made horse, interested, attentive and willing to give his all. Blake says Duelly is one in a thousand," say the Vielocks.

Duelly's beauty, his glistening black coat and spectacular motion are the reasons people are initially attracted to him, his owners say. "They pull over on the side of the road to take his pictures and just watch him."

But get to know him, and "the real thing that draws you to him is his love of himself, life and the people who care for him. There is always a nicker and a quick, soft bump with his head, to either be rubbed, scratched, or given a carrot," they add. "Our grandchildren and everyone else love him, and ask about him as though he were a real person. He's fun, he's a clown, and we sometimes sit and watch him move and just get goosebumps.

"To us, he is what every breeder dreams about, an example of the breed that brings converts and makes us proud to say we had a hand in his life."

*AN Malik

My horse *AN Malik is a Taurus like me," says Dorothy Stream. "His birthday is May 11, 1970," she continues, "he is 15 hands tall, flea-bitten grey and he is a proud Arabian stallion."

He is also so gorgeous he looks as if he had just stepped out of the illuminated pages of a medieval storybook – the horse the knight prince rides to rescue the princess and to slay the dragon.

This leading Spanish sire of champions came into the lives of Jay and Dorothy Stream in 1972 at the first Spanish National Arabian Horse Show in Jerez de la Frontera, Spain.

Foaled by chance the only Arabian on a Thoroughbred farm in the north of Spain, he was named "Malik," meaning king. But his rightful kingdom was far away in California, and fate was about to enthrone him there.

The Jerez show was planned to exhibit the Spanish Arabians to prove that their quality was as unquestionable as their records. The two-year-old *AN Malik stole the show and was the first National Champion Stallion of Spain. "He pranced into the show ring and it was love at first sight for me," says Dorothy. "His beauty, elegance, balance and motion were our hope for the future. He has more than fulfilled our dreams.

"When *AN Malik finally reached Greengate Farms, our ranch in San Luis Obispo, California, we bred him to a few mares to test his breeding ability. We were astonished and elated at the quality and temperament of his foals. The rest is Arabian horse history. Since 1974, *Malik has sired an impressive number of champion horses for us and for a vast number of people who began bringing their mares to our breeding barn.

"*Malik changed our lives because we became a very busy ranch with the correspondence, phone calls and staff to handle a top breeding stallion," she continues. "*Malik made us many new friends, and his well-deserved popularity brought in fees which paid a lot of ranch expenses over the years.

"We are breeders and have been for over thirty years. It all began because our daughter, Linda, wanted an Arabian gelding. Jay and I became so interested in Arabian bloodlines after horse-shopping in Scottsdale that the interest grew into a lifetime of Arabian horses." The Streams even moved from Illinois to California in search of better and greener pastures for their growing number of horses.

"*Malik is our family horse and the first love of all the dedicated girls in our barns," adds Dorothy. Greengate Farms has an all-girl staff handling its horses. "Linda Stream, our daughter, is farm manager and Laurie Thomsen has been stud manager for over eleven years; her assistant Mona Schlageter has been with the farm for eight years."

Many years after *Malik was imported, Dorothy and Jay purchased his grandam in Spain. After three years of piroplasmosis treatment cured her of the infection, *Zalema was imported to the U.S. at the age of twenty-three. "As a barren mare she was to be killed in Spain, even though she was beautiful and famous as the dam of Galero, *Malik's sire," says Dorothy. "The lovely *Zalema lived another eight years with a pasture next to her champion grandson, *Malik. To see those two beautiful horses trot up and down their rolling hills was a thrill for us and for many visitors.

"*Malik is our riding horse, our good-natured breeding giant who passes on his great disposition to his progeny, the clown who will wear a Santa Claus hat at Christmas or a top hat for New Year's Eve. The stallion people come to see and who has kept us in the horse business for the past twenty years," says Dorothy.

"Our lives have definitely changed because of Arabian horses. Jay and I have traveled all over the world because of his presidency of the World Arabian Horse Organization. We have been received by reigning monarchs and we have seen places and met people we never could have known, except through the horses. Our friends worldwide are horse breeders, and sending *Malik sons and daughters to many countries has brought us additional lasting friendships."

Fadjur

Much has already been written about the "Fabulous Fadjur," a horse whose legend looms so large it seems impossible to try to constrict it into a few words.

Fadjur was the American dream, acquired by a farmer's wife as a weanling colt, who would grow up to become one of the most popular Arabian stallions ever to set hoof on the planet, a hero to thousands of horse lovers.

His was a "look," a type which transcended many show fads of size, color, shape and form. Those came and went over the years, but Fadjur won top awards everywhere he showed over a span of twenty-three years. He was a Class A Champion Stallion twenty-two times, the last time at age twenty-three at the prestigious Santa Barbara All-Arabian Show. At the incredible age of sixteen, he was named U.S. National Reserve Champion Stallion for the second time, competing against sixty champions from the U.S., Canada, Poland, Egypt and England. He also was named U.S. Top Ten Stallion three times and Canadian Top Ten Stallion once.

While he lived, Fadjur earned the honor of Leading Living Sire of Champions, and after he died, the title was passed to his grandson, Khemosabi+++.

Fadjur had a long, full life; foaled February 12, 1952, he died in February, 1983, 31 years old.

He was a leading sire of "Aristocrats," mares who have produced four or more champions. He sired twelve, among them the divine Jurneeka++ (the dam of Khemosabi), said to be his truest daughter for the charisma she inherited from him.

That was the public Fadjur, the stallion of celebrity and acclaim.

In private, his story was one of immutable love and faith on the part of his owner, Marjory F. Tone.

She had wanted that bold blood bay colt with left hind sock and a bursting star on his forehead, with that shiny black mane and tail, from the moment she first saw him at six months old.

"It took four months of apple pie, special dinners and much persuasion," she says, to convince her husband Jack Tone that Fadjur should be part of the Tone family. He finally broke down and presented Fadjur to Marge as a birthday gift.

"To me, Fadjur was everything I ever wanted in an Arabian," Marjory recalls. "He fit exactly the mental image I had, the description of what I knew an Arabian should be. He had the huge dark eyes, small, tipped ears, extra width between his eyes, low-set eyes, small muzzle, fine skin with veins close to the surface, large nostrils. Also, a finely chiseled head, a high-set arched neck, and high tail carriage.

"He was the epitome of Arabian type and proudness. Fadjur with powerful, slow prance, his neck highly

arched, his tail proudly held high, nostrils flaring, chewing the bit, is an image burned forever into the memory of everyone who had the privilege of seeing him show off for a crowd. He loved people and they loved him back," she says.

Fadjur thought of himself as the boss stallion in the world's corral, but he might be an obscure gelding today if it weren't for the belief of the good woman who loved him.

When one of the top breeders and showmen of the time saw Fadjur, he told Marjory she should geld him. Or sell him. He had concluded that Fadjur, already 15 hands at two years of age, was going to be too big to be a top stallion. His words were "as if he had knifed me," says Marjory. The stallion's first foals were already on their way, and if they were what she expected, she would not follow his advice. "Many people have told me that poor man will never live down his recommendation to geld Fadjur," she says.

"Fadjur's ability to sire world class offspring who compete in virtually every way in which good horsemen use the blood of Arabian horses is what everyone remembers Fadjur for the most," adds Marjory.

"The look and heart and pride of Fadjur are carried on and will continue to be for many generations to come."

*Nariadni

When WAHO (The World Arabian Horse Organization) accepted the Russian Arabian Stud Book at its 1978 meeting in Hamburg, Germany, an event followed a few months later with Registry acceptance, that meant Russian-bred imports could be shown. Owner Howard F. Kale, Jr. was ready and waiting. His *Nariadni was one of the first Tersk-bred horses to win a championship when he took the Champion Stallion title at the All-Arab Horse Show of Washington at Yakima in July, 1979.

Today, *Nariadni belongs to Rick and Paula Taylor of Taylor Ranch in Preston, Idaho. The Taylors had first fallen in love with a beautiful *Nariadni daughter, then bought the sire. "We actually never dreamed of having the great *Nariadni in our barn, but as fate would have it, we were able to acquire him from Howard Kale, Jr. who had imported him from Russia," says Rick Taylor. Rick owns twenty Taylor Maid Beauty Supply stores thoughtout Utah and Idaho and breeds Piedmontese cattle as well as horses on his 500-acre ranch. "He is simply everything we dreamed of in the Arabian horse. Elegant, huge dark eyes, magical disposition," he says.

*Nariadni was high on the list of horses for which

Howard Kale, Jr. negotiated long and hard with the Russians in 1975. The beautiful chocolate chestnut Arabian stallion, foaled in 1973, is an Arax grandson. "He reinforced all I had learned about the Arax line," Kale said.

Kale saw *Nariadni's sire Nabeg as the most refined and typey of all the Arax offspring.

"I felt that *Nariadni's big black eyes, gorgeous head, and long neck would be ideal with many of the *Silver Drift and Tornado daughters," says Kale.

After four trips over a year's time, Kale finally was able to cut a deal with the Russians and on May 17, 1976, *Nariadni and two other stallions, including his full brother *Nanam, and twelve mares arrived at the Kale farm in Washington.

Gladys Brown Edwards, who had visited Tersk in 1974 herself, was one of the first persons invited to see *Nariadni, and she noted his beautiful topline, typical of his sire line, his compactness, and his typey head. Michael Byatt, head trainer at the Kales' Karho Arabians at that time, showed *Nariadni to Reserve Champion Stallion at Pomona in 1986 at age 13. He commented, "If someone wants to write the definitive criteria for the Arabian head, *Nariadni should be the model. He has the most beautifully uniform face and eyes and ears of any horse alive."

Respected by horse breeders as one of the great horses of the world, *Nariadni has, since that first historic win, won many championships in English pleasure; he was Top Five Stallion in 1981 and 1982 in Region 7, and 1983 Scottsdale Top Ten Stallions of 1977 and Older.

*Nariadni was at one time syndicated for $2.4 million dollars, and he has sired over 450 offspring, with close to 900 grandget, says Rick Taylor, who adds that the majority of *Nariadni's offspring carry his chestnut color. Among them are four National Champions or Reserve Champions and other of his get have won championships in Canada, South America, Europe and the USSR as well as the United States.

Howard Kale, Jr. himself used to ride *Nariadni, and commented on the experience: "He's a very attentive, easy-going horse, a great gift from Arax, and a wonderful ride. He's a very happy horse, almost like someone who has music in his soul and is moving to music all the time. Even walking, he has that extra little bounce. He's also very curious; his reaction to something new is to stick his nose out and find out more about it. It follows that he is not scared easily and there has to be some reason for him to do something. He's easy to train and very willing to please, but don't use coercion, and don't demand slavery. He is not a good slave." Kale claims that his concept of Arabian horse perfection lies somewhere between *Nariadni and *Muscat.

GH Muscateer

"GH Muscateer, when seen in person, sends a certain excitement through you that cannot be described or written down – only experienced," says Rick Taylor, owner of this straight Russian stallion. "You can line up four or five stallions in the center of a ring," continues Taylor, "and Muscateer will be the one who makes the hairs on the back of your neck stand up."

Sired by *Muscat, the breed's first Triple Crown Stallion – Scottsdale Champion, Canadian National Champion and U.S. National Champion all in the same year – Muscateer is out of the beautiful *Nahodka, the 1974 Dutch National Reserve Champion Mare, and the only imported Russian mare to produce five champions. They include Akshyon, Raxx, and Barodd, as well as the Canadian Top Ten Gelding Baarod. *Nahodka is a daughter of Arax, sire of five National Champions worldwide.

Muscateer, a 1981 bay, is many times a champion himself and has sired champion offspring. He has five full siblings all of whom have been National Champions or Reserves in Canada, United States, and South America. A full sister is Reserve Champion Mare in Brazil, and he has sired New York Futurity Champion sons and Texas Futurity Champion daughters.

"At this point, he's being used strictly as a show horse. This will be the last year we will show him," says Taylor.

Taylor owns Taylor Ranch, a 500-acre spread in Preston, Idaho, "with mountains, rivers, valleys and streams...the horses love being here," he says.

Rick has had horses since he was two or three years old, starting with a Shetland pony. When he was sixteen, he bought his first Arabian stallion, Sardare, whom he owned until he died at the age of twenty-two. "When my family couldn't eat, he did. He sold me on Arabians and we've had them ever since," says Taylor, who also raises Piedmontese cattle on his ranch.

"Horses are part of my life," says Rick. "I can't imagine not having at least one. When you have as many as we have, they become part of the family." Everyone feels so connected he says, that when a new foal arrives, all the horses are aware of it and whinny to one another as if to pass the message, "All right, fellas, we got this one out."

"Both *Nariadni (who also stands at Taylor Ranch) and Muscateer have led us to national recognition for having top quality Arabian horses," says Taylor. "Without them and our fine broodmare band it would have been a much longer time coming, if at all. Much of the credit goes to Howard Kale, Jr., for opening the door to Russia and bringing to the United States such fine horses as *Nariadni, *Muscat, *Nahodka and others and in being so free with his time and knowledge in helping us."

"Howard Kale, Jr. bred Muscateer," says Rick, "then sold him to Georgian Hills, a farm in Scottsdale, which showed the stallion quite extensively for a time. Then followed a period of about three or four years when he was not shown at all."

Two years ago, Rick and Paula Taylor purchased Muscateer, along with Lady Topaz, a Canadian Top Ten Mare, and another mare named Desert Topaz at a sale of Georgian Hills stock. "Two and a half months after we bought Muscateer he was a Champion Stallion," says Taylor.

"He is a wonderful horse, a typey Arabian, but also an exciting horse. He's also a unique horse," he adds. "I've got fifty horses and only one like him. We have had absolutely no problem with the horse since we got him. But I think people get intimidated by his growl. He's loud and noisy and very deep-throated. I've got one of his foals in the barn that sounds like a tiger.

"Muscateer will have about thirty-one foals on the ground this year. His get go like hotcakes," says Taylor. "The first foals born this year were sold within five weeks of being born.

"Along with the internationally-known stallion *Nariadni, Muscateer complements our Russian Arabian breeding program, utilizing our straight Egyptian, pure Polish, and Crabbet mares," adds Taylor. "We are well on our way to producing some of the most beautiful Arabians in the world."

Beau Shannon

After a prolonged illness that caused life to lose a lot of its sparkle for Jennalee C. Thompson, she was advised by her doctor to find something that might interest her, and do it!

When she attended the Arabian National Show in 1979, she discovered Arabian horses, finding them so exquisitely beautiful in the show ring and lovingly friendly and inquisitive in their stalls that she lost her heart to them, then and there. She had found what the doctor had ordered. She vowed to look for the barn with the most Arabians in it and to take riding lessons there, just to be near them.

Beau Shannon belonged to the owner at the stable she chose. Though the 14.2 black bay Arab stallion was a show horse, because of his willing and gentle nature, he was used on occasion as a lesson horse. On her very first visit she was allowed to ride him.

It took Jennalee's husband two months to say yes when she asked if she could have Beau. The morning after he did, she raced to the barn to tell the owner, only to learn that the night before, a man had called to say he was flying in from Tucson to see Beau. He bought Beau, who was to stay on to be trained for six weeks to compete in a show in Albuquerque. After that, the new owner would take him home with him.

At first Jennalee wouldn't go near Beau, but after three days she realized that if six weeks was all that was left to them, then she'd make the best of them. She walked him, groomed him, rode him every chance she got and when the day came to deliver him to the show grounds, she rode along in the truck with her heart in her throat, determined to see if the man would consider selling him to her. He said no, but he did give her right of first refusal if he ever decided to sell Beau.

Jennalee went home and cried for three hours, believing she would never hear from that man. "Why would he want to give up such a wonderful, push-button, Western pleasure horse?" she asked. Beau Shannon had been a Region 1 Western Pleasure Champion in the late 70's.

Five months later, however, the man called her with the news he was going to take Beau to Scottsdale and sell him if she did not want him. Later Jennalee heard that Beau had spooked with the owners' daughter on board in the show ring.

One week later, Beau was delivered to Jennalee's house. When he came out of the trailer she could hardly believe her eyes. The color was right, the blaze and socks were right, but instead of the calm, sweet, heavy-set fellow that left in July, there stood a slick-as-a-whistle, high-as-a-kite, snorty stud. She altered his diet, and in about a month he came back down to earth and was the calm and gentle horse she once knew.

Jennalee thought Beau might enjoy a new challenge—dressage. "We tried it and both loved it," she says. "Beau became the keeper of all my hopes and dreams and fears, as I became a twelve-year-old child again," she says. "Did we turn each other's lives around? Yes! Our lives went from the boredom of a hum-drum housewife and barn-sour horse to the adventure of exploration into the mind and spirit of another being, and as different as we were—male and female, horse and human—finding a common ground based in trust, loyalty, integrity, and love, and sharing the joy of living in the world together.

"Beau Shannon showed me that the dream of unconditional love in this world is true, and he taught me to take hold of that dream and share it, no matter what the source might be."

On January 16, 1989, a broken shoulder claimed Beau Shannon. "I don't know that I will ever know another being of such nobility and inner beauty and though I shed a tear over my great loss, I never regret a moment of knowing him," says Jennalee. "He was my fondest joy, my dearest friend, and it is my deepest longing and hope that when it is my time to leave this reality, his will be the first face I see on the other side."

Juan De Shawn

"Take Juan Leap Ahead," "Juan Forward Step," and "Juan Decision," reads the ad copy for Weidel's Boxwood Farm in Pennington, New Jersey, beneath an alabaster horse leaping exuberantly into the air.

The delightful word plays are on "Juan" great horse, the Arabian stallion, Juan De Shawn.

He belongs to Pamela Weidel, who had a childhood fantasy that remained a longing even into adulthood to own a famous or important white horse.

She acquired her own horse at age 12, then entered the Arabian horse business in 1978, and began racing in 1985. But it wasn't until seven years ago that she was lucky enough to find Juan De Shawn, the 15-hand grey stallion who has fulfilled her fantasy.

"Juan De Shawn absolutely put us on the map. He is a well-known sire and grandsire of successful race and show horses and his get and grandget are scattered around the world. He is a special horse in more ways than one," she says.

An athlete, he sires athletes. His winning 1991 get include Juan's Karita Ku, Kentucky Stakes and multi-winner; Shawn's Kandi, multi-winner in California; Shawna Flame Ku and Juan And Only, both California multi-winners. Coming on strong for '92 are Juan De Kon, Juan For The Money and Shawndelle.

Pamela originally purchased Juan De Shawn in partnership to breed to her racing stock. He had already sired many winners including the IAHA Horse of the Year and California Race Horse of the Year, By Golly, and his daughter Shawna Dew had started to win big.

By the following year, she bought her partner out of his share, and since then has turned down substantial offers for Juan, who has become the main focus of Boxwood Farm.

Juan De Shawn is a stakes winner of the heart as well. Foaled in 1971, he was eight years old and into his own racing and dressage career when he put his foot through a fence. Veterinarians said any other horse would have had to be destroyed, as Juan's pastern bone was multi-fractured. His then-owner Robbie Rogers agreed to surgery, and a metal plate was placed in the stallion's foot.

"This 'wonder horse' has never taken a lame step since," says Pamela. "He has quite a strong will and high level of courage which he prepotently passes on to his offspring. I strongly feel his attitude and strength which he passes on to his offspring are largely the reasons for their continued success in racing."

Although Juan De Shawn is not a family horse, Pamela and her husband Richard derive great enjoyment from owning him. "He is sweet enough that from time to time we let someone sit on his back, including children. Otherwise, he is too valuable to ride.

"He is also all stallion. Although he likes people, he is most concerned about his broodmare band. He knows that when a trailer pulls up, the mare inside is for him," Pamela says. Yet she can go into his pen anytime and he will stand for her with no ties or halter and let her do anything to him. "Juan is a perfect gentleman," she says.

"Sometimes we watch his foals walk up to his pen and sniff him. They know they're related. It is as though they say 'We want to grow up to be like you, Dad,' colts in particular."

Pamela, a professional horsewoman, breeder and equine professional consultant, says, "Horses have been my salvation. I turned to horses when things didn't seem good to me in my adolescent years. And now the business and professional equine involvement has given me purpose and a focus on new challenges and goals."

Finding and owning Juan De Shawn, she adds, has taught her, "more than anything, that I don't have to settle for less.

"See you in the winner's circle, more than Juan time," she couldn't resist ending her conversation with me.

Huckleberry Bey++

"Bay-Abi++, Bay El Bey++... who is next?" Sheila Varian mused in the early 1970s, naming the two magnificent breeding stallions that had been superhorses of the breed and the strength of Varian Arabians for so many years.

Varian Arabians, then officially in its twentieth year of Arabian horse breeding, had just enlarged its facilities in Arroyo Grande, California, and was planning a show barn; and Sheila, who had established herself as a breeder and trainer to be reckoned with, was anticipating a third-generation sire line colt.

"In a way, I knew who he was, how he would look," she recalls today. "He was out there, and I knew I was going to get him. And that's the important part, the knowledge that we had the wherewithal to produce him. He could have come from any number of breedings."

But it was Taffona, a bay 1966 daughter of Raffon out of Waneta, that was instrument of the creation of a horse that would newly embody Varian's ideals...a horse that would beome a third-generation *World* Sire of Significance and a second-generation *World* Legacy Sire, a landmark horse for Varian Arabians as a breeding stallion who would sire champion sons and champion daughters, both performance and halter champions, and be breathtakingly beautiful.

"Just as I kept rolling the athletic ability through the horses we produced, I kept bringing in the pretty," explains Sheila. In line with that philosophy, Taffona was

bred to Bay El Bey++ Canadian National Champion Stallion, National Reserve Champion Stallion, Scottsdale Champion Stallion, Legion of Merit and sire of National Champions. Bay El Bey++ is the son of Bay-Abi++, National Champion Stallion, National Top Ten English Pleasure, National Top Ten Western Pleasure, Legion of Merit, and sire of National Champions in halter and performance.

As a result of that mating, on March 19, 1976, Taffona foaled a black-bay colt with a little boy sparkle in his eyes that made only one name possible: Huckleberry, for his adventuresome Huck Finn attitude, and Bey for his sire.

Huckleberry Bey quickly established his prowess in the halter ring by winning the Cal-Bred Futurity and U.S. National Reserve Championship Futurity Colt. Sheila then set out to prove Huckleberry Bey in Performance. As an English pleasure horse, Huckleberry Bey brought in the titles of 1984 U.S. National Reserve Champion English Pleasure, and 1980, 1982, and 1983 United States Top Ten English Pleasure and 1982 Scottsdale Champion English Pleasure.

The United States and Canadian National wins of his offspring kept pace, and Huckleberry Bey has been recognized as a sire of national winners each year since 1984.

The record for Huckleberry Bey as a sire of winners through the 1991 Nationals is twenty-one winners with a collective score of seven National Championships (three in halter, four in performance), nine Reserves (two in halter, seven in performance), and thirty-six Top Tens (twelve in halter and twenty-nine in performance).

The National performance wins are varied in disciplines: pleasure driving, western pleasure, native costume, park, formal driving, English pleasure, and country English pleasure.

The Huckleberry Bey prepotency is easy to spot. "Walk into a halter or performance class, anywhere in the country, and pick out the Huckleberry Beys," says Sheila. "The first clue is a beautifully arched neck, then the way they move. The willowiness, the freedom, the fluidity, will tell you you are looking at a Huckleberry Bey.

"Bay-Abi++, while he sired some wonderful daughters, had more lasting influence through his sons, as has Bay El Bey++," continues Sheila. "They were sires of sires. Now we have this third generation stallion that sires sons and daughters equally well.

"It's not an easy chore for a young stallion to come up through a legacy of that magnitude and deliver what his ancestry demands of him. But Huckleberry Bey has more than proven himself worthy of that role," concludes Sheila.

Bay-El-Bey++

Crowned as the "king maker," sire of a dynasty of champion-siring sons, Bay-El-Bey++ might never have existed had his grandam not planted her hooves firmly into Polish soil and refused to go to Russia.

It was long ago, September, 1939, at the Janow-Podlaski State Stud in Poland. As Nazi forces spearheaded toward Janow from the west, the Stud was evacuated toward the east in an effort to get the horses to safety. Stopped at every avenue of escape, the Poles were forced to return to Janow. As the horses turned in at home, they were met by the Russians occupying the stud. Two weeks later the troops left, taking with them about 180 of Janow's best Arabians. But not Najada.

Najada, a pretty grey mare, refused to be haltered by a Russian soldier. She struck at him, injuring him, and he abandoned his efforts. Najada stayed behind, and became a Polish national heroine.

Her daughter, *Naganka, foaled in 1952, became a "mail-order mare" in 1961, when California breeder Sheila Varian of Varian Arabians in Arroyo Grande, California, gambled on what she considers the best bargain she's ever made; she purchased three Arabian mares sight unseen from Poland through an English agent. One of them was the tall, willowy, snow white *Naganka, "more beautiful than you could bear," says Sheila.

On April 25, 1969, bred to Varian's National Champion Stallion Bay-Abi++, *Naganka produced a bay colt, neatly trimmed with a small star and two fetlock-high socks – Bay-El-Bey++.

Due to family illness, Sheila could not spend much time with the colt while he was growing up. Destiny, however, kept tabs on its favorite.

She sold Bay-El-Bey++ when he was two. He was to be delivered at the Scottsdale show, but injured himself and was dead lame. Sheila made every effort, but the day before she was to leave for Scottsdale, the veterinarian declared him unsound. Sheila returned the buyer's money at Scottsdale. Within a week Bay-El-Bey++ healed and went sound. Sheila Varian accepted what was meant to be; he was never offered for sale again.

As the young stallion matured, Sheila saw that Bay-El-Bey++ was the realization of her breeding ideals in one glorious bay package combining power and refinement.

Tall, with a beautiful natural arch to his exceptionally long neck, he has very long hips, powerful muscling running down into the gaskin and forearm, and well set, correct, good-sized knees. He has a large, soft eye with a lovely expression set in a magnificently sculpted head.

As for character, like his sire, Bay-Abi++, he is very sensitive and concerned about doing the right thing. Sheila says she relates to Bay-El-Bey++ on a very inner level of vibration. "It's unspoken," she says.

At the age of three Bay-El-Bey++ began to win and never let up, stockpiling the awards – 1977 Canadian National Champion Stallion, 1974 and 1976 U.S. National Reserve Champion Stallion, Scottsdale Reserve Champion English Pleasure, six times U.S. National Top Ten Stallion, Legion of Merit.

The recipient of so many desirable characteristics from his ancestors, Bay-El-Bey++'s ability to consistently pass those traits along was like having your cake and eating it too, Sheila says.

Bay-El-Bey++ has sired more than one hundred champions, and his thirty-one National winners have won more than eighty National performance and halter titles. Other sons have created dynasties of their own. To name a few: Huckleberry Bey++, Barbary+++, Bey Shah+, Moonstone Bey V, Talisman Bey, Cinco Bey, Moonlight Bey, Bay Dubonnett++, Balajkar Bey V, August Bey V, Woodwind V.

Sheila Varian, "with humility intended," calls Bay-El-Bey++ "a true superhorse of the breed. I look at Bay-El-Bey++ and he's just what a horse is supposed to look like as far as I'm concerned. He's stately, dignified, a grand horse, and he's quiet in his grandeur. He is to me what this breeding business is all about."

Imperial Phanilah

There is something about the regal grey Egyptian-bred mares which reminds me of the lovely, graceful, enchanted swans in Tschiakovsky's "Swan Lake Ballet." Imperial Phanilah is one of those – a true beauty queen whose superiority has been paid homage since she was very young.

She was a Champion at the IAHA Yearling Breeders Sweepstakes, a Champion Straight Egyptian Two-Year-Old Filly at the 1986 Egyptian Event, European Champion and World Reserve Champion Filly at the prestigious Salon du Cheval in Paris in 1986. After which she was crowned 1987 U.S. Top Ten Futurity Filly in Albuquerque, New Mexico.

Today Phanilah is a broodmare in the green pastures of Valour Arabians in Smyrna, Delaware. Howell

and Margo Wallace had heard casually, over Sunday evening dinner in March, 1990 from trainer Eileen Verdieck that perhaps Phanilah might be available for purchase. By the following Wednesday morning, Howell Wallace was on his way to Bishopville, South Carolina to pick her up from Whitehaven Farm.

"I had always watched her, always rooted for her and had always wanted an Ansata Imperial daughter," says Margo. "I couldn't wait to get Phanilah home so I could put her in our barn and just look at her. I wanted to see her in our pastures."

Margo reports that like many top show mares who become broodmares, Phanilah is seductively charming with people. With loud, trumpeting whinnies, she welcomes admirers as she races across the pasture to greet visitors. She obviously has never forgotten how wonderful it was to get all that attention before an audience. So busy does she get with her "career," making sure no one goes ungreeted at the farm, that often *Wadeea, with whom she is turned out, babysits her foal for her.

From the start, the beauty and elegance of the Egyptian Arabian horse captivated Howell and Margo and sold them on the breed. As the couple began to establish Valour Arabians in 1981, their dream was to own a straight Egyptian mare.

"Back in 1982 and 1983, straight Egyptian mares were so highly priced that we hoped to someday own ONE," explains Howell, the president of the Pyramid Society since 1990.

"Today we have fourteen, and think highly of all of them," he adds. "Three, however, are extraordinary by anyone's standards: *Wadeea, who produces performance horses, Flying Tessie, (also profiled in this book), and Imperial Phanilah...each a queen in her own right. Without these particular mares we would never have accomplished what we have and in so short a time."

Imperial Phanilah's pedigree is as regal as her appearance. Her sire, Ansata Imperial, was a U.S. Top Ten Stallion and sire of National winners in performance and halter, including 1988 U.S. National Reserve Champion Stallion Imperial Imdal+, the leading sire at the Egyptian Event for the past three years. Phanilah's grandsire on the paternal side was U.S. National Champion Stallion Ansata Ibn Sudan. Phanilah's dam, Imperial Phanadah, the producer of three other champions, is by U.S. Top Ten stallion *Ibn Moniet El Nefous, and Phanilah's second dam is the gorgeous *Pharrah, dam of 1989 Canadian Top Ten Futurity Colt Royal Mikhiel. Phanilah herself produced the exquisite 1991 filly Valour Saphina by *Ibn Safinaz, for the Wallaces, and will be bred again in 1993 to the same stallion.

Soon those pastures will be populated by a whole corps de ballet of lovely "swans"...

Flying Tessie

Howell and Margo Wallace got their first look at Flying Tessie in September, 1986, at an Arabian racehorse sale at Delaware Park Racecourse. Bob and Pam Halbrook, owners of top racehorse and top race sire, By Golly, had brought their superstar race mare to the auction to sell her 1987 unborn foal sired by By Golly.

"I thought she was the neatest mare. The auction was held right off the saddling paddock and the horses were paraded for over an hour," says Margo. "All that time, Tessie continued to prance and rattle her teeth, even though she was heavy in foal; she thought she was going to get to race."

Margo had heard some of the legends about Tessie. In her first Delaware start of one mile and seventy yards in 1984, Tessie was carrying 113 pounds. She jumped out of the gate, took the lead and won by thirty-one lengths, still a record today at Delaware Park for both Arabians and Thoroughbreds.

That was but one of the races that made Flying Tessie probably the greatest Arabian race mare in modern history. Named 1985 Race Mare of the Year and 1985 Delaware Filly of the year, she earned her title in a series of thrilling contests which culminated with her victory in the Delaware Arabian Oaks on September 2, 1985.

In that race, she carried a whopping 130 pounds over the one mile and seventy yards, but Tessie was perfectly conditioned for that day. The minute she stepped onto the track on her way to the starting gate, her tail was curled over her back, her foxy little ears were up and she was just dancing on her toes. She led wire to wire to win by five and a half lengths in 2:00.

Throughout her brilliant racing career, Flying Tessie proved that speed doesn't come from size alone. Tessie stands just barely 14.1-3/4 with her shoes on, and when she's in peak racing shape, she tips the scales at a lean, mean 830 pounds.

Bred by Beverly Thomas, trained by her husband Darrell, Tessie even as a little filly had a thing about wanting to be the leader.

"We had Flying Tessie and her dam NZ Ababa out with the Quarter Horse and Thoroughbred mares and their foals and that filly would run from daylight to dark," says Beverly. "They'd all take off together and first the Quarter Horse foals would quit, then the Thoroughbred foals would quit, but Tessie would still be trying to get somebody to run with her."

At the end of her first season in 1983, Darrell entered her in the six-furlong California Derby at Los Alamitos. The only filly in a field of colts, she won it by five lengths in 1:07.3 carrying 115 pounds, edging out colts who had outrun her earlier in the season when she was green. With that victory, Flying Tessie was named 1983 California Filly of the Year. "I knew she had it in her, because I raced her daddy, Tiki Tessar, and he was one of the greatest. He still holds records for both five furlongs and one and a half miles," says Darrell.

The Halbrooks of Rehoboth Beach, Delaware, then bought the filly. She started nine times in 1985, finishing in the money in eight of those races. At the end of the season, the Halbrooks retired Tessie.

In 1991, five years after they first saw her, Tessie was bought by the Wallaces, breeders whose broodmare farm, Valour Arabians at Smyrna, Delaware, is based on fourteen straight Egyptian mares. The Wallaces bought Tessie "primarily because there is no mare with a race record like hers in the Egyptian gene pool," says Margo. "Additionally, our friendship with the Halbrooks is such that when they moved to Tucson, Pam couldn't stand to see Tessie, who had been raised on green grass, standing in the desert, and she wanted her to come back to Delaware."

Tessie to date has been a very successful producer and will be bred for the remainder of her life to straight Egyptian race sires like Moniet El Nafis (who sired 1989 Armand Hammer Classic winner Imperial Na Laseef) to match their heart and speed with her indomitable desire and determination to win.

FF Summer Storm

When Betty Zekan went to her first all-Arabian show in Ohio in 1978, her neighbor was the only person she knew there. So naturally, after the show was over, Betty went back to his stalls to visit. There she found the two show judges inquiring if her neighbor's mare, FF Summer Storm, was for sale.

"She wasn't," Betty remembers, "but I thought if she's so good the judges are interested, we'll have to keep our eyes on her." Betty and her husband Bill had established Zekan Arabians at Hickory Lane Farms at Richfield, Ohio in 1973, and they were always on the lookout for superb stock.

So, the Zekans asked their farm manager to inquire occasionally about the mare and finally one day Betty learned she was indeed for sale. The mare was FF Summer Storm, a 1974 bay daughter of *Bask (National Champion Stallion and National Champion Park) and out of Zarahba.

"So I had to get Bill up there to see her. He hadn't even attended a horse show!" says Betty. "But he went to see her, came home a bit later and said, 'Guess what? I bought a horse!' From that day on, Bill became one of the biggest fans of the Arabian breed and over a hundred horses later, Summer still remained his favorite.

"Shortly after the purchase of Summer Storm, she was sent to Gene LaCroix who put the finishing touches on this naturally gifted mare," Betty continues. "In 1979 Gene and Summer won the Arabian Triple Crown in performance: Champion English Pleasure at Scottsdale, the Canadian Nationals and the United States Nationals.

"After taking off a few years for motherhood, Summer Storm returned to the ring and won Scottsdale Champion Pleasure Driving and the 1985 United States National Champion Informal Combination," says Betty.

"Those were the golden years for Bill and me. Through Summer Storm, we met a great many people we would otherwise have missed in our lives. When you have a horse as great as Summer, people seek you out to tell you how much they enjoy watching her perform. I received letters and phone calls from admirers, and she seemed to be everyone's favorite. Summer loved to compete and her way of going was so exciting – though she always made it look easy. Competing trainers told me they could always tell when Summer entered the ring, because 'it sounded like a freight train!' She was truly a once-in-a-lifetime show horse."

Farm manager Kristen Cusac, who cared for Summer on a daily basis at the Zekans' farm, always felt Summer was actually happier before her retirement from the ring. She never really seemed to enjoy the long, lazy, hazy days of being a broodmare, and could frequently be caught longingly watching the horse trailer as it departed for the horse show.

FF Summer Storm died in 1989 at the age of fifteen, just three weeks from delivering her sixth foal. Her memory lives on at Zekan Arabians through her son, Storme Warning, a bay stallion sired by the many-times National Champion Park Horse, Zodiac Matador.

"Stormy most closely resembles his famous dam and is following her footsteps in the performance ring," says Betty.

Bill Zekan passed away in January, 1991. At his request, Betty continues to follow her passion for horses and she is showing and breeding, keeping the legacy of FF Summer Storm alive through her descendants.

*Witez II

At age ninety-seven, Earle Hurlbutt, who owned the great Arabian stallion *Witez II from 1949 to 1965, maintains that *Witez' greatness came from good breeding and the trials of his life, but what truly set him apart from all other horses was the amazing effect he had on the persons with whom he came in contact.

That effect continues to take hold even now, more than twenty-five years after *Witez' death, so inspiring is his life story.

It begins in Poland, where *Witez was foaled at the Janow-Podlaski State Stud in 1938. The Poles reared him and the Germans cared for him as he endured the hardships of World War II. In 1945, personnel of General George Patton's Third Army rescued this gallant stallion and brought him to the United States. He was sold at a U.S. Army Remount auction in 1949 to Earle and Frances Hurlbutt in whose stewardship he established himself as a show champion and legendary sire of champions. *Witez sired more than 200 foals in this country, and his descendants continue to make their mark in the show ring, on the racetrack, and in distance competition.

In 1985, Kaethe Ellis-Williams of Carbondale, Colorado, came across the story of *Witez, put down in the book *And Miles To Go* by Linell Smith. Kaethe has not been the same since.

"The story touched me deeply and because the book was out of print, I was determined to get it republished," she says. "More people needed to enjoy this special tale and I felt it had all the right ingredients for a great motion picture as well."

Kaethe, who has dedicated many years to "Project *Witez," succeeded in getting the book republished by the Arabian Horse Trust (Denver, Colorado) in 1986. Then in 1990 she was able to get two-time double-Oscar winner Robert Wise, producer and director of *Sound of Music* and thirty-eight other films, to read the book. Although Mr. Wise is not a "horsey" person, he loved the story and immediately recognized the dramatic potential of the story. To hear him tell it, *Witez showed him the war as he had never seen it before.

"Not long ago I found a copy of the book *And Miles To Go* at my vacation door in Aspen, Colorado," comments Wise. "Before I knew it, I was being held captive by a young Arabian horse and a Polish boy named Stasik Kowalski in the middle of World War II, somewhere between war-torn Poland and the Russian border. We were running and hiding between the forests and swamps, soldiers and gunfire. We carefully made our way through the dangerous countryside, fearing for the horses and dodging enemies from two directions. The hunger and terror were overwhelming and the tragedies mounted. The young horse *Witez would be of much interest to both the Russians and Germans and Stasik and his sister Stacia were willing to risk their lives for the horse and their country. The greatness of *Witez had been predicted and once foaled he was immediately given the name that meant chieftain, knight, prince and hero, all in one..."

Wise realized this was no ordinary story and *Witez no ordinary horse, but rather the common denominator to all who came in contact with him. The miles he traveled, the borders he crossed, the languages he heard—this was a horse who had lived history, made history, and to some extent, even changed history. "This was a horse that earned every aspect of his name," Wise told Kaethe.

Since that snowy day in Aspen, Robert Wise has acquired an option on *And Miles To Go* and is currently in the process of seeking investors who would show their support by funding the project.

Horse heroes are few and far between these days, as are good family movies with the qualities found in the magical story of *Witez. Wise is a proven producer of classics and a movie such as this could well be one of the best horse films ever made. Kaethe continues in her quest to find supporters for this film about a horse that was real, a horse with a message to share and a spirit that lives on.

Medalion

"Medalion is *Bask born all over again," says Mike Villaseñor, staff member at Colonial Wood Arabians, in Arlington, Texas. "He's a mirror image of *Bask – the bay coat color, the star, the four little white socks, the motion, the length of neck. The only ways he differs from *Bask are to his credit. He's bigger than *Bask, about 15.1, and has more hip than *Bask. Genotypically he's tailor-made to breed to the *Bask daughters. Medalion is a Comet grandson, so you can breed him back to *Bask-bred mares that are out of Comet-bred mares; you can breed him to *Bask daughters of course for a super cross, and you can breed him to double *Bask-bred mares. The crosses are consistent and his foals are very *Bask-looking; if the world thought we'd lost *Bask, we've just found him." Mike, a lifelong horseman, sold Colonial Wood owner, Paul Wood, some of his very first horses in 1976.

*Bask, of course, needs no special introduction – he remains the all-time leading sire of champions and National winners in Arabian breed history. His accomplishments as a sire remain the standard for breed records.

Medalion is a great grandson of *Bask through his dam Marushka, who was sired by Negatraz (*Bask x *Negotka by Negatiw), *World* Sire of Significance and sire

of thirteen National winners. (His sire, *Dar, was a Regional Reserve Champion Stallion and halter champion.)

Medalion came to Colonial Wood in 1982 as a yearling. Paul and Dody Wood and Johnny Downing, their farm manager at the time, were at Patterson Arabians in Sisters, Oregon, looking for broodmares. It was Johnny who spotted Medalion in the yearling pasture and immediately recognized his quality. Dick Patterson reaction however was: "Not for sale. We've been breeding for that one for twenty-five years." He didn't even want to talk about it.

It took three or four months of negotiations before a deal was struck, says Paul. He and Dody had collected a lot of good *Bask daughters by that time, and it seemed they would be a good cross with Medalion. They saw *Bask several times in the last few years of his life, and he was just a phenomenal stallion to them. "The fire, the long neck, the vitality, the look, and the demeanor. When we saw Medalion as a yearling, he reminded us of *Bask, and today he looks so much like *Bask, it gives you chills," they say.

Medalion, like *Bask, consistently sires both halter and performance winners. More than twenty Medalion offspring had collected champion or reserve titles through mid-1991.

Medalion has the distinction of having been bred to five National Champion English Pleasure mares: Firenella, Lite My Fire, Afire, FF Summer Storm, and Basquelle. "We don't believe any other stallion has done that," says Mike.

Rick Moser, manager/trainer at Colonial Wood, schooled Medalion, but says, "There never was a thought of getting him in the show ring; he had become too valuable as a breeding horse."

Medalion has some of his finest moments when the Woods entertain their insurance company managers at Colonial Wood. About 100 or 150 people gather around the rail, and Medalion is turned loose. He runs and throws his head up and trots around and shows the crowd how an Arabian stallion should look and move. After he's shown off for a while, he invariable spots Dody in the crowd and runs directly to her for her recognition. Medalion occasionally decides that he doesn't want to be put away. The more grooms out there trying to catch him, the more fun he has. He's in his glory in those moments.

"A definite personality at Colonial Wood," adds Rick. "His attitude seems to be, 'This is my place. You may approach me.' He's a gentleman at all times, very easy to work with, and not a mean bone in his body. But turn him loose for a crowd and he's the cockiest horse in all of Texas." But what else would one expect from the heir apparent to *Bask?

Bask Melody

Paul and Dody Wood, owners of Colonial Wood Arabians in Arlington, Texas, had seen Bask Melody named United States National Champion Mare at the 1976 United States Nationals. The announcement that the mare would be offered in the Lasma Sale III at Scottsdale in February, 1977, came soon after, with pre-sale rumors that as a National Champion Mare she would go for about $250,000.

Paul was geared up to bid on another horse in the sale, and when he didn't get that lot, he felt down, Dody remembers. "But he didn't have much time to be disappointed, because Bask Melody was next on stage. 'Either you bid, or I will,' I told him. He didn't raise his hand until $80,000. We got her at $140,000, the best buy we ever made, because Bask Melody set the mood for Colonial Wood. From then on, every horse we acquired or bred had to compare favorably with her."

Like many an Arabian breeding farm, Colonial Wood, a fifty-acre facility, is the realization of a dream. It all started back in 1976, when Paul Wood bought his wife Dody a present of an Arabian stallion.

Dody was a typical horse-crazy girl who grew up without a horse of her own. She rode green-broke horses for a trainer who lived down the road, and found that a Half-Arabian pinto she met there meshed with her daydreams. Books on horses were read and reread and dreams of ownership persisted into young adulthood. "When you're young, you create your ideal in your mind and I created that beautiful horse," says Dody.

"When I discovered a pure white Arabian stallion I knew I had found my dream," Dody remembers. "He had the pretty short head, the big dark eyes, and beyond that I didn't care."

Paul had asked Dody to check out library books on other breeds and to consider them as well. She dutifully checked out the books, but never cracked a one. Paul, with some sort of presentiment, began to build a fourteen-stall barn that was soon filled to capacity.

That was about the time they bought Bask Melody, with the intent of establishing a superior broodmare band, primarily of Polish bloodlines.

Bask Melody was one of the fourteen offspring of Susecion, a mare who was such a super producer she was called "a golden hen." Owned by Dr. Fred and Florence Ragland of El Cajon, California, Susecion went to *Bask for nine of her foals, becoming one of his most durable mates.

Bask Melody, Susecion's pretty bay filly, was foaled in May, 1972. She was sold to Lasma where she was shown to her 1976 Scottsdale Reserve Champion Mare and Buckeye Champion Mare titles. That fall at the United States Nationals, she went National Champion Mare.

The second highest selling mare in the Lasma sale, Bask Melody carried the bonus of a breeding to the stallion *El Paso; she foaled Dear Melodie in April, 1978. But first, in the Woods' ownership she went on to add the 1977 Canadian National Championship Mare title to her record, thus giving her dam, the memorable Susecion, her second double National Champion Mare; Fire Music, her full sister, was the other.

At Colonial Wood, Bask Melody produced fillies by *Aladdinn in 1980 and 1982 (Love Melody and Enchanting Melody) and a filly, Memorye, by *Eukaliptus in 1983. Bask Melody died in August, 1983 when Memorye was just three months old.

Thanks to the nature of Paul and Dody Wood's early purchases and the early National wins of mares such as *Bask Melody, Colonial Wood was established early on as a source of high quality stock.

Heritage Emir++

The horse sale had an interesting twist to it in that a "mystery horse" was going to be auctioned. Without any introduction, the curtain was raised just enough to reveal the legs of a horse trotting across the stage. It was as though the animal were moving in suspended animation, with each hoof rising to an incredible height before touching the earth again. The horse was no mystery to Deedie Wrigley-Hancock, who was sitting in the audience with then-husband Tom Chauncey. She had watched that same motion daily at Chauncey ranch in Scottsdale, where the rangy, black bay two-year-old colt, Heritage Emir++, had been brought to be conditioned for the sale, and Deedie knew she was seeing nothing short of the exceptional. Deedie had tried to convince the colt's owner and breeder, Ward Weaver, to let her buy Emir before the auction, but to no avail.

Deedie sat anxiously beside Chauncey, who was equally mesmerized and was bidding furiously. When the dust settled, Heritage Emir++ went back to the Chauncey ranch to stay.

During the early 1980s, Heritage Emir++ racked up an impressive number of championships in the driving and park horse divisions, but a National title eluded him. In 1983, it was decided that Deedie's daughter, Misdee, would show him in the amateur division.

This was a dream come true for Misdee, who was riding before she could walk and began showing horses when she was eight. She had always admired Emir and fervently wished she could ride this horse who seemed to fly without wings. When she first sat on him, some-

thing magical happened – a bond was cemented. It was as if both horse and rider realized they had been meant to be a team. An electrical current seemed to flow through the reins as she put him through his paces. Misdee knew she had found that "once in a lifetime" horse. Over the next couple of years they were almost undefeated, and together Misdee and Emir won the elusive National Champion English Pleasure AAOTR title. However, in an ironic quirk of fate, the pair's triumphant victory pass was the last time they would be together for several years.

When Deedie and Tom Chauncey were divorced it severed many ties, one of which was Deedie and Misdee's involvement at the Chauncey ranch. Misdee was no longer able to show horses, and she moved as far away as she could, to Florida, to try to dull the painful loss of the magical hours spent with Emir. Not just in the show ring, but quiet moments in the stall where the stallion would doze with his head in her lap, or beg his favorite treats, red grapes and Oreo cookies.

Then one September evening in 1986, Deedie called Misdee in Florida with a simple question: "Would you like to ride Emir in this year's National Championships?" Things had settled in the divorce. Misdee headed back to Arizona. There was a scant five weeks before the Nationals and neither horse nor rider had been in training. They couldn't have chosen a tougher year to get back into competition. Over ninety horses, including five former National Champions were vying for the same title, but Misdee and Emir emerged with National Reserve Champion English Pleasure AOTR 18 and Over.

After a decade in the ring, it came time to retire Emir to stud. Misdee and her mother decided that the 1988 National Championships would be his last show. On a crisp October night in Louisville, Kentucky, Misdee and Emir headed into the show ring for one last time. The coliseum was packed and the stallion sensed the importance of this particular competition. With ears pricked and tail held high, he put in a flawless performance. When the announcer finally took the microphone, he named Heritage Emir++ as the National Champion Ladies Side Saddle by unanimous decision.

When the award presentation was over, the lights were dimmed and Misdee and Emir were alone in the ring in the spotlight. With his neck wreathed in red roses, the stallion made his triumphant turn around the arena, his legs driving in that beautiful motion which had thrilled so many.

Emir's story does not end there. He still enjoys red grapes and Oreo cookies and lives a life of leisure at Kaaba Arabians in Scottsdale. There he relives his show ring days through his get, today taking their own victory passes.

Eagle NA+

Some horses pass only briefly through the lives of the people who love them, but the impression they leave is indelible and everlasting. Such is the case with Eagle NA+, who belonged to my friends Karen and Neil Wood of Myerswood Arabians in Lincoln, California.

I had met Neil in Spain, when he bought some sketches from John Fulton, the artist for this book. We share very special memories of such singularly Spanish events as the running of the bulls in Pamplona.

Shortly after their marriage, Neil and Karen decided to satisfy their separate and now converging childhood dreams to have horses as part of their lives. After much evaluation and study they formed Myerswood Arabians in 1980, with the goal of breeding Arabian horses in the tradition of the Polish stud farms – beautiful, athletic animals with willing dispositions.

One stallion stood out as their ideal, both physically and genetically – the dark bay stallion Eagle NA+, bred by film director and actor Mike Nichols. Eagle NA+ was by *Elkin++, the Canadian and United States Champion Stallion in 1972. His dam *Elzunia was considered to be one of the most beautiful mares in the world by her importer and owner, Mike Nichols. She left a permanent legacy to U.S. breeding programs in 1975 when at the age of 24, she gave birth to her last foal, Eagle NA+.

The Woods already had the nucleus of their broodmare band by the spring of 1989. By October of that year, they convinced Ken and Charlene Robinson of Sweet Home Arabians in Olympia, Washington, to sell them Eagle NA+ (whom they had bought from Nichols in 1981).

"What arrived on our ranch in the pre-dawn hours one frosty October morning in the guise of this stallion, was a rare and special friend," says Neil. "Eagle NA+, with his unique personality, far exceeded our expectations."

At Myerswood, Eagle NA+ literally lived with the Woods. He spent his nights in a large box stall attached to their house, adjacent to the office where Neil and Karen spent most of their evenings. Plexiglass windows allowed Eagle NA+ to look into their office and "keep tabs" on them.

The most special moment of the day for Neil and Karen was late at night when they'd go into Eagle NA+'s stall to say good night. At these times, the stallion, who was extremely talkative during the day with visitors, was as quiet and gentle as he could be animated during the day.

It was his habit to take one of their hands between his teeth and very gently massage that hand, a look of absolute contentment in his eyes. "I believe this was Eagle NA+'s equine version of holding hands," says Karen.

Tragically Neil and Karen had but one year with this personable, magnificent stallion. On October 1, 1990 he died as a result of a coronary artery aneurysm. But in that too-brief year he gave the Woods the gift of his friendship and many memories, as well as the camaraderie of the many people they met through owning him.

Last but not least he gave them anticipation and joy in the arrival of his 1991 foal crop, his last, which are all they had hoped to create when they chose Eagle NA+ as their ideal Arabian.

Those who shared the life of this special horse, whose lineage can be traced so far back through time, have not only become a part of history, but perhaps also of eternity.

Mafier

The elegant grey Arabian stallion Mafier is one of the newest additions to the state-of-the-art stables of Bill and Julie Wrigley, Wrigley Arabians, in Lake Geneva, Wisconsin.

"We purchased him in December, 1991 for our breeding program for two reasons," explains Julie Wrigley. "First we have a goal of breeding athletic Arabians. That in fact has been the goal of the Wrigleys since 1930. To us, this stallion exemplifies a very athletic horse – and for too long the breed got away from breeding good athletes."

Mafier has already proven himself, in athletic ability and in temperament, to be a superior show horse. Foaled March 29, 1986, as a three-year-old in 1989 Mafier dominated the English Pleasure Junior Horse division by being named both United States and Canadian National Champion English Pleasure Junior Horse. He added another victory with 1990 United States National Champion English Pleasure horse. Then in 1991, he became United States National Champion Informal Combination.

His accomplishments in National competition are no accident. His sire, Zodiac Matador, won 1984 Canadian National Champion Park and 1985 and 1987 United States National Champion Park, and his dam, Fierina, traces to many generations of National winners. Zodiac Matador is a son of *Bask++, himself a National Champion Stallion and National Champion Park horse, and sire of more National winners than any other Arabian stallion in the history of the breed. Fierina is by Gai Champion, the 1975 Canadian National Champion Stallion and sire of multiple National winners. Gai Champion's sire, Gay-Rouge, was twice Canadian Top Ten Stallion and once Top Ten English Pleasure as well. Fierina is out of Fiera Blanca, a daughter of *Naborr, well known as a sire of National Champions. She gives Mafier a second cross to the valued blood of *Bask++ through her dam, Arabask, a producer of National winners and full sister to two National Champions in performance.

Julie Wrigley knew Mafier from watching him in the show rings, mostly at the U.S. Nationals. (The young Mafier was owned by Helen and Stanley Fried of Las Vegas, Nevada, and shown by Raymond La Croix.) Which brings us to the second reason she bought him. She intends to show him herself in English Pleasure Amateur Owner To Ride.

"The nice thing about Arabian horses – stallions or mares – is that we who are not professionals can ride them and show them," says Julie, who has been showing them since 1988. As a child she showed Quarter Horses and hunters and jumpers. Then, when she was in high school, she met Deedie Wrigley, whom she calls her "mentor." "Deedie and her family had had Arabians since 1915 and I was enamored of the horse, and of the people who loved horses. They were very family-oriented," she says.

"Mafier is not a big horse," Julie adds, "Just 14.2, but he's very dynamic. You'd think he'd be snorty and blowy, but he's very easy to ride, very quick to bond with the rider. Another thing that's special about the Arabians is they're very people-oriented. They are responsive to the rider. It's more than training; it's the breed. Mafier has a big eye, very strong back and hip and loin. He's won four National Championships and we're hoping for more," says the pretty, petite Julie, who married Bill Wrigley in 1981 and set about re-establishing Wrigley Arabians in Lake Geneva.

"We started with Russian bloodlines. Now I find the origin of the horse isn't so important, but the quality of the individuals is," she says. "We in America are breeding the best Arabians in the world today, whereas historically the Russians and the Poles were considered the top breeders. Especially, Americans are breeding the best athletes, which is what each generation of Wrigley breeding has accomplished."

Duel

This utterly stunning true black Arabian stallion exceeds even the creative imagination of novelist Walter Farley. Perhaps the glorious looks and charisma of Duel can be attributed at least in part to the fact he is double *Bask++. He is sired by a *Bask++ son, Gdansk, and is out of a *Bask++ daughter, Joule.

Apart from that, tell me he sprung from the night-sea when the horse-god struck his trident in the waves, and I will believe it. A star perfectly placed between his eyes and a rakish snip on the nose illuminate a fabulous head sculpted in the most pleasing proportions. A long, upright neck, an intelligent, intense look in his eyes, and four white socks are some of the details.

Duel was foaled March 25, 1982, bred by Jerry and Joan Smola of Sweetwater, Texas. He now belongs to one of the luckiest horseowners in the world, Julie Wrigley. She first saw him in the show ring in Scottsdale, and the impact on her was such she knew she had to have him.

"This guy was so beautiful in the show ring, though he makes you feel the same way when he's in his stall. He wasn't really for sale, but he was by the time we made an offer," she says with a Mona Lisa smile, remembering the occasion.

Under the ownership of Bill and Julie Wrigley, Duel had a short but brilliant show career. He was twice Scottsdale Reserve Champion English Pleasure (1989 and 1990), Buckeye Champion English Pleasure, and United States Top Ten English Pleasure.

Then somehow he injured an ankle in his stall. "He went back to Scottsdale that next spring and we realized the injury was permanent," says Julie. "The vet told us that if we gave him a lot of medication, he could go back to the show ring. We said no." Instead they brought him to Wrigley Arabians in Lake Geneva, Wisconsin, where he has been used for breeding. (His oldest son, Firepower W, has just been started under saddle.)

At Wrigley Arabians, Duel is Julie's favorite riding horse. "I ride him all the time. He's perfectly sound," she says. "We just don't want to stress him in the show ring. On weekends I just saddle him up and ride him around the farm, which he loves." She regrets she did not get to show him.

When Duel was in the show ring, Julie recalls, "He was the prettiest horse to look at, every child's dream of the Black Stallion. Now he's my own private dream come true. He is the kindest horse, and a perfect gentleman. Even though he's a stallion and I'm a woman, there's never a concern for my safety. Both Mafier and Duel are pets. They don't nip. They don't bite."

Right now, she says, the plan at Wrigley Arabians is to breed all their mares to these two stallions, Duel or Mafier, "because we think they're such great athletes and they'll complement each other."

Duel, Julie notes, "is a very strong *Bask++ horse, with his greatest strength the flexibility in his neck. Duel is very balanced, so it is easy for him to be an athlete. He's an English horse, but he could be a stock horse. Arabians are supposed to be versatile!"

Horses are an enormous part of Julie's life. "I've been riding since I was two. I said 'horse' before I said 'Mom' and 'Dad.' I lead a somewhat stressful life in that it is busy, but I can go out and ride a horse and all the troubles of the world are gone."

How could they not, riding an ebony stallion who is kind as a kitten and more beautiful than a myth?

Talisman Bey

"I have many fond memories of my family and our horses. but the memory that will stay with me forever is my fifteen-year-old son, Steven, bringing Talisman Bey up from the pasture. The tall, slender Steven is running full speed, yelling out 'Yea, hah!' as Talisman gallops beside him with his mane and tail flowing in the wind. Both of them abounding with the joy of life and showing it, both glad to be with one another," says Steve Pekary, who with wife Myra owns and runs Tyra Arabians in Rapidan, Virginia.

"You know, a talisman is something magical, a good luck charm," adds Steve. "And in that respect, Talisman Bey was certainly well-named. He's brought us through the horse business to the point where he's supporting us. He's built this business around us and lets us make a living in something we love.

"Talisman Bey came into our lives in 1979, while we were visiting our good friends in Santa Maria, California, Mark and Ginny Fagerlin, who bred him," he recalls.

"When we saw him, he was a yearling growing up in the pasture, half-wild with his mane and forelock blowing in the wind. Every time we walked out to see him, his tail went up over his back and in playful fashion, he blew and snorted at our presence. At that point in our lives we had been involved with Arabians for several years, and were already leasing a stallion from the Fagerlins. Common sense would have dictated we didn't need another stallion. We were raising a family, had recently bought a small home, I was fairly fresh out of college and starting a new job and, most importantly, we couldn't afford him!!! His price was about twice my annual salary at that time.

"This horse, however, was so special that he became all-consuming in my thoughts. I secretly determined that somehow I was going to have this horse at home in Virginia! Or at least I thought it was my secret. On the plane ride home Myra and I sat in silence. I was trying to figure out how to convince Myra that we had to have Talisman Bey. Suddenly, out of nowhere, Myra turned to me and declared, 'We have to have Talisman Bey!'"

Help with financing and much moral support from the Fagerlins solved the problem, and in late 1980 Talisman arrived at his new home in Virginia.

"At this point, our lives took a major turn," says Steve. "In the next few years Talisman easily paid for himself and helped put us in the Arabian horse business on a full-time basis." By 1984 the Pekarys had purchased their farm, and that same year, Steve left his job with the local power company to work with horses.

His major focus soon came to be the showing of Talisman's offspring. They began winning on a consistent basis and soon became serious competition in the Arabian show arenas in the East. To date, he's sired sixty champion offspring out of 180 purebred registered foals, including eleven IAHA Breeders Sweepstakes Champions and four Reserve Champions, all shown by Steve Pekary.

"In short, Talisman Bey has given us our livelihood, our way of life, and a sense of pride that we have made a positive contribution to the breed. Our children, Allison, Ariana and Steven have all grown up with Talisman. With all the ups and downs of the business, all the highs and lows of showing, there is nothing to equal seeing your children riding or showing the get and grandget of our magical horse, Talisman Bey," says Steve.

"Making a living entirely in the horse business will not make anyone rich," he adds, "but the lifestyle that Talisman Bey has given me and my family has made us rich in many other ways. The dream I had as a small boy growing up in Cleveland of being a horse breeder and trainer has been fulfilled; the dream I had of raising beautiful horses and a beautiful family in a country setting has been fulfilled."

*Haracz

To John and Peggy Yates of Pay-Jay Arabians, beauty means white horses with big, black eyes.

The Yates have a breeding program at their ranch in Artesia, New Mexico, in the foothills of the Sacramento Mountains, unique to the Arabian horse world. Its goal is "to create a gene pool of Negatiw blood which we and other breeders can tap into, to improve the quality of Arabian horses when outcrossing," says John.

Why Negatiw? "Through our studies we discovered that great old stallion (by Naseem, a son of the immortal Skowronek) consistently sired horses not only in our favorite color, grey/white, but more importantly, with beauty, size and outstanding athletic ability," says John. "Now that he has died, the only way to preserve these genes is to linebreed or inbreed his sons, daughters and grandget; we have chosen to linebreed," which means breeding closely-related animals to concentrate good qualities.

The Yates had been seeking something special in a Palas/Negatiw cross for several years. The cross of Palas (bred at Tersk Stud in Russia and imported to Poland) and Negatiw daughters is considered by Polish breeders to be consistently excellent, and is known as "The Golden Cross."

"We set a budget as to what we would spend," says Peggy. "Then when we actually saw the stallion of our dreams (at the 1986 Polish Prestige Sale), the budget went right out the window. He was just the most beautiful Arabian stallion we had ever seen in any show in any country. We were both thunderstruck."

They had never had a horse affect them the way this charismatic, silver-white stallion with huge black eyes, called "the ideal cross between power and elegance," did when they first saw him.

John was determined to have *Haracz, says Peggy. So were several other people. When the gavel finally came down at a record $380,000 price, *Haracz's lead shank was handed over to the very happy Yates.

"After the hammer fell, we were walking on air" recalls Peggy. "In fact, we never came down out of the sky. We are still flying when it comes to *Haracz."

*Haracz has that effect on lots of people.

A race champion in Poland, his halter wins include the coveted European triple crown: 1983 National Champion of Poland, (European Reserve Champion that same year), 1985 Swedish National Champion, 1985 European Champion stallion.

In addition to these wins, he won numerous halter championships once he arrived in the U.S.

He was foaled January 27, 1976, sired by the Aswan son Palas, out of the alabaster *Harmonia PASB (Negatiw x *Harfa), considered by *Haracz's trainer Michael Byatt one of the five most beautiful mares in the world.

The Poles called him "a spectacular, brilliant individual, a phenomenal and powerful mover, perfect in conformation, a proven sire."

Under saddle he is described as being "full of fire and ready to go." In or out of the show ring, he is "presence personified."

Life has never been the same at Pay-Jay Arabians since he arrived. He has been a favorite of all visitors, and is considered a local celebrity.

Peggy Yates had a deep love for this beautiful animal, and the Yates' grandchildren are very attached to him. But John Yates is still the most taken by him.

Beyond the Yates' personal feelings for him, *Haracz, now chief herd sire at Pay-Jay, has brought worldwide recognition to their breeding program. His popularity has brought mares of diverse bloodlines from all over the U.S. and Canada to the farm.

"We have always desired a stallion with his credentials, and the ability to reproduce his qualities. *Haracz has culminated these dreams. We feel fortunate just to be a part of this great stallion's life," says Peggy, who is one of the warmest and kindest ladies that it has been my good fortune to know.

THE DUTCH WARMBLOOD

The modern Dutch Warmblood has made a meteoric rise to prominence as a sport horse in the international equestrian world in recent years.

The success of the Dutch horse is no accident. The stated goal of the Dutch breeding program is that of producing the best sport horse in the world. Good conformation, good gaits, excellent character, performance ability and soundness are some of the characteristics for which the Dutch horse is selectively bred.

The organization which supports, regulates and promotes Dutch breeding is the Royal Warmblood Studbook of the Netherlands or KWPN (*Koninklijk Warmblood Paardenstamboek in Nederland*), formed in 1969 as a private group by combining a number of independent regional organizations into one national breeding association. The affiliated breeding organization in North America is the North American Department of the Royal Warmblood Studbook of the Netherlands, or NA/WPN.

Members of the Royal Warmblood Studbook, 25,000 strong, are firmly united in their efforts to produce the best sport horses in the world for top international competition in jumping, dressage, eventing and driving as well as top horses for people who ride for recreation. Perhaps part of this bonded effort is traditional. Dutch horse breeders have been organized since 1887 when King William III recognized the first studbook, thus stimulating the breeding of registered horses.

The modern Dutch Warmblood evolved from two native Dutch breeds, the Gelderlander and the Groningen. The Gelderlander, developed on the light sandy soils of central Holland, was a stylish horse of medium stature, frequently chestnut with flashy white markings. The Groningen evolved on the heavy clay soils of northern Holland into a larger and heavier horse, frequently black. These horses became the ancestors of the modern sport horses of one of today's foremost horse-breeding countries and regions.

As farming became more mechanized after World War II, the breeding goal was redirected toward producing sport horses for pleasure. During this process of modernization, there was considerable influx from other countries – Thoroughbreds from France and England and Holsteiners and Trakehners from Germany. Even today, Dutch horses continue to be influenced by imported blood.

Today in Holland, three distinct types of horses are bred. The most numerous and internationally important is the *Rijpaardtype* or riding horse type, a distinctly modern, elegant sport horse bred for athleticism, good character and soundness. International jumpers, dressage horses, combined driving and vaulting horses are selected from this category.

Second is the *Tuigpaardtype* or show driving type, a stylish, high-stepping carriage horse shown rather like the American Fine Harness Horse. These horses are of mostly Gelderlander blood, with an infusion of Hackney.

Third is the *Basistype* or basic type, a stylish all-around horse reminiscent of the earlier Gelderlanders, useful for riding, driving, and farm work.

In Holland, only "Approved Breeding Stallions" may be used for breeding; mares are inspected and performance-tested. The Dutch stallion testing is said to be the most rigorous in the world. Stallions are not approved for life; offspring are constantly evaluated, and breeding licenses may be withdrawn.

The system is built around *Keurings*, evaluations of the horses, important events in the lives of Dutch breeders and riders and exciting spectator events for foreigners.

The mares qualify for a National Mare Show, but the highlight of the year is the Stallion Show, a spectacular extravanganza held in mid-winter in Utrecht, at which new breeding stallion prospects are selected to undergo the 100-Day Stallion Test in the spring to attain "Approved Status." This exciting event plays to a packed house of enthusiastic spectators. The VIP stands are filled with representatives from all the major studbooks of the world, as well as representatives of foreign Olympic teams and equestrian federations, all looking for the next "Dutch treat."

Consul

Consul is one of the superhorses at Iron Spring Farm in Coatesville, Pennsylvania, a farm owned by Stuart and Mary Alice Malone.

Consul's sire, Nimmerdor, holds the prestigious predicate of "Preferent" stallion from the Royal Dutch Warmblood Registry of the Netherlands, and is the leading sire of jumpers in Holland, just as Mary Alice's Roemer, who has also earned the predicate Preferent from the Dutch Warmblood Registry, is the leading sire of dressage horses.

Foaled in Holland in 1984, a 17-hand, dark bay with white markings, Consul is "Λ" rated by the KWPN (Dutch Warmblood Registry of the Netherlands) and is approved by the Oldenburg Registry and the International Sporthorse Registry.

For Mary Alice, Consul's bloodlines were an important addition to the Iron Spring breeding program. "Consul was in such demand as a stallion that in his first year at the farm in 1989, he was fully booked for the season," she says. Consul was a successful and popular sire early on.

"His foals have been exceptional," notes Mary Alice. "He seems to throw his best traits in both Warmblood and Thoroughbred crosses – very elegant, balanced types with long necks, good shoulder angles, and nice hips. Like many Warmbloods, he's slow to mature. He'll probably be eight by the time he's fully grown."

As to what Consul means to her as a rider, Mary Alice says, "When I first looked at him in Holland, I saw an excellent mover, a super jumper, and a horse with a very sensible attitude. I saw him ridden early in the morning by a young jumper rider. It was misty, and they were hacking alone through a rough-cut cornfield and he was impressively good and quiet, mental qualities that are much valued in the sport horse world".

Fulfilling that early promise, "Consul's proved to be a very steady fellow," says Mary Alice. "He loves attention and seems to like my children a lot. He's pretty careful with them. He always had his head out of the stall, looking for treats. And he knows how to ask, almost as though he's speaking English. He likes crisp apples the most."

Trained by Mary Alice, Consul is now performing at fourth level dressage. In 1990, his first year in performance in the U.S., he earned nine first place wins at first and second levels, including the Bengt Ljundquist Memorial Championships. He also qualified for a USDF Performance Merit Award with nineteen scores over sixty percent.

"He was just four when I got him, and he's settled down quite a bit," Mary Alice continues. "He's steady but sensitive to ride. He's the kind of horse who's always thinking. He's unhappy until he figures out what's required of him at each level; now he understands what's involved in the fourth level and Prix St. Georges tests.

"Consul has been wonderful to train. He really tries to do what I ask him to do, and he's upset when he's reprimanded. He wants to do it right! Like Winston, he has taught me to be careful and tactful," she says. "He's one of the best rides I have all day." High praise indeed considering who his stablemates are!

Roemer

Roemer has far surpassed the dreams and hopes held by Mary Alice Malone, owner of Iron Spring Farm in Coatesville, Pennsylvania, one of the most prominent sport horse breeding centers in the United States.

This 17-hand-plus liver chestnut Dutch Warmblood stallion possesses the rare combination of extraordinary success as a performer and a breeding sire.

"When I first saw Roemer, he looked like what I thought the ideal dressage horse and stallion should be," says Mary Alice. "I had the feeling that this was the horse for me – there was no question. I've always known what an incredibly special horse he is," she continues. "The rapport we have is very important to me. Out of all my wonderful horses, I enjoy riding Roemer the most. He makes me feel like I'm riding the best horse in the world."

Roemer is special to Mary Alice because he was the horse to help her achieve her professional goals – what is often an elusive dream for many dressage riders. "Roemer helped me become a Grand Prix competitor," she says. "Though I had some help, I trained him mostly on my own," a testimony not only to her skill but to his cooperative nature.

Roemer had been a Grand Prix jumper on the European circuit when Mary Alice brought him to the United States. While he was already ten at the time, she found him easy to train in dressage. So much so that in only a few months he was ready for Prix St. Georges. By 1990, he had won a United States Dressage Federation Performance Merit Award at Grand Prix level for achieving ten scores over sixty percent, fifty-five being "average." He won numerous USDF All-Breed Awards in 1989, including fourth in Grand Prix, and second place in the Grand Prix Freestyle, and he won the Grand Prix at the 1989 AHSA Eastern Regional Finals in Lexington.

"Roemer is always kind and considerate, a true gentleman," Mary Alice says. "Yet he knows, as do the other stallions at Iron Spring, that he is the Numero Uno Stallion in the barn."

Roemer is also number one in the minds of other breeders striving for an all-around sport horse. Foaled in Westphalia, Germany in 1975, he was named a "Preferent" stallion by the Royal Dutch Warmblood Studbook in the Netherlands, the highest honor of the breed. Roemer is only one of two riding-type Dutch Warmblood stallions living today who have earned his predicate of Preferent, and he is the only such-designated stallion outside of Holland. This title acknowledges the great number of his offspring that are scoring exceptionally well in sport and breeding competitions – Roemer has been the number one sire of dressage horses in the registry's stallion index for four years.

Roemer is the foundation of the breeding program at Iron Spring. "Through his get, he has surpassed anything I could have imagined in the advancement of our farm," says Mary Alice. "His ability to pass along his conformation, temperament and athletic talent has been recognized internationally. His foals win top premium awards from the Dutch registry every year.

"Roemer is not just another horse. He is one of my most treasured friends. If I need cheering up, I go out and ride him, and that does it! From him I've learned that some horses are a gift, never to be taken lightly."

Winston

"Winston's meant a lot to me professionally, because he's the horse I've gone International with," Mary Alice Malone says. "We were invited to the 1989 North American Championships in Canada, a high point for both of us."

Winston is currently competing at Grand Prix level, and last year at the 1990 AHSA Eastern States Finals, he won the Grand Prix Freestyle Championship. He also won the Bengt Ljundquist Memorial Finals at Grand Prix level and was Reserve Champion in the FEI Freestyle. (Ljundquist was a distinguished dressage judge, clinician, and mentor to many American riders.)

The prestigious *Chronicle of the Horse* magazine noted on November 23, 1990, that this was the third consecutive year that Mary Alice and Winston won the finals class in the Bengt Ljundquist Memorial show. Other important wins were the Prix St. Georges Championship in 1988 and Intermediare I in 1989, giving Mary Alice a total of six BLM titles, more than anyone else.

A horse with such winning ways is the stuff of dreams for a dressage rider. Mary Alice found him when she was looking for a Grand Prix prospect in Holland.

Mary Alice founded her Iron Spring Farm in Coatesville, Pennsylvania in 1976. As she moved up the levels of dressage, she and her husband Stuart knew they wanted high quality performance stallions for Iron Spring that could further her competition goals.

During several buying trips to Europe, Mary Alice searched for "Mr. Right," a stallion ready to bring in show ribbons and to sire excellent foals.

When she heard about the Royal Warmblood Studbook of the Netherlands and its reputation for extreme selectivity in its breed registry, she and Stuart visited the Netherlands in 1985.

On the van Teul farm, the Malones found Winston, a young 16.1-hand chestnut stallion, who had passed his 100-Day Stallion Test with an "Approved" rating, the highest possible. He was just beginning to compete at the very basic second level dressage, but Mary Alice saw enormous potential in him.

"I thought he was breathtaking," she recalls. "He was only five, but I knew he'd fit into our plans."

And he did. "He turned my life around," she says. "Within six weeks we went to our first show, and he did well without giving me any of the grief I had been used to (from other horses). He was cooperative and so eager to please.

"He's such a generous horse, wonderful to ride, though he's never been a 'pal.' He's too sophisticated and a bit proud. He has such presence and self-awareness. I think it's those qualities that make him want to try hard. If he doesn't do what's asked of him, I know he's trying to tell me there's a problem somewhere, such as an uncomfortable saddle."

A few months after they acquired Winston, the Malones heard that Winston's sire, Roemer, was for sale and bought him.

"Winston has been slightly overshadowed by a famous father," says Mary Alice. "We limit his outside bookings, saving his offspring for our program. His foals are lovely, winning first premiums in the Dutch inspections. I'm sure that, as time goes on, Winston will be one of the top stallions in our barn."

Elastique

Elastique is a very exciting horse to his owner, Louise B. Edelman because, she says, "I just can't go in there and sit on him in the show ring. I have to ride him. Maybe because he is a stallion, he likes to look around. When we win, it isn't that I sat on him...I got it out of him, I had to ride him and I won."

Elastique is a beautiful, very typey Dutch Warmblood. The 16.3 chestnut, foaled May 18, 1986, has the breeding which destined him for athletic success. His sire is Cor de la Bryere, the finest sire of jumping horses in Germany today; his grandsire, Duc de Normandie; his dam, Ida Utopia.

Libby Edelman's husband, Samuel, found Elastique in his native Holland. "He was purchased from friends who raise Warmbloods in the Netherlands," she says. "Samuel did not buy him for me. Samuel loves to buy horses, train them, take them from the beginning."

A friend watching this process with Elastique made the comment, "This horse is going to make a great hunter." And suggested he would be a wonderful horse for Libby to ride in competition in the amateur division.

Among the reasons this thought occurred to the friend are, first of all, "Elastique is just gorgeous, looks to die for," says Libby. "Then to he jumps very well. He covers the ground so elegantly and beautifully. Just a beautiful picture with every jump he takes. He's quiet. If I don't get in his way, he's perfect."

Elastique was purchased in June, 1990. A professional showed him for a while and then he became Libby's responsibility. "It took me a while since I was learning to ride again," says Libby, the mother of three.

Her first show with Elastique was at Del Mar near San Diego. Libby was a little nervous. "Being at home is different from going to a show. After the first round I knew we would be a great match. This is the greatest horse I've ever had," she adds.

The only real obstacle Libby had to face with Elastique, apart from those in the show ring, is her insecurity about riding a stallion.

"Elastique likes to look around a lot when I'm first riding him. We used to think he had a thing with pink flowers--'Hey, what are these, flowers?' He's like a great big lovable dog. He's very easy."

Libby is riding with trainer Hugh Mutch who says, "Elastique is a real gentleman for a stallion. He's very well behaved and has quite a regal look about him. He carries himself like a real man," says the well-known professional.

Elastique has been doing extremely well in Hunter classes in which the numbers of competitors can be daunting. He was the winner of the $10,000 Regular Working Hunter Stake at the Oaks Fall Classic in 1991.

The Edelmans, of Woodside, California, did not consider themselves breeders until they bought Elastique. "Because the horse is so beautiful and is doing well in competition, many owners want to breed their mares to him," says Libby. "His first two foals, a colt and a filly, are only a month old.

"Because of Elastique," she adds, "I have a new confidence in riding and it has spilled over to my riding other horses. And he's fulfilled another dream – I've always wanted to have a horse that responded to me only...in the show ring and in life."

THE FRIESIAN

"You can have any color you want as long as it's black, just as Henry Ford used to say about the Model A Ford," joked a fan of the Friesian horse.

The monochromatic Friesian, an ancient Dutch breed, once carried knights into battle wearing heavy plate and armor. The breed stood the test of time through the rise and fall of empires and survived near extinction more than once. Only three stallions survived World War I.

Gentle, honest, and sober but highly-mettled and clever, the Friesian fortunately is now regaining popularity worldwide as a breed suitable for sport and recreation, both as carriage and riding horses. North America, where this rare animal now thrives, is no exception. The popularity of the Friesians increased tremendously as a result of the 1985 Warner Bros./Twentieth Century Fox film *Ladyhawk* in which actor Rutger Hauer rides the Friesian horse Goliath.

Worldwide, there are about 6,000 Friesians today, with about 550 of these in the United States. Because of the small numbers "they're very expensive," said a spokesperson for the Friesian Horse Association of North America, located in Grand Rapids, Michigan. Foals sell for $5,000 and up, a yearling may cost $8,000, and mares sell from $6,000 to $15,000, depending on bloodlines and premiums.

Physical characteristics of the breed are neat, small ears set into a relatively upright head; the back is strong with a low-set, very thick tail; the barrel is deep and well-rounded; legs are correct and strong, with heavy feathering, often to the knees and hocks. Average height is 15 hands; average weight, 1,200 lbs.

Historically, the Friesian horse goes back to 500 B.C., when the Friesian people settled along the borders of what is now known as the North Sea in Friesland, one of the eleven provinces of the Netherlands.

The breed is descended from a large statured horse, *Equus robustus,* and has many draft horse characteristics. Armored knights of the Middle Ages found the Friesian very desirable as it had the strength to carry great weight and still maneuver precisely in battle. Its suppleness and agility gave the Friesian horse qualities that made him sought after later on in the riding schools of Paris and Spain in the fifteenth and sixteenth centuries.

Before the sixteenth century Reformation, horse breeding was done in the monasteries of Friesland. There, the Friesian was refined to a lighter body frame, high knee action, smaller head and upright neck, differentiating him from his *Equus robustus* cousins.

Throughout Europe, the royal courts sought the Friesian as a coach horse. France, Austria, Prussia and Holland are known to have had Friesians in their royal stables. The Friesian knows few equals pulling an elegant carriage. The Friesian also was known as an excellent trotter in Friesland, for the short distance of 300 meters, the winners of races being awarded silver and gold whips. A fine collection of these prize whips is in the museum at Leeuwarden, Holland.

Very little is known of the history of the Friesian horse in the United States. It first arrived in the seventeenth century when the Dutch settled New Amsterdam (now New York), but soon dissolved through crossbreeding. The Friesian horse played a role in the breeding of American Morgan Horses in this country, as well as in the English Norfolk Trotters and the Russian Orloff Trotters abroad.

After an absence of several hundred years, Friesians returned to North America in 1974, reintroduced by Thomas Hannon of Louisville, Ohio, who imported four mares, and Frank Lyendekker of California who brought several mares and a stallion from Holland. Since the Friesian horses' return to North America, they have become a familiar sight and consistent winner in all phases of carriage competition. In 1984, a pair of Friesians owned by Mr. Lyendekker won the North American Pleasure Driving Championship, including a victory at the Canadian Carriage Driving Classic.

Today in Friesland there are many carriage events in which these black horses are the stars. The Friesian *sjees* can be seen in these events. The *sjees* is the Friesland form of the French word *chaise,* the name for the vehicle after which Friesian carriages are patterned. This unique two-wheeled cart can be drawn by one or two horses and is driven by a gentleman accompanied by a lady, both dressed in traditional costumes of the 1860s.

Four-in-hand carriages are commonplace in Friesland and as many as ten-in-hand can be seen pulling light carriages. These large and unusual hitches for demonstration purposes are becoming more popular with drivers.

Friesians are also widely used as riding horses, most often for dressage, and they have enjoyed a rich history in circuses around the world because of their excellent temperaments and handsome presence.

Sir Lancelot

Both John and Anita Mellott, breeders of Friesian horses, were raised with horses, but in very different parts of the world. John's first experiences with horses were in Colorado on his grandfather's farm and on an uncle's dude ranch.

Anita's parents raised coffee and rubber on the island of Java where Anita had a pony-sized Arabian stallion at a very young age. When the Dutch were asked to leave Indonesia, Anita and her family returned to the Netherlands, where she saw her first Friesian horse.

But it was John who was really impressed with Friesians when by chance he happened to see them in a driving clinic in Pomona in 1981. "Anita knew what they were," he says, "a native Dutch horse." The Mellots at the time were into Arabians. They saw Friesians again when they went to the World Driving Championships in Apeldoorn, Holland in 1982, and while they hadn't intended to horse shop, they decided to buy three excellent mares.

The mares were followed in 1984 by the Qualified Stallion, Sander 269. Additional mares were acquired at various times, for a current count of twenty-three Friesian horses on their ranch.

The Mellotts were among the founders of the Friesian Horse Association of North America and John served as its President for several years. They are owners of the California Carriage and Harness Company in Harbor City, California.

The Mellotts have chosen to honor the young stallion Sir Lancelot in this book, as being "among the most beautiful of Friesian horses, and the first horse of this quality that we have bred."

Sir Lancelot, a 15.3-hand black, was foaled May 1, 1986, a son of their imported, Sander 269, and out of the imported star mare Aaf.

"Lance was outstanding from the first day, and had a look that was special," says Anita Mellott. "He has created substantial interest in Sander 269 and our breeding program.

"Lance has always been very personable and easy to handle," she adds. "He received lots of personal attention, and as a result his temperament is outstanding and he has no stallion vices."

However, when the day came to apply his tongue tattoo, he changed! In accordance with the rules for Friesian horses, the foal must be tattooed while at the mother's side. Arrangements were made with the Association and an official came to apply the tattoo. "Lance would have none of it; he fought us every way he could," says Anita. She found herself mouthing the same phrase she'd heard other horseman say in similar situations: "He never acts this way. I don't know what got into him!"

As Lance was growing up, says Anita, a ranch employee often scratched Lance's rump, just above the tail. So Lance learned to present his backside for a friendly scratch. "Although this practice was stopped, Lance will sometimes turn his tail to you, which can be a little startling when you don't know that what he wants is a scratch," she says.

In physical appearance, Lance is very refined for a Friesian stallion. He has a nice head and arched neck. He has the pride and action of a Friesian with conformation similar to that of a Warmblood.

"Lance rides, drives and is willing over fences. He is quick to learn and is suited by temperament, intelligence and athletic ability for training in most horse activities," says Anita. "We love to show him; everyone is impressed. He catches your eye."

"Lance has won every Friesian halter competition available to him. He has been first in his class at every age in every National Friesian Horse Show he has entered. In 1991 he was judged Champion Unqualified Stallion," Anita notes.

"Our goals in showing and breeding Friesian horses are to enjoy the performance, expose the breed to horse lovers, and create a successful business. A horse like Lance brings pride to your breeding program."

Frans 289

"Everybody dreams of having a black stallion. Well, Frans certainly fits that description and much more," says Carolyn Sharp, who with husband Johnny, owns Midnight Valley Friesians, Inc. of Fort Collins, Colorado.

"Not only is he incredible to look at, but add his personality and you have nothing short of an angelic individual. He has a very special soul," adds Carolyn, whose love for this rare creature entrusted to her care radiates from the very pages on which she wrote to me.

There are only forty qualified Friesian breeding stallions in the entire world, and only nine in North America, Frans included, Carolyn told me. He is the only one in the United States from the rarest "middle" line; only five stallions from this same line are breeding in their native Holland.

Frans, foaled on April 15, 1983, came into the lives of the Sharps three years ago, arriving at their breeding farm two days before Christmas, when he was only five.

After the Sharps had searched unsuccessfully for over a year for a stallion approved for breeding, a friend called to say that a "mystery" stallion had come up for sale in Holland. The Sharps immediately flew to see him. "He was all we had hoped for. So beautiful and magical, he brought tears to our eyes. We bought him on the spot from his wonderful owner, Auke Frankena," Carolyn recounts.

Frans, who stands 16 hands, is solid blue-black. He has a muscular, well-arched neck, a beautifully shaped head, and his shoulder has a good angle which aids his distinctive way of going. Very animated both in front and back, he is wonderful to watch in motion, his luxurious shoulder-length mane and ground-level tail and feathers flying in the wind.

The outstanding characteristic of his personality is his gentleness. "Quiet and affectionate, he would like to be a lap horse, despite his size," says Carolyn. "Frans is so kind and loving, it makes every minute we spend with him important."

Frans has exquisite table manners. He loves to dip every bite of hay in his water bucket before he eats it. Legendary Dutch cleanliness is obviously bred into him; he will sulk at a show if his stall is not spotless. But he's not a wimp. He also loves to prance down the aisle of the barn and strut his stuff for the ladies.

"Just his presence in our lives makes such a difference. It's hard to look at such a beautiful creature and not know that God has a hand in everything. Only God could make anything so fantastic in every way. We are truly blessed to have him in our lives," Carolyn says.

The Sharps started out in Friesians five years ago by breeding their mares to other qualified stallions. They show their horses both in harness and under saddle – Frans has been trained in dressage as well as carriage driving and is talented at both.

"Our purpose in breeding is to produce the finest Friesian horses in the country--Friesians so good the Dutch would want to have them back in Holland," says Carolyn. "And of course, we would love to produce the first qualified stallion foaled in North America." Frans is already the only stallion in North America who has the honor of siring a stallion approved for breeding in Holland. In April, 1991, his son, Melle, was given permission to breed and, at the stallion show in January 1992, was Reserve Grand Champion.

"Frans has fulfilled our greatest expectations for our Friesian breeding operation," Carolyn adds. "He has made our breeding farm known nationally as well as in Holland and has opened many doors for us. Because of him and our lovely mares, we have a professional reputation for producing the finest Friesian horses."

"Frans is important to us, not only as the sire of our foals, but as a member of our family. Our lives just wouldn't be the same without him," Carolyn concludes. "He has opened our hearts because he has such a big heart himself."

THE HANOVERIAN

Deister, a horse foaled in 1971 and still alive at the time of the writing of this book, is often referred to in his native Germany as "The Horse of the Century." He is certainly the most successful show jumper in the world to date. His owner/rider, Paul Schockemohle, won the European title with Deister three consecutive times, and while he has had other victories with other horses, Schockemohle acknowledges that no other horse in his life has come close to this living legend.

Deister is a model of the combination of ingredients that make the Hanoverian horse: ability, stamina, persistence, and a natural love of performing. Even in his old age and retirement (with his own pony to keep him company), Deister becomes upset when all the other horses in his barn go to competitions and he is left behind. So Schockemohle loads him up with the others and takes him along. While everyone else is warming up horses for competition, the world-renowned German jumping ace takes Deister out, warms him up a bit and pops him over a few jumps. Strangers who don't know the story of this great horse often ask, 'What is Schockemohle doing with that old horse?' Just humoring a great old champion who deserves to be happy.

Deister is only one of the great Hanoverian horses that have established a reputation for the breed by winning in the upper echelons of showing. Other winners of major events are Mehmed, ridden by Dr. Reiner Klimke; Warwick Rex, ridden by Alwin Schockemohle; Slibovitz, ridden by Dr. Uwe Schulten-Baumer, all three of Germany; and The Natural, ridden by Katherine Burdsall of the United States.

At the Olympic Games in Seoul in 1988, twenty-two Hanoverians competed in various disciplines. Walzerkoenig on the German show jumping team and Sherry and Shamrock on the eventing team won gold medals, and Dynasty, ridden by Cindy Ishoy of the Canadian dressage team, won a bronze medal.

That year Hanoverians were rated top breed in the world by *L'Annee Hippique* in its International Equestrian Yearbook World Ratings, based on placings in show jumping, dressage and eventing for the six major events of 1988 including the Olympic Games. The Hanoverian received the American Breeders Award as "The horse best representing the ideal of sport horse breeding in the United States."

The breed's historic home is in Lower Saxony, in northern Germany, the former Kingdom of Hanover, where a flourishing horse-breeding industry has existed for 400 years. The State Stud, founded in 1735 by the English King and Count of Hanover, Georg II, is in Celle, southeast of Verden.

Around 200 stallions stand at the State Stud at Celle and are available to breeders at affordable prices.

The guarantors of the breed are the stallions; they must pass a rigorous selection and licensing process. At the age of three they must go to the stallion performance test in Adelheidsdorf near Celle and prove their worth under the rider before being accepted as breeding stallions. Only the stallions with the best test results will be taken into active service at the State Stud.

In February, at the beginning of the covering season, the stallions are distributed to fifty covering stations within the Hanoverian breeding area, and they remain there until the middle of July.

The Hanoverian Horse Breeding Society (*Verband Hannovescher Warmblutzuchter*) is a private organization with about 8,500 active members, mostly farmers, who own about 12,000 registered mares. The Society traces its roots back to its forerunner, the Hanoverian Mare Registry, founded in 1888. The Society's director is answerable to the Department of Agriculture in Hanover. The registry office is based in Verden, where the building complex, *Niedersachsenhalle*, also houses a training and marketing sales center.

Twice a year at the Elite Auction of Hanoverian Riding Horses held in Verden, more than one hundred three- to six-year-olds, offered as potential winners, find their way from the breeders' hands into those of top riders from equestrian teams all over the world.

The stated aim of the Hanoverian breeders is to produce a "precious, well-proportioned, correct and talented Warmblood horse with elevated, forward-going and elastic movement, which based on its temperament, its character and its rideability, is especially suitable for riding purposes of any kind."

At the time of the founding of the Celle State Stud, a robust coach horse was favored. During most of the nineteenth century, more and more English Thoroughbreds and Warmbloods were used. After World War II, the breeding of working horses for agricultural purposes was abandoned and the demand for improved riding horses was recognized. Thoroughbreds and Trakehners (such as the great Abglanz) were introduced into the bloodlines, as were Arabians, to a lesser extent.

The American Hanoverian Society, headquartered in Woodinville, Washington, was incorporated in 1978 for the purpose of gathering the Hanoverians in North America into a registry and of preserving and promoting the breed. While the AHS is an independent organization, it maintains a close relationship with the German Hanoverian Horse Breeder's Society regarding inspection, registration, licensing procedures and educational activities.

Nebelhorn

The noble, kingly demeanor of the Hanoverian stallion, Nebelhorn, reveals his specialness – an eye and an expression that simply say, "Love me!"

"Everyone involved in his daily care is in love with him," says owner Priscilla L. Hanford of the Nebelhorn Partnership of California. "Above all, he's kind. I think it is this quality which captivates those who see him."

The 16.2-hand deep chestnut stallion with white markings was foaled in March, 1978, an outstanding example of the Hanoverian breed. Hanoverians originated in the Lower Saxony area of Germany, the breed studbook established in 1735 by George II of England, Duke of Saxony of the House of Hanover. The historic town of Celle, where King George's original brick stables still stand, is the official state stud, and that is where Priscilla found Nebelhorn. His extraordinary qualities were recognized when he was chosen as a stallion of the state stud.

The Class 1A Hanoverian stallion was the champion of his three-year-old performance test with one of the highest scores ever given.

Nebelhorn's dam, the Hanoverian State Premium Mare Dorella, through her sire is from the foundation D-line, highly-sought after by the world's top dressage riders because the line is known for producing great stars in this discipline.

Phyllis, an amateur dressage rider, had not planned to buy a stallion, but her close friend and former sister-in-law, Kamila du Pont, a top competitive rider and trainer, told her she knew of several prospects through the eminent judge and clinician, Hermann Friedlaender.

"Mr. Friedlaender's aim was to bring over to this country a top-quality stallion to improve the breed in the United States; his intervention on our behalf was crucial to acquiring Nebelhorn," says Priscilla.

Through Friedlaender's reputation in Germany, arrangements were made for du Pont to try two young stallions at the state stud. After trying Nebelhorn, an ecstatic Kamila phoned Priscilla from Celle. "I found him!" she declared, and the Nebelhorn Partnership was born.

The stallion was flown to the United States in January 1985, and his training with du Pont began the next month.

Kamila competed "Nebs" to outstanding success, winning with him the USDF Gold Medal as the highest scoring Hanoverian in the United States from 1985 through 1989, Third Level through Intermediare 1. He won the Individual Silver Medal in the Olympic Sports Festival in 1987 and was short-listed that same year for the Pan American Games.

In 1990, the decision was made to concentrate on the breeding aspect of Nebs' career. He was already a successful sire of dressage horses in Germany, consis-

tently ranked in that country in the top ten percent of his age group of stallions siring winning offspring.

"His first three crops of United States-bred foals fulfill our dreams and those of their owners through their success in breed shows," says Priscilla. "Nebelhorn stamps his foals not only with his color, markings, beauty, elegance, presence, and fluid and elastic movement, but also his kindness, willingness and trainability."

As for what makes him special to his now-sole owner, Priscilla says: "Nebelhorn is a business interest as well as my great pleasure. I look forward to a long, rewarding partnership with him. And every spring I have the joy of seeing his youngsters and sharing the delights with their owners."

THE LIPIZZANER

The very word *Lipizzaner* is an electrical sound in the heart and soul of horse lovers and those who appreciate art and beauty. The word immediately sparks a vision of the "dancing white horses" of the Spanish Riding School in Vienna, where for 400 years they have safeguarded and kept alive the beauty of an art that dates back to Xenophon.

The miraculous escape of these beautiful, intelligent creatures during the destruction and chaos of World War II became the subject of a Hollywood film *The White Stallions of Vienna*, a film that popularized the breed worldwide.

Now their fame so precedes them that when the Spanish Riding School Lipizzaners perform before audiences in Europe, the United States and Canada, these splendid, powerful horses with their large, dark liquid eyes, proud carriage and graceful movements are consistently met with great love and respect.

High school (or *haute ecole*) is divided into the exercises of airs on the ground and the airs above the ground. While the exercises on the ground are required in the dressage test at the Olympic Games, the airs above the ground are exclusively preserved in all their purity by the Lipizzaner stallions of the Spanish Riding School, the ultimate shrine of the art of classical riding.

Other Lipizzaners outside the Spanish Riding School are every bit as regal. Ordinary persons enjoy Lipizzaners as riding and driving horses, as well as extraordinary companions that form strong attachments to human friends.

Many opinions are proffered on the origin of the Lipizzaner breed but, according to Alois Podhajsky, for many years Director of the Spanish Riding School, Spanish horses were trained from about 1560 in the "Spanish riding stables" at the Imperial Court of Vienna as mounts for the Imperial family and members of the Court.

For many centuries, the Spanish horse, a crossing of Berber stallions with native Andalusian mares, was bred with the same care and importance as the Thoroughbred is today. When the Moors were driven out of Spain, the breeding of horses, which had reached a very high standard during their 700-year reign, began to decline.

In following years, attempts were made to continue the Spanish breed in a number of European countries, including Austria. The Imperial Court in Vienna ordered stallions and mares to be bought in Spain and transported to Lipizza, a small village near Trieste. Here the Imperial Stud Farm was founded in 1580 to make a new home for the Spanish horses, a place where their breeding was continued on the same principles as in their homeland.

The horses bred at this new stud farm were called Lipizzaners.

The Spanish horse had also been transported to many other parts of the Austrian monarchy and was also bred in the royal stud farms of Denmark and Germany. Of all these ancient breeding farms, only the stud farm of Lipizza has been preserved to the present.

Although, in the beginning, Lipizza was founded for the purpose of furnishing the necessary horses for the Imperial Mews in Vienna, the newly-established breed had a considerable influence on horse breeding in general in the Austro-Hungarian Empire.

The breed developed peacefully for the first 200 years and it survived the Napoleonic Wars and the breakdown of the Austro-Hungarian Monarchy in 1918.

After World War I, Lipizza became Italian territory. Italy was allotted half the breeding stock, and breeding of the Lipizzaners continued according to tradition. After World War II, Lipizza was ceded to Yugoslavia and the stud farm was renamed Lipica. Today the farm is a favorite tourist attraction.

The other half of the Imperial Stud Farm stock was allotted to Austria, and in 1919 the horses were taken to the mountain village of Piber (in Styria in the south of Austria). From then on it was the task of the Piber stud to provide the necessary horses for the Spanish Riding School in Vienna. Formerly a property of the Imperial Court, the School was placed under the control of the Republic of Austria.

Lipizzaners can also originate in Lipica or stud farms in Italy, Hungary or Czechoslovakia which were established with stock from Imperial breeding farms after World War I..

Private breeding farms have sprung up in other countries. Among the most renowned is Tempel Farms in Wadsworth, Illinois, established by steel entrepreneur Tempel Smith, after he was stirred by a performance of the Lipizzaners in Vienna during a post-World War II trip.

The Tempel Lipizzaners have been seen by millions on television as they participated in presidential inaugural parades. At home, they continue to give performances echoing those of their cousins in Vienna.

Neapolitano Santuzza

"The capriole is a natural movement in the purest sense of the word," says George Williams, Director of the Tempel Lipizzan Corporation at Tempel Farms in Wadsworth, Illinois since 1988. "Young horses will do caprioles in the pasture, sometimes when frightened, but more frequently just for the sheer joy of it."

One such horse is Neapolitano Santuzza, the capriole specialist at Tempel. Foaled March 27, 1964, he seemed destined by his breeding to achieve some sort of distinction.

Santuzza's Hungarian-bred sire, Neapolitano Alnok, was trained at the Reitschule Frendenau on the outskirts of Vienna by *Oberbereiter* Johann Irbinger and Peter Szalle. There he learned the capriole under saddle before being imported to the United States by Chicago businessman Tempel Smith.

Santuzza's dam, 12 Santuzza, was one of the original mares purchased by Tempel and Esther Smith in 1957 from Piber Stud. She was foaled June 13, 1948 at Piber, a pure specimen of Lipicca/Piber breeding, and her first foal, a colt by Pluto V Presciana, entered the Spanish Riding School in 1956. In 1958 she was imported, in foal, to the United States.

These two horses joined Pluto Ancona in Northern Illinois as the beginnings of Tempel Farms and what would eventually become the largest herd of Lipizzans in the world.

Neapolitano Santuzza began training with Riding Master Alf Athenstaedt as a young stallion in 1968. By 1971 he was performing the capriole in hand as part of special performances that were held during the 1970s — at the National Horse Show in Madison Square Garden in 1977, at the World Three-Day Event Championships in Lexington, Kentucky in 1978 and at the Washington International Horse Show in 1975, 1977 and 1979.

Through his great, breathtaking leaps, Neapolitano Santuzza helped to bring classical horsemanship to the attention of thousands of Americans, thrilling audiences of thousands, horse people and non-horse people alike.

After the death of Tempel Smith in December, 1980, Tempel Farms came into a new era. While it had always been the hope of Tempel Smith to bring the beauty of the Lipizzans and classical horsemanship to the American people, this was not fully realized until 1981, when regular summer performances modeled after those in Vienna were opened to the public at the farm.

It was then, at the age of seventeen, that Neapolitano Santuzza started a new career as a mounted capriole horse. With a rider on his back, usually George Williams, Neapolitano Santuzza performed regularly in the summer performances in the mounted "Airs Above the Ground" segment.

The two seemed to have a special chemistry together. George began his classical dressage training with Egon Von Neindorff in Germany as a young man, and upon his return to the United States followed his mentor, Karl Mikolka, to Tempel Farms in 1981.

Williams and Neapolitano Santuzza also performed at the twenty-fifth Annual Washington International Horse Show in 1983 and at the United States Dressage Federation National Championships in Kansas City in 1984.

In 1985, the stallion was officially retired to a small private farm in Pennsylvania. At the age of twenty-eight, Neapolitano Santuzza is still sound as he trots and canters around the fields of his new home.

"According to the principles of dressage, the training will increase the useful life and longevity of a horse. If one believes that, then it must be said that Neapolitano Santuzza is still enjoying a long and happy life," says his friend Williams.

Conversano II Belvedera

"The Lipizzan breed has certain characteristics; among them are the extremely well-developed neck, the very intelligent eye and, in some cases, the high knee action. Put all three together, then you have Conversano II Belvedera, a horse who represents the younger generation of Tempel Lipizzans," says Karl Mikolka, former *Oberbereiter* (senior or chief rider) of the Spanish Riding School who joined the staff of Tempel Farms in Wadsworth, Illinois in June, 1980.

At sixteen years of age, "Moose," as he is known to his friends, is still considered a young specimen within the breed.

In 1981, Moose began his training with Mikolka, who was impressed with his size, beautiful grey color, his big

movements, especially at the trot, and his gentle character. During the training, Moose normally demonstrated what Mikolka describes as "a certain laissez-faire attitude."

One morning, however, Moose managed to buck his rider off and stormed directly toward Tempel riding master Alf Athenstaedt, who was having his morning snack ringside while keeping an eye on proceedings. This so startled Alf that he swallowed the plum he was eating, pit and all, while Karl, the trainer, slowly collected himself from the sand.

Moose matured fairly quickly and soon he was performing in the Young Stallion segment of Tempel Farms' summer performances for the public.

He learned to tolerate well the various challenges of a show environment. His size and presence were two elements highly desirable in a competition horse. Therefore it was only logical that Conversano II Belvedera represent the Tempel Lipizzans, first in local dressage competitions and later in national competitions up to FEI level.

"Competing against Warmbloods which have very different conformation was not always easy for the stallion whose ancestors were famous for entertaining royalty with their 'airs above the ground' such as levades, courbettes and caprioles," says Mikolka. Mikolka's knowledge of the Lipizzan, its breeding and training is well complemented by his experience with international dressage as a coach, trainer and judge.

"But Conversano II Belvedera overcame those obstacles of having to deal with judges' preferences, their likes and dislikes," he adds, "by improving steadily in competition and getting the necessary mileage in the arena, a must for flawless performances."

Moose became the "schoolmaster" or equine learning vehicle for Jennifer Leffingwell, granddaughter of Tempel Smith, the founder of Tempel Farms.

On the show circuit, they competed against some of the better upper level Warmblood competition horses in the country, many loaned to the young riders for the occasion by the senior riders/trainers who had trained them. But, Moose gave Jennifer such fluid, steady performances in her dressage tests at the North American Junior Rider Championships held at Tempel Farms in 1990 and 1991 that the pair won the Team Gold Medal in 1990 and the Team Gold and the Individual Bronze in 1991.

George Williams, Jennifer's coach, will continue to compete Moose at the Grand Prix level on a national as well as an international basis, making a reality of the dream of Tempel Smith, that of Lipizzan horses taking part in public performances as well as in high level competition.

Pluto Ancona

Pluto Ancona was the first Lipizzan to arrive at Tempel Farms and also the first Tempel Lipizzan to be trained to Grand Prix level dressage. He was only three years old when Tempel and Esther Smith found him in Illinois, following their Lipizzan-searching trip to Vienna in 1958. Pluto Ancona belonged to a woman in the Chicago suburbs who was the devoted owner of his dam, Ancona, and had raised him from birth. The young horse was the last ungelded son of Pluto XX, the stallion presented to General Patton by Austria in gratitude for his role in saving the Piber herd after World War II.

Pluto Ancona proved to be a talented and brilliant performer when introduced to upper level dressage training by Riding Master Alf Athenstaedt. The latter began his long association with Tempel in 1966. He had received his early training in Germany near his native city of Hamburg, at the stables of distinguished German rider Rosemary Springer. There he worked directly for seven years with her trainer, Willi Schultheiss, one of the premier dressage trainers of this era, and himself a student of the legendary Otto Lorke. Mr. Schultheiss made annual trips to Tempel Farms from 1966 through 1978, during which he rode and trained a number of the Lipizzans. Mr. Schultheiss recommended that his student Athenstaedt visit the farm. He came for "a short visit" and never left.

Pluto Ancona and Athenstaedt presented numerous exhibitions of classical dressage at business and charitable gatherings at Tempel Farms and at many horse show events in the Chicago area and across the country. In 1966, they gave solo exhibitions during the International Livestock Exhibition Horse Show in Chicago—all at a time when dressage as a riding discipline was almost unknown in the United States.

Athenstaedt spoke of Ancona and their work together: "If the dressage horse is trained well, then the horse and rider should be completely together. They should move together as a unit. Not all horses, even the Lipizzans, have the quality of the movement in extended trot which Pluto Ancona has." The extended trot, Ancona's forte, is the fastest tempo of the trot, elongated in perfect rhythmic cadence.

Another highlight exhibition of Pluto Ancona was in 1967 at the opening of the American Dressage Institute in Saratoga Springs, New York. There his demonstrations of classical dressage movements such as pirouette, piaffer, and passage were compared to the ballet movements demonstrated by three ballerinas from the New York City Ballet.

In addition to an exhibition in 1968 at the Rolling Rock Races in Ligonier, Pennsylvania, he was one of the Tempel Lipizzans who led the 1969 Inaugural Parade of Richard Nixon, moving up Pennsylvania Avenue in half pass and passage.

"We were extremely proud that the 1969 Inaugural Committee invited us to send our Lipizzan stallions to lead the parade," said Tempel Smith. "A Presidential Inaugural is a memorable event, witnessed by millions through the medium of television. When our Tempel Lipizzans stepped off at the head of the parade, it was an occasion we remembered for years. They made Tempel Farms and Tempel Steel Company better known across the nation."

Pluto Ancona also became an important sire at Tempel through his son, Pluto Platana, who, sired over one hundred foals.

"Pluto Ancona served as an ambassador for the Tempel Lipizzans and classical horsemanship, introducing both to many audiences across the country," says Linda Smith Buonanno, daughter of the founder of Tempel Farms. "The beauty of his accomplishments was a source of great pride to his owners."

Maestoso II Primavera

The late Walt Disney himself couldn't dream up a plot with as dramatic a turn of events as the real life story of Maestoso II Primavera, an American-bred Lipizzan stallion who had the distinction of performing with the Spanish Riding School when it made a rare tour of four East Coast cities in the fall of 1990.

The wife of the Austrian Ambassador, Mrs. Claire Barclay Hoess, interested in promoting handicapped riding programs, asked the School to take part in a fundraiser performance, and the officials agreed, a first in the 400-year history of the world-renowned riding school.

As part of the plan, a member of one of the local therapeutic riding programs was to ride one of the famous Lipizzan stallions. Then came the "glitch." By Austrian law, only Spanish Riding School employees may ride the stallions. Johannes Willenpart, an Austrian who owned the Sommersberg Lipizzan Farm near Annapolis, Maryland, saved the plan with his suggestion that Maestoso II Primavera be used for the handicapped rider

The stallion, owned by Leonard and June Boardman of White Horse Vale Lipizzans in Goldendale, Washington, was boarding at Johannes' farm while competing in the East. "M" had taken a few spins in the turnstile of fate since he left Tempel Farms in

Wadsworth, Illinois, where he was foaled in 1976. When he was three, Tempel donated him to the Living Waters Wilderness Corporation's Shiloh Ranch in Idaho, a nonprofit organization where the Boardmans found him in 1987.

M was ridden western by June until Sigrid Soors, a young Belgian tourist, paid a visit. Sigrid, a lover of Lipizzans, had trained with Hans Riegler, a Spanish Riding School *bereiter* or trainer. The change in M when Sigrid rode him was remarkable, and she stayed to show him that summer of 1989, winning at first and second level dressage. When fall arrived, Sigrid asked to take M back East with her for the rest of her visit (which she would spend at the horse farm of her friend Johannes Willenpart) so that she might train and show him the following season.

The 1990 show season opened with M competing at second level in the USDF's Region 1, one of the toughest in the country. By mid-summer he and Sigrid were bringing in wins at third level after only eighteen months of dressage training. The end of the summer found M First Place Lipizzan in the USDF All-Breeds Awards at second level.

By this time the pair had quite a fan club, and M seemed a natural as a stand-in for his royal cousins from Austria. He was booked for the Spanish Riding School's special free full-performance matinee for all the handicapped riders and special education students in the Washington, D.C., Maryland and Virginia area. Mrs. Marilyn Quayle, wife of the Vice President, was the honorary chairperson and introduced the performance. At the end of the program, M was led between the pillars decorated with Austrian flags in the center of the arena, and stood beside a low bench. Wendy Shugal, a victim of cerebral palsy, entered the opposite end of the arena in her wheelchair, was helped onto the bench, then onto M's back. To the strains of "One Moment in Time," Wendy and Maestoso II Primavera danced before thousands of admirers. Video footage of their performance was shown on five area television stations and in Austria.

The performance was so successful that it was repeated in New York, where M was ridden by a Downes Syndrome child and in a special musical ride by Claire Newman, daughter of actor Paul Newman.

Following that performance, M was taken backstage where Herr Arthur Kottas, renowned *oberbereiter* or senior trainer of the School, offered him a lump of sugar from the special sugar lumps pocket in the coattail of his uniform. M politely refused this materialistic reward. He already knew he'd done his job well.

M is back home now, after proving his nobility and giving of his gentleness and spirit in a way special to him and to the many people that love him.

Pluto II Balmora III

"So much of life today is a struggle, it is nice to know there is one place I can go and not have to fight for everything," says Kathie Parker Brown, referring to her relationship with her Lipizzan stallion, Pluto II Balmora III.

"Piber" is without a doubt the easiest horse she has ever broken to ride and drive, she says. She did both in three months.

"He offered almost no resistance to anything that was asked of him and seemed to enjoy the work. It is this quality that makes him very special for me," says Kathie, owner of Tegleaze Lipizzans in Winters, California.

Competitive carriage driving is Kathie's main interest and the intended use for the grey stallion. "It is a very demanding sport requiring enormous trust and understanding between horse and driver. A successful driving horse must not only enjoy the work but be willing to give that little extra that will make the difference between winning and losing. From the very beginning Piber has shown a willingness to try, lending the sparkle that only a stallion possesses," she says.

Kathie spent a great deal of time looking for her special horse and set standards she knew would not be easy to meet. "Conformation and movement are important and must be sufficient to meet the task at hand, but more important for me is disposition. Lipizzans live a long time and I would hope that Piber will be with me for the next twenty years. But no matter how talented he is, if I don't actually like the horse and his disposition, twenty years is a very long time!

"Piber showed me a very tractable temperament with a mind open to new ideas and a very gentle manner. When one meets a horse for the first time, it is really no different than meeting a new person. Some you like and some you don't; with some you feel an immediate affinity and others nothing. When I first met this horse, I knew he would become a major part of my life."

Piber was foaled June 13, 1986, sired by Pluto Bona II, who was rated the top stallion in the United States by Dr. Jaromir Oulehla of the Spanish Riding School in Vienna during his 1986 visit to the U.S.

Piber's show record includes 1990 U.S. Lipizzan Registry Halter Champion, 1991 North American Lipizzan Federation Halter Champion, and North American Lipizzan Federation English Pleasure Champion.

He is a classical Lipizzan in looks, with a broad forehead and a slightly Roman nose, high set neck and powerfully built body. "For me his most distinguishing feature is his eyes--large, dark, with an incredible gentleness and a twinkle at the same time. Half the time he looks angelic and the other half you know he is looking for trouble. At shows many people remark on his expression," says Kathie.

Piber's eyes have expressed deeper emotions. "Three years ago he choked on something out in the pasture and required surgery to clear the blockage. The greatest fear was that he would develop pneumonia, which could have killed him. I remember sitting in the stall at the University Veterinary Hospital watching him struggle to breathe, and praying we would both be there at the end of the week. A strong bond developed between us," says Kathie. "As I entered the stall he would move over to put his head close to me wanting his neck scratched and as he relaxed his eyes would close. But each time I left, his big dark eyes followed me until I was out of sight, making leaving very hard indeed. He is, needless to say, very much a one-person horse.

"I have had a great many competition horses in my life and have ridden many for other people," adds Kathie. "I believe that if you involve yourself with animals you will find both enormous heartbreaks and rewards along the way. But if you are lucky, there will be one or two very special animals in your lifetime. For me, Piber is certainly one of those rare creatures."

Conversano Brentna I

Most horses have a quirk or two contributing to their charm. Lipizzan Conversano Brentna I has quite a few eccentricities which make him an especially vivid personality.

"He must be greeted first at the barn or he pouts if he perceives he's being ignored, turning his back to you and refusing carrot treats for up to two hours," says his owner, Susan Castle. "He is jealous of some of his sons and will shake his head angrily if even their names are mentioned out loud. He listens for and watches for airplanes and helicopters, turning his head skyward as soon as he hears the whirr of a motor, often well before his human companions hear it."

In fact, he is so fascinated by airplanes that his rider always prays for no air traffic during outdoor dressage tests. "Bret" has been known to halt, salute, and look up...to search for planes. This behavior is a little difficult to explain to the judges.

Bret shows in upper level dressage tests and musical kurs throughout the demanding New England circuit

with rider Carol Popp, a USDF candidate for the Silver Medal and winner of seventeen USDF championships. They train with Dr. Max Gahwyler, United States Equestrian Team coach, author and international-rated judge.

Bret seriously loves being scratched under his chin and on his withers. When he sees a likely scratcher he will stretch his neck and twist it like a sea serpent, begging to be scratched. When he gets a taker, he twists his head and neck to about a thirty-degree angle above the horizontal, almost falling over in ecstacy. Cleaning his stall takes longer than most, since scratching him is part of the procedure.

The 15.1 stallion, so shimmeringly bright he is almost silver white, is descended from Lipizzans imported solely from the Piber Stud. His most illustrious ancestor is Maestoso Borina, the subject of Marguerite Henry's book, *White Stallion of Lipizza*.

Royally finicky about treats, Bret limits them to carrots, never sugar or apples. He dunks his hay in water. He is typically neat, generally won't roll in mud or dirt. Clean sawdust, on the other hand, is acceptable.

As a riding horse, he takes a lot of personal pride in his work and visibly puffs up when praised lavishly for a job well done. He is quick to learn entire dressage tests. Medium trots are his favorite, since he can "open up" and really show off. He likes shows and adores the attention he gets from the audience.

Conversano Brentna I is not the first horse that Susan Castle has owned, but he's been the most significant, her life having changed dramatically. Prior to Bret, "owning a horse was a pleasurable but manageable part of my lifestyle," she says. She was a fast track environmental manager for a Fortune 500 corporation, and owning a horse simply meant boarding her Morab gelding and visiting him/riding him after work. Life had few wrinkles. All that changed once she bought Conversano Brentna I as an unbroken five-year-old. "I came to understand that owning Bret meant that I had to learn more about horses than ever before and learn it quickly." She became dissatisfied with boarding her stallion in public facilities and realized he needed his own home where he could be out all day and handled with gentleness.

Leaving her sixty-plus-hours-per-week job, she settled down with her "significant other" and started a horse farm, Castle Lipizzans, in the scenic hills of Litchfield County, Connecticut.

"Conversano Brentna I, patriarch of Castle Lipizzans, now has the farm and the broodmares we imagine he's always wanted," says Susan, who focuses on keeping unbroken the connection from Piber to Connecticut and from Maestoso Borina to Bret, raising her young Lipizzans with affection and understanding.

Neapolitano Astra

Earline Dacus of Bullard, Texas was looking for a trained dressage horse to help her advance in her riding career. She wanted a dark bay or brown Thoroughbred type, at least 16 hands, something very well trained at second level. Gelding or mare didn't matter, but NO stallions.

Her instructor, Lisa Brown, told her about a few horses that she had at her farm, including a young Lipizzaner mare, green-broke, not trained like Earline wanted, but a magical Lipizzan! It was worth the trip just to see one.

The mare turned out to be just too green and much smaller than Earline had expected. In fact, none of Lisa's horses fit what Earline wanted. They had pretty much gone through them all when Lisa said she had one more and walked her to a back paddock where a short, grey, heavy-set stallion stood – Neapolitano Astra, known to his friends as "Inci."

"Just what I didn't want," says Earlene. "I had never been near a Lipizzaner stallion before, but I expected something more – more grand, I guess. He walked over, lower lip hanging loose, head low, looking one hundred years old. I was a little disappointed. Here was my first Lipi stallion looking like an old grey mare."

Lisa led him into the arena and put him on the longe line. Suddenly he was transformed. Earline had never seen a horse move like that. Bowed neck, graceful, high steps. THIS was the Baroque horse of Vienna!

"When I climbed into the saddle, I knew I had found my horse," says Earline. "I had reached a point in my life that I didn't believe in dreams any more," she says. "Yet here I was, an eight-year-old girl again. Inci was a unicorn, My Friend Flicka and Pegasus all wrapped up into one. I was in heaven, just sitting on his back."

The trip home was the longest four hours of Earline's life. Inci was way out of her price range.

"No horse could be that great," her mother told her. "Keep looking." But the more Earline looked, the more she realized Inci was the one.

She had given up, when her brother Rex called and asked if Inci was the horse she really wanted. Earline said yes. "Don't worry about the money," he said, "Buy him!"

"My dream of owning a Lipizzan came true, and surprisingly enough, he was also a second level dressage horse," says Earline. It wasn't until a year later that Earline found out where the money had come from. Her brother and his new wife's house had burned down a few months before, and Rex had given her part of his insurance money. Four years later, he still refuses to let her pay him back.

Earline would like to breed purebred Lipizzans, but until she can afford quality Lipizzan mares, she is trying to breed Paint and Appaloosa Lipizzan crosses at her Plum Crazy Originals farm.

Inci, however, seems to love pears almost more than mares! "He is very laid back and rarely gets excited about anything," says Earline, "but when he sees me coming from the direction of the pear tree, he runs to the fence and nickers and will actually chase me down the fence line."

Inci has further enriched Earline's life by inspiring her bronze sculptures. "His head and neck have had a profound effect on them. They all have a classical look about them now," she says.

The most special moment with Inci remains her first ride. "I never knew anything would be able to make me feel that way. Even if things had not worked out and I could not have bought Inci, I would never have forgotten my first ride on him," she says.

"Inci and I have not burned up the local dressage scene, but I still get that wonderful feeling when I climb in the saddle. Looking down at his beautiful flowing mane and feeling his springy trot, I know that sometimes dreams do come true."

Favory II Bonasera III

Charlie Horse Acres in Graham, Washington, "runs a double track" in that Cele and Tony Noble raise a select crop of Lipizzan foals each year, because they love their characteristics, but devote the other half of their energies to showing people how to have horses with wonderful manners – a method they call Equine Technics. They put on an average of two clinics a month, demonstrating how to train using classical driving and riding methods.

Their stallion, Favory II Bonasera III, exemplifies the way people want their horses to go under saddle and to act in hand. "He serves as a figurehead for what Charlie Horse Acres stands for – the message we want to convey to other horse owners," says Cele.

This Mr. Manners of the horse world comes from the proper aristocratic background to be a role model. Foaled at Tempel Farms at Wadsworth, Illinois on February 11, 1979, he comes from the rarest line of the six Lipizzan lines in the United States, and is a superb example of the classical characteristics of the breed in that he possesses fluid movement, a superior disposition, and excellent bone. His maternal grandsire, Pluto

Ancona, was the first Lipizzan purchased by Tempel and Esther Smith, and was a son of Pluto XX, a Lipizzan given to General George Patton by the Austrians in gratitude for his role in saving the Piber herd at the end of World War II.

"FB" came into the Nobles' lives in 1986 through a phone call. He had been sold by Tempel Farms and wound up confined to a small, spare stall for a year and a half. He was sold again as the result of a divorce proceeding to his next owner, who sold him to the Nobles, because he was going on vacation in two weeks' time.

The arrival of FB that spring created a major lifestyle change for all three. The Nobles and FB found themselves on the road to large and small stallion shows and dressage shows all over the Pacific Northwest.

FB's forte is, not surprisingly, dressage. His piaffer, the trot in place, has been called world-class caliber, and he's been performing it for two years, while his passage is still developing. Cele Noble has also shown him in English pleasure classes.

To date FB has won the following: in 1989, High Point West Coast Stallion, and Pacific Northwest Lipizzan Association Champion Stallion, Pacific Northwest Lipizzan Association High Point Dressage Award; in 1990, Second Place First Level in the United States Dressage Federation's All-Breeds Awards, and a First Level Performance Certificate.

FB is teamed with well-known Pacific Northwest area rider and competitor/trainer, Debbie Noble-Perry, who is now schooling him at third and fourth levels. Debbie, who studies regularly with Charles deKunffy, distinguished dressage judge and lecturer, conducts her horse training business from Charlie Horse Acres.

FB has also been used for breeding, and his offspring inherit his kind temperament and his fluid movement, says Cele. Two of his colts, Favory II Amorosa, foaled in 1987, and Favory II Materia, foaled in 1988, are part of the Lipizzan Show at L-W Performance Horses in Las Vegas, Nevada.

Cele had the fun of riding Favory II Amorosa in November, 1991, while she was in Las Vegas, and says his movement is a carbon copy of his sire's. A daughter, Nadia, foaled in 1987, is trained to drive in long lines, is broken to cart and saddle, and did her first trail course as a three-year-old. Cele feels she exemplifies the versatility of the breed.

"FB remains a very special part of Charlie Horse Acres, conveying the wonderful temperament of the breed to visitors, living proof that horse and man can work in harmony. 'The Breed of Emperors' is now the horse of a lifetime for the North American Continent," says Cele Noble who, despite her last name, doesn't live like royalty, but certainly rides like royalty.

Pluto Bona II

The Lipizzan stallion, Pluto Bona II, almost like the fabled "Black Beauty," had been sold again and again and again. Then he met Carole Jessup, whereupon each turned the other's life around, and he found his true home.

"First a kind woman owner, then a famous horse trainer, then a home where he wasn't appreciated for his true worth," Carole chronicles Beau's misadventures. "That's about the time we discovered one another. Beau needed me at that time in his life and I found out that I needed Beau to give me new direction in the horse business and to keep me from retiring," says Carole, who with husband "Skip", owns Starmount Lipizzan Stable at Bridgeport, Michigan.

"Within three days of buying him, I knew this was the most athletic and most intelligent horse I had ever worked with in my twenty years as a trainer," Carole says. "He has three perfect gaits and the rhythm and balance that come only from the 400 years of selective breeding behind the Lipizzan breed."

Beau's ancestors are some of the most famous in the world of Lipizzan horses. His grandsire, Pluto Theodorostra, was called "the greatest exhibition horse of all time at the Spanish Riding School of Vienna, Austria," says Carole. "Beau's sire, Pluto Calcedona, was imported in utero from Austria, and later ridden by Paul Newman in a movie about the life of Buffalo Bill. Beau's dam, Bona, was also imported from Austria and is from a famous mare line dating back to 1782."

Beau was foaled in 1969 at Raflyn Farm in Washington. Luckily for both him and those who love him, he was sold the first time before the tragic flood that swept through Raflyn Farm in 1975, drowning twenty-nine of thirty-four horses there, including Beau's sire and dam.

After Carole acquired Beau, she rode him for five years in exhibitions, demonstrations and clinics, searching all the while for Lipizzan mares of his quality.

Then Tempel Farms in Wadsworth, Illinois put some of its good mares up for sale. Carole drove all night to be first in line there on sale morning. She chose Granella, Balmora, Dixana, Fabricia, Almerina II, Delphinia and Primavera.

"All the mares have proven to be excellent choices, and with Beau they have produced some of the best Lipizzans in the country today," says Carole. "Each of his offspring is in turn producing offspring worthy of the title 'Royal Horse of Austria.' We think Beau will go down in history as one of the best sires of pure Lipizzan type."

No less an authority than Dr. Jaromir Oulehla, Director of the Spanish Riding School, thought that Beau was the perfect example of the breed in this country, and that, when bred to the mare Dixana, would sire a superior breeding animal. When the Director saw Pluto II Dixana at the age of three, he confirmed this and said, 'Never sell this horse;' Beau now shares the breeding duties with his son," says Carole.

One of Beau's first foals was Crescendo, owned and ridden by Sharon Rowe of Okemos, Michigan. In 1989, he was named the U.S. Dressage Federation "Horse of the Year" at Grand Prix, over all breeds of horses. "Crescendo was the first Lipizzan horse to achieve this honor, but he won't be the last," says Carole. She helped to found the U.S. Lipizzan Registry, was its president for two years, served on the board of directors, and is now chairman of fund-raising.

"My whole life evolved toward this one goal; perhaps all of my experiences in the horse world have been toward this one breed, to help save it for eternity. All because one horse named Pluto Bona II happened to come to Michigan," says Carole.

"Even though we have thirty horses on our farm now, the highlight of my day is seeing Pluto Bona II, first of all each day. I can't imagine what my life would be without his being a part of it!"

Siglavy II Dulcibella

Kit Young Knotts had a feeling 1990 was going to be a good year. Her Lipizzan stallion, Siglavy II Dulcibella started the show season doing an acceptable Grand Prix with few mistakes. But it was in performing early versions of her musical freestyle ride that Kit began to realize how really well he was beginning to do.

"That freestyle was so exacting, it would be impossible to do it without complete harmony between us," she says. "Then came the test that was so light, so effortless, so confident, such a joy to ride, that I realized we had done it. We had achieved a level of performance I thought I was destined only to read about."

By year's end, Duce (Doo-Chay – a play on his prominent Roman nose) and Kit had achieved one of the more ambitious of the dressage rider's dreams. With Kit training Duce herself from green horse to Grand Prix, the pair won the USDF Horse of the Year Championship at Grand Prix level. Duce also came in in the Grand Prix Freestyle Champion and was first in the All-Breeds Awards (Lipizzan) both at Grand Prix level and in the Grand Prix Freestyle.

It was the payoff for nine years of a roller coaster ride up the levels of dressage competition.

"Our relationship over the years has been like a tem-

pestuous but passionate love affair, up one day, down the next, wonderful one season, awful the next. And more than once, I have almost given up." says Kit.

She fell for Duce from the start, acquiring him sight unseen as a green-broke six-year-old from Tempel Farms. When he arrived at Kit's Pegasus Farm in Orlando, Florida, she looked beyond several conformation problems to see that Duce was very athletic, flowing in his way of going, and above all, had "it" – that elusive charismatic "something" that might be the sign of a star.

"Duce is not a big horse, not a fashionable breed, not a spectacular mover, but he was and is a nice size for me, of the breed that I love, and a good and honest mover," says Kit.

"Yet for nine years, Duce sorely tested my conviction that in the final analysis, a special partnership can overcome more obstacles and bring more rewards that all the fancy, expensive or push-button horses in the world.

"Duce has the temperament of a Russian ballerina: sometimes sweet/sometimes haughty, anxious to please/devastated by correction, absolutely sure of himself/painfully insecure" as Kit describes him. "And he's a vocal, sometimes aggressive stallion, to boot."

She started Duce in Grand Prix when he was eleven. "Our difficulties were largely in our communication and the level we showed wouldn't have changed that," she reasoned.

"After two fairly awful seasons, but with him showing more and more ability, I decided I had to take control of our relationship and convince him a correction was a help and not the end of the world."

Kit and Duce spend five months doing walk, trot, and canter each way of the ring in a nice frame with Kit in charge of each step. When they started to show again, she had a Grand Prix horse. The rest is dressage annals history.

Kit believes many factors contributed to Duce's final metamorphosis. "Duce at fifteen was finally physically mature enough to take more and more weight behind and mentally willing to let me direct him," she says. Homework from coach Jessica Ransehousen, advice from judges, and the support of her husband, Ben, helped too.

"This may not have been the easiest way to achieve goals in dressage, but I would not trade the years of back-breaking work, the disappointment or the tears for anything, if the result is the ultimate sense of accomplishment I have in making this horse from the beginning," Kit says.

"Though Duce's being USDF Horse of the Year is a wonderful honor, it is secondary to the thrill of riding him everyday, feeling him get stronger and better and knowing we have many years ahead of us."

Siglavy Gaetana XXII-II

Bold, floating movement, as if he is Mozart's magnificent music come to life, a powerful presence, near-mythological beauty, and the gentle docility of a kitten. These are the essence of the classic Lipizzan horse, and the stallion Siglavy Gaetana XXII-II has all these qualities in generous measure.

At one show, his owner, Laura Leafgren of Leafgren Lipizzans in Sylmar, California, says she overheard the lady behind her comment, "He is so beautiful, he belongs on a carousel." Carole Jessup, a prominent Lipizzan breeder in Michigan, tells everyone "Sigi" (whose bloodlines date back to the original Siglavy Arab stallion introduced into the classic stallion lines of the breed in 1816) is the most beautiful Lipizzan stallion in America today. His trainer says Sigi is the only horse she knows who could be a unicorn.

Laura experienced a strange feeling when she first set eyes on Sigi, then only a few hours old. "That is my horse. I know that horse. We were together during another lifetime" were the thoughts that went through her mind. "I believed it, and knew that he was mine. There was really no decision to make," she says. "I'd have him and that was that. The little colt belonged to me." Laura, a registered nurse by profession, was an amateur rider. For a year she had been riding at a friend's barn where the beautiful Lipizzan mare, Gaetana XXII-II foaled Sigi.

"Love is a driving force," as Laura says, "and it was not long before I became quite proficient at handling a youngster." She presented him in several open breed competitions as a yearling and two-year-old, returning with ribbons, firsts among them, every time.

But eventually, Laura says, "Because I knew he deserved and needed consistent training if he was ever to develop his potential, I decided to place him with trainer Creeky Routson in Walnut Creek, California.

Routson has been showing him in three star dressage shows, those approved by the California Dressage Society, the USDF and the AHSA, and this splendid milk-white stallion, a living dream out of Austrian antiquity, has won many silver trophies.

A thrilling moment came in 1987, when Dr. Jaromir Oulehla, the director of the Spanish Riding School in Vienna, placed Sigi third in the senior stallion class, against considerably older and more developed stallions. He also won all his dressage classes at the event, judged by Dr. Rolf Vlatten.

Sigi has fulfilled Laura's childhood dream of owning a horse. "But I didn't bargain for such a fine animal, nor one that I felt would have to 'go to college,'" she says, adding that owning Sigi is somewhat like having a genius child that one must do right by.

"My life has been made more beautiful for having loved Sigi," she says. "He has expanded my experiences on this planet. The material aspects of life have become very unimportant to me. I would sell my possessions to do right by this magnificent being. I have become more patient, more gentle. Learning to communicate with a horse opens up a whole new world for the intellectual, left-brained person I have had to be. Inside, I am right-brained, and Sigi has allowed me to express this part of myself."

Maestoso II Sabrina

"For the true horseperson looking for the ultimate in communication and trust, no other breed equals the Lipizzan," says Laura Wiener, whom I've gotten to know as an exceptionally perceptive person – able to tune in on high frequency bands of communication with horse or human.

Laura has told me and written to me of many of her private feelings concerning her grey Lipizzan stallion Maestoso II Sabrina, or "Smokey," of whom she is justly proud.

"When I first met Smokey and stood in his presence our eyes met and I knew he was the horse I was supposed to have – not to own, but to be with and share a journey in life," she told me. "I was overwhelmed with inspiration and an unexplainable sense of understanding,"

Their relationship has been a richly rewarding one in many ways, but above all, Smokey has inspired Laura to overcome many obstacles in her life.

Even purchasing Smokey presented obstacles. His price was twice that of the previous record price at which Tempel Farms had ever sold a horse. Miraculously, Laura found the money.

Even purchasing Smokey presented obstacles. His price was twice that of the previous record price at which Tempel Farms had ever sold a horse. Miraculously, Laura found the money.

There were psychological barriers as well; her first attempt at breeding Lipizzans ended sadly when the nineteen-year-old Tempel stallion Pluto Belornata dropped dead of an aneurysm one month after she'd purchased him.

When in 1983 she announced her plans to bring home a seven-year-old stallion that had run wild until he was five and a half years old "for a riding horse and a friend," the local experts were aghast. "They warned me I did not have enough experience, strength and assertiveness to handle a stallion, that I would be injured or killed.

"Then when I mentioned that my plans included showing and breeding this stallion, horse friends warned me that a stallion cannot start out breeding and showing at the same time, that it would produce a dangerous, unmanageable monster."

But Laura paid heed to the inner voice which urged her to trust.

In 1984, Smokey began competing at nationally recognized shows against the best and most experienced riders in the country on the best horses Europe had to offer. He was breeding mares every season, while training sometimes two levels at a time.

By the summer of 1988, with Jennifer Roth as trainer, Smokey had reached Prix St. Georges level, taking third place at the California Dressage Society Annual Championships, and winning the USDF All-Breeds Award at Third Level.

Smokey and Jennifer spent the month of August 1989 showing Intermediare and doing a freestyle performance which brought standing ovations as they danced in perfect harmony to the music. In September, they placed second in the nation in the USDF Horse of the Year Awards for Intermediare Freestyle, also winning the USDF All Breeds Award for Intermediare and the Intermediare Freestyle. "I believe only a Lipizzan could earn this type of recognition with only eight weeks of Intermediare training," Laura says.

In 1990, Smokey placed second in the AHSA National Finals for the Intermediare Freestyle and third in the Intermediare and Grand Prix Freestyle Open, with a score of 69.275%, only four-tenths of one percent from first place. He was the only horse who received deafening applause and a standing ovation from a thousand people that night. A very famous and respected European judge sitting in the audience that night was overheard telling his wife that Smokey's performance was what dressage is all about.

To Laura, Smokey represents hope: "The white horse of hope vanquishing the dark horses of depression and bursting into the light in a capriole of pleasure...he has inspired me to follow my dreams in spite of obstacles and negativity from others."

Pluto Balmora

Sandra L. Heaberlin of Silver Meadows Farm in Johnstown, Ohio began her riding career at the age of eighteen, after she received her first paycheck. She progressed from saddleseat to hunters to dressage, but never forgot her attraction to the Lipizzan horse, which began when she was ten years old and saw the Disney movie, *Miracle of the White Stallions*.

"I never thought I would ever be able to own a Lipizzan and knew that there were very few outside Austria," says Sandra. "Finally I discovered the Raflyn Lipizzan Farm in Snohomish, Washington, owned by Evelyn Dreitzler. Mrs. Dreitzler knew she was corresponding with a child, but nevertheless sent sales lists and Christmas cards every year up until the time that her farm was almost all destroyed in the 1970's when a dam broke. I remember that Evelyn Dreitzler once wrote in response to one of my cards that 'Someday you will own one of my horses.' She was right!"

Pluto Balmora, Sandra's Lipizzan stallion, is the grandson of one of Dreitzler's stallions, Pluto Calceldona.

Before Sandra purchased Pluto Balmora, she owned a fifteen-year-old broodmare that gave her a purebred colt. But when Sandra's husband died, she desperately needed to ride to distract herself, and began the search for a riding horse.

"I had absolutely no intention of getting a stallion; I was not set up to keep a stallion. I did and still do board my horses," Sandra says. A breeder offered her a choice of Pluto Balmora or his full brother. Pluto "chose" her.

"Although not the largest of the colts, he was very powerful and could be a handful. Heaven knows his trot is so animated that sitting is work for the rider, but the horse possessed the most expressive eyes and willing disposition of any horse I have encountered," says Sandra.

Pluto Balmora's barn name is "Nipper," she says. "No, he isn't a biter. His breeder said he looked so much like his sire, they all remarked, 'Oh, look at the little Nipper,' and the name stuck. The nickname isn't dignified, but then again neither is Nipper, on occasion. He can look down the length of his nose and give you an affronted 'So what's not to admire' glare, but most of the time his large dark eyes hold a mischievous sparkle, especially when he up-ends a full manure bucket."

Nipper has very large, expressive eyes, well-shaped ears, a long, arched neck, powerful quarters, large flat joints, and substantial bone. He obtained his silver coat at a very early age and is becoming a proven competitor at dressage, winning his class at the first show in 1992 and placing second in another. Currently he is schooling second level.

Several years ago, Nipper was a co-mascot for the Central Ohio Lung Association's "Celebration of the Horse." As co-mascot, his duties included a television appearance and exhibition on the lawn of Battelle Park in downtown Columbus during rush-hour traffic. Nipper was also persuaded, although reluctantly, to enter an army tent where he could be viewed at the Celebration, but only after two people raised the poles of the tent's entrance to accommodate his size. "The horse was too royal to bend his neck to enter the musty tent," jokes his owner.

Nipper's versatility – halter, suitability, English pleasure, hunter under saddle and dressage – gave him the high point Lipizzan trophy at the regional Lipizzan-Andalusian Show held at the Kentucky Horse Park in Lexington, Kentucky.

"Partner, companion, friendship based on mutual respect and affection. These words come to mind when describing our relationship," says Sandra. "The same arrogant horse that can puff up and grow three inches to impress another horse is the same one that snuggles his nose under my arm when I finish riding and enthusiastically greets me when I walk out into the pasture to say 'Hi.' I've learned patience, and certainly have no idea of who is the senior member of the partnership and don't really care. The only sad thing is that we will probably only have another twenty years together."

Siglavy Deja

Fate deposited the Lipizzan stallion Siglavy Deja into the safekeeping of television celebrity and animal trainer Joan Embery when his previous owner became seriously ill.

Siglavy Deja, whose barn name is Gallo (meaning "rooster"), was part of a three-horse liberty act which toured for several years with the Circus Vargas, one of the last of the traveling tent shows.

It was the winter of 1981, and the late Don McLennan, owner/trainer of Siglavy Deja and two other horses in his act (Diamond, a half-Lipizzan, half-Arabian, and Jason Gali, an Arabian gelding) were in San Diego with the circus when Don suffered a heart attack. From his hospital bed, he called Joan Embery, animal ambassadress for the San Diego Zoo, and asked if she would keep his horses while he recovered, because the circus was moving on without him.

"I brought the horses out to my ranch," says Joan, "while Don was in the hospital. In time he recovered from his heart attack, but he was unable to go on the road again." While convalescing, Don came to Joan's ranch and coached her on how to work liberty. After a while he offered to sell Joan the horses, rather than haul them back to Oregon, where he lived.

"I was having such a good time with them, I decided to buy the three animals," Joan says. "I wondered how they would act when I was by myself, since by then I realized that working a liberty act is not as easy as it

looks. Once Don McLennan left town, I envisioned those three horses standing there staring at me and asking, 'Well, what do you want?'"

No need to worry. Joan, who made seventy appearances on the Johnny Carson show with three hundred animals over a twenty-two-year period, mastered the liberty horse techniques in short order.

Along the way, she got to know Gallo better. Gallo, now twenty-one years old, takes his work seriously, Joan says. "He's a short, stocky strong horse, with good action, and he's level-headed. He is the center horse in the No. 2 slot, and also the horse who does the capriole. It's amazing how he can really get himself airborne and kick out."

Though she's worked with all breeds, from Thoroughbreds to draft horses, Joan likes the mentality of the Lipizzan. "They're very quick to learn. Gallo is so smart. At the time I bought him, he knew his routine better than I did. Everytime I would get out of place or do something wrong, the horses would let me know.

"For one thing, if you step back in liberty, it drives the horses toward you. If you step toward them, you drive them to the rail. If you do the wrong thing when they come in and run in front of you, it is possible to get run over. One wrong step can spoil the whole routine," she says.

"Liberty work takes a lot of finesse," she continues. "If you're overly powerful or too pushy, it interferes with the horses' concentration. If you get excited, you lose control. You must maintain a balance between controlling the horses and giving them the freedom to do the movements."

The horses worked so well that Joan has given exhibitions with her act at the large indoor "A to Z" horse show in Phoenix, Arizona, as well as at the Del Mar Horse Show. The liberty act was also one of the segments on her syndicated television series, "Animal Express." On camera, she taught actor John Ritter how to work liberty, "and it was a riot," says Joan. "It looks so easy, but he would make one wrong move and everything went. 'Oh, no, I broke the act!' he would say. But John was a good sport and actually did quite well."

Joan has worked with creatures from hummingbirds to elephants, aardvarks to zebras, but horses are her favorites. "Whether it's liberty or jumping or dressage, what happens between horse and trainer or rider is the ultimate cooperation between man and animal," says Joan. "The ability to have that kind of give and take rapport is not as easily achieved with other animals as it is with the horse. It is hard to find anything that comes close to that. Perhaps only the mahouts who work the elephants in the teak forest have the same kind of rapport."

THE LUSITANO

Both the Spanish or Andalusian horse and the Portuguese or Lusitano horse stem from the same ancient root, the Iberian horse.

Early in the twentieth century, it was determined essential for the future of the breed in Spain that it remain absolutely pure and that all future outcrosses with other breeds would not be entered in the Spanish studbook. Spain imposed strict controls and requirements for acceptance in the studbook, and disassociated itself from the Portuguese horse, whose breeding was guided by less restrictive parameters.

Because of this basic philosophical difference in the recent evolution of the Iberian horses in Spain and Portugal, it is now necessary for them to be categorized as two separate breeds and for the respective studbooks to be separated.

To realize what the differences are, one must understand that the Lusitano's breeding traditions are inextricably tied to the breeding of brave bulls for *rejoneo*. The Lusitano's function as a working horse has remained of greater importance, whereas with the Spanish horse, the emphasis has been placed more on the physical grace and beauty of the animal and its purity of bloodlines.

The Lusitano's use for hunting the wild Iberian bull goes back to pre-history on the Peninsula. The terminology comes from the Spanish word *rejon*, meaning spear. *Rejoneadors* or spearmen mounted on hot-blooded horses have practiced this dangerous sport down the centuries. Wild bulls were hunted with great ceremony on special occasions, such as a royal marriage or a religious festival, but probably any excuse would do. Even foreigners such as Julius Caesar got caught up in the excitement of the sport; Caesar himself fought from the back of an Iberian horse in the Coliseum of Rome.

When the role of the horse trained for war diminished, Portuguese and Spanish knights found it only natural and great sport to turn to the hunting of the wild Iberian bull. This activity properly exercised their mounts and kept them in shape for battle conditions, if needed.

Equestrian bullfighting was a passionate pastime in both Spain and Portugal through the seventeenth century. The horses bred for this purpose were bred mainly in the southern part of the Iberian peninsula. Horses bred in Portugal were called Lusitanos or Lusitanians; in Spain, the Spanish horse.

But so many young nobles were being killed in bullfighting that their distraught families petitioned the Pope, who laid down an edict, enforced by the Bourbon Dynasty. *Rejoneo* was forbidden and eventually disappeared, replaced by bullfighting on foot by serfs.

This is when the schism in breeding philosophies actually occurred, as the Portguese continued to breed for *rejoneo* while the Spaniards did not.

In 1763, the art of *rejoneo* was more popular than ever in Portugal and the Marquis de Marialva, a brilliant horseman, introduced new methods of attack and defense and laid down rules that hold to this day. Traditional Portuguese horsemanship is called *A Marilava*, and *rejoneo* is essentially a Portuguese art.

In Spain, equestrian bullfighting was revived relatively recently, but often the *rejoneadors* go to Portugal to buy trained horses. Breeders, however, do the reverse. There are larger numbers of horses in Spain than in Portugal, and pure stock of ancient Spanish bloodlines is at times infused into the Portuguese stock in order to improve and strengthen the breed.

When the Portuguese go to Spain to look for breeding material, they search for a horse that is specifically athletic. This is because most of them will go into bullfighting, working in the country with the bulls, or into producing bullfighting horses. The latter has to be very athletic, quick to react, quick on its feet, and very responsive to the rider. Its cat-like agility makes riding the horse the equivalent of driving a Ferrari with a sensitive accelerator.

The Lusitano is long-legged and short-backed, which usually means it can get its hind end under it easily. The robust strength in the Lusitano's hindquarters gives it superb natural impulsion, a great potential for dressage. This impulsion and its ability to step under behind, combined with the relaxed swinging of its back and flexing of its joints, can make a superb Lusitano the envy of German Warmblood fanciers.

Most Lusitanos are good-sized, 16 hands and up. Bulls in Portugal are a ton and a half in size, and the *rejoneador* has to be able to lean over – not reach up – to place *banderillas* and *rejon* into the bull.

The guesstimate is that there are about sixteen purebred Lusitano stallions in the United States, plus a few in Canada. The International Andalusian Horse Association registers them with "P" for pure Lusitano next to their names, and "S/P" if they are a cross with the Spanish. The American Andalusian Horse Association registers them with an "L" for Lusitano next to their names.

La Cobista

In Spanish *la cobista* has this delightful meaning: "a girl who flirts and uses her feminine wiles to get whatever she wants." This approach is true of the personality of La Cobista, the ever charming and eager to please Lusitano mare owned by Patricia Akkad of Swan Farms at Acton, California.

La Cobista was foaled February 16, 1978 at Ramona, California, at "El Cortijo Andaluz," a breeding farm owned by Budd and Mary Boetticher. The mare is unusual in that she works as a polo pony, and more than holds her own in a discipline dominated by the Thoroughbred.

Actually, "Cubby" has shown at amateur levels in almost every discipline, from dressage, stadium jumping, cross-country jumping, and parade work to team penning. However, of all La Cobista's awards, owner Patty is most proud of the polo recognition of December, 1991, "Best Playing Pony of the United States Women's Open," a title won against a field of about 200 horses, mostly Thoroughbreds.

Patty ensured the announcer told the crowd Cubby is a Lusitano.

Another exciting moment in Cubby's career occurred when Patty loaned her horses to Tommy Wayman, the only ten-goal American polo player. (Ten goals is the highest handicap possible; there are only ten so-handicapped players in the world.) Wayman played several of Patty's horses, including the Thoroughbreds, and declared Cubby "quick and handy."

"This mare is a superlative horse for low goal polo," says Patty who, together with a partner, was the first woman in the country to own a United States Polo Association member club. "La Cobista is so athletic and loves the game. She may not have the running-on speed of the Thoroughbred, but she is as handy and brave in a ride-off (bumping another horse off the line of the ball) as any horse on the field."

Patty's daughter, Rima, now twenty-one, and rated one of the top women polo players in the United States, began to play polo on Cubby when she was eleven. "When Rima plays Cubby, the mare is described as 'awesome,'" says Patty.

Patty first noticed Cubby being ridden across a field from the boarding and training stable she managed. The sensation was similar to the time when "one is startled to meet the eyes of a true love for the first time," she says.

"Cubby was only two years old and very green broke, acting naughty, nearly unseating the young lady who was trying to ride her. But what beautiful movement and she had that most unusual color of greyish-gold or ermine. With her flaxen mane and tail flying, I was smitten in that first moment.

"It was somehow meant that she was to be mine. Cubby's owner was unable to pay the board bill for several months, and simply abandoned her. So I paid the delinquent bill of $500 and she was mine! I was intrigued by the unusual brand on her hip and, in tracing its origins, was elated to learn of her breed, as I have always had a special place in my soul for Iberia," says Patty. From the Boettichers, Patty learned that La Cobista was sired by the great bullfighting stallion Califa, out of the mare Destinada, which must have had something to do with her bravery, quickness and handiness on her feet.

"La Cobista's life of capriciousness changed radically when she had to learn the very rough game of polo," says Patty. "But Cubby has consistently given me more than any of the other hundred or so horses I have owned over many years. In essence, she taught me more than any other horse of that special understanding between horse and owner.

"Amazingly intelligent and cooperative, La Cobista always seems to live up to her name—she flirts and endears everyone to her," continues Patty. "I am currently reducing my numbers of horses and playing less polo. But one thing is sure. I will keep this mare to her last day, sound or not. She has earned our special care for life."

Moro

Though the grey Lusitano Moro was "the least flashy, least pretty" of all of the horses that Edith Evans-Williams, the American *rejoneadora*, was selling, he was the only one who interested movie actress Bo Derek.

Bo, known for her roles in movies such as *10* and *Bolero*, in private life is an accomplished horsewoman and a great friend of mine. Besides being the most beautiful woman I have ever known, she is natural, accessible and very bright.

"I was brought up on the beach in Southern California, but I was horse crazy. I think there's a genetic code for it," Bo told me. "I read all the horse books that little girls do, and my father got me an old retired rental horse."

By the time she traveled to Spain to film the movie *Bolero*, Bo had graduated to an Arabian gelding. Within hours of arriving, she was riding some of the best bullfighting horses of Alvaro Domecq and Angel and Rafael Peralta. That changed forever her ideas of what constitutes a "10" of a riding horse. It also influenced her choice of the twenty horses at the Evans' sale.

"Moro was the only one she rode for me," says Bo. Evans had trained him to spin and to do sliding stops (moves from her Texas upbringing) which she demonstrated for Bo.

"I saw the way he got excited when she came around him. There was something about him...and the way he treated Edith as against the other people who handled him. He's one of those rare horses that does recognize you and with whom you can develop a relationship," Bo recalls.

Bred in Mexico, the then twelve-year-old Moro "also was not a giant like a lot of Spanish horses, only 15.1," Bo notes. "He was strong in the hindquarters and collected all the time, which I knew would make him easier to ride."

Once she tried him, Bo thought Moro "just incredible, a very, very special horse" and bought him along with two-year-old dark bay-black Spanish stallion, Centauro, who was "a lot flashier, a fantasy horse come to life in looks," she says.

But Moro remains her favorite. "I like the smaller compact, quick, really athletic horse," says Bo. She describes him as having an "old, classic profile with really fine bones in his face, a beautiful wedge-shaped diamond when you look at it from the front. Short coupled, with a short back and hind end set under tight. He's really a beautifully balanced thing. Leggy, but shorter than most Iberian horses," says Bo.

Moro was fully trained when she bought him. His repetoire includes pirouettes, caprioles, passage, piaffer, Spanish trot, and the slides and spins. "I can take him on cattle gatherings and brandings. He loves it," Bo says.

He is Bo's personal riding horse, though he is often full of himself. "He's the most proud, noisy, showy thing!" she laughs, "but if I can mentally say, 'Please, not now,' somehow he understands and behaves," she says.

Asked how many horses she has on her California ranch, she replies "Oh, lots," in her whispery sweet voice. "I think we're a real inconvenience in their lives," she says of the horse/human relationship. "We take them away from everything that is natural to them. Everything we get from them comes from their pain. When you're horse-crazy as a little girl, it is kind of depressing to think that you're putting this painful bit in their mouths in order to ride them. But when I got to Spain and saw those horses, how they moved and how they acted, the horse-craziness started all over again for me!" She was convinced that to own the kind of exciting horses she saw in Spain, she would have to import them – until she learned of the Edith Evans sale.

Bo now has an heir apparent to twenty-year-old Moro, his son Morito, who is out of a half-Lusitano mare, Lanca, sired by the Westmoreland's Leopardo III.

Morito is two years old and "living up to his sire. It is wonderful to see the same personality and physical traits," says Bo of her new "dream horse."

THE MORGAN

America grew from the muscle of the Morgan horse, one of the most noble, historically important breeds that nature and man have ever collaborated to create.

The Hollywood film, *Justin Morgan Had a Horse*, the story of the plucky, prepotent little bay stallion who founded the breed, and the many books published on Morgans provide an abundance of material on the breed.

A seemingly bottomless source of intriguing, controversial, quaint, and often humorous data exists to offer insight not only into genetics of the breed, but the history of our country.

From the start, Morgans could be picked out on sight from any and all other breeds. They were small, symmetrical, plump and pleasing in outline, tough, clever, nimble saddle horses, as sure-footed as a goat and as hardy as hickory, full of life and spirit, but so tractable that women and children could handle them, and as intelligent as they were good-tempered, according to John Hervey, one of the historians of the breed.

The original Morgan, known as "Figure" in his lifetime, was about fourteen hands high and weighed about 950 pounds. His color was dark bay with black legs, mane and tail; his mane and tail were coarse and heavy.

Posthumously, Figure came to bear the name of Justin Morgan, in honor of the schoolmaster, singer and composer who first brought him to Vermont.

Figure was a horse from which legends would be built; his history is given a romantic flair by the unknown, like a painting left half in shadow. During the lifetime of Justin Morgan, the man, no account of his horse's pedigree was put into writing, and verbal accounts are as disparate as each individual's memory.

Even the year he foaled is disputed. One researcher gives his foaling year as 1789, which seems more reasonable than the alternate 1793, as he was first advertised at stud in 1792 in the *Hartford Courant*: "Figure, a beautiful bay horse, will cover this season at twenty shillings the season or Two Dollars for the Single leap."

The ad noted that Figure "sprang from a curious horse owned by a Col. De Lancey of New York, but the greatest recommendation I can give him is, he is exceedingly sure, and gets curious colts." (Curious, in its archaic use, meaning "fashioned skillfully.")

Figure was an uncommonly sturdy animal who survived a lifetime of hard work and may have lived until 1821. The early days of his life were occupied with carrying Justin Morgan to and from school, plowing, stump-pulling and pulling wagons. He was often leased out to farmers who used him for the most grueling of labors.

In spite of lack of pampering, this phenomenal little stallion was found to have few rivals when it came to stamping his own likeness on his descendants. As his fame spread from Vermont to Tennessee, he became the founder and progenitor of a distinct type of horse.

Researchers have documented and identified a dozen or more sons of the bay stallion that perpetuated their sire's image and were instrumental in the foundation of the breed. Six stand out more than others: Sherman, Woodbury, Bulrush, Weasel, Young Traveler (or Hawkins Horse) and Revenge, the last three less widely known.

In addition to leaving his imprint so deeply on generations of Morgans, Figure and his descendants mingled his blood with other outstanding breeds of American horses.

Morgans were used to perfect the modern Tennessee Walking Horse and the Quarter Horse. Several Morgans of outstanding quality, tracing back to Justin Morgan through his sons Black Hawk, Sherman and Woodbury, made tremendous contributions to the American Saddlebred. Standardbred experts consider Morgan influence important in the development of that breed.

When the Morgan horse, supplanted by the automobile, found itself in precarious position at the turn of the century, it was able to make the transition from eighteenth century plow, pack, stagecoach, army and parade horse to twentieth century hobby, trail, police and show horse.

Early in the 1900s, the Morgan Horse Farm near Middlebury, Vermont was established. It has gone through various incarnations, but today students of the University of Vermont and State Agricultural College continue to work with, care for and show the Morgans. Presided over by the famous statue of Justin Morgan, the farm continues to be a mecca for horse lovers. Morgan horse judging schools are held there, while riding clubs and 4-H groups come for information and demonstrations.

Today's Morgans are a tribute to old Justin's prepotency and multi-faceted attributes. Modern breeders continue to strive to produce a horse with the conformation, disposition and performance of which Justin Morgan, the man, would have been proud.

Lord Appleton

Can you imagine a stallion whose attractiveness was of such magnitude, a horse of such rare charisma and aesthetic perfection that its one-time owner allowed no one else to see and be witness to its brilliance?

Because the owner's greatest pleasure in life was the overpowering beauty of his horse, he built an arena especially for it with state-of-the-art lighting and sound systems. In the evening, as the lights played on the stallion and classical music filled the air, a sole spectator– the stallion's owner– would sit in the darkness of the empty building, delighting in the extraordinarily beautiful animal before him.

The dark stallion of the story later went to live where he could be viewed by the many people who know of his extraordinary beauty– at Nemours, the Delaware farm of Martha and Henry du Pont.

"Muffin" du Pont's joy in having shared part of her life with Lord Appleton is a reflection of her passion for North America's oldest breed of domestic equine.

"I know that this may sound crazy to some people, but Lord Appleton is not an ordinary horse," says Muffin. "He is one of the few American Morgan horses left that is built very much like Justin Morgan, the founder of our breed.

"Appleton is on earth, we believe, to remind people of what the Morgan breed looks like and to share his essence as a horse. We are simply his fortunate keepers and safe-guarders. Our responsibility is taken very seriously, particularly when it came to breeding him. At Nemours farm we are producing a very uniform crop of Morgans who look like Morgans and will not be mistaken for any other breed.

"We decided to get into raising Morgans because they were America's first breed, used to help develop this country," says Muffin. She is the originator of the Morgan Horse Breeder's Association and president of the Morgan Horse Development Institution, which promotes the American Morgan horse internationally, funds research grants, and sponsors breeders' seminars, and other related projects.

For me, photographing Lord Appleton was much like photographing some legendary creature of Greek mythology. He fell naturally into every pose that showed his beauty without the slightest interference or direction from the artist. I can honestly say that never in my life have I been so impressed by a horse's presence and what seemed to be his own opinion of himself.

But if I was impressed with Lord Appleton in person, later I was literally startled when I opened a book to find an engraving depicting the stallion Justin Morgan– a mirror image of the horse I had recently stared at through the camera viewfinder.

Only fate could have put such a horse into the hands of the du Ponts. They have the love and means to ensure that the Morgan horse will not only be remembered as an important part of America's past, but will continue to be ridden and driven with pride into America's future.

(Since this profile was written, Appleton died. It was my good fortune to know him and to number myself among the admirers of his bold beauty.)

Rake's Progress

Salem Farm in North Clarendon, Vermont, is home to numerous World Champions and many famous Morgan horses reside there, but one horse in particular stands out for owner/trainer Peggy Alderman – the chestnut stallion, Rake's Progress.

His is the story of a horse who finally found someone to "listen" to him and allow him to do what he was best at.

Rake came to Salem Farm in September, 1976 and spent the next three years growing and learning his lessons to harness and saddle. He made his show debut in the spring of 1979 at the Northampton Fairgrounds in Northampton, Massachusetts. For the next several years he won many prestigious classes, competing in Park Saddle and Park Harness. "He also lost many classes as he was extremely volatile," says Peggy. Many saddle classes were lost when he refused to canter. In harness Rake disliked the slow, elegant ways of a top Park Horse, and was difficult to rate. Rake also displayed a nervous temperament, disliking change in his routine and often colicking under new circumstances. "For these reasons I always felt protective of him," says Peggy, who acquired a half-interest in Rake in 1985, when he was nine years old, this in return for assuming responsibility for his care. It was then that Rake was retired to stud and turned out in a paddock to exercise.

"Rake HATED retirement and became surly and ugly whenever I walked by his stall," says Peggy. "Rake always demanded to be worked first on our daily schedule. He would fuss and kick and carry on until taken out. I finally put him back to work, for everyone's sake. Rake's previous work involved slow, lifting animation, and he was difficult as he always wanted to go on. Also, he hated to canter. As he was not in serious training, I said to myself, 'Fine, go ahead!' I was astounded by the speed he exhibited at the trot. A light bulb went on in my head and I decided to develop him for the roadster division, where style is important, but speed is the major criterion. In hindsight, it was the division he should have been in all along."

Rake debuted that spring and defeated not only Morgans but Saddlebreds and Standardbreds to win the Championship. He won and won and won at every show. He won the Stallion and Geldings qualifier at the World Championship. He lost only once in the World Grand Championship to a great mare, the reigning World Champion. In 1987 he did much the same. "1988 was the year I judged the World Championship, and Rake was worked but not shown," says Peggy. In 1989, at age thirteen, he won every class he competed in and was the World Champion Roadster to Bike. Peggy became the first woman driver to ever win this award, as the Roadster Division is a fast, thrilling, macho type of class, dominated by men. Rake did not lose a class in 1989, 1990 and 1991, and was World Champion those three years. Rake will show one more time in 1992 at Northampton Fairgrounds where he started, and where he will be retired with fanfare, at age sixteen.

"I have shown and trained hundreds of horses and I can safely say I have never worked a horse as competitive as Rake," says Peggy. "He knows several days ahead that we are preparing to go to a show and his demeanor changes. He becomes expectant and anxious. When we wash his tail, he starts glowing. He knows his routine and when he is not worked the morning of the competition, he stands at his door waiting. By the time he is brought out of his stall to prep for the class, he is already 'high' and he looks through you and not at you. By the time we hitch him, he is on full alert, ears straight ahead and oblivious to his handlers.

"He lives to compete and I have mixed feelings about retiring him, but he has won everything a horse can win and more. I have enjoyed showing Rake more than any other horse and have turned down numerous offers for him – remember I'm in business! I feel a lot of loyalty to Rake and know he would not thrive with a new owner and handler," says Peggy. "Rake still looks and acts like a youngster and I will enjoy speeding down the dirt roads of Vermont with him for a few more years."

Treble's Willy Wild

July of 1977 was to have a profound impact on Treble's Morgan Manor in Reddick, Florida. A twist of fate would close the final page of one chapter of the small breeding operation and open a new one. Quaker Acre Treble, the farm's founding horse, was laid to rest after an extended illness. Treble had made the childhood dreams of owner Carol Bailey Hudson come true. "My small farm was named after this wonderful chestnut stallion," she says. "When he died, I vowed to never love another horse so deeply that a part of my heart would be broken forever."

But then a new page in her life began to be written as, within days of Treble's death, a little bay colt was foaled. "I avoided any emotions when this precocious colt demanded my attention," says Carol. "I tried to ignore him, but something set this one apart from all the rest." Intuition told her the colt was destined to be a star, but she would not let her heart be involved. She resolved to keep the breeding operation on a strictly business level.

But the more time she spent with Treble's Willy Wild, the first colt to carry the "Treble" prefix, the more she realized this colt had a special charisma. "He was becoming another dream," she says.

"Willy Wild drew the attention of everyone who came to the farm. His seahorse-shaped head was like none other seen in the Morgan breed. Horsemen, no matter their breed affiliation, would remark on his glorious head and huge eye," she continues. "Willy Wild quickly developed a fan club. Morgan fanciers enjoyed his attitude; trainers appreciated his athletic ability; artists, his sheer beauty. Author Walter Farley was fascinated by the depth of Willy's eyes. Artist Angela Conner of Great Britain came to the farm to select a son of Willy Wild to continue the Foundation Morgan Farm in her country. One of my treasured pieces is a sketch of Willy that Angela sent after her Willy Wild colt arrived in London."

Willy enjoyed a successful show career in park saddle as well as in hand. As his show career was winding down, his breeding career blossomed. Carol says his first two foal crops were so well received that Willy was set on his new course as a sire. "Willy Wild stamps his offspring with that unique 'Willy' look," says his owner. "His get and grandget continue to have a significant impact on the show ring today, winning World and Grand National titles."

She feels that as Willy matures he seems to become even more beautiful. "When he was ten years old his trainer, Cheri Barber, along with Conky Price, decided to show him one last time," recalls Carol. "They chose the prestigious New England Morgan Regional Championship in Northampton, Massachusetts. After years of retirement, it made me nervous!" But Cheri and Conky believed that he never looked better. Show shoes were made, his bridle was dug out of storage and the anticipation began. "The excitement that was in the barn that week cannot be put into words," says Carol. "Then reality set in. What if he gets beaten at the largest show in the country with the largest audience? By the time we reached the show, my nerves were shot!"

No one knew Willy was there until he went through the gate. The crowd tried to figure out who the mystery horse was. It didn't take long. Willy made a show to remember, tail flying over his back. Treble's Willy Wild was named Grand Champion Stallion. "We had wanted to show this wonderful horse just one last time so everyone could admire what we enjoy on a daily basis," says Carol.

"Living with Willy, you admire his striking beauty but, beneath the skin and bone, there is a rare dimension of love that sets this one stallion apart. Willy's love made me open a part of my heart which I was firmly determined to keep closed."

Courage of Equinox

It is normal for a young stallion to begin his adult life with a performance career to introduce his abilities to the horse world at large. In that way people who see him can become familiar with his attributes, and Courage of Equinox showed a great potential for the show ring. His pedigree on both sides is loaded with show ring champions and he appeared to embody the best of all the genes behind him.

Impressively tall for a Morgan (15.3) his build is an elegant blend of substance and refinement; his long upright neck blends smoothly into a deep, strong shoulder and his hindquarters show depth and strength.

However, his owner, Orrin Beattie, a Vermont state legislator, had different plans for this extraordinary young stallion. He had originally sought out Courage as a junior herd sire for his Morgan horse farm, East of Equinox, in Manchester Center, but became so attached to him, he decided to keep him for his own personal riding pleasure. He didn't want Courage "ruined" by the high pressure world of the show arena. And so it happened that this elegant, high-stepping athlete became the fanciest trail horse to ever grace the hills of Vermont.

Orrin Beattie found the three-month-old chestnut colt in Connecticut in 1972. Over the years Beattie had become infatuated with the elegant show mare, Kay

Bennfield, and when he found out she had a two-year-old son sired by the prominent stallion, Chasely Superman, he had to see the colt. The colt exceeded all of his expectations, and Orrin quickly struck a deal for him. "Courage came to the beautiful valley lying east of the famous peak of Equinox Mountain in the fall of 1972, there to embark upon the most incredible career ever achieved by a Morgan," says Ivan Beattie, Orrin's son. "We had no idea of the impact this young stallion would have, not only on our lives but on the Morgan breed in general."

While Courage was trotting down maple-shaded country lanes, his full sister, Special Kay, was burning up the show ring. She became the only mare in Morgan history to win the title of World Champion Morgan Mare twice (a distinction she still holds today).

Morgan owners became interested in breeding to Courage because he is the only son of Chasely Superman and Kay Bennfield. More important, Courage of Equinox offspring were starting to hit the show ring and were dominating their respective divisions.

Sadly, in 1978, Orrin Beattie died of a sudden heart attack and his son Ivan and his wife Sandy decided to attempt to make East of Equinox Farm a profitable business. At its center, of course, was Courage of Equinox.

"Even without a large bankroll to promote him, by 1983 Courage of Equinox was ranked third among living sires in the breed, and in 1984, he became the youngest sire to ever top the Morgan sire ratings, besting all stallions living or dead, and he topped it by a commanding margin," says Ivan. The rating is determined by points gained by a stallion's offspring in competition.

The offspring are testimony to traditional Morgan versatility, winning championships in dressage, carriage competition, harness racing, competitive trail riding, even western reining.

As of this writing, Courage of Equinox has sired more champions than any other stallion in Morgan history. He has well over 250 offspring throughout the United States, Canada, England, Sweden and Germany.

Still never shown, Courage has set another record that Ivan says may never be eclipsed in the Morgan breed. In 1985, a single breeding to Courage of Equinox sold for $27,000 at public auction to benefit the American Morgan Horse Association.

People have traveled from all over the world to see Courage of Equinox at home in the Vermont Hills. At twenty years of age, though graying a little on his temples, he still gives viewers goosebumps when he strikes a pose.

And he is still Ivan's favorite trail horse out of sixty-some horses on the farm. "My son Matthew, age eight, loves to climb into the saddle with me and hit the trails," says Ivan.

Legacys Viking

Through all her horse-dreaming years, through high school, college and medical school, Dr. Lisa A. Duval-Kennedy had decided from which breed she would distill those dreams. "I knew that I wanted a Morgan," she says with finality. "I had known several when I was younger, and they all had lovely temperaments and were good friends."

Finally the moment came – in 1983. Lisa had finished medical school, was entering her residency training program and would be earning her first paycheck. The choice before her was a common one for horse lovers: "Whether to trade in and upgrade my 1971 Ford Pinto or buy a horse. It was no contest." She took a vacation, visiting Morgan farms in New England, and finally purchased UVM Leader who still lives at Lisa's Fox Meadow Farm in Springfield, Maine. But Leader was just the initiation to an undreamed future, a horse of the caliber she had never planned or hoped to own.

It was November, 1990 and Lisa attended a sale in Kentucky. Her accountant stood beside her. Lisa had already bought the young breeding stallion she had come for. The sale was nearly over, with only two or three horses to go.

Then Legacys Viking made a spectacular entrance into the ring. Lisa had heard that Legacys Viking was a World Champion many times over, and that he had been owned by several people over the years, but that was all she knew.

Lisa turned to her accountant and asked, "Do you think I should buy him?" The auctioneer's gavel was raised and he was asking, "Last call. Any more interest?" The auctioneer's assistant however picked up the vibes from Lisa's corner and, keeping an eye on her, motioned to the auctioneer to hold up. The accountant's answer finally came: "It's only money." Lisa nodded once, held her breath through a pregnant pause, and the gavel slammed down. "Sold for $16,500!"

Lisa was dumbstruck. What had she done? Her trainer/agent, who had so carefully screened horses for her, spending countless hours on the phone with various breeders across the country to track down the right horse for her, was a sea of faces away, totally unaware of her move. Then suddenly she was at Lisa's side, craning to see who the runner was approaching for a signature.

"Who bought him?" she asked. Lisa's heart pounded: "Your client here!" she answered, watching the trainer's face for signs of what was coming next. The trainer was speechless, fumbling for words that finally came: "It's all right. Maybe we can make an amateur horse out of him."

"I think my heart pounded for at least another two hours," says Lisa. "Would I do it again? In a minute!"

In the past year or so, Lisa has learned more about "Mac," who now stands at Fox Meadow Farm.

"He's a show horse through and through," she says. "He loves to be in the ring. He is a horse who epitomizes all that is revered in the equine world! He has a singular commanding presence, a bold and willing spirit and an unrivaled power in performance, driven by a grand and noble heart."

Great horse that he is, however, he does have his weakness, says Lisa. "Nacho Cheese-Flavored Doritos. And don't try to pass off those ranch-flavored chips."

As for his favorite person, "It would have to be Tom Caisse," says Lisa. "Together they dominated the Grand National Show Ring from 1979 to 1984, accumulating a show record few if any horses have ever come close to, including 1987 World Grand Champion Park Saddle Horse and 1983 World Champion Park Harness Horse.

"Tom thinks the world of Mac, and I think that feeling is mutual," says Lisa. "Horses do their best for those they love the most. As for me, I can only hope that the way to Mac's heart is through his stomach, so I keep those Doritos coming!"

Mapleridge Sonatina

In 1981, Mapleridge Sonatina put on the show of a lifetime and was named World Champion Two-Year-Old Park Harness at the Grand National Morgan Horse Show held in Oklahoma. After her spectacular showing, she was brought back to her home state of Illinois where she was bred to Cajun Pepper, the only surviving son of Brown Pepper.

Dr. Linda Ehlers first saw her at a 1983 sale. "When she came into the ring, I realized I was looking at the kind of horse you only dream about owning. She had action, presence and the sense of power that belongs to a Morgan horse."

But at that time Linda had just opened her chiropractic office and felt she could not afford another horse, time or money-wise, so she only watched the bidding, which did not reach the reserve. She recalled thinking that the owners must have been relieved to have an excuse to keep the mare, and went home to focus on her work and to ride the Morgan gelding she already owned.

Then in May, 1986, Linda encountered the mare at

another sale. "This time there was no reserve on her. This time I could afford to own another horse. And this time I bought her. And suddenly I was in the breeding and showing business," she says.

She placed Tina, who had been bred back to Cajun Pepper, into training with a well-known trainer in the southwestern suburbs of Chicago. Linda went out to watch one Sunday afternoon. "He had her in harness and was driving her around the outdoor arena. I stood on the fence and got goosebumps watching her travel around that oval. She had her head held correctly, her knees coming up high in the air, and the wind flying in her mane. She looked like she was enjoying herself, the trainer was as cheerful as a lottery winner, and I knew I made the right decision when I bought her. It was a perfect moment."

After her filly was weaned, the trainer worked Tina back into show shape. "As she got stronger she taught me the beginnings of the art of driving, an addiction I have to this day," says Linda. By that fall Linda was eager to get into the show ring and entered her in the Morgan Park Harness Class at a Milwaukee, Wisconsin show. But Tina began to act oddly as soon as she entered the arena in her patent leather harness. At first her work in the ring was smooth and well-executed, but then she stopped, suddenly pranced in a great deal of agitation, reared onto her hindquarters and then fell down between the shafts of the buggy. Fortunately she was not hurt and Linda walked her out of her last appearance as a harness horse.

As Linda recovered her composure, some of the other Morgan show people came up to her and related Tina's history. How she had never again shown as well as she had in Oklahoma and how after a few more shows in which she'd done poorly, she'd been placed in broodmare status.

"I believe she soured on showing because she'd been pushed too hard as a young horse," says Linda, who retired her from the show ring, and bred her to a fine Vermont stallion, Equinox Benn Adam, one of the leading sires of Morgans. "Tina is producing the kind of horses I have always wanted, dream horses," she says. She has had five fillies as of 1991.

"Owning this horse has taught me a lot about the breed and the show world," Linda admits. "She introduced me to the realities of showing and helped to clean out the fuzzy-headed thinking most neophytes possess. Tina's a once-in-a-lifetime horse. She's beautiful, yes, even now with a saggy, pregnant belly. She's kind and she's still a people horse. She taught me that even though I pay the bills, she does the work and the kind of work she wants to do is far from the ego trips and pressures of the modern show world."

ATMF Superstition

"Superstition is the smartest and most communicative horse I've ever known," says Patricia Hitt of Autumn Twilight Morgan Farm in Salem, Oregon. "He doesn't let you wonder what he is thinking; he makes sure everything is very plain and obvious, much like a mime. He gets impatient when we don't seem to understand and will try a different explanation, as in charades. His eyes dance with humor and intelligence. His most famous expression is 'Who me?' Especially when he's caught red-handed. It's hilarious."

Patricia bred this horse herself, naming the 15.3-hand black chestnut stallion for the magical faith she had when she was a fifteen-year-old girl. "At that age I was awestruck by a two-year-old colt named Rapidan Apollo," she says. "Upon sight, I knew Apollo would become a world champion and that someday I would own one of his finest sons." With an absolute image of her colt in her mind, Patricia bought a Top Flight daughter, and bred her to Amaster. Apollo's future mate was foaled in 1977 and named ATMF Twilight Tryst. The rendezvous for which the mare was named finally came to pass, and on St. Patrick's Day, 1987 she fulfilled her destiny by producing Patricia's fantasy colt. Top horsemen confirmed her belief that he was a future world-class stallion; now his foals have earned him the honor of standing as a breeding stallion.

"From the beginning, Superstition had a haunting aura of intelligence and dignity," says Patricia. "An undeniable presence, an essence of quality and self-assuredness that commands respect. He still has the curious expression of a colt and is intensely interested in everything.

"Sometimes I feel sad that Superstition's tremendous intelligence, heart and spirit are imprisoned within his domestic lifestyle. But I know he thrives on attention, learning and praise. I challenge his mind and body and he really thrives on that. He likes interacting with me.

"Free-play time is Superstition's opportunity to think of new ways to entertain himself. Most of his favorite games involve buckets or traffic cones. He runs full speed with one firmly gripped in his teeth, banging it loudly against the walls, then tossing it into the air and striking or kicking at it before it hits the ground. He also likes stacking and restacking the cones in a sort of relay race, and tossing them to humans so they'll toss them back to him. He gets so intense with these games, he will run until I have to take away his toys so he can cool out," says Patricia.

Riding Superstition evoked more sublime emotions.

"From the moment I first got on his back, I felt plugged into his electrical system. I could feel his tremendous, surging power, just standing still. For the first time in my years of professional training and riding, I felt that deep sense of honor and humility I knew as a girl, the first time a horse let me touch her and I felt her breath on my cheek. I became fully aware of how Superstition allows me to ride, and teach, and direct his movement and energy. He is so intensely responsive he challenges me to be my best every second I am on him, and he always tries his best for me. All the trophies he has collected and will continue to win will never equal those gifts he has given me. He has given me back that magical sense of awe and wonderment I felt as a little girl reading Walter Farley's books and dreaming of a horse of my own.

"Superstition challenges me to be the best I can be," concludes Patricia. "He expects a lot from me. I don't want to disappoint him."

Christmas Hymn

His photograph hangs on the wall of the office of his veterinarian, who describes him as a "perfect gentleman." He is so calm that he usually falls asleep in cross-ties waiting for his class to be called at the shows, but performs with a unique exuberance and charisma. In his younger days, that enthusiasm frequently resulted in a ballotade in harness upon entering the show ring, and again when called from the lineup to receive the championship award.

The black bay stallion, Christmas Hymn, is one of the most enduring and popular horses in the Morgan breed. Kathleen Koch, who received Christmas Hymn as a wedding present from her husband Jonathan, says the stallion is without question the most successful horse in the history of the Open Pleasure Driving Division at the Morgan Grand National and World Championship at Oklahoma City. Twice the Pleasure Driving World Champion in 1989 and 1990, Christmas Hymn was Reserve World Champion in 1991. He was voted Pleasure Driving Morgan of the Decade (1980s) in the Horse World Readers' Poll and has been Pleasure Driving Morgan of the Year

three consecutive times in the same poll. He has numerous regional championships in the Open Pleasure Driving Division and, in only two outings under saddle, won the Open English Pleasure Stallions and Geldings Stake at the Jubilee Regional in 1990 and 1991.

"He is a horse whose talent and quality is apparent even to people who know nothing about horses," says Kathleen. "This was evident to us at the first horse show either of us ever attended, when we returned from our honeymoon in 1986." Trainers Gene Olesen and Jim Stevenson of Travelers Rest, South Carolina suggested that the Kochs attend a multi-breed show at the Florida State Fairground to learn about the different classes and versatility of the Morgan breed.

"The show was held outdoors, and the horses warmed up in a large field adjacent to the ring," Kathleen continues. After several hours of watching classes and speculating on the winners, Jon's attention wandered over to the Saddlebreds, Paso Finos, and Morgans warming up in the field for the upcoming classes. Pointing to a black horse in harness at the far end of the field, some 200 yards away, Jon said, "Look at the black horse pulling the cart. He's different than the others. He looks better." As the horse drew nearer, Jon declared, "That's the one I want someday." As the horse came still nearer, they recognized trainer Gene Olesen in the buggy. The horse he was driving, Christmas Hymn, went on to win the Open Pleasure Driving Championship as a brand new four-year-old. He was Jon's favorite from that day on. Six months later the couple, who met when they both went to work for the same Tampa law firm, had the opportunity to buy him. Kathleen got her wedding present, and the Kochs' life with a legend began.

Since that fateful day, says Kathleen (who is very happy she didn't ask for pearl earrings when she married), many other newcomers at Morgan shows have seen Christmas Hymn and decided that they, too, want a Morgan driving horse.

"As Steve Davis, Director of the University of Vermont Morgan Horse Farm and a noted Morgan judge and breeder, stated after observing one of 'Sam's' regional championships, 'Christmas Hymn would have been chosen as the winner even by someone who had never seen a horse show before.' Sam is a true representative and ambassador for the Morgan breed," says Kathleen.

While Christmas Hymn does not live with them at their Evensong Morgans farm in rural Valrico, Florida, the Kochs breed at least two Christmas Hymn foals each year. "We former 'city folk' are both practicing lawyers who make time to raise our horses, as well as to enjoy our children," says Kathleen. "Christmas Hymn has introduced us to the diverse and welcoming world of the Morgan horse."

Rose Valley VIP

Always, in the back of Dr. Teresa Krieger's mind was a nagging, apparently unrealistic dream – a World Championship. Unrealistic because the first attempt at it had failed. Teresa and her family, Dr. and Mrs. Norman Krieger, Norman, Jr., Kristen, Karen and Teresa had scraped together the cost of the hauling, the stabling, the equipment, and entry fees with the expectation of a win at the Nationals in Oklahoma. Their "home-grown" Morgan Park Harness horse, Rose Valley VIP, affectionately called "Danny," had finished a remarkable three-year-old season and was primed to win in Oklahoma. But on the trailer ride there, the horse in the adjacent space broke his tie, reached around the partition and inflicted a nasty bite on Danny's neck. Although he was able to compete, Danny's neck was very stiff and sore, and he was not true to form. "He finished a disappointing third in the nation," says Teresa.

"The dashed dreams were something that stuck with us for quite awhile," says Teresa. Danny would make no more trips to the nationals for quite some time. The Kriegers competed him locally, in and around the state of Michigan, where their Rose Valley Farm is located. No matter where the show, no matter who the competition, Danny nearly always left the ring with a park harness or a park saddle win. "Some of my most memorable classes were those where I rode or drove Danny," recalls Teresa. "The power that exuded from him to me through the lines in the harness classes was indescribable. Under saddle, the thrill of having his knees popping so high that I could easily see them from atop his back was incomparable.

"But I still felt it was foolish to dream beyond our means. How dare we believe that we could, with our home-grown foal, out of a plain-looking, $500 mare, compete with the best in the nation? The competition at the Nationals each year consists of the top Morgans from coast to coast. They come from the best farms in the country, many of which have generations of breeding Morgans to their credit. There was no way for us to compete in that kind of ball club, so we gave up," says Teresa.

After the 1986 season, Danny was brought home from the trainer, his shoes pulled, his blankets removed. And he was gelded and turned out to pasture. Nothing could ever remove his show attitude, however. Whenever visitors came to the farm, he would flag his tail and put on a show for them, strutting around the field.

During 1987 and 1988, Teresa pulled him out of the pasture on a couple of occasions and took him to local shows. One day in 1988 she received a phone call from an Ohio trainer, John Hufferd, who had seen Danny at a smaller Michigan show that year and wanted a chance to work with him for a while. It was understood that if Hufferd received a reasonable offer for Danny, the Kriegers would sell him.

By the time the 1989 show season came around, Danny was back in form, and with Hufferd's input, the Kriegers came to the conclusion he would, after four long years' absence, return to the nationals. When October 1989 arrived, he was headed for the second time in his life to the Morgan Grand National and World Championship show in Oklahoma City. Teresa was the only family member able to go to watch Danny, and her heart sank as once again he pinned third in Ladies Park Harness Geldings Championship. His performance, however, was solid enough to justify bringing him back into the World Championship class.

Danny was in near-perfect form that night. As the class went on, he kept getting better and better. Just when he was set up and trotted higher than ever before, he took his performance up yet another notch. "I can remember the exact tone and slightly Southern accent of the show announcer's voice that evening. I can vividly recall the exact smell of the arena, the exact cheering of the crowd, and the exact spot where I stood, peering over the in-gate," says Teresa. "And I can recall the exact position where Rose Valley VIP stood in the lineup as he was called out as the new Ladies Park Harness World Champion! The proudest, happiest moment of my life was when Danny made his electrifying victory pass, with a blanket of roses draped around his neck and his tri-colored World Championship ribbon flowing from his bridle. A fairytale DID come true!"

Noble Flaire

Noble Flaire was a horse with an attitude right from the start—one which inspired his prophetic name, for this Morgan is considered the most thrilling horse to enter the show ring in many years.

His extravagant beauty, charisma and way of going have made him one of the most popular horses of the decade, with a total of twenty World or Grand National titles.

He began by becoming the first junior horse to win the title of World Park Harness Champion.

In 1991 alone, Flaire won the titles of World Champion Stallion, World Champion Senior Stallion, World Champion Park Harness Horse, Grand National Champion Five and Older Stallion, and Grand National Champion Park Harness Stallion, duplicating 1989's record.

It was his show attitude that caught the eye of a renowned trainer when he was just a weanling colt in 1984 at Whitney Stables at Cox's Creek, Kentucky. Mr.

and Mrs. Herbert V. Kohler, Jr., owners of Kohler Stables in Wisconsin and their manager and trainer, Tom Caisse were visiting, looking for a replacement for one of their farm's foundation mares.

The colt caught Tom's eye, and he decided to "spook" him a little, test his mettle. The weanling trotted off a few steps, then turned to face Tom and struck the ground, as if to say, "This is my turf!"

"He had the vigor and brilliance we were looking for," Herbert Kohler says. "He is the second stallion I have bought in my life (the first was the legendary Vigilmarch), and I think I paid the highest price for a weanling at that time in a private sale. There has never been a day that I regretted it," he adds.

Noble Flaire's charisma was intriguing to all who laid eyes on him. "I have never witnessed a performance horse like him, even from his earliest days," says Tom, his life-long trainer. "From the beginning, it was obvious to everyone in the barn that he was unusual."

And so began a life filled with blue ribbons, not only for himself but his offspring.

Flaire, the result of the "golden cross" of Noble Command and Lost River Sanfield, has also proven himself as a breeding sire at a young age. His first foal, HVK Courageous Flair (out of Val's Christy) was World Champion Four-Year-Old Park Harness Horse, Grand National Champion Four-Year-Old Park Harness Horse, Grand National Two-Year-Old Park Harness Stallion Champion and the Reserve World Two-Year-Old Park Harness Champion. HVK Make Em Cry was Grand National Yearling Champion Colt and Reserve World Yearling Futurity Champion Colt. There are many, many other winners across the country, and even abroad.

One wouldn't expect a performer like Flaire to be ordinary at home either. His trainer says "he's unbelievably smart." Flaire, whose bloodlines go back to government mares, is also tough and strong, and is worked twice a day.

Nor does he have any problem with self-esteem. "That horse takes possession like no horse I've ever known," says Tom. "He's the first one we work in the morning and if he sees the groom in a stall with another horse before his turn, all hell breaks loose. Flaire is not into sharing. People come out to the farm and ask, 'Why isn't he wearing a hood? Why isn't he wearing a bustle?' I just tell them, 'What Flaire doesn't like, he don't get.'"

At a young age for a stallion, Noble Flaire has become a horse for all time. "He is the most talented Morgan I have seen in my judging career," says horse show judge Lewis Eckhard. "He is a beautiful individual with a lot of charisma. That's what show horses are all about." And what Noble Flaire embodies as the ultimate expression of show horse.

Vigilmarch

Vigilmarch, who lived from 1957 to 1980, was one of the great sires in Morgan history, creating a profound impact upon the breed. His ability to sire top offspring has resulted in incredible numbers of winning horses in every aspect of the Morgan breed.

Ironically, the story of this stallion in its turns of fate resembles that of Justin Morgan, the foundation sire of his breed.

Herbert V. Kohler, Jr., the innovative Chairman of the Board and President of Kohler Co., the nation's leading manufacturer of plumbing and specialty products, went to the Whitney Stables auction at Cox's Creek, Kentucky, hoping to buy a pleasure gelding for Mrs. Kohler, or a filly or two. operates several unique hospitality and land development businesses in Kohler, Wisconsin, Kohler Stables being one of them. Today it ranks as a major Morgan show stables, a premier training facility that is highly successful in the show ring, one of the most respected Morgan breeding operations in the nation and as influential in the development of the Morgan breed.

However, at the time of the Cox's Creek auction, Kohler Stables as a breeding operation was far from Herb Kohler's mind. But when Vigilmarch, considered one of the three best horses in the breed, came on the block at what appeared to be a bargain, he bought him and became a serious breeder.

Vigilmarch became the cornerstone upon which a strong foundation for the breed was built; he also came to represent everything excellent that Kohler Stables stands for.

Vigilmarch, like Justin Morgan, was not big by the stick, only about 14.3, but his lofty front end towered over handlers. When in motion, he was transformed into dynamic symmetry, balanced with a great masculine air of elegance. A great show horse, he always turned in a spectacular performance. He won his first blue ribbon as a foal at the 1957 National show, and was shown for the last time two weeks after Herb Kohler purchased him, at the 1970 Gold Cup, where he won the Sire and Get Class. In between he won many Grand Championships and Harness Stakes.

Greatness was bred into Vigilmarch. His sire was Orland Vigildon, a successful show horse descended from a long line of noted producers. The outstanding matron Mayphil was his dam. Had Vigilmarch been her only foal, his achievements and popularity would have been more than enough to assure her a place in the Morgan Hall of Fame. But Mayphil and her seven other foals earned their own fame by winning more than twenty-five times at the Eastern Nationals.

Vigilmarch was bred to breed on and, after his triumphant return to the show ring, he began a leisurely life at stud. Kohler Stables provided him with a loving atmosphere which gentled him. He was loved, adored and treated like the royalty he was. Herb Kohler brought only the best mares to his court. In short time, his sons and daughters began to enter the show scene and have remained in the limelight ever since.

In December, 1980, Vigilmarch developed colic. Surgery to remove a tumor was successful and he recovered normally from the anesthetic, but the next morning the great heart stilled and he was gone.

He left his mark as a sire of versatility, siring countless National and World Champion horses, prepotent sires and broodmares that play an important role in the success and growth of the Morgan horse today.

Hailed as an all-time great, the name of Vigilmarch will be read in the history books for years to come.

Poco Aljoy

Poco Aljoy, affectionately known as "Corky" throughout his lifetime, was a dark bay gelding who seemed to have an intuitive ability to look over his rider's clothes, check the saddle and tack, and shift gears from an easy, gentle western jog to the high action needed for a saddle seat horse; from a rocking horse canter to the fast dash and sliding stop of a stock horse; from a quiet slow walk to an extremely fast flat walk that passed every other horse on the Rancheros Visitadores Trek.

However, his flawless ability to move into a canter from a standing position with no transitional steps could be totally humiliating to an unsuspecting rider on a loose rein. For when that tense moment arrived at the end of a class when the announcer takes the microphone to announce "the winner of such and such," Corky would break directly into a canter from the lineup to pick up the blue ribbon he naturally assumed he had won.

More often than not, he had. For five consecutive years he was the High Point Performance Morgan in Southern California.

On many occasions he participated in trail, western pleasure, stock, English pleasure, hunter hack, saddle seat, and driving classes as well as pulling contests, handled by as many as five riders in a row, including owner Malcolm McDuffie of Rancho Campo Verde in Santa Barbara, California, his wife Mary, and their daughter.

On one memorable occasion at a Morgan show, he won eleven ribbons, including six blues, in a single day, says Malcolm. "He was tired, but quickly revived with Coca Cola and bourbon, both of which he adored. On another occasion in an open show, he participated in thirteen of the seventeen classes offered in one day, with four different riders, placing in all classes and winning five blue ribbons, beating Thoroughbreds in the hunt seat classes, Saddlebreds in the saddle seat classes and Quarter Horses in the western classes. At the end of the show, the announcer made a little speech, 'in tribute to the big little Morgan, the hardest-working and most versatile horse in the show.'

"Often after such a performance, we were approached by people wanting to arrange a breeding. Alas, it was not to be!" adds Malcolm.

"Although gelded early in his lifetime, Corky developed into the perfect prototype of a classic Morgan stallion. He became Justin Morgan personified. He was dark bay, with black points; he was blessed with a big eye, small ears, a large jaw, an arched neck, a wavy double mane and a long wavy tail. (His head was used as the model for the Southern California Morgan Horse Association logo.) He was small, but strong, proud, and spirited, with an athletic body and a loving disposition.

Corky was foaled February 17, 1955 in Ventura County, California. Sired by a popular Morgan stallion of the period named Red Gates, he was tenderly delivered by his lovely dam, Almond Joy, a mare owned by Malcolm's friend, John Newman, a prominent Ventura County rancher, and an ex-Presidente of the Rancheros Visitadores. "One of our favorite pictures is of Almond Joy, lying in an upright position, with her head turned, looking proudly at her newborn, Corky, just as he poked his head out of the sac!" says Malcolm.

"As his show years waned, and our daughter went on to the thrills of jumping Thoroughbreds, Corky happily carried me and my wife for many years over many miles of mountain trails and in many parades," Malcolm adds. "Always a good companion, he seemed to enjoy human company more than that of other horses, so naturally he endeared himself to all those fortunate enough to have known him. He safely carried me on many week-long treks of the Rancheros Visitadores in the mountains behind Santa Barbara. As I celebrate my forty-second year with that well known horsemen's organization, my friends still ask about 'that great little Morgan' I rode. I sadly advise them that in 1989, in his thirty-fourth year, he lay down for his final rest under a sycamore tree at Campo Verde where he spent most of his wonderful life – a life which brought so much happiness to so many people."

Triton Wells Fargo

The classic bay Morgan stallion, Triton Wells Fargo, represents the culmination of a love for Morgan horses which began sixty years ago.

Growing up in the early 1930s on his father's farm in Adams County, Pennsylvania, young Bob Morgan worked with his father's three Morgan horses, which were used to cut hay, cultivate corn and pull the hay wagons in from the fields. From the very beginning, Bob learned that Morgan horses were a breed of unique ability and stamina.

Bob's Red Fox Stables in Gilroy, California originated in 1960 with Bob's purchase of his first Morgan, Princess Victoria, and flourished from that point on with the support of his wife, June, and their two children, Marilyn and Robert H.

"When I started breeding horses," he says, "we were concerned with California blood and the Morgan stallions that had come to the West Coast. These stallions were brought from Vermont. They included Morgan stallions that raced as trotters here, and then went on to travel throughout the United States, winning stallion classes in shows.

"I'm like most breeders in that I've gravitated toward the bloodlines that succeeded," he adds. "I started out with Lippitt blood in Lippitt Pecos, and Cornwallis and Bed Don Blood in Applevale Red Fox. I had Uledon blood with Orcland Bold Fox and Great Hill Atlantic. I became very interested in Bed Don Blood over the years.

"I would say that this farm is basically a Cornwallis and Bed Don farm with some Lippitt. We like high heads, strong necks, and lots of type with a flare for elegance."

Triton is now the uniquely metaphoric prefix name for Bob's horses, adopted for its meaning in Roman mythology. Triton was the demigod, half-man, half-fish who blew his conch shell trumpet at the command of Jupiter to summon all the gods to Olympus. Usually Triton was pictured riding in a porpoise-led chariot, but when he walked on land, every place his staff touched the ground, a horse would spring up.

Triton Morgans are now in their third generation. "With each generation," Bob said, "we have been able to breed prettier horses. Morgans today are prettier than they were twenty-five years ago. Our number one requirement is a good head. We like to breed for Morgan type as opposed to Saddlebred-looking horses.

"Wells Fargo, foaled March 20, 1987, is the son of Dandy's Diamond and Triton Susan, both of whom were bred at my farm," he says. He describes Wells Fargo as tall, with perfect conformation and excellent temperament. His forte is English Pleasure Driving. As a breeder, Bob is proud to have produced such an excellent Morgan stallion, one he believes has a great future as a sire.

Triton Ellen and Triton Suzanna are now in foal to Wells Fargo. Red Fox Stables trainer Shannon Storma will show Wells Fargo throughout California and at the National Show in Oklahoma this year.

Bob and his wife June also enjoy collecting works of art, especially Morgan horse art. In their home hangs the original George Ford Morris painting of Justin Morgan, as well as Walter Dennis's illustrations for Marguerite Henry's book, *Justin Morgan Had a Horse*.

In 1965, Bob established the Triton Museum in Santa Clara, California, an art museum consisting of four pavilions on seven acres of ground, on which a life-size bronze of one of his first stallions, Lippitt Pecos, stands.

History is also a great interest of Bob's, especially that of the Morgan breed, and he has reprinted numerous old books that contain rare and valuable background information on Morgans.

Topa's Krystal

As old horse trainers say, "If you're lucky, you might own one great horse in your lifetime." The luck of the McLemore family of Apple Flat Farm surfaced with the purchase of Topa's Krystal in 1987.

Foaled March 6, 1983, the chestnut mare, sired by Foxmoor Captivator, her dam Black River Sioux, is "Ms. Sophistication," says Robert V. McLemore. Krystal has won twenty-two Grand National and World Championship titles so far and shows no inclination of slowing down.

One of the greatest old horse trainers around, Bob Whitney of Kentucky, told the McLemores in 1991, "You may not know just how wonderful Krystal is. She's the greatest!"

Krystal, whose forte is park harness, was purchased

"to fulfill the dreams of a grand lady to compete nationally," says Robert, referring to his wife Linda.

"Krystal is a great talent that never quits. She will give her all every performance, a true show horse. She loves to show for anyone. My wife has a similar personality: GO FOR IT!" Robert notes.

"Krystal is nine years old this year and if the way she is performing now is any indication of her future, she may never quit. Our guess is that the day she dies she'll be giving everything she has at that particular moment and it will probably be equal to a World Championship effort. We've tried to slow her down by a relaxed work schedule and the finest treatment a horse could have. She continues to throw her tail over her back and to trot around the exercise paddock as if she had 5,000 spectators cheering her on," Robert told me.

"This is part of what horses are all about...the love affair most horse owners have with their horses. I don't know exactly why people become so involved with horses. Maybe the sheer size of them. The ability one has to temper their wildness and become a part of the animal. To ride the beast through the fields and experience the thunder of a 1,000 pounds of muscle galloping in the wind.

"I watched my wife become attached to her first horse and know very well how much she cared for it. What I know about horses, I learned through Linda's eyes and ears. She told me, just after winning her first World Championship title, 'When the spotlights were turned on me and Krystal, it was one of the greatest moments in my life.'

"Our daughter Libby found this love at age six, and in no time became a great horsewoman. Linda and I have watched her and her horse become one as they so gracefully perform together. Libby wants her horses to feel free in their own way, with her on their back. To control the horse removes the thrill she experiences as she and her horse appreciate each other and trust each other. No wonder she's so successful as a junior exhibitor in world class competition. She and her horses hold more National and World titles than any other junior rider. She pleases herself and her parents in the process, along with a lot of loyal supporters. This equine love story continues with our oldest daughter, Kristy, and one of our twin sons, Thad, as they both enjoy the excitement and rewards of competing at horse shows," Robert says.

"As for Krystal, she will compete as long as she wishes. She has given enough joy to so many, she should have full control of her destiny. More important, Krystal and the other wonderful horses at Apple Flat Farm supply the common means for an entire family to share the joys and heartaches of life's stages together."

Cedar Creek Harlequin

"A young stallion with that something that separates him from the rest," is what Robert V. McLemore calls Cedar Creek Harlequin, who stands at his Apple Flat Farm in Charlotte, North Carolina.

The bay Morgan, foaled April 8, 1983, was sired by I Will Command out of Serenity Anna Rose. "He stands tall and possesses the fineness of a great breeding horse — long neck, a thin throatlatch enabling him and his off-spring to place their heads in a manner that will thrill any horse show enthusiast," McLemore adds.

Bob had always wanted a stallion at Apple Flat Farm to breed to his mares. He had always liked Cedar Creek Harlequin, 1987 Reserve World Champion Four-Year-Old Park Saddle, and 1987 Grand National Four-Year-Old Park Saddle Stallion Champion. So the McLemores purchased him three years ago, and are pleased with the foals he is siring.

Linda McLemore showed him in 1989 in the Amateur Park Harness division and culminated the season with the Grand National Amateur Park Harness Stallion Championship title in Oklahoma City.

"He will continue to be shown as breeding demand allows," says Bob, whose eighteen-year-old daughter Libby desires to ride this horse someday at World Level Competition.

The McLemores are a typical "horse family," with all the varying degrees of involvement one would expect from any random roundup of individuals.

Though Bob doesn't show, he gives everyone strong support, and can offer many helpful comments, as he spends hours watching his family practice and compete. He especially enjoys studying prospective new horses.

Bob says he first experienced "the value of people expressing themselves through horses" twenty-eight years ago, when his wife, Linda, got her first horse. "I shared the joy she expressed winning a World Championship in Oklahoma City. A great experience. A delight for me," he says.

Owning and showing Morgans and Saddlebreds and winning three World Championships is a dream come true for Linda McLemore. (The neon lights above the entrance way to the Apple Flat Farm stable area spell out the words "Childhood Dreams.") What makes horse ownership even more special for Linda is that her husband and their four children enjoy the horses too.

"Libby, like her mother, is a true horse lover," says Bob. "She has created so many wonderful moments for Linda and me. She inherited her mother's desire to be around horses day and night and has already won two World Championships. Libby, too, enjoys the spotlight experience."

Kristy McLemore Cariker shows in Western Pleasure and enjoys pleasure riding at home.

Thad loves the fast-paced roadster classes and has also been successful in pleasure driving.

His twin brother, Chad, is the hunting and fishing buff of the family, but attends a few shows each year in support of his family's endeavors. He has spent many hours setting up stall decorations at horse shows.

"Chad, too, has experienced a spotlight. One fell on his head and he thought his brother hit him with it," his father jokes. Chad says, 'Horses are too expensive. Save some money for me. I need a new bass boat. Horses smell, step on your toes, and will kick you.'

"'Things are getting out of hand,' is Chad's favorite expression around horses," his father says.

"After twenty-eight years of sharing my family's horse stories, it is simple to me," concludes Bob, a house builder. "This horse thing is a way for me to know what I wish to be doing and where I wish to be.

"There couldn't be a better way for me to grow older than with my family's love and sharing their goals at Apple Flat Farm, making any thoughts of slowing down at work impossible."

Serenity Flight Time

Jackie Millet, owner of HyLee Farm in Cannon Falls, Minnesota, professional trainer and judge, was planning for her future in the horse business and wanted a breeding program. She had not owned a stallion for several years and had been sending most of her mares outside for breeding.

She went to the Kohler Sale of the Future II in May, 1987, and when the gavel fell, she owned Serenity Flight Time, a Morgan stallion who is one of the last living sons of Fleetwing, one of the great Morgan family sires, and whose dam is by Kohler Stables' immortal Vigilmarch.

"I didn't fully realize what I had done until I went back to his stall and there were so many people looking at him saying what a great stallion I had purchased," Jackie says. "Of course, then I was in tears."

The golden red chestnut with a light mane and tail is twenty-one this year. "He has brought attention to my farm, HyLee, and contributed to the promotion of my horses in the show ring and in sales," says Jackie. "I have a great deal of respect for the horse's capabilities and the individual he is," she adds.

He is the sire of National and World Champion Mor-

gans, and grandsire of World Champions, "but his greatest contribution is his daughters who have produced many, many world champions, and champions who have remained reigning in their divisions for multiple years," Jackie continues. "He has sired the World Champion Park Saddle stallion, Master's Touch. He has also sired horses who have excelled in carriage competition, western, hunt seat, saddle seat and pleasure driving.

"Because of the investment there is in a breeding program, I always tell people that "George" (as Flight Time is known around home) owns the barn," she says. "That he is the boss, so treat him like a CEO. I think what is special about our relationship is that for a breeding horse he has not been a disappointment as an individual."

"He stands about 15.1 but most people think that he is much taller because of his long neck which is set high on his shoulders. When we have blankets made for him, we have to have the neck cut back another two inches, even when it already has a cutback. He has a beautiful big eye and a whinny that sounds as if he is singing, it is so soft. He likes to stick out his tongue so that you will rub it, and when you are slow to do so, he will push his way around you until you comply. He has taught the horses next to him (and there have been several) how to stick out their tongues, and you have to rub theirs, also. He likes red licorice and loves to share apples with my Gordon Setter, Ali," she says.

"Owning Flight Time has introduced me to many new people in the Morgan business, as if they are 'his friends,' as he has quite a following of admirers. It is not unusual for me to get a call from someone who asks 'How is Flight Time?' or 'I'm in the area and would like to stop by and see Flight Time. It's been awhile since I have seen him.'

"And of course, George takes it all in with his dainty bites of apples, and his tongue exhibition, and then he's led out and stands up like he expects to go into the show ring. And when we turn him loose, he snorts, flags his tail, and trots with so much motion everyone asks how much shoes we have on him. And are surprised to find out that it is only a plate weight shoe.

"Flight Time gives me a great deal of satisfaction. With him I felt I could contribute to the Morgan breed in some areas that were very important to strengthen and maintain—length of hip and loin, attitude and temperament, cadenced trot, and balanced hocks," says Jackie.

"He has taught me to believe even more strongly that if you are going to own a stallion for profit that there is only one kind to own, a good one, one who has a good disposition, and one in whom you respect the characteristics he passes on to enhance or stabilize the breed."

Dolly Mae

When Jackie Millet was a little girl, the chestnut Morgan mare, Dolly Mae, was the horse on whose back her parents would let her sit while chores were being done. Or they would put Jackie in her manger with the hay while Dolly was eating. "They say that I was one of the few people to ever ride her," says Jackie. "That was when she found the gate open or a hole in the fence and would decide the grass was greener down the road. My folks could holler 'Dolly Mae, get home!' and she would turn around and come back.

"She had a definite mind of her own," Jackie continues. "When it was time to eat, if the barn door wasn't open and the feeding had begun, she would knock the door off its hinges and go into her stall and wait, though not with any patience. Also the drawing in this book represents the only photo we took of her. She was of the attitude 'I raise foals and do a good job. I don't do pictures, and you are ridiculous for all the strange things you are doing, trying to get me to put my ears up and wear this halter.' My mother opened an umbrella in her face to get her attention. Note that the ears are up and there is a surprised look in her eye. After that, she dragged my father, who was holding her, back to the barn, with a walk so determined it might have been easier to stop a freight train!" says Jackie.

Dolly Mae was there waiting when Jackie was born. "My parents, Bob and Jane Behling, purchased her the year they were married, 1947. She was carrying a foal, a filly, HyLee's Lady Justin, who was foaled in 1948, the same year I was born."

Dolly Mae remained on HyLee Farm in Cannon Falls, Minnesota, until she was put to sleep, well into her twenties.

Dolly Mae, foaled May 16, 1942, came from very old Midwest Morgan bloodlines, good foundation stock, and she imprinted on Jackie the ideal way a broodmare should look like and how it should produce. That first foal she had for the Behlings, HyLee's Lady Justin, was Grand Champion Mare in three different states for three years in a row. She had many others. In 1959 at the Illinois State Fair, the Grand Champion Mare and the Grand Champion Stallion were both out of Dolly Mae. "She would put such beautiful bodies and bone on her offspring, no matter who sired them," says Jackie.

"Those offspring that were fertile went on to produce and sire great horses in their day. So a great deal of my breeding program today is credited to my parents and to Dolly Mae, who truly created HyLee Farm in 1948," she adds.

Dolly was never shown or really trained to do anything special other than have foals, "and for us that was enough," Jackie says. Jackie had the fortunate experience of watching Dolly, her daughter and a few granddaughters imprinting their foals as they went outside with them for the first time.

"The mares are all so consistent, it can't be coincidence," she says. "The mare walks around her paddock with her foal and the foal is between her and the fence. She will occasionally bump the foal's nose against the fence, telling the foal why the fence is there. After making the trip completely around the paddock, she will go to the center and lie down and roll over three times. Then she gets up and gives a little buck and trots off, looking for something to eat. This is the routine of all Dolly's daughters and granddaughters. They also have this insulting look about them when you offer to help in any way with the foaling or the foal nursing: 'If you think you can do it better, then why don't YOU have them!!!'"

"It is obvious that Dolly Mae has given me great insight into the power a good broodmare can have on a breeding operation," says Jackie, "as well as a unique opportunity to observe three generations of mares whose dam's imprinting at an early age has carried through. It makes me more convinced of the positive effects of the owner imprinting on the foal."

Fletcher Banjo John

Fletcher Banjo John is a horse with an attitude — show horse attitude. "That attitude has to be there, it cannot be made," says his owner, Dolores Nickel of Kingsgrove Morgans, a.k.a. Bittersweet Farm in Somis, California.

"Banjo John is the ultimate show horse," she continues. "He is happiest coming through that gate into the show ring and as the spectators cheer, his adrenalin flows and he says 'Watch me get better' and he does. He loves it. He is a special Morgan. I believe a horse like Banjo John doesn't come along once in a lifetime, but only within generations of lifetimes, if you are lucky."

Dolores and her daughter Michele got lucky in 1987. They had been searching two years for an amateur park horse. Banjo John was almost three years old when they purchased him from Fletcher Farm of Peoria, Arizona, where he had been introduced to the show ring by John Williams. About four weeks after their trainer Gerry Rushton of Norco, California had gotten Banjo John in training, he called Dolores and Michele into a meeting and advised that in his opinion "BJ" had the potential to be an open stake horse. "Michele, being the consummate horsewoman, agreed, and BJ was on his way under Gerry Rushton's guidance and care to becoming our World Champion," says Dolores.

"The true measure of talent is meeting with great competitors," she continues. "Banjo John has met great competitors and compares well."

He was Reserve World Champion Four-Year-Old Park Harness horse in 1988, Reserve World Champion Park Harness horse in 1989, and by the judges' unanimous choice, the World Champion Park Harness horse in 1990. In 1991, he was once again Reserve World Champion Park Harness horse.

Banjo John also has seventeen in-hand wins. As a two-year-old he was the Junior Champion Stallion and Reserve Grand Champion Stallion at the Regional Medallion in Santa Barbara, California. He also won the Two-Year-Old Sire Auction Sweepstakes Championship at the Grand Nationals in Oklahoma City. He was Junior Champion Stallion and Reserve Grand Champion at the Golden West show in Monterey, California, and as a three-year-old, Banjo John was the UPHA Classic Reserve Champion Park Harness Horse at the American Royal in Kansas City, Missouri.

The handsome bay stallion, a Waseeka's Nocturne/Beamington cross with many world champions in his pedigree, stands at stud at Kingsgrove Morgans/Bittersweet Farm, a modest breeding operation with a small broodmare band. "This makes every outside mare bred by Banjo John very important and gives us the opportunity to evaluate crosses on a variety of family bloodlines," says Dolores. "Banjo John currently has a yearling colt being readied by Gerry Rushton for the 1992 show ring. His foals are eligible for the Medallion Futurity Cup and the World Futurity Cup.

"Banjo John passes on extraordinarily beautiful heads, long necks that come straight up from the shoulder, and that marvelous attitude," says Dolores. "My goal down the road is to breed a World Champion. Banjo John is the root of that hope. Each year, Banjo John's place in Morgan history is in my foaling stall, and I am smiling."

UC Ringmaster

When that one moment in time comes along for a human or equine athlete – when they are more than they or anyone else thought they could be – the occasion becomes an indelible memory for all who witness it.

Such was the case at the Nineteenth Annual Grand National and World Championship Morgan Horse Show in October, 1991 at Oklahoma City, Oklahoma. There the most exciting moment of the show was unanimously judged to be the stirring, brave, dauntless performance of the great red stallion, UC Ringmaster, and his trainer Leslie Parker.

The Waseeka's Showtime son, foaled in June 1978, was given a daring, all-out ride by Parker, who frequently dropped his curb reins and urged his willing mount to greater heights while maintaining the horse's beautiful collection. At times he rode with one hand patting the stallion in whom he had so much confidence. The pair blazed past all competition to become the World Champion English Pleasure Horse of the Year. Maybe the decade, maybe forever, say those who were there.

Owned by a sublimely happy Cheryl G.W. Orcutt of Juniper Hill Farm in Peterborough, New Hampshire, "Wing" has been shown for the past three seasons by Leslie Parker.

They met when Wing was sent to stand at stud at a farm in Connecticut where Leslie was employed as trainer. "From the moment Leslie first laid hands on the horse to merely exercise him, I could see a metamorphosis taking place," recalls Cheryl. "Something very unique and strange occurred between man and horse. Their souls touched and bonded in one brief, shining moment. The horse was transformed into something we had only dreamed he could be. There was no decision to make – only to go forward. So, there's Leslie waiting in the wings for his turn in the spotlight and beside him, his equine counterpart."

Observing them on the brink of their future, Cheryl wondered, "Can they fulfill each other's destiny, now one and the same? From the moment the pair hit the tanbark, they made history. A horse no one had really SEEN before, a man whose talent few realized. Hearts in the crowd missed a beat as they charged through the ingate. Spectators witnessed communication at its highest level – no words, just thinking, and response and motion. Was there anything the great red horse would or could not do for the tall, black man? Few doubted it," says Cheryl.

"Crowds rose to their feet to cheer magnificent pass after pass as man and horse called on each other. They became the stuff journalists' dreams are made of, as Wing gained national acclaim with titles heaped upon titles.

"Our World Championship was not won by influence, political power, slick advertising or wealth," Cheryl continues. "It was just a horse and a man whose talents could finally not be denied...Leslie, from a family of talented horsemen; Wing, a good horse become great, the pleasure horse of the decade, maybe even the century. It was truly their day."

Initially, Wing was not thought to be a show horse. Cheryl acquired him in the fall of his four-year-old year, from the University of Connecticut when the school had its funding severely cut and some horses had to be sold to feed the herd for the winter. Wing was bought as a breeding horse, "but as we exercised him, we soon realized he wanted to be a show horse," says Cheryl. She allowed him to fulfill his destiny.

She and the stallion have an unusually close relationship. "Feelings, emotions, moments are shared between us. Qualities are shared between us: Never give up. Give it your best. If it is meant to be, it will be, and if it isn't, stop looking back and go on. It is really the story of both our lives. Most of all, I am him and he is me," says Cheryl.

"Of course, everyone dreams of having a World Champion, but this is not what we are about," she concludes. "We are about hard work, honesty, loyalty, and integrity. Leslie believes in these values as well, and for all of us, Wing's World Championship is one of the rewards for a lifetime of adhering to these principles."

Intrepid Marlene

This Morgan mare, who had the look of a champion from birth, was named after the actress, Marlene Dietrich because of her great legs, says her owner, Arthur L. Perry, Jr. of Intrepid Farms in Carpinteria, California.

Art planned for her, bred for her, and she "turned out to be all I hoped she would be," he says. "One of the best mares ever produced at Intrepid Farms. She represents the ideal Morgan mare and every breeder's dream."

Many times local, national and World Champion in-hand mare, Intrepid Marlene was foaled at Intrepid Farms in March of 1976. By the time she reached four years of age, she had grown to 15.1 hands with distinguishing dapples in her beautiful bay coat. Her sire is the National Champion, Bar-T Invader, and her dam is the great producing mare, Ware's Mar Lisa. Both of these horses, along with several other broodmares, were the foundation stock of Intrepid Farms, established in 1968.

"The sole purpose of this venture was to produce Morgans of quality that would be a credit to the Morgan breed," says Art. "Horses have been a part of my life since childhood. I guess it runs in the blood. My great grandparents on both sides of my family had horses. My mother's grandparents raised purebred Clydesdale horses in Nova Scotia, Canada."

At the age of twelve, Art first saw Marlene's grandsire, Orcland Leader. "He was the Morgan who was responsible for my lifelong interest in the breed," he says. "Marlene is the result of the image and dream I had when I started the breeding program. I am looking to her to be the producer of other Morgans like herself."

Marlene was shown from her second year through her ninth year, during that time capturing many local, national and world titles in pleasure harness, pleasure saddle and in-hand classes. She was shown by Judy and Bob Whitney during her second, third, and fourth years and by Harold Angle during her fifth and sixth years. "She has been shown by me for many of her recent years," says Art. "We always seem to work well together and she always seems to put on a better show when I show her."

Art has shown Marlene in many parade classes, and she has led the Morgan Horse Equestrian Group in the Tournament of Roses Parade on five different occasions.

Marlene has also produced three foals to date, two of which have been outstanding show competitors, Intrepid Marialana, and Intrepid Sovereign. Both are champions in their divisions.

"Marlene is also queen of the stable," Art reports, "and lets you know when she feels she isn't getting her fair share of attention. She loves to be scratched on the withers, and positions herself for the scratch," says Art.

Horses continue to be a passion with Art, who has devoted his life to the Morgan horse not only as a breeder, but as a director on the board of the AMHBEA. He is its Western Vice President and serves as Chairman of the Archives and Museum Committees. "The history of the Morgan breed is very important to me, and I have dedicated myself to seeing that the story is passed down to others in their own quest to know and love the Morgan horse," he says.

"Marlene has given me the inspiration to go on trying to produce Morgans that will be a credit to the story of the Morgan breed."

Apollo's Reflection

At a Kingston, New York, sale in 1970, Mr. and Mrs. V. Watson Pugh purchased and brought back to their Tara Farm in Raleigh, North Carolina, a mare in foal and a Morgan yearling colt named Empyrean Apollo.

As a two-year-old, the colt, who became known simply as "Pete," won all his in-hand classes. The following season, Pete collected three Top Ten Stallion awards at the Grand National Morgan Show, and word of Tara spread throughout the Morgan horse world.

"He really got this place going," says Cindy Noble, Mrs. Frances Pugh's trainer. "He had what Morgan people want, a beautiful neck and head, with bay color. When he appeared at a show, a lot of people stood along the rail watching him. He even had a fan club."

Unfortunately, in August, 1974, midway through his four-year-old show season, Pete developed colic, and two surgeries later died. He is buried under an oak tree at Tara.

Nine months later, on May 26, 1975, Pete's son, Apollo's Reflection, a bay with white markings, was foaled, out of the mare Bar T Regina. As occurs with some reflected images, the projected result was magnified.

In a lovely double portrait of sire and son in show ring spotlights, artist Denise Peterson captured the memorable beauty of Apollo's Reflection, as well as his remarkable resemblance to Empyrean Apollo.

"Reflection's head and eye are unsurpassed. His extreme and naturally high head carriage and depth of hip are no less than exceptional. They are all qualities that are greatly sought after by today's connoisseurs of fine Morgans," says Mrs. Pugh.

"Apollo's Reflection marked the turnaround of our breeding program to national standards," says Mrs. Pugh, a trustee of the American Morgan Horse Institute. Shown to a host of victories in hand, under saddle and in amateur park harness classes, his show career culminated in his winning, in 1981, the title of World Champion Morgan Stallion, a very special moment for his owners.

"Now seventeen years old, he is truly the highlight of Tara Farm, and he's fulfilled a special dream," says Mrs. Pugh, "a World Champion of our own that we can enjoy daily."

He's also brought special fulfillment to Mrs. Pugh's love for horses – "the pride of having bred my own stallion and mare to produce this World Champion and their subsequent offspring," she says.

Mrs. Pugh's maiden name was Frances Plimpton. She is a distant cousin of the famous author George Plimpton, and the granddaughter of the founder of Plimpton Press. She married a Raleigh, North Carolina pediatrician, V. Watson Pugh, who gave her a Morgan stallion, Millers Bendel, for their third wedding anniversary in September, 1960. That was the beginning of their horse farm, Tara, now home to forty Morgans, two of which have actually been named Rhett Butler and Scarlett O'Hara.

"As a breeding stallion, the name Apollo's Reflection has become synonymous with type and attitude," says Mrs. Pugh. "We have found Apollo's Reflection's get to be some of the most trainable, intelligent, and enjoyable Morgans with which we have ever worked.

"He stamps each foal with his inviting disposition, correctness of conformation, and a certain quality that makes each of his owners love them dearly. We cannot say enough good things about 'Floyd.' He is a breeder's dream and a dear friend to us all. His sons and daughters are proving to be superior breeding animals in their ability to pass on those most desirable traits of their grandsire, Empyrean Apollo, no matter with what bloodline they are crossed."

Indian Creek Jade's Joe

Indian Creek Jade's Joe "is a sweetheart, friendly and even-tempered from the start," says Jeanette Quilhot. "Joe" welcomes all visitors to Indian Creek Farm in Columbia City, Indiana with typical Morgan good manners. "Overcast skies and gloomy weather, however, tend to make him mope a bit," adds Jeanette. "When the sun shines, he responds with a brighter, livelier attitude and eagerness to work. If he were human, he would probably be one of those people who just wants to stay in bed and keep the covers over his head on a gray day."

Joe (by Trophy's Jade out of Swingtime) was initially a case of "mistaken gender." He was foaled on Mother's Day, May 14, 1989, a beautiful bay with a white star and a white sock on his right hind leg. The phone call to report the birth of the second Indian Creek foal informed Jeanette that the new arrival was a filly. "So we named 'her' after my husband Russell's mother. After a call to Florida to tell my mother-in-law of her new horse namesake, we rushed to the farm to see our brand-new filly. There we discovered that our 'she' was a 'he' so the foal was renamed 'Jade's Joe.'"

Indian Creek Jade's Joe began life on the show circuit in 1991 as a two-year-old pleasure horse. "He had some high and then not-so-high show results that first summer," says Jeanette. "Most of the time, he was in the shadow of Indian Creek Payday, his two-year-old stablemate, foaled just two months before Joe. Payday is a flashy park horse who won the blue whenever he competed, but our trainer, Kurt Hufferd, knew Joe's potential and kept working and showing him in his capable, wise way."

Finally, at the 1991 Morgan Grand National in Oklahoma City, Indian Creek Jade's Joe came into his own. In fact, the entire farm seemed to come into its own and the Grand National was a horseman's fantasy come true for the Quilhots and for Kurt Hufferd. They had entered three homebred two-year-olds and left with four World Championships and one Grand National Reserve.

Indian Creek Jade's Joe swept the honors with the World Champion Pleasure Driving Two-Year-Old, and World Champion Futurity Pleasure Driving Two-Year-Old titles. Indian Creek Payday took World Champion Park Harness Two-Year-Old and World Champion Futurity Park Harness Two-Year-old. Southview Super Megan took Reserve Grand National Park Harness Two-Year-Old Mare or Gelding.

Added to this already stunning cluster of victories was the setting of a record. For the first time in history, both the World and Futurity World Championships were won by the same farm and/or trainer in the Pleasure Driving and Park Harness Two-Year-Old events.

The Quilhots were especially proud of Indian Creek Jade's Joe, who in every class looked and acted like a champion. "He was steady, consistent and a beautiful World Champion," says Jeanette. "One of the best things about Jade's Joe, besides his good looks and temperament, is that he just keeps getting better and better. Kurt is riding him now and his word to describe Joe under saddle is 'Wonderful!'

"We are looking forward to Joe's competing as a three-year-old," adds Jeanette, "but the thrill of seeing his name twice on the winner's marquee at the Grand National Morgan Horse Show as a two-year-old will never be forgotten."

Joe is an affirmation of the goal of Russell and Jeanette Quilhot – to breed, raise and train champion Morgan show horses that they and the industry can be proud of and, at the same time, provide family-oriented enjoyment for themselves and their children and grandchildren.

Indian Creek War Chief

The Morgan involvement all began, as these things sometimes do, when Russell and Jeanette Quilhot's youngest son, John went off to college in Hanover, New Hampshire. Russ, feeling his own version of the "empty nest" syndrome, looked for a new activity for his spare time. The couple had been introduced to horses through their children. The two oldest sons, Charles and David, had gone to summer camp at Culver Military Academy in Culver, Indiana, known for its Black Horse Troop which marches in many presidential inaugural parades. The Quilhot's daughters, Dru, Sally and Anne, had attended a variety of horse camps. Russ decided to keep up with them by joining the Shrine Horse Patrol. He bought a Palomino Quarter Horse and enjoyed it so much that he wanted his wife to share in the experience and offered to buy her a horse. Jeannette had never forgotten learning about the Morgan horse from the book, *Justin Morgan Had a Horse* and, from having seen the Disney film version of the book. She wanted a Morgan.

When the Quilhots took their son, John to college, they decided to take advantage to the opportunity to visit the nearby University of Vermont Morgan Horse Farm at Middlebury, Vermont.

"When we saw all those beautiful Morgan horses, we knew our dream would become reality!" says Jeanette. "And when we saw the legendary UVM Promise, we began to dream again, this time of some day owning a foal by that great stallion."

That experience set off a series of events. The Quilhots were recommended to Dale Redding of Southview Morgans. Through Dale, in the fall of 1986, they purchased Shamrock Banjo, bred by Rob and Juliane Wilson of Shamrock Morgan Farms.

Next, Russ and Jeanette purchased Southview Commander, their second Morgan, and placed him in training with Mark Mason. Southview Commander was named Park Harness Two-Year-Old Reserve Champion at the New England Regional, and in 1987 was Three-Year-Old Pleasure Driving Reserve Champion at the New England Regional. "This win really whetted our appetites," says Jeanette.

Subsequently the Quilhots purchased more horses from trainer Larry Bolen of Cedar Creek Farm. Among these was Cloisonne, a Trophy's Jade daughter, purchased in 1989. "The next time we saw UVM Promise, it was at the 1991 Grand National, and we were expecting his foal out of Cloisonne," says Jeanette.

"On April 13, 1992, Indian Creek War Chief arrived! A stretchy, stunning little bay who already loves to strut, has a long, upright neck and his hock action is something to see! Of course he has that wonderful Morgan temperament – friendly, curious, and already a character," Jeanette adds. "We noticed that his white star is al-most identical to that of our Jade's Joe, sired by Trophy's Jade. So our Trophy's Jade son and Trophy's Jade grandson have a similarity that's always fun for breeders to see. We're looking forward to a bright future for this little one."

War Chief is one of more than two dozen Morgans on Indian Creek Farm, where the Quilhots and their trainer, Kurt Hufferd, are dedicated to breeding and raising champion home-breds that will be competitive on the national level. Their goal is to raise, train, and present the best possible examples of the breed – not simply win blue ribbons. "When we sell horses, our primary goal is to match horse and rider and to have a happy customer," says Jeanette.

The entire Quilhot family is enjoying the Morgan experience. Son David, and daughter-in-law, Vicki Quilhot have become addicted to pleasure driving with HPS Cool Commotion. The Quilhot's four grandchildren ride, and one is taking riding lessons from Kurt Hufferd.

Indian Creek Farm – with its green and blue colors representing the green hills of Vermont where Justin Morgan lived and the blue waters of Indian Creek near the Quilhot Farm in Fort Wayne – is all the Quilhot family dreamed of, and more.

Charlestown Czar

There was something about the rather dark photo in a small breed newsletter that caused Robert and Leslie Raven of Raven Ridge Morgan Horses in Brooks, California, to inquire about and to visit the Morgan stallion, Charlestown Czar.

"As we rounded the corner at his stable and saw him standing there with that beautiful head and neck over the partition, we lost our hearts to him. Then we saw him move, and we were sold," says Robert.

They were looking for a trained horse for their daughter, Marta, to show, and found Czar to be an exciting horse in action. "His hindquarters are powerful and he uses his hocks very well. When he moves, the viewer sees this upright, high-stepping, forward-driving horse. When he goes into his road trot, he seems to sink down and drive off his hindquarters. It's like flying!" Robert says.

There was one consideration, one caveat. The 15-hand black-brown Czar was still a stallion.

"At first we thought we would geld him, but he was so wonderful it seemed a waste of genes. It was a bit of a gamble as, at the age of four, he had not been used for breeding, even though his bloodlines were impeccable."

Charlestown Czar, considered "the old-type Morgan," was foaled on June 10. 1981, sired by HVK Fieldmarch, who was by the great Vigilmarch and out of Julie Bennfield. Czar's dam, Futurama's Empress, was by UVM Highlight, out of Paramount's Futurama.

Since Czar was the kind of horse they intended to breed anyway, the Ravens just bought a stallion a little earlier than they had planned. "Since he is so gentle and kind, it worked out well," says Robert. "A green stallion and a green handler make for a potentially disastrous situation. But Czar is a terrific breeding stallion, a wonderful riding horse and a good friend."

Charlestown Czar was originally purchased from Charlestown Morgans by Barry and Jeanine Leonardini. He was trained and shown in the Morgan Park Division by Bob Lewis, a well-known Saddlebred and Morgan trainer.

After the Ravens bought Czar, Marta showed him in the Pleasure Division, and they were usually in the ribbons, Marta learning a great deal and Czar looking good.

"Czar's kindness and gentleness at home also deserve mention. A hen once made her nest and raised her chicks in his feed manger. He never hurt them. He took his afternoon nap with his head hanging over the manger, almost guarding the hen and her brood. Czar also has his own personal cat, the black and white 'Half-Cat,' who believes herself to be the manager of the barn. One can often see her in Czar's paddock or stall, winding herself around his legs and purring. He never chases her out of his territory as he does the farm dogs," says Robert. His only obnoxious habit is banging on his stall door at feeding time. Fortunately, his clock is pretty accurate.

"How we feel about Czar and what he has done for us must be split into two parts," says Robert. "First, he is a very fine stallion as measured by the quality of his get. They have all been excellent. The Czar offspring have that 'something extra,' that spark that is so important. As such, he has been a boon to the farm.

"Second, as our daughter, Marta, does most of his handling and riding, her feelings toward Czar are important, and she adores Czar."

Robert has observed that "No matter what a horse looks like or how it moves, there is something spiritual about the connection between horses and their people. Perhaps we are led by fate to take certain steps. Certainly something led us from the ad offering Czar for sale to buy him, show him, stand him and, above all, love him."

Taproot FlagShip

Can a Morgan horse be a competitive dressage horse? Yes, as the proud Morgan stallion Taproot Flag-Ship is proving. He is the third generation of Taproot Morgan Horse Farm horses to hit the dressage arena and prove that this American breed of horse has what it takes to compete against the big guys, the imported European Warmbloods.

"Taproot FlagShip is sired by the sire of sires, Deer Run Command, and out of the mare Taproot SweetFlag, a daughter of the *grande dame* of Taproot — UVM Harmony. FlagShip was bred and is owned by Charles and Charlotte Ross, owners of Taproot Morgans in Hinesburg, Vermont. She's trained by Jackie Qua of QUA-lity Stables, Inc. in Oneonta, New York.

Little did the Rosses know that with their purchase of the Morgan mare UVM Harmony that history was in the making for their Taproot Morgans and that they were far ahead of their time in Morgan history. During the 1960s, Harmony and the Ross's daughter, Jackie, competed successfully in the hunt country of Maryland and Virginia in Combined Training at the preliminary level and in straight dressage competitions. Harmony's offspring have continued in her footsteps of excellence, and now the third generation is doing the same.

Foaled on April 1, 1985, FlagShip romped and frolicked with his friends in the green pastures at Taproot. As he exhibited much charisma and showed a talented way of movement, his owners Charlie and Charlotte decided that this special colt should be watched carefully. As the seasons came and went, FlagShip slowly changed from that leggy young colt into a large, handsome young stallion who continued to show great promise. Through his young years the Rosses' daughter, Jackie Qua and her husband, Ben, also kept their eyes on this young stallion. During his fourth year, Charlie and Charlotte decided it was high time for FlagShip's formal schooling to begin. FlagShip was loaded into the Taproot trailer and headed off to Oneonta, New York, where he would reside at Ben and Jackie Qua's QUA-lity Stables.

Under the direction of Jackie, who had trained his grandam, FlagShip began his education. He had the mind, the conformation and the way of going to be a dressage horse, but a lot of hard work lay ahead to prove that he was indeed going to be competitive.

Taking to his lessons well, this maturing young stallion and his trainer and friend, Jackie, were soon ready to leave the quiet hilltop dressage arena where they had spent many hours perfecting their skills and to venture forth into the world of competition.

The bell has now rung many times for the two of them to enter at A, halt at X, salute the judge, and proceed accordingly. In a very short time, FlagShip exhibited to the dressage world that a Morgan stallion has

what it takes not only to be a competitive dressage horse but also a winning one. In 1990 Taproot FlagShip won first place at training level in the USDF All-Breed Awards sponsored by the American Morgan Horse Association. He is presently showing at third level.

Taproot FlagShip has proven and is continuing to prove that a winning dressage horse need not be an imported Warmblood but indeed can be the original American Warmblood, the Morgan.

FlagShip continues to carry the banner for Charlie and Charlotte's Taproot farms. The Rosses know that FlagShip and his daughters and sons to come will continue to excel, for the Morgan is a kind, athletic, talented and competitive horse whose talent shines in many disciplines.

Century Free Spirit

"Nothing can describe the feelings one has for a special person, place or animal; I have this feeling for 'Guy,'" Kelli G. Ross says of her Morgan stallion, Century Free Spirit. "He is irreplaceable in my life. For me, there will never be another like him.

"I've had two very special moments with Guy.

"When the show announcer called out: 'Ladies and Gentlemen, the 1988 World Champion Stallion is number 554, Century Free Spirit,' it was the thrill of a lifetime. He was the best and he deserved it," says Kelli.

The other moment occurred after her horse farm, Liberation Morgans, was founded in Anchorage, Kentucky, in 1988. Kelli was inspired to create the farm by her many visits to see Guy when he was being trained in the Blue Grass State. "Once Liberation was underway, we had a barn opening party and when presenting Century Free Spirit to the guests, I was overwhelmed by a feeling of pride in my stallion and my farm—both dreams come true," says Kelli.

The flashy red chestnut colt with a white blaze,

foaled on April 9, 1984, was destined to become "one of the winningest Morgan stallions in history," says Kelli. Guy is by Wham Bam Command, a son of In Command, who in only a few years' time became the sire of the largest number of world champions.

Kelli found Guy as a yearling on the grounds of a sale connected with the New England Regional Morgan Horse Show. Kelli asked if she could inspect him and as he parked out on the grass one wonderful July morning, it was love at first sight.

"I had to have him," she says. "I tried to buy him then but for a variety of reasons I was not to have that satisfaction until the beginning of his three-year-old year. I had no choice but to root for Guy for the next year as if he were mine, during championship after championship."

By the end of Guy's four-year-old show season, this remarkable Morgan with the great heart had won thirteen World Championships and eight Grand National titles, including 1988 World Champion Morgan Stallion, plus regional titles too numerous to list. He was also the UPHA Classic Three-Year-Old Park Harness Champion. "He does it all," says Kelli, "World titles in hand, in harness and under saddle."

Guy has been trained from birth by Joan Lurie, one of the most distinguished trainers in the breed, who has shown him in hand, in harness and under saddle. She sums up his athleticism as "deliciously threefold." As she says, "He can position his neck to permit balance and cadence and moves with this balance and cadence with the smartest and most sincere attitude you could hope for."

Kelli says "Guy is extremely photogenic and a ham to boot. His extremely long neck, upright conformation, high tail set and beautiful head and ears help him strike a pose that, once set, does not alter. As if he knows the camera is on him, Guy doesn't move a muscle or an ear."

Peppermints are his favorite treat and he certainly gets his share. A neck scratch, which makes him extend his neck like a crane, and his peppermints make his day. After breeding or training or both in the early morning, it is time for his nap and by ten a.m. each day you will find Century Free Spirit flatout, asleep in his stall. He has been known to save a bit of morning hay and to put it in a pile on his stall floor for use as a pillow for his nap."

Come night, the situation is somewhat reversed as the barn cat, Serina, sleeps on his back, using the cordovan-colored stallion as a giant pillow.

"The small moments of joy in one's life make it all worthwhile," says Kelli, "and one of those joys for me is having a red chestnut stallion who always puts a smile on my face."

Liberation Starbrite

"Having had incredible success with the Wham Bam Command son, Century Free Spirit, I wanted to repeat those bloodlines," says Kelli G. Ross. "Unfortunately for me and the entire Morgan world, Wham Bam died in the fall of 1987.

"In 1988, I found a sale ad for Austin Flying Cloud, a mare I was familiar with and liked, and she was in foal to Wham Bam. There was no hesitation. I bought Bobbie (her barn name) immediately. Little did I know this purchase would result in my star of stars, Liberation Starbrite," Kelli continues.

The elegant bay filly was foaled on April 1, 1988. While waiting for her Liberation Morgans farm in Anchorage, Kentucky to be ready for horses, Kelli boarded the mare and foal at the Brattleboro, Vermont, farm of a veterinarian friend, Dr. Al Grass. The first hint the filly was something special was his comment to Kelli, "That's quite a filly you've got there."

Several months later, Star and Bobbie made their way to Kentucky. When they stepped off the van, Star's soon-to-be trainer, Joan Lurie, commented that this filly was the best she'd ever seen. She was shortly proven right.

As a yearling, Star was Reserve Grand Champion Mare at the New England Show; as a two-year-old, Park Harness Champion at the New England Regional, and Grand National Mare at the Gold Cup Regional Show. She went on to win two-year-old World Champion Futurity Mare In-Hand and was the 1990 World Champion Mare as a two-year-old. With that win, Star set a precedent, as no two-year-old had ever been named Grand Champion Mare.

Her debut under saddle as a three-year-old was equally impressive – Junior Park Saddle Champion at the New England Regional Show; World Champion Three-Year-Old Futurity Park Saddle; World Champion Three-Year-Old Park Saddle. By the end of her three-year-old show season, Star had collected five world titles.

"When she is determined to be her best, nothing can look like she does," says Kelli. "Star has a long neck with a fine throatlatch, a keen ear and beautiful eye. She moves as squarely and as athletically as any that have entered the show ring.

"As with most animals, Star has her own personality," adds Kelli. "Sometimes she is temperamental as all mares are, sometimes demanding, causing some heart-stopping moments when she shows.

"One of the greatest moments for me with Star was during the 1990 Gold Cup Regional Show. Given her temperamental nature, it was with great trepidation that I awaited her entrance into the two-year-old mare in-hand class," Kelli says. "She was last into the ring, in an entrance that brought gasps from the crowd. 'Look at me, look at me,' Star seemed to be saying. Elegant, alert, athletic, attitude to spare. She went on to be Grand Champion Mare."

Liberation Starbrite spends most of her time at Liberation Morgans where she is trained. When Century Free Spirit is off showing, the barn cat Serina – a finicky cat with world-champion taste – sleeps on Star's back.

Kelli expects Star's show ring successes to continue as a four-year-old. "It is an extremely satisfying feeling to have raised this mare – the first World Champion to carry the Liberation prefix. What a thrill!" she says. "My one experience on her back was incredible. She loves to move and feels as square and as athletic underneath as can be imagined. It would be a dream to show her myself one day!"

Schiaparelli

"In the dim light of a foaling stall, a mare labors to give birth to a new life, and one has the pleasure of watching the emergence of a miracle. It was my pleasure to be present at the birth of a filly that would become the love of my life in the horse world, and I knew before she was even dry that she was a remarkable individual," says Louise Brandon Shane of Glen Arden Farm in Alpharetta, Georgia. "The fire and heart that would form her inner strength were present from the first moment she was on her feet. I was also privileged to be the first to witness her display the trot that has become her hallmark."

The filly was to become the World Grand Champion Schiaparelli, proving herself beyond all expectations in the show ring. The extremely talented trainer, Billy Parker, started 'Scap' in her show career. Under his expertise she made history by becoming the first weanling in the Morgan breed to be voted World Grand Champion Mare. "That year was one of the most exciting and agonizing of my entire nineteen years in Morgans," says Louise. "It was such a thrill to watch the development of a filly that I felt so much for, and more so to watch her become a World Champion and to have been fortunate enough to have raised her. She was so thrilling to watch move and show the world that she was, and knew she was, an exceptional individual." All this was proven again when as a yearling she won Junior World Champion Mare.

Sired by the immortal Wham Bam Command, and out of Vagabond Donachime, Scap has two full sisters, Carillon Command (tragically deceased) and Wham Bam Thank U Mam, and a full brother, Suite After. Schiaparelli and her siblings were predestined to be great, whether in the show ring, the breeding paddocks or both. "It was a stroke of luck for me to have had the opportunity to lease 'Chime' (Scap's dam) then to have the opportunity to purchase her before the first foal belonging to me was born," says Louise.

After those first wins, another chapter in Scap's life began. "I had always respected and admired the talents of trainer Glenn Bouvier and it was by providence that 'Scap' and I had the opportunity to become part of his elite stable," says Louise. "Under Glenn's watchful eye and caring demeanor, Scap would only get better and better.

"Glenn campaigned her brilliantly in her four-year-old year, and the entire Morgan world was witness to the inexhaustible talents of this remarkable filly. Scap was definitely meant to be part of Glenn's world, as he was meant to be a part of ours.

"In Scap's five-year-old and final show year, we decided to present her in the Ladies' Park Saddle Division under the talented rider Ashley Wilson. In 1991 Scap

ended her career as she began it, a World Champion. The road was not easy, but anything worth having is worth whatever it takes to get there. Scap never made a bad showing. Some were better than others, but none were less than the best she had to offer at the time.

"Schiaparelli has now entered a new arena of life as she has joined the broodmare ranks. Bred to the incredible Dancity Ala Bam this spring, 1993 will find us waiting for the first foal that will carry forward its dam's noble heritage. We are expectant and thrilled over the possibilities, but no matter what happens in this new endeavor, Schiaparelli will always be the love of my life, an individual born of nobility and possessed of an inner strength we would all feel privileged to experience."

Suite After

Suite After was foaled six months after the death of his sire, the noble Wham Bam Command, and it was immediately apparent to his owner, Louise Brandon Shane of Glen Arden Farm in Alpharetta, Georgia that the dark bay Morgan colt was extremely special.

"Bold, athletic and fiery, Suite After is the epitome of the Morgan horse. While he was still at home roaming the pastures, the thrill of watching him show off would send chills down your spine. He knew he was special and he wanted the world to know it," Louise says.

Louise sent the colt to Kentucky to be put in training with the talented Glenn Bouvier, joining his full sister, the legendary Schiaparelli, and other champion stablemates.

"Glenn is known for wisely refusing to make grandiose statements of any kind about the horses he has in training, so there was very little conversation about Suite After's progress. The only word would come from other clients and friends who had visited the farm and happened to be privileged enough to see him work."

Finally, the long-awaited call from Glenn came, and what he told Louise made her feel thrilled to have raised a colt so highly regarded by his trainer. It was an indirect but very meaningful compliment.

"Glenn was so impressed that he presented Suite After with the nickname Tommy," she says. "Glenn had always wanted to nickname a horse Tommy after his dear friend and multi-talented Saddlebred trainer, Tom Moore, but until he met Suite After, he never felt he knew a horse deserving of this honor. His expectations of Tommy were well-placed.

"In the Two-Year-Old Stallion Futurity at the 1990 Grand National, Tommy leapt into the ring as if a fire had been set underneath him," says Louise.

"He snorted, pranced and blew all the way down the ring, and when the time came for him to be judged in the lineup, he blew at the judges and seemed to be daring them, 'Don't take your eyes off me, 'cause you ain't seen nothin' yet.' He was thrilling and won the class, much to the delight of the audience for whom he had put on such a spectacular show. He continued his education over the next year, and Glenn felt that he definitely was ready to challenge the best in Oklahoma City.

"Unfortunately, just three weeks prior to the Grand National in Oklahoma City, nearly half of the horses in Glenn's barn, including Tommy, were taken ill. The trainer opted not to ship Tommy to the show unless he was 100% well. He noted that there would be many other shows, but there may never again be a Suite After. Although heartbreaking for me, I was in complete agreement with this decision," says Louise.

"In the course of time, we had also decided to breed Tommy to a very small and select group of mares, believing that his heritage would enable him to be a world-class sire like his own sire, Wham Bam Command," says Louise. Tommy had the good fortune to be bred to four World Champion mares, one the only full sister to Wham Bam Command.

The months waiting for his first foals to arrive were agonizing, and the question was in Louise's mind as to whether he would pass on his genes as believed. Finally, Louise remembers, a call came from Trudy Case of Century Farm to say that the foal out of Appleton Baroness was the best foal ever to be born on her farm. As if that wasn't enough to make her feel ecstatic, "All those who have seen the filly out of Lady Bird Command say she is the best of the foals at Stonecroft Farm," says Louise. "We are still waiting with bated breath for the arrival of the last two out of WC RRG Promises Promises and her dam, HRH Trophyette.

"We hope that Suite After will be able to fill a part of the void left by the death of Wham Bam Command. We are firm believers that he will be able to accomplish this feat. It's horses like Suite After that make us remember that dreams really do come true on this side of the rainbow."

Century Enjolie

For the first time ever, in 1991, a yearling filly wore the roses as World Champion Morgan Mare. She was Century Enjolie, belonging to John Scheidt and Don Spear of Stonecraft Farm in Shelbyville, Kentucky. When Larry Bolen, the judge presiding over this unprecedented event, was asked for comment, he replied: "I don't make decisions like this to be known as a trendsetter. I may have been a bit hesitant at first, but if I hadn't felt she was the best mare there, she wouldn't be World Champion."

He offered some additional tribute to Enjolie. "She's very beautiful and conformationally correct. In addition, she has pizzazz and moved along the rail with an even, effortless cadence. Above all, she never let down. Enjolie is an outstanding representative of the breed."

This filly who took the in-hand division by storm at such a young age was bred by Michael and Trudy Case at Century Farm in Osceola Mills, Pennsylvania, out of one of their great mares, Appleton Baroness.

Baroness, an outstanding individual, was bred to Tedwin Topic. The resulting lively bay filly born in March, 1990, was christened Enjolie, which means "joyful" in French.

Trudy felt Enjolie was special from the beginning, a gorgeous foal who had her dam's leggy looks, and the same huge eye and beautifully chiseled head that typify Lord Appleton offspring. The looks coupled with her show attitude made a package that Trudy knew would only get better with time.

Enjolie was only two days old when John Scheidt called. He and partner Don Spear were interested in purchasing a Tedwin Topic foal. They had seen and loved Enjolie's half-sister, Century Celebration, in the show ring. "It seemed logical to call Trudy when I heard of the match. It looked so good on paper that I couldn't pass up the chance that the foal might be for sale," says John.

Excited by Trudy's judgement and description of the filly, John wanted to see her, but his busy schedule prevented any immediate trip, so he asked for a videotape. Trudy, knowing the growth pattern of Baroness's foals (which made them a little chunky at a few weeks of age), discouraged the idea. She invited John to wait awhile and come to see the filly in person at six months when she would look more sleek.

For the next months, John phoned Century Farms regularly for progress reports on the filly. Each one made him more determined to see her, and finally he made the trip to Pennsylvania.

When the stall door opened, Enjolie's head went up, her tail curled over her back, and she snorted. "That incredible attitude was all it took to make up my mind," says John. "I fell in love."

The deal was made that night and Enjolie was shipped to her new home in Kentucky. She was sent to Whitney Stables for some charm school lessons, and it was agreed that the filly would be campaigned selectively. Enjolie debuted at the Gold Cup Regional, going first in a competitive nine-entry Yearling Fillies class. She went on to capture Junior Champion and Grand Champion Mare titles and made history as the first yearling to become a Gold Cup Grand Champion mare.

The next stop was the Grand National, where Enjolie was named 1991 Grand National Yearling Filly Champion, and went on to win the World Junior Champion Mare title before her final victory pass as the 1991 World Champion Mare.

As to the future, John doesn't see much point in showing Enjolie in-hand again. Judge Larry Bolen supports that decision: "Once a horse has been a World Champion, there's no reason to bring it back. It's a bit sad that Enjolie's in-hand career is over so soon, but she's got a long life ahead of her and there are so many horizons open as both a performance and breeding horse."

New fields of conquest this fabulous filly is sure to make her own.

Starwood Heritage

"I have often joked about 'Taj' being my foundation gelding," says Katana Dembicki-Rubenstein of her Morgan, Starwood Heritage.

"Taj was really responsible for starting my farm. Horses are an addiction for me. I couldn't stop at just one. Taj was followed by Alta, my first Andalusian, and on down the line." Now Katana has twelve Morgans, thirteen Andalusians, and what she calls "two random extras," plus four cats, two dogs, two sheep and a goat at her Shadow Fax farm, founded in 1988 in Erieville, New York.

"I had been looking for a horse for some time," Katana tells how it all began, "but none had impressed me. I was looking for a feeling, a horse that would somehow make me feel the same as the horse of my childhood did."

Taj, a dark chestnut with white markings, and a pure Lippitt line Morgan, bred by Noel W. Drury of Randolph Vermont, had been for sale for a long time.

"I had heard about him, and had been warned not to buy him," says Katana. "He was a bit of a rogue. But my curiosity overcame me. I had to see this 'monster Morgan' for myself. I drove the sixty-some miles to the farm where he was stabled and peered into his stall. His dark eyes glared back at me from a black corner. He was brought out on cross-ties. He looked so small (14.2, and I had been used to tall, lanky Thoroughbred types), but so arrogant. As I watched him move, I was overwhelmed by his grace and beauty."

Katana was allowed to try him. "As soon as I settled into the saddle, I knew I had found my horse! The feeling was just so right."

But they didn't just ride off into the sunset together in a fairy tale ending. Katana believes Taj had been abused at some time. "For that reason he has only disdain for humans. He could not be intimidated, and he did not really care if he pleased people."

But that appealed to Katana as she saw herself in him – "Almost as arrogant as he, at least as bull-headed, and even if I could be intimidated, I was very stubborn.

"I have a great deal of respect for Taj's spirit. I sometimes feel that our personalities are the same, although I hope I am more tractable. I saw in this horse a regal free spirit where everyone else saw dog food," she adds.

Shortly after she bought Taj, Katana was in a very serious car accident. Through the long months of recovery and years of physical therapy, she refused to give up, drawn on by the overwhelming desire to ride Taj again. "Through this recovery period, he was the only one that could make me laugh. He would chew on my crutches, 'slime' on my arm and make silly faces. He kept me going, and I never stopped believing he could be a star – we would do it together," Katana told me.

The incredible dream came true. "We have won numerous awards in jumping, eventing, and especially in our forte, dressage, winning many championships and receiving numerous AMHA and USDF awards," she says.

It wasn't always easy. "Taj is so smart that he is hard to deal with. He anticipates everything, to the point where I swear he can read my mind."

Like many of his breed, Taj is totally convinced of his own self-worth. "He is a clown, often a brute, and always a free spirit!" says Katana. "I get angry, frustrated, and often end up laughing as he outwits me all the time." Lucky Katana and Taj to have found each other.

Ulterior Motive

Ulterior Motive was only one and a half years old at the time this book was written, and already he had made a powerful impact on the lives of Daniel and Janet Unrein.

The Unreins were trying to heal from the tragic loss of their stallion, Spice O Life Alliance, who was euthanized in September, 1990 for severe kidney failure. Alliance had been named Reserve Senior Champion Stallion the previous August at the Jubilee Regional Mor-

gan Horse Show, despite the fact, unknown to them, he was seriously ill.

"The loss of Alliance was almost unbearable," says Jan. In fact there was a question in both their minds about whether they wanted to continue in the horse business. This extremely impressive stallion was to have been the future herd sire for their Chimera Morgans in Tualatin, Oregon.

Their trainer, Pam Ellingsen, however, urged Jan to inspect a young stallion in Kentucky, a half-brother of a former World Champion Morgan.

As often happens, it wasn't the colt Jan went to look at that won her heart, but a younger half-brother. "Though only nine months old, this colt had a presence that made it impossible not to pay attention to him. A dark bay, with only a small white star, he was quick to flag his tail and show off when turned loose in the paddock. He possessed natural athletic ability and, in the opinion of Pam, a top-rated Morgan judge, had the most correct conformation of any Morgan weanling she had ever seen," says Jan.

However, Ulterior Motive's breeder, Peter Schwartz of Foal's Paradise Morgans in Burlington, Kentucky, had no intention of selling Motive, sired by his popular breeding stallion, Ultimate Command. Both Motive's sire and his dam are by the great Morgan stallion, Waseeka's In Command, whose get and grandget have generated millions of dollars in sales and won countless championships. The breeder saw in Motive a realization of his breeding that far surpassed his expectations.

But the Unreins finally convinced Peter to sell, and Motive came to the Ellingsen's stable late in 1990. Pam spent the winter and spring getting to know him, and as she puts it, "becoming much too attached to his captivating personality."

When Motive became friends with the colt in the adjoining stall, for example, Pam started finding Motive's toys in the latter's stall every morning. Motive had thrown them over an eight-foot wall to share them with his friend.

When two colts who were his pasture buddies were returned to the pasture after being gelded, Motive spent a long time sniffing their incisions. Then, when it was time for the youngsters to go back into the barn for the night, Motive, usually the first one in the gate, refused to be caught for almost an hour. It wasn't clear to him what had happened to his pals, but he sure wasn't going to let it happen to him!

Although the Unreins will never forget Alliance – his only son, conceived one month before his death, now stands in their pastures as a living reminder – they have refocused their dreams and expectations now on this super young horse, Ulterior Motive.

His Royal Highness

"I always wanted the best Morgan trotter and in His Royal Highness I got just that–the modern day world record holder (2.33), and the gentlest horse a man could ever want!" says his owner/driver, Leo Tancreti.

His Royal Highness first came into Leo's life when he saw him race at the New England Regionals in 1989. The bay Morgan gelding by Evenmist Commander and out of Vega Sweet Scarlett, foaled April 14, 1984, had never raced before. "But could he fly! I liked him immediately and knew that we had to be a team," says Leo.

Leo first became interested in horses a few years ago when he went to a farm auction expecting farm equipment to be on the block. Instead the auctioneers were selling Morgans. "Before I knew it, I was leaving the auction with two wonderful creatures," he says. "I've been hooked ever since!"

"I began my involvement with horses for the simple pleasure of it and enjoyed it so immensely that I decided to start my own stables shortly thereafter, in 1986," he adds. Tancreti Stables in East Haven, Connecticut offers boarding, training and breeding services under trainer Allan Rutledge.

"Since we have our own trainer, facility and staff, I can still manage to say that I'm in it for the pleasure. They take care of the rest! And since I hold a strong interest in trotters and roadsters, we breed Morgans with speed and athletic ability in mind," he adds.

His Royal Highness is shown strictly in the Morgan Horse Trotting Division and is virtually undefeated. His record speaks for itself: New England Regionals, Northhampton, Maine, Champion Mile Race, Champion Half Mile Race in 1989, 1990, 1991; Vermont Spring Classic, Northhampton, Maine, Champion Mile Race, Champion Half Mile Race in 1990, 1991; The Governor's Justin Morgan Classic Horse Race, Tunbridge, Vermont, Champion Mile Race, Champion Half Mile Race in 1990, 1991; The John D. Phillips Memorial Trot, Meadowlands, New Jersey, World Champion Mile Race in 1989, 1991, and World Reserve Champion Mile Race in 1990.

His Highness set his 2:33 record on August 3, 1991 at the John D. Phillips Memorial Morgan Trot World Championships at Meadowlands.

Chances were he would have won the 1990 race as well, since two of the other drivers inadvertently boxed him in at the start. "Leo was told to protest the race – by the winner, of all people--so that the championship could rightly go to His Highness, but my father refused to do this and accepted Reserve instead," says Leo's daughter, Cheryl Tancreti.

Leo says his favorite win, notwithstanding, was the Vermont Governor's Classic Road Race in Tunbridge, Vermont. "It wasn't our first race won and it certainly wasn't our last or biggest, but for some reason this race will always be my favorite. It was 1990 and we were racing where it all began–Justin Morgan, the founder of the breed was from Vermont. His Royal Highness won the half mile and the mile by more than a quarter lap against some of the best Morgan trotters in the country."

"Off track, His Royal Highness is big and bold with a heart even bigger than he is. He is very gentle and always a gentleman. Whenever you mention him to anyone, the phrases, 'He's a big teddy bear,' and 'What a puppy dog,' or simply 'Sweetheart!' keep coming up," says Leo.

"The special relationship we have enables us to be one as we control great speed around the racetrack," he adds.

"I do have two young grandchildren who think His Highness is a great big teddy bear. The younger likes to ride in the sulky with me and is always saying to me, 'Make him go faster, Pop!'"

"His Royal Highness certainly made me a very proud owner of a beautiful animal!" says Leo.

Prince Of Highland

Prince Of Highland was rotting away in a damp, dark stall in Indiana, past days of glory a distant memory. He was fed, but no human gave him any comfort beyond that. One wonders if at that low point he ever dreamed of what used to be.

Bob Skiles who had once owned the Morgan gelding and the farm, showed Highland as a park horse and rode him right into the record books at the Gold Cup Morgan Show in 1975. The four-year-old Highland won the Park Harness Amateur Championship, then the same evening Bob, an amateur, showed him in the Junior Park Saddle Championship Class against professional trainers. Bob and the 15.2-hand Morgan took home the tricolor ribbon for the second time that day.

A couple of years later Bob saw his favorite horse shown at the Indiana State Fair for the last time. Bob, who had throat cancer and was not strong enough to show himself, sat in the stands and saw Highland win the Morgan Park Saddle Championship. A few months later when Bob passed away, his son put a photograph of Highland in the breast pocket of his father's coat, and Bob was buried with a picture of some of his best memories.

Fast forward to 1982, when trainer Larry Bolen was working for Linda Fu Wylie of Dragonsmead Farm in Perrysburg, Ohio. Linda was searching for a park horse to compete at the World Championship level. Larry remembered a young horse at a farm in Indiana where he had worked starting out as a trainer in 1972. Larry found Highland in the same barn where he had worked years ago. The barn had aged and was falling apart, but in a dark, filthy stall, there stood Highland. "Even then," Larry said, "the horse was regal." Larry told Linda that Highland was just what she was looking for.

"Little did we know what was in store for us," says Linda.

Highland won the World Championship Amateur Park Saddle Class in 1983, 1984 and 1985, probably the oldest horse ever to compete for the Championship, let alone win.

"We got Highland when he was eleven years old. By most show horse standards, this is considered a little old. However, Highland has a heart the size of a large Midwest city, and an attitude that most horse show people would kill for. Now he is twenty-one years old and he still thinks he is the neatest thing since Hershey made chocolate kisses," says Linda.

"What makes Highland wonderful is what he is on the inside. His attitude is unbeatable. Anytime we had a workout in a class, Highland acted as though it was the first time he had ever been around that ring.

"On the ground, however, Highland is somewhat aloof," Linda adds. "He isn't even very friendly to other horses, which is very strange, considering he is a herd animal. I believe this is from being alone for so long after Bob Skiles died. This is just one thing that makes me love the horse so much. He had to draw on his inner strength to survive.

"I may be very biased but I believe that Highland was the best Park Morgan of his time. I truly feel that he upgraded the standards set for the Amateur Park Saddle division if not the whole Park division. Highland was always a challenge to ride. He was not difficult, but boy, did he keep me on my toes. He made me become a better rider. He taught me to ride using intuition more than just sitting there and pushing the right buttons.

"He demands the best from himself and his rider," continues Linda. "With Highland you were never a passenger; he made you work as hard as he worked himself. He improved my riding by making me ride using my heart instead of my head. It seemed he felt that if you thought you were good enough to ride him, well, be prepared for the ride of your life."

Stoneholm Taliesin

One good horse often leads to another, as happened with Tracy Fietz and James Hangley of Morgan Ridge Farms in Culver City, California. They had a couple of young horses which they had brought to Rock Walker Stables in Goleta, California, after having seen Walker, a well-known Morgan trainer, and his partner, Robert Hughes, at several horse shows.

At Rock Walker Stables Tracy and James saw Dancity Sojourn, a horse registered as brown but who looks like he's all black. "He has lots of charisma and show horse attitude," says Hughes. "Tracy saw him work and she wanted him."

"From the first time I set my eyes on him, I knew he would be mine," Tracy agrees, and in 1988 she and James purchased Dancity Sojourn.

Sojourn had had an incredible show year as a two year old which culminated in his winning the 1988 Grand National Champion Two-Year-Old Park Harness Stallion title at the Oklahoma City Nationals.

Tracy was so delighted she bought Sojourn's sire, Stoneholm Taliesin, in partnership with Rock Walker and Robert Hughes. The 15.1 bay stallion with a white star, then owned by Mark and Linda Hansen of Canyon Country, California, was also in training at Rock Walker Stables.

"'Tali' is a horse that wins your heart from the first moment you see him," says Tracy. He was an irresistible colt with a gorgeous Arabian-type head when he was purchased as a six-month-old weanling by the Hansens. Tali, bred by Anita and Frederic Anderson at Stoneholm Farms, was foaled June 3, 1983, sired by Waseeka's Showtime, a popular breeding horse, out of Wales Farm Gidget.

Tali also won the votes of horse show judges. He was Yearling Colt Futurity Champion, Yearling Colt Open Champion and Reserve Junior Colt Champion at the 1984 Western States Futurity; in 1985, he was Two-Year-Old Colt Champion and Reserve Junior Stallion Champion at the California Crystal Classic, and Two-Year-Old Colt and Reserve Junior Champion Stallion at the Morgan Medallion Regional in Santa Barbara. Returning to the Western States Futurity in 1987, Stoneholm Taliesin was named Grand Champion Stallion and Four-Year-Old Champion Stallion.

"He hasn't had a long career, but what he's done in the time has been outstanding," says Hughes.

In 1991, Tracy first drove Tali, whom Hughes describes as a relatively easy horse for an amateur in that he loves to work. The more you work him, the happier he is. He goes as long as you want him to go," says Hughes.

Tali went right to the top with Tracy. Their first time out they got a third, and then moved into high gear. Tali won the 1991 Reserve World Championship in Amateur Pleasure Driving and the 1991 Grand National Amateur Pleasure Driving Stallion title, both in Oklahoma. At Santa Barbara, Tali won Regional Amateur Pleasure Driving Champion and 1991 People's Choice Amateur Pleasure Driving Horse of the Year in a special balloting held by *Horse World* magazine.

"Some people have driven years and years and don't have what Tracy has won in one year," Hughes describes her achievements.

"This was the thrill of my life. Tali seems to improve each year; 1991 promises more blue and tricolor ribbons," was Tracy's reaction.

"He has a genuine love for the show ring and turns on all four burners when he hits the ring," as Tracy describes the sensation of showing him. "He has a big heart, true Morgan stamina. Tali consistently gives his all, has unending confidence. He is proud, bold and has impressive athletic ability."

This spirited stallion continues to sire championship get in his image of beauty, conformation, athletic ability and heart. "All his offspring are easy to work with, and all have really good dispositions," says Hughes. "He's a very special horse to all of us."

THE NATIONAL SHOW HORSE

This pretty, leggy, athletic, long-necked animal has caught the imagination of the American public. One of the newest breeds, it is an inspired combination of two others, the Arabian and the American Saddlebred, for a result that is nothing short of electric.

The sense of excitement generated by the National Show Horse is even written into the breed standard: "When observed at rest or in motion, the horse must exhibit a natural presence and when animated, extreme brilliance. The horse must exhibit high carriage when showing or relaxed."

Knowledgeable breeders had for many years recognized the potential in crossing these two breeds to accentuate the outstanding qualities of both. In 1981, the National Show Horse Registry, with headquarters in Louisville, Kentucky, was formed.

One goal of the NSHR was to create a registry that would allow breeders a systematic means of refining and improving the cross to create the ideal show horse, one which combines the beauty, refinement and stamina of the Arabian with the long neck, high motion and show ring brilliance of the Saddlebred.

The bloodline content for the National Show Horse may range from 75 percent Saddlebred to 99.9 percent Arabian, but can never contain less than 25 percent Arabian blood.

Very often, the most distinguished bloodlines of both the American Saddlebred and the Arabian are used with excellent results. In a relatively short time, breeders have produced significant numbers of horses representative of the type and high quality outlined in the breed standard.

The breed has grown rapidly, for in 1988 more than 6,400 horses were recorded in the registry books. The American Horse Council reported that the only breeds of horses in this country to have increased registrations in 1988 were the Peruvian Paso, the Paint and the National Show Horse.

A crowd favorite, the National Show Horses are consistent winners in Half-Arabian performance and halter classes. Underlying the NSH's popularity is its versatility, which makes it appealing as a horse with which the whole family can become involved. These horses can easily switch from pleasure driving, with one member of the family showing, to three-gaited or equitation, with another exhibitor, or from showing in hand with a professional trainer in an early morning class to a performance class with an amateur exhibitor in the evening.

In no other breed is the amateur owner and exhibitor given more support and importance. The National Show Horse has developed a reputation as an excellent mount for young equestrians and equitation classes for riders seventeen and under are given special attention.

The extraordinary success of the National Show Horse in such a few years is also a testament to the industry of those horsemen and horsewomen dedicated and courageous enough to be pioneer forces in establishing a new breed. Arabian enthusiasts such as Deedie Wrigley, Dr. Dean Tolbert and Mike Nichols have offered their support to the emerging National Show Horse, and from the Saddlebred side, Bob Ruxer, Tom Galbreath, Marsha Shephard and Arthur Meyerhoff have contributed their efforts to this new and very exciting horse.

DW Tempting Fate

The operative word in the breed name "National Show Horse" is SHOW, and it was apparent from the beginning that the filly DW Tempting Fate would live up to that designation. She immediately dominated the other foals as she strutted around the pasture, her long elegant neck held high, her powerful legs gracefully propelling her.

The bright chestnut filly was one of the first National Show Horse foals produced at Kaaba Arabian Enterprises in Scottsdale, Arizona, owned by Deedie Wrigley-Hancock and her daughter, Misdee Furey.

My good friend Deedie was one of the founding board members when the National Show Horse Registry was established in 1982. The thought of producing a horse that is as beautiful as it is athletic and being on the ground floor of creating a new light horse breed in America had enormous appeal for her.

Mother and daughter embraced the idea of combining the blood of the Arabian and the Saddlebred to create a cross of extreme hybrid vigor, and they believed their Arabian stallion, Heritage Emir++, would be the ideal sire to produce National Show Horses. Since they had spent their lifetimes breeding Arabians and did not own any Saddlebred mares, they decided to lease several. One of them, Eve's Temptation, a chestnut mare of classic Saddlebred pedigree would become the dam of Tempting Fate.

Deedie and Misdee felt the need to test their breeding program in the field of competition and decided to show the filly as a yearling at the National Show Horse Finals. From the moment Fate entered the show ring, she displayed the charisma and attitude of a champion. "There is nothing that can quite compare to watching a horse that you have bred and raised capture the hearts of the audience and judges," says Deedie.

Deedie and Misdee knew their breeding program was indeed on track when Fate left the Finals with the title of Grand National Champion National Show Horse Filly.

The win confirmed that Tempting Fate had correct conformation, but the true test was to see if she could be a performance horse as well. As a two-year-old, Fate began her performance training with Robb Wallen, and by the time the Finals came around again, it was decided she would not only defend her halter title, but compete in two-year-old driving as well, the ultimate test of form fitting function.

Like her sire, Fate loves the show ring and seems to thrive on the competition. She possesses a quality about her unlike that of other young horses. She never frets, never seems nervous, but is aware of the excitement around her. She has a habit of occasionally throwing her head up high, her eyes taking on a distant look, her nostrils flaring, as if some ancient genes were telling her that she must prepare herself for battle, even if it is the modern-day battlefield of the show arena.

Fate responded to the call, winning both the Driving National Championship and the Halter National Championship by unanimous decision of the judges.

As a three-year-old, Fate continues to set a standard for National Show Horses. At the prestigious Scottsdale Arabian horse show, she repeated her halter and performance championship wins, the first Half-Arabian mare in a decade to achieve those honors. As of this writing, Tempting Fate continues her record, adding six more unanimous championships.

Fate has no doubt as to her celebrity status. In the barn she is intensely jealous of any other horse receiving attention. If she is ignored too long, she will toss her head impatiently at the stall door until she receives a pat or a carrot.

"If one horse could confirm the belief that man might attempt to be a 'co-creator,' that he might aspire to help put a creature on earth that is truly special, all the while realizing that he was tempting fate to do so, then a bright chestnut filly foaled on a clear spring morning gives us that hope," says Deedie.

Cameo King

When Cameo King arrived at his new home in Edmond, Oklahoma, and his new owner, Terry Papa first laid eyes on him, she recalls, "I knew in my heart he would have some kind of impact on our lives for years to come."

Terry had spent most of her childhood days with horses, but like most girls soon discovered boys, cars, and then college and work, and put aside her dream of owning one. When her oldest daughter, Jenny, was seven, Terry discovered a love of horses in her, although she had never been exposed much to them. Terry and her husband Ron decided to begin a business related to horses that she and Jenny could enjoy together.

"Through Ron's medical supply business, we became acquainted with the Dr. Jack Howard family in Ada, Oklahoma, and began admiring their National Show Horses, a breed that was fairly young. We felt that by getting involved in the National Show Horse breed, we could enoy a thrilling and beautiful horse and possibly run a profitable business due to the lucrative prize money offered by the National Show Horse Registry," adds Terry. The Papas' search for a young horse to show

led to Cameo King, who was named the National Champion English Pleasure Amateur Horse the day they purchased him.

Foaled on March 3, 1984 at the Ruxer Farm in Jasper, Indiana, the 15.1-hand chestnut gelding, registered as both a NSH and a Half-Arabian, is well-named, as he has an especially pretty head.

King showed well during the remainder of 1988 and finished the year with six National Championships. "We came to the realization that what we had was more than just 'a good quality amateur horse,'" says Terry, referring to the "order" she had put in with the trainer who did the equine star search.

Terry began riding King herself during the winter of 1988-89 and worked on building up her confidence to take this great horse into the show ring. "As a complete novice in this type of riding and showing, the stress at times felt tremendous because I certainly did not want to make him look bad. Just as I started to feel a little sure of myself, my riding career faced a slight setback, though not an unhappy one, as Ron and I found out we were expecting another child."

King continued his career with trainers Bill Addis and Dee Brown until Terry was ready to get back in the saddle again. "The highlight of my show career with this magnificent horse had to be the 1991 season," she says. "King won three District Championships in Three-Gaited Amateur, three District Championships and one Reserve Championship in English Pleasure Amateur and one District Championship and one Reserve Championship in English Pleasure Open. At the 1991 National Show Horse Finals in Omaha, Nebraska, my dream of riding King to a National Championship came true when he was named the National Champion Three-Gaited Amateur. The following night, Bill Addis rode him to a unanimous decision Championship in English Pleasure Open.

"After four and one-half years of owning Cameo King, Ron and I are still in awe of him and thankful that we are blessed with owning him. He is truly a pleasure to ride, drive or just hang around with, always willing and able to do what you ask of him. He usually captures the heart of at least one groom in the barn who remains his friend for life," says Terry.

Terry and Ron have also been able to realize their business aspirations with this National Show Horse. Cameo King not only has performed at the top level in both of his breed registries, but has won $69,000 in show earnings from both registries to date!

"I would be comfortable riding him anywhere and I trust his instincts sometimes more than my own," says Terry. "When he hits the show ring gate, though, he truly comes alive and in our opinion he is and always will be 'The King of the Ring.'"

CH Obsession

CH Obsession is most distinguished by her coloring, which is essentially bay and white. But where the bay stops there is a shading or a border before it turns white. "I would point out that Someone with just the right touch had a hand in her markings," says her proud owner, Crete B. Harvey of Harvey Arabian Farm, Stanwood, Washington.

Obsession was "the ultimate Mother's Day gift," says Crete, who admits "I have always liked pretty pinto horses and ponies." Tim Fredericks, her partner in a pinto Saddlebred stallion, The Northern Lights, had to take back a mare for lack of payment along with her two-year-old black and white tobiano pinto purebred Saddlebred filly. Both were in neglected condition.

Crete bought the filly from Tim and named her Key Dancer. With proper feed and care she began to grow and blossom into a wonderful broodmare. She first produced a National Reserve Champion Park Horse gelding, Andre Dancer. Then Crete decided to breed her to Al-Marah Canadius, a Legion of Merit Arabian stallion.

"So, on May 10, Mother's Day in the year 1987, CH Obsession was foaled. I had asked to be called if it was a filly, no matter what time of day or night. So at two in the morning, even by flashlight, one could see the perfect Half-Arabian pinto filly," she says.

Crete bought her first Arabian on July 15, 1959 as a riding horse. However, curious as to what kind of horse she had bought, she took him to an Arabian show where he won a championship. And from there on, "the 'disease' spread," she says. "In all my years of showing Arabian horses, I had never had a National Champion. I guess it is fair to say that I had never felt I had bred the perfect Arabian. However, from the moment Obsession was foaled, I felt I had produced the perfect Half-Arabian pinto."

Crete sent the weanling filly, registered with three registries (Half-Arabian, National Show Horse, and Pinto) to trainer Jeff Schall. "I told him that I did not want one untoward or inauspicious thing done to Obsession. That when he showed her, if she won, that was wonderful. If she didn't, I didn't care. Jeff found it took very little time to show her what he wanted and that she only kept improving. She was always happiest to do what she was supposed to do without being pushed. Jeff showed her to 1990 U.S. National Champion Half-Arabian Mare.

"Her trot was full of life and extremely airy. She did have one year of performance training and went to one show, winning first place in English pleasure. She did have her days of brilliance, but she did not want to be pushed. She knew that she was doing her best and to push her further would make things all wrong," says Crete.

"It would be very difficult to try to explain what sets Obsession apart from other pintos, if you have not seen her," she adds. "Her presence and the aura that she gives off endear her to everyone who sees her."

"Obsession definitely has a special personality. In the stall and in the barn she will come right up to the threshold of the door and stand waiting for you to pet her, open the door and give her attention. She is incredibly forward in that manner. Out in the paddock she will follow you around with her head right by your shoulder just to be near you and enjoy your company. She has a heart of gold."

With Obsession's National Championship, Harvey Farm gained in stature. Recently Crete has concentrated on Half-Arabians, primarily trying to produce beautiful pintos. With Obsession's help, she is bound to succeed.

The mare was bred to the great stallion Khemosabi+++, and is due to foal in June, 1992. And once again, Crete is "anticipating with great expectations in every aspect the future of Obsession. It is hard not to, and I will say no more," she adds, leaving us with tantalizing visions of special spotted newcomers.

Irish Cream

"We call her Bailey," says trainer Joey Canda of the National Show Horse, Irish Cream. "She's one of those special horses that has a great show horse attitude."

Joey, of River Ridge Farm in Auburn, Washington, believes Bailey and her owner/rider, eighteen-year-old Stacie Stewart, are the ideal combination. "The horse has a very sporty way of going and Stacie is very petite. They look very good together," says Joey.

Stacie and her family have shown purebred Arabians for many years. Stacie showed Lakesides Kubal all the way to the Nationals, but when he reached his twenties, she wanted something younger. Following Kubal, Stacie had "a very moody mare, and it wasn't working between us," she says. She began to look for another horse.

It was about two years ago that Stacie learned that Irish Cream was for sale. The dark bay National Show Horse mare is by the Arabian stallion Promotion (a *Bask son) and out of the American Saddlebred mare, Kalarama's Funburst. Stacie went to Santa Ynez, California to have a look.

Stacie could see Bailey "was extremely talented and had motivation, a lot of get up and go."

The pair have gotten up and gone to a number of shows since they joined forces.

Last year at the U.S. Nationals in Albuquerque, New Mexico, Stacie and Bailey were Reserve Champion English Pleasure Junior Owner to Ride. In 1990, in Louisville, Kentucky, they were U.S. National Champion English Pleasure Junior Owner to Ride; also in 1990 they were Canadian National Champion English Pleasure Junior Owner to Ride, and Canadian National Champion in Equitation, Junior Owner to Ride. That same year at the National Show Horse Finals, they went Reserve Grand National Champion, Equitation, Junior Owner to Ride; and same year, same Finals, National Champion English Pleasure Age 14 to 17.

"There's not a whole lot she hasn't won," says Bailey's owner laconically. "She loves the ring. I don't think there's anything about showing she doesn't like."

Asked what it is that makes them such a great team, Stacie replies, "Her attitude. She's just as aggressive as I am. Not a whole lot stops her because she's a lot bigger (16 hands) than most of the other horses, and has a muscular look to her and kind of a cocky attitude to go with it."

Bailey is also "really pretty," says Stacie, "though she has more of a Saddlebred look to her." Stacie thinks Bailey inherited her motivation from the Arabian side.

"We hit it off right from the start," says Stacie, "Just kind of sat down and got to work. When I first got her, she hadn't done any equitation, and that's what I really wanted to show. She didn't resist any of the maneuvers," adds Stacie, referring to the patterns of circular figures and figure eights for which a horse must slow down. There was no frustration, no fighting, no arguments. Bailey just said, 'I'll try. Okay, I can deal with this.' She is real positive about doing things. She likes to truck, and she is BUILT! We get up and move.

"She just waits for that gate to open so she can get out there with those other horses. I couldn't have found a better horse. When you're competing like Bailey and I are, you've got to be a team. If one's off pace, the whole picture is off," adds Stacie. The pair's immediate goal is to finish off this year with the National Show Horse Nationals and the U.S. Nationals in Louisville, Kentucky, where this high-powered pair will hopefully continue to blow their competition away.

Dream On An On

At the present time, the National Show Horse is not as popular in Ontario, Canada, as it is in the United States. Shari Wilson of Brantford, Ontario, is not only certain this will change, but that her bay stallion, Dream On An On, will be instrumental in bringing the breed to prominence in her country.

Shari first discovered "On An On" when she was at the National Show Horse Finals in 1990. She was searching for a stallion to breed to her National Show Horse filly, and she was impressed with On An On's looks, attitude and temperament. A short time later she contacted Patricia Carleton, his owner breeder, and booked a breeding to him, and went to watch him show as a two-year-old at the National Show Horse District 1 Show in Columbus, Ohio.

"When his handler trotted him into the ring, I don't think I have ever been more excited in all my life," says Shari. "I was completely overwhelmed with the way On An On had developed. He went on to win that class as well as the one in the District 2 show in Syracuse, New York, a couple of months later. I decided this was the horse I was looking for. For quite some time, I had been considering purchasing a stallion of my own, but had not quite found what I wanted. It was almost a full year later, in March, 1992, that mine was the name appearing on On An On's papers as his owner. At that same time, his first son was born to my own mare. The foal was everything I had hoped for and more. He possessed the same temperament and attitude his dad has as well as the athletic ability we look for in the National Show Horse."

On An On comes from a championship background. His sire, Dream On, was a Champion National Show Horse in both halter and performance. His half-brother, Dream On Dreamer, is a three-time National Champion Halter Stallion.

Shari hopes to prove that Dream On An On is a great performance horse as well as a halter horse, and toward that end, he will remain in training for the next few years with Ralph and Jo Brown of Joral Stables in Chagrin Falls, Ohio. Eventually Shari will bring him home to stand at stud at her farm, located on fifty-six acres of rolling farmland in rural Ontario.

Shari has been riding horses since she can remember, and had the good fortune to own her own horse at the age of eleven. Ten years later she began riding an Arabian mare for a friend. "There was an instant bond between this small mare and me. Although only 14.1 hands high, she had more quiet spirit and spunk than any horse I had ever known," Shari remembers.

"A couple of years later, I purchased this mare, and bred her to an Arabian stallion. The resulting foal still resides at my farm and last year was a Regional Champion Amateur Owner to Ride Hunter Pleasure Horse."

Through her Arabian interests, Shari began to notice the National Show Horse. In order to develop breeding stock for this exciting new English pleasure type horse, she bred her Arabian mares to Saddlebred stallions. "My little 14.1-hand Arabian mare produced a filly that eventually became the mare I bred to On An On," she says.

"My biggest wish is that someday I will be able to get on this incredible young horse and ride him in the amateur division at the National Show Horse Finals," she adds. "I have been very fortunate to have produced a number of wonderful horses in the past that have brought a great deal of pleasure to a number of people as well as myself. I am certain On An On will continue in this tradition. The National Show Horse is an exciting new breed, and I am honored to be part of it.

"Horses are meant to be ridden, driven and loved. Not necessarily in that order, though," she concludes. "There is a certain group of us who have horses, not because we want to buy and sell something, and not because we like to show off in front of other people, but because we have a passion for their beauty."

Love Key

Shannon Ryan, of Boulder, Colorado, actually wasn't looking for a National Show Horse when she came across the mare Love Key, a solid chestnut with a white star, at the 1986 NSH Sale at Lasma in Kentucky.

"I was out to buy a purebred," says Shannon. "But I saw her at the sale and fell in love. It was her personality mostly, and the fact she is beautiful." Love Key is by Key Largo, a Pinto Saddlebred stallion and the first nominated NSH stallion. Her dam was Esser Valley Isis, a purebred Arabian.

When Shannon saw Love Key at the sale, she was very big (16.2) but not quite grown into herself. "All legs, but not sure how to use them. Just broke, but knew how to walk and trot in a straight line, and that was it," Shannon remembers.

"We took Love Key to her first show that spring, not knowing if she was really ready. And she won both her qualifying class and the Championship in Amateur English Pleasure. The championship ride was the most unbelievable ride I have ever experienced. We made it to the in-gate, with many distractions, and I gently urged

her toward the ring, hoping we would get into the ring without any real catastrophe. As soon as she hit the ring, she was all business. I burst into laughter a couple of times during the class. I couldn't help myself. Here was my horse, who is so timid about everything, going around the ring as if she owned the place!"

Love Key's short but successful show career came to an end in 1987 when she was diagnosed as having a lameness which required immediate retirement with no hope for returning her to the show ring. In 1989, Love Key was bred to Hucklebey Berry+, the 1989 and 1991 U.S. National Champion English Pleasure Horse.

"Love Key produced a beautiful colt in the spring of 1990," says Shannon. "Very big and bright and much more courageous than his mother had hoped for. Love Key chased him around the pasture, stopping just for a bite of grass when she had a chance. Unfortunately, his bright little life came to an end four months later, after a week-long battle with colitis.

"He found the will to live that most horses find only as the years go by, and he fought to stay alive until he could fight no more. I spent many days in the stall with Love Key just sitting next to her, talking to her, consoling her as if she might understand that I was sorry. When I left, she hung her head outside the stall door, as if she were waiting for the colt to come home," Shannon says.

"In 1991, I decided to try to ride Love Key again, but this time we started out riding dressage from the very beginning. It seems now as if she missed her calling as a young horse, as she is now sound and happy and doing very well in dressage. Every new thing we do, she becomes excited about. Perhaps she was bored with English pleasure; it wasn't enough of a challenge. She is a joy to ride, and she's smarter than I am — sometimes. She lets me know in her own little way when I am doing something incorrectly — a schoolmistress of sorts.

"What I like and respect most about Love Key is her personality. Everytime she sees me, whether it is the first or tenth time of the day, she runs to the fence, calling to me the entire way. When I leave for work in the morning she follows my car along the fence line to the end of the driveway and watches as I drive away. The other horses now follow her; they seem to think they are missing out on something grand."

Shannon didn't have Love Key with her for a couple of years — the years she was turned out to pasture. When the two were reunited, it was a scene right out of a Disney movie. "I hadn't seen her for two years, but when I called her, she came running through the pasture from two acres away. I've had quite a few horses that I grew up with but I've never been as close to any of them as I am to Love Key."

THE OLDENBURGER

Although the Oldenburger is one of the oldest Warmblood breeds, going back some 400 years, it was in the 1960s that it was "recycled" and redesigned into the modern sport horse of today.

Count Johann XVI von Oldenburg, who ruled from 1573 to 1603, established many breeding farms in the sandy regions at the far north of Germany for the purpose of producing warhorses, using imported Turkish, Neapolitan, Andalusian, and Danish stallions to improve his large, strong Friesian horses. By 1600, the Oldenburg was well established as a heavy, elegant carriage horse.

Johann's successor, the legendary Count Anton Gunter von Oldenburg (1603-1667), found a considerable breeding base with which to work as he set about making the Oldenburger horse famous throughout Europe. A painting portrays the Count, an excellent rider, sitting in grand dignity on his favorite horse, Kranich, a dappled grey. Kranich had his own portrait done in 1650, showing a groom carrying his interminably long tail as reverently as if it were the train of a wedding gown.

Regardless of cost, the Count collected breeding stallions from Naples, Spain, Poland, England, Tartary (Turkey), and Barbary (North Africa), and founded a stud farm, breeding stations, a riding school and royal stables. The Oldenburger brand became established as an elongated "O" surmounted by a royal crown.

The Count completely controlled the horse trade in his realm. A natural public relations man, he presented horse experts in many countries with "beautifully-built and colored riding horses" and the somewhat heavier carriage horse. Soon horses of Oldenburg origin were sought after and admired throughout Europe.

In the seventeenth century, Leopold I, King of the Holy Roman Empire, rode through Vienna on his wedding day astride a black Oldenburg stallion. Other great kings and rulers were soon eager to obtain the tall, attractive, mostly-black carriage horses for the honor of their stables. Even today, three centuries later, the royal stables of Queen Elizabeth of England includes black Oldenburgs to draw her ceremonial carriages.

Some landmarks in the development of the Oldenburger breed were the holding of the first of the stallion testings and founding of the studbook in 1820 and the beginning of hip and neck branding for approved, registered horses in 1861. Soon the breed proved itself in agriculture, the cavalry and the horse-drawn mail service that ran between Oldenburg and Bremen, known as one of the fastest connections in Germany, barely four hours driving time.

During the time of the Counts, the breeding of Oldenburg horses was restricted to the royal studs. However, in the nineteenth century, the Counts passed the responsibility for breeding these horses to private breeders, an important move which allowed the Oldenburger to evolve to its present state.

In their determination to survive, Oldenburger breeders banded together in the 1960s and decided to "recycle" the breed and to change its type from a work horse to a riding horse. Their goal was to develop an animal full of temperament and character suitable for any kind of riding – a sport horse. Unlike many other Warmblood breeds, the modern Oldenburg horse is the result of utilizing the best of all European bloodstock.

Fortunately, decisions on breeding were made by private breeders who could afford the very best. They traveled throughout Europe to select new stallions to remodel their breed. Several stallions were imported from France, among them the Anglo-Arab, Inschallah, and the Anglo-Norman, Furioso II.

The quality and reputation of these stallions caused many mare owners from the surrounding breeding areas to bring their mares to Oldenburg, despite the fact that breeding fees were often twice those of government-owned stallions. Over the years the modern Oldenburger developed into a slightly taller, lighter and more elegant horse than many other German Warmbloods.

Most Americans got their first look at an Oldenburger in 1978 at the World Championships in Lexington, Kentucky, when a beautiful raven-black stallion named Volturno, ridden in the three-day event by German team member Otto Ammermann, galloped away with their hearts. Since then, the breed has greatly influenced sport horse breeding in the United States.

Today the modern Oldenburg sport horse holds its own internationally, but Oldenburg is still the center for the breed. At the annual Elite-Auktion in the little village of Vechta, in the province of Oldenburg, one can find some of the most famous faces in the sport horse world, as buyers review the prospects for their next Olympic or World Champion.

Grand Slam

The Oldenburg Grand Slam, another Iron Spring Farm stallion, has also been very special to Mary Alice Malone's career. "He's one of the few horses in this country who have been given a USDF Performance Merit Award at every level from Training through Intermediare II, the last level before Grand Prix – a great feeling of accomplishment for me," says Mary Alice. "With every new test I do, every new level to which I graduate, I say, 'This is a horse I started as a youngster and trained myself.'" Which is possibly one of the proudest feelings of satisfaction a dressage rider can have.

Grand Slam, foaled in Germany in 1982, was found by Mary Alice when she went there in 1984 to look for Iron Spring's first serious performance prospects. "I kept looking at a snapshot we'd taken of him. A fuzzy little fellow, just two-years-old, but there was something about him. We ended up buying him. I've brought him up and he has developed into a wonderful animal," she says.

The 17-hand bay "has an upbeat, outgoing personality," Mary Alice, says. "When he was three, I watched him go through his stallion test for breeding approval at the Oldenburg Registry Inspection in Germany. After the performance part, the audience applauded, and he turned his tail up over his back, which he always does when he's especially excited or pleased with himself. (Many of his offspring do the same.)"

Grand Slam is a very dependable and reasonable character to deal with, and to handle in general, despite being a stallion. "Sometimes when I'm training him, he gets nervous and pretends not to know what I've asked him to do...so he simply ignores the request. But he's definitely talented and a ham, and loves to perform. His favorite show classes are the musical 'kurs,' dressage movements choreographed to music. I've had some of my most fun rides in performance with him. He loves the music," Mary Alice says.

In 1990 Slam was Reserve Champion in the FEI Musical Freestyle at the Bengt Ljundquist Memorial Championships (BLM), and took several USDF All-Breed awards including third at Prix St. Georges, and first at Intermediare I. He was fifteenth in the country at Prix St. Georges and tenth at Intermediare in the Horse of the Year Awards. He was named second alternate for the 1990 Olympic Festival and was put on the United States Equestrian Team's Developing Horse list for up-and-coming-horses, which entitles him to participate in special clinics at the USET headquarters in Gladstone, New Jersey.

"Grand Slam is competing at Intermediare II now, and he's very good under saddle," says Mary Alice, "as well as becoming a very steady and consistent breeder, siring outstanding premium foals."

For three years, Mary Alice has offered Grand Slam's stud fee at a special rate, less than half his regular fee, to Pony Club or 4-H members with qualified mares. More than forty young riders have taken advantage of this opportunity and have high quality foals.

"I get to share what I got out of Pony Club as a child, while helping today's youngsters get a good horse to bring along," says this generous benefactress of her sport.

Lehndorff

This young stallion is a prime example of what the Oldenburg breed is about – bred to be a rideable, versatile athlete, Lehndorff has been shown successfully in both dressage and show-jumping.

He started off his career with an impressive performance in his native Germany in the rigorous 100-Day Stallion test there, placing in the top ten with 119 points. No less than one of America's top dressage riders, Olympian Robert Dover, picked Lehndorff as a prospect for Mike and Anna Dorazio of American Performance Farms in Rancho Santa Fe, California. There his jumping talents were brought along by another great American rider, Hap Hansen, who showed him over fences.

Early in 1991, about the same time American Performance Horse Farms was changing hands, Terry and Pamela Ratto arrived there to look at some young Oldenburg and Hanoverian colts which were for sale.

"Lehndorff came into our life totally by accident," says Pamela. "Fortunately, it was one of the best accidents that we could ever hope for.

"While waiting around the ranch, we saw Lehndorff for the first time. As a dressage rider and enthusiast, I had been following Lehndorff's career since APHF had imported him. I was impressed with Lehndorff's performance in Medingen, Germany in the 100-Day Stallion Test. His dressage accomplishments were fantastic. In California, Lehndorff was the California Dressage Society First Level Reserve Champion in 1988. In 1989, while maintaining a successful jumping campaign with Hap Hansen, Lehndorff was USDF third place at Second Level Oldenburg Horse of the Year. In 1990 he placed among the CDS Top Five at Third Level. I was familiar with some of his foals such as Louisiana, owned by Kate and Sam Ross of San Juan Capistrano, Lenny, owned by Mike and Anna Dorazio, of Rancho Santa Fe, as well as others."

But the thing that REALLY impressed Pamela about the young stallion was how much her husband Terry liked him.

"Terry owns and shows cutting and reining cow horses," says Pamela. "He was really taken by Lehndorff's impeccable conformation and his incredible athletic ability. Above all, he was so well-mannered, that it's not immediately obvious that he is a stallion."

One Sunday in December 1991, Terry had a long phone conversation with Mike Dorazio of APHF. "After hanging up, he told me we were the new owners of Lehndorff. I was shocked. We never even rode or handled him. Nor did I even dream we would own a horse like him," says Pamela. "Terry bought Lehndorff primarily as a dressage horse for me though we are excited about his present offspring and the ones to come."

Pamela is very lucky as an amateur dressage rider to have a horse like Lehndorff on which to learn and gain mileage in the show ring. When it comes to special competitions and exhibitions, German-born and internationally-recognized trainer and rider Jan Ebeling will be in the saddle.

"We have so enjoyed owning him. He is athletic, exciting, a great dressage horse and a superior sire," says Pamela. "He truly lives up to his pedigree, which is so royal." (He is a grandson of the phenomenal Furioso II.)

"Lehndorff has been a dream come true to us. If we never own another horse, owning Lehndorff has fulfilled all our equine needs. To us, he exemplifies the following: 'Hast thou given the horse strength? Hast thou clothed his neck with thunder? Cans't thou make him afraid as a grasshopper? The glory of his nostrils is terrible. He paweth in the Valley and rejoiceth in strength; he goeth on to meet the armed men. He mocketh at fear, and is not affrighted; neither turneth he from the sword.' (Job 39:19-22.)"

Atlanta

"I will never forget my first sight of Atlanta," my friend Mary Daniels, author of the biography of *Morris the Cat* and feature writer at the *Chicago Tribune* told me. I will let her tell the rest of this story in her own words:

"It was Mother's Day, 1989, just slightly more than a year since my only child had died in a mysterious and unexplained fire. Deeply traumatized, I was trying to escape from all evidence of Mother's Day celebrations, agonizing reminders of my loss.

"So very early that morning, I drove to Wayne, Illinois to the breeding farm of a friend of mine, Edith Kosterka, a legendary horsewoman who has had more champions in her barn than anyone I've ever known. I knew I would be distracted by her fabulous Trakehner horses and Mother's Day could pass by without my having to take note.

"Edith was putting her broodmares out to pasture for the day when I arrived. But first she wanted to show me something special, a three-month old filly named Atlanta, out of one of her best broodmares, Austria, who had been imported from Germany. Austria had been bred to Frohwind, a young Oldenburger stallion who won his 100-Day Stallion Test in California and was making a name for himself.

"My heart, broken as it was, was taken at first glance.

"Atlanta was exquisite, an unusual golden lion-color with a dish face that bespoke of the Arabians in her pedigree. Beautiful as she was, it was her personality that was even more engaging. Bold and unafraid, she came immediately to me and gently tasted my hair, chewed on my scarf and on my jacket sleeve. She untied my shoe laces, and when I tied them up again, untied them once again. When I scolded her, she gamboled about to the other side of her mother, and peeked at me around her chest.

"When the stall door was opened for mare and foal to walk down the aisle and out the big door to the pasture, Atlanta quickly stepped out ahead of her mother and bravely and confidently walked far ahead of her, knowing exactly where she was going. I could see she felt the world was made for her, a quality that reminded me very much of my talented and beautiful daughter.

"I kept my eye on little Atlanta out in pasture. I saw she was a showoff, too. All the other foals gathered about to watch her as she cantered in a small circle, doing a series of flying changes every second stride as perfectly as a Grand Prix horse.

"'That's my flying change horse!' I heard myself exclaim out of the blue. I love doing flying changes above all the other dressage movements, though it takes a talented horse with excellent balance, and I had been looking for one for some time.

"I went home and thought and thought about the little filly, and a few weeks later I told Mrs. Kosterka I would like to buy her. Normally her horses go to riders setting their sights on the Pan American or Olympic Games, or to outstanding breeders and I am just an amateur rider, though I know a good horse when I see one.

"Mrs. Kosterka said she had been thinking too – that a very sad thing had happened to me and that if she sold me the filly, then 'she perhaps would be like your child.' It was an act of thoughtfulness for which I will always be grateful.

"A few months later, in September, my judgment of Atlanta was validated at the Annual Oldenburger Evaluation at St. James Farm. Dr. Roland Ramsauer, Director of the *Oldenburger Verband*, named Atlanta Premium and High Point filly, and her dam, Austria, High Point Mare.

"Atlanta is still a pasture horse, as Warmbloods mature slowly. But these past months, watching her develop mentally and physically, as Mrs. Kosterka carefully raises her for me, I have changed too.

"Atlanta has brought me joy again, the joy that only the young can bring to life. Although I can't ride her yet, her bold spirit has already carried me far, farther than anyone can imagine."

Frohwind

Dr. Roland Ramsauer, the United States representative of the Oldenburger Breeding Association of Germany and the breeding director of the International Sporthorse Registry, has called Frohwind "one of the outstanding young Oldenburger stallions in America."

This horse seemed marked by destiny to be extraordinary from his conception. Frohwind was the first Warmblood foal born in the United States from a breeding using frozen semen imported from Germany, an innovative process introduced by a visionary breeder, Michal McClure of Lake Forest, Illinois.

Foaled March 17, 1984, Frohwind was sired from across the Atlantic by Furioso II, a "once-in-a-hundred years" legend who has sired phenomenal numbers of winning offspring, mostly in jumping.

Frohwind's dam is Windstille, an Oldenburger mare imported by McClure who won a Devon breeding class as a two-year-old. Windstille's sire was Weltmeister, who sired some excellent horses, mainly in dressage, including Walzertakt, Robert Dover's world class mount.

Windstille's dark bay foal, a playful character, always full of himself, was named "Frohwind," the German for "happy wind."

Jorg Stockinger, owner of Meadow Brook Farm in Schaumburg, Illinois, bought Frohwind as a two-year-old, and committed himself to the work and expense of the next step. To become fully licensed as a stallion, Frohwind had to go to the 100-Day Stallion Test at Rancho Murietta, California.

The exacting Eugen Wahler, who conducts the major stallion test for Trakehners in Germany, was head trainer for the 1988 test in California; among world-class guest riders rating the stallions were Bernie Traurig, Rudy Leone, and Oliver Luze (a German Grand Prix rider).

Eighteen stallions were competing. But put to the test, Frohwind scored above average in willingness to work, character and temperament; one of his highest scores was 9.0 for rideability, and he received a 9.3 for his elegant walk. His final score, making him the winner of the 100-day test, was 137 points. (His actual score was 142, less a five-point handicap, because he was slightly older than the other horses.)

After the test, Frohwind returned to Illinois and continued his training with Margret Schrant, Jorg's daughter, and her husband, Helmut, who became his new owners. Helmut evented him at training level, rode him in jumper shows and continued to work him in dressage.

Approved for breeding by the ISR, the *Oldenburger Verband* and the Canadians, he began his career as a stud at three. For the first two years all his foals were premium and now, with the numbers greater, ninety percent are premium. One yearling Frohwind filly in Washington State, owned by Charlene Summers of Summervale Farm, prompted Dr. Ramsauer to remark, "That's the type of horse we're trying to breed in Germany today."

In the fall of 1991, the Schrants went into a partnership called "Equiventures" with Vanessa Carlson of Woodridge Farm in Claremore, Oklahoma. Frohwind went to Oklahoma to stand at stud there and to further his dressage career.

One of his strongest points continues to be rideability. "He's so easy. He's not TOO sensitive, but sensitive enough, so he makes for a great ride," says Margret. "He's intelligent, learns quickly and has presence. He's very proud. You can just tell he knows he's special. He has that little extra something," she adds.

Vanessa fell in love with Frohwind while searching for a stallion for her outstanding Oldenburg mare. "I went to the East Coast, I went to the West Coast, and I just couldn't find one with that something special Frohwind has," she says. "The Schrants didn't want to sell him. Why would anyone ever part with such a creature?" And so the partnership ensued.

"To me, Frohwind is close to the ideal for which we're breeding," says Vanessa. "He has the bone and substance of a Warmblood, but he has that extra athleticism that you don't often see in the Warmblood. You look at him and know that, apart from being beautiful, he's an athlete."

THE PASO FINO

In 1493, on Columbus' second voyage to America, he brought with him a few hardy horses and settled them at Hispaniola, now Santo Domingo. These horses were a mixture of Barb, Andalusian and the Spanish Jennet, the latter a smaller, ambling-type horse considered suitable as a lady's mount during the Middle Ages and known for its extremely comfortable saddle gait.

Later, explorers brought more horses, and these together with the original stock were blended to produce a horse that was uniquely suited to the demands of the new land. These hardy horses could travel vast distances without tiring, and were easy keepers, maintaining their stamina on the available vegetation.

But most importantly, these horses possessed and transmitted to their offspring a natural four-beat gait that provided an extremely comfortable ride, a desirable trait to the explorers who spent endless hours in the saddle. These horses came to be known as "Los Caballos de Paso Fino," the horses with the fine walk.

A major remount station was established on Santo Domingo for the conquest of the New World, from which point horses spread out to the other islands and eventually to the mainlands.

Different regional groups developed on the basis of environment or function eventually consolidated into the breeds we now recognize as Colombian and Puerto Rican/Dominican Paso Finos and Peruvian Pasos. Each took its own course until the beginning of the present century, when in the Caribbean, two-way contact between Puerto Rico and the Dominican Republic maintained a common breed standard and type until approximately 1970. At that time the first contacts between the Caribbean and Colombia were made. The introduction of Colombian blood into the Dominican stock was intense from 1972 until approximately 1978, resulting in considerable modification in the horses's size, speed of execution and style.

The Paso Fino's "fine gait" is what makes this breed unique. It is an evenly spaced four-beat lateral gait, with each foot contacting the ground in a regular sequence at precise intervals, creating a rapid, unbroken rhythm. Executed perfectly, the four hoofbeats are absolutely even in both cadence and impact. Footfall is in this sequence: left rear, left fore, right rear, right fore. The power of the hind leg drive is demonstrated in beautiful contrast to the stunning restraint of the forelegs, which move forward in inches.

The Paso Fino gait is performed at three forward speeds and with varying degrees of collection. In all speeds of the gait, the rider should appear virtually motionless in the saddle, and there should be no perceptible up-and-down motion of the horse's croup. The impact of the horse's motion is absorbed in its back and loin.

First in order of speed is the Classic Fino gait, executed fully collected, the forward speed very slow, and the footfall extremely rapid while the steps and extension are exceedingly short. Those horses that demonstrate superb execution of the Classic Fino Gait compete in classes where the ultimate test of the even footfall comes with the horse traversing a board to the hushed silence of the audience. As each hoof strikes the board, the quickness and even rhythm are communicated to judge and audience in a clear report. A champion generates a rapid staccato rhythm.

In the Paso Corto, the forward speed is moderate and ground-covering but unhurried, executed with medium extension and stride. This is the average trail gait. Collection varies with class requirements.

Paso Largo is the fastest speed of the gait, executed with a longer extension and stride and varying degrees of collection. Forward speed varies with the individual horse, since each horse should attain its top speed in harmony with its own natural stride.

Other qualities are bred into the Paso Fino, such as its striking beauty, with luxurious mane and tail. Hooves are durable and it is seldom shod. Size varies, with the average being slightly over 14 hands. Every equine color can be found with or without white markings. The Paso Fino is people-oriented, enjoying human companionship and striving to please. Willing and spirited, it is gentle and easily handled.

Paso Finos can be ridden and trained English or western. Many owners use stylish tack from one of the countries of the horse's origin. They demonstrate their versatility not only in the show ring, but on competitive trail and endurance rides, in dressage work, at barrel racing and gymkhana events, and back at the ranch working cattle.

With its remarkable disposition and willingness, the Paso Fino can be the first horse for a child, or the last horse for one's autumn years. It is the premier choice for those with back and neck injuries or arthritis. And it may be the horse that can bring the pleasure of horseback riding to the handicapped or disabled.

In 1972, the Paso Fino Horse Association, Inc., with headquarters in Bowling Green, Florida, was established to promote, protect and improve the breed, giving breeders an opportunity to join in an effort to publicize the availability of this once rare breed.

Juan Miguel Del Prado

Individual horse names, I have found, often mean more than something that suits the personality of the bearer.

Such is the case with the Paso Fino stallion Juan Miguel Del Prado, described by his owners, Art and Lee Glatfelter, as "the quintessential result of careful breeding and an uncompromising devotion to horses.

"The special qualities of this colt were so evident at foaling that this horse was christened with a name being saved for one that would embody the hopes of the stables where he was foaled," the Glatfelders told me.

Juan Miguel, foaled May 2, 1989, is named for John Michael Rudisill, the grandfather of Lee Glatfelter who, with her husband Art, owns and operates Fieldstone Meadows Horse Farm in Dallastown, Pennsylvania. In keeping with the tradition established in the American Paso Fino breed, the horse took the Spanish version of Lee's beloved grandfather's name. The addition of the suffix *Del Prado* follows another custom of the breed that in which the origin of the horse is reflected in its official name. *Del Prado* means "of the meadows" and is reserved for horses born at Fieldstone Meadows.

There is another sentimental meaning behind the choice of Lee's grandfather's name. Lee's love affair with horses began when her grandfather, a gentleman farmer, lifted her onto the back of "Mack," a Clydesdale.

The horse which merited the traditional naming honors is a stunning bay stallion with a perfect star on his forehead, a right hind sock and light hairs in his tail. From the first impression, his conformation, balance and intelligent head suggest a champion. His vitality and willingness to please human beings point to his regal past as well as to his bright future.

Juan Miguel is the high point in the Glatfelter's love affair with Paso Fino horses, an affair which began in the early 1970s when Lee developed a back problem and was told she would have to give up riding.

Friends told her about the American Paso Fino breed, and upon investigation, she learned that many people with physical limitations ride Paso Finos comfortably, while they could not sit the gaits of other breeds.

Art and Lee visited a Paso Fino breeder in Puerto Rico and purchased two Paso Finos. Their operation has since grown from those two horses to a stable of approximately seventy horses today.

Within those years, Lee became a widely-recognized authority on the bloodlines of the Paso Fino, and she and her husband started a breeding program focused on the very best Paso Finos available. Their trainer, Robert L. Kilgore, became nationally known for turning out award-winning horses year after year, and by the late 1980s the Glatfelter farm was home to a number of regional and national champions.

But it was only when the Glatfelters produced Juan Miguel by breeding their mare Margarita Del Prado, who traces to the legendary Paso Fino Hilachas, to the stallion Nevado, who traces back to Resorte III, one of the most prestigious Paso Fino names, that they achieved a new high point in Paso Fino history.

The careful efforts and the vision of their breeding program were recognized at the National Paso Fino show at Asheville, North Carolina in September, 1991, when Juan Miguel Del Prado was named 1991 National Champion Two-Year-Old Colt.

"Juan Miguel, from the beginning," says Lee proudly, "was a crowd-pleaser. When this horse is in the show ring, he adopts a clearly superior attitude. It's almost as if he is standing there saying to the crowd, 'Here I am, one of the most handsome horses ever foaled. Come see me!'"

Dulce Melodia D4R

Dulce Melodia, foaled in October, 1991 and six months old at the time of this writing is the youngest horse in this book, symbolizing her breeder's hopes and investment in the future.

"We think she's kind of special. We expect great things out of her," says J.D. "Spud" Maulsby, manager of the Diamond 4R Ranch in Citra, Florida, a breeding and show operation owned by Ronald O. DeCuba. The farm is home to fifty Paso Finos. Dulce Melodia was foaled there, sired by the ranch's senior stallion, Dayan D4R.

The filly, nicknamed "Raven", is dark bay or seal brown, "though for a while she 'threatened' to turn black," says Spud. "Latins are very fond of the dark colors, black and seal brown."

Raven's dam is Finesa Alqueria Rocinante, imported from Colombia in 1988. Finesa was a show mare there, but is used as a broodmare at Diamond 4R Ranch.

"The interesting thing about Finesa is that her lineage traces back to the immortal Colombian stallion, Resorte III," he says. "He was Finesa's great grandsire, and the cornerstone of the better show horses in America. Dayan's grandam is the dam of Resorte III," he adds, which means that Raven is closely linebred, for an exquisite result.

"Our intention with this filly is to show her," adds Spud. "Of course, she was foaled late in 1991, so she needs time to catch up to her year group. We hope to have her in the show ring in late summer or early fall of 1992, and she will definitely be our show filly for next year."

Meanwhile, back at the ranch, Raven is a "barn pest," laughs Spud. "She is one of these really friendly foals--wants to have her nose into everything and anyone who comes in and around the barn. She's very people-oriented. We spent extra time with her when she was very small and it seems to have paid off. She has no reason to be afraid."

"She was the tiniest thing as a foal," says trainer Cathy Keeley. "I had to go to the local Miniature Horse show to find a halter than would fit her."

"Raven is very refined, very delicate; we think she will be quite striking," says Spud. "She has all the attributes of a Paso Fino show horse – the elegance, the looks, and a very honest gait."

Spud explains the gaits: "The Paso Fino has three different gears of the same gait, essentially a walk. The classic Fino, probably the one people recognize most, is a short rapid step with limited practical use, but a way to demonstrate purity of gait; second is the Corto, which is trot speed; and third, the Largo, similar to the rack on the gaited horse, with a speed of fifteen to sixteen miles per hour. In all three gears you strive for the same rhythm of footfall, an absolutely evenly spaced four-beat gait," he says.

"Foals demonstrate the gait running loose with their dams. The ones that are honest-gaited are born with it.

"Latins want the horse to have what they call *brio* – animation and fire – as much horse as they want to ride under saddle, yet gentle as a house pet in hand. They want the horse to be very manageable, but also want it to look as though it is ready to bust out of its skin. The Paso Fino is actually a very kind breed of horse. Just about anyone can get along with it.

"Raven, like other Dayan offspring, has his disposition," says Spud. A Dayan son, Canciller was sold to a retired physician from Michigan as his first mount. We sold another Dayan son to a woman with a back condition bcause she can no longer sit horses that trot.

"Our idea is to breed a horse the owner can use as a pleasure horse or as a show horse," Spud adds. Raven is likely to be a prime example of that usefulness.

Dayan D4R

"Dayan D4R is a true elder statesman of the Paso Fino breed. He carries himself with the nobility of an older stallion who is sure of himself and has nothing left to prove," says J.D. "Spud" Maulsby, manager of Diamond 4R Ranch in Citra, Florida.

A dark bay stallion, Dayan was foaled on April 30, 1973 in Colombia, South America. He is by Delirio III and out of La Ninfa De Besilu. His grandam, Guala, is the dam of the immortal Resorte III.

"I believe Dayan looks like Resorte III as portrayed in the painting by R. A. Morales-Hendry," says Spud.

Dayan went from Colombia to the Dominican Republic, where he became a Champion in Fino and Bella Forma (a competition in which the horse is judged sixty-five percent on conformation and thirty-five percent on gait) and stood at stud.

Ronald O. DeCuba saw Dayan and bought him after evaluating his bloodlines, conformation, performance and get. DeCuba kept the stallion at his farm in Aruba, then shipped him in 1989 to his breeding operation and show barn, Diamond 4R Ranch, in Citra, Florida, where he is senior stallion.

"My fondest memory of Dayan is riding him for the first time," says Cathy Keeley. She is the trainer for the ranch in Florida established in 1988; its sister ranch in Aruba is about twenty years old.

"When I was hired in February, 1991, the ranch did not have a riding ring," she adds. "It was an exercise in trust to bridle this immensely powerful stallion with the mildest bit I had and then ride him through the fields. Like the fine gentleman he is, he never put a foot down wrong.

"Paso Finos seem to be small horses, yet they absolutely swell with pride when mounted and have no difficulty performing when carrying a quarter of their own weight. Under saddle, Dayan is no exception. It's like sitting on a locomotive that handles with the precision and elegance of a dancer," she says.

"This is a horse that is extremely strong, extremely bold. But anybody can catch him, lead him and handle him," Spud testifies to his character.

"I admire Dayan's ability to adapt to whatever is thrown his way without showing any outward sign of disturbance. He holds no grudges," says Cathy. "I have had the privilege of training and showing his get, and we have had no difficulty getting them to perform whatever is required of them.

"We are raising horses with a social attitude toward people that retains the Paso Fino breed's natural qualities of self-carriage, smoothness of gait and inherent toughness. These horses are definitely not 'hothouse flowers'," says Cathy. "We are also starting a program of breeding gaited mules," she adds, whereupon we come to one of Dayan's little quirks.

"We try not to take it personally, but Dayan's favorite 'person' is Walter the mule, with whom he lives in a two-acre paddock," Spud relates. "Walter gives him someone to swat flies with and somebody to tell lies to in the summer."

Dayan is retired now and his get have claimed his place in the limelight. His son Grano De Oro has won several championships in pleasure with three different riders and is currently showing in performance and versatility. Carnaval is winning in both pleasure and performance. Canciller won half of his show classes as a three-year-old and was shown to a Reserve National Championship in Three-Year-Old Geldings, Bella Forma and Fourth Grand National Gelding.

"The sons and daughters of Dayan have the extraordinarily kind disposition and brilliant gait we strive for in our breeding program. The end result allows us to build a comfortable relationship with our clients and to be successful in the show ring ," says Cathy. "Dayan has given all of us at Diamond 4R Ranch a positive future. For me, the fairy tale came true and it's called Dayan."

Petrolero Del Juncal

"This horse reminds me of my childhood days in Cuba, where I first had the pleasure of riding a Paso Fino," says Dr. Ciro S. De Las Casas of his grey Paso Fino stallion, Petrolero del Juncal.

"I first became interested in horses as a child," he continues. "I was brought up on a ranch in Cuba where horses were a part of our everyday life. They were used for transportation, running fence lines, checking cattle on the range, driving the milking cows into the barns, and for competition. And usually the fellow with the nicest horses was given more attention·by the best-looking girls."

Today Dr. De Las Casas is a breeder of quality show horses based at two ranches, one in Agua Dulce, California, founded in 1971, and the other in the beautiful Willamette Valley near Eugene, Oregon, founded in 1968. The original goal for these ranches was to raise cattle and horses. Today the main focus is on Paso Fino horses.

The show horses are kept in California for training and showing purposes, while the broodmares and foals are kept in Oregon, where they are able to run free on 329 acres of green pastures.

However, it wasn't until he bought Petrolero Del Juncal in 1990, that Dr. De Las Casas felt a dream within a dream was being fulfilled, that of owning a champion stallion.

"The dream of owning the best Paso Fino stallion in the country is becoming a reality," he says. "I never expected to acquire a stallion of this type in such a short time. Some breeders wait ten to fifteen years before they can produce or obtain an animal of this quality. Because of his bloodline, his show record and his appearance, Petrolero is now in great demand for breeding."

Petrolero, who has a large star on his forehead, a three-quarters stocking on his right hind foot, a white coronet band on his left hind foot, and a small brand on his left hip, has a long, flowing mane and tail which add to his regal appearance. "Petrolero under saddle is very fiery, proud and exciting to watch," says his owner. "Because Petrolero is consistent in his performance as a smooth, balanced, classic fino-gaited stallion, he can always be depended on to win. He makes the adrenaline flow."

Among the numerous championship titles won by this beautiful stallion to date are these: 1990 Reserve Grand National Champion Schooling Fino Colt, 1990 Grand Champion in Arizona, 1991 West Coast Champion, 1991 Grand Champion in Ocala, Florida.

Petrolero, foaled May 10, 1987, was sired by Postin, and is out of Contrasena Del Juncal. He is a grandson of Bochica on his sire's side, and of Contrapunto on his dam's side. Dr. De Las Casas has owned him since he was a three-year-old schooling colt.

Petrolero is extremely spirited, says Dr. De Las Casas, but at the same time is a very responsive, gentle animal. He has had an even, gentle temperament all of his life, and can be handled by anyone. He loves his carrots and gets them as a special treat. He has a friendly disposition, and whenever Dr. De Las Casas walks through the barn Petrolero calls out a greeting to him.

"A horse is a companion, partner, pet, something of great value and something that keeps life from becoming dull. I hope I never find myself without a horse," Dr. De Las Casas asserts.

Ensueño De Colombia

"The best way for me to describe this outstanding stallion, Ensueño De Colombia, is to look back on my history with the Paso Fino horse in the United States," says Alvaro Iriarte of Startown Stables in Newton, North Carolina.

"In 1973 I came upon my first American Paso Fino horse show in Tanglewood, North Carolina," Alvaro continues. "Being a native of Colombia, South America, and a fourth-generation Paso Fino breeder and trainer, I was well-knowledged in the Paso Fino horse. After two years of training Quarter Horses for a living, I was so excited to even see a Paso Fino, I could hardly believe it.

"In 1971, when I first came to the United States, I did not know why or how I had come to find myself in a new and totally different country. I only knew America was a land of opportunity, a place where dreams could come true. Now, for the first time, I could clearly see why and how I would make my American dream come true. I saw the opportunity to develop and promote the unique Paso Fino breed that was so unknown and yet so full of possibilities for the American people. From that moment on, I began to form an image of the American Paso Fino, an image that would most appeal to the American people. I set two goals for myself: one, to promote that image of the American Paso Fino and, two, to produce and market the champions that would fulfill that image.

"Through the years," continues Alvaro, "we have been fortunate and privileged to introduce the Paso Fino horse to many new enthusiastic horse lovers. We have been successful in producing and marketing several national champions, and today Startown Stables offers a variety of services, including breeding consultation, training, clinics and seminars for amateurs and professionals alike.

"Much of our success can be attributed to Ensueño," he says, referring to Startown's dark bay Paso Fino stallion with a beautiful white star, a marking that he passes on to his offspring with great regularity.

In 1982, Alvaro was looking for a foundation stallion that would continue improving and developing his breeding program...Ensueño turned out to be an excellent choice. Among his many honors, he was awarded 1984 High Point Conformation Stallion, 1984 and 1985 Reserve Grand National Champion of Champions Conformation Stallion, 1985 Reserve National Champion Get of Sires, 1985 Title of Proficiency, 1985 Piedmont Overall Champion, and 1986 Junior Grand National Champion Classic Fino Youth.

"Ensueño and I have shared many exciting moments together," says Alvaro, "but by far the most memorable to me was in 1984 when he won the National Champion Classic Fino Stallions Award. The class had over twenty-five of the nation's top quality Classic Fino stallions in it. As Ensueño crossed the Fino board I could hear the crowd go wild with excitement as his solid, symmetrical four-beat gait created a rhythmic beat – TACA-TACA-TACA-TACA!" Later, as the judges called for the grueling Figure Eight, Ensueño performed perfectly, curving his body around each turn and making his turns tighter and tighter without missing a beat!

"It was with great pride and exhilaration that we accepted that 1984 Grand National Classic Fino Stallions Award and took our victory lap around the ring, as the roaring crowd gave a standing ovation, a rare and cherishable honor," says Alvaro. "In that moment I knew that I was riding my image of the American Paso Fino Horse!"

Since that time, Ensueño has gone on to the National Top Ten Sires List in 1988, 1990, and 1991, each year moving a little closer to the Number 1 spot.

Ensueño, whose name means "dream" in Spanish, has signified a lot to Alvaro, his family and Startown Stables. "He has brought me closer to fulfilling my goals and he definitely has made MY American dream come true!"

Bravado Wind Song

One of the great pleasures for me in writing this book was learning that extraordinary friendships between children and their horses exist not only in fiction, but in real life.

Tiffany Garamella and Bravado Wind Song, a spectacular dapple grey Paso Fino stallion with a thick silvery mane three feet long and a forelock that touches his nose, live one of those friendships.

"Bravado has been very effective in the reputation and image of our Wind Song Farms, the upper Midwest's oldest and largest breeder of the Paso Fino horse," says Tiffany's mother, Jacqueline Garamella, "But on a personal level, he is the dream horse of my daughter's childhood."

Tiffany was nine years old when Bravado was foaled in the summer of 1979, at Wind Song Farms. "My parents and I tromped out through the mosquito swarms and tall grass to find him," she recalls. "He was a day old; a small, black colt sleeping beside his dam in the warm Minnesota sunshine. I crawled eagerly toward him, and he watched with increasing curiosity as we came face to face. As we touched noses, we knew a friendship had begun."

Tiffany spent every day that summer following Bravado, the other foals and the rest of the herd around the Farms' one hundred acres of pastureland. Although the other foals grew shy with age, Bravado and Tiffany remained close. "We ran and napped together. He was always 'The Brave One,' hence his name. During the evening, we sat apart from the herd on the hillside and watched the sky above turn deep shades of fuchsia in the wake of the setting sun. As we listened to the music of the marshes below, we shared a language far beyond words. He would nibble my hair and nuzzle my nose until Mom rang the dinner bell and I had to go in. Bravado and I have always been equals. We are playmates and friends who fight and love as brother and sister," Tiffany told me.

Their relationship changed when Bravado began his basic training under the expert handling of a rugged northern Minnesota cowboy, Joe Thompson. When he was three, Bravado began competing regionally in the Classic Fino Schooling Colt and Gelding classes. That same year, he was taken to the National Paso Fino Horse show in Atlanta, Georgia. While his grandsire and grandams — Sin Verguenza, Mar De Plata LaCE and Bolero LaCE — were among the first Paso Finos to be brought into the United States, Bravado was virtually an unknown at the time. During his appearance at the Nationals he came on with "the rushing, powerful effect of a Midwestern summer storm," says Tiffany. "His quick natural fino shocked competitors and captivated anyone who watched him."

In his National class, Bravado was breathtaking, his performance flawless, and everyone cheered and screamed as he made his victory pass through flying hats and finoed down the fino strip.

That was only the beginning for Bravado. "Once an entire class was dismissed except for Bravado," says Jacqueline. "The judge asked the spectators to leave the stands and stand at the side of the asphalt road so they could listen, to appreciate and understand the cadence of the true fino gait as performed so naturally, and to perfection, by Bravado Wind Song."

Although Tiffany has had great experiences of her own showing Bravado, the strength and beauty of their relationship is rooted on their farm. "My fondest memories with Bravado are of our crazy adventures together, our levels of communication, and his interpretations and subsequent reactions to the people around him," she says.

The idyll continues. "I look forward to spending this summer with him," says Tiffany. "Once more we will race up our favorite hill. I will drop my reins and reach toward the sky, and I will listen again to the thundering echo of his hooves."

Quintessa Wind Song

On one of those soft, sunny Indian summer afternoons that Minnesota can have in October, Beverly Tesch first saw the Paso Fino mare, Quintessa Wind Song.

Beverly was looking for a top quality broodmare that would also be her personal mount, one that had excellent gait, outstanding conformation and a willing personality.

As she watched the trainer take Quintessa around the outdoor ring, Beverly knew the search was over. Quintessa fulfilled all of the requirements. She had a very smooth four-beat gait and was very responsive to leg aids and voice commands. She was very well trained in hand, under saddle and in manners. And she had the chiseled classic beauty that is a distillation of the Andalusian, Barb and Spanish Jennet.

Her breeding was also impressive. Foaled April 23, 1984, she was by Bola Negra Wind Song and out of the mare Primera Wind Song, making Quintessa a full sister to the multi-champion Bravado Wind Song.

Campaigned only one year, Quintessa had proven herself as the Regional Bella Forma Champion and Performance Champion.

Quintessa was scheduled to be sold and shipped to Germany within ten days of the time Beverly first saw her. "I didn't need ten days; I needed only one to make the decision to buy her," says Beverly. "From that day on, other than my family, she was the most important part of my life." Beverly owns a small breeding operation, Greenwood Farm, in Olivia, Minnesota, founded in 1976 and named after the 1876 farm of her immigrant grandparents.

Quintessa was truly a lady's horse, her hair as fine as silk and raven black except for her four white stockings. She was as refined and as feminine as her brother, Bravado Wind Song, is strong and powerful.

"Quintessa taught me so much about being alive. When I was grooming her I felt grounded to the earth, and connected to the stars," Beverly says. "I felt a stream of light of connectedness between us. I felt a sisterhood with her in giving birth and in loving and nurturing that new life."

A grandmother herself, Beverly says the most special moments she remembers with Quintessa were the births of her two foals at Greenwood Farm.

"In 1990 she gave me a refined, sparkling black colt, Poetica De Greenwood, sired by Poema De Colombia of Wind Song Farm, a National Champion and son of National Champion Ensueño De Colombia of Startown Stables in Newton, North Carolina.

"Part of the excitement of Poetica's birth was in Quintessa's allowing me to lift him out of the birth sac. He bonded first with his dam and then with me. He spent his early months racing circles around his dam, being mischievous and teasing. He now lives as a stallion at Ren's Ranch in Elizabeth, Colorado. We can picture him being 'king of all he surveys' there. Hopefully he keeps a small memory of his early life at Greenwood Farm," says Beverly.

In July, 1991, Quintessa gave birth to another foal, this time a longed-for filly by Poema De Colombia. She also was raven black, very refined, with a small star like her dam's and alternate, very short white socks. "Poema also enjoyed racing circles around her dam, imitating her, and showing more signs of independence than did her brother. At the time I didn't know how important this bit of independence would be," says Beverly.

For on November 4, the day planned for weaning Quintessa dos, Beverly went out to do the morning feeding and found Quintessa dead in her box stall. Her untimely death at eight years of age was a shock and severe loss to everyone. Beverly is consoled by knowing Quintessa passed on to her filly all of her intuitive qualities, and that she (Beverly) has the responsibility to build on them.

"Quintessa gave me everything she had to give, now Quintessa dos de Greenwood and I must continue her heritage," she says.

Dorotea De Prodeco

Dorotea De Prodeco is widely known as one of the finest performance Paso Finos ever shown. Foaled October 9, 1979, the 14.2 chestnut mare with a small star and three small socks, is the daughter of the now deceased Resortes IV, sire of many champions. Her dam is Diosa de Prodeco, who is also the dam of champion Pandora de Prodeco.

Dorotea was purchased in 1986 by Sweet Water Paso Finos, a ranch which breeds, trains and sells Paso Fino Horses in Agua Dulce, California. Sweet Water has four owners: Dan and Stephanie Livingston, both of whom are involved in other professions as well, and Charlie and Milda Minter, professional horse trainers and breeding and health care managers.

Dorotea was previously owned by Herbert Sutton, and she won Performance Schooling Fillies at the Nationals in 1982. She was also the winner of Reserve Grand National Performance Champion in this same year. From 1982 to 1986 Dorotea was used as a broodmare and was not in competition. Still in all, when it was announced that she was for sale, her reputation preceded her and there was a rush to buy her.

When the dust settled, she belonged to Sweet Water. "She turned our lives around for many reasons," says Stephanie. "We were a young ranch trying to get established. Within a year of the existence of Sweet Water Paso Finos, Dorotea brought prestige and credibility to our ranch."

The Sweet Water partners started to show Dorotea and she began to win championship after championship. "In 1987 we took her to Asheville, North Carolina where not only did she win National Champion Performance Mares, but went on to win Grand National Performance Horse, a much revered title," continues Stephanie. "Her ears are always up and she has the appearance of a happy horse. In the show ring, she always has a look that says, 'Look at me' and spectators knew she loved the competition."

Since Dorotea is such a wonderful mare, one can imagine the consternation when on July 3, 1988, she caught her head under a railing in her stall and was severely traumatized. When she was found at 5:30 a.m., her temperature had soared to 105 degrees and she began to have seizures and appeared near death. Charlie Minter sat with her head in his lap for nearly thirty hours, refusing to let her go. Neighbors and close friends joined forces in a round-the-clock vigil to help keep her alive. As she began to recover, one neighbor devised a sling to help get her up on her feet.

"With the help of about twelve friends and the sling, we were able to get her up," says Stephanie. "But she was unable to stand on her own so we supported her weight and massaged her muscles until she could. By mid-afternoon on the Fourth of July she was able to walk down the barn aisle."

Dorotea has had recurring health problems since then, although the incidents appear to be unrelated. In 1992, she had colic surgery at Alamo Pintado Equine Clinic at Los Olivos, but recovered well.

"The vets are truly amazed at her strong will to fight as well as the trust that she has developed toward her human friends that have encouraged her," says Stephanie.

"She is still as alert and determined as ever. She has taught me about perseverance and that life is worth fighting for," adds Stephanie.

"Through the experience of horse ownership, I have a new way of experiencing the universe and the essence of God. There is no assurance of how many tomorrows Dorotea de Prodeco may have, but we feel very honored to have an animal of her stature in our presence. I question if there will be another one quite like her in our lifetime."

Pandora De Prodeco

So extremely special is the grey Paso Fino mare Pandora De Prodeco in her ability to produce future champions that it is not at all unusual for some of her foals to be sold in utero. "Some people are even interested in leasing her belly from us," says Susan Neri. She and her husband Joseph are small breeders in Agua Dulce, California. Their ranch, founded in 1990 when they married, is named Rancho Nuevo Comienzo, signifying a "new beginning" for both.

Of course, their main mare is Pandora De Prodeco, sired by the legendary Bochica, one of the best Classic Fino stallions in the Paso Fino breed.

"As a breeder, Pandora has been extremely special to us," says Susan. "In 1990 Pandora made No. 10 on the Top Ten Dam List of the United States in our breed. Most breeders and trainers know her and what she is capable of producing."

Her first son, Dios Del Mar Bravo, a beautiful stallion owned by Sweet Water Paso Finos in Agua Dulce, has won many championships, including 1989 West Coast Classic Fino Grand Champion and many wins in Bella Forma. Pandora's daughter, Semilla De Corazon Bravo, owned by Royal Oak Ranch in St. Louis, Missouri, was the 1990 National Champion Classic Fino Mare as well as Reserve Grand National Classic Fino Champion, and the High Point Horse of the show. In 1991 Semilla was Reserve National Classic Fino Mare, Grand National Bella Forma Champion Mare, and also won the High Point Horse of the Show Award. Another daughter, Caliope Bravo, owned by Charles and Bonnie Minter, Sr. of Agua Dulce, is a newcomer to the show ring who has placed high in her Classic Fino filly classes.

Pandora has had an extensive show career herself. In 1982 at the National Show, she won first place in her Classic Fino Schooling Filly class, then went into the Classic Fino Grand Championship Class and took Reserve Grand National Champion as a filly competing against mares, stallions, geldings and schooling colts.

However, the moment the Neris remember best of her show career was in July, 1991 at the West Coast Championship Show in Monterey, California. Ridden by Johnny Lanier, one of the top Paso Fino trainers on the West Coast, Pandora took first place in the Classic Fino Mare class and went on to win the West Coast Champion Classic Fino Mare Award. It was an especially sweet win because Pandora hadn't been shown all year and had to compete against another mare that had just won at the National Show. "We were planning to retire her from the ring and wanted to give her one last chance in a show. We couldn't have asked for anything more," says Susan, of the win.

"Pandora is now retired from the ring to have foals, give us pleasure in riding her and enjoy the rest of her life," says Susan.

"To us, Pandora is like a daughter," adds Susan. "She has a gorgeous face with nicely tipped ears and a very gentle look about her eyes. My relationship with Pandora is special in that she seems to really listen when I talk to her. I call her 'My Lady.'"

Susan has always dreamed of one day owning a famous racehorse like Secretariat, a dream which took a change of direction when she saw the Paso Fino breed. "Although Pandora isn't a racehorse and may not be famous to the world, she IS famous in our breed, and has fulfilled my dream of owning a famous horse," she says.

Leyenda

"From the stallions to the mares, you won't find a more solid foundation anywhere in the United States," says Millie Martinez. She believes the foundation mare Leyenda is the reason her husband, Dr. Alfonso Martinez, owner of Los Arrieros de Casta Paso Fino Farm in Ocala, Florida, is such a successful Paso Fino breeder.

Leyenda means "legend" – appropriate since she seems to be one in the making. She was imported from the Dominican Republic for a very good sum. Foaled in September, 1979, her show career as a youngster was spectacular. She won every class in which she was entered and was AHSA Horse of the Year in 1983.

Dr. and Mrs. Martinez bought her in 1985, after seeing her perform at a show at the Los Angeles Equestrian Center, in which she won the Fino class. Unfortunately, she was foundered after that show, which is the reason she was for sale and Dr. and Mrs. Martinez were able to obtain her. "Leyenda was shown again after her founder, but she was never the same," says Millie, and so she was retired from the ring.

"In any case, we knew she'd be a good producer," adds Millie. Leyenda's pedigree backed up that knowledge. "Her sire is Ladrillo, and Leyenda is considered his best daughter," says Millie. "Her dam, Sotileza, is one of the top mares in Puerto Rico."

At the time they bought Leyenda, Dr. and Mrs. Martinez already had two horses: a 1969 stallion, Lucimiento Del Pino, who had once belonged to the President of the Dominican Republic; and the mare Rica. Both were purchased as pleasure horses. "We started out as a hobby and it grew into more than that," says Millie.

"In a relatively short time, Los Arrieros has become the largest breeder of Paso Finos in the United States with a herd of close to ninety. It must be about ninety. I just got a $4,000 feed bill," she jokes.

"Today, even though Leyenda is busy being a broodmare, she still looks as though she could walk right out of the fields and go to a show," says Millie. "When you see that, it's *raza*, good race, good blood. Most horses who are out in the fields look rough."

She adds that Leyenda has a wonderful temperament, has lots of *brio*, is very *fino* with beautiful conformation. Mrs. Martinez enjoys riding her, and says that under saddle, Leyenda is very powerful and very smooth, and looks very elegant in the show ring.

As a broodmare, Leyenda has produced Los Arriero's stallion, El Pica Flor de Casta (also profiled in this book), sired by Capuchino, and the filly Jacaranda, also by Capuchino, one year younger than El Pica Flor and now beginning to enter the show ring. She has also produced Leyenda II, foaled in 1989, by Castellano, a brother of Capuchino, and two young colts.

"Everything she has given us seems unbeatable," says Millie. "I call her the goose that lays the golden eggs.

"Other breeders say it's the stallion that makes the offspring," says Millie. "I feel it has to be the mare. No matter the sire of Leyenda's foals, the result is incredible. That goes to prove the point right there: on every good farm there's an incredible mare."

El Pica Flor De Casta

Just ask Dr. Alfonso Martinez what the driving force is in his successful breeding operation, Los Arrieros de Casta Paso Fino Farm in Ocala, Florida, and he will be glad to tell you: the love of the breed.

Dr. Martinez, a California dentist who commutes to his Florida farm, grew up with Paso Finos in Colombia, South America.

From his youth, and through the years he spent struggling to establish himself as a professional in this country, the desire to take the old bloodlines of the Paso Fino and develop them to recognition as "the most refined gaited animals in the world" became his passionate quest.

"He wanted to introduce to America these wonderful, graceful animals, the smoothest riding horse in the world, and bring only the best blood to his farm here in Ocala," says Dr. Martinez' charming wife, Millie. "His desires have been accomplished, without a doubt."

At the time of this writing, Millie reported that the Martinez farm had just sold five horses to breeders from the Dominican Republic, who through word of mouth had heard of Los Arrieros. "They came and had breakfast with my husband, and then went out in the fields to look at the horses," she says, "They were astounded to find this quality in Paso Finos in the United States, and by the time they left, they had bought five horses."

As recounted in the profile on the mare Leyenda, Dr. and Mrs. Martinez were careful to choose good foundation stock for their farm. On May 21, 1987, Leyenda produced their future stallion, El Pica Flor de Casta, one of the first Paso Finos foaled at Los Arrieros.

Now five years old, El Pica Flor is taller and larger than most Paso Finos and a red chestnut with "bleached blonde" mane and tail. "He is extremely striking in the show ring," says Millie. "You can have twenty horses in the ring and you will see only him.

"He's an extraordinary horse, one of the top horses in this country. I've been told he's the best offspring of Capuchino," adds Millie. "He proved himself in 1990 as High Point Fino Colt. He's siring outstanding foals and has approximately twenty offspring on the ground at Los Arrieros.

"They show the qualities that Dr. Martinez has worked for and researched for years to achieve," says his wife. "My husband's mind is like a computer with the bloodlines."

When he is in Florida, Dr. Martinez is a hands-on horse owner. Millie reports that he is at the barn usually by six a.m. and seldom leaves before six p.m. "He is out in the fields, checking on the young ones, worming, giving shots, watching the training, overseeing the staff, never leaving the care of the horses to chance. I think you have to have a love for horses, because you're not going to put in twelve hours a day if you don't," his wife adds.

When her husband is in California, Millie runs the farm, while caring for the three Martinez children, ages eight, eleven and twelve. "It is no easy task as this is a busy working farm with two trainers and three grooms," she notes.

Millie compares learning how to run the breeding farm with learning to run her husband's dental office in California. "I knew nothing about dentistry, either," she says. "I've done well with the horses. I like the breeding part of it best, figuring out which mare will be good with each stallion."

Her husband's goal is "breeding for the ultimate Fino horse, and the farm has come a long way toward accomplishing that in a short time," she says. "I don't think anybody in the country has done what we've done, starting from scratch. Other farms may have imported horses, paying a lot of money for them, but they didn't breed them or make them and that's the trick."

Manuela Del Conde

disposition and at the same time a super producer." Zaemis is a daughter of the stallion Aramis, a very renowned Colombian stallion imported to Puerto Rico in the 1960s.

"Manuela is a solid dark bay mare, very *fino*, very elegant. She is now in foal to Cancionero, a Colombian stallion.

"She's really special to all of us. She takes Mrs. Macdonald out on trail rides, and though both Macdonalds like Manuela, she is Mrs. Macdonald's favorite," Jaime continues.

Mr. Macdonald describes Manuela: "Gentle as a lamb but a fierce competitor. She is in fact the barn mascot and comes when called. Her favorite treats are apples and carrots which she loves to have hand-fed to her as she takes one small bite at a time."

As for her show attitude, "She's ready to go out and do it," Jaime Suarez says. Shown by him, Manuela was National Champion in the United States as a two-year-old. She also won her class and the championship at the International Show in Puerto Rico and is considered one of the top Fino fillies in the world, says her owner, John Macdonald.

The Macdonalds, who began their operation as a hobby, first bought pleasure horses, and then progressed to better and better horses and eventually turned their hobby into a business. They bought Manuela in 1990.

"JLM Stables purchased Manuela after she won the National Championship as a filly," says Macdonald. "It is probably safe to say that because we purchased her Jaime Suarez decided to join us as a trainer."

Suarez is now farm manager of the newly-built JLM Stables in Ocala, Florida.

"The new Macdonald farm is a beautiful facility, even by Florida standards, which are already lavish. It is pure class all the way," says Dennis Kesseler, who handles JLM public relations. The 130-acre farm consists of two barns, a riding arena and a circular training pen for the training and maintenance of twenty show horses and broodmares.

Before the new farm was built, Suarez ran the Macdonald's Paso Fino operation out of the farm, Four J's Paso Finos, that he co-owns with his three brothers, José, Jorge and Javier. Each of the brothers trains for his own clients. Between them they have sixty horses at their Ocala farm, and they own another farm in Puerto Rico.

"The relationship between Jaime Suarez and JLM Stables is a special one, and the combination makes us one of the best stables in our breed," says John Macdonald. "Manuela is one of the cornerstones of our farm and one of the reasons we became more heavily involved in breeding and showing."

Manuela Del Conde, a dark bay mare with a star, was bred, raised, and trained by top Paso Fino trainer, Jaime Suarez, and is extremely special to him.

"From the first day I put a halter on her she showed she was a good horse and had a very good gait," he says. "Manuela," he explains, "comes by her talents naturally, having the same bloodlines on the paternal side as JM, the JLM Stables stallion."

Foaled August 1, 1987, Manuela was sired by the stallion Capuchino, the son of Resorte IV; her maternal bloodlines are different from JM's, however. She is out of Zaemis, who is owned by Suarez. The trainer describes Zaemis as "a big, grey, very refined horse, with a super

His bloodlines, his show record, his temperament, everything together – that's what makes JM neat," says trainer Jaime Suarez of the five-year-old Paso Fino stallion who belongs to Mr. and Mrs. John L. Macdonald of Stamford, Connecticut and Ocala, Florida.

The pedigree of this powerful, macho-looking light bay stallion seems to have predestined him for greatness.

"His sire, Capuchino, in three years' time changed the show world when he was shown here, because he was very different, very collected," says Suarez, considered one of the top trainers of Paso Fino horses. "He won everything in Colombia, in Puerto Rico, and in the United States.

"Now his foals are out," Suarez continues. "Out of twenty, seventeen are extraordinary. Capuchino is a son of Resorte IV, a stallion who is the best sire in the history of the Paso Fino. JM's dam, Miss Cayey, is a daughter of Plebeyo, a son of Kofresi, the best of the Puerto Rico Paso Finos, and undefeated for eight years. The best horses in the breed are either sons or grandsons of Kofresi," adds Suarez, a native Puerto Rican who has been living and working in the United States for nine years.

JM was bred in Puerto Rico, Suarez says, by breeder José Miguel Miranda, and was purchased and imported to the United States in March, 1991 by his current owner, John L. Macdonald.

John Macdonald and his wife, Derry, saw JM's performance at the Caribbean International Open. "His performance excelled all others and brought the crowd to their feet cheering. JM won his class and our hearts that day," says Macdonald.

Since then, JM has won his class as National Champion Fino Colt at the United States National Show as well as the International Caribbean Show in Puerto Rico. He will be shown this year as a stallion by Jaime Suarez, who in 1991 garnered the most national horse show championships on the Paso Fino circuit.

JM has already begun his breeding career. "JM bred fourteen mares in 1991. Some foals are on the ground already, and they look very good," says Jaime.

"JM is ranked among the top three Paso Fino stallions in the United States," says his owner, John Macdonald. "The horse is alert, has lots of *brio* and high action. He is the cornerstone of our breeding stock, and his success in the show ring has given stature to JLM stables, making us one of the top competing show stables in our sport.

"Regarding the horse's personality, he easily adapts to any situation," says Macdonald. "As a stallion, he can be ridden by a child on a trail ride and, upon his return, give an outstanding performance in a national show."

Macdonald and his wife were first introduced to the Paso Fino breed during a vacation in Florida. Macdonald owns JLM Industries in Stamford, Connecticut, the largest producer of liquid petro-chemicals in the world.

"I originally became interested in Paso Finos after a serious spinal injury," says Macdonald. "In order to continue riding horses, a sport which I have always enjoyed, I now needed a smooth ride, and I turned to gaited horses. Paso Finos gave me the look and the feel I wanted. I enjoy trail riding and above all showing these horses, whose versatility is always a source of amazement to me."

Ladrillo

Ladrillo is one of the happiest stories in this book as he, by one of the merest quirks of fate, narrowly escaped a dreadful death.

The 14-hand chestnut was foaled in Colombia in 1973 and imported as a two-year-old to the Dominican Republic by Manuel Diez, owner of Rancho La Joya in Jaruboca.

During his show career in South America, Ladrillo won numerous Championships and Champion of Champions out of competition, meaning he had won so much he no longer was allowed to compete. One of his major wins was Reserve Champion Stallion in the World Cup of 1986 held in Sidra, Puerto Rico, with the best Paso Finos from seven countries competing. Sired by Guazipungo, out of Mireya, his bloodlines are considered the foundation lines of the Paso Fino in the Dominican Republic.

Ladrillo had sired numerous champions, including Joya La Joya, two-time winner of the World Cup in 1985 and 1986 in Puerto Rico; Dinastia La Joya, who won U.S. National Champion Fino Mare in 1989; Armonia de Graubo, U.S. Reserve Performance Champion in 1989, and many times Fino Champion in the Dominican Republic; and Rebeldia de Besilu, 1983 U.S. Champion Schooling Fino Filly.

To say the least, he was a very valuable horse to the breed and to his owner. In the spring of 1988, Diez decided to send Ladrillo to the U.S. to stand at stud at J Sol Reye, Nancy Moffitt's farm at Frankfort, Illinois.

"I had bought a couple of daughters by the horse, Mr. Diez' son was attending school in Illinois, and the horse was a little bit sick," Nancy lists all the reasons Ladrillo came to the Chicagoland area. "The vets in the Dominican Republic couldn't see anything wrong with him," she says.

Within two weeks after he arrived, Ladrillo became very dehydrated and was taken to the Illinois Equine Hospital and Clinic in Naperville. Dr. Margaret Mac Harg, a brilliant young red-headed veterinary surgeon who specializes in equine colic surgery, took the case.

"The horse presented with a bowel obstruction. Basically what was wrong was a section of small intestine, about eight feet of it, had strictured shut," says Dr. Mac Harg. "He was severely distended upstream from there. He certainly would have been dead the next day."

Dr. Mac Harg remembers Ladrillo as "a neat horse," attended by a groom who had been with him since he was born. "The poor man didn't speak any English and here's this horse he's never been separated from, dying. He was there when we were anaesthetizing the horse, and he was there when the horse woke up." A good thing, as Ladrillo didn't think too well of the situation and sick as he was, was hard to catch in his hospital stall. But as soon as his groom appeared, he went right over to see him.

From the tests and x-rays, Nancy was sure "the horse had cancer because the intestine was so closed off and appeared to be full of tumors.

"When Dr. Mac Harg was doing the surgery we kept hearing 'beep, beep, beep,' and when it stopped, I thought 'Either Ladrillo was dead or the doctors were finished,'" Nancy adds. "Ladrillo's great heart pulled him through this major operation. He recovered very well."

Tissue slides from the eight feet of intestine that were removed were sent to laboratories all over the country in an attempt to determine the cause of the stricture.

"It looked like a rare type of coccidia," says Dr. Mac Harg. "Our best conclusion is that this type of coccidia was pathogenic. The horse had been wormed when he came to the United States and got a big die-off of the coccidia, which caused inflammation and the stricture. Everything was resolved."

Ladrillo's recovery was so successful that he has since sired many foals, and by the time this book is published he will be back in the Dominican Republic carrying on his career as a stallion there.

Dinastia La Joya

Dinastia La Joya, a lovely buckskin mare with a star, was foaled in February, 1984 and, in 1986, she completely charmed Nancy Moffitt, her present owner, when Nancy visited Rancho La Joya in the Dominican Republic. "I looked at five different fillies. I liked her best. I liked her bloodlines," Nancy says.

Ladrillo, the chestnut stallion owned by Manuel Diez of the Dominican Republic, was her sire, and he is known as a sire of good producers. Her dam was Mensajera, who came from Colombia. Mr. Diez bought Ladrillo, Mensajera, and a few other good mares to start his Rancho La Joya in Jaruboca.

Nancy imported Dinastia to her J Sol Reye ranch when it was still in Frankfort, Illinois. She has since moved the ranch to a sunnier climate in Ocala, Florida. "We had a heated barn in Illinois," Nancy says, "but the horses liked the snow of a Chicago area winter."

The plane carrying Dinastia from the Dominican Republic landed in Miami and Nancy had her sent immediately to Capuchino, a stallion standing at Hacienda Castañuela in Bell, Florida, before she resumed her journey to Illinois.

Capuchino and Dinastia's colt, Bolivar, when only two weeks old got to meet Dr. Margaret Mac Harg at Illinois Equine Hospital and Clinic in Naperville. Bolivar colicked after eating plastic in the pasture. "My son's kite, which had been caught in a tree forever, blew down," says Nancy, and Bolivar thought it was horse treats.

"If I cut him, he's going to die," said Dr. Mac Harg when presented with the colicking foal, "He's just too young." Through nonsurgical treatment, she was able to save him, and Bolivar is now four years old and hopefully more discerning about his diet.

Dinastia was just starting under saddle when she was shipped to America. "She was just broke, not trained at all. She just wasn't bucking, went forward but didn't know how to turn," says Nancy.

After Bolivar was weaned, Dinastia was shown and won Fino Fillies and Championships at regional shows in Illinois, Minnesota and Ohio. In 1989, she first competed as a mare. Shown by trainer Jorge Suarez, she won High Point Fino Mare and many Championships at larger shows in Florida, Texas, Kentucky, Illinois and Ohio. She won National Champion Fino mare, High Point Fino Mare, and Third Grand National Champion Fino horse that year. Since then she has been semi-retired, and in 1992 was bred to the Colombian stallion Cosmos through artificial insemination of frozen semen. "Cosmos has been siring very well; and he's the same bloodlines as hers," says Nancy.

As for the mare's personality, "Dinastia is a very friendly mare," Nancy says, "but she is a very hot mare when you ride her. She is all business, wants to work all the time, and very eager to please. She is very fino and has great back-end action. That's one of the things Ladrillo does pass on really well, his back-end action.

"Once the latest foal is weaned, hopefully we will get Dinastia back," says Nancy, "and we'll have a good year to show. I hope that she'll be competitive. She will stay in Fino classes. I don't know if I'll ride her or Jorge will ride her in the future. Jorge, who was with me in Illinois, likes Dinastia a lot and he's very proud of her."

Nancy started as a breeder in 1979; "I liked the Paso Fino breed, but the horses are also a business," she says. "My goal is to breed quality horses and produce quality offspring."

Coral LaCE

When Clifton W. and Barbara Preiss bought the Colombian Paso Fino stallion Coral LaCE in 1981, he brought them instant fame.

"We suddenly became known as his owners. He was famous – not us," says Barbara. Coral LaCE had won the National Top Sire of the Year title the previous year.

Actually Coral LaCE had been outstanding from his foaling on December 23, 1964, in Medellin, Colombia, South America. Bred by a well-known Colombian breeder, Alberto Uribe Sierra, the majestic mahogany bay with blaze and two white hind stockings was imported by George LaHood of Valdosta, Georgia.

Today Coral LaCE's name is in the pedigree of many American Paso Fino show ring superstars. He has sired numerous National Champion Paso Finos and many Reserve Grands and Third Grands in multiple divisions such as conformation, performance, pleasure, versatility and trail classes, says Barbara.

So many winners have been sired by him, his offspring have won him a Reserve National Get of Sire award. He is also a Grand National Champion in Performance in the Paso Fino Horse Association.

"At age nineteen, he was superbly ridden by our daughter Diane, a Paso Fino trainer, judge and rider, in a special Parade of Past Grand National Champions. He performed beautifully, even though he had not been ridden in many years," says Barbara.

"Under saddle he is powerful, proud and perfectly gaited," she says. "Ridden western reining horse style, he is as agile as a cat on complete 180-degree turns, whether to the left or to the right. Ridden English, he is an agile dressage horse and responsive and eager to please. He would die under you before he quit."

Serious athlete that he is, Coral LaCE too has his quirks.

"This horse loves chocolate," Barbara reveals, "and he loves little calves. They come to him across the neighbor's fence and he enjoys them. In the barn, he prefers a smaller stall in the middle of the mare barn to the twelve by twenty-four stall in the stallion barn, and behaves like a gentleman living there.

Breeders of the Paso Fino since 1977, the Preisses, owners of La Caballeriza Farm in Weirsdale, Florida, started out primarily with Puerto Rican Paso Finos. When they saw how beautifully Coral LaCE crossed with these mares, they bred Colombian/Puerto Rican type Paso Finos, "which is predominantly what the American Paso Fino is," Barbara says.

"We do have a special obstacle in owning Coral LaCE," Barbara admits. "A horse of this caliber should be owned by a wealthy person. I have given much of my time and resources to this horse. However, he did drive us to bigger and better goals in life. We have acquired more land, which has kept our son and three daughters and the grandchildren on the farm with the horses, dogs, kittens, and other creatures."

Like many horseowners who work to support their passion, Barbara regrets that she cannot spend much time with Coral LaCE. "I have to work many hours to maintain the prestige he deserves," she says.

But Barbara has no complaints. "I love and admire this horse enough to work to care for him for the rest of his life," she adds. "This horse is an animal for which my whole family has respect and love. His presence on our farm has made it somewhat of a tourist attraction for Paso Fino enthusiasts from various parts of the world. I have been privileged to meet many fine people from all over the United States who have bought his offspring.

"As a little girl, I had a dream of owning a beautiful stallion and a horse farm," she says. "Coral LaCE has fulfilled my utmost dreams."

Presidente Con Vivo

Some horses provide a special dimension to family life, as did Presidente Con Vivo.

Beverly Sheriff bought him in 1984 as a charming three-year-old bay gelding with soft brown eyes and a luxuriant mane and tail. He quickly became her 13-year-old son Christopher's horse. From the first time Christopher rode Presidente Con Vivo, they shared a bond few people ever experience with a horse. Vivo even seemed to be able to read Christopher's mind at times.

Christopher began showing the animated, classy Vivo in Performance Youth classes and won almost everywhere they went, repeatedly taking High Point Youth Awards.

"Every show was a pleasure to us," says Beverly. "Vivo seemed to know when he was in the lineup that he had won again, and became excited when the numbers were called."

In 1985, Beverly purchased a beautiful bay gelding, Regocijo Con Vivo, a half-brother to Presidente Con Vivo, for Darian, Christopher's twin. "'Reggie' was a good performance horse, but not consistent," says the twins' mother. "He was hardheaded and difficult to ride, so Darian always placed second or third to Christopher. This made Christopher sad. He always wanted to give Darian his ribbon."

As a good horse show mother, Beverly always taught the boys from the beginning of their first show, "We are here to enjoy our horses, not just to win a ribbon. And always, Christopher would say, 'I don't care if I win or not, I know I have the best horse here with or without taking home the ribbons.'

"The boys and I attended the shows together, usually taking their friends along. These years were the most pleasant of my life," says Beverly. "I hooked the four-horse trailer to our dual wheel truck and took them anywhere they wanted to go. The boys and I have always been very close. Their father, Leonard, is a heavy utility contractor and often out of town on business. So it has always been up to me to take care of the farm."

Sundown Stables and Kennels was begun in 1957 with registered Black Angus cattle and a few pleasure horses. After attending their first National Paso Fino Show and Auction in September, 1982, the Sheriffs purchased three broodmares, which evolved into their present count of thirty-five registered Paso Fino horses. They also raise beef cattle and pointer bird dogs.

"We live on 300 acres with trails throughout for riding. The boys ride everywhere, even swimming their horses in the lakes. Vivo especially loves the water, doing anything to please Christopher," says Beverly.

Then in 1987, the Sheriffs purchased Forest Cabin Erectorita, a "fino" mare many times National Champion. Chris began showing her in amateur owner classes, winning both regional and national awards. He stopped riding Vivo, and Vivo became depressed.

"Tim Carroll, Sundown Stables' barn manager, told me one day that Vivo didn't seem the same," says Beverly. "Chris was working in the summer and didn't have as much time to spend riding. I decided Vivo needed something special, so every morning after he is fed, he is turned out to roam free around the barn and out the drive. He wanders around visiting the mares and the weanlings in the smaller pastures. Sometimes he ambles into the barn to aggravate the stallions. But when he sees one of us, he scoots out as if he knows he's creating mischief. At noon, when Tim leaves for lunch, Vivo goes to his stall to rest, then comes back out when Tim returns. In the evening, he is stalled until morning."

Lucky Vivo, and lucky Christopher and Darian, who have a special mother like Beverly, one whose fervent wish is: "I hope I am never without horses."

Madonna

Like the rock star for whom she is named, the Paso Fino mare Madonna is a public figure of high visibility. Her image, complete with the blue ribbon she won at the Nationals around her neck, is on ten billboards on the highways into Ocala, Florida, where she lives.

The billboards advertise the Ocala Hilton in a part of Florida filled with such an intense population of horse farms that it is called "The Kentucky of the South."

Madonna is the most popular of the performing stars at Young's Ranch, a beautiful 20-acre facility which in the last few years has become one of the U.S.'s leading Paso Fino farms, as well as a favorite tourist attraction.

Barbara Young has created an effective way to promote the Paso Fino breed. Her farm welcomes and puts on shows for group tours. She also makes her facilities available for special events such as charity benefits, in order to acquaint people with the breed's remarkable temperament, smooth gaits and irresistible beauty. She gives as many as three or four shows a week to audiences of hundreds of people.

"The Ocala Hilton caters these affairs, which is why Madonna is on the billboard. The Hilton brings its large groups out here," says Barbara.

Madonna's stall is near the barn entrance, where her friendly manners and charm make her one of the farm "hostesses" and official greeters of visitors.

"People fall in love with her," says Barbara Young. "She is a magnificent horse. First of all, she is an unusual color, a rose grey. She loves to be loved." And once they see Madonna 'onstage' in performance, they find her unforgettable.

"One of the things Paso Fino horses are judged on in competition is the ability to turn on a very, very tight circle," explains Barbara. "Two people stand back to back in the ring and then take three steps apart. The horse (with a rider) is asked to do a figure eight." One person then steps in with each turn until there's only one step left between the two. "Madonna will go between them and never touch them. She is so delicate and dainty."

Foaled March 25, 1985, Madonna was imported on October 21, 1987. Mrs. Young bought her when she was four, the day after the grand opening of Young's Ranch.

Madonna has done very well in competition, having won National Schooling Fino Filly and Reserve Grand National Filly in September, 1989 in Memphis, Tennessee.

"Madonna is one of the top Fino mares in the nation that demonstrate the Classic Fino gait. The classic show ring gait is a rapid steady unbroken rhythm of the hooves with slow forward speed, performed with the horse fully balanced and collected," Barbara explains. "She has been classified as a finely-tuned ballerina on the (fino) board."

Madonna gave one of her most memorable performances late in February, 1991, at "Mystery Under the Stars," a charity event hosted by Barbara. The event benefited the Association for Retarded Citizens and provided Madonna one of her largest audiences.

"We put Madonna on the board (48 feet long and four feet wide), so everyone could hear her footfalls, then asked people to count each footfall as she moved across – 140 steps.

"On Madonna, it will take you all day to go from the farm's back gate to the front gate," Barbara adds jokingly.

Barbara has turned down an offer of $750,000 for Madonna. After one woman saw her perform, she presented Barbara with a blank check and said, 'Whatever you want, I want that horse!'

"I couldn't sell her. She's one of my top horses, my building blocks," says Barbara.

Madonna will be bred this year, and motherhood should give a whole new meaning to her name, making her even more lovable, if that is possible.

Emisario

"Arthur called this God's Country," says Barbara Young, recalling when she and her late husband first passed through Ocala, Florida in the early fall of 1987. "He said he'd love to have a horse ranch." At the time the Youngs had designed and were running four golf courses in another part of the state.

By October, 1987, they had taken possession of what is now the beautiful 20-acre facility called "Young's Ranch." Two months later, on December 12, 1987, Arthur Young died of an incurable disease he had been bravely battling.

His wife had to make the decision whether to go back to Stuart, Florida where she had family and friends, or stay in Ocala and carry on with the legacy and new life her husband had left to her. Matching his courage with her own, she stayed, learned the horse business in a remarkably short time, and has become extraordinarily successful at it.

There are now thirty-eight Paso Finos on Young's Ranch, where Barbara breeds, trains, boards and sells Pleasure, Performance and Classic Fino horses.

Chief stallion at the ranch is Emisario, foaled May 10, 1982 and imported from the Dominican Republic on March 31, 1988.

Emisario has striking good looks. He is a golden bay with a thick jet black mane and forelock framing a handsome head which speaks of long-ago Barb ancestors in his pedigree. His mane has a curly effect to it that makes him even more arresting in his appearance. "We braid their manes," says Barbara. "Everybody thought for the longest time that we gave perms to the horses, but it is all natural."

Beyond his sheer physical impact, "Emisario is one of the top Classic Fino horses," continues Barbara. "The Classic Fino is the top of the line; they're considered the Rolls Royce of the horse industry because they're so smooth-gaited and their temperament makes them even more special."

In the formal show ring, Emisario has won many titles as Top Classic Fino Stallion; he is also a Champion in Bella Forma. The latter is a division of horse show classes, explains Barbara, in which the Paso Fino horse is judged "sixty percent on conformation, thirty percent on natural gait, and ten percent on the grooming and manners of the stallion or mare. As for *brio*, he's got the fire, but it's controlled," she says. "You can do anything with him."

One of Emisario's most outstanding wins was the 1991 Florida State Championship in Classic Fino. 1990 was also a good year, as that's when this stallion won his T.O.P. or Title of Proficiency, which means he earned 500 points in a show season. He's also won many additional championships in Georgia, North Carolina and Florida.

Emisario is also proving to be an excellent sire who passes on his most desirable qualities. "You should see some of the foals he has and their temperaments" says Barbara. "You go out to the pasture to see them and they put their heads on your shoulder. He also throws his wonderful gait. That is the true meaning of a fantastic sire, when you can see the beauty coming from the stallion to the offspring. One of his sons, Bozanova De Young, is also breathtaking, and he's very special on the fino board," says Barbara.

Barbara has involved her entire family, including daughter Betty Ann, grandson Christopher Arthur ("Skipper"), and sons Donald and James, in the horses and the shows and tours hosted by the farm. Her son James rides Emisario and the other champion horses at the ranch and all shows pertaining to the ranch.

"It is kind of neat to watch your son riding the ones that are carrying my Arthur's name," says Barbara, a woman who took up the challenge facing her to find an absorbing, compelling and ultimately fulfilling new life for herself and the family her husband left behind.

"My husband knew he had two months to live, you see. He said there was a future with this horse. We had to hold our head high and just go forward," says Barbara, who has done it with the same *brio* and championship style of her wonderful horses.

Plebeyo

Plebeyo is the cover boy of the Paso Fino Horse Association's official brochure. Milky white with shadings of silver, huge dark eyes and a velvety grey muzzle, he is a stately spokes-stallion for his breed.

His owner, Codelia (Dee) Torcise, of Tijodee Farms and American Classic Fino Horses, Inc. in Ocala, Florida, found him in Colombia, South America in 1982. "I went to Colombia in search of a Classic Fino that I could bring to the United States," says Dee. "There were no breeding stallions here at that time. I needed a herd sire for myself and to improve the breed.

"Through his own reputation, I knew the horse before I went to Colombia," says Dee. "I had heard a great deal about him from Paso Fino *aficionados*."

But after traveling all that way, "I really didn't get to see the horse," she says. "He was well-guarded. I saw him only through a peephole." But it was enough. She made arrangements and imported him into the United States that year, and began to show him the following year, 1983.

The outstanding career of this twenty-two-year-old stallion, foaled February 24, 1970 includes the 1980 Colombian Get of Sire Award; the 1981 Document of International Champion in Bogata, Colombia; numerous international, national and state championships; the 1983 U.S. National Champion Classic Fino Stallion Award; the U.S. Champion of Champions Award; the U.S. Top Ten Sire Award in 1989, 1990, and 1991.

"Having won the highest national and international awards, Plebeyo was retired, his legend continuing through his magnificent progeny," says Dee. "Plebeyo has been heralded as one of the breed's foremost stallions." His offspring are marked with the same winning talent, beauty and conformation, she says. "His great attributes have had a major impact on the Paso Fino breed.

"He has sired more national champions than any other Paso Fino stallion," she says. His son, Tito Livio, a seven-year-old bay, won the Nationals in 1990.

"One of the highlights for me," adds Dee, "was when a Plebeyo daughter, Zarzamora, won the Amateur Owner class under saddle in 1989." Dee was riding her. Zarzamora, also a grey, is now a broodmare.

Dee calls Plebeyo, who was sired by a very famous Colombian stallion, Chucuano, out of the mare Pandereta, "the backbone of a very special breeding farm." Her goal since 1980 has been to produce the best. But she also enjoys a "very endearing relationship" with the stallion. "He enjoys human companionship," she says. "He is not hard to handle and he passes on to his get his personality. Quite often I ride him myself. He's controlled, but he's all fire under saddle. He has a perfect fino gait, and he's very famous for passing on his hock action."

Horses in general have been very important to Dee, not only professionally, but emotionally. "I enjoy them so very much. I don't know what else I would do with my life," she says. "I saw a Paso Fino horse in a parade when I was showing Tennessee Walking Horses. I converted immediately. I lived in Miami at the time, and I started looking at Paso Fino farms and bought my first mare."

Plebeyo got to be a cover boy, by the way, the same way he got to be one of the breed's top horses. "Everyone sent in photographs of their horses, and Plebeyo won," says Dee.

Mi Stolen Moment

Two friends, Joane Parkin and Priscilla Bowman, escaped their worries by going to the farm where they kept their horses. The grooming and riding sessions were great therapy for them, and renewed their strength for the test they were mutually facing. Both their husbands were critically ill.

Joane would often say, in consolation to Prissy, "These are our stolen moments." In the back of her mind Joane decided that some day she would use that phrase as a horse's name, as metaphoric tribute to what they meant to her psychologically.

In time, both women's husbands died. Joane stayed on her farm, Watson's Landing, in Crescent City, Florida; the property her late husband, Bill, had bought for them in 1983 after they had married. She hoped to "close the gate and shut the world out," creating her own sanctuary.

Born in Brooklyn, New York, Joane had lived in Miami and worked on a cruise line before marrying Bill Watson. There was nothing country about her, but she fell in love with a white horse, so Bill bought the horse along with the property for her. Soon Joane was looking around for someone to teach her about horses, how to groom, saddle, and care for them. That's how she met Priscilla, who started giving her lessons.

Joane began riding Paso Fino horses because she couldn't take the jarring trotting motion of other breeds. Soon after Bill's death, she bought two more horses: Flor de Lisboa Caje, a big, beautiful black mare, and Casimia, a caramel-colored, pure Puerto Rican mare, both in foal. Two other mares at the farm were also in foal. All four were due around the same time.

In the interim, Joane met Priscilla's brother, Elmer Parkin, and they were married. Foaling time arrived and a camper was set up near the barn to await the new arrivals. Every little nicker made them jump to see if they were needed. Two foals were born with no problems. With two more to go, Joane took "a stolen moment" to go to the house for a cup of coffee. When she returned, there was a bundle of black, nickering to its mother.

Joane knew that this was the filly she had been waiting for, that this indeed was her "Stolen Moment."

Stoli grew up to be a barnyard pet. She loved people and aggressively sought out attention, though there was no meanness in her. Joane went through a period of bad health and, unable to work with Stoli herself, hired a trainer. Seeing Stoli after a three-month absence, Joane was surprised to find she had undergone a metamorphosis. The romping filly had become an elegant swan. She was still a pet, but she knew she was in show business and was now well-behaved.

"Stoli's elegant bearing serves her well in shows," says Joane. "Taller than most Paso Finos, she steps out confidently and portrays an easy grace in the ring, win-ning pleasure classes with her new trainer, Josue Perez." In the future, Joane plans to be in the saddle herself.

Stoli's sire, Alegria de Blanca, is still siring winning show stock; her grandsire, Coral LaCE, has been Top Ten Sire many times. Her dam still resides at the farm, and this year produced Stoli's brother, Alegre Momentos, she reports.

All horses foaled at Joane's farm now have "Alegre" as a prefix to their names, "To reflect the Spanish background of the breed and to speak for their happy, outgoing natures," she says.

"The training at Alegre Watson's Landing is gentle and accomplished with love. No harsh tactics are used and training is at the horse's individual pace. Pasos usually train very quickly and seem to have an inborn desire to please. It's all in the natural gait," says Joane. "You can ride forever."

THE PERUVIAN PASO

The Peruvian Paso is a unique breed of horse that has become more familiar to Americans only in the past decade. Yet within a few short years, the breed has gained tremendous recognition and popularity.

This marvelously versatile breed is in use for show, pleasure, trail, endurance and parade riding.

There is something for everyone in this smooth-riding elegant animal: comfort and stamina for the avid trail rider; a calm, tractable disposition so important in the family horse; arrogant, flashy presence and action which set the exhibitor and parade rider apart from others, plus an investment potential supported by its relative rarity and increasing popularity. Breeders here are already exporting horses to Europe, Australia, the Orient and Canada.

The Peruvian Paso had its origins over four centuries ago in South America. The ancestors of the present-day Peruvian horse came from Spain with the conqueror Pizarro and were of Andalusian, Friesian, African Barb and Spanish Jennet blood. These horses were largely credited by historians with the fall of the centuries-old Inca Empire, as they gave the Conquistadores a distinct advantage over the natives. Horses were reportedly so valuable that many were shod with silver and young foals were carried by porters in "hammocks" during the long, forced marches.

As Lima became the Vice Royalty of New Spain, the owners of Peru's large haciendas favored horses with fast, smooth gaits.

The Peruvian's unique gait is a broken pace which gives the rider neither the vertical movement of the trot nor the lateral motion of the pace. It is said to be the smoothest ride in the horse world.

Another trademark characteristic of the Peruvian horse is *termino*, the outward rolling of the front limb during extension, much like the loose outward rolling of a swimmer's arms in the crawl. This showy action gives the Peruvian horse the appearance of always being "on parade" and is completely natural, due to selective breeding. It is not a wing or a paddle and originates in the shoulder, giving the horse the ability to swing the leg forward with minimum vertical force to the back.

Generations of strict selection have genetically fixed these traits. Once established the Peruvian Paso was maintained in its native country as a closed population, isolated by geography and the dedication of its creators from the influence of outside blood. For this reason, the breed can guarantee one-hundred percent transmission of its gaits to all purebred foals.

A major principle with Peruvian breeders is that great Peruvian horses are born, not trained. Training is designed to bring out the animal's inherent ability, but not to modify it artificially.

If a horse will not collect properly or can't be managed with a mild bit, it is not deemed suitable for breeding. If a horse lacks *termino*, exercises to increase *termino* are not used as this would only prolong the fault in future generations. The guiding philosophy of breeders is that it is easier to cull undesirable qualities immediately than to deal with them in future generations. To help insure retention of completely natural action and gait, no horse is allowed in the show ring with hooves longer than four inches.

Yet the Peruvians did not breed exclusively for gait. Disposition was equally important. The horses were used for transportation and riders did not want to deal with temperamental, stubborn or nervous horses.

For horsemen, the Peruvian Paso is an enigmatic blend of extremes. They have the fire of the old Spanish warhorse, yet are noted for tractability. For many, the disposition of the Peruvian horse is its most appealing virtue, although the smooth gait is probably more renowned. As a result of strict selection, the Peruvian horse is intelligent, tractable and eager to please. Nevertheless, it has retained the *brio* or spirited presence and arrogance of his warhorse ancestors. The modern day Peruvian horse still "travels like a conqueror."

The Peruvian Paso comes in all the basic colors: chestnut, black, bay, chestnut, grey, palomino, buckskin and roan, with the solid and darker colors considered most desirable. Peruvians boast a long, luxurious mane and tail with hair that may be curly or straight. Size ranges from 14 to 15.3 hands with the average being about 14.3.

Since their importation to North America, Peruvian Pasos have proven their ability to adapt to all climates and are easy keepers.

Fenix

On May 8, 1979, a dark brown Peruvian Paso colt was foaled, shortly after the untimely death of his full sister, the champion mare, Madrilena. The colt was so strikingly similar to her, he was given the name "Fenix," the Spanish word for "Phoenix," the mythological creature which rose newborn from its own ashes. Fenix is the son of a National Champion and the linebred grandson of Caramelo, Rey De La Solana. His dam, Mariangola, was by the Champion Carnaval out of the great broodmare Faraona.

Fenix would more than replace his sister. He would become a living legend in international breeding circles and one of the most popular and renowned stallions of the Peruvian Paso breed.

His list of achievements was long even before he was acquired by his present owners, Bryan and Jeanelle Anderson of Pecan Valley Ranch, Arlington, Texas.

At the Solana Classic Sale in 1981, Fenix became the first Peruvian Paso stallion to be syndicated, and he set a new record price for a two-year-old colt. He became a National Champion at an early age, and for several years stood at stud in northern California, siring many outstanding foals, including the 1991 National Champion Stallion, Favorito, to whom he passed on his outstanding conformation, gait, *brio*, personality and charisma.

A strong, dynamic stallion, Fenix is gentle as a lamb when youngsters come to admire him. He will stand for hours and savor their attention and affection, letting them stroke his mane or muzzle, noble as a monarch before their inquisitive awe and curiosity, but gently accepting offerings of hay from their small hands.

Posters of Fenix are a favorite with children who hang them on the classroom walls at school. Because of his popularity through the years, Fenix receives many cards, presents and toys on his birthday and at Christmas.

"His impact is amazing," says Jeanelle, who has perhaps felt it far more than anyone else.

Raised in cities, she was always drawn to all animals. "With the tales in one particular novel and a vivid imagination, I soon envisioned owning and caring for a spirited but gentle black horse, one not unlike 'Black Beauty.' A romantic fantasy for countless young girls, this became my dream, one that was to come true many years later," Jeanelle recounts.

After trial and error experimentation with several breeds, Jeanelle concluded that the Peruvian Paso horse satisfied her expectations best, and she began raising, breeding and showing them exclusively.

"The next sequence of events in this dream-come-true love story" she says, "occurred a few years ago. I was looking for new bloodlines and purchased a breeding to one of the best stallions in the Peruvian horse world – Fenix."

The Andersons were rewarded with a beautiful new colt and that remarkable experience inspired them to travel to California to visit the sire. "It was the beginning of the realization of my childhood dream," says Jeanelle. "There he was, an incredibly gorgeous black stallion, a fantastic storybook incarnation, perhaps even more spectacular than anything I'd imagined. Fate and good timing were on my side because Fenix soon came to his new Texas home, and the Black Beauty of my hopes was now real."

Jeanelle hopes the new foals by Fenix will become National Champions like their sire and will make someone else just as proud and happy to own a Black Beauty.

Franqueza

Although Rita Apsley wrote me that her Peruvian Paso, Franqueza, is "truly a wonderful mare, worthy of better words than my husband Richard and I might put together," their tribute to her is as eloquent as any professional wordsmith's, coming as it does directly from their hearts.

Franqueza, whose name in Spanish means "frankness" or "candor," is a bit of a flirt, one who had decided to pick her own human, rather than waiting for a human to select her.

The Apsleys purchased their first Peruvian horse from breeder Naomi Baker, Rita recalls. "While visiting Naomi's ranch to watch the training of our new gelding, we noticed this little filly who would place her head against the stall door and watch. Nosey! She seemed to think she was a person and never failed to show off when Richard was around."

"We were unable to resist her wiles, and Richard bought her, an act that would alter our lives adding enrichment and changing our future plans," says Rita.

"We originally planned for a maximum of four horses. Trail riding and just simple things were our maximum aspirations."

But because of the quality of Franqueza and the love of the Peruvian horse she inspired, the Apsleys purchased more land, added more barns and changed their lifestyle considerably.

They now own more than thirty horses, and have a trainer and ranch help at their Rider Ridge Farm in North Vernon, Indiana. There they breed, show, train, sell, trail ride and thoroughly enjoy their horses as well as the other horse people they meet through them.

But more about "Frannie."

Foaled June 12, 1985, the striking chestnut with a Farrah Fawcett fall of flaxen mane was sired by Regio, who in turn was sired by Polomo, a stallion noted for his outstanding gait. Frannie's dam was Bello Amandalina, a mare with an impressive show record and a producer of superior foals; her sire is the magnificent Destello.

Frannie was a yearling when she came to the Apsleys. Already a strong personality, the chestnut filly continued her attachment to Richard. They spent many hours "just fooling around, playing frisbee, or kick the bucket." Another favorite game was hide and seek around the shelter in her paddock.

By age three, Frannie was ready for the more serious business of school. However, the woman trainer who had agreed to break and train her was expecting a baby, so Richard decided to step in and do the job.

Despite their great relationship, training was no simple feat, as Frannie had a mind of her own. The hardest part was getting her to accept the saddle. "But once done, her gait was as natural to her as breathing and her willingness to 'go' was remarkable," says Rita.

"Fran's great heart has pulled her through some bad times. The way she responded to an injury to her legs at a horse show taught us that this is a horse you never have to push," adds Rita.

Fran is an expectant mother now, due to foal in early spring, 1992. She was bred to another great Peruvian horse, Excelente.

"If this foal is as good as its parents, you will see its name around," says Rita.

"We believe in the future of the Peruvian horses," she adds. "Their loving character, beauty, and smooth ride make them a desirable item in today's rough, push-and-shove society.

"A Peruvian horse is not just a possession, because the horse also possesses you." Franqueza certainly seems living proof of that notion.

*Lindero+

A horse who has his own pet snake can't be expected to have normal drinking habits.

Years ago, the Peruvian Paso stallion *Lindero+ had as his "compadre" a very old and very large rat snake named Sydney, who lived in his stall and usually could be found wrapped around *Lindero's feed dish, sharing grain, or coiled in an out-of-the-way corner of the stall, resting.

The snake stayed home during the years that *Lindero+ was on the show circuit; but perhaps influenced by Sydney, the stallion felt accustomed to doing things in a more exotic way.

*Lindero+ was a good traveler, never lost a pound. But he refused to drink water from a bucket on a trip. "Consequently, we would have to pull into rest areas, unload, and lead him to the nearest drinking fountain where he would drink his fill," says Pam Boswell, who with Lee Johns owns Rancho Puesta Del Sol in Palm City, Florida.

Weird as he was about what he drank on the road, it was worth the trouble. In 1981, *Lindero+ was a winner in every show he entered. During his show career, he's won over twenty major championships throughout the United States, an achievement that very few Peruvian horses have approached. His crowning achievement was becoming United States National Champion for 1981 as well as High Point Breeding Stallion that year.

*Lindero+ came into their lives when Pam and Lee decided to find a special stallion to complete their Peruvian Paso breeding program and to complement the Sol de Oro bloodlines they wished to use. Verne Albright, who had been involved with the importation of Peruvian horses into the United States for many years, advised them that without question they should consider *Lindero.+ (The asterisk denotes that *Lindero+ was imported to the United States from Peru; the plus indicates he is a Laureado Champion, having won the title Champion of Champions Breeding Stallion in 1984.)

At that time, the deep copper chestnut was owned by Dr. Curtis Boyd at Cypress Ridge Ranch in northern California, about three thousand miles from Rancho Puesta Del Sol in southern Florida. Lee called Curtis and struck a deal on April 15, 1981, the day before a Canadian group tried to buy *Lindero+. At that time, *Lindero+ was relatively unknown and expecting his first foals that year, so Pam and Lee were basing their purchase on bloodlines alone.

*Lindero+ is by the famous Peruvian stallion, Regional and out of the mare, Tajahuana, with a closely-bred Sol de Oro Viejo heritage.

"*Lindero+'s greatest asset is his ability to consistently sire many excellent offspring, particularly colts," says Pam. "His colts have consistently won under a great

number of judges in all areas of the country, and in regional area shows as well as National Championships.

"*Lindero+ has an enormous amount of *brio*, a word that means spirit, strength, heart, energy, tractability, charisma, presence, and willingness; plus he has excellent bone and superb conformation. His gait is smooth, wonderfully coordinated and eye-catching. He has exceptional *pisos*, which is the manner in which he executes his gait. As a breeding stallion, he passes on all these traits to his get. We call it 'The Good Housekeeping Stamp of *Lindero+,'" says Pam.

"We have never had a single doubt that we made the right decision in purchasing *Lindero+," she adds. "Without him, we would not have the strength and consistency that we get with nearly every foal. Lee and I feel deeply that we are just the caretakers of a very special stallion with phenomenal bloodlines. History will prove him to be one of the premier breeding stallions in the Peruvian breed."

Serenata De Los Piños

Ray and Sandra Chesney's ranch name, "Rancho de Los Sueños," means "ranch of dreams" in Spanish.

Those dreams, of owning and breeding quality Peruvian Paso horses, were helped to realization by Serenata De Los Pinos.

But not until the Chesneys saw "Sera" through a nightmare of her own.

In 1987, when she was six, Sera suffered a puncture wound to her right rear leg at the joint between her pastern and fetlock. She somehow injured herself while out in pasture at the Chesneys' ranch at Falcon, Colorado, just outside of Colorado Springs.

The veterinarian recommended immediate surgery to avoid infection. He predicted that after 120 days of shots and confinement Sera still might not have sufficient use of her leg to carry a foal to full term or to be ridden to any extent.

Though the Chesneys were disappointed, since they'd had big plans for Sera in the show arena, it was more important that she be healthy and pain-free and they proceeded with treatment. On the 120th day of shots, they woke up to find she had reopened her wound and was unable to put the slightest bit of pressure on the foot.

Back into surgery she went, her owners very concerned that the anesthesia might have some negative effect on the foal she was carrying.

This time the vet was quite certain Sera could never be ridden again.

Sera's show career was definitely postponed, but gradually she recovered to the point where she had no residual lameness. She was finished in the bit, and in the last few years has accomplished what few mares accomplish in a lifetime. She has several championships to her credit, including two Champion of Champions wins in the breeding division, Laureada Pleasure Mare (three Champion of Champions wins at one show), numerous Merito Zootecnico (conformation) firsts, plus many sidesaddle ribbons.

Foaled April 24, 1981, this good-sized (15 hands) black mare, sired by José Antonio TB and out of *Colona, was purchased at the age of two from a small breeder on the eastern slopes of Colorado. "She helped us make the decision to go into business breeding Peruvian Paso horses," says Sandra. "She had excellent *brio* and conformation."

The first year they owned Sera, Ray Chesney, a professional trainer, broke her to ride and entered her in a national show in Denver after only a month under saddle. Sera received an honorable mention, and was the only Colorado horse allowed to stay in the arena for the judging.

Sera is flexible. Ray can ride her in breeding classes and make her take on the look of a fire-breathing stallion. Novice rider Sandra rides her in sidesaddle and pleasure classes. Their son Chris, now twelve, has shown her since he was eight and has many High Point and Reserve High Point Junior Awards to his credit, with Sera to thank.

"She is loving and very easy to manage, standing quietly while she is groomed and saddled," says Sandra. "However, she's a raving maniac in the pasture if you are late with her dinner. She has been dubbed 'Sera-Lee' for a good reason."

Sera has had four foals which have done well in shows. Her oldest, Sueno Bonita, is just starting her show career and doing well.

Sera obviously means a lot to the whole Chesney family, but especially to Ray who has launched his training career through her. He is now well-respected nationwide for his training.

"Sera has taught all of us to share feelings with the animals that mean something to us, and they will give you love in return," says Sandra. "We have learned that even though things may look bad at times, you must hang on to your dreams and with hard work and lots of love, they will come true."

Conmovedor R&BM

The name of this stallion, Conmovedor, means "moving, touching," in Spanish. His appearance and his story are both.

Shortly after losing their lead stallion, Igneo, to natural causes three years ago, Roger and Dale Williams visited a central California Peruvian Paso breeding farm, looking for a suitable replacement.

They noticed a striking young golden stallion stashed away in a back stall. Upon inquiry, they were advised that not only was the three-year-old grandson of Mantequilla expensive, but that he was considered unmanageable.

"On closer examination we found that the horse not only was dispirited, but needed serious attention in the manners department if he was ever to live up to his famous bloodlines," says Roger.

Nevertheless, one thing was certain, Conmovedor responded immediately to Dale's overtures of affection.

After serious negotiations and with some trepidation, the Williams family brought Conmovedor to their ranch, Rancho De Los Establos Verdes in Carmel Valley, California.

There he was immediately put onto a regimen of food supplements, exercise, gentle discipline and good old-fashioned loving care. "Suffice to say, it all worked, and now the horse is a pussycat around people, but still a knockout in the show ring," says Roger.

Dale became the "bonded other" to Conmovedor, who responds emotionally when Dale returns to the ranch, any time of night or day. Conmovedor's loud and drawn-out whinny is heard when Dale is within a mile or so of the ranch. No other human is favored with this greeting. On the ranch, Dale may be completely out of earshot or downwind, and the horse will still call out his hello.

Conmovedor also displays an especially attentive response to Dale, the ranch manager at Rancho De Los Establos Verdes, when they enter the training corral. "It is almost as if he recognizes that this is HIS human who has lifted him from loneliness and despair and transported him into sunlight, loving care, good feed, grooming and the freedom to run, breed and be admired and appreciated in the beauty of the Carmel Valley," says Roger.

In regard to Conmovedor's stunning color, which never fails to provoke comment, Dale has some interesting background on its history in the breed. The golden Palomino in Conquistador times was usually reserved for royalty to ride and own. In later years in Peru, the animals were reserved for priests and clergy. In contemporary times, due to political upheaval, Palominos came to represent oppression by the church, and the people of Peru disposed of many of the magnificent Palomino bloodlines. For many years, the preferred colors were browns, blacks and chestnuts. Mantequilla, Conmovedor's grandsire, was one of the first golden Palomino Peruvian stallions to be recognized by Peru as a National Champion.

Dale adds, "Conmovedor is proving to be one of the cornerstones of our breeding stock. Conmovedor's first offspring is Estrellita Contenta REV, a chestnut yearling filly with golden overtones in her coat. She is of exceptional quality and calm judgment.

"Conmovedor provides color contrast for the discriminating client, and breeding a Palomino can provide some interesting color surprises. It's really a roll of the dice," says Dale. A jackpot of "gold" is worth the gamble, however, just as it was for the Williams.

RDS La Quesadilla

RDS La Quesadilla, the top breeding and show mare of Rancho Cerro Gordo in Haworth, Oklahoma, where Peruvian Pasos of the best selected bloodlines from Peru are bred, is an outstanding example of the pure Southern line.

"The Southern-bred horse of Peru was admired for its qualities of conformation," explains Renato Catanzaro, Cerro Gordo trainer, "Long manes and tails, beautiful heads and well-developed hindquarters which make them very powerful. The Southern-bred horses excel in qualities of temperament as well – such as *brio* – the willingness to go forward constantly, giving the impression of restlessness."

"In contrast, Northern-bred horses," Renato adds, "are recognized as excellent gaited horses with lots of *termino*, over-reaching well with their rear legs; they are foaled with the natural Paso Llano gait, three feet touching the ground at all times, an extremely smooth gait."

La Quesadilla, was foaled in the United States, and acquired by John and Marlowe Cochran, owners of Cerro Gordo, in the winter of 1991-92. She is a daughter of HNS Domingo, Peruvian Champion and United States Champion Breeding Stallion, the sire of more than forty-four titled offspring. Also in her bloodlines is Caramelo, a son of Sol de Oro V, the modern day foun-

dation sire; her dam is the daughter of the Peruvian champion, Mantequilla.

The 14.2 seven-year-old grey mare was trained and had established her impressive show record before the Cochrans purchased her:

In 1987 she was Champion Junior Mare in the Southern California Championships; in 1989, she won First Place Mares, Gait, and Reserve Championship Pleasure Mare at the Los Amigos Championships; in 1990, she was Champion, and Champion of Champions Pleasure Mare at the Los Amigos Championships, Champion and Champion of Champions Breeding Mare at the World Championships, Champion of Champions Pleasure Mare at the Silver State Reno Championships, Champion and Grand Champion Breeding Mare at the Southern California Championships; in 1991, Champion of Champions Breeding Mare at the Los Amigos Championships, Reserve Champion Performance Mare at the PPHRNA Nationals, Champion of Champions Pleasure Mare at the AAOBPPH Nationals, Reserve Champion Breeding Mare, Champion and Champion of Champions Pleasure Mare in the East of the Rockies Championships.

While La Quesadilla was relatively new to Cerro Gordo, Renato discerned that she has very good temperament. Anyone can ride her. "She is always gentle in the stall or pasture. The first week she was here she was put in pasture with a younger mare and there was no fighting or kicking at all, which speaks very well for her."

So pleased have the Cochrans been with the mare that Cerro Gordo's latest acquisition is RDS Contigo Peru, her two-year-old son by RDS Me Llamo Peru, the U.S. National Champion of Champions Breeding Stallion and Laureado, purchased from the same farm from which La Quesadilla came.

"We were looking for a young stallion with especially strong hind legs. The son of Quesadilla has that conformation, and the disposition," Renato says.

While the Cochrans are new to the breed, John Cochran, seventy-five years young and a successful attorney in Tulsa for more than forty years, has bred and trained other breeds of horses for more than sixty years. It was his wife Marlowe's love for the Peruvian Paso that focused them on that breed.

"Presently Cerro Gordo has approximately forty head of horses with more due as spring arrives," says John. "We are developing a program which mandates a constant improvement of its horses. High on the list of requirements is the development of more strength and stamina, while keeping the other traits--the outcome of more than 450 years of breeding, stamping on the breed an exquisite imprint of smoothness, beauty, and willing temperament."

AHT El Capea

"No breeding program is complete without outstanding stallions," says John Cochran of Rancho Cerro Gordo in Haworth, Oklahoma, where four-year-old AHT El Capea, a bright chestnut Peruvian Paso, is transmitting his excellence to his offspring.

"We started using him for breeding last year," says Peruvian Paso trainer Renato Catanzaro. "He has sired a filly and a colt, both excellent, so we have used him more than any other stallion this year."

AHT El Capea is a grandson of AV Sol de Paijan and SR Chilcal, both Peruvian Champions of Champions. His dam lines have four Laureado Champions. A horse that wins Champion of Champion title three times in a National Show is officially retired from competition classes, the highest honor a Peruvian Paso horse can receive. The four Laureados in El Capea's maternal lines are the legendary AEV Regional, FPC El Cid and the mares AV Andauza IV and AV Ximena.

"El Capea has inherited the best of all of them, his superb lift, his *brio* and stamina, making him a top contender wherever he is shown," says John.

El Capea also has the remarkable temperament of the breed. "Stallions are very particular in their ways of being," trainer Renato poetically describes an equine truth. "But AHT El Capea is quite gentle for being a breeding stallion. He's easily managed. He won't make any strange or unexpected movements. But he is a horse that must be ridden by a knowledgeable rider. If he is, he will give much of himself. He's very responsive and he's so happy when you work him," says Renato.

Renato describes the way a Peruvian Paso's training begins – in the bozal, a kind of hackamore that works on the noseband area. After six months in the bozal, the trainer works on four reins, two from the bozal and two from the bit, "so you don't make an abrupt change," says Renato. "You are working him in the bozal and playing with the bit, and then finally you work the horse on the bit alone. The horse thus trained needs only a very small movement of the reins, and he will obey."

El Capea was imported from Peru as a yearling. His outstanding show career began here in 1989 and includes these wins: in 1989, Reserve Champion Junior Stallion, Central and East Championships; First Place Colts, Two Years old, Southwest Championships; in 1990, Third Place Stallions Bozal, Southwest Championships; in 1991 First Place Stallions Bozal, Southwest Championships; Second Place, Stallions Bozal, East of the Rockies Regional Show, and First Place Stallions Bozal, Lone Star Championships.

The Cochrans, whose first date was a day-long trail-ride in New Mexico leading to true love and a new start in life for both, consider El Capea and their other Peruvian Paso stallions, mares, colts and geldings, their "pride and joy."

Rancho Cerro Gordo is the place "where the romance of horses begins and continues," John wrote to me, opening the gates of his private feelings regarding this very special breed.

"The inspirational influence of our horses leads us to wonder. Has Pegasus then visited this earth, borne on great wings, lyrical with thunder and are these his foals? This breed of wonder, fearless, free and sensible of worth. With flash of eye, strong of girth they change, now lifting high, then wheeling asunder with quivering sides, their gait without blunder. Wide nostrils blowing in pride of birth, sired from the skies. Chestnut and brown and the high-lifting dun. Swiftly they flow across the great plain, eagerly they come, afire in their run. The get of Pegasus, gentled to rein, these brothers and sisters of the wind and the sun."

Ojos Azules

As his name, Ojos Azules ("blue eyes" in Spanish) might indicate, the most distinguishing characteristic of this chestnut Peruvian Paso gelding is his clear, azure-colored eyes. They seem to stand out even more against the very large white blaze that covers most of his face.

As one might suspect, Ojos Azules is an attention-getter on looks alone.

"But gait is his forte," says owner Nancy Johnson, "and he does it beautifully. His four white socks accent his every move."

The 14.2 gelding, foaled May 16, 1986 and sired by AV ORO Puro out of Lancerita, is affectionately known as "Big O" at home. He came into Nancy's life as though he were a living incarnation of her thoughts.

Nancy already had an idea of what she wanted a Peruvian pleasure gelding to look like. When she saw Ojos Azules, Nancy had an equine "eureka experience." "I immediately knew that was my horse, even before I rode him!"

Nancy and her husband, Sam, established their El Gato Grande Stables in Murfreesboro, Arkansas in 1989 as novices with no other idea in mind, they admit good-naturedly, than to breed for long manes and tails. "The established breeders rolled their eyes when they heard this. Our breeding philosophy has since matured, and we are now dedicated to raising the finest, best-gaited Peruvian horses in America," Nancy says.

While the Johnsons are breeders, they own Big O solely for pleasure. He is the mascot of their show string, and "an excellent calling card," says Nancy. Spectators cheer for him by name and the Johnsons are frequently asked, "Where can I find one just like him?"

Above all, Big O is special to every child who visits El Gato Grande Stables. He has a large fan club of local children who all call him, "MY horse – Big O!"

Something else very special about Big O, says Nancy, is that he adjusts his personality to fit the ability of his rider. With a child, he turns it down to "gentle" and gives a wonderfully easy ride. Two minutes later, in the show ring with his trainer, he's the king turning himself to "high," showing his flashy gait with the air of the champion that he is.

He's also versatile. At a show, Big O is entered in perhaps eleven classes, including luxury gelding classes, gait classes, bareback classes, pleasure gelding classes and junior equitation classes.

Big O's many awards reflect that versatility. He won First Place in gait classes for geldings at the 1991 Atlantic Regional in Asheville, North Carolina, plus First Place Open Novice Class (bit or bozal), First Place Pole Bending, First Place Open Champagne Class, plus Reserve High Point Horse Junior Exhibitor at the 1991 Rocky Mountain Regionals in Colorado Springs, Colorado. Not to mention a great variety of second, third, and fourth placings.

One ring steward, after seeing Big O at several shows, remarked that if there were an award for the horse that had been ridden the most miles in a show, Big O would surely win.

The biggest obstacle in the life of this great character has been "learning to walk over a green garden hose," jokes Nancy.

"Although Big O has such strength that you can ride him for hours at a time and never feel like you have been riding at all, he is totally trustworthy," says Nancy, who was able to ride in competition with him, and to win, a few months after an accident in which she fractured her pelvis.

"Big O is a dream come true; he's the horse I always longed for as a child," concludes Nancy, whose pretend horse then was a broom with a string around its head.

Perhaps, in his total predictability and trustworthiness, Big O is a bit of Everyman's dream horse come true.

Encobrado RPS

In the summer of 1991, while showing at the Rocky Mountain Regional Championships in Colorado Springs, Colorado, Sam and Nancy Johnson watched the Peruvian Paso stallion Encobrado RPS enter the arena with such presence and arrogance that it took their breath away. At that very moment they knew they were interested in owning this stallion.

Sam, who rode many a mile in his dreams as a child, sitting on a small saddle perched on a stool as he watched television cowboys, says he'll never forget the moment. "Encobrado was literally gliding around the arena, head held high and chest thrust out with arrogance."

It was an equally lucky moment for Encobrado, a solid liver chestnut foaled May 2, 1984, the outstanding son of the National Champion Breeding Stallion, *Lindero, and the mare Amara Del Sol, a daughter of of Sol De Oro CRR.

Encobrado was National Champion Gaited Stallion in 1988 and National Pleasure Champion the same year, as a four-year-old. He'd won many regional awards, including the Rocky Mountain Regional Breeding Stallion Championship in 1991.

However, at the time the Johnsons first saw him, Encobrado was a confused, homeless horse. His original owner went through a ranch liquidation a year before, and his second owner decided to go into another breed and offered him for sale.

The Johnsons started their own ranch in 1989 because of a dream of Nancy's. All she wanted was a quality Peruvian gelding and a run-in shed.

Sam admits to a tendency to overreact and they bought three bred mares. They had no intention of showing or getting into breeding as a business, only to raise a few Peruvians for their own pleasure. Somehow that desire escalated into the building of their own stables in Murfreesboro, Arkansas and the purchase of nine more horses.

Nancy chose the name "El Gato Grande Stables" for their operation because of her love for cats—a large orange cat Dalton is the "barn manager"—and because of the cat-like gait of the Peruvian horse. "Besides," she notes, "the breed needs a little humor."

In two short years, the Johnsons acquired twenty-two Peruvians, and with Encobrado as their senior stallion they are on their way to reaching their goal of breeding the best-gaited Peruvians possible.

"Encobrado," they told me, "has the most muscular, masculine body of any Peruvian stallion. One of his outstanding features is his long, thick flowing mane which falls below his shoulder and his long forelock which goes nearly to his nose. His gait is fluid, with a driving rear end that creates a gait which gives one the sensa-tion of gliding on air.

"Encobrado's personality commands respect," says Sam. "His *brio* or contained energy appears on the verge of exploding. He requires affection and lots of attention. Earlier, without this special attention, he began to mistrust humans," says Sam.

"Since his purchase, we have shown him affection, and he has shown us loyalty and a willingness to please."

Things are still escalating at El Gato Grande Ranch. "The acquisition of Encobrado marks the beginning of our breeding program on a higher level than we had ever dreamed," says Sam.

Amoretta DC

Jeri Kimmel grew up in the late 1940s and 1950s, a fan of all the movie cowboys, with a dream, deep down in her heart, to own a Palomino horse. The pale-maned golden horse of her dreams, however, always seemed elusive, waiting on the far horizon of reality.

"Palominos are not common in the Peruvian Paso breed, and most of those for sale did not fit into our breeding program," says Jeri. "I decided to set a personal goal – to breed my own Palomino. Mare, stallion, gelding – I didn't care!"

Jeri had a head start, since she and her husband Gary have been breeding and showing Peruvian Pasos since 1983. Their 45-acre ranch, Rancho de Colores, is located between Monterey and Salinas, California, in an area the author John Steinbeck called the "pastures of Heaven."

By 1986, Jeri had solidified her image of the perfect horse that she wanted to breed. The Rancho de Colores' stallion HNS Iqueño (now deceased), a beautiful chestnut with flaxen mane and tail imported from Peru, was strong and well-built with lots of refinement, arrogance and *brio*, as well as good gait.

After a nationwide search, Jeri found and bought Mantineza, an older golden Palomino mare. The bloodlines of this Mantequilla daughter were a wonderful match with HNS Iqueño, and she was guaranteed preponent with her color.

"Mantineza and Iqueño did not disappoint us," says Jeri. On April 29, 1987, "Manti" gave the Kimmels a filly that at first appeared to be chestnut. "For a long time we were not sure what her color would be. What a glorious surprise when she eventually was transformed into a deep chocolate color with white mane and tail," says Jeri. "We named the filly Amoretta DC.

"So I had my Palomino – or did I?" asks Jeri, for this stunningly beautiful, exquisitely feminine mare seemed to have a destiny of her own.

Through the skills of their trainer, Dante Mazzi, son of a renowned Peruvian judge, Amoretta won the 1989 Harry Bennett and Medallion de Plata awards for High Point Junior Mare, and the Reserve U.S. National Championship.

"It was clear to me that this would not be my horse after all, at least not for several years," says Jeri. "Amoretta would stay in Dante's hands for competition."

About this time Amoretta took time out to foal a beautiful buckskin colt named Hijo de Reyes, or "Son of Kings", sired by a black stallion named *RyR Galileo.

During Amoretta's last months of pregnancy, when she was too heavy for hard work, Jeri was at last able to have the mare as her own, and they became close friends.

But after weaning her foal, Amoretta went back to work, learning to carry the bit. Her first show in the bit in 1991 was a very important one in Reno, and the judge, Sr. José Risso, one of the best in the world. Captivated by Amoretta, he named her Champion of Champions Breeding Mare. "My baby was queen for a day!" exulted Jeri.

At the last show of the year, the U.S. National Show in Los Angeles, Amoretta carried herself elegantly through her qualifying class and won. In the Championship class, proving herself against more mature and experienced mares from around the country, she triumphed as the 1991 U.S. National Champion Breeding Mare. "What a celebration! What jubilation!" recalls Jeri.

At the time of writing this book, the Kimmels were awaiting Amy's second foal, this one by Lindero, a chestnut stallion.

"Maybe this time I'll get a Palomino for me," Jeri told me wistfully, but resignedly, "because surely Amoretta will not be all mine for many years. Oh yes, I've ridden her, and she is a powerhouse. She is also elegant and beautiful and makes heads turn, but she belongs to many people and lives in the spotlight."

Ramaje

Phil and Nanci Leslie's introduction to the Peruvian Paso stallion Ramaje had a profound affect on their lives.

"This wonderful horse has enabled us to fulfill a number of our special dreams," says Phil. "He was the catalyst for our finding and acquiring Quail Valley Ranch, an event which almost completely changed our lives. His talent, appearance, and disposition have enabled him to win a second Champion of Champions award since we acquired him--a remarkable accomplishment for two neophyte horse people. We have also enjoyed riding in nationally-televised parades in which Ramaje and the other Peruvian Pasos have never failed to please the crowd with their flashy and spirited appearance."

Ramaje, a 15.2 chestnut with flaxen mane and tail, was foaled in the United States, June 6, 1983. He was sired by Real, the first Peruvian Paso Stallion to be named "Laureado" in the United States, the ultimate award for a Peruvian Paso stallion. The award signifies that Real won "Champion of Champions" awards in three national shows. Nothing is known of the lineage of his dam, Princessa De Los Andes, a beautiful Peruvian mare found running wild in a valley in Peru.

Phil and Nanci purchased Ramaje from Joe and Nelma Epple, owners of the JNE Ranch in Dallas, Texas. Ramaje had already won his first Champion of Champions Breeding Award at the Annual Southwest Peruvian Paso Horse Show in Fort Worth, Texas. The extraordinary appearance of this horse and his wonderfully easy-going disposition so impressed Phil and Nanci that they decided to look for some acreage so that they could acquire five more of these wonderful animals. Their inquiries into land ownership led them to a fabulous 124-acre ranch in LaRue, Texas, seventy-four miles southeast of Dallas. (They also maintain a home in Dallas where their business, The Leslie Companies, is located.)

"After we acquired Ramaje, it became apparent that he had two distinct obstacles to overcome," jokes Phil. "Their names were Phil and Nanci Leslie, as we had no previous equestrian training of any kind."

The Peruvian horse, however, is bred with some apparently contradictory traits – the spirited presence or *brio* and an extremely gentle personality – traits which served him well in his new home.

Nanci has now ridden Ramaje in sidesaddle competitions and has performed with the nationally-acclaimed Texas Ladies Aside, a sidesaddle drill team. Ramaje is the only stallion in this ten-horse drill team and performs intricate drill maneuvers alongside mares and geldings. He is also a wonderful trail and endurance horse.

"He is without question the most gentle and most cooperative horse with which we have had the pleasure to be associated," says Phil. "Because of this wonderful combination of qualities, Ramaje is known and loved throughout the southwest Peruvian Paso world."

Ramaje is a unique and outstanding example of the best qualities which have been bred into the bloodlines of the Peruvian Paso for more than 450 years, and as such he truly deserves the tribute paid him in this book.

Exotica

Patricia C. Loewy decided to ride the Peruvian Paso mare, Exotica, her husband's personal riding horse, for the first time on the three-month anniversary of his death. "She was superb for me. Our bond began that day," says Patricia. "Since then, I ride her whenever possible."

Pat and her late husband, Frederick, started their Hacienda de la Esperanza northeast of Santa Rosa, California, after their retirement in 1989.

Pat had ridden very little since her school days. Because of her serious back injuries, she was very attracted to the smooth gait of the Peruvian Paso horses, and in February, 1988, the Loewys purchased their first two mares and a filly.

"One of them Exotica, then seven, was obviously outstanding, with exceptional gait and elegant appearance," says Pat. But due to a recent knee injury, Pat was unable to ride. "My husband took over Exotica for his personal riding horse and shared her only with the most special guests to the ranch," she says.

On May 23, 1989, Exotica foaled a lovely filly, Carlotta, sired by Principe De La Solana. "She was the richest chestnut imaginable with white-white blaze and socks, great conformation and presence from her very first day," says Pat.

Exotica, shown that year with her foal at her side, was always in the ribbons. At a show in Reno (with her foal left in the barn), Bonnie Perica, daughter of the farm trainer, rode Exotica to win the High Point Junior Award of the show.

The event was very special, but also a sad turning point for the Loewys. Upon their return, it became apparent that Pat's husband was not well. He died ten days later, of cancer, without ever leaving the hospital.

"It seemed unfair for him to be taken away from a new lifestyle he was so enjoying. For me, at that time, the horses were my salvation. They were very therapeutic," Pat says.

Pat began taking her horses on day trips to the coastal areas of Bodega Dunes and Point Reyes National Seashore. "These are our favorite rides," she says. "Once we are on the beach, tide permitting, I allow Exotica to set the pace. She loves to be out front and the beach riding suits us both.

"In September, 1991, we started working Exotica for the National Show of the Peruvian Paso Horse Registry of North America in Santa Barbara. To our happy surprise she took second in performance and first in her breeding class. She was also in the ribbons in Amateur to Ride, Ladies to Ride and other classes, placing higher than the 'show horse' I had recently acquired," recalls Pat. "Our junior rider took first place in all of the Junior Classes Thirteen and Under, riding Exotica. Exotica, who loves attention, enjoyed her victory passes."

But the most rewarding experience for Pat came after the 1991 National Show, when she had a chance to share her horses as a healing experience. "Ann, a young woman, friend of a friend, confined to a wheelchair after an illness, came out to see the horses. She'd had a great love for horses while growing up. We arranged for Saturday lessons and I put her on Exotica. The thrill of seeing her ride after putting the wheelchair up to a mounting bench, then boosting her up on the bench and into the saddle defies description," says Pat. "Ann is all smiles and the one-hour lesson easily stretches to two, which even then she is reluctant to end.

"My horses are all show quality but Exotica stands out among the rest. She is my favorite, but they all have distinct personalities and are wonderful in different ways," says Pat. "They have added a dimension to this time of my life that I would not previously have considered possible."

WRR Benjamin

WRR Benjamin had a most rude and violent entry into this world. His dam, Bella Paloma, suddenly panicked in the process of delivering, got up and started running across the pasture. The foal's head, neck and chest had emerged, and the mare began to kick in order to rid herself of the unknown "thing" hanging from her body.

"Poor Benji, he was catapulted into the air, and landed in a heap," says his owner, Susan M. Pascoe, of White Rock Peruvian Paso Horse Ranch in Forney, Texas. "I was in an absolute tizzy. I thought he was dead. I ran to him and tried to 'unravel' him."

Susan took off her jacket and tried as best she could to dry the colt. Then his dam walked over, sniffed at her first foal, licked him, and in a few minutes everything was all right.

"But what happened," continues Susan, "was the foal had immediately bonded with me, creating a special relationship which continues to this day."

Bella Paloma has since delivered several foals in a more sedate fashion.

Benji, no worse for his rocket arrival, grew up without further incident on 100 acres of rolling grasslands, wandering creeks and swan-graced ponds of White Rock.

Now five, he is a 14.3-hand, dark bay gelding and Susan's personal riding horse, as well as a blue ribbon show winner. He is especially attached to her, and answers to his name when she calls him, though he won't let one of the helpers catch him very easily.

Susan shows Benji herself. "There's nothing spectacular about his looks," she says. "He's just a very nice package – a very reliable, very consistent, very willing and extremely even-tempered horse. He's just superb. He weighs 1,100 pounds, and he's an extraordinarily well-balanced horse, which is very unique in this breed, because Peruvian Pasos tend to have better-developed front ends than back ends. His front and his back ends fit together just perfectly," says Susan.

Early in his show career, and while still in the bozal, Benji came in fourth in the Fort Worth Nationals against seventeen horses, says Susan. In 1991, he took first place in Pleasure Gelding at the Lone Star Show in Houston, as well as the Reserve Champion Pleasure Gelding title.

"He's a very, very special horse," says his owner. "He has very good conformation and terrific motion. He has a very nice gait, with perfect timing. In short, what it takes to be a phenomenal Peruvian Paso show horse. He is very close to the quality we want to produce."

Susan and her husband are involved in horses more as a hobby rather than a business - -both are medical doctors – but they are very serious about offering an outstanding, sound family of linebred Peruvian Paso horses.

Susan breaks and trains many of the horses. "Training requires patience and more patience. The process is much like polishing a precious jewel. You do a little every day. A marvelous experience.

"Peruvian Paso training is very much like the training the Lipizzan," Susan explains. "The spirit isn't broken, so the horse is always very perky, very interested in what is going on."

The Peruvian horse stays in the bozal (horse hair hackamore) six months to a year. Then it is graduated to the four reins, after it has learned to collect from the rider's legs and weight, and without any force.

"The bit is only an ornament," says Susan. "In Peru they do some fancy things – sometimes they put ribbons instead of reins on the bit when they show the horse."

As for Benji and White Rock, she says, "We're planning to continue his show career and we want to be in the marketplace as a provider of trained, well-balanced horses."

Antares

Like his astronomical namesake in the constellation of Scorpio, the stallion Antares is a star of the greatest magnitude in the Peruvian Paso breed.

Millions of television viewers have seen this charismatic, mahogany bay stallion in several Tournament of Roses parades.

While his ancestors traveled in their smooth gait across Andean valleys, Antares' kingdom is now the 186-acre Meadow Springs Ranch in Moorpark, California,

where he is the senior stallion. Formerly the thoroughbred farm of Bing Crosby and Lindsay Howard, Meadow Springs Farm is currently owned by premier Paso breeder Vivienne Lundquist.

Antares burst upon the show scene at an early age and set enviable records from the start in both the classic breeding divisions and the performance arena. A decade on the show circuit netted him an impressive thirty-three Champion of Champions, Champion and Reserve Champion titles and High Point Awards, plus seventy-two first place wins.

In the prestigious get-of-sire competition in which three offspring by the same sire compete as a unit, Antares entries have captured the winning blue ribbons an impressive thirty-one times. Offspring wins, both at halter and under saddle, totalled enough points to repeatedly earn Antares the "Sire of the Year" Award presented by the Southern California Peruvian Paso Horse Club. All of which contributes to Antares' standing as one of the first great American-bred foundation sires of the breed.

Genetically, Antares offers a pool of the best bloodlines from Peru. Foaled in California in 1976, his sire, Burlador, was a handsome chestnut stallion imported to the United States in 1965; his dam, Estrellita del Sur, the magnificent Sol de Oro (V) daughter, is still considered by many *aficionados* to be the finest producing mare ever imported to this country.

Commenting on the cross that produced Antares, Meadow Springs Ranch owner, Vivienne Lundquist, says, "This combination contributes beauty, extra strength, and correct conformation to the Meadow Springs genetic pool. Antares seems to be making a major impact in one specific aspect of the Peruvian horse which bears improving – the rear assemblies of our horses. He himself personifies the drive and power for reach and efficiency of forward movement combined with the high action and extreme *termino* so desirable in a show horse.

"He executes his correct and fluid gait with ease, efficiency, and economy of motion, while exhibiting the pride and arrogance so necessary in a great breeding stallion.

"He also radiates an unusual inner quality," Vivienne continues. "Antares' love and respect for the people in his life is uncanny. His foals reflect this special quality. Our trainers all comment that his youngsters are very intelligent, eager to learn and use their abundant *brio* in an energetic yet easily trainable way.

"For me, the great superstar Antares stands at the forefront of Meadow Springs Ranch's contribution to the Peruvian Paso breed," she concludes. "His legacy will stand virtually unrivaled in the breed's 'History Book of the Future' in the United States."

Britania MSR

Britania MSR's story is one of the most touching accounts of equine courage I have ever come across, since she had to battle for her life from its very beginning.

Today she is perfect, the outstanding daughter of Antares, a very famous stallion profiled elsewhere in this book. She is a very beautiful, rich liver chestnut, extremely elegant with big, beautiful dark velvet eyes. She is also a great performance mare.

"In the Peruvian Paso breed, where the wonderfully smooth and fancy gait is everything, the mare Britania MSR has one of the most phenomenal and exciting gaits ever seen in the show ring," says Vivienne Lundquist, owner of Meadow Springs Ranch in Moorpark, California, and one of the most respected breeders in the Peruvian Paso breed for almost twenty years. "Her timing is flawless. The footfall of her gait is very exciting to listen to. You can hear her coming down the road with a perfect cadence – like the finest drum tattoo of a British marching band."

But when this great mare was foaled on February 19, 1982, there was a little lump on her hip. At first the veterinarian wasn't sure if the filly would survive surgery to remove the growth. But major surgery had to be performed and she came through it better than anyone had hoped. At first it was touch and go and then she started getting better. Then the growth returned and Britania had to have surgery again five days later. (When the growth was discovered, one veterinarian's opinion was that it might have been the site where a twin had started to develop on the embryo of the other foal, and then was walled off.)

No one had any hope for the little filly, but she pulled through the second surgery. It was a very special moment for Vivienne when little Britania came out of the anesthetic after the second surgery and made a faint nickering sound. "Just to let us all know that she hadn't given up; so we didn't either."

Vivienne nursed the filly around the clock after both surgeries. Britania came out of the experience with a long scar on her right hip, but grew up to become one of the most beautiful and exceptional mares in the breed, winning many ribbons on her way to becoming United States National Champion Junior Mare twice and later winning the title of Champion of Champions Mare in the Breeding Division.

Another result of her early experience is that Britania is very closely bonded with Vivienne, remembering how she nursed her around the clock while she was fighting for her life in those fragile first days.

And as if she appreciates being alive, Britania hates to be kept in a barn. Instead, she loves the feel of sunlight. Even in the pouring rain, she will stand outdoors as though constantly celebrating life, exhilarated by experiencing the wind and the rain on her beautiful body.

Trained and ridden part of the time by Andres Salinas, one of the top trainers in the breed, Britania has an enviable show record. Given her initial struggle, Vivienne was most excited and gratified when Britania took the show ring by storm. "She has done it all, from a baby not expected to live to Junior Mare Championship through Best Bozal in Show titles, all the way to the top, to Champion of Champions Breeding Mare of the Show, always going forward and gathering momentum as she won everything in sight. She holds fifteen titles, four high-point awards and twenty-seven first place blue ribbons. She has also participated in twenty-one first place get-of-sire competitions, winning the blue ribbons with two other Antares-sired offspring for their famous sire.

The personification of a professional breeder, Vivienne, a woman of great vitality and good looks and a long time friend, shows most of her horses herself and rides for pleasure as well. To date her 186-acre Meadow Springs Ranch has bred over ninety champions which have won over 400 titles and awards, but one of the farm's greatest stars remains Britania.

*Labriego

"We had a friend who said, 'Come see this horse I have.' It happened to be a Palomino Peruvian Paso gelding," says Alice Nunes, a partner with Dorothy Owens in Poso Creek Ranch of Bakersfield, California.

"Shortly after setting eyes on the gelding, we bought him. And then we bought a mare. And now we have thirty-five horses. Isn't that how farms usually get started?" Alice asks goodhumoredly.

King of the hill and foundation stallion at Poso Creek is *Labriego, a chestnut stallion both Alice and Dorothy describe as "gorgeous and very macho."

"He loves to talk to his mares," says Dorothy. "Like other Peruvian Paso horses, he is sweet-tempered and people loving. Much like having a big dog with you.

"But he also has plenty of *brio*. He appears as though he will explode at any moment. He has an excessive amount of energy, and before he's taken into a class at a show, he must be ridden for thirty to forty minutes."

*Labriego was bred in Peru at the ranch of Alfredo Elias, and foaled March 21, 1978. He carries Southern blood through both his sire and his dam, Rosita.

"*Labriego is one of the few remaining sons of the legendary stallion Regional, winner of the highest honor Peru awards to stallions, the title of Champion of Champions Stallion at the Peruvian National Show, which made him 'Laureado' there. Regional is known for passing *brio* to his get," says Dorothy.

*Labriego's grandsire, Sol de Oro (V), is considered the most important Peruvian Paso sire in modern history. Every National Champion of Champions Stallion in Peru since 1961 has carried his blood and, since 1973, every National Champion of Champions in the United States has his blood in his veins.

*Labriego was imported from Peru to the United States in 1981, by Vivienne Lundquist of Meadow Springs Farm in California.

"We were always attracted to *Labriego because of his beauty, presence, arrogance, *brio* and gait," says Dorothy. "He is an exciting horse to ride and to watch perform. His many championships and Champion of Champions Awards attest to his show career.

"*Labriego has a quality that is undefinable," adds Dorothy. "Once we saw *Labriego, the experience became a haunting melody that continues to run through your mind, one you can never quite forget. After seeing *Labriego, all other stallions were compared to him and, in our eyes, none measured up to him.

"No matter how many horses were in the show arena when *Labriego entered, all eyes turned to him, such was his presence. The extreme action of his gait only added to the excitement of watching him. Even though he appears to be fiery and explosive, he is a joy to work with. Always very calm and does what is asked of him.

"We were thrilled in 1985, when *Labriego was seven, and we unexpectedly had the opportunity to purchase him.", says Dorothy.

Fortunately, *Labriego had already established his show record by this time, as he had a serious accident while being conditioned in a swimming pool. "He fell getting out of the pool and injured his suspensory ligaments, but he is sound enough to breed," says Dorothy. "He also would never quit in the show ring," she adds, "and so, out of love, he must be protected from his own drive to win."

Though his own show career was cut short, the *Labriego get continue to prove his legacy in the show arena. *Labriego has sired many Junior Champions, Champions, and Champions of Champions, says Dorothy.

"Having *Labriego as our chief sire gives us the opportunity to have one of the great bloodlines from Peru in our breeding program. He has helped Poso Creek establish its reputation for breeding and showing quality horses and to become recognized by the most distinguished breeders in Peru as one of the top ranches in the breed," Dorothy concludes.

Marisa Mia PCR

Marisa Mia PCR is considered a prima ballerina of the Peruvian Paso horse world.

"It has been said of her that to watch her move will take your breath away," says Dorothy Owens, owner and breeder. "She just floats in the show ring, her bay body gleaming, her long mane and tail flowing, her front legs lifted high, her toes pointed, her arrogance and *brio* showing – sheer equine poetry in motion."

The 14.2 bay mare was only four years of age when she won the United States National Championship, then went on to be crowned United States Champion of Champions, competing in very large classes.

Marisa was foaled March 23, 1984 at Poso Creek Ranch in Bakersfield, California, co-owned by partners Dorothy Owens and Alice Nunes. Her terpsichorean talents come to her naturally, for her sire is the famous Antares, a winner of many championships, a Champion of Champions himself and the sire of many champions. Her grandsire is the well-known Burladero; her grandam, Estrellita Del Sur, a show ring legend and Laureada in the United States.

Marisa's dam is Mechita PCR, one of the best producers at Poso Creek Ranch. Mechita's sire Erial, was named the best gaited horse in the National Show in Peru, as was her grandsire, Solidario. Mechita PCR's dam, Lecuma, is considered by many to be the best of Solidario's offspring. "Solidario is best-known for his gait and for passing along that trait to his get," says Dorothy.

For the first few years of her life, Marisa was allowed to play and grow in the pastures. At the age of three, her saddle training began. At our ranch, all training moves at a slow, easy pace that the horse is comfortable with," says Dorothy. "With Marisa, this was a necessity, because of her high spirits and *brio*."

Marisa "never quits, keeps going," adds Dorothy.

Her partner Alice Nunes describes Marisa as "very elegant, very proud of herself, and very feminine."

Both Dorothy and Alice are attracted to the Peruvian Paso breed because these horses love people. "Marisa's not attached to anyone, however. "She's a little standoffish," says Dorothy. "She's actually very gentle, but she looks as though she might explode anytime."

Marisa was first shown in the bozal at a few shows in 1987. She finished that first year of showing at the United States National Show by placing third in a large bozal class. The next year, Marisa competed very successfully in bit classes, and won her Champion of Champions title.

For Marisa's first breeding, the legendary stallion AV Sol de Paijan (Laureado in Peru) was chosen.

"The stallion has been recognized as the best sire in Peru for the past ten years. The result of this breeding was a colt named Aristo," says Dorothy. "We think Aristo has the potential to carry on the legacy of his dam and sire and that he will be a great champion and noted sire.

"Visitors to the ranch are all drawn to Aristo. Peruvian Paso breeders who have visitied the ranch believe Aristo is outstanding. We are anxiously awaiting Marisa's next foal.

"Marisa Mia PCR is not only a great beauty, a great competitor and a great champion, but is also a great producer; one who is a wonderful asset to our Poso Creek Ranch breeding program," says Dorothy. "With all of her talents and traits, Marisa Mia PCR is truly a Champion of Champions!"

Santisima P.R.

Denise Messina was picked out as her future owner by the Peruvian Paso mare Santisima when the latter was only five days old.

Denise had had three spinal surgeries for injuries sustained in a fall down a flight of stairs. "Steel rods were put in my back, and I was told I could never ride a horse again," she says.

Trying to ride the trot or canter of the Quarter Horse or Thoroughbred she then owned would have been injurious, she adds. After reading an article about Peruvian Pasos, Denise, a Staten Islander, visited Phoenix Ranch in central New York State.

"Santisima was five days old, running around in pasture," she says. "She left her dam and came flying over to me just to say 'Hi, how are you?'" Denise remembers with delight.

Denise liked the filly "because of her arrogance," which she still has.

"I pointed to Santisima and said, 'I'd like to buy her.'" Sonja Wirth, owner of Phoenix Ranch, told Denise, "Nobody buys a horse at five days old."

Sonja tried further to dissuade Denise by telling her to pick a filly, if that's what she wanted, but one that didn't have all the white markings Santisima has. Peruvian Paso judges do not like a lot of white markings on a show horse, and the filly had four white stockings and a white star and strip the length of her face.

But Denise did not budge, and Sonja promised her the filly would not be sold to anyone else and that she would have first priority when she was weaned.

"I said I was going to own her, and she worked out exactly the way I thought she would," Denise recalls.

When Santisima, a liver chestnut foaled March 3, 1988 (by Phoenix Ranch's herd sire, Sagrado and out of AF Peseta) was four months old, Sonja sent Denise a videotape of her. "She was absolutely gorgeous!" says Denise. She saw the filly again at the Northeast Peruvian Paso Show in Bloomsburg, Pennsylvania, when she was five months old, and bought her.

Santisima has been shown twice; she came in second at the Bloomsburg Show, and in 1991 at the age of three she won the bozal class in Indianapolis in an extremely large class of twenty-two horses.

"It is unusual for a horse with all that white to have beaten all those horses. The show uses a three-judge system so all three judges had to pick her," says Denise. Santisima's other merits obviously outweighed the white in the judges' mind.

"This horse has a great deal of her sire in her," adds Denise. "He gives his offspring of himself and even more. He has great arrogance and presence in the show ring.

"Santisima is sweet as can be, very docile. And when you put the saddle on, the *brio* and arrogance come out. She will go and go and go till her heart gives out, a trait observed in Sagrado."

Santisima has now been bred to RYR Insolida, a solid black and a son of RYR Galileo, a famous Peruvian Paso stallion owned by Raul and Barbara Risso.

"My plans are to show Santisima in the future, perhaps showing the mare and foal together in August 1992," says Denise, who grew up in Brooklyn where there were very few horses beyond the produce peddler's wagon horse.

Denise still rides her Peruvian Paso gelding, Condor, taking him out on two-hour trail rides and having no negative effects on her spine.

"I am dying to ride Santisima," she says. "I've only been on her a few times so as not to interfere with her show training, but I've tried her a few times at shows. Like riding a cloud. I've ridden her sire and I've ridden her. Both are like sitting on our couch and commanding 'Just float me away!'"

*MVM Sagrado

"*MVM Sagrado was bought by me by accident," says Sonja Wirth of Phoenix Ranch, twenty-eight miles north of Ithaca in the Finger Lake region of central New York state. "I went to California to lease two stallions of a particular bloodline. When I arrived, there was this little horse penned up next to a cow."

After asking a few questions, Sonja learned the horse belonged to a man who had gotten himself into a difficult political situation in Peru and was spending some time in jail. She also learned the man had only been able to make partial payment for the horse before he ended up behind bars. "This horse was sitting there in limbo. I didn't know what he was or who he was," says Sonja. "It was romantic instinct, love at first sight. I became so attracted to him I ended up taking him to New York."

Sonja was able to obtain ownership of the "orphaned" horse through another bit of luck. "I knew relatives of the original gentleman who contracted to buy him," she says. "Another person's misfortune was my fortune."

Sagrado himself – "a liver chestnut so liver, he's almost purple," as Sonja says – seemed to have something of a disguise or false identity.

"I thought he was much younger than he was," Sonja says. "I also thought his name was Cimarron." Later on, when she obtained his papers, she learned he was bred by a rather famous breeder in Peru, Miguel Vilches. He was a year older than she believed, foaled November 30, 1983 and his real name was "Sagrado," which means 'sacred one' in Spanish. Most importantly, she says, "I found out he had the exact bloodlines I wanted."

He was linebred to a famous Peruvian Paso horse, Piloto, both on the top and the bottom, and is the grandson of another distinguished stallion, Sol de Pajan.

Sonja was one of the first Peruvian Paso owners and breeders in the United States. She bought her first horse in 1969, from Bud Brown in Arizona, after reading an article in *Western Horseman Magazine*. She now has sixty-five Peruvian Pasos on her farm, with six stallions.

"Sagrado is the senior stallion," she says, "Numero uno."

When Sonja brought Sagrado home, she imagined that he was going to be her personal riding horse. She had lost a mare who played that role in her life the summer she found him. But Sagrado had other ideas.

"He turned out to be quite exceptional. Twice he has won Championships in the breeding divisions at the Northeast Show in Bloomsbury, Pennsylvania, and at the Franklin, Indiana Show in 1988 and 1989," says Sonja. "He has a very photogenic face, with a very soft, big eye. His forte is Zootécnico, which is strictly modeling, be-cause of his excellent conformation, which he throws.

"Most important he throws the gait," adds Sonja. "His oldest daughter Santísima ('very saintly') is also exceptionally well-gaited.

"I've been so fortunate that it turned out this way. I had no idea what I was bringing up," Sonja says. "Sagrado has something that I think we have sort of lost in the United States, and we're working at getting it back. Although he's a very small horse, he's got great extension, reach, as well as good timing and good looks. Extension is something the horses have been lacking awhile and that's one of Sagrado's strong points," says lucky Sonja.

Bartolo

Bartolo's story is "Black Beauty" retold, with a Peruvian Paso as the protagonist.

"Bartolo is probably the most celebrated gelding in all the Peruvian Paso breed," says his present owner, Robert Dale, of Cypress Spring Farm in McKinney, Texas.

"For nearly five years Bartolo was the dominant gelding in the breed. He was the U.S. National Champion Luxury Gelding in the years 1979, 1980, and 1981, and Laureado at the U.S. national level as well as at most major shows. In most shows he would be Champion of Champions Pleasure Gelding as well as Champion of Champions Luxury Gelding. In 1980 he won eleven major championships as well as the U.S. National Show. Under distinguished trainer and rider Juan Gallegos, Bartolo was campaigned harder and longer than any horse before or since. He is a member of the American Association of Owners and Breeders of Peruvian Paso Horses (AAOBPPH) Hall of Fame, and is still remembered for his heart in the ring," adds Robert.

"In 1984 he was sold and dropped out of sight until we stumbled onto him in California in 1988. We were committed to the breed at the time, but had not found a horse that really touched us in a special way. All that changed when the 'old man' was led out for us to see.

"The 15 hand bay with star and socks was thirteen years old and was in pretty bad shape," continues Robert. "He was off his weight, and his legs were in bad condition, but the old flame could still be seen when he was led around for us to look at."

Robert's wife Terri fell in love and had to have him. "Her excuse was that although he had leg problems and was older, he would be an ideal horse for the kids. The fact that she is terribly sentimental and could not stand to see this grand old champion in that condition was not something she would have admitted. She felt that with proper love, and care, he could be nursed back into condition."

Bartolo arrived at the Dales' farm a short while later and assumed command of the place. He was pastured with the mares and young geldings and quickly took over as tribal leader of that group. "He has a bad habit of falling in love and wanting to be with the same mare, and will 'pine' for his 'sweeties' when they are taken away for breeding and foaling. He tolerates the geldings, but will quickly put them in their place if they become too presumptuous," says Robert.

"Terri was certainly right about one thing," he adds, "and that was that Bartolo would teach the girls to ride. Heather and Chelsea were ten and six at the time and took to Bartolo like he had always been part of their lives. They rode him everywhere, at all times, in all kinds of tack, and always had a big time. Generally you could see them going across the pasture bareback with nothing but a halter draped around his neck. On occasion, Heather, the oldest, would ride him without even a halter, just holding onto his mane. He became the horse that everyone wanted to ride on a trail ride, or just around the farm. People always like to see Bartolo when they visit the place.

"There are many who would acclaim Bartolo the greatest show horse of all, if all the variables are considered," continues Robert. "Others talk of his arrogance and pride and heart that kept him going when others would have quit. We, of course, never saw him in those conditions. Yes, we have all the old videos and show records, but I don't know that this is our Bartolo. Our Bartolo is the sweet, gentle old man who resides in the front pasture. He is always ready for a carrot, or a rub or a romp if you demand one. Yet none of us ever lose sight of the fact that he is after all seventeen years old and has had some tough, tough campaigns.

"And so, if sometimes he wants to be haughty and arrogant and ignore us, then we forgive him, and if sometimes he stands alone looking off to a place we can never go, then we understand. After all, just think of the joy and excitement he has to remember."

THE QUARTER HORSE

The modern American Quarter Horse is promoted as "The World's Most Versatile Horse," and the statistics back up that claim.

Gentle-natured but athletic, the Quarter Horse can be found as a top performer in an incredible variety of athletic contests including western and English pleasure, jumping, dressage, calf roping, barrel racing, trail classes, pole bending, reining, cutting, working cow horse, team roping, hunter under saddle, hunter hack, working hunter, chariot racing, stake racing and driving. Along with all of that, the Quarter Horse is still used as a working horse on ranches.

This versatility makes the Quarter Horse one of the world's most popular breeds; more than three million horses from all over the world are registered with the American Quarter Horse Association. There are more than one million Quarter Horse owners in this country, as well as sixty-four other countries, making this the breed enjoyed by more people than any other on earth.

This breed of many uses originated in Colonial America in the early 1600s when it was used primarily for sprint racing because of its quick acceleration and muscular build.

On Sunday afternoons, the town populace would gather on the main street to witness a race between two local favorites. The starter would shoot off a gun, and spectators screamed their encouragement, as most had bets on the outcome. Little more than twenty seconds would pass as the two speedsters ran the quarter mile down the village street. A new champion would reign. Until the next Sunday!

The origins of the Quarter Horse go back farther than Colonial days, to the stallions shipped to the Americas by Spanish explorers and traders. These stallions were crossed with mares that arrived from England in 1611. The cross produced a compact, heavily-muscled horse which could run short distances faster than any other.

As the new country developed and more and more Englishmen arrived, they replaced the quarter mile races with longer distance races which were not suited to the stocky Quarter Horse. With a decreased interest in short distance races, the Quarter Horse began to change from a sporting horse to a working horse.

When the pioneers moved westward, so did the Quarter Horse. In the 1800s, vast cattle ranches stretched across the plains and it was there the breed established its strongest reputation. The Quarter Horse proved to have cow sense, a natural ability to judge the actions of cattle, making it the greatest cattle roundup and trail driving horse in history.

With the approach of the 1900s, mechanization and the settlement of the western states caused a decline in the number and size of the massive cattle ranches. Fewer horses were needed for cattle operations.

In the 1930s, a group of ranchers became concerned that the Quarter Horse breed might not survive. Consequently, in 1939, at the Southwestern Exposition and Fat Stock Show in Fort Worth, Texas, a handful of breeders met to lay the groundwork for an organization to represent and preserve the Quarter Horse.

One year later, representatives from several states and the Republic of Mexico met in Fort Worth to formally establish a registry known as the American Quarter Horse Association. Eight hundred shares of stock were sold at $10 a share to finance the operation. Present Quarter Horse owners and admirers are indebted to these individuals who traced bloodlines and established a strong base for the breed's registry.

Registry founders determined that the Grand Champion Stallion at the 1941 Southwestern Exposition and Fat Stock Show in Fort Worth would be assigned Number 1 in the registry studbook.

Many of the Southwest's top ranches entered their prized stallions in the competition, but it was Wimpy, owned by the King Ranch of Kingsville, Texas, who captured the honor. Sired by Solis, out of the mare Panda, Wimpy's bloodlines trace back to Old Sorrel, Hickory Bill and Peter McCue, three of the most famed foundation sires of the modern Quarter Horse. Foaled in 1935 on the King Ranch, Wimpy became one of the most noted Quarter Horses in the world. He died in 1959, and a statue of him was placed at the entrance to AQHA's international headquarters in Amarillo, Texas, the nerve center for Quarter Horse owners and enthusiasts worldwide.

Tio's Fancy Bikini

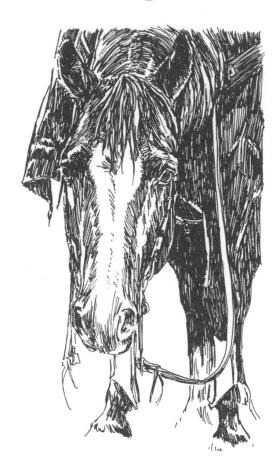

In a barn filled with twenty-four horses of various breeds, including Arabian, Lipizzan, Clydesdale, Thoroughbred, miniature and even a zebra, Tio's Fancy Bikini is a standout, says my friend Joan Embery, ambassadress of the San Diego Zoo, television personality and Alpo spokesperson. "Not many visitors pass by without stopping to admire her," Joan adds. "A people horse with personality plus, she is quick to nicker to anyone approaching her and expects the pampering she always receives."

Joan purchased Tio, a Quarter Horse, in the parking lot of a cutting horse show. She happened to strike up a conversation with a fellow cutter and mentioned she was looking for another horse. After listening to a description of Joan's ideal prospect, the man said he had just what she was looking for inside his trailer. "The mare was of course more money than my husband had agreed to spend, but I liked her the minute she stepped out of the trailer," says Joan.

The 15.2 seven-year-old copper chestnut mare with four white socks and a blaze was prettier than most cutting horses, which are prized more on their "cow sense" than their beauty. Joan had been determined to find one that was both talented and pretty.

"Tio was definitely a looker and her owner said she was equally talented in the cattle pen. He suggested I saddle her up and enter her in one of the remaining classes that day," Joan told me.

"As I entered the herd and pushed forward, the cattle began to peel off and Tio sensed we were about to select a single calf to control, keeping it from returning to the rest of the herd. Her calm, casual demeanor transformed as her muscles tensed in anticipation. Ears forward, eyes riveted on the remaining calf, she began to 'read' its every move. The power and speed as she dropped back on her hindquarters and pivoted to block the calf was awesome. I knew she was exactly the horse I was looking for. In my first year of showing her, she won four silver buckles for me and taught me more about cutting than any trainer. It's a humbling experience to ride a horse that knows its job better than you do."

Those buckles were for the following awards in 1991: Pacific Coast Ladies Reserve Champion, San Diego Cutting Horse Association Non-Pro/Novice Champion, Ladies Champion and $2000 Reserve Champion.

In that first year together, Joan found that "Tio has that rare combination of looks, style and ability that make her a joy to be around."

However, a special bond with one's horse can be an incredible relationship not often assessed until parting becomes a reality, as Joan learned in January, 1992. "I was anxious to start a new show season, to test our talents among the best. To my alarm on our first class in competition, something felt wrong. Tio strained at every move, not able to respond to my cues. I walked out of the show pen and immediately called a veterinarian," Joan said.

"Her heart rate and respiration were extremely elevated and erratic. After treatment, with the cause still unknown, tests were to be run while she rested in her stall. I tended to my other horse in the adjacent stall and returned to find my mare lying on her side, unconscious and unresponsive. I tapped her eyelid with no response and broke into tears as someone approached and asked, 'Is she dead?' I ran for the mobile phone to call the vet. When I returned, I was panicked. I couldn't accept losing her. I realized how totally attached I had become. It was frightening!" The mare must not have been ready to give up either. She miraculously rallied to her feet after being stimulated with massage. The veterinarian and Joan sat with her throughout the night, administering fluids and drugs. When she seemed relatively stable, Joan hauled her home. After a few tense days of further veterinary care, she gradually improved.

"We missed the first two months of shows, but I was so thrilled to just hug my horse and know she was all right. We would be showing again soon," said Joan, for whom the world once again was wearing a smile.

Pecho 2 ("Watermelon John")

As a child, Donna T. Johnson read *Black Beauty* until the covers fell off the book. Now an adult and a talented writer herself, she's lived a friendship with "Watermelon John," a 29-year-old registered Quarter Horse gelding as moving and memorable as that literary classic.

"John is semi-retired these days, and is dignified in his old age, but there's still a spark just beneath the surface," says Donna, whose commercial beef operation in Sarasota, Florida is named Middle Age Spread.

The sorrel with white markings is grizzled now by the years. "But he still has a sly bone and now and then will still try to surprise me with a whole hearted buck or two," says Donna, who claims it was John who "convinced" her to own her own cow-calf commercial operation.

John is the typical old-time Quarter Horse, sired by Poco Pecho; his great grandsire was Poco Bueno. There's a freeze brand on his left hip for breeder John King of Cleburne, Texas. Only 15.1, even today John's powerful hindquarters propel him forward like a bullet.

His nickname was justly earned in his youth during a midnight raid on a watermelon patch in which he and a two-legged culprit fled the scene, leaving their fellow raiders to fend for themselves. He hasn't lost his sweet tooth, having recently devoured a good three-quarters of a watermelon left in the back of a truck.

Donna met up with John when he was thirteen, considered a good age for a roping horse. He had been trained for working cows and for arena roping of steers or calves. She was twenty-eight, learning to ride at a stable where John was used for riding lessons during the week.

Donna bought John shortly thereafter, in 1977, and decided to learn to team rope on him. Her first effort as a total neophyte is the stuff of high comedy.

"Hub Hubbell, my mentor in this endeavor, nodded to the chute man, the steer jumped, John came out of the box as if shot from a cannon. I saw sky, my feet were alongside John's head, the stirrups were flapping and we were off!" Donna remembers.

Though not literally. She was still alive, still on ol' John, who was exactly where he was supposed to be, and she finally roped that steer, although by only one foot and long after the cowboys had stopped timing them.

Donna and John finally became a working team as she became better and better with a rope. "When all was said and done, we were truly one. One mind, one body," she says. For the first two years Donna owned John, she did not miss one day of riding him, even in rain, cold, and humid Florida heat. "I loved him and the challenge of getting to know one another," she says.

"John is his own horse, to be sure. He owes his mind and body to no one, his soul to no one. John does what I ask, simply because he has decided he wants to. Others have ridden him in the arena to work cows and to rope and they have all wondered how I could get him to do what I want."

Beyond the fun they've had together, Donna says it was John who led her down a different path in life than the one she might have taken. "He opened doors and introduced me to people I might never have had the pleasure of knowing," she acknowledges.

When Donna got her first newspaper job, her slot was as a business reporter, a beat that included agriculture. "I gradually made contacts in the world of ranching and farming," she says. "The fact that I owned a horse, could work cattle and was familiar with roping and similar skills helped me to be accepted into what at times could be a very closed world. Soon, some of my best stories came from the world of agricutlure." Donna's column and features became so popular she won third place in the features division of the Florida Society of Newspaper Editors Annual Writing Contest.

And it was John who "convinced" her to own her own cow-calf commercial operation.

"All of these things, events and occurrences I have described lead back to John. He is the center, with all things radiating from him," says Donna.

"My life might have been consumed by a pointless quest for material things, a quest both seductive and subtle, swallowing you before you know you've been swallowed. Instead, John opened the doors to a world designed by God, and led me into a new appreciation of nature, of life itself, and of beauty. I shudder to think that, but for John, I would have missed it all. Someone has said, 'In every true friend is a glimpse of God.' John is my friend."

THE SPANISH BARB

Today's Spanish Barb horse is the result of extensive historic and genetic research, selective breeding, and economic sacrifice by a unique group of owners and breeders.

The equine descendants of the Iberian Barb strongly reflect their ancient ancestry in the substantial bone, conformation and movement inherent in other Iberian breeds, such as the Andalusian and Lusitano, even though five hundred years now separate their lineage. Since the Barb was the root stock from which the Peruvian Paso was developed, there are also distinct similarities in conformation with this breed and, to a lesser degree, with the Paso Fino. Some of these breeds may have longer recorded pedigrees, but none has a longer history than the Spanish Barb.

The blood of today's Spanish Barb comes to us through old Spanish land grant breeders and a handful of western ranchers who came to appreciate the breed for its outstanding disposition, endurance and ability in all types of ranch work, especially working with cattle. Twenty years ago, a small group of people realized it was imperative to preserve what they could of the remaining pure Spanish Barb horses.

The ultimate goal of breeders was to not only save and retain the athletic abilities and acute intelligence of the breed, but to return the horses to the beauty and elegance for which they had been known in centuries past.

However, individuals working with a limited number of horses simply did not have access to the genetic diversity necessary to restore the breed as a whole. An undertaking of that nature required the efforts of a group which could utilize all the existing bloodlines to insure the continued survival and sound expansion of the breed.

With their goal of restoration firmly fixed, the organizers of the Spanish Barb Breeders Association (with headquarters in Lyons, Colorado) carefully chose the best of the remaining horses to begin the program.

Some documentation was available on horses from the old Spanish land grants, but only oral histories existed on the horses that had been continuously bred by the ranchers. Under those circumstances it would have been impossible to establish a standard registry in the beginning of the restoration process, as there were no written pedigrees upon which to rely. The only avenue left to breeders was to begin breeding based on Spanish phenotype. So, the Spanish Barb Registry began as a phenotype registry and later evolved into a blood registry.

The early years were hard. The registry of necessity differed from every other registry in that each foal produced had to meet strict requirements before it could be registered. If several foals out of a particular cross failed inspection, then the parent breeding stock was either mated differently or no longer bred. This worked an economic hardship on some breeders, but it was the only way to achieve authentic restoration. Only the stock which could consistently produce Spanish Barb conformation and type was retained; others were removed from the breeding program as the purity of their genetic heritage became suspect.

Early Iberian Barb horses were never large in terms of height, but were horses of great substance, depth, stamina and agility. The size and conformation of the Spanish Barb remains constant and in that respect the breed has faithfully adhered to the mold of early ancestors.

Today's Spanish Barb stands at an average height of 14.2 hands. The breed is noted for a clean, well-defined head carried on a deep, strong neck which blends smoothly into a long, sloping shoulder. The back is average to short in length, the croup and hip are rounded, with excellent depth and strength to the chest and body. The legs are clean, with short cannon bones, springy pasterns, and substantial bone. The mane and tail are normally long and full. The carriage of these horses suggests the same pride displayed by all Spanish breeds.

The descendants of the original Spanish Barb must still be classified as a rare breed with a small gene pool. The population remains small and expanding the numbers has been a slow, careful process. In 1975 only fifty-six horses were numbered in the SBBA registry, but by 1990 that figure had increased to 326.

In anticipation of future breeding needs, a program to selectively infuse the blood most closely related to the Spanish Barb – that of the non-gaited Iberian breeds and the African Barb – has been incorporated into the association's breeding and registration regulations. The goal is to reinforce the ancient heritage of the breed without altering its original size or conformation.

While the 1970s were devoted almost exclusively to breeding and building the foundations of the SBBA Registry, the 1980s attracted a different type of Spanish Barb enthusiast, one interested in a versatile performance horse. Individuals have chosen various fields of endeavor for themselves and their horses, and from "Tally ho" to "Pas de Deux," the Spanish Barb has excelled in all facets of competition and sport.

Spanish Gambler

"Owning horses is more of a forward-looking venture than anything else I know of, except for having children," says Peggie W. Cash of Afortunada Farm in Lyons, Colorado.

Peg and her husband, Will, and daughter, Julie, certainly got an opportunity to find that out when they acquired the Spanish Barb stallion, Spanish Gambler, a horse that brought them a change of luck.

They first saw the 14.2-hand stallion, foaled May 6, 1977, and coal black except for a white left hind coronet band, on a freezing wet spring day in 1984 at Bob Evans Farms in Ohio. The Cashes had traveled there to help arrange for the Spanish Barb Breeders Association's upcoming show.

"Black horses are scarce among the Spanish breeds...for this reason alone, Spanish Gambler stands out from his peers," says Peg.

The Cashes were instrumental in forming the association when Julie was a teenager. Although they had reluctantly sold their horses a number of years later because of severe financial difficulties, Julie never lost her love of horses, and Will and Peg continued to be in-volved with the breed.

They saw Spanish Gambler again at the Festival of Spanish Horses in the fall of 1987 at Culpeper, Virginia.

"Julie was totally captivated by this relaxed, thoroughly agreeable and attractive stallion who possesses a world of presence, and while her resources were limited at the time, she made up her mind then and there to bring him West," says Peg.

One year and one month later, the Cashes' "Black Stallion" arrived in Colorado, changing their lives. They looked for property that would accommodate them and their horse, then began searching for just the right mares to complement him in order to produce Spanish Barbs that would bring credit to the breed.

Since they were starting all over again with horses they named their small farm, "Afortunada," or "lucky" in Spanish--"Something of a talisman for Gambler and his two ladies, and for the future," says Peg.

On the four occasions when Gambler was shown in competition, he won the following: in 1981, Reserve Champion Performance Horse at the SBBA Annual Show; in 1984, Grand Champion Halter Horse, also at the SBBA Annual Show; in 1987, Open Performance Division Winner at the Festival of Spanish Horses; and in 1988, Second Place Most Classic Spanish Barb; Champion Western Pleasure; and Grand Champion Western Performance Division, all at the SBBA Show.

"Gambler is an extremely sensitive, responsive horse," says Peg. "His gentle behavior around children and his patience with amateur riders are wonderful traits in a stallion, but he does have his quirks. He hates being tied while being groomed, or at any other time, and considers it a challenge to untie any of the various knots we have used. We haven't found one he can't manage to undo. However, Gambler will stand quietly for grooming (if we don't take too long and bore him) or for saddling, if we simply drop the rope.

"One other little quirk that causes both comments and chuckles from others is Gambler's penchant for sucking his tongue whenever he is bored or, in his mind, unjustly chastised. He is like a small child with a pacifier in these instances," Peg adds.

Gambler's most distinguished offspring at this time is a yearling son who appears to have his sire's disposition and intelligence and the conformation that promises a performer. "We all look forward to seeing 'Magic' at maturity," says Peg.

"Spanish Gambler has presented us with the opportunity to get back into breeding, with one of the best Spanish Barb stallions available. To me, horses are a constant source of pleasure and I hope to be surrounded by them and to be closely involved with them for the rest of my life," Peg notes.

Rivendale's Wildfire

Rivendale's Wildfire started earning his name in utero.

"He was a very active fetus, causing his mother great anguish. We could see his hooves pounding her sides from within the womb," says Jim Graziano who, with wife Lynn, breeds, trains and competes top-quality Spanish Barbs on their Rivendale Farm in Platteville, Colorado.

"Our favorite story of Wildfire, which shows his bold nature and indomitable spirit, and which was the basis for selecting his name, goes back to his foaling," Jim told me.

The cream dun Spanish Barb Stallion, the last and possibly the best son of Rawhide, the great permanent foundation sire of his breed, was foaled, unexpectedly at that, on May 9, 1984.

The Grazianos and probably his dam, Tawa Tashena, were just happy that he was finally on the ground. Their veterinarian arrived a few hours after the birth and he, along with Lynn and Jim, boldly entered the stall to provide the little unnamed foal with his first vet check.

Jim held Tawa Tashena. As Lynn and the vet approached the foal, he wheeled around and blasted between them. Lynn and the vet pursued the newborn but were led on a merry chase around the stall.

Finally Lynn managed to grab the foal, prematurely shouting with glee. Undaunted, Wildfire exploded skyward, kicking Lynn in both shins, and virtually bowling the vet over as he rocketed away. Made wary by the foal's unwillingness to cooperate, Lynn and the vet trapped him in a corner of the stall and tackled him as he made his next headlong charge at them. The two managed to wrestle him to the ground, where he lay silently, glaring defiantly at his captors. The panting vet then remarked, "Why are we bothering to check this foal? He is without a doubt the healthiest damn newborn I've ever seen!"

That's about when the name Wildfire occurred to Jim and Lynn as being descriptive of his temperament.

As a youngster, Wildfire was an equine version of Dennis the Menace. When he was three weeks old, the Grazianos took him and his dam out for air and exercise. Wildfire quickly took off through their yard, up to their house, and through their patio. In response to his dam's hysterical whinnies, he bolted to her side by leaping off a retaining wall surrounding one side of the patio.

Having learned their lesson, his owners confined the mare and foal's exercise area to the riding arena where Wildfire, upon seeing Tawa Tashena roll for the first time, proceeded to jump with all four hooves on her now-exposed belly. "Mom was displeased to be used as a trampoline," Jim says dryly.

Wildfire managed to grow up to become a 14.3, handsome macho-looking stallion, a prime example of his breed in conformation, disposition, and athletic ability.

Through loving but firm handling by Jim and Lynn, Wildfire learned to view humans as friends and companions, and he is now a faithful companion who gives his all when Lynn calls upon him.

Nevertheless, he continues to think very highly of himself and believes himself to be "top dog" at the farm.

Though shown on a limited basis, he was named Reserve Halter Champion Stallion at the 1988 Spanish Barb National Horse Show. He is now in training for Western Pleasure and Combined Training competition.

Riding Wildfire is an exciting experience, Jim says. "Wildfire gives you the impression that he has endless energy, that you have harnessed a source of tremendous power, available to you at your command. You have the feeling of utter freedom and invincibility while riding Wildfire."

It was a joyous feeling for me to learn that a horse with Wildfire's spirit exists in real life, not just in fiction. "Wildfire has fulfilled my childhood dream of owning a noble, free-spirited horse who willingly gives his friendship and allegiance to people," Lynn told me.

El Torbellino

All the horses at Aramore Farm in Terry, Mississippi, are special to her, each in its own way, says Jean Walsh, but she decided to pay tribute in this book to her Spanish Barb stallion, El Torbellino, for three reasons. First, his presence on earth is just short of a miracle, since he's cheated death twice; second, he was the first colt foaled on her farm that succeeded in passing the stringent testing qualifying him to stand at stud; and third, as a show horse, he's a legend in his breed.

El Torbellino arrived in the world in 1982 "like some genie emerging from its magic container," says Jean. "One breeds horses with great hope, aspiration, and expectation, but we also know for all the research-supported variables we factor into a given mating, some foals exceed earthly breeding efforts."

And so it was with Torbellino, a 14.2 dun, whose name means "the whirlwind."

"ET," as he is known to his friends, spent his early days living a charmed life, frolicking in his pasture by day and resting in his stall at night. Until one day when he was six months old. While racing with his pasture mates, he looked over his shoulder to check the distance by which he was leading and crashed through a fence.

Jean feared he would bleed to death in her arms before the veterinarian arrived. ET, however, made a remarkable recovery, though he was left badly scarred. Two cosmetic surgeries left only a hairline scar which is hidden by a carefully-fitted halter.

ET was successfully shown in hand for two years, winning many halter championships. But Jean could not forget how close she had come to losing him and did not want to send him out-of-state to the trainer she usually used. Instead she placed him with one four miles away where she could keep an eye on him.

Her premonition was warranted. One day she looked up to see a helper from the training facility speeding down her driveway. He had a speech impediment which was worsened by the excitement. The only two words Jean could understand were *ET* and *vet*.

By the time she got to the training facility the vet was extracting something from ET's throat. A load of hay there had a few bales containing some strange sticky seed husks, and ET was fed some of the bad hay by mistake. He was catatonic and choking to death when the vet got to him.

"Once the crisis was over," says Jean, "the vet turned to me and said, 'This colt must have a guardian angel. Twice we have come so close to losing him.'"

Despite his overworked guardian angel and the early rocky road, all led to a zenith never before achieved nor since surpassed by a modern-day Spanish Barb, says Jean, currently president of the Spanish Barb Breeders' Association, and an inspector for the breed.

After his first two years of competition, ET was inducted into the SBBA Legion of Honor, the youngest horse in the history of the registry to achieve that honor. He also won the breed's Versatility Championship, an honor he holds to the present, having never been defeated in that competition. In 1987, he competed in the Festival of Spanish Horses and swept the breed division championships, completing the festival as the Grand Champion Halter and Grand Champion Performance Horse. In 1989 ET finished the year as the first Supreme Show Champion in the history of the registry.

"Life with ET has never been dull," says Jean, "given his history and what I sometimes call his artistic temperament. He can challenge you to distraction one moment and charm you out of anything you own the next."

In January, 1990, El Torbellino was retired from the show ring. "The past two years have afforded ET and me very special time together," Jean says. "As I watch him at pasture, I have a warm and peaceful feeling that all is well with the world. A *Vuestra Salud*, El Torbellino – to your health!," she concludes, and we can all echo that!

THE SPANISH MUSTANG

The American mustang is the horse that made America.

The story of this breed begins when some of the hardy Andalusian stock which Columbus and later the missionaries, and still later the settlers, brought to America managed to get free. Some of the horses broke lose during military battles or expeditions and joined their wild cousins, greatly enjoying the free life. In time their numbers multiplied until the sound of their hoofs was like the roll of thunder across the plains. In the middle of the last century, Mustangs numbered in the millions, roaming free from the Mexican to the Canadian border.

The Spaniards called these wild ones *mesteños*, meaning strayed or running free. The word was bastardized by English-speaking peoples into the word *mustang* which stands for something as tough and hardy as the breed itself.

Some of the horses became Indian mounts. As soon as Native Americans overcame their fear of the "big dogs" on which the white men rode, and realized it was not necessary to be white to ride such an animal, they began to acquire some for themselves. From the hands of the Indians, the Mustang came into the hands of mountain men, trappers and explorers, and thus helped to forge the new country. Mustangs helped open up the Santa Fe Trail, leading the way for gold seekers, fur traders and the moving caravans of freight to market. On the very roughest segments of the Pony Express route, the Mustang was used as the priority mail deliverer of the day.

Then the tides of history turned, and this great American heritage was threatened by greed. Thousands of mustangs were rounded up to end their lives on the battlefields of the Boer War and World War I. Hundreds of thousands more were slaughtered to manufacture pet food and fertilizer. Ranchers wanted the grasslands for their livestock and treated the Mustangs as a nuisance, killing them by the thousands.

As late as 1925, more than a million mustangs and burros roamed nine western states; this number had dropped to 17,000 in the 1950s. By that time, a demand for canned horsemeat had made killing the mustangs very profitable.

The horrible cruelty to which the Mustangs were subjected galvanized into action a horse lover nicknamed "Wild Horse Annie," Mrs. Velma B. Johnston of Reno, Nevada, in real life. For over a quarter of a century, until she died in 1977, Wild Horse Annie fought to preserve what she believed to be the most beautiful, spirited and inspiring creatures ever to set foot on the grasses of America, the wild Mustangs of the West.

It took Annie seven years but she finally got Congress to pass a law protecting the Mustangs. She was helped by her enlisted army of school children in what came to be called "The Pencil War." They wrote thousands of letters to Washington pleading for the protection of the Mustang.

Lovers of the Mustang have carefully tried to conserve and breed stock with true Spanish ancestry. The Spanish Mustang Registry (the oldest of several registries) was established in 1951 by nine families that didn't want to see the Mustangs vanish. Almost all registered Spanish Mustangs of today trace back to the horses of those nine families.

The standard for Mustang conformation today includes a convex-type head, or ram nose, with eyes that are large and wide-set. The nostrils are large for the size of the head, and the chest cavity is deep. The temperament is quieter than that of ancient ancestors, the Arabian, though they, like the Arabian, are said to have one less rib. Rarely do they attain 15 hands in size, the average being 12.3 to 14 hands. Some have very smooth and syncopated motion in their gaits, much like a small Andalusian.

Immigrants naturally brought their own horses with them, and they too helped make our country grow. But it was these feral descendants of the Spanish horse, manes and tails flying in the wind, that through time have symbolized the romance of early America.

Steens Kiger

Here is a fascinating story of living legends – the story of the Kiger herd, thought to be the most representative band of Spanish Mustangs existing in the wild today.

Kiger Mustangs were discovered in the mid-1970s during a routine gathering by the Bureau of Land Management (Department of the Interior) of wild and free-roaming horses on public lands in southeastern Oregon. During the roundup of an isolated band of horses on the high desert south of Burns, Oregon, government officials realized they had happened across a very different and special kind of horse. Consequently, they introduced the small band into another isolated area on the north end of the Steens Mountain near Kiger Gorge, from which the horses derived the name they bear.

Through the BLM, Rick, Judy and Rob Littleton of Bend, Oregon adopted Steens Kiger, foaled in the spring of 1987 in the wild. "He is a registered Kiger Mustang, with Spanish blood," says Judy Littleton.

"'Mesteno,' the original foundation stallion who still roams free with his Kiger herd, is our stallion's sire. His dam is unknown. We adopted Kiger as a weanling to be the Kiger stud for our ranch. If it weren't for him, we would not have all the horses we have today at our ranch. Because of Kiger, we are directing all our time and money to increase our own herd and to educate the public on these horses' existence in the wild and in captivity.

"Kiger Mustang Ranch was founded in 1987 with the one stallion and three mares. Today we have forty-plus horses for the purpose of introducing the Kiger Mustang to the world," says Judy.

Dun in color, Steens Kiger bears the distinct characteristics of the dun factor, which Judy explains refers to the zebra striping of the knees and hocks, dorsal stripe, outlined ears (the top one-third of the back of the ear is darker than the rest of the body color), fawn color inside the ears, and multi-colored mane and tail.

"Kiger is not only special to the Littleton family but to everyone who has met him," continues Judy. "Coming from the wild, he has very strong herding instincts. We were concerned about his well-being, but he has favorably made the transition from the wild to captivity. His physical attributes, personality and his distinctive relationship with people make him stand out among all horses. Kiger seems to have a power over everyone in our family and the people who have met him. There is a special aura about him," she observes.

"The most memorable moment we remember occurred when we took him back to Steens Mountain, where he came from. A special dedication ceremony, with a bronze plaque to be mounted there, honored the Kiger Mustangs. ABC Special Events with commentator Pat Wilkins was there to cover the proceedings. The Chief of the Division of Wild Horses and Burros from the BLM made a special trip to Oregon in honor of the occasion and was very proud of the accomplishments of the wild horse program in Oregon. It was a special moment when Kiger was led back to the land where he once roamed free. We realized his destiny was now in our hands.

"Our stallion has given us offspring that are sought after throughout the world," Judy adds. "On March 21, 1991, Mamba Productions of Paris, France came to our ranch to film Kiger and his herd for a television special that will be aired in Europe. Through Kiger, we have met people from all walks of life, people who are as intrigued as we are with this special horse.

"Through Kiger, we are inspired to commit to continue to tell the world of this rare breed, to pursue the preservation of Kiger Mustangs in the wild, and to breed them in captivity so as to continue their bloodlines.

"Our family history has been dominated by Kiger, and now we can see a dream coming true for all of us."

Mustano

Mustano is one of the most fascinating horses in this book, a true wild Mustang who represents a rare link to the past.

Robin Keller, the person who now shares Mustano's life – for one hesitates to say "owner" when dealing with so regally autonomous a horse – believes Mustano and the other horses she raises on her Laguna Seca, California ranch are among the few direct descendants of the horses Columbus brought with him to the New World.

Foaled about 1974, 14.2 hands, a gorgeous black-gold buckskin with an abundant mane and tail, Mustano looks as though he could have stepped down from a sixteenth century Velasquez painting.

"Spanish Mustang in phenotype, his blood work shows up several rare markers, most of which indicate Andalusian ancestry," says Robin.

Mustano was gathered from the open range on the California/Nevada border in February 1985, which is when Robin first saw him. He was held in the Susanville Bureau of Land Management pens in Northern California. He was the only senior stallion in the herd of twenty-two individuals, the rest mares and foals. Years

later, Robin learned cowboys tried to ride Mustano and failing, shipped him to Cottonwood to the livestock yards to be sold by the pound for slaughter. Unable to attend the sale herself, Robin sent a friend to bid on Mustano for her. The friend purchased Mustano, his lead mare, and several of his band of offspring from the slaughter yard.

"It is fair to say that we have had considerable impact on each other's lives," says Robin. "I saved his and he changed the whole focus of mine. After his capture, Mustano's life was upside down. All he had known was taken from him – his independence, his job and his freedom. All was denied him after ten wild years. It was clear he had to adapt or die."

Robin, who shares my fascination with equine social behavior, deeply felt the responsibility for Mustano's life and the quality of that life when it had been so altered in ways almost too immeasurable and profound for humans to really understand. "Few, if any of us, have ever known such freedom," says Robin. "It wasn't my task just to help him try to adapt to new surroundings, but to grant him self-esteem and to replace his noble position in a world of confinement, a world void of his subjects and his realm.

"Due to his wild beginnings, he was approachable only by his standards," she says. "He visits with me voluntarily and I truly believe he considers me a friend.

"Mustano's personality is deep, sensitive, complete, confident and just," she says. "He is willing to attempt to comply with any fair request. For someone who used to make all the requests, this is quite a statement. He is always vigilant, totally aware of his surroundings, and he is a great band or herd manager, overseeing each individual with love and care."

Mustano's unique qualities brought him to the attention of Dr. Phil Sponenburg of Virginia, who found him rare, not only because it is highly unusual to find a true Spanish horse on the range today, but also because of the stallion's color. Dr. Sponenburg, a scientist who has written a book on equine color, has seen only one other horse close to Mustano's black-gold color. All of which makes Mustano an important horse for breeding.

Because of Mustano, Robin's focus of horse involvement has changed radically – from the horse show world to developing her Wild Horse Discovery Center which features wild horses with special cultural, historical and genetic values. As Robin was in the process of developing this Center, she was notified of a rare find in Arizona: horses that had been isolated on a ranch for a very long time, and which had come from the Spanish Mission Chain – the Wilbur Cruce horses. That story is told on the following page through Francisco, Robin's other stallion.

Francisco

"While in pursuit of appropriate Spanish-type mares for Mustano, the herd of Wilbur Cruce horses was brought to my attention by Dr. Phil Sponenberg and Marye Anne Thompson, breeder of the Cerbat Spanish horses in Arizona," says Robin Keller of Carmel, California. In July 1990, Robin was able to obtain eighteen horses from the Cruce herd including five stallions, nine mares and a couple of youngsters.

Again these wild horses' lives were turned around, especially that of the Paint stallion, Francisco, as he was the premier leader of all the bands on the ranch. He alone left the gathering process totally unscathed. "He was extremely solitary and formidable, separate from the rest," says Robin. "For him to relinquish his position and his authority was very hard.

"My first strong memories of this horse are of an aloof individual who denied everyone interaction of any kind. He would not even recognize you with his eyes (one blue, one marble). A distant resistance.

"He spiraled into a very deep depression the first two months," she adds. "At times he looked as though he was fading away emotionally. He would reject all our efforts to be friendly, to offer him gestures of goodwill or to share our company in any way."

Robin saw that he was uniquely beautiful. Foaled on the Wilbur Cruce Ranch in Arivaca, Arizona in about 1982, he was 15.2 hands high, an overo roan sabino liver chestnut Medicine Hat Paint.

"His ancestors were purchased from the Mission Chain, Mission Dolores, in Magadalena, Mexico. He represents sixteenth-century Spanish horse genetics. He has been confined all his life on the ranch, as were the other members of his herd, for generations. He is not a feral horse, but a pure Spanish horse, descended from the original bloodlines brought over by the Conquistadors," says Robin.

"This horse's personality appears to be a contradiction," Robin continues. "His composed exterior hides the warmth and depth of a loving, care-taking individual. He is a family man in every way. He is a nurturing, loving partner to each mare, his courtships are lengthy and complete according to her desires and he is a doting father. He plays boisterously but patiently with the colts, endearingly and nurturingly with the fillies. He must be coaxed to interact or display himself, except when he is being the nurturing family man."

The special part about Robin's own relationship with Francisco is that "he accepts me as his own and I am free to interact with him and his band at any time, under any circumstances."

After approximately six months of ground work and ground socializing, including being tacked and given the foundation for riding, and with thirty days of actual saddle time, Francisco's education has reached a level where a rider can work cattle from him, rope steers and dally. After approximately thirty days ranch work, Francisco was returned to the breeding program at Robin's farm.

"The offspring he has sired are tractable, bright, sensible, very athletic and all colorful," says Robin. They perform liberty work at her Wild Horse Discovery Center.

"As with Mustano, this horse creates dreams — dreams of another level of understanding, compassion and success. A success in our helping one another to make the world a better place," says Robin.

"As we all strive to become wiser and better-educated, let us not forget the wisdom and the education that these wild species have learned through the art of survival. By studying these societies, we are allowed to witness the one constant in life, Mother Nature, as a harsh ruler, generally with ways to bring things back to balance. Perhaps by studying a society such as that of the wild horses, we will better find the balance of life," says the already-wise Robin.

Choctaw Sun Dance

In 1991, a bridge in the Kisatchie National Forest nearly cost Choctaw Sun Dance his life. The bridge was constructed of one-by-sixes treated with creosote for survival in the Louisiana rain forest, and Vickie Ives Speir's stallion was stuck between its boards. His little hooves, greased with slippery clay, slid between the boards—one hind leg to the fetlock, the other to mid-cannon—and he just sat down gently like a dog. He struggled only once, but when he did, he fell off the side of the bridge, dangling by his imprisoned hind legs with his nostrils below the water line in the flowing creek.

For nearly an hour, Vickie held his head out of the creek to keep him from drowning, before rescuers were able to ride to get tools, and to pull up enough boards to free Dance.

"God's hand and his Spanish courage held him until he fell free," Vickie recalls today. "If he had struggled he would have fractured both hind legs and been destroyed right there."

Perhaps the Great Spirit spared Choctaw Sun Dance for his rarity—he possesses the rarest combination of Mustang color genes in existence, according to Vickie. Choctaw Sun Dance, now eleven years old, 14.2 hands, and about 800 pounds, is a red roan Medicine Hat Appaloosa stallion with blood-sweating, lightning strikes, and parti-colored eyes. "He is the color of clouds, grey-silvered with the distant storm; he is the color of lightning in an early dawn sky; his eyes contain all the sky and all the earth and the place where they meet; he walks on ivory hooves and wears the flecks of the spotted eagle on his hips," Vickie has written in a poem about him.

He was bred by Nanci Falley, AIHR president, on her Rancho San Francisco at Lockhart, Texas. She had crossed the leggy and elegant Choctaw Ghost Dancer, a grey overo, with the chunky and snorty little Rosario, a red roan Appaloosa.

In 1981, when Dance shed his foal coat, white hairs began to appear throughout his red paint spots. Vickie had driven to Lockhart to see him, pulling a horse trailer even though she had promised herself that she would not bring the yearling colt home unless he was a stallion prospect. "The long, clean legs, the smooth, floating trot and the magic parti-colored eyes that flashed like cat's eye marbles in the central Texas sun said things to me that rivaled or even surpassed the rare color," she says. "Besides, my dad had taught me that a good horse can't be the wrong color," she adds.

She gambled that his coat would not gray out completely, and won. The roan worked its metamorphosis. The white hairs sprinkled through all the paint spots but not the Appaloosa spots. His mane became white, black and silver. The dark stockings of the latent bay darkened three legs so that his lightning strikes shone like ragged ribbons. When he was a two-year-old, the bloodsweating began to appear, running down his sides from the faint road spots and the roaning that traced his dorsal stripe.

Registered with the Spanish Mustang Registry, the Southwest Spanish Mustang Registry, the American Indian Horse Registry, and the North American Mustang Association and Registry, Dance has more awards than any other Mustang alive today.

He is the Spanish Mustang Registry's only Grande Conquistador stallion, with additional Conquistador awards in Show and Games; Horse of the Year Awards in Show, Games, and Competitive Trail; winner of the AIHR Hall of Fame and Supreme Hall of Fame Awards; and the American Indian Horse Registry's Premier Sire #1.

But most importantly, "This magic horse has changed my life and the direction of our breeding farm. Karma Farms (in Marshall, Texas) originally bred Quarter Horses and Appaloosas," says Vickie. "Today we breed Spanish Mustangs and American Indian Horses exclusively. The Plains Indians believed that the Medicine Hat horse made his rider invulnerable in battle and in the hunt. My Medicine Hat has made Karma Farms one of the best names in the annals of the Spanish Mustang."

Choctaw Star

Who hasn't had childhood fantasies of their own Indian pony, a pony splashed with spots a leopard could envy, wild as the winter wind, but a loyal friend to the one who tames him with love?

Leana Westergaard has been lucky to live the fantasy with Choctaw Star, who is registered with both the American Indian Horse Registry and the Spanish Mustang Registry.

Foaled on April 21, 1971, in the Kiamichi Mountains of the Old Choctaw Nation in southwest Oklahoma, Star was raised by R.R. Crisp, a Choctaw Indian breeder of authentic Choctaw Indian horses for seventy-five years.

A clear bay in color, she has roan hairs widely dispersed through her coat, accented by a "mealy nose" and by her famous star, usually hidden beneath a forelock which falls to her nostrils. She also has black-tipped ears, a black mustache, and yellow flanks and britches, and she carries a large "45" brand on her left shoulder, for Leana's "45 Outfit" in Waskom, Texas. Star's very small, almost non-existent chestnuts are also characteristic of her ancestry. Round cannon bones and a short back, typical of her breed, help give Star her tough reputation, and a well-earned one at that.

In October, 1983, Choctaw Star became the first Mustang to earn the 1000-Mile Award in the North American Trail Ride Conference, Inc. Through all the conditioning and competing, from Padre Island in the Gulf of Mexico to blistering 102-degree July trails in central Oklahoma, Star remained unblemished, finishing 1000 competitive miles with legs as sound as the day she began.

Leana's shelves and walls display many trophies, but the 600-Mile Jubilee Overlanders Ride in the fall of 1985, commemorating the 150th birthdays of South Australia and Texas, "is still our most treasured accomplishment, our ultimate dream come true," she says. Along with Kiamichi Wildfire, her trusty grey paint gelding companion, Star, traveled from the Alamo in San Antonio, Texas (Leana's birthplace), to Fort Leaton, Presidio, Texas, in twenty-six days, with a total of ninety-two consistent miles under saddle for Star on the most rugged stretch.

Gentle but spirited when fired up, Star has inherited the homing instinct common in the Spanish cowpony, says Leana. She had a reputation for swimming the Little River and going back to her home range or *querencia* in the heart of the Old Choctaw Nation whenever she could escape from her first owners. "Like the Indian who returns time and again to his ancestral home, Star was strongly attached to the ranges of her forebears," says Leana.

Leana bought her as a bedraggled and undernourished three-year-old raising a large colt. Leana had to travel quickly to pick her up on very short notice to keep her from escaping to her *querencia* again.

Once bonded to her new partner, however, Star has always stayed close on the trail. Once when her halter gave way, she slept through the night in a strange campground lying down outside the door of Leana's tent.

Star has a long list of other firsts to her name, including the AIHR's first Hall of Fame Award (200 versatility points), followed by the first AIHR Supreme Hall of Fame Award (1,000 versatility points).

A tribute to the hardiness and intelligence of her now rare breed, Choctaw Star "has shown a lot of people what a real Mustang looks like and what it can do," says Leana. She has been featured three times in the All-Breed Issues of *Western Horseman*.

"Drawn to the Mustang because of its unique heritage and traits, along with the rarity of the breed, I have had every dream fulfilled," says Leana.

"Whenever travails surround me, all I ever have to do is swing up on the back of my horse to be carried above life's cares and woes, corraling in my mind just what horses have meant in my life. Tragedy is no match for a couple of soft brown eyes and the feel of warm horsehair between my fingers. A long, flowing mane can soak up a lot of tears. Sharing my little sorrows and my happiest moments, my horses have always been there for me."

THE SWEDISH WARMBLOOD

Great elegance, combined with effective gaits, jumping ability, a positive attitude and the ability to absorb training, has made the Swedish Warmblood highly regarded as a performance horse both in the United States and Europe.

Unlike many of the other Warmblood breeds, Swedish riding horses did not evolve from heavier agricultural types. The main objective of the Swedish breeding program has always been to produce light riding horses, initially to mount the Swedish cavalry, and more recently, to create a horse ideal for dressage, show jumping, eventing and driving. One difference, however, is that the modern Swedish Warmblood is larger than the cavalry horse of the 1800s.

Riding is the second most popular sport for young people in Sweden today, leading to a growing demand for high quality horses. In 1989, just over 7,000 Warmblood mares were covered in Sweden in contrast to about 2,000 in 1970.

Swedish Warmbloods have had an open studbook, maintained since 1812, allowing the introduction of selected stallions and mares from other countries, including Germany, France and England. There is now an exchange of breeding horses between Holland and Sweden, helping to bring new desirable characteristics to the breed. However, four out of five stallions in the current Swedish Warmblood breeding program are in Sweden. Imports are mainly made to introduce more international show-jumper blood into the breed. Thoroughbreds are also important in the breeding program. Currently about twenty Thoroughbred stallions are licensed to serve Swedish Warmblood mares, and in the pedigree of many top dressage Warmbloods, the second or third dam or sire is often a Thoroughbred.

Swedish horses are particularly known for their success in the dressage arena. They have been medalists in dressage in every equestrian Olympic Games since their foundation in 1912.

Zorn and Garrant, two of the four stallions honored by the United States Dressage Federation for the success of their offspring in the 1990 Horse of the Year Awards, are Swedish.

Zorn's success with rider Dennis Callin at the international level is well known to dressage enthusiasts. Juvel is another well-known Swedish performer who competed in Europe under Robert Dover and was a member of the 1988 Olympic dressage team. Swedish horses, in fact made up twenty percent of the dressage horses competing in the 1988 Olympic Games.

Gaugin de Lully ridden by Christine Stuckelburger, considered the world's top equestrienne, won the individual bronze medal in Seoul, and helped win the silver medal for the Swiss team. The gold medal-winning Germany team counted one Swedish Warmblood, Courage, ridden by Ann-Katrine Lindsenhoff. The bronze medal-winning team, Canada, included two Swedish Warmbloods.

Despite the fact there is no official North American organization controlling breeding and registration of horses, the Swedish Warmblood is a popular sport horse in this country. Control remains within the auspices of the Swedish Warmblood Association headquartered in Flyinge, Sweden. The breeding of horses in Sweden has been under rigid government control since 1874. It's only been since 1985 that breeders' organizations have taken over the responsibility of regulation, and even now, approval from the Swedish government is required. Tours of the United States by an inspection team from Sweden occur every two years. The evaluators travel across the country to examine foals, mares and stallions for approval and branding.

Entheos

The five-year-old Swedish Warmblood stallion Entheos is just starting out on a show career, which given his background and talents promises to be an exceptional one.

His first time in a dressage ring, Entheos scored an impressive 72.50%. He won top honors at the 1990 Dressage at Devon Show and made a very successful debut this past winter during the Florida show season under the training of Betsy Steiner, a world class competitor from Illinois.

The 16.2 bay, whose name means "enthusiasm" in Greek, certainly has an owner filled with that quality. Kathy Klammer of Summerfield Farm in Aurora, Illinois says, "His breathtaking movements and elegance will enhance his abilities to become a world class dressage horse, which is the direction of his career. Entheos also seems to show a very natural ability in jumping. After only being schooled eight times, he completed his jumping courses for the eventing portion of his stallion approval, stopping at nothing. This diversity in talent gives him the potential to become a world class sire of remarkable Swedish Warmblood horses."

Entheos, foaled April 20, 1987, comes from a line of world class equine athletes. His sire Elektron was long-listed for the 1984 Olympic Games. His grandsire Gaspari represented Sweden in both the Tokyo and Rome Olympics. His grandam Kalmia is known as one of the world's finest broodmares, having produced five approved stallions.

Kathy has owned Entheos since he was a yearling. He was bought as the first stallion to stand at Summerfield Farm, established in 1987 for the purpose of producing premium quality performance horses.

"Entheos was hand-raised by me," says Kathy. "He learned about people, how to love and how to respect them. This makes for a very special kind of bond between us. He is a very kind horse, very social, but can be very mischievous and has a special playfulness I hope he never grows out of. He has a 'Me first, I'm Number 1' kind of attitude. The other woman in his life is his groom, JoAnn. He knows he can depend on one of us to be around almost all the time. He is one happy stallion when the two of us give him our undivided attention! He knows our voices, our smells, our moods. He knows when to play and when to stand at attention. He knows exactly how far he can push us before he gets punished! We know just how much stallion he can be and we respect that.

"His personality quirk?," she adds. "He is a space invader. Most horses will approach you, neck stretched and muzzle to your hand. Entheos will walk up to you and literally put his face to your face. His first daughter Elsa does the exact same thing. And he will always look you straight in the eye – and so will she."

In November, 1991, Entheos was one of twelve stallions presented to the Swedish Warmblood Association for approval, which involved his receiving a Certificate of Recommendation for Breeding (CRB). This certificate is awarded to stallions who are approved for breeding purposes; a registry is kept of approved stallions and their offspring for registration and branding. These stallions must have a pedigree of at least four known generations recorded in the Swedish Warmblood Studbook. They must be of proper type, well-proportioned, and sound, have good movement, good temperament, and be free of any genetic unsoundnesses or defects. The stallions were also asked to satisfactorily complete an eventing test. Out of the twelve stallions presented, only six were approved.

Entheos was the highest-scoring stallion with a score of eight (out of a possible ten) for all his gaits. "To date, this was our most special moment," says Kathy. And another step in the direction of the heights to which Entheos seems destined.

THE TENNESSEE WALKING HORSE

The pages of American history reflect the strong influence of the Tennessee Walking Horse in the building of our country and in the daily lives of our forefathers. The ancestor of the modern Tennessee Walking Horse was the Southern Plantation Walking Horse or Tennessee Pacer. Its bloodlines included famous equine families, such as Copperbottoms, Gray Johns, Slashers, Hals, Brooks, and Bulletts.

This old plantation-type horse gained wide popularity for its ease of gait, swiftness and ability to stride faultlessly over the hills and through the valleys of the rocky Middle Tennessee terrain. Its gaits were not trained, but were naturally inherited.

In its early days this horse was also used as a utility animal for all types of farm work as well as family transportation and recreation. On Sunday, the horse that had plowed fields from sunup to sundown during the week was groomed, hitched to the Sunday buggy and drew the whole family, dressed in their best, to church.

During the Civil War (1861-1865), new bloodlines impacted the breed, as movement of horse transport gave occasion to the cross-breeding of Confederate Pacers and Union Trotters.

In 1886, a cross of the stallion Allendorf, from the Hambletonian family of trotters, and Maggie Marshall, a Morgan mare, resulted in a black colt with a white blaze called Allan F-1.

Allan F-1 arrived in Middle Tennessee in 1903. It was the cross between Allan and the Tennessee Pacer that produced the Tennessee Walking Horse. Allan was later designated by the Tennessee Walking Horse Breeders' Association as the foundation sire of the Tennessee Walking Horse.

Early breeders of the Walking Horse were for the most part farmers; Walking Horse colts soon became a money-producing crop in the Middle Tennessee area.

Proud as they were of their Walkers, these breeders of Middle Tennessee were smart enough to realize they were in keen competition with their Kentucky neighbors. While the Tennessee Horses had their free and easy gait, they looked like country bumpkins by comparison with the elegant and stylish American Saddlebred.

In 1914, with the idea of remedying this situation, Henry Davis brought the American Saddlebred stallion, Giovanni, from Kentucky to Wartrace, Tennessee, the cradle of Walking Horse breeding. This Saddlebred blood, crossed with the Allans, brought quality and refinement to the breed.

Middle Tennessee breeders wasted no time in beginning to promote their breed as the "World's Greatest Pleasure Horse." Its distinctive way of going has set it apart from other breeds and made it famous worldwide. Its flat-footed walk, four-cornered running walk and rocking chair canter are natural, inherited gaits which can be seen even in a young foal as it follows its dam about in pasture.

In 1935, the Tennessee Walking Horse Breeders' Association was formed in Lewisburg, Tennessee. (In 1974, the registry's official name was expanded to the Tennessee Walking Horse Breeders' and Exhibitors' Association.) One hundred fifteen horses were selected as foundation stock. During the first year of the association's existence, 208 horses were registered.

By 1950, some 30,000 Tennessee Walkers had been registered from more than forty states, and the United States Department of Agriculture recognized Tennessee Walkers as a distinct breed. By 1989, more than 250,000 Tennessee Walking Horses were registered.

Selective breeding has added polished touches, while continuing to maintain the muscular vigor, unexcelled disposition and calmness, size and structural soundness sought after in the modern Tennessee Walking Horse.

Top examples of today's breeding can be seen at the many annual one-night horse shows which are very much a part of community life in Tennessee. One of the top events of the year on the show roster is the fifty-year-old Tennessee Walking Horse National Celebration in Shelbyville, Tennessee, held just before Labor Day and billed as the "World's Greatest Horse Show."

But this horse is not just a pampered pet of the show ring. It is usable as a pleasure, trail or work horse. The breed gives great pleasure to persons (including aged and timid riders) who like to take their exercise and recreation in a temperate manner.

The Tennessee Walker is found in all fifty states, in Canada, and several foreign countries. Today more and more South American plantation owners are turning to the Tennessee Walking Horse.

All that seems to sustain the statement frequently made of Tennessee Walkers, "If you ride one today, you'll own one tomorrow."

The Pushover

When there are heartaches and obstacles in life, horses seem to be able to carry those who love them through these difficult passages to new and expanded horizons.

That's how it was with Looking Glass Farm in Gallatin, Tennessee, which Dr. Bill and Alliene Varner say "was not so much a dream come true, as the natural outgrowth and development of a family's needs."

It all started, says Dr. Varner, a psychiatrist, when their older daughter Susan was diagnosed as having an audio-perceptual problem. At the same time their younger daughter Sarah was diagnosed with acute lymphocytic leukemia.

Susan overcame her difficulty through a lot of hard work and sheer grit, undergoing special speech and education training. During this period of intense work, it was suggested to the Varner family that horseback riding was a wonderful way for a child to gain self-confidence and self-awareness.

Susan was seven when she began riding lessons. "It grew from there, and then kept growing," says Dr. Varner. "My wife got into it too, partly to keep Susan company, but because of her own interests as well."

Their first horse was "an old racking horse that had been out in the pasture for several years," he says. "She was a Tennessee Walker and she awakened a family heritage. I had had some family back in Alabama that had Walking Horses," says Dr. Varner, "and I knew I didn't have time to learn how to hunt-jump!"

"Over the years we found that Tennessee Walking Horses were much to our liking," adds Alliene. "They were calm animals and everyone was able to be involved, whether they could ride or not."

Alliene obviously could – on her show horse, Generator's Pro Am, she won a blue ribbon at a major show, the International at Murfreesboro, Tennessee. After that, she was hooked.

"By that time we wanted to get into horses even more, and began looking at several different stallions," says her husband.

One of them was The Pushover, sired by The Pusher and out of Pride's Super Dawn S, a Pride of Midnight mare, foaled on May 5, 1979. The Pushover won at some really good shows on the Tennessee Walking Horse circuit and was a great crowd pleaser.

"He's a really, really charismatic horse. One of the most popular horses of the breed – certainly he's in the top two or three," says Dr. Varner. "He is the classic image of a stallion; he believes he's the top horse wherever he is."

On the advice of the Varners' trainer, Alliene bought The Pushover at the Montgomery Horse Show in 1986, this without her husband seeing him, for fear of losing out to one of several other interested parties. The Varners' trust in their trainer's opinion paid off.

On September 1, 1990, before 28,000 screaming fans, The Pushover was named the fifty-second Tennessee Walking Horse World Grand Champion. He had been Reserve World Grand Champion in 1989, and International Reserve Grand Champion in 1986.

The Pushover was retired last year at the Tennessee Walking Horse National Celebration, in Shelbyville, Tennessee, and on August 31, 1991, was retired to stand at stud, and, as Alliene puts it, "be forever a celebrated member of the Varner family."

THE WESTPHALIAN

A Westphalian horse is a guaranteed Olympic medal, say the breeders of this German Warmblood. It is difficult to argue with that statement, one which no longer seems like hyperbole when one looks at the list of Westphalian horses that have been winners in international sport.

Rembrandt, who won individual and team medals for Germany in dressage in the 1988 Olympics, with his pretty young owner/rider Nicole Uphoff, is probably the most famous Westphalian horse currently. Admirers say one sees a horse-and-rider team like this one once in a hundred years.

Then there is Ahlerich, World Champion in 1982, and Olympic Champion in 1984 and 1988 in dressage, ridden by German amateur competitor Dr. Reiner Klimke, one of the most adulated figures in the discipline today. Ahlerich's expressive personality made him an audience favorite in the Los Angeles Olympics.

Ganimedes was also an Olympic dressage champion in 1988, under Germany's Monica Theodorescu. Starman, ridden by the USA's Anne Kurzinski, won an Olympic silver medal in 1988 in show jumping.

On the German jumping team that same year, Wolfgang Brinkman rode Bugatti's Pedro to an Olympic gold medal, and Malte, under Gina Smith, won an Olympic bronze medal in dressage for Canada.

"The Westphalian is the most winning horse internationally," says Lucy Taylor Parker, President of the Westphalian Warmblood Association of America. The association was founded in 1987 with the goal of recognizing the Westphalian Sport Horse's achievements in American competition and to promote the Westphalian breed. To this end, the WWAA, with headquarters in Penn Valley, California, is a member of the All Breeds Council of the United States Dressage Federation and sponsors awards for the horses registered with the WWAA for each competition year.

In 1991, WWAA was able to present 135 awards, even though the numbers of this breed are still small in the United States. The Association has about 150 members scattered all over the United States, says Parker. Only about ten approved stallions are in the United States, and the German Westphalian organization keeps tight controls over all activities in the U.S. All registration and foal approval is done in cooperation with the German studbook.

The formation of the Westphalian Horse Breeder's Association in Germany in 1904 and the founding of the Westphalian National Stud in 1926 represent the beginning of the Westphalian breed as we know it today.

The Westphalian horse has primarily been farm-bred and raised, pedigrees often dating back to the beginnings of the farmers' own families. There are currently about 8,625 registered mares, and about 192 breeding stallions in the Westphalian region.

Breeders are justifiably proud of their horse. Their careful selection and testing throughout the years has produced a riding horse well-respected for its talent, good character, reliability, and rideability.

Like other regional Warmblood products, the Westphalian is another "cocktail mix" breed. As with a martini, everyone creates it with subtle differences. The Westphalians breed for a horse that can perform in dressage and jumping, rather than for a uniform physical type. The dressage types are usually elegant and light movers, resembling a good-sized Thoroughbred, while the jumping types are often more robust.

The breed comes from the upper west central part of Germany, one of the most important horse-breeding areas in Germany. Headquarters are in Warendorf, where on a daily basis one can see horses being ridden and led up and down cobbled streets in an old village, one which seems populated by nothing but die-hard horse people. Here in Warendorf are the immense ivy-covered barns of the Westphalian Stud and the German National Riding School (*Deutsche Reitschule*).

At the edge of Warendorf lies the state-of-the-art complex of the German Olympic Riding School and the offices of the powerful "FN," the German National Equestrian Federation, Europe's most highly developed equine bureaucracy.

Most dressage grand masters are based in Westphalia, along with a show jumping superstar or two.

Rolls Royce

At Iron Spring Farm, Rolls Royce was an instant breeding success, booked to sixty mares in his first season at the farm. "People took one look at him and fell in love, just like I did," says owner Mary Alice Malone.

In 1972, Mary Alice, who can't remember a time when she didn't love horses and want a farm, founded a small breeding business which has grown to one of the most outstanding in the country. Her facility in the lush rolling countryside of Pennsylvania includes an Olympic-sized indoor training arena, broodmare barns, a breeding shed and state-of-the-art laboratory for frozen and fresh cooled semen. But the 200-year-old barn housing the stallions is the focal point of the farm, and the most recent arrival – Rolls Royce, a Westphalian, imported from Germany in 1991 – has the greatest personality of them all, says Mary Alice.

"Rolls Royce is stunningly beautiful, a real heartbreaker," she says. "He's very mature-looking for such a young horse. Here at the farm, he's the new kid on the block, so he makes sure he's noticed. He's a favorite with the kids, and they like to pet him. He loves the attention and knows how to ask for more."

But he's not just another handsome face.

The 17-hand dark brown stallion with white markings, was foaled in Westphalia in 1986 and comes from some of the best bloodlines in Germany. He is approved by both the Westphalian and Oldenburg Registries.

Rolls Royce's grandsire, the famous Romadour II, an outstanding mover, won Warendorf's 100-Day Stallion Test, an important and rigorous examination that evaluates temperament as well as way of going. The Westphalian Studbook said of Romadour II: "One of the greatest sires that Germany ever produced, a stallion who could improve the faults in any mare." Rolls Royce's sire, Rheingold, also placed first in his Stallion Test. At age three, Rolls Royce followed this generational tradition by winning the 1989 100-Day Test at Warendorf.

The following year Rolls Royce won thirteen firsts and seven second places in Germany in the varied disciplines of conformation, riding horse and jumping classes. He also received a first in dressage at "A" or advanced level, and was chosen to go to the national championships for young riding horses at Warendorf.

"All my horses are not only athletically brilliant, but they're exceptionally fast and cooperative learners," says Mary Alice.

"Rolls Royce is incredibly comfortable to ride, quite athletic and balanced. He has a great feel and he's a smooth and powerful mover. He's always thinking too. I try to understand what he's thinking about or worried about or playing with. I stay one step ahead, psyching him out," she says.

"In training, Rolls Royce is still developing. Even though he looks grown up, he's really an adolescent. He has a lot of presence in the ring, and he likes to be the center of attention, to be the one-man show. Basically, he needs and wants to know at all times who is in charge. He keeps asking, keeps testing, but then, like an adolescent, he asks, 'Do you still love me?'"

The answer, of course, is yes.

THE TRAKEHNER

The story of the Trakehner breed – the horse with the elegant elk antler brand on its left hip – is one of matchless courage in the face of near-annihilation.

Forced to leave its land of origin – the cool forests and cobalt lakes of East Prussia – the predecessors of the present specimens of the breed made one of the greatest and longest treks in history, enduring incredible hardship and suffering on their desperate flight through the inferno of war.

The East Prussian horse of Trakehner origin (as it is properly called) perhaps owes its very survival to the hardiness and stamina it inherited from its long-ago ancestor, the Tarpan horse that lived in the forests and steppes of northern Russia, existing on very little food and in the harshest climatic conditions.

These small, dorsal-striped ancestor horses were used as draft animals by medieval farmers. They were later crossed with Crusaders' warhorses, with Oriental breeds the knights brought back as spoils, as well as with Friesians, Spanish horses, and heavy types of horses from north and central Germany.

It was King Frederick Wilhelm I who organized the varied stock from breeding centers in 1732, and formed the Royal Trakehnen Stud. Set in beautiful surroundings, it became the "Lexington" or "Newmarket" of Warmblood horses in East Prussia. So useful were the horses bred here that they were exported in great numbers all over the known world.

The famous seven-point elk antler brand first appeared in the year 1787. Horses from Trakehnen were branded on the off thigh with a single antler. Since herds of elk had roamed the emerald forests of the province since its earliest history, not surprisingly the antler became the symbol of the breed.

Another great landmark for the breed was establishment in 1888 of the original East Prussian studbook for Warmbloods of Trakehner origins. The family tree now includes a great deal of Arabian and Thoroughbred blood. The first formal infusions were around this time. In 1903, a Thoroughbred stallion, Perfectionist, was introduced; his son, Tempelhuter, became the main stallion in Trakehnen from 1916 to 1933 and, in turn, the legendary supersire of the breed.

Other landmarks were use of the new double antler brand on the near side in 1922 by a new East Prussian organization, and establishment in 1926 of the first stallion test, approving for breeding only those horses that met rigorous criteria.

But life itself would give the Trakehner its toughest test.

After 200 years of development, the breed was nearly destroyed in World War II. As Soviet troops advanced upon East Prussia in the winter of 1944-45, about 700 mares and 32 stallions with their human caretakers set out on a 900-mile flight to West Germany in an emergency evacuation. The courageous horses made the journey on foot, most of them unshod, many pulling field carts and wagons driven by desperate women, old men, and children. Most of the mares were in foal. Often the horses had to spend the night still harnessed to their wagons, in the freezing cold, most of the time unfed.

They trekked through ice, snow, storms, axle-deep mud for hundreds of miles, the mares bearing foals that had starved to death in utero, but never giving up and finally bearing their human burden to safety. Only a few hundred survived. (One and a half million horses are said to have died in World War II.)

Even after the trek, many Trakehners were expropriated by, or handed over to, the Russians when the agreement that Russia would occupy East Germany was enacted. The fate of these horses is unknown.

The present-day *Trakehner Verband*, or breeding association, was established in 1947 in Schleswig-Holstein. It dedicated itself to keeping the breed alive through the difficult post-war years and did eventually rebuild it.

A tribute to Trakehner resilience is that Perkunos, a horse of that breed, helped win the silver medal in dressage for Germany in the 1956 Olympics.

A regal bearing, medium height, a dished face (from its Arab ancestors), great sturdiness, a long, arched neck, a powerful, floating trot, and a willing disposition are characteristics of today's Trakehners.

Azurit

A trainer refers to Azurit as "the Rhodes Scholar of the horse world." One of his breeding handlers calls the stallion "a real gentleman, tried and true."

His exceptional intelligence and sterling character make this Trakehner stallion endearing to his owner, Tracey Hodges, on a personal level.

But Azurit (pronounced Azur-eet) is also special to the world as one of its highest-achieving Trakehner sport horses. When he arrived at Tracey Hodges' Royal Oaks Farm in the Twin Oaks Valley in San Marcos, California on April 26, 1986, Azurit had already been trained to Grand Prix level in dressage and competed by the famous five-time Olympic Gold Medalist, Christine Stuckelberger of Switzerland. He was already a star, having finished second in the 1982 World Championships in Switzerland and won over twenty FEI (international) level classes in Europe.

Foaled July 28, 1973 in Wetterade, Germany, the accomplished Azurit stands 16.2 hands, a liver chestnut with a golden cast to his coat that makes him shine in the sun as if he were a bronze sculpture come to life.

"He literally takes your breath away," says Tracey who I found shares my love for Nature when I spoke to her.

"Soon after Azurit became a resident of our farm, he began competing in top level dressage classes," says Tracey. "As the winner of twenty-two major Grand Prix and Grand Prix Specials in the United States, he achieved the status of the most winning Grand Prix horse in the United States."

Azurit was shortlisted for the Olympic trials in 1988 at Gladstone, New Jersey, and while he was not chosen to represent the United States in Korea, nevertheless 1988 was still a very good year for him. At its end he received two major awards: the ATA's (American Trakehner Association) prestigious Palmenblute Award presented to the purebred Trakehner that has contributed the most in competition to promote the breed on the North American continent, and the German Trakehner Verband Award, a similar award presented in Europe.

"The original purpose in our purchase of Azurit was not only to show him in competition, but also to help improve the Trakehner horse in America. Never did we dream he would be so honored by the ATA and the German Verband. We were thrilled and you can be sure he received extra carrots and apples that day," says Tracey.

"Azurit is very noble, expressive and sensitive; good face, well-set neck, big shoulders and withers; a very beautiful, expressive way of going in all paces; truly a brilliant specimen, full of masculinity. From his very first stride, he impresses you with his proud bearing and his long, elastic way of going. Azurit's fan club always compares him to a master ballet artist," says Tracey.
says Tracey.

Azurit is now retired to stud. His offspring are already winning awards as yearlings and two-year-olds, for he passes on his movement and good looks. His impeccable bloodlines are the top lines being used currently in German breeding programs. He is sired by My Lunaria xx (the two x's mean Thoroughbred breeding) and is out of Arietta (by Coriolan), from the top mare line in Germany.

"Azurit is with me for his lifetime," says Tracey. "He loves it when I just sit in his stall and talk to him. He nickers softly as though he understands this difficult time in my life." (Tracey was recently widowed.)

"Azurit, in the years I have owned him, has brought great joy, heart-stopping thrills, plus a lot of tense moments in his competitive career," she concludes. "In difficult times, his great heart never failed him. Now he looks and acts like a two-year-old, cavorting in the pasture, and seems very happy with his new life which includes a lot of new lady friends. I am so thankful this very special horse became a part of my life."

Leggiero

It was equestrian matchmaking in the electronic age—one videotape of the great Trakehner dressage sire, Troubadour, made Isabel Ballerna fall in love with the stallion and his bloodlines.

After a year and a half of searching for a Troubadour son, another videotape led Isabel (in 1985) to Leggiero, then owned by a German couple in South Carolina.

"They produced a very cute video," says Isabel, an Argentine-born interior designer and artist from Carefree, Arizona. "Leggi was a three-year-old stallion and hadn't been handled very much. One person was pulling him, the other was pushing him, and the woman was saying, 'Do so and so, because that is what the lady wants to see.'

"Through it all, Leggiero was docile and forebearing. I thought, 'What a gorgeous temperament! I have to have him!'" says Isabel. "His way of going was what I was looking for, and so was his color—I had always dreamed of owning a dark mahogany bay stallion."

Leggiero, however, was not in the best physical condition. He was 16.3 hands at the age of three, and three South Carolina veterinarians said he had a disease which affects the joints of big horses that grow too fast. Another group of vets said Leggiero did not have the disease.

Isabel's intuition told her the horse was healthy, and she bought him. Just to make sure, she sent him to the topmost authority in the country for this condition, the University of Colorado Veterinary School. After Leggi's exam, the vets there informed Isabel he was healthy and advised her to put him to work. "Once he started building up his muscles to support his skeleton, he was fine," she says. "And I was one of the happiest human beings!"

Leggiero, by Troubadour out of Lensroze by Mikado, became the foundation for Isabel's Carefree Sporthorses, a small breeding farm dedicated to the beautiful and intelligent Trakehners and Paso Finos.

When Leggiero was four, he was approved as a stallion by the North American Trakehner Association, as well as the Oldenburg and International Sporthorse Registries.

He has already sired a magnificent son, Darlego, now three, whom Isabel is starting under saddle with hopes for a show career.

Leggiero himself has followed his sire's lead by proving himself successful in the dressage ring. He was High Point Champion Fourth Level Dressage in the 1991 Arizona Dressage Association Fall Show, which qualified him to compete for Region 5 Championships at Fourth Level in the Open Division.

Leggiero is now schooling Prix St. Georges. "He has been shown by professionals since he started his career, but starting with the 1992 season, I shall be showing him in amateur adult classes while the trainer will show him in open classes," says Isabel. "I have waited a long time and have sacrificed much to have him in training with the best of instructors. This often meant he was away from home. Now we are ready for each other."

In order to prepare herself for Leggiero's return, Isabel bought another Trakehner, an imported gelding named Lenard, on whom she was able to learn all the dressage movements. With Lenard she won the AHSA Adult Amateur Championship in Region 8.

Isabel's relationship with Leggiero has been a very rewarding one from the start, she says. "He's very willing to please. Even for me, a very small person, he is extremely easy to ride. His gaits are very comfortable; he's like riding a sofa."

Isabel also owns one of the Top Ten Paso Fino geldings in the country, Merlin Cabal, whom she shows in Bella Forma, Performance and Pleasure. "Paso Finos are ridden with a dressage seat and a dressage saddle," says Isabel, "so it's not so different. But I do go from the giant, 16.3, to the midget, 14.3," she laughs.

"Dressage is so difficult and time-consuming, and the Paso Finos are fun," she says.

Troubadour

A hundred years ago, the tiny village of Wayne, Illinois was famous for breeding the best Percheron horses in this country. As times changed, the need for work animals diminished, replaced by the demand for sport horses. Today Wayne is known as the home of one of the largest herds of Trakehner sport horses in the country, and the home of Troubadour, Trakehner dressage sire, and producer of top competition horses.

A massive black-brown stallion, Troubadour is the dressage rider's living dream, perfection on four feet. He is himself a proven competitor at the ultimate level, having gone to the Seoul Olympics in 1988 as the reserve mount of Christine Stuckelberger, Swiss equestrian star, Olympic medalist, World Champion and many times Swiss National Champion.

But his greatest fame is for consistently siring dressage horses, many of which are already competing at high levels in the show ring.

One of his sons, Triomphe, with owner/rider Jennifer Miller, won the individual bronze medal and helped win the silver team medal at the 1991 Pan American Games in Cuba. Another son in Texas, Trabour, was one of the top horses in the nation at Intermediare Level, and is now doing well at Grand Prix. Other sons — Leggiero in Arizona, Amadeus in Virginia, Montenegro and Tulare in California, and several others in Europe — are talented up-and-coming performers.

Lowell Boomer, Executive Director of the United States Dressage Federation headquartered in Lincoln, Nebraska, said of Troubadour's impressive output, "That beautiful stallion is definitely a valuable asset to the United States dressage program."

"Every horse he sires is a good mover, and with a good trainer could become a top dressage horse," says Troubadour's owner, Edith H. Kosterka, a great and legendary horsewoman who has devoted her life to her goal: "to produce an American-bred sport horse for the American rider aiming at the Olympics."

Edith acquired Troubadour in Germany when he was not quite five, through the famous breeder and trainer Eugen Wahler, owner of Klosterhof Medingen.

"When I first saw Troubadour, he was breathtaking and different from any stallion I'd ever seen; in my mind I knew he'd make it to the top. He is the kind of stallion that comes along once in your lifetime," Edith says.

"In general, a stallion does not pass on to any great extent all of the talents needed for dressage," she continues. "Besides natural good movement and good looks, these talents include mental stability and the ability to learn easily. You seldom find all those qualities in one horse."

Troubadour, however, has them all in good measure. "His own training came easily to him because he had extremely good character and a clear mind, along with his athletic ability," says Mrs. Kosterka. "Without fail he passes these on to his get."

Because he is so outstanding, "Only the best have been on his back," she adds.

Apart from Stuckelberger who competed Troubadour in Europe, Melle von Bruggen, former coach of the United States Equestrian Team dressage squad, had him in training in California, bringing him up to international level; American Olympian Robert Dover rode him in a special exhibition at the American Royal Horse Show in Kansas City in 1989, bringing a standing ovation from 9,000 spectators. Christian Plaege, one of Germany's top young trainers, exhibited Troubadour both under saddle and in long lines at the 1991 American Trakehner Association's Annual Meeting in Columbus, Ohio.

"It takes time, money, patience, and a lot of work to breed horses, but I finally have the satisfaction of seeing my efforts rewarded," says Mrs. Kosterka, "and I am very proud that my stallions have sired so many sport horses that win."

She stands two other stallions: Traum, whose jumping bloodlines go back to the legendary Morgenglanz, sired by the famous Trakehner stallion Abglanz; and Troy, a talented, versatile youngster, already named Canadian Reserve Champion Hunter and Grand Champion in the Performance Division of the Canadian Breeders' Show, both of whom will follow in Troubadour's hoofprints in the future.

Amiego

Amiego, the great grey Trakehner stallion, was the hero of an inspiring story of courage comparable to those of the greatest horses of history.

Amiego was marked by destiny never to be ordinary. His bloodlines were brilliant; his sire was Handel; his dam the legendary mare Abiza, dam also of Abdullah, Olympic gold and silver medalist.

Amiego himself would win the bronze medal in eventing at the Pan American Games in August, 1987. In 1990, he had the honor of being the first North Ameri-

can-bred Trakehner stallion to be approved by the German *Trakehner Verband*, or breeding association.

Amiego left no doubt as to why. At his first public performance at the approvals, namely the free jumping phase in the indoor arena, Amiego decided to jump the five and a half foot wall dividing the riding hall, on the other side of which spectators were standing. After calmly flying over both wall and spectators, without disturbing one of their hats, Amiego waited quietly for one of the handlers to retrieve him. His feat was greeted with great enthusiasm, and his tale has been told endless times on both sides of the Atlantic.

During the time he was in Germany, Amiego bred 120 mares, which made him most popular stallion of the year. He had returned to stand at stud in Canada at the farm of his breeder, Gerhard Schickedanz, when he died of a heart attack in 1991, at the age of 17.

It was a great loss to the breed, but to John Krenger, custodian of the legend, it meant losing a close personal relationship that filled his life with extraordinary events and memories.

"He was my buddy and my friend," John sums up the relationship. "When I bought Amiego as a yearling, I didn't know what I was doing. I got caught up in the Trakehner breed, but didn't even know what an extended trot was." Warmbloods and dressage were new to the United States then.

"But when I saw Amiego for the first time at Schickedanz', he was a foot off the ground when he trotted, and I understood what it was all about," John adds.

Amiego's strength of character was tested early on, when he slipped and fell on ice in his paddock in the winter of 1977. He spent six months in a tight supportive stall with a sling under his belly, while his fractured pelvis healed. John spent a lot of time with him, and to keep up his morale, groomed him with a child's bamboo rake.

Amiego's great heart brought him through the ordeal, and he recovered completely, physically and mentally.

While John always engaged the best professional riders to show Amiego, as an amateur rider he showed the stallion in dressage, and he foxhunted him, always winning many compliments on his regal bearing and pleasant personality.

"He could almost talk," says John. "When you were handling him in the breeding shed and said something to him, he would understand."

A legend in the sport horse world while he lived, Amiego now lives on through his offspring. Late in 1991, John traveled to Germany and bought home a weanling Amiego son, now at his exquisite Sanctuary Farm in Woodstock, Illinois.

Pregelstrand

"The color of a highly-polished piece of mahogany furniture; the agility, coordination and balance of a superb athlete; the beauty and harmony of a work of art; the intelligence and character that allows communication with man – Pregelstrand is a very special stallion," says his owner, Vanda Werner of Mile High Horse Ranch, Inc., in Parker, Colorado. "He wears his feelings, moods and thoughts on his face and one knows what is on his mind or what he is going to do at first glance," she continues. "As a human he would be the prankster, the braggart, definitely a brute of a man physically who would think it's macho to get dirty, but whose feelings could be hurt by the slightest insult, a man with some tender thoughts, but who would never get caught expressing them. No couch potato, this one. He would like activity."

The 16.2 mahogany bay Trakehner stallion, foaled February 13, 1970 in Germany and Reserve Champion at his stallion performance test, was imported by Vanda in December 1976. Sired by the legendary Morgenglanz (who qualified for the West German Championships in eventing), Pregelstrand's grandsire was the great Abglanz, a stallion bred in Trakehnen and the founder of one of the most important lines in the Trakehner and Hanoverian breeds, after being saved from the ravages of World War II and confiscation by the Russians.

"Was I lucky!" says Vanda. "After discovering the Trakehner breed in 1975, long before the 'Warmblood Rush' in North America, I spent the summer on a Trakehner farm in California and decided this was the breed for me. Deciding to go into the breeding business, I bought a ticket to Germany and left home with a suitcase and a list of breeders to visit. I traveled around Germany and looked at ten stallions, none of which really struck me." Upon visiting Klosterhof Medingen, the owner directed Vanda to the indoor arena. In came the six-year-old Pregelstrand under saddle. "Shivers went down my back," says Vanda. "It was an immediate decision. This was the stallion I was looking for."

The Trakehner was then relatively new to the U.S. and unheard of in the West at the time. "As my cowboy/rancher brother asked, 'He's real purty, Vanda, but what the hell ya goin' to do with him?' I enjoyed feeling that I was breaking new ground," Vanda says.

Between 1976 and 1986, when he was retired, Pregelstrand had a very long and outstanding show record. He qualified for the USET World Championship team tryouts at Prix St. Georges and Intermediare I in 1982; that year he finished tenth nationally at Intermediare I. In 1983, he competed in the National Sports Festival V hosted by the U.S. Olympic Committee and placed fourth individually at Intermedaire I and was a member of the Silver Medal Team.

As a sire, in 1989, Pregelstrand had more offspring that won USDF Awards at all levels than any other stallion of any breed. His son, Titan, out of a Thoroughbred mare, was the USDF's Fourth Level Horse of the Year and is long-listed for the 1996 Olympic team.

"From a breeder's point of view, a stallion's success as a sire is more important than his success as a performance horse," says Vanda. "I am, however, still waiting for a colt that would be worthy of keeping as a stallion; he has been mainly a sire of fillies.

"Turned my life around, at least in a different direction, and that's an understatement," Vanda says of Pregelstrand's effect on her life. From a high school French teacher and single mare owner, she was suddenly immersed in all the myriad tasks of running a breeding farm. Mile High today stands four Trakehner stallions and feeds about fifty young horses and mares. Vanda spends seven days a week there. "Although I was raised on a farm and always had a horse in my life, never did I ever dream that I would be up to my eyebrows in horses!" she says.

Martini

One of the most difficult movements to train in dressage is the flying change of lead at every stride. The Trakehner stallion Martini and his owner/rider Jean L. Brinkman of Wellborn, Florida, had accomplished flying changes every four, three and two strides, and had worked long and hard on the singles. But it seemed she could not get the timing right and they were only able to get two or three changes in a row. This was the last movement the pair needed to learn to compete in the Grand Prix test, in which fifteen "ones" are required.

"We had been working on this several months and on the morning of my birthday, I expressed to Martini that the best possible birthday present would be to accomplish this very difficult movement," says Jean. "To our absolute astonishment on our first attempt we accomplished ten changes in a row and, from that day on, had no more trouble with the changes every stride. You can imagine my excitement and particular pleasure that this goal was reached on my birthday."

While some may be skeptical, this anecdote is indicative of the close, symbiotic relationship which develops between dressage rider and horse. Martini is a wonderful example of the Trakehner sport horse that brings so much to such a relationship.

"Martini's elegant type and gorgeous expression bring attention wherever we go and his exemplary dis-

position has brought many fans to the Trakehner breed," says Jean. Competing on him, she earned her USDF Gold Medal for competition at the Intermediare and Grand Prix levels; they also competed in the Olympic Sports Festival and were on the Silver Medal Team.

The 16.3 mahogany bay, foaled March 19, 1978, was an unexpected bonus for Jean. In 1977 she and her husband Roy traveled to Germany to observe the Trakehner Stallion Test, which all Warmblood stallions must pass to receive breeding approval. At the following auction, Jean was quite taken with a large, very attractive mare with tremendous gaits and a special look. "Very calm and somehow above the whole proceedings," she recalls. When all was said and done, they found themselves the unexpected owners of this wonderful mare, Maranja, who was in foal to a stallion named Coktail and due in about four months. Little did they suspect what far-reaching results this purchase would bring, for Martini was the foal she was carrying.

Martini arrived early one evening and was spectacular even at birth even though he arrived with one ear plastered over his head and the other pressed down on his cheek, giving him a rather rakish appearance. "If love at first sight is a possibility, it is without doubt that I knew I had received a very special gift that evening," says Jean. "Almost from birth, Martini became the center of our lives. His temperament is very special, exceptionally kind and as he grew, it became very apparent that his stallion qualities were abundant. He was just the type I wanted in order to develop my Warmblood breeding program.

"He was raised in a very ordinary fashion, turned out with other colts to play and grow. However, my connection with him was always very strong and he showed his strong feelings for me in an unusual horse fashion one day."

It was Jean's habit to walk out each day and retrieve the colts from their pasture an eighth of a mile from the barn. Since they knew this meant dinner was ready, they would gallop to the barn as quickly as possible, leaving her to walk back to the barn by herself. "However, Martini, acting in unusual horse fashion, ignored his companions when they left. He stayed by my side to walk quietly with me all the way to the barn. Very unusual colt behavior," says Jean. "From the time Martini reached riding age, he has been my constant companion and competition mount. I am rarely apart from him and even manage to organize vacations that include him.

"Martini is a special gift from God for someone as committed to horses as I have been my whole life. I realize I will never own another horse so special in so many ways. He is very much responsible for the success of our breeding farm, as his offspring are much in demand as competitors in the fields of dressage and eventing and as hunter/jumpers."

THE THOROUGHBRED

There are few horsemen, no matter what their personal preference is as breeds go, whose souls are not touched by the sight of a beautiful Thoroughbred horse pounding down the home stretch of a racecourse to victory.

Born to run, this breed of horse is engineered for speed. The fastest are considered the best, and a whole lucrative international industry of breeding and racing has thrived on this one quality.

Not only does the Thoroughbred horse dominate the racecourses of the world today, it has influenced countless other breeds and continues to do so actively today in the "cocktail mix" of bloodlines used to produce all high-performance European Warmblood breeds, such as the Trakehner, the Oldenburger and the Swedish Warmblood. In America, the American Saddlebred, the American Standardbred, and the Morgan trace their ancestry to Thoroughbred foundation sires.

The Thoroughbred is a relatively new breed, though its antecedents go back centuries.

Horse racing was a favorite pastime in England going back to the Roman occupation, when chariot races were held at Epsom, the site today of a racecourse of great traditions. By the Middle Ages, there were races in England organized around 14-hand Galloway ponies, some of which had already received infusions of Oriental blood to increase their speed and endurance. Pony mares of this type which had already proven their speed for generations provided the female foundation stock for developing the Thoroughbred. The male foundation for the breed consisted of the legendary three Oriental stallions known as the Byerly Turk, the Godolphin Barb and the Darley Arabian. Their progeny have been recorded in the *General Stud Book* since 1793.

The Godolphin Barb, also sometimes referred to as the Godolphin Arabian, is probably the best known of the three, thanks to Marguerite Henry's book, *King of the Wind*. This bay stallion was sent to the stables of Louis XV of France as a gift from the Bey of Tunis. Legend has it the horse was so ugly, King Louis either sold him or gave him away. The horse went from hand to hand, his luck turning blacker, until he ended up pulling a water cart through the streets of Paris. An Englishman named Edward Coke saw him in a miserable state and bought him for reasons which remain unknown. When Coke died four years later, the stallion was inherited by Roger Williams, owner of a coffeehouse. He in turn sold him to Lord Godolphin, who admitted him into his breeding establishment on trial. The Barb was so ugly, mares were said to refuse the stallion. Once he managed to mate, however, the results were so promising, he was allowed to continue his breeding career. When his offspring began winning on racetracks, their owners came to the conclusion that looks are not everything.

Little is known of the Byerly Turk other than that he was a Turkish stallion ridden by a Captain Byerly in William III's Irish Wars whose speed was said to have helped his rider elude capture at the Battle of the Boyne. In 1691, the stallion was retired to stud in Yorkshire.

The Darley Arabian came into the hands of a racing enthusiast named Richard Darley through his brother who went to the Middle East on a business trip. He bought an Arabian stallion for his brother, importing him into England in 1704. This stallion, however, showed little apparent talent for racing and was crossed at first with only second-rate mares.

Then in 1715 a mare named Betty Leeds, owned by a Mr. Childers, was sent to the stallion. The resulting foal was named Bartlett's Childers, or Bleeding Childers (he was a 'bleeder,' bursting blood vessels in his nostrils while running). He sired Squirt, who in turn begat Marske. Marske became the sire of one of the greatest Thoroughbreds of all time, Eclipse, who ran twenty races leaving all his challengers far behind each time. Many of the Thoroughbreds thrilling crowds today with their speed and athletic prowess trace their ancestry to Eclipse.

Descendants of those long-ago Galloway ponies and the three great Oriental foundation sires today are outwardly arresting to look at – sleek and slender-legged, with powerful shoulders and thighs, a barrel that has plenty of room for lungs and other internal organs, a sculpted head with a large intelligent eye containing the "look of eagles", and a long flexible neck.

But just as important are the Thoroughbred's inner qualities needed to compete against all comers on the flat racecourse and the event course, in the steeplechase and the dressage ring. The Thoroughbred is saluted for its fighting spirit, great heart, and noble character.

Revelation

Revelation's story reveals so powerful a lesson of courage, one wishes there were more than a page to tell it. It began in 1967 in New York. Bred by Dr. George Holton, the grey, 16.1 Thoroughbred, sired by My Prince II was registered with the Jockey Club and originally named "Mr. Wrong." Bought in a cheap claiming race in Florida by a jumper trainer known for his finds, the horse bombed out of a jumping career as well, crashing through everything.

Cynthia Bishop learned about him from another hunter trainer. "Jeane Kovacs told me she had a beautiful-moving horse that absolutely would not jump, but would be a real nice horse on the flat. It turned out to be Revelation," says Cynthia. "And sure enough, he had been a problem. His papers had twenty-one transfers on them. He had been a real bad actor, refusing and rearing at the in-gates, kicking out at any noise, and finally being banned at the show grounds for rearing and kicking. All this I learned after I bought him. I wondered if anyone could turn 'Mr. Wrong' into 'Mr. Right.' I didn't count on it. I bought two more horses to bring along at the same time," adds Cynthia, who was trained in the French method in Guayaquil, Ecuador (where she lived as a child) by Col. Galo Gomez Mancheno. She won her first

Grand Prix Medal at the age of eleven, and set a children's record, jumping 6'3".

"By the time I bought Revelation I had trained many national champions in many different disciplines – reining, dressage, hunter, jumper, walking horses, Arabians," says Cynthia. "Reve was a special challenge to me. After I got home and found out all the negatives, I felt there must be something wrong with Mr. Wrong. A skull X-ray showed he had an astrocytoma, a brain tumor that prevented the optic nerve from sending signals to the brain." He was blind.

"The decision to keep him was purely a sentimental one," Cynthia says. As she began training him, he offered a lot of problems, but instead of fighting him, "I just fed him treats and steadied him. After a while, he decided we weren't out there to fight and from that point on, he was the easiest horse I ever had to train."

Their first year out, Revelation was undefeated in training level dressage, winning the high percentage ride at every show. Their second year out, he won the year-end award for first and second level, competing in Florida.

"Reve was totally dependent on me to tell him everything and I didn't want to betray that trust," says Cynthia. "Riding Reve was like climbing into a horse suit – he did everything I asked, even if it was wrong. No one knew that he couldn't see. He did his tests with his ears pricked so tight, trying to hear every sound. Riding that horse developed me as a rider and as a person. I became aware of every step and the preparation it took to make even the simplest transition."

The next year the two won the Southern States Dressage Championships at third level, qualifying for the finals in North Carolina where they came in fifth.

"The thing to remember is that this horse could not even find the feed tray in his stall," says Cynthia. "These shows were in different states and different places and yet Reve never let me down. I won the fourth level Southern States Championship with Reve the next year. I kept wondering when he would take a turn for the worse, but every year he got better, so I kept the training going. I kept him home for a year to put the *piaffer* and the *passage* to him.

"He died eight years after I bought him, at age 17, and two weeks before his Grand Prix debut. He had a massive stroke and passed quickly," she says. "I sat with him through it all and I miss him to this day. Revelation was a true gentleman and my closest friend. The time we spent together molded my life. He WAS a true revelation – he showed me the wonder as well as the responsibilities of the horse/human relationship. He finally became Mr. Right." Cynthia now trains horses "who have no problems" at Mile High Horse Ranch in Parker, Colorado.

THE CROSSBREEDS

We have seen from the other breed profiles in this book how, over millions of years, the descendants of the primitive little *Equus przewalski* spread over Europe, Asia and North Africa and evolved into the several hundreds of very useful breeds and types of horses we know today.

Over these millenia, the breeder has functioned as a true artist, creating, through the mingling of genetic material in stallion and mare, living works of biological art which are able to serve humans in very specific ways.

Many of the breeds which have been around for hundreds of years, as we have seen in the other breed essays in this book, are a result of the merging of other breeds and types:

The Andalusian horse, crossed with native Italian and Austrian mares created the royal Lipizzaner.

The Spanish Barb formed the foundation for newer breeds such as the Peruvian Paso, the Paso Fino, the Mustang, the English Thoroughbred.

The American Saddlebred evolved out of the crossing and re-crossing of English Throughbreds, Canadian and other pacers with Hackneys, Morgans, and others for one of horse history's most beautiful show animals.

The Morgan is the result of the crossing of Thoroughbred, Arab, Hackney, and Fjord bloodlines.

The Quarter Horse was produced by crossing Arab, English, Spanish and other breeds to develop an animal that could run fast over a quarter-mile track.

The Trakehner or East Prussian Warmblood has crosses with Arab and Thoroughbred stallions.

Looking back, we can see that over the past half century or so, the equine race began a new phase in its evolution.

With the invention of mechanical vehicles, the horse no longer was necessary as basic transportation in war and commerce, and horse numbers plummeted in the era before and after World War II. There were doom-sayers who prophesied domestic equines would be practically extinguished from the earth, except for a few kept in zoos.

But that wasn't the case at all. Something radically different and quite wonderful began to happen. More and more people began to keep horses for the sheer pleasure of association with them, as we can also see from the profiles in this book.

People around the world began to take a new focus on the art of breeding horses. Apart from those persons whose interest lies in breeds which have a special athletic skill, such as the Thoroughbred and Standardbred, the goal of most breeders has become one of creating a versatile sport horse/companion animal.

The Oldenburger is a classic example of how a very old coaching breed, based on Spanish, Italian and old Friesian bloodlines, was recycled and brought up to date in the last twenty years or so with infusions of Thoroughbred and Anglo-Norman bloodlines to create a fabulous riding horse.

The process of evolution continues today as breeders and individuals seek to create their own ideal of the perfect pleasure horse.

A cross of the peacock of the show horse world, the American Saddlebred, with the ancient, noble and elegant Arabian gives us the exciting National Show Horse.

Breeders crossing the Andalusian with the Quarter Horse have given us the handy Azteca; the Andalusian crossed with the Arabian gives us the Aralusian or Hispano Arabe.

Nearly across the board, the modern German and other European Warmbloods have had infusions of lighter Thoroughbred and Arabian blood to create a lighter, taller, more athletic sport horse.

The Anglo-Arab was developed by crossing English Thoroughbreds with the Arabians to harmoniously combine the good features of both breeds – the size of the Thoroughbred with the beauty and stamina of the Arabian. The French Anglo-Arab is considered the ideal type and has been used as an "improving" breed in further crosses, especially the modern Warmblood sport horse.

Crossbreeds have and will continue to give horsefolks the best qualities of two or sometimes even three or more breeds, as one can readily determine by reading the profiles of horses in this book.

Clyde Jones

Clyde, the colorful "Chairhorse" of "Carriage Tours of Savannah" has always seemed eager to return the favor of getting a second chance at life – given him by his owner, Diane Brandt Brannen.

Kentucky-born Clyde, now thirteen, was bought as a three-year-old in 1982 by a man in southern Georgia looking for a heavy hunter prospect. Clyde's Clydesdale, Thoroughbred, Appaloosa ancestry produced a very tall, blond, sinewy youngster with white on his belly and side, a big blaze and stockings.

As part of his training, the new owner began teaching Clyde to pull logs about on the farm. On one occasion he was working Clyde next to a mule, skidding logs in the woods, when the mule stumbled and pushed Clyde onto a stump. Poor Clyde was impaled.

When Diane first saw him, he was still suffering from this injury. He stood quietly in the corner of a dark stall, gaunt, and rough-coated. Infection had obviously set in. Clyde's owner considered it a losing battle and planned to sell the horse at auction, thinking that only the slaughterhouse would be interested.

"There were other horses there that would probably have been suitable for the carriage trade," says Diane, who conducts carriage tours of beautiful historic Savannah. "But for some reason I just kept coming back to Clyde. Maybe it was the look on his face. He looked like a gawky teenager who, in spite of his miserable state, had a cheerful, almost comical demeanor and was interested in what we were up to."

Diane decided to take a chance on Clyde, and bought him for $750. She took him back to Savannah where she cleaned and disinfected the wound daily, hoping he would improve. He didn't, and she called in the veterinarians. They determined that Clyde still had pieces of the stump embedded in his abdomen and required surgery to remove them. During surgery they found more and worse – the intestinal tract had ruptured, and hay and grain were spilling into his body cavity, causing severe infection. After the vet patched Clyde up, he told Diane, "The horse has at most two days to live. Call us when he stops eating."

The veterinarians prescribed Gentocin, a new and very expensive drug. Diane supplemented it with penicillin from her physician father's stock. "Then we waited," she says.

"Clyde never stopped eating. Although he appeared to have trouble breathing at one point, he began to improve after a few days. A week later, the vet returned and said it was a miracle. (To this day a bulge as large as a fist can still be seen on Clyde's belly where he was impaled). Soon Clyde was bouncing off his stall walls, clamoring to get out for a run. He was no doubt glad to be alive."

After recovering fully, Clyde began his career as a carriage horse. He quickly became a favorite of the drivers. Early in his career he had his first and only accident where he hung up a carriage wheel on a dumpster. "When I arrived at the scene, Clyde's driver was steadily asserting that the accident was not Clyde's fault. As if to bear out what the driver was saying, Clyde was hanging his head dejectedly as if to say, 'Please don't fire me. It wasn't my fault!'" says Diane.

Today Clyde is the "flagship of the fleet." New drivers typically begin by driving reliable Clyde.

As Clyde gained in notoriety, Diane began using him in her promotional literature. In time, he became the company's Chairhorse. "I added the last name 'Jones,' an old Savannah name, because it seemed to fit and gave distinction to his character," she says.

Clyde gets a lot of fan mail, especially from Girl Scout Troops – Savannah is their national headquarters. "We get a kick out of it," says Diane. "Sometimes people even phone and ask for Clyde Jones. We usually play along by saying, 'He's out now. Would you like to leave a message?' Clyde always leaves his fans chomping at the bit for more."

Tegdim+/

Tegdim+/, better known as Gidget, is a beautiful dapple-grey registered Half-Arabian mare who reflects the best of the Arabian working horse. Eleven years old and twice a National Champion Trail Horse, Gidget is a great performer, one who "paved the way for Megan Callan as a competitive rider and for her farm, Calarab," says Megan's mother, Joanne Callan.

"Gidget, with her calm attitude and her athletic ability, proved to be a horse with the talent to take herself and her junior rider to the top and she has the personality to make the journey challenging and fun."

Gidget carried Megan to United States Top Ten Stock Seat Equitation in both 1990 and 1991, and the pair has also claimed many championships at Regional and Class A shows.

Gidget comes from a long line of horses who have excelled in National competition. She is by Ephraim, an Arabian who was Canadian National Champion English Pleasure and out of Midget, a registered half-Appaloosa/half Quarter Horse. Her maternal grandsire was Blue Admiral, a World Champion Trail, English Pleasure and Western Pleasure performer who twice tied for all-round top Appaloosa in the United States.

Ephraim's owner was so impressed with the versatility and personality of Blue Admiral's daughter, Midget, that she arranged a breeding with Midget's owners, Frank and Bette Evans, well-established breeders and trainers. That breeding produced Gidget, foaled at Rancho Santa Fe, California on May 15, 1980, at the Evans' Buckeye Ranch.

Frank Evans co-founded the highly-celebrated Del Mar National Horse Show in 1946, where some forty years later, Gidget won the Challenge of the Breeds Championship by giving top performances in Trail, Western Pleasure, Driving, English Pleasure, and Hunter Hack. Shown by Lou Roper, nationally-recognized trainer, Gidget demonstrated her impressive versatility with high style.

"She can come out from winning a stock class and move directly to a winning performance in trail," says Joanne Callan.

How does she do it? "She requires her riders to be precise and to tell her exactly what is wanted," says Joanne. "Once a clear command is given, she will carry it out. If the rider doesn't remain focused, however, Gidget will stop and wait for direction. This kind of composure is one of the qualities that has enabled her to be such a successful trail horse."

The Callans first leased Gidget from the Evans and she joined their very first mare, Jhe La Mia, also a registered Half-Arabian, at their Calarab ranch at Solana Beach, California.

They were so impressed with Gidget as a talented, safe and well-bred mare, they decided to purchase her. Frank Evans had refused many prior offers to buy her, but was persuaded to sell by the love that young Megan Callan had developed for Gidget.

Since then, Gidget has been a partner in two special combinations: With Lou Roper, Gidget won the National Championship in Half-Arabian Trail at the United States National Show two years in a row, in 1989 at Albuquerque, New Mexico, and in 1990 at Louisville, Kentucky. She also won a National Top Ten Trail in 1991 with Megan, the only junior rider in the competition among professionals.

"Without question, Gidget is special!" says Joanne Callan. "There are not that many horses that have the special combination of talent and disposition that she does.

"She has a loving look about her. People seek her out. When charity events are held, celebrities want to ride Gidget. They feel confident and safe when riding her, and she's fun – she loves to be treated to carrots, apples or watermelons after a great ride.

"She looks at you with her deep dark eyes and there is that sense of special connection between man and animal, a sense of universal oneness. She will always be a special member of our family and a special horse to anyone who knows her."

Colonel

Colonel represents those fortunate few horses who live out their lives with their original owners and families, with the shared love and trust creating memories that somehow make the loss of such a friendship a bit more bearable.

Bill Raftery's face was both the first and the last that the paint horse ever saw. There were twenty-eight full years between.

The bond between Bill and Colonel was special from the start. Bill bought Colonel's dam, the Half-Arabian Dulce, from Everet Bowman, World Champion

Team Roper at Madison Square Garden when she was in foal to Bowman's famous stallion, Hillside Little Man, a World Champion roping horse. On February 4, 1947, a cold winter morning in North Phoenix, Arizona, Colonel tried to make his first appearance in the world. But he was presented in breech position, and Bill had to turn him around, forelegs first, before he could emerge.

"What a prize he was!" recalls Bill. "A beautiful sorrel and white tobiano paint with the prettiest little Arabian head." Thereafter, Bill always said, "Mine was the first friendly face the Colonel looked into. After all, Dulce had her back turned."

Thus began a nearly three-decade partnership between man and horse. With Bill as his trainer, Colonel learned how to cut cattle, calf rope, team rope, even do a little jumping and driving.

Colonel was ridden in both the Phoenix and Tucson parades, and participated twelve times in the 120-mile, five-day Los Charros rides. Many of these miles he was ridden without halter or bridle, so accomplished was his training.

Colonel even earned some of his keep, winning over $11,000 in cutting competitions when $100 was the standard winner's share. Even when the competition was stiff, Colonel could be expected to come out on top because he could cut without bridle or halter.

There were heartaches in his life as well.

Colonel twice survived being bitten in the face by rattlesnakes. The first time occurred in the years before cortisone was available to help reduce the swelling caused by the venom. The veterinarian placed hoses up Colonel's nostrils to keep his air passages open, and Bill fed him by sliding mesquite beans into the side of his mouth. The vet said Colonel was saved by the antivenom shots, but Bill's devotion was just as powerful.

Another morning, Bill found Colonel standing in his pasture with a shattered sesamoid bone. The veterinarian shook his head and recommended Colonel be put down. But Bill insisted that Colonel should be allowed to live out the rest of his life in retirement--if he could be made comfortable. Bill designed a shoe with long metal straps that went around Colonel's leg, around which the veterinarian built a cast.

Colonel pluckily got around this way for a year and made a full recovery. Retirement would have to wait. Colonel completed five of those 120-mile rides after that injury. For many more miles still, Colonel carried each of Bill's children, teaching them to ride, on into his old age.

In the late summer of 1975, Bill had to say goodbye to his old friend and had him humanely put to sleep.

Colonel's family hopes that, as his spotted spirit gallops across the heavens, he remembers them as fondly as they remember him.

Rum 'N Coke

Some horse stories give you a natural high just hearing them, such as that of Rum 'N Coke, a non-registered chestnut gelding, a Morgan/Quarter Horse mix who has reached the venerable age of twenty-six.

"Coke" is Barbara Wozencroft's dream come true. Barbara, of Wish It Were Farm at Medford, New York, had, like so many others, wanted a horse since she was a little girl.

At twenty-eight, all she had to satisfy her horse cravings was an occasional hour-long ride on weekends with her friend Sue at the local livery stable where Sue boarded her horse. When Sue decided to move to a more pleasant atmosphere at a distant backyard barn, despair overswept Barbara, as there were no horses at the new place for her to ride.

Sue realized Barbara's plight and phoned her with information on Coke, an eighteen-year-old barrel racer up for adoption to a person who could give him some much-needed TLC.

Barbara and Coke first met face to face on Mother's Day May 8, 1983, in Bohemia, New York at Dottie McCue's barn.

"Even though I was numb and shaky as I rode him, I was convinced he was the horse for me," says Barbara. "He was a terror to ride, but I can't explain the thrill I felt when Dottie grumbled to me, 'Here, YOU groom him. He's YOUR horse now!'

"It didn't take long to find out that we were perfectly matched," jokes Barbara, "Me, inexperienced, and Coke, unmanageable."

Coke seemed to be a four-legged textbook of all the bad habits a horse can collect. Dottie's gruff instructions to Barbara included: "He'll never trailer, so don't bother trying. Don't pick up his feet, he'll kick. Don't saddle him alone, he'll rear. Don't go near him with a hose, a spray bottle or electric clippers, he'll rear. Don't put a blanket on him, he'll eat it. Always ride him with a tie-down and don't let him lope too fast, or you'll never stop him." And all that was if Barbara could catch him in the first place.

Understandably, the first few months together were not always the most enjoyable. Barbara wondered if she'd made a huge mistake as she chased Coke around the paddock with a halter in her hand.

The first real improvement started when she changed to riding him English style, which seemed to make Coke happier. "While he was never asked to jump over two feet, three inches at his age, convincing him to go OVER fences instead of around them was no easy task, especially since I'd never jumped before either," says Barbara.

But something must have clicked, because one year later, at their first show, at the Fall Show of the Islip Horsemen's Association of Long Island, New York, Barbara and Rum 'N Coke placed Reserve Champion in the Adult Maiden Equitation Division. Since then they have won several more division championships and in 1991, Coke had his best show season ever, by winning Division Grand Champion and/or Reserve Champion in every English class he and Barbara entered. The pair also earned these end-of-year awards: Reserve Champion Adult Novice Equitation Division and Grand Champion Pleasure Division.

But showing is but a small part of Barbara and Coke's relationship. "He's my best pal and we've enjoyed many a happy day just spending quiet moments together, sharing Snickers and granola bars under a tree," says Barbara. Now the former renegade follows Barbara and her husband, Rick, around like a huge puppy, happy to do anything they ask of him.

Since 1985, Coke has been a member of the Islip Horsemen's Association Drill Team. He gave his proudest performance ever when the drill team was invited to perform at Belmont Racetrack's 1990 Horse Fair.

"Yes, my dream of owning a horse has been fulfilled," says Barbara. "But more than that, I've found a special friend with whom I share a unique trust that few other owners and horses know. Rum 'N Coke has helped me to learn about myself and what I'm capable of. He has given me confidence and the opportunity to make some pretty terrific friends. There really isn't much that Coke and I can't enjoy together. If that's not special, then I don't know what is."

INDEX